I0814468

DEVOURING TIME

TODD GODDARD

DEVOURING TIME

Jim Harrison, a Writer's Life

Published in 2025 by Blackstone Publishing
Cover and book design by Alenka Vdovič Linaschke

Printed in the United States of America

First edition: 2025
ISBN 978-1-7999-0236-2
Biography & Autobiography / Literary Figures

Version 3
Blackstone Publishing
31 Mistletoe Rd.
Ashland, OR 97520

www.BlackstonePublishing.com

To my mother and father

Devouring Time, blunt thou the lion's paws,
And make the earth devour her own sweet brood;
Pluck the keen teeth from the fierce tiger's jaws,
And burn the long-liv'd phoenix, in her blood;
Make glad and sorry seasons as thou fleets,
And do whate'er thou wilt, swift-footed Time,
To the wide world and all her fading sweets;
But I forbid thee one most heinous crime:
O! carve not with thy hours my love's fair brow,
Nor draw no lines there with thine antique pen;
Him in thy course untainted do allow
For beauty's pattern to succeeding men.
  Yet do thy worst, old Time; despite thy wrong,
  My love shall in my verse ever live young.

—William Shakespeare, Sonnet 19

CONTENTS

Preface xiii

1. The Legend of Little Jimmy 1
2. Haslett 17
3. On the Road 34
4. Something to Tie Me to Earth 48
5. Black Thickets 64
6. Operation Stony Brook 82
7. Locations 103
8. Wolf 119
9. The Sporting Club 145
10. Zen and the Art of Tarpon Fishing 165
11. Farmer 178
12. Legends of the Fall 191
13. The Theory and Practice of Hollywood 216
14. Up in Michigan 240
15. Dalva 260
16. Patagonia 275
17. Entre Chien et Loup 294
18. The Shape of the Journey 314
19. The Roving Gourmand 332
20. Mortality Is Gravity 352
21. Antelope Butte 372
22. Parts Unknown 390
23. Counting Birds 406

Acknowledgments 423
Notes 427
Index 493

Illustrations follow page 252.

ILLUSTRATIONS

The author and publisher would like to thank the following for permission to use photographs: Michael Abramson (20); Russell Chatham (15, 18); Dan Gerber (13, 14, 16, 17); the Harrison family (1–12, 21, 23, 24); Cynthia Lord Harrison (33); Stanley Krohmer (32); Dan Lahren (27, 30); John Schulz (19); Douglas Seifert (28); Don Usner (29); Guy de la Valdène (22); Bob Wargo (25); Laura Wilson (34). Photographs 26 and 31 were kindly provided by Lea Chatham and Robert Dattila, respectively.

1 Winfield, Norma, John, and Jim Harrison, circa 1938
2 Jim Harrison in Grayling, Michigan, 1938
3 John and Hulda Wahlgren with John and Jim Harrison, Rodney, Michigan, 1938
4 Jim Harrison, summer 1940
5 John, Winfield, and Jim Harrison in Haslett, Michigan
6 Jim Harrison, circa 1948
7 Jim, John, Mary, David, and Judy Harrison at home in Haslett, Michigan, circa 1954
8 Judy Harrison, circa 1956
9 Jim Harrison playing for the Haslett Vikings, circa 1956
10 The Harrison family, circa 1956
11 Linda King Harrison at the Kings' house, East Lansing, Michigan, 1959
12 Jim, Jamie, and Linda Harrison, Haslett, Michigan, circa 1960
13 J. D. Reed and Jim Harrison, Stony Brook, New York, 1966
14 Jim and Linda Harrison, 1968
15 Guy de la Valdène, Tom McGuane, and Richard Brautigan in Key West, early 1970s

16 Jim Harrison's Soviet visa, 1971
17 Jim Harrison, France, 1971
18 Tom McGuane on a skiff in the Florida Keys, 1972
19 Jim Harrison at his writing desk, 1972
20 Jimmy Buffett and Dan Gerber on Deep Creek, Montana
21 Lake trout catch, Lake Leelanau, early 1970s
22 Jim Harrison and Pat Paton, circa 1973
23 Jim Harrison on the running board of Russell Chatham's truck, mid 1970s
24 Jim, Jamie, Linda, and Anna Harrison, circa 1977
25 Joyce Harrington Bahle and Jim Harrison outside the writing studio in Lake Leelanau, Michigan, early 1980s
26 Russell Chatham and Robert Dattila
27 Dan Lahren and Jim Harrison on the banks of the Yellowstone River, 1987
28 Jim Harrison and Guy de la Valdène hunting in Michigan
29 Jim Harrison and Peter Lewis at the Lannan Foundation's Readings & Conversations series in Santa Fe, New Mexico, 2002
30 Dan Lahren, Jim Harrison, and Peter Matthiessen at Pine Creek boat launch on the Upper Yellowstone River, September 2003
31 Jim Harrison and Robert Dattila, Paris
32 Jim Harrison at the estuary at Grand Marais, Michigan
33 Jim and Linda Harrison at the casita in Patagonia, Arizona, circa 2010
34 Jim Harrison in Patagonia, Arizona

PREFACE

Grand Marais, Michigan, was fifty-three degrees, a damp seaway cold, in mid-July. I had a room at the Superior Hotel on Lake Avenue. The hotel was one of Jim Harrison's regular stops when he was staying at his nearby cabin in the state's Upper Peninsula. From his cabin steps, you can hear the flow of the Sucker River, itself the color of a dark golden ale, and the roily, sliding surf of Lake Superior in the distance. After a dinner of whitefish—one of only a handful of meals available in town—and a few beers at the Dunes Saloon (another of Jim's hangouts), I hurried to bed. I was meeting Jim's friend Mike Ballard, the former owner of the Dunes, in the morning. He had agreed to show me around.

The next day, I climbed into Mike's pickup truck. His old black Lab, Wilson, slept on the middle console between us. Mike took me to see Harrison's former cabin, and he drove me out to the Kingston Plains, a vast "stump prairie" south of Grand Marais. It was one of Jim's favorite places to walk and hunt. The Kingston Plains is eerily beautiful. The countless tree stumps, like memento mori, memorialize not fallen soldiers but the forests of old-growth trees clear-cut—some fifty million board feet of white pine—by an avaricious lumber industry. The area is still home to plenty of game birds—sharp-tailed and ruffed grouse, American woodcock, and so on—and seemingly endless miles of good walking.

Somewhere in this vast landscape was what Jim Harrison called his sacred place, the hollowed-out stump of a large white pine, probably moldering in some leaf-strewn gully, and we aimed to find it that day. Jim frequently searched out the sacred in the physical, nonhuman world, looking for what he called "small gods," and he often found it in unlikely places, like in the Chihuahuan ravens that once followed him on his walks, or among old logs and tree stumps in the backwoods. Jim's poetry editor at Copper Canyon Press, Joseph Bednarik, once suggested that Jim had more tree stumps in his poetry than all other American poets combined, and I think he's right. Stumps were a material fact and potent metaphor for Jim—places of revelation and re-creation imbued with the spiritual: "My place of grace on earth, my only church," as he once described his stump in the Kingston Plains. "The gods live there."

The Upper Peninsula was my first of many stops for this book. Throughout his life, Jim established rich associations with places: Lake Leelanau and Grand Marais, Michigan; Patagonia, Arizona; Livingston, Montana—all places he lived for many years. I would also follow Jim, so to speak, to Nebraska, Mississippi, Florida, California, New York, and Paris, and the list goes on. Jim visited these places often, and he wrote about them, though the "dream coasts," his name for Los Angeles and New York City, wouldn't typically fare well in his novels and poetry. Jim preferred remote rural places—locales proximate to wilderness with meandering streams and rivers, places for trout fishing and bird-watching and hunting, with a few good bars and restaurants thrown in for good measure. The cities of France were another story. There Jim imagined he could live, if he weren't so "addicted to wild natural beauty," as he once wrote to a friend, "shooting birds and catching fish, the grand pelvic gorges that rivers cut in the fleshy earth."

The son of a former schoolteacher and an agricultural agent in Michigan, Jim clung to the memories of his rural upbringing, and he returned to them often in his work. Time spent on his grandparents' farm, at the family's cabin on Wells Lake, in Reed City as a young boy, and fishing and hunting were formative. But he was also restless and eager for experience. He hitchhiked at the age of sixteen to Colorado and, later, to Boston, New York City, and San Francisco. As an adult, he loved to drive with friends around the country, taking mostly back roads, with a Best Western hotel map as a guide. Still, despite his wanderlust, his first and last books of fiction are set in Michigan. Many of his poems are anchored in these early memories—the farms, rivers, and woods, surely, but also the loss of sight in his left eye at age seven and the untimely, tragic deaths of his father and sister in an auto accident. Those events would forever change the way he viewed the world, quite literally, and his place in it.

Jim built vast networks of friends and associates, a fact that kept me steadily interviewing people: more than one hundred separate interviews, many of them conducted in far-flung places, from the Sierra Mountains in Nevada to Arkansas and Marseille, throughout the writing of this book. Many of them I did while carefully navigating Covid protocols, and I traversed large swaths of the country at least a dozen times, driving myself through a mostly emptied landscape. Friendship was one of the defining features of Jim's life. From a young age, he fearlessly sought out connections with other writers, such as the poet Denise Levertov, who served as an early mentor to him. One friendship led to another, but Jim was always open to meeting new people, and he was willing to put himself out there. While he generally avoided literary politics, which he mostly resented and associated with New York City, he cultivated a powerful and influential group of loyal friends, and despite his exhausting pace of work, he almost always made time for them.

Jim and his wife, Linda, regularly hosted and cooked meals for friends. Jim fished and hunted with friends; drank, traveled, and visited with friends; and he wrote volumes of letters to them. The collected papers of Jim Harrison, housed at Grand Valley State University near Grand Rapids, where I spent nearly six solid months, include more than seventy-six boxes of personal letters alone. That number excludes correspondence to book and magazine publishers and film producers, many of whom also became friends. Jim seemed naturally inclined to collapse the distance between the professional and personal, as he often did with his publishers and editors. Indeed, he forged lasting friendships with some of his medical doctors and even his psychologist (his "mind doctor," as he called him), Larry Sullivan.

Throughout this book, I opted to keep a special focus on Jim Harrison's poetry, though the fiction and nonfiction are here in spades. Poetry was Jim's first love. If he was remembered at all, he thought, it would be for his poetry, and time and again, in moments of distress and depression, the writing of poetry helped pull him through it. Remarkably, during his most difficult times, he was often most productive. Jim thought of poetry as "the true bones of my life," but he would also take on what he referred to as a quadria-schizoid existence, which meant he wrote not just poetry but journalism, fiction, and screenplays. The addition of the latter three was to feed his family, he would say, something he couldn't quite do on poetry alone. That's only partly true. In fact, Jim had an early interest in fiction and began penning stories in his early twenties. Jim's close friend, the writer Tom McGuane, led the way in journalism and screenwork, and Jim would follow in his footsteps. Those endeavors helped pay the family's bills, even as Jim cultivated more lavish tastes, and those bills mounted alongside his success. The more he earned, the more he spent, and the more he felt he had to stray from his poetry to make ends meet.

Jim published his first book of poetry in his late twenties, and while he was well regarded for it, his renown grew from his journalism. His work for *Sports Illustrated* in the 1970s, especially, as well as *True*, *Playboy*, *Esquire*, *Outside*, and other publications—deep-pocketed magazines with their own literary aspirations and broad circulations—provided Jim with a forum to introduce himself: his outsized personality, appetites, the overall persona of Jim Harrison that he would create in those pages and cultivate for a large readership. That journalism, and later his screenwork and fiction, expanded Jim's recognition beyond the tight poetry circles where he'd solidly established himself. Jim's poetry sold well because people liked it, and they liked Jim Harrison, but those readers came to his poetry from elsewhere. Very few people came to the poetry *through* poetry.

But the same renown that attracted readers arguably held him back and tended to estrange him from the relatively smaller community of poets. Jim's literary agent, Bob Dattila, told me how he once stood at the back of a room during one of Jim's poetry readings and noticed a man next to him almost scowling. That man, a poet himself, admired Jim's poetry, but he thought Jim Harrison had "sold out" to the magazines and novels and Hollywood. That idea, that Jim had somehow sold out or moved on from poetry, had sometimes kept him from being considered for awards and anthologies and other opportunities. Some of that stemmed from resentments, some from the simple fact that other poets overlooked him, intentionally or not. Nonetheless, Jim never stopped writing poetry, and until his death in 2016, it remained the central fact and driving force of his life. Copper Canyon's marvelous *Jim Harrison: Complete Poems*, a 931-page tome, is a powerful testament to Jim's astonishing poetic achievement.

Jim was quick to admit, if not always to his publishers, that he was paid more for his fiction and poetry than most writers. That he knew. But he would never obtain the kind of purchase on the literary world, particularly with poetry, that he desired and almost certainly deserved. Jim was not a professional poet, a phrase he would have likely despised. While he published often, he didn't lecture or teach. He didn't work to make inroads into the academy and didn't attend writing conferences. Many of Jim's readings focused on his fiction, with a poem or two tacked on at the end. He readily targeted MFA programs, where poetry increasingly resided then and mostly does today, with some of his most withering criticism. He also eschewed cliques and schools of poetry, the kinds of tribal associations that might have allowed others to better label and promote his work. Jim's geographic remoteness from the center of the publishing world didn't help him much either, as he well knew. A writer's reputation, as such, he'd say, depends on "social contiguity," and that mostly meant socializing and living in or around New York City.

It might be hyperbole to say that the author of *Legends of the Fall* was a contradiction of a man, but he certainly was a unique combination of things: a serious, critically acclaimed writer who hung out with the likes of Jack Nicholson and the Hollywood set; a hard-living, hard-drinking outdoorsman who crafted exquisite poetry; a wounded man whose epic depressions threatened the well-being of his family but fueled his writing. While Jim actively promoted and encouraged young writers, and he was quick to help out friends—"Jim would give you his last nickel if you needed it," said Ballard—he could be impatient, demanding, unyielding, and all-consuming. Behind his back, a few of his friends had nicknamed him "the General" because it was Jim's way or the highway, and one could quickly find oneself the focus of his ire.

Jim was a loving husband and father who adored his wife and family, but he was also highly sexual, an aspect of his poetry and fiction that is readily apparent, and at times in his life, he pursued women with an almost voracious appetite. He was prone to fits of self-pity and depression, and he could be self-involved without necessarily achieving introspection. He was extremely ambitious, though he rarely let on to it, and at times, he was capable of consuming everything and everyone in his path in service to his work. Jim's writing, perhaps as it needed to be, was paramount. He adopted early on Faulkner's dictum that the writer's only responsibility is to his art; and that art, which saved him on more than one occasion, would also come close to destroying him.

Still, Jim managed to bring beauty and joy into people's lives and enrich them with his innate warmth; his endearing, self-effacing charm; his wit and intelligence; and his seemingly inexhaustible store of humor. Many of my interviews for this book—with friends and colleagues, women and men alike—ended in tears, sometimes from a complex mixture of emotions. Jim took up a lot of space, and his death in 2016 left an equally large absence. Few writers have enjoyed such a loyal following of readers.

Despite Jim's large public persona, much of his life remained protected and private. Indeed, the Falstaffian figure he was happy to project tended to hide and obscure his more private self, one he reserved mostly for his poetry. It was arguably in his poetry where Jim was most candid. Other aspects of his life he kept entirely to himself, though, like his immediate family and his marriage. Linda Harrison was as private a person as Jim could be a public one. She preferred to remain out of the spotlight, and she devoted her time to her family, her dogs, her garden, and her close friends. She rarely traveled with Jim, especially when it involved work, and she seemed at peace with letting her husband perform Jim Harrison on a public stage. When Jim was off to Key West, New York City, Montana, or Paris, he often seemed like a lone planet in a public universe—no family, no attachments, grounded only in his sense of himself and his art. But Linda was always present in his life, even if not physically so. Because Jim and Linda mostly spoke on the telephone, there are relatively few letters between them. Her absences in this book can thus seem magnified out of proportion. She was always the first true reader of his work. The two of them shared an understanding that kept their marriage intact for more than fifty years, while many of those around them ended. In many ways, theirs was an extraordinary love story.

Mike Ballard and I searched the Kingston Plains for the stump that day, but we didn't find it. On several occasions, Mike jumped out of the truck and crawled into gullies, scouting the area, trudging along, talking as he went—me following him with a recording device in hand. Wilson stayed in the truck and napped. We eventually gave up looking and went fishing, and we chatted about Jim as we trolled the nearby Grand Sable Lake. Perhaps it was better that we didn't find the stump that day, I thought, mostly in retrospect. Others have found the stump over the years, though it must now be well on its way to becoming nutrients for the soil. It will soon help to grow other plants and thickets for people and critters—the small gods in the area. Jim would have liked that.

1

THE LEGEND OF LITTLE JIMMY

(FALL 2003; FALL 1937 – FALL 1949)

Go, my songs
to the young and insolent,
speak the love of final things—
do not betray me
as a dancer, drunk,
is dumb to his clumsiness.

On a cool, misty morning in November 2003, a hungry Jim Harrison paced the gardens of a manor house in the medieval village of Saint-Père-sous-Vézelay in Burgundy, anticipating the beginning of a thirty-seven-course lunch. "Life is a near death experience," he'd later write, "and our devious minds will do anything to make it interesting." Despite being sixty-five years old and suffering from painful bouts of gout, hypertension, and kidney stones (he'd soon add chronic shingles, postherpetic neuralgia, type 2 diabetes, spondylolisthesis, spinal stenosis, and hip arthritis to the list), Jim had traveled from his home in Livingston, Montana, to Paris two weeks earlier. "Devouring time," a phrase from a poem Jim liked to quote, would eventually do its worst.

At noon that day, twelve invited attendees crowded into the Michelin-starred restaurant of Marc Meneau, L'Espérance. The grounds included the restaurant and a hotel, a small gift shop, and parklike gardens of flowers and herbs crisscrossed by little streams and walking paths. The restaurant's dining room overlooked the gardens, and that morning, it had been amply appointed with fresh flowers. It lay just a few miles from Vézelay's cobblestone streets and its Benedictine monastery—now the Basilica of Sainte-Marie-Madeleine—Jim thought the village and the cathedral the loveliest in France.

The attendees included Jim's friends Guy de la Valdène, a French count, and restaurateur and writer Peter Lewis, plus a mix of gourmands and chefs, mostly French. The organizer of the event was Jim's friend Gérard Oberlé—an unquestionable genius, he thought him (add book dealer, writer, and scholar of French food)—who resided in a manor house in nearby Nivernais. For this hours-long meal, Oberlé had crafted a menu drawn from seventeen cookbooks published between 1654 and 1823. As the diners filed in, Chef Meneau, a brilliant but "tempestuous French chef of the old school," stood by, wearing a crisp white uniform with a blue apron. His job and that of his wife, Françoise, along with thirty-nine members of his staff, was to keep the thirty-seven courses coming throughout the day.

The first service of the lunch began with Meneau exclaiming simply, "Courage" (or "coo-rahj," as Jim would write), followed by a grand assortment of nose-to-tail dishes: tartines of foie gras with truffles and lard; a "velvet cream of squab with cucumbers, served with cock-crest fritters"; oysters and cream of Camembert on toast; a "jellied loaf of poultry on sorrel cream"; "a tart of calf's brain with shelled peas"; and an omelet of sea urchin. Later came a stew of suckling pig, "a warm terrine of hare with preserved plums," and "a poached eel with chicken wing tips and testicles in a pool of tarragon butter." Coo-rahj, indeed. A selection of celebrated French wines, Jim would note, "rained down on us as if from the world's best garden sprinkler"—by one account, nineteen different bottles.

Before departing Montana, Jim had queried editor Deborah Treisman at *The New Yorker* about the possibility of a write-up for the magazine: "I am going again [to France] tomorrow and one of my duties is to attend a 37-course lunch (yes, 37) of 17th & 18th century food down in the country. I've developed a pretty good access there to aspects of their culture that don't appear in *The New Yorker.* Of course the approach would be comic." If she didn't want the story, he wouldn't bother taking notes—"Vaguely thinking that a doctor should be in attendance." Treisman was interested and agreed with Jim's latter concern, hoping afterward that he had survived the meal, and thought it "a thrill to have [the piece] in the issue."

The result, "A Really Big Lunch," was included in the magazine's September 6, 2004, issue and would earn "a certain notoriety," as one critic put it, for its unapologetic description of excess, about which Jim remained thoroughly unrepentant. His defense, what little there was, relied mostly (and characteristically) on humor: While the lunch "likely cost as much as a new Volvo station wagon . . . none of us twelve disciples of gourmandise wanted a new Volvo. We wanted only lunch and since lunch lasted approximately eleven hours we saved money by not having to buy dinner."

"It's a long road from a childhood in rural Michigan to being the sort of man who gets invited to a thirty-seven-course lunch," Jim would write in *The New Yorker*, though he'd return again and again in its narrative to his childhood memories as if pausing to measure the distance he had traveled. He took pride in his Midwestern upbringing, and it affected him permanently. He'd recall his astonishment as a young boy growing up in northern Michigan at the limitless appetites of his grandfather's pigs and the "Gospel" assumption in the Calvinist Midwest that "we eat to live, not live to eat." In describing a torte of pigs' noses once prepared for him by Oberlé, he observed how such food is usually only for the extremely curious or those with an agricultural background—Jim was both. He remembered his grandmothers boiling pigs' heads with herbs and onions to make a headcheese of the cheek, tongue, and neck meat. It was a family specialty worthy of Oberlé's menu. As a private joke, Oberlé had arranged to have Meneau serve fresh Baltic herring with mayonnaise, a staple food of Jim's Swedish relatives, because everyone knew that Jim had relished it since age two.

As for his mother, Jim informed the reader she was "a Swedish Lutheran, [who] liked to ask her five children, 'What have you accomplished today?' If I'd told her, 'I have eaten thirty-seven courses and drunk thirteen wines,' I would have been cast into outer darkness. But then this was the Iron Mom who also said, with a tiny smile, in reference to my life's work, 'You've made quite a living out of your fibs.'" If his mother's comment seems barbed, she wasn't entirely wrong. At the time of his death in 2016, Jim counted over thirty books of fiction, nonfiction, and poetry to his name. He had traveled a very long road indeed.

—

James Thomas Harrison was born on December 11, 1937, in Grayling, Michigan, in the one-time home of a lumber baron. The ornate mansion then served as the town's hospital. French doors opened to the second-story balcony. Polished wood and wallpaper adorned the rooms. Wooden bassinets sat at the foot of the beds. As was common at the time, Jim's mother, Norma, was confined to her bed there for two weeks. The opulence reflected the boom times of Michigan's recent past and served as a monument to the lumber industry that had transformed the state.

Grayling had been named for the once-abundant Arctic grayling fish that inhabited the nearby Au Sable and Manistee Rivers.* When Jim was born, it was still a lumber town, though the dense virgin stands of Norway and white pine that once covered Crawford County had largely been replaced by second-growth forests and fields. Jim's parents, Winfield and Norma Harrison, relocated to Grayling from Big Rapids in July 1935. His father had taken a job with the Resettlement Administration, a New Deal agency dedicated to rescuing failing farms. The glaciated landscapes of the northern stretches of the state's Lower Peninsula proved inhospitable for agriculture. Small amounts of nutrient-rich humus, left over from the white pine forests, rested on beds of sand, and once the topsoil eroded, it was difficult to make a living from crops. Winfield's task was to purchase

* By 1936, unregulated harvest and predation of the Arctic grayling, along with destructive logging practices, had completely extirpated the fish from the area's rivers.

submarginal land from local farmers on behalf of the government and relocate the farmers to more promising tracts. He had graduated from the Michigan State College of Agriculture and Applied Science (later renamed Michigan State University), becoming the first member of his family to go to college. Winfield and Norma had their own roots in Midwestern farming families, where money was almost invariably scarce. Both came from generations of plain working-class folk who farmed or labored in low-paying jobs. Their forebears were not written about; they weren't on the member rolls of clubs, nor had anyone attended university. For generations, Jim Harrison's ancestors had fought simply to get by.

Norma Olivia Wahlgren, the "Iron Mom," was born on November 24, 1914, in Chicago to Swedish parents and raised on a farm in Rodney, Michigan, a farming village of "Germans and Swedes (with a Dane or two thrown in)," she'd say. Founded by the Hood & Gale Lumber Company in 1879 as a railway hub, Rodney had changed little since then. Mostly farmers and some leftover lumbermen lived there, and the town boasted only a handful of businesses. To attend high school, Norma had to move to the larger town of Big Rapids, where she cleaned houses to pay for room and board. Norma excelled at school, graduating fourth in a class of 105 students; her sisters, Inez and Grace, were valedictorians. Norma remembered finding her English classes ponderous, mostly because of a lackluster instructor. Her favorite teacher, Roland Faunce, taught speech and debate, and she fondly recalled how he introduced her to "ideas, to argument," and taught her to "speak clearly and best of all to think." After graduation in 1932, during the worst years of the Depression, she attended County Normal, a training program for rural schoolteachers, and she was lucky enough to find a job.

Norma and Winfield began dating on a summer night in 1934 at the River Gardens, a dance hall on the banks of the Muskegon River. When they met, Winfield was working as a beer-truck driver and deliveryman. He had just graduated from college, but as Norma would put it, "there was no money and the whole process was one of hanging in there and taking whatever jobs he could to survive." The couple had to keep his job a secret from Norma's aging landlady, a strict Free Methodist who would not have looked kindly on it. "Win," as his friends called him, was twenty-five, handsome, obsessively hardworking, and often clad in a black-and-red mackinaw, rubber boots, and a black knit cap. Norma, just twenty, had brown hair and large blue eyes and, like Winfield, was driven and ambitious. The two fell in love and sensed their compatibility from the start. They were married during the summer of 1935. Inez and Grace pitched in to find suitable clothes for Norma to wear on her honeymoon at nearby Houghton Lake. What money was left over went to purchase a secondhand Chevy.

Less than a year later, in April 1936, Norma gave birth to John Arthur Harrison—the couple named him after his two grandfathers, John Wahlgren and Arthur Harrison. Jim arrived the following year, delivered at Mercy Hospital, and soon after, the Harrisons relocated to a cottage on Lake Margrethe, just outside of Grayling. Only two doctors then lived in the town, and both oversaw Norma's pregnancy. The bill was thirty-five dollars, a hefty sum considering that the Harrisons had another mouth to feed on only one income. The couple had never discussed Norma finding work, in part because married women were typically restricted from doing so during the Depression.

"Using the word work that way is ridiculous, of course, as being a homemaker was surely very real work," as Norma would often point out. While friends and family helped with childcare and knitted garments, Norma prepared food at home and washed and ironed clothing using a method that took most of a couple days' time. Meanwhile, Winfield agonized over the family's bills. On Sunday nights, he'd sit down with a yellow legal pad—Jim would later use similar pads for his writing—and methodically list each bill, trying to make it all add up. Still, Norma would remember these years fondly. "Everyone doted on the new baby," she'd say of Jim. "It was a time of relatives as we considered family best friends and spent all available spare time with them."

—

Jim did not have the unhappy childhood of many writers. He loved his parents and siblings, and he spent a great deal of time with extended family, as he did on Norma's parents' farm in Rodney. When Winfield's job in Grayling ended in the fall of 1938, he moved the family to the farm, and over the years, as the family visited, Jim latched on to his experiences there and never let go; his poetry and fiction would grow from the seeds planted there. The house, which smelled perpetually of tobacco, had only two bedrooms, and people slept where they could. In the evenings, everyone played pinochle, the adults sipping whiskey.

Norma's father, John Severin Wahlgren—a "true Swede autocrat," as Jim referred to him—reportedly got along well with Winfield, though Jim thought his father happy to get away from him. Wahlgren and his wife, Hulda, had six daughters—Inez, Grace, Norma, Irene Dorothy (who died soon after birth), Evelyn, and Marjorie—and he was happy to have a son about the place, at least for a season. While the family joked that with six daughters, John Wahlgren had nothing to fear from the draft, neighbors thought it a grave misfortune for a farmer. But the fact was that the daughters were all strong and capable, like their mother, and contributed physical labor. Along with Norma and Hulda, aunts peopled Jim's early world. From the start, he was surrounded by strong women.

Jim's Grandpa John had been born Johan Svensson in 1874 in the port town of Halmstad, Sweden, to Hannah and Sven Olsson, a laborer and tenant farmer. Nineteen years later, he sailed to New York City and made his way to Chicago, where he met his wife, Hulda, and where his sister and older brothers already lived. There he'd work as a streetcar conductor, and he'd boast that Robert Todd Lincoln was once a passenger. Many Swedes, like John and his family, had been attracted to Chicago because of its expanding labor market and role as a gateway to the arable lands of the Midwest.

But John had had something else in mind, at least at first. From Chicago, he headed west by train into South Dakota and Wyoming with the intention of becoming a cowboy. (Jim later claimed incorrectly that John went westward in 1890, the year of the Wounded Knee Massacre, but John didn't arrive in the US until 1894.) Like the cowboys he admired,

John was laconic. Jim's sister, Mary Harrison, exchanged hardly more than a dozen words with him in his lifetime, she reckoned. John was stubborn and liked to take risks. When he played pinochle, he would drive everyone crazy, recalled David Harrison, Jim's youngest brother. John was always "trying to make too much of a crap hand." Later in life, Jim would remember John in several poems, including "John Severin Walgren, 1874–1962"* and one of his first, "Sketch for a Job-Application Blank":

> From my ancestors, the Swedes,
> I suppose I inherit the love of rainy woods,
> kegs of herring and neat whiskey—
> I remember long nights of pinochle,
> the bulge of Redman in my grandpa's cheek;
> the rug smelled of manure and kerosene.
> They laughed loudly and didn't speak for days.

Hulda Severina Elliason, Norma's mother, had been born in Centerville, Iowa, a Swedish colony in a major coal-mining region. Her parents, John and Charlotte, had immigrated from Gränna, Sweden, a small, crowded city known for its quaint wooden houses and steep streets. Hulda's grandfather, Israel, worked there as a farmer, and her father may have opted to leave the country after a series of crop failures. Iowa promised uncrowded open spaces, but John made his living underground as a miner. He died when Hulda was just seventeen. Hulda was more personable than her husband but far from indulgent. She was an "exquisite quilter with an incredible eye for color," noted Mary, and she was athletic and strong. In old age, when her legs began failing her, she crawled up and down her garden rows on her hands and knees.

John and Hulda had signed the deed on the farm property in April 1915. It came with forty acres and an unpainted clapboard house with

* Jim used an earlier spelling of the Wahlgren family's name for the poem.

no indoor plumbing, a large bedroom and storage area upstairs, and a master bedroom and kitchen downstairs. (Winfield would later install imitation brick siding and, with Jim's help, an indoor bathroom and electric water pump.) John would settle into general farming: He'd plant corn, potatoes, and oats; raise pigs, cows, and horses; and sell milk and cream, the family's cash crop. The soil was a rich, productive loam, but it was stony and filled with old tree roots and prone to swampy flooding. Despite the family's hard work, the farm would survive only on the margin for years to come. Norma would remember her father as a "sunup to sundown worker" who literally whistled while he worked, but he had no experience managing a farm. Near her death at age ninety-six, Hulda put it bluntly: "Your dad was never a farmer." Winfield would eventually bail the family out and save the property from foreclosure.

The farm paid other dividends, however: Jim learned life lessons there—aspects of rural labor and the sometimes blood-and-bone facts of life. "I grew up within that framework," he once told a reporter from the *Detroit Free Press.* "It's whatever you get your juices from, your ideas from. My ideas seem to be rural in nature." Jim would remember the privy "out near the pigpen and the granary full of corn and wheat," Grandpa John's draft horses being put out to pasture, the "vivid energy" of pigs eating slop, and the whirl of a cream separator. It imbued him with an appreciation of the countryside, farm animals, outdoor labor, and rural simplicity, though his view of such things was never romanticized. He learned the violence of pig butchering that led to the pleasures of pork sausage on the family dining table, as well as matter-of-fact lessons about sex. "Farm children then, before artificial insemination, had a built-in sex education in the barnyard," he once observed, and he felt his own sexual stirrings there, aroused by his attractive Aunt Marjorie, the youngest daughter, whom he'd sometimes spy bathing in a tub in the kitchen. Overall, he absorbed the particulars that come only from close firsthand experience, like "Smoking in a barn was a taboo on the level of incest" or "Pigs don't forget."

After a brief stint working at Michigan State back in Lansing, Winfield accepted a full-time position as an assistant agricultural agent for the state. The job required him to advise farmers throughout northern Michigan about modern science-based farming practices, and it meant the family had to relocate almost every ten months—to Boyne City, Gaylord, Harrisville, and Cheboygan. The frequent moves exposed Jim to different places and people at a very young age. In Cheboygan, the family lived next door to the local Works Progress Administration office, and Jim and his brother often mingled with men who hung about the grounds, all of them down on their luck, and some a rough bunch. Two men in particular, Frank and Dumby, regaled the boys with stories and fed them Vienna sausages with soda pop. The men were middle-aged—Jim was four. Dumby, a thin gray-haired man with wire-rimmed glasses, had been exposed to mustard gas in World War I, and his mind had suffered from it. The time amounted to just a blip in Jim's childhood, but he would remember these men for the rest of his life. His mother took a photo of the two men standing next to the WPA sign. More than fifty years later, Jim would write that they reminded him of his father's brothers, Walter and Arthur, who had fought in World War II and who he sensed, even then, had somehow suffered long-lasting wounds.

The Harrisons moved next to Reed City—a homecoming of sorts for Winfield, whose family lived in nearby Paris. They would remain there for almost a decade. "Finally we were to stay in an area long enough to feel like we were home," wrote Norma. Jim would measure all other places against it, and he'd attempt to re-create the feeling of his childhood in Reed City time and again. The family purchased a house at 442 Upton Avenue, at the corner of Upton and State Street, close to the center of town. It had windows on all sides, an upstairs loft with a gabled dormer, a two-car garage, and a wide grassy lot. In the backyard, Winfield planted a garden that included huge raspberry bushes. A morning glory trellis hung next to the front porch. The house was spacious, though it looked smaller in comparison with some of the larger, lumber-industry-era houses on the block.

At the time, Reed City felt like "the nineteenth century in a small county seat," and he'd remember it (and romanticize it) as an idyllic place with something akin to the nostalgia of Tom Sawyer's St. Petersburg (or Twain's Hannibal, Missouri). In truth, the town was bustling, mostly because of a boom in oil and gas exploration and production (the Reed City oil field, the state's largest single strike of the 1940s, stretched over 5,300 acres) stimulated by World War II, which felt ever present to the Harrisons. Families rationed food and used blackout shades on their windows and slotted covers on vehicle headlights while airplane spotters kept watch atop the town's fire station—such was the concern of a bombing, as unlikely as one might have been in the middle of the country. At nine o'clock each night, a siren marked the beginning of curfew, and the Harrisons would huddle around their radio to listen for dispatches and news that might affect Jim's uncles, Walter and Arthur, who were fighting in the Pacific. As a joyful interruption to their concerns, the family welcomed Judith Ellen Harrison into the family in July 1943. Jim would grow very close with Judy, and the two would share a special relationship, almost like twins, despite their age difference.

During the seven years the family lived in Reed City, which covered Jim's elementary education, he reportedly didn't stand out as a student. In an interview in 1977, he described himself as "basically an obnoxious child," not the "least bit creative at all," and without "particularly good grades," though his classmates remember him differently: as uncommonly "smart" and "very intelligent." Teachers in Reed City tended to broadcast the success of students, as well as their failures, and everyone knew where their classmates stood, said Marylin Jones, a classmate of Jim's who still lives in Reed City. Jim's sixth-grade math teacher, Mrs. Raab, would pick out the worst student in class and "lift him up by the ankles" (or so Jones insisted) to illustrate how to invert and multiply fractions. Jones, who was at the top of her class, remembered "Jimmy" as the only student who beat her in a "spell down"—he won on the word *biscuit*, and she never forgave him for it. Indeed, reading held a special place in the Harrison household. Winfield was an obsessive reader and "something of a populist" who treasured John Steinbeck's *The Grapes of Wrath* and would regularly take Jim to the public library—really just a room in the basement of the community building—every Saturday throughout the winter. Jim relished Ernest Thompson Seton's *Two Little Savages*—a 1903 book about two nature-loving boys who learn to live in the woods, as Seton claims, "as Indians." The book would later appear in more than one of Jim's novels and inspire his lifelong interest in Native Americans.

Besides his prodigious reading, Jim's upbringing in Reed City was largely unremarkable. He went to the movies with friends, played marbles, listened to ball games, participated in 4-H, which Winfield supervised, and attended services with his family at the Congregationalist church. A few blocks from the Harrisons' house, the town maintained two ice rinks in the winter and a sandlot for pickup baseball games in the summer. Jim could fish in the Hersey River or the millpond, and he could easily walk to the end of town where the woods and fields began. More than anything, what set Jim's childhood apart were his visits with his father to local farms, where he'd learn about the private lives of rural Midwesterners as well as new farming practices, which Winfield considered an applied science and his job that of a missionary. Winfield dispensed advice to "farmers in a hopelessly unfertile countryside of jack pine, scrub oak, cedar swamps, and fields where gravel, sand and marl lurked altogether too close to the surface." With lessons derived from the Dust Bowl, Winfield taught crop rotation and terrace and contour planting, and Jim watched his father become part of these people's lives, sometimes in intimate ways. On one of their shared visits, he helped his father deliver a calf. Another time, his father left in the evening to help the family of a farmer who had hanged himself in his barn, a story Jim would borrow years later for *The Road Home*. In the novel, a fourth-generation farmer hangs himself in a barn he no longer owns after his cattle and equipment are sold at a bankruptcy auction.

—

In April 1945, a seven-year-old Jim Harrison walked a long block on Upton Avenue past residential houses to the hospital on the corner. In the parking lot behind the building, Jim played with Mary Jo, a young girl from Saginaw who was then visiting her aunt and uncle in Reed City. As the two set about "playing doctor," Mary Jo struck out at Jim's face with a broken beaker she had picked up from the hospital junk pile. The stab was sudden—the effects permanent. With one sharp shock, the left side of Jim's world disappeared forever. The shards of glass cut into his left cornea, and blood leaked out from his eye. The Harrisons' family friends Dr. David Kilmer and his wife, Vera, lived across the street. Vera, a nurse, immediately recognized the seriousness of the injury.

Why exactly natural curiosity and experimentation turned to violence is unclear. Jim never speculated about the girl's reaction or reasons, but he never forgot the details, like the "mosquito-bite scab on the dirty knee of the little girl," the Major League Baseball standing of the Detroit Tigers ("third place") at the time, and even the fact that Hal Newhouser was starting as pitcher for them that day. On the drive to the doctor's office, his parents' car smelled of fish because he had earlier left a bluegill in the trunk behind a tire. It was his "first sexual experience," or so Jim called it, an incredibly unfortunate one that would leave an indelible mark. And the physical effects of the trauma were clear. At the age of seven, he had lost vision in his left eye, and it would never return. He spent the next two weeks (it felt twice as long to him) in Blodgett Hospital in Grand Rapids. The doctors covered both of his eyes for almost a week to keep him from moving them. He'd later write that for months afterward, "the blind eye shone like a red sun in my head." Winfield and Norma visited often, and they'd bring him pickled herring, the smell of which apparently repelled the nurses. There was at least some good news: no infection was present, and the eye itself would remain intact—a tremendous relief to everyone. But the injury had immeasurable long-term consequences, and it would shape Jim's view of the world and his place in it.

With a damaged eye that would sit askew and angle outward, Jim worried that people would view him differently. Combined with his buckteeth, as he referred to them, a cowlick, and his swarthy complexion, this would lead to a sense of himself as the "one-eyed goofy," a feeling he would never fully shake. Yet the injury afforded him certain advantages, including an outsider's view of things, which he would credit with contributing to his sensitivity as a writer and his motivation to become an artist. He would eventually embrace the disfigurement, so much so that he would build it into a caricature of himself that served as a shorthand signature. But beneath it all, there was also the possibility of a subtler sexual trauma caused by the injury, one Jim never discussed, and one that's freighted with all the complexity of childhood sexual development. The stabbing, whether brought on by fear or anger or both, interrupted his prepubescent experimentation, as Jim would characterize it, in a violent and unforgettable way.

Jim's children's book, *The Boy Who Ran to the Woods*, published in 2000, focuses narrowly on these events and reads like a personal mythology and origin story, complete with the hero's journey. The book identifies the injury and its aftermath as one of the single most formative moments of his life. The character Jimmy spends a month in a hospital far away from home, endures surgery, and has both of his eyes covered for an entire week. Nurses strap him to the bed at night to keep him from wandering. One of the only things that gives the boy comfort is his ability to see the brightness of the moon, a talisman of sorts, with his blinded eye. In the months that follow his discharge, Jimmy becomes "wild and unruly," certain that his peers are staring at him. He refuses to learn to read and "pee[s] on the cloakroom floor" of his school. It isn't until Jimmy undergoes a kind of rebirth through his immersion in the natural world that he begins to truly heal.

Notably absent from *The Boy Who Ran to the Woods* are any adults counseling Jimmy about his trauma or answering his many urgent questions, and he's unable to communicate his pain to them. His parents are understandably exhausted and overwhelmed by the situation. Jimmy eventually returns to school (though he remains "wild at heart") with a renewed interest in himself and the world, but he has developed habits that will stick with him into adulthood, like walking through untracked woods and sitting still to watch the wildlife. This is where his questions are answered. He has also learned that running fast and far away (or driving, as Jim Harrison would later do) is a natural response to feelings of anger, pain, confusion, and claustrophobia—like that of being strapped to a hospital bed in darkness.

The consequences of Mary Jo's simple, violent gesture, Jim would write elsewhere, "were long-range, to use a euphemism."

In the late summer, Winfield's brothers, Arthur and Walter, returned home from the navy and the South Pacific, which allowed Jim to temporarily free his mind from the traumatic events of the previous months. His grandparents threw a big party for them. Even better for Jim, the two brothers helped Winfield build a cabin on nearby Wells Lake (one of the larger ones in the area, at about forty-two acres and more than eighty feet deep in spots). The Kilmer family had gifted the Harrisons the lakeside lot in return for Winfield's having planted white and red pines on their property. The cabin would become a tremendous source of solace for Jim. It was a "very simple cottage" with one room, a loft, no electricity, and an outhouse. Painted white and green like the few others in the area, the Harrisons' cabin was surrounded by trees and perched directly on the shoreline. For the next half dozen years or so, the whole family—including two more children added to the clan, Mary (February 10, 1947) and David (December 3, 1947)—would spend most of their summers there.

The cabin provided Jim with freedoms incomparable to those in town. Behind it stretched a seemingly endless expanse of virtually unpopulated land to explore, about twelve by fourteen miles. Jim rambled about the dunes and oak savannas, over hilly ridges covered by birch, oak, maple, and beech trees, and through the fens and fields where white pine stumps lined old logging roads. When Winfield gave him Audubon cards, Jim searched their subjects out—grouse, woodcock, herons, ravens, bluebirds, kingfishers, loons. It was at the cabin that Jim, along with his brother John and friend David Kilmer, became "expert" swimmers. "They would take the rowboat to the center of smallish Wells Lake," Norma remembered, "and swim over and under 'with time up for air.'" The lake brimmed with largemouth bass, perch, panfish, and rainbow trout, and Jim fished it often. Full of abundance, these were halcyon days for Jim, but such days never last.

On September 15, 1949, the Harrisons relocated to Haslett, Michigan, 130 miles south of Reed City, where Jim would later graduate from high school. Winfield had accepted a position in resource development at nearby Michigan State College.

The move meant that the family found only snatches of time to visit the cabin, and so it marked a goodbye not just to Reed City but to Wells Lake. Soon the summer retreats to the cabin, which Winfield sold to one of his brothers, ended almost entirely. On what is perhaps one of their last trips there, Jim, John, and little Judy posed for a photo: The boys hold a stringer of a dozen perch and panfish. The day is cloudy. Jim wears jeans and a brown shirt with white stripes, and both brothers have crew cuts. Between them, Judy grips the tip of a fish's tail. With his chest puffed out, Jim looks happy and more than a little proud of the catch, staring at the fish instead of the camera. As Jim would write in *The Boy Who Ran to the Woods*, this was "a world where he felt he belonged. And he did."

2

HASLETT

(FALL 1949 – SUMMER 1956)

A little life,
Not much,
But enough,
For our passion.

The Harrisons' new home at 1930 Haslett Road sat on three acres of land, but at roughly 1,200 square feet, it was relatively small for a family of seven. A coal-burning stove in the basement heated the home in winter. Jim shared the upstairs bedroom with John, while David, the youngest, slept in the hallway. Judy and Mary shared a room downstairs next to Winfield and Norma's. There was only one bathroom, a living room, and a small kitchen, where the family spent much of their time. Winfield took advantage of the ample acreage and planted a half-acre garden beside a large wooded marsh behind the house.

Jim struggled with the relocation, which he would later replay in his fiction and autobiographical writings as an "unhealable rupture"—a kind of paradise lost, a move from the Edenic natural world of his childhood to the suburbanizing, middle-class town of Haslett, which was quickly becoming, according to him, a mere extension of the more metropolitan Lansing and East Lansing. The truth was that the area was still very rural—Jim would attend Haslett Rural Agricultural High School, a name that speaks for itself. Yet the move uprooted him at a vulnerable time, separating him at age eleven from close friends; it would prove an easier transition for the younger Judy, Mary, and David. Jim later saw it as a trade-off between the nature surrounding Reed City and the cultural opportunities of nearby East Lansing, since Haslett's proximity afforded him access to a symphony orchestra, theaters showing foreign films, a good bookstore, and because of his father's job, the college library.

For Jim's parents, the change was a good one. Winfield's new job as an extension specialist and the assistant secretary of the state Soil and Water Conservation Committee amounted to a significant promotion. He'd now work with conservation groups throughout the state. Funded by both the college and the United States Department of Agriculture, it was a respected position, especially at a land-grant college that saw agricultural research as part of its mission, and the school integrated him into its faculty as an adjunct assistant professor. It was an astounding success for Winfield. And the job came with the added benefit of securing college educations, or so Winfield and Norma hoped, for their children.

—

Jim Harrison's forebears on his father's side had lived in the United States since the seventeenth century and hailed originally from West Kirby, England, a town about twelve miles from Liverpool. Jim's grandfather, Arthur Harrison, was born in Mecosta County, Michigan, in 1873 and grew up on a farm owned by his parents, Sprague and Mary Harrison.* In his twenties, Arthur—or Carty, as everyone called him—had worked as a head cook for a timber company and, for seven summers, traveled by raft with a crew of men who brought logs downriver. An old photo

* Sprague Harrison, Carty's father, was born in Milwaukee around 1838. During the Civil War, he enlisted with the Seventy-Second New York Volunteer Infantry Regiment and was quickly promoted to sergeant in the Union Army. During a battle at Gettysburg, he was wounded in the thigh. After the war, he packed up his family and moved to Michigan, where he and his wife, Mary Gamage, set up a farm in Mecosta County. On March 20, 1873, Mary gave birth to Carty Harrison. Sprague died of consumption in 1891 at the age of fifty-one.

shows him with a thick mustache and a white chef's apron, surrounded by twenty lumbermen. Carty could be tough and irascible, and he reportedly liked to drink and fight, or so Jim wrote. Others remembered Carty as good-natured and humorous.*

In 1905, Carty married Amanda Diller, known as Mandy, who was twelve years his junior. Mandy's father was a Mennonite from Lancaster, Pennsylvania, and her mother had grown up on a farm in Michigan. After their wedding, Carty and Mandy settled on the forty-acre farm of his parents, and within five years they had two children: Lena (1907) and Jim's father, Winfield (February 4, 1910). Carty's father had died years earlier, and his mother passed a few months after Winfield's birth, which left the farm entirely to the young couple. The farmhouse was quite small, with open bedroom spaces upstairs and a small living room and kitchen downstairs. Despite its size, the family did a lot of entertaining, often hosting suppers and dinners for friends and relatives. They kept cows and chickens and always had a large garden with vegetables and berries. One year they canned more than ninety quarts of blackberries. They also hunted rabbits and fished and bartered for what they needed, as did many of their rural neighbors. Winfield grew up on that farm, and he would carry those experiences with him into his professional life.

By 1920, Carty and Mandy had added three more children to the family—David, Walter, and Arthur—and they would remain on the farm for another fifteen years. By 1935, they decided to give up farming entirely and move into a larger house in Paris, Michigan, where Carty would work as a mail carrier. David Harrison, Jim's brother, remembered the family as a close-knit and boisterous group, though Mandy was known for her moodiness. In later years, Winfield would enjoy visiting with his siblings, and the whole family would often gather together at Wells Lake.

What motivated Winfield to value reading and attend college isn't

* Carty's son, David, never recalled his father getting into fistfights or drinking to excess, and after reading Jim's description of him in *Off to the Side*, wrote to Jim and told him as much.

exactly clear. Books weren't a part of Carty and Mandy's household, and higher education was certainly not common in rural Michigan. "These were hunters and fishers and people who did work for a paycheck and enjoyed living in a rural area," said David Harrison. "I think the quest for education and for a somewhat different life than that probably grew out of [my] father's love for the land." Winfield knew that he wanted to study soil science, and he may have had the idea of working as a county agent in mind from an early age. Coming from a failing farm himself, he may have been attracted by the idea of becoming something like a farm doctor. That he had joined FarmHouse, a fraternal organization of students who shared agricultural backgrounds, reflected his commitment to his roots. He would later serve as president of the Michigan State chapter.

—

Winfield and Norma were the best-educated members of their families and proud, not so much of their accomplishments per se but in their shared confidence that together they'd succeed as a family, an assurance that extended to their children. This involved fostering a climate in the home where education and ideas were honored. Both of them were avid readers: Norma had eclectic tastes and preferred novels, attending to them religiously; Winfield ("widely if erratically read" in general) liked Westerns. During Jim's childhood, the family subscribed to a range of publications, including the *Lansing State Journal*, *Detroit Free Press*, *Life*, *Time*, and *The Christian Century*. Despite their lack of money, they also managed to accumulate a small library's worth of books. In the seventh grade, Jim's brother, David, did a book tour of his house for a class assignment. Some of his classmates were saying, "Well, we have eighteen" books, he remembered. "Our family had more than two thousand." The differences were vast and revealing.

The Harrisons also valued good food, which played an outsized role in the household. For Jim, the future food writer and gourmand, his early experiences at home were formative. Typical meals might include side pork and cornmeal mush, rolled rib roasts, homemade bread, grilled chicken, meatloaf, sauerkraut and sausages, venison, and beef roasts with gravy. Bone marrow was highly prized. Much of it was extremely fresh, and many of the vegetables, picked and prepared seasonally, came directly from Winfield's garden, which was less a hobby than a second job that put food on the table. With his great-uncle Nelse—"a wonderful smelly old bachelor who live[d] in the woods" and drank to excess—and his other Swedish relatives, Jim reportedly ate possum, beaver, raccoon, and of course, herring, salted and fresh. While the quality of the food the family ate didn't necessarily stand out from that of other rural families, the energy the Harrisons gave to it did. Their meals required planning and knowledge, and Jim absorbed these lessons as well as an appreciation of process and of food that came directly from the land.

The Harrison household was traditional in its division of labor. For one thing, Norma did almost all the cooking. When girlfriends and wives visited, they'd help her in the kitchen with the preparation and dishwashing. Norma was almost entirely in charge of the homemaking: She cleaned the house, washed and ironed clothes, and oversaw basic childcare. She did not drive until much later in her life. While she fitted the 1950s mold of a wife and mother in some ways, she broke it in others. She couldn't abide small talk, and she read extensively about politics and other contemporary issues; she'd fearlessly confront people about their own views, particularly those who might be on the other side of an issue. Her interest in conversation and debate harked back to her love of speech and debate in high school and was tied to her Christian faith, which she believed demanded taking informed positions on societal issues. She had high expectations for her children too, and she was particular about how they would spend their time, insisting that it should always be meaningful in some way. Years after Mary Harrison left home, she said her mother's typical telephone sign-off was "Now get to work!" Not "Have a good day" or "Talk to you later," but "Get to work!"

Winfield's role in the home was otherwise conventional for rural families in the Midwest. He was the breadwinner, and he alone made major decisions. Like his father, Carty, he had a clever sense of humor and a facility with language—Jim would later remark that the verbal wit of his father's family, often bawdy, had a strong influence on him. Winfield was nurturing and had, by all accounts of the family, a positive, generous personality. He would support and encourage Jim's interest in writing despite its apparent lack of practicality. Both parents disciplined the children, and although Winfield could get angry at times, he was never severe. Indeed, it would be hard to overestimate his importance to Jim and the entire family. He had a close, loving relationship with all the kids, and his marriage to Norma was loving, steady, and solid. David Harrison remembered him as "the emotional center of the household."

Winfield joined the school board of Haslett High—he'd eventually serve as president—and he led the local Boy Scouts troop. Jim and John were in the Scouts, and Winfield would continue in a leadership position long after Jim dropped out. He imparted his love of hunting and fishing to Jim and John and took them on annual deer-hunting trips in the Upper Peninsula. On the weekends, he would spend the morning in the garden. In the afternoon, after the family purchased a television, he liked to watch the Detroit Tigers, smoke Lucky Strikes, and drink Stroh's beer. He hardly ever drank during the week, and he sometimes joked that he would have been a drinker like his brothers, Walter and Arthur, if he could have ever afforded it. No one in the family drank wine or cocktails, and whiskey was reserved for special occasions.

The Harrisons regularly attended church in Haslett. At first, the family went to the local Baptist church but switched to the newly organized Congregationalist church, which they helped found. Jim and John chose to remain at the Baptist church, mostly for social reasons, since it was by far the best attended and established one in town—attractive girls and friends were there. Winfield and Norma chose the Congregationalist church because it more closely accorded with their understanding of Christianity: Both thought the Baptist church far too severe for their tastes and not sufficiently focused on God's love and social justice. The

Harrisons were New Testament Christians and held liberal beliefs about religion that emphasized forgiveness and tolerance, and they believed that the church should be a font of good works. Norma would become an early and vocal supporter of Martin Luther King Jr., and her politics would become increasingly liberal.

Winfield's interest in the church was based less on faith and a deep belief in God than on the lifestyle of the church and its social programs. He served as church treasurer and believed, like Norma, that it should promote social justice. Norma was intensely curious about theology, as she would be for the rest of her life, and serious about her faith. She read daily devotions every morning and was widely known among local ministers for initiating intellectual discussions with them. Martin Marty, the American Lutheran scholar, was one of her heroes. Her Christianity, while deeply felt, was not overbearing, and she rarely imposed it on her kids, though she held out hope that one of her children might someday become a minister. Jim would certainly come the closest.

Writing to the poetry editor of *The Christian Century* in 2015, Jim recalled the strong presence of religion in his childhood home and how that "religion stuck fast" into his old age and kept "coming up in [his] poems." In the winter of 1951, after claiming to have been saved at a revival meeting, Jim became more serious about religion than anyone in the family, and he would remain spellbound for more than a year. He became president of the Baptist Bible Club, preached at a fundamentalist youth fellowship, won a countywide Bible quiz competition, and vowed to abstain from sex until marriage. The whole affair was a shock to his parents and a sharp departure from their more liberal, civic-minded Protestantism, amounting to a teenage rebellion of sorts. In *True North*, Jim would write that his character David Burkett's religious conversion was driven by a desire to "piss off [his] parents."

By becoming "a Bible-thumping fundamentalist," Jim essentially made an intractable break from his otherwise conventional upbringing and adolescence. He later blamed the religious upheaval on the family's move from Reed City and the tepidity of his life in Haslett. Religious conversion fulfilled for a time his need for ecstasy, and it gave him "actual emotions that were the equivalent of Beethoven's Ninth Symphony." At times, he reported having spiritual visions that came to him during prayer or on the verge of sleep—mystical experiences he attributed to a Christian God.

Jim's attraction to the church had more than a little to do with the devout Caroline Buxton, a pretty girl and Baptist whose father was a minister. Jim would date Buxton off and on until high school. Chuck Roost, the charismatic leader of the local chapter of Youth for Christ, was another attraction to the church. "Everybody loved [Roost]," said Ralph Morr, another attendee of the church. "He knew how to treat young people, and he knew how to get into their inner being." Roost had persuaded Jim to participate more actively, as did Jim's close friend Gary Raymond, who later became a pastor in Grand Rapids. Youth for Christ met at least once a month on Sunday evenings and organized events and outings along with the Haslett Baptist Church, which held retreats at the Christ-centered Camp Barakel in northeast Michigan—Jim sometimes attended these.

—

Jim's years at Haslett Rural Agricultural High School, where many of the students were fellow Baptists, were active ones. He excelled in English, speech, and debate, and he participated in more school-related activities than many of his peers. With a broad chest and strong arms, he played left guard and middle linebacker for the school's football team, the Haslett Vikings; nonetheless, the team ended their season sixth in the conference during his senior year. The team won only one of six games. In his sophomore year, Jim served as class president, and he participated in multiple extracurricular clubs throughout high school. For the Dramatics Club, Jim directed a play, *Drums of Death*. The school described it as "suspense, death and comedy all tied into one terrific package of fun"—a blurb that could apply to any number of Jim's later novels. The fact that Katherine Sgouris supervised the play—she was a popular English teacher, as well as "young and pretty and well built," explained a fellow student—may have persuaded Jim to take the job. Jim would one day write about the play in a letter to actor Harrison Ford, explaining that directing it was "real hard as my leading man couldn't quite read the [script] and sort of made it up as he went along."

Jim was reserved and quiet in school, though his peers thought him "highly confident," "very popular," and "extremely intelligent"—when his name came up among former classmates, the superlatives flew. It was an odd combination, even contradictory. (By contrast, Jim's best friend, Roger Wilson, who lived next door to the Harrisons, was loud and gregarious.) "I did not know anyone who did not like Jim Harrison," recalled Morr. When Jim spent time with fellow student June Marr (not to be confused with Morr), a popular cheerleader, she felt intimidated by his intelligence: "I liked him. A lot. But in a way, I was afraid of him because of his intellect," she said. "I mean, it was readily noticeable to me that he was way above [others] intellectually." (Jim and June's dating status remains unclear, though Jim apparently had strong feelings for her. He reportedly once told a friend that she was the one who got away.) Morr, too, insisted that "[Jim] was head and shoulders above the rest of his classmates—intellectually. Everybody knew that—that was accepted—but he didn't flaunt it. He was just plain smarter than the rest of us."

Jim was also witty: For the graduating class's senior will, Roger Wilson bequeathed his athletic ability to a friend. Jim willed his wisdom to the school's administration.

While Jim read deeply and vigorously on his own, two teachers helped to broaden his reading and encourage his writing. The first, James McClure, was a stylish and popular teacher of social studies who recognized something in Jim right away. A POW in Germany during World War II, McClure introduced him to the writings of social critics and labor leaders like Thorstein Veblen, Walter Reuther, John L. Lewis, and Eugene Debs. The second, Bernice Smith, an English and debate instructor, read Jim's work carefully and seriously, and she helped to bolster his confidence. Like McClure, she recognized Jim's unusual intelligence. The gray-haired Smith was serious and strict—she wore a suit to school every day, which was then atypical—and she seemed older than the other teachers. She was also more educated, with a BA and MA, than most of her colleagues. "I don't know if I ever saw her laugh," remembered Jean Marr, June's twin sister, "maybe a time or two and only with Jim, because they got along so well. I think she felt freer with him—he was more her caliber." Smith introduced Jim to Willa Cather, Trollope, and the English Romantics Keats and Byron—Jim's favorites—and she lent him copies of *The Nation*, *Harper's Magazine*, *The Atlantic*, and *Saturday Review*. He would remember her powerful influence long after leaving her classroom, and the two would remain friends.

In his final term of high school, Jim wrote a lengthy essay on Thomas Wolfe for Smith's second-semester class on American literature. Following a discussion of novels with well-defined literary forms, Jim questioned the tendency of critics to look to form as a measure of a work's success: "Critics are continually harping on form. Is this a logical criteria [*sic*] for judgment? Obviously, no. Life is infinitely formless." It was a telling insight for a future poet who would frequently eschew traditional forms. Besides her frustration with the absence of apostrophes in Jim's paper, Smith wondered, "Maybe we don't have enough perspective to perceive the form or pattern of life."

When Jim's brother David was about fourteen, he found a pamphlet, "The 100 Greatest Books of All Time," in Jim's bedroom. Jim had checked off ninety of them. "He figured if those were the one hundred most important books, by God, he would read them," said David. It demonstrated remarkable drive and ambition. In high school, Jim devoured Walt Whitman, Walter Edmonds, William Faulkner, Erskine Caldwell, John Steinbeck, Sherwood Anderson, and James Joyce as well as Romain Rolland's *Jean-Christophe*, a ten-volume biographical novel, all alongside the New Testament (he "could recite any verse in the Bible," remembered Morr)—wonderful training for a writer.

"I finally realized only last year that writing, or art as I'd just as soon call it, had absorbed the transference of all my religious impulses at age sixteen," Jim told an interviewer in 1985. "Up to sixteen I wanted to be a preacher, and then one day I did a whirlwind: I jumped from Jesus to Keats in three days." Jim would overstate the abruptness of the transition: His religious impulse, even his conservative brand, remained with him well beyond the age of sixteen, but Keats likely prompted the change. So too did his growing interest in classical music and the visual arts, which Norma helped to foster. His mother listened devotedly to classical music and opera on the radio, and Jim and Judy joined along. Jim developed a lifelong appreciation for Beethoven, Grieg, Berlioz, Stravinsky, and Mozart, and he increasingly admired artists like Van Gogh, Gauguin, and Modigliani. The idea of becoming a professional painter would compete in his mind with writing for years to come.

—

During sophomore year, when he was sixteen, Jim grew restless with Haslett and the "pallid and drudgery-ridden confines" of his life. He planned to travel during his summer break and visit what he hoped were exotic locales. He would begin with mountains, he decided, and after misrepresenting his age as eighteen on job applications at several western resorts, landed a job as a busboy at the Stanley Hotel in Estes Park, Colorado. After arriving there by Greyhound bus in June 1954, Jim wrote to his parents on hotel letterhead. He assured them that he was far from homesick and that the hotel was the most beautiful place he'd ever seen. It had four hundred rooms, a swimming pool, horse stables, and "about the nicest looking girls" he had ever seen. A month later, though, he'd grown "quite lonesome for home and church." He hadn't been to church since he arrived, he told them. But he tried to make the best of it. He swam, played tennis, rode horses, and hiked Longs Peak, a nearby mountain with a summit of over fourteen thousand feet (overwhelming for "a flatlander"). He saw Dean Martin and Stan Kenton perform at the hotel; shook hands with Chief Justice Earl

Warren, a guest; traveled to Laramie with a group of friends; and saw "the world's biggest rodeo" complete with "real cowboys" in Cheyenne.

Colorado was a transitional time for Jim, and in letters home, he still frequently mentioned his Baptist faith. In one, he assured his parents that he was being "very thrifty" and avoiding entertainments that included drinking and dancing. He generally kept to himself and roomed with a fellow Baptist. While he corresponded with girls from back home, he discussed his relationships openly with his parents. He had just broken up with a girl named Sue Ann (with whom he had had a "little affair") because he didn't believe in dancing, as she did. He exchanged letters with June Marr and discussed saving money with an eye to getting more serious with her. In this version of events, Jim was the dutiful, observant son, still guided by his faith.

Years later, he described a very different summer. At one point, he reportedly got fired for throwing an egg in the hotel kitchen that hit a cashier and for ordering prime rib—forbidden to staff, who generally ate for free. After apologizing, he was promptly rehired. Later, he threatened the hotel's management with a labor strike and negotiated better food service for his fellow employees. He got into several fistfights and drank a lot of beer. When a bellhop introduced him to a waitress, a college student from St. Louis, she "resolved his virginity," and he prayed afterward for forgiveness. Jim's summer surely fell somewhere between the two accounts.

Jim had also decided to hitchhike back to Michigan ("just for the fun of it" and against his parents' wishes) to better experience the countryside. He departed Colorado in early August, planning to travel through Nebraska, North Dakota, Minnesota, Wisconsin, Michigan's Upper Peninsula, and then south to Lansing. In Nebraska, he reportedly slept in a pasture on the banks of the Platte River, where he was awakened by Hereford calves. In Duluth, when a policeman caught him slipping a blackjack into his boot (he had bought the weapon from Roger Wilson), his adventure ended abruptly. Jim was detained and taken to jail and even interrogated about a robbery. The police, who didn't at first believe he was sixteen, telephoned the Harrison home in Michigan, and Winfield wired money for a bus ticket. It was an unfortunate cap to the summer, and although Jim later explained that it was humiliating having to return home by bus, there was nevertheless some romance and excitement in his brush with the law.

—

When he returned from the West, Jim declared his intention to become a poet. He was now a junior in high school, and his experiences in Colorado had managed to shake him mostly free from the Baptist faith. His parents weren't surprised by his announcement, though the idea of his becoming a poet was quite far outside their range of experience. To his credit, Winfield encouraged his son's ambitions and later purchased a twenty-dollar typewriter for him. Norma, while generally supportive, harbored a range of concerns and worried, as she would continue to do for some time, that Jim would never be able to support himself and a family by writing poems. "Not only did we not know writers," David Harrison explained, speaking of his family, "we didn't know people who knew writers." For Norma, there simply was no recognizable economic model associated with being a writer—much less so a poet. Hers wasn't an unreasonable response for someone who grew up on a marginal farm and came of age during the Great Depression. But her feelings were tempered by her understanding of Jim's willfulness and intensity.

Jim's declaration was soon accompanied by a resolve to travel again, if only briefly, during his summer break in 1955. This time he planned a trip to New York with his friend Randy Scott in his '49 Ford. Before visiting Scott's cousins in Albany—the ruse for the trip—the two made a detour to New York City, where they stayed in a hotel in Greenwich Village, which they both recognized as a bohemian capital and mispronounced as "Green Witch Village." The two stayed at the Hotel Marlton on Eighth Street, and both slept with the same redheaded prostitute. (Jim would later claim that *she* took his virginity, rather than the college girl in Colorado.) Imagining themselves as bohemian artists, like the depictions they'd read of Van Gogh in Irving Stone's *Lust for Life*, they all drank Cognac together (the prostitute humored them and joined in the revelry). "We were more immediately taken with Pierre La Mure's *Moulin Rouge* about Toulouse-Lautrec," Jim would write, "who drank a lot but frequently bedded 'sensual' whores."

They also managed to get out of the hotel room. They visited the Metropolitan Museum of Art and listened to chamber music in Washington Square. Jim would remember the program as Telemann, Buxtehude, and Monteverdi, a delight for the young men, both classical music lovers—the nearby Washington Square Arch evoking Paris and their Lautrec fantasies on a warm summer evening. It was another eye-opening trip for Jim, and more than anything, it left him longing to return to the city. He arranged to go back in just a little over a year's time.

That year, however, his senior year of high school, proved a long and painful one. In the spring of 1956, Jim suffered a deep depression, the first of his life, attended by thoughts of suicide. It followed in the aftermath of a failed operation on his damaged eye in early March, just a few months before graduation. It left Jim in the hospital for several days and cost him and his family almost $1,200 out of pocket, including the money he had saved for a trip to Paris. His parents couldn't afford medical insurance, although it is questionable whether the sketchy procedure would have qualified for coverage. The doctor, a fraud, had assured the Harrisons that, along with the operation, a thick plastic insert—sort of an early version of a contact lens, though huge by today's standards—would return his eye to its pre-injury capabilities and appearance. Following the operation, Jim worked diligently at a series of prescribed eye exercises with the lens and a clunky stereoscope, the latter of which entertained young David and Mary, who would play with it. When the lens failed utterly to restore his sight, Jim tossed it into the marsh behind his house. It was a plot fit for a Flannery O'Connor story—full of the grotesque, gothic, and absurd—and a crushing blow to Jim that was made even more devastating by the hope it had engendered. He would later revisit the experience at the beginning of his poem "Sketch for a Job-Application Blank," where he would depict the doctor as a kind of traveling snake-oil salesman peddling false promises and gore: "My left eye is blind and jogs like / a milky sparrow in its socket," he'd begin the poem. Jim's friends had called him "pig eye," and he feared "the salesman of eyes, / his case was full of fishy baubles, / against black velvet, jeweled gore."

During the summer after his graduation, Jim Harrison, still angry and reeling from the letdown over his eye, made his first foray into the world of publishing. In July 1956 he wrote a letter to John Ciardi, the poet and poetry editor of the *Saturday Review*. The impetus for his letter came from an article Ciardi had written for the same magazine, "Poverty on Parnassus: The Economics of Poetry," in which he argued that the reliance of poets on universities for financial support was productive and necessary. According to Ciardi, contemporary poets were already deeply embedded within higher education, and after endorsing this relationship, he dismissed calls that poets should get out into the real world as silly: "Thus, exhorters of the spirit will be heard crying: 'Go out and swing a pick! Or go sell groceries! Or go drive a truck! But get out where life is!'" The trick to survival for a university poet, he explained, was to "resist being swallowed up" by the institution's orthodoxies.

Ciardi's article so rankled Jim, just eighteen years old, that he felt compelled to respond. Almost immediately after the article's publication, Jim sent a blunt, handwritten letter that began simply, "Your article was depressing."

> The discouraging point is that a so-called poet follows a vogue instead of the nature of his emotions. Those that would follow in obeisant awe their obscure or simple predecessors deserve their inevitable destiny; that of forgotten copyists writing

> in periodicals published in a situation similar to a tax write off . . . They are poets only to undergraduates and fools.

Jim's letter, while vehement, wasn't necessarily responsive to Ciardi's claims, though it adequately conveyed his distaste for them and for academic poets. It also showed Jim beginning to articulate his ideas about what a poet is or should be. Poets err if they follow the popular trends in poetry, ones promoted and perpetuated at the universities, instead of pursuing a singular examination of what Ciardi had called "those irrationalities we call the emotions." What Jim found most depressing was likely Ciardi's challenge to Jim's romantic ideas about the life of a poet.

Jim's position wasn't merely impulsive intolerance or a one-time outburst but rather an early expression of a conviction he'd hold for the rest of his life—that poets should get out into the world. Arguably to his professional detriment, the writer Jim Harrison would rail against academia and MFA programs, which he considered harmfully insular, the latter akin to "Ford Motor Plants." Better to work as a "truck driver, a proctologist, a stripper, a dishwasher, a furrier, a cowboy, an unlicensed plumber," and so on, he would later write. An ideal writing program, he once told an interviewer, should "require one year of manual labor in the country; one year of life in the city; one year of life spent reading, and only then would anyone return and begin writing. How else would anyone know anything?"

Ciardi was kind enough to reply to Jim's letter. He acknowledged the young man's "strong opinions," asked if he weren't being unnecessarily harsh, and then cautioned him about being too readily dismissive of other poets: "The fact is that our best poets have in fact stayed close to the universities while turning out good poems. The abuses of some are certainly not the destruction of all nor are they an open license to attack all."

In a follow-up letter to Ciardi, Jim dropped his argument entirely. Apparently stunned that Ciardi had written back at all, and sensing an opportunity, he admitted that his previous letter was a product of youth

("I am eighteen") and, hoping for publication, included a poem of his own, "The Existentialist," inspired by Sartre and Kierkegaard. Ciardi declined to publish it, and Jim never forgot it. Many years later, he would describe Ciardi as part of "the tweed school" of university poets, a "very catty bunch." As Jim prepared to attend Michigan State University that fall as an aspiring writer, his convictions about proper occupations for poets did not bode well for his own academic success.

3

ON THE ROAD
(FALL 1956 – FALL 1958)

Hot, hungry, eighteen and reading
Lorca's Poet in New York.
. . . .
I walked three months
until my soles became paper and
I finally understood Poet in New York.
Homesick, I went home and worked on a farm.
Homesick, he went home and got murdered.

On a morning in late September 1956, a passerby might have seen Jim Harrison standing outside a pleasant four-story building with red brick facing and Lake Superior sandstone at its base. The neoclassical building, known as Morrill Hall, housed the liberal arts division of the Michigan State University of Agricultural and Applied Science, as it was then named. The Religious Studies Department occupied the first floor, English the second, and History the third. Jim would have passed the fountain in the courtyard, climbed the wide steps to a portico framed by Doric columns, and walked the broad hallways, trimmed in dark wood and lined with benches, to his first college class. Jim's brother John had just returned to the university after a stint in the navy, and his arrival on campus, combined with Jim's, was an important milestone for the boys' parents. But Jim felt little of the magic and excitement likely shared by other freshmen on the first day of school. His years in college would not be a love story.

He began by declaring a major in art history, in part because he enjoyed sitting in the dark and viewing slides of paintings and places he wanted to visit, though he would eventually change it to English. He preferred the art students because they "had a lively wildness to them not shared by students of literature who mostly planned to be schoolteachers except for a few aspiring writers who were mostly drunk on a daily basis." He also liked the prefabricated steel Quonset huts that then housed the art department and the classrooms' "rich stew of oil paints" and abundant easels. In his first quarter, he enrolled in a whopping twenty-two credits' worth of classes, almost twice the load of a typical full-time student: among others, "Introduction to Prose Fiction," "Survey of English Literature," "History of European Art," and "Conversational French" as well as physical education classes, such as "Individual Tumbling," "Track and Field Activity," and "Advanced Swimming"—he was already an exceptional swimmer from his summers at the lake. Overall, his grades were mixed, mostly Bs, although he received a D in Natural Science during the winter term before retaking and finally failing the class in the spring. Before the end of his freshman year in 1957, just prior to final exams, he resigned from his job at the university library and dropped out of college entirely. He was nineteen years old.

Quitting school was the first of several such breaks he would make with MSU, and it marked the beginning of a string of uncertain, convulsive years for him. His depression had worsened and refused to let up, as he revealed to his parents that he not only hated the university but himself "for not feeling good about living." His reaction to his freshman year highlighted just how much things had changed for him. The former class president of his high school vehemently rejected formal education and, specifically, the institution that employed his father. For starters, aside from the Art Department, he disliked the campus itself with its institutional feel, including plastic tile floors and rooms painted beige and pale green, as he remembered it, like a "mental torture barracks."

He wanted to become a poet, and poets, in his mind, as he had made clear to John Ciardi months earlier, should avoid academia and get out into the world. He "couldn't stand college," he later reflected. "Of all the writers I admired, like Sherwood Anderson, Faulkner, Hemingway, I didn't notice any BA's attached to their names, you know? None. Hart Crane, Rimbaud, García Lorca. Where are the BA's?" By comparison with his experiences the previous summer in New York City, college in the Midwest felt cloistered and suffocating, and he feared that it meant "sitting inside insides," as a friend had phrased it. "Stay in your fool proof college study. Don't meet too many people or life may become too complex." It was the "inside insides" that Jim desperately wanted to avoid.

In late June, Jim packed a handful of his things: a stack of volumes wrapped in cardboard and bound with rope; a few changes of clothing; a pre-tied tie, compliments of his father; and about fifty dollars split between his sock and wallet as a hedge against theft, and he hitchhiked the nearly seven hundred miles to New York City, where he rented a room on Valentine Avenue in the Bronx—that it was near the Edgar Allan Poe cottage gave it a literary feel, though he quickly realized it wasn't exactly "the center of cosmopolitan activity." When he wasn't riding the D train or trekking by foot to Manhattan, he sometimes babysat for an older waitress down the hallway who turned tricks. "She was blond and frowsy and chain-smoked," as he described her in *Wolf: A False Memoir*, an explicitly autobiographical novel and the fruit of his travels from these years. She once offered to lay him for ten dollars, but he had to decline. "What are you, queer?" she carped. He was just broke. Several weeks later, he moved to 21 Grove Street, a brick building between Hudson Street and Seventh Avenue in the Village. It was a dingy place worthy of a Dostoevsky novel: dark, no windows, and cockroaches, which, as he informed his parents, are sensitive to light. While money remained an ever-present concern for him, he found a job as a car wash attendant and then as a clerk at Marboro Books, a discount store on Forty-Second Street. While the job allowed him easy access to books, he hated it—the cheapness of the store offended him. "No more than a supermarket for trash," he wrote home. "Always some preposterous sale going on."

He did little writing that summer and had no idea where to begin, but he read night and day—he would gain a meaningful education on his own, without school—and enjoyed the more affordable entertainments of the city, like walking and people-watching. He read the Italian poets Giuseppe Ungaretti and Gaspara Stampa; the French writers Paul Valéry, Louis-Ferdinand Céline, and Arthur Rimbaud; Aldous Huxley, Hart Crane, Rainer Maria Rilke; and the Russians Ivan Turgenev, Nikolai Gogol, Aleksandr Blok, and Sergei Yesenin. He immersed himself in James Joyce and "drowned" in *Finnegans Wake*, a book he likened to "a vast night ocean." As he would later phrase it, he was "quite drunk with language," and more than a little of his oversized determination to educate himself came from a sense that, as an aspiring "future great poet," he needed to somehow compensate for his rural Midwest upbringing. And so by reading voraciously and through disciplined writing, he thought, he would defy some people's perceptions of him as merely a "yokel, a clyde," as he'd write in *Wolf*, whose skin was "the color of cocoa from working on construction." Few things made him angrier than condescension.

Even at that point, Jim's sheer intellectual force ruled out "yokel" and "clyde" entirely, but he was still something of a country mouse in the big city. This was the first time he had lived in one. He was fascinated and felt "good about being in a place so huge and interesting." He learned from an Italian neighbor how to make real marinara sauce with garlic and herbs, a relatively exotic dish—many Americans still equated Italian food with Chef Boyardee. He flirted with politics, attending meetings of the Young Progressive Socialists, and reportedly signed up to fight with Fidel Castro and Che Guevara in Oriente Province but was rejected as an "obviously daft *poet*." Art rather than politics was his priority, and he would discount his motives by noting the presence of "free donuts [and] radical ladies" at the meetings. Nights he walked the empty streets of the Financial District and the East and West Side waterfronts—his watch and money left in his room—and he relished the diversity of the city. "I am not especially looking for 'congenial' people," he once corrected his parents. "I am interested in seeing people, all different kinds." In Greenwich Village, he was surrounded by "millions of Jews and Italians. In a sense I feel invisible as no one seems to notice me. I enjoy that part." Such anonymity, wherein Jim could simply observe the world unnoticed, was unheard of in Haslett.

He also fell in love with Billie Meisner, a pale-skinned red-haired Jewish girl from the Bronx. Meisner had recently graduated from New York's High School of Music & Art, a public school in the Hamilton Heights neighborhood of Harlem, which, along with its Gothic Revival building known as "the Castle" and specialization in visual and performing arts, could not have been more different from Haslett High. Nor was Meisner like the girls from Jim's hometown. She was a handsome girl with poise and a confident countenance. For her senior yearbook quote, she chose one from the Danish philosopher Søren Kierkegaard: "Put me in a system and you negate me—I am not just a mathematical symbol—I am." "She is undoubtedly one of the brightest girls I have ever met," he rhapsodized in a letter to home, "and one of the most profoundly moral beings I have ever known." The two had apparently met at a concert in Washington Square, or so Jim later explained, and they spent nearly all of their time together that summer. "I am getting involved but I do not care as I feel very deeply about her."

In *Wolf*, Jim would lightly fictionalize Meisner as "Laurie" and recount their first meeting, though in the novel they meet in Bryant Park behind the library, where he bought a sandwich during his lunch hour:

> First three doubles at a White Rose on Sixth then a sandwich in the park. I was reading Henry Miller's biography of Rimbaud and she was with a group of a half dozen young people who were obviously what the press like to call 'beatniks.' She came up to me and said directly into my face, 'I've read that book.'
>
> I was so startled I couldn't answer. She was very pretty and you usually have to approach pretty girls, they don't approach you.

While *Wolf* takes liberties with facts, the character Laurie accords closely with Meisner. Like Meisner, Laurie is bold, smart, and uninhibited. Laurie invites the protagonist, Swanson, a stand-in for Jim, to Central Park, while he talks with her friends about Henry Miller, Céline, and Jack Kerouac. If Meisner, like Laurie, had read Henry Miller's book *The Time of the Assassins: A Study of Rimbaud*, the fact would have impressed Jim mightily, as did Meisner's fluency in French. Although she was younger than Jim by a year, he thought her "way ahead of [him] intellectually."

Meisner was a sophisticated and apt companion for Jim, and they met at a time when he really needed company. With little money between them, the two made seemingly endless trips to "everything that was cheap." They visited the Metropolitan Museum of Art, the Cloisters, and the Museum of Modern Art, where they saw a Picasso exhibition, as Jim wrote home to Judy, who, more than anyone else in the family, shared his interest in art. "It was wonderful. Also saw Van Gogh's Starry Night[.] Originals of course—also Gauguin, Modigliani, Pollock and many others." That he pointed out they were originals spoke both to how special it was for him to see the paintings and the distance he had come from the dark rooms and slide projectors at MSU, the "inside insides." One night, the couple attended Bertolt Brecht's *Threepenny Opera* at the Theater de Lys in the West Village. Another night, they dined on smorgasbord at a Finnish restaurant. And they shared sexual adventures: The two made love against Cleopatra's Needle in Central Park and on benches and behind rocks and in the grass on the Great Lawn.

Meisner was one of only a handful of Jewish people Jim had ever met and the first Jewish woman he had dated. In letters home, he struggled to describe her background, writing that "she is Jewish not Orthodox though, so I suppose one should rightly say she is Hebrew." The Meisner family was less than happy with Jim, mostly because he was not Jewish and looked like a "shabby beatnik." After months in New York, by his own admission, he looked bedraggled: His clothes were dirty and stained, his hair had grown long, and he was unusually skinny, down to 135 pounds on his five-foot-ten-inch frame. On top of that, his nerves were "completely shot" from drinking ten to fifteen cups of coffee a day. Meisner's grandmother expressed her disapproval openly and spoke only Yiddish when he visited the family's Bronx home. At the end of the summer, the couple decided to break things off, though they would stay in touch. While Meisner planned to attend Barnard College in the fall, Jim's plans were still uncertain.

Winfield and Norma were understandably concerned about Jim's decision to abruptly abandon college and live like a bohemian. Almost every letter between them included some mention of the issue. For Jim's part, his letters often mixed contempt or indifference for school with vague reassurances. In one, he upbraided his parents for somehow suggesting that his homesickness extended to missing the university: "Do not be so absurd as to ~~equa~~ mention MSU. I will attend, but I am coming home because I wish to be with my family. I do not equate organizations with people." In another, he alluded to how his travels had helped him temperamentally: "I think you shall find me more sufferable or even tolerable." (Given his sometimes condescending tone, his parents must have hoped for this outcome.) "I can't say I am especially concerned," he wrote of his poor grades. "I am only concerned with displeasing you and I was hurt in learning that papa was that dissatisfied. Please don't make any more references to escaping the 'parental thumb.' I would rather be with my parents than anywhere else." At other times, he seemed less certain of his bearings and agreed to return home and resume his studies. While he insisted that he wouldn't attend school if he lost his scholarship, because "paying the place seems preposterous," in yet another letter he vowed to make a new start: "I shall try to compensate for the work I have missed when I arrive. I intend to regularize my study habits a bit and show you a Harrison performing. As for the past—~~my~~ all issues are dead."

Jim kept his promise and returned home in time for school that year, but his issues were not dead. MSU had reinstated his tuition scholarship, and he reenrolled as a full-time student in the fall of 1957. He finished the quarter, completing eighteen credits and classes in elementary Italian and the humanities, and he finally passed Natural Science. But before the winter quarter began, he dropped out and hit the road once again.

This time, Jim hitchhiked to Boston, which he had heard was the "St. Petersburg of the United States" and thus sufficiently literary, with the hopes of writing and publishing. He rented a room in nearby Waltham and then a dingy, cold room on St. Botolph Street, a few blocks from the Boston Public Library, where he read Dostoevsky for weeks on end. He took a job at the Prince Spaghetti House in the city's North End, and although the cooks treated him to Neapolitan specialties, he despised the job and generally disliked Boston. He squabbled with the waitresses and made little money. In *Wolf*, he'd write that his room was so ill-heated that he wore his father's overcoat for an entire month and even to bed. He paid about five dollars a week for the place. The wino next door, as he referred to him, pissed out the window to avoid walking downstairs to the toilet. It was all miserable but literary and bohemian in its squalor and reminiscent of Jack London's *The Road* or Orwell's *Down and Out in Paris and London*. He was earning his stripes and learning something about urban hardship and poverty, unique from that of the rural farmers he knew growing up.

Despite his efforts, Jim struggled to put words to the page, and he was very anxious to publish, a pressure that, at that point in his development, couldn't have helped the writing. Doing so would almost certainly have helped validate his questionable choices to his parents—and to himself. Perhaps he could manage to live like Kerouac or Miller or London, but could he write? His work schedule and commute kept him busier than he had imagined, and he sought to reassure his parents that he wasn't wasting his time. He worked on his writing for at least six hours one day, he recorded in one letter, but his writing journals from the time remained mostly empty, and he feared—even worse—that he might have nothing to say.

His efforts would have other payoffs. He worked at his craft, read actively with an eye to the stylistic and formal aspects of literature, and rehearsed what would become his own writing process—the daily routines, the physical and mental labor of it, the sustained exertions of imaginative energy. It was important, necessary work, undertaken alone and without the benefit of mentorship and reassurances. With little explanation, he had also shifted his focus from poetry to fiction. He had begun work on a novel and some short stories (none of which now survive), and he strategized about how to get his work into print. "My story is completely ready to be sent, all I lack is the 50 cents for two manila envelopes and postage," he explained. "I have another story almost ready. I want to get several circulating at once so I'll have a better chance at getting something published. I never thought that the lack of 50 cents would delay my entrance into the American literary scene."

His parents occasionally sent money and care packages to help, and despite assurances from Jim that he felt very well mentally—with no self-analysis or despair, as he told them—they were concerned for their son's future and emotional well-being. Winfield had been more tolerant of his travels than Norma and even a bit envious, but he worried about his son. In February, he penned a letter urging Jim to reconsider his current plans and return to Michigan. He offered "wisdom based on experience" and asked him to use his "extra fine intellect" to some purpose, even "some lesser goal at least temporarily until you were better prepared." He continued:

> Years ago you said "don't tell me what to do & what not to do—let me find out for myself." So I have, within reason accepted your statement. I have had no reason to regret it. I have never attempted to direct, at least very forcibly either John or you. I do get concerned however by the tone of your letters, both now and when you were in New York. I wouldn't expect to hear that you are terribly happy in ~~New York~~ Boston. After all you don't know exactly what you are looking for do you[?]

The letter is an excellent example of Winfield's parenting style—suggestive, light-handed, loving, humorous. That Winfield rarely wrote letters to Jim without Norma or the family joining in emphasized this one's importance. He feared that Jim was stuck and making little progress toward any goal, and he recommended that he do something—anything—to better set himself up for the future: "And that something could be digging ditches, carpentry, going to college etc." At some point, he reminded Jim, with some fatherly foresight, "a dame will enter [your] life that will really send [you]. That will mean that [you] should be prepared to marry, support her & all that comes with marriage."

Jim had plenty of his own misgivings, and Winfield's letter rattled him even further at a vulnerable time. On a snowy morning, he replied ("Dear Dad") that he had reread the letter for the eleventh time, and he felt sure that his father was right. He admitted that he actually had less time now for his writing than he had had at home—at most two hours a day, and less as he got tired. "If I had wanted to write as bad as I thought I did," he confessed, "I could have written last fall while I was not studying. I neither studied nor wrote, just generally sat on my ass. I am saying all of this as recently I have abandoned some of my grandiose conceptions of myself." Jim *was* floundering, as Winfield suspected, and his candor to his father suggested that he wasn't simply humoring him. He acknowledged that he hoped to get married in three or four years, and he promised to return in six or seven weeks, save money, pay off debts, and attend summer school.

His resolve didn't last long, however. Instead of returning home, Jim went back to New York City. Norma was furious; Winfield stayed silent, which was perhaps worse, as Jim wished for something from him, "even if it wasn't condonement." But he wasn't apologetic either. He loathed Boston, he explained to his parents, wanted to see O'Neill's *Long Day's Journey into Night*, playing on Broadway for one last month, and he missed Billie Meisner, who was on his mind and in his letters. Most of all, he wanted to wander more and work out his restlessness, at least temporarily, so he could have the patience to go back to school and earn a degree, or so he told them. Remaining in New York also bought him more time for writing, at least without the hassle of school, but whether it was put to use is questionable. And then, returning to Haslett—studying, living at home with room and board—would amount to an admission of failure.

That March, Jim hitchhiked to New York City with a friend he had met in Boston, Peter Snyder, and he rented a place on MacDougal Street, a twelve-by-seven room with a kitchen and a genuine rathole in the corner (or so he claimed), where he pinned two pictures to the wall—Rimbaud and Dostoevsky (poetry and fiction, the two sides of him that would never go away). His first days back in the city were lean ones. He pawned his watch, sold his field jacket to Snyder, and ate nothing but cheese and salami sandwiches for a week, but he made good on some of his promises. He got a job at Brentano's, a fashionable bookstore on Fifth Avenue ("awfully snobbish"), and he drank at the Five Spot Café, a renowned jazz club in the Bowery, where he twice hung out with Jack Kerouac ("the first actual novelist I had ever met"). Kerouac's *On the Road* had been published six months earlier, and the then famous author was hopelessly drunk and wearing a rumpled corduroy suit jacket. At the Met, Jim viewed an exhibition of Winston Churchill's paintings—he didn't think much of them—and, with money from his new job, practiced cooking. Notably, he had begun describing his meals with the detail and gusto that would characterize his later food writing. "I am developing into an excellent cook!" he announced in a letter to his family. "I just finished a meal of ronzoni, italian style rigatoni 27, made of enriched durum wheat, high protein no. 1 semolina macaroni with buitoni meat beef sauce, harrison bread and ballantine beer." The bread was sent to him from home.

The return to the city provided him with a fresh start, and he was committed to writing as much as possible. He would work at a job for about thirty hours a week and try to discipline himself into using the remainder of the time for writing. If he didn't have at least two hundred pages of a novel written or a short story published by summer's end, he assured Winfield that he would return to school. It was a good plan in theory, but Meisner tended to draw him away from his work, and he wound up spending many days walking the city with her instead of writing. He also hadn't counted on a string of inevitable rejections from his submissions. "I am sick of trying to write a salable short story," he griped in one letter to home, but he remained remarkably undeterred, even defiant. In the same letter, he added a bold postscript, a quotation, slightly paraphrased, from William Faulkner: "A writer's sole responsibility is to his art." It was like the planting of a flag, and it contrasted sharply with his disappointment. And it was also a maxim that would seemingly guide his conduct, perhaps more than any other, for decades to come. Few principles would wind up defining Jim Harrison, for better and for worse, more than this one.

Jim would eventually shape his world around that sentiment—an unwavering commitment to his art above all else—but even then, back in New York, it did not go unchallenged. Jim spent a lot of time in the city with Snyder, a student at Yale and an aspiring poet, whose father (Jim bragged to his sister Mary) published *The Atlantic*. Jim had become close with both Snyder and his girlfriend, Carol, whom Snyder would marry in April after the couple returned to Boston. Jim and Snyder would regularly discuss art and literature (writers like Hesse, Pound, Lawrence, and Camus, who had appeared on the cover of *The Atlantic* that May), and over the coming months, they would debate the role of the artist vis-à-vis his work. Snyder thought that Jim was "much too IDEALISTIC regarding that only important relationship, i.e., between yourself and your art." On this point, Snyder worried for Jim, and he told him as much:

> Still, I cannot value the expression of him whose sole occupation is his Art, over and above his Life. And I think there IS this distinction and that you make it, subconsciously. And I think that you have a far more terrible force against you than mediocrity and this is the possibility of isolation, abnormality,

> unnatural and un<u>real</u> perspective. Shitty neuroses. Hell. nuf, nuf, nuf!!!

Jim's reply to Snyder is lost to time, but Snyder's note is revealing. Jim's view of the writer's life as subordinated to (or inseparable from) the work resembled his earlier impulse to give himself over completely to the Baptist faith. From early on, Jim inclined toward intensity and extremes, and his great fear was mediocrity. Snyder chalked it up to Jim's age and his romantic aspirations and thought he'd grow out of it.

Within a month, Jim's relationship with Meisner had mostly ended, though the two kept the door open for a possible future together. When Jim had first arrived in the city, they had spent nearly every day together, and she helped to lift his spirits ("I would be very morose now if it were not for her," he had told his parents), but both felt that there were strong forces working against them; for one, Jim had committed to his parents to return home to Michigan. Jim's romantic relationship with Meisner was the most important one he had had to this point in his life, and their separation hurt him deeply. In *Wolf*, Swanson admits to feeling "overwhelmed with love for [Laurie]," a feeling that Jim surely felt for Meisner and one he never fully admitted to his parents. Swanson even talks of marrying Laurie, and toward the conclusion of the novel, just before he leaves for Michigan, he promises to return to do just that. Jim had promised Meisner that he would return to New York City at Christmastime, but the two would never see each other again. In one of her last letters to him, Meisner asked Jim to explain what had happened between them, adding only, "I feel as though I am writing to 'the Dead.'"

By the beginning of April, Jim had fallen into a serious funk, and if it was not exactly the "terrible force" that Snyder had warned him about, it seemed nonetheless inescapable. On March 31, Carol, Snyder's fiancée, recognized a serious sadness in Jim, and she was alarmed enough to plan a trip from Boston to New York to see him, arranging a visit at Brentano's on the following Saturday: "Would like to talk to you, Jim, and have you talk to me, please." A day later, Snyder wrote and expressed deep concern for Jim's well-being. He thought it better for Carol to see Jim alone, and he urged him

> to be perfectly honest with her and with me. You must realize that the three of us are infinitely bound up with something or other and that you are terribly important to both of us as a person . . . We simply must know what the problem is—<u>whatever</u> it is, whether it concerns us (Carol and me) or whatever . . . Simply, if you can talk about it we want you to, terribly.

Whatever "it" was that troubled Jim went unexplained, but it almost certainly involved his breakup and a subsequent deep depression. The meeting with Carol never happened—Jim had left the city before she arrived—and he was evidently not doing well. In one letter home, he complained of growing "more morose and inward every day," and in another, he admitted to feeling "quite homesick," adding that his health was not good. He confessed to having recently lost "full possession of my reasoning powers." The dislocation and time away from family had almost certainly worn on him, as had the flophouse rooms, heavy drinking, busted relationships, and perhaps most of all, the feeling of failure regarding his writing. He was heading home with little to show for his time, nothing tangible that would impress his family and friends, and the upheaval he had made of his life the previous year. As he wrote to his parents, he hoped and trusted that "I am, as one of your sons, still welcome."

When he returned to Haslett, Jim reportedly slept away most of the days that summer before eventually reenrolling for the fall semester at MSU. He would not drop out again, nor miss another semester, though in the coming months his life would change in momentous ways. That fall, Jim met Linda May King, a girl from East Lansing, who really sent him, as his father had predicted, and she came into his life sooner than anyone had expected. In just a little over a year, the two would be married, with a child on the way.

4

SOMETHING TO TIE ME TO EARTH

(FALL 1958 – FALL 1962)

The boy followed the girl to school eating his heart with each step. He wished to dance with her beside a lake, the wind showing the leaves' silvery undersides . . .

Jim first saw Linda King standing outside of her parents' suburban home on an affluent street in East Lansing. An avid horse rider, she wore jodhpurs and hit a riding crop against her leg as she waited for a ride to a nearby stable. It was 1954, and Jim wouldn't forget that image of her. He'd remember it four years later when the two met again at a party and started dating. He had just returned from New York and still had Billie Meisner on his mind, but not for long. Linda was seventeen, two years younger than Jim, intelligent, attractive, with shoulder-length brown hair, curled bangs, and shrewd, enigmatic brown eyes, like a young Natalie Wood. Linda would later joke that what really caught Jim's attention was her 1956 Sunliner, a robin's-egg-blue-and-white Ford Fairlane convertible: "He was only attracted to my car," she'd tell friends. But the attraction was all her.

Jim, for his part, was handsome and intense, and the two "just really, really fell in love," said their daughter, Jamie Harrison. They would love each other "with the desperation one is capable of only once in a lifetime, a childhood version of *Wuthering Heights*," as Jim would write of one of his fictional characters. Linda easily played Catherine to Jim's young Heathcliff: Linda, poised and introspective, came from a well-to-do family; Jim was wildly intelligent, dark complexioned, ungovernable, mostly broke, and more comfortable on the moors than in parlor rooms.

Throughout his life, Jim would stay uncharacteristically tight lipped about his courtship of Linda and their marriage. He would casually fill dozens of magazine articles and essays with manifold details of his life, but what he publicly said or wrote about Linda would hardly take up a single page. She was the private part of his life—a part few would ever get to know. He once declined to answer an interviewer's questions about their relationship, responding only that "marriage is, and should be, a mystery to all but the two in it," a feeling Linda shared. She was an intensely guarded and private person and could be aloof, but once she got to know and like someone, she became warm, welcoming, and even confiding. Later television shows and documentaries featuring Jim Harrison would show only fleeting glimpses of her, usually cooking or dining with Jim but never examined. When Jim would travel to Los Angeles, New York, Paris, or around the country for book tours, Linda chose to stay at home, far from Jim's public light. A note in a letter from Jim to Tom McGuane in 1984, offered without further context or commentary, would concisely sum it up:

Journalist – "We'd like to have a photo of you with Jim."
Linda – "No."

Linda May King grew up in a prosperous middle-class family that, while not wealthy, could afford to give their daughter—their only child—a car like the Sunliner. Linda's father, William "Bill" Ludlow King, a slender, handsome man with sandy gray hair and a professorial air about him, had long worked for the state of Michigan and directed its Transportation Division. Friends remembered being impressed with how Linda and the Kings would sometimes get chauffeured about by the state police and, although Bill King reputedly avoided graft, by the fact that Jimmy Hoffa would send extravagant gift baskets to the family at Christmastime. Bill King's was a relatively well-paid and prestigious position, and the family were active members of the community.

The family's standing and wealth (or what was left of it; the King family would lose much of their money in the Great Crash) originated a few generations back. Bill King, who had graduated from Dartmouth College in 1933, hailed from a well-to-do northern Michigan family. Photos of his father, Harry King, who had himself grown up with money and managed to make even more of it in the insurance business, show him posing with chauffeurs and fancy cars. But the family fortune came from William Alfred Ludlow, Linda's great-grandfather, a Cornish immigrant who had made his money in the mining business—this Ludlow would partly inspire Jim's "Legends of the Fall."

Linda had a strong, loving relationship with her father, who "really was a wonderful person," as Jamie remembered him. He was patient and polite and tended to put people at ease. He was also reserved, clever, humorous, and part of the country club set and, as an old-school Republican, despised unions (despite the gift baskets from Hoffa). Jim would describe Bill King fondly as "essentially a kind man whom I always thought of as 'the last gentleman.'" A friend of the family, Penny McClure, knew that Linda adored her father. He was "very kind and very supportive" and "loved Linda to death." Linda's relationship with her mother, Margery (Moulton) King, was a different story. Margery, "Mimi" to her grandkids, grew up in Menominee in the Upper Peninsula, had three sisters, and lost her father to a car wreck at age sixteen. She was smart, very pretty, fantastically charming at times, and plagued by mental illness. Throughout Linda's childhood, Margery suffered frequent breakdowns. She was often hospitalized in asylums, sometimes for many months, and subjected to shock treatments. Margery was also a "really, really difficult woman," Jamie clarified, lest there be any doubt. She quarreled intensely (and unreasonably) with her husband and daughter, and she was apt to make off-color remarks about Jews and Black people. She could be an assortment of waspy, snobby, snooty, emotionally abusive, and horribly bigoted.

—

When Jim connected with Linda in the spring of 1958, she was set to begin her sophomore year that fall at Stephens College in Columbia, Missouri, the second-oldest women's college in the country—and one that offered her plenty of opportunities for horse riding. Although many of her friends had opted either not to go to college or to attend ones closer to home, Linda's decision to go to Stephens had provided her with much-needed distance from her mother, but it now also put distance between her and Jim—after they had grown very close very quickly, having spent all their time together during the lazy summer months. In *Wuthering Heights* fashion, the separation was agonizing, and their torment played out in letters.

"I wish that you would ask me some of the things you would like to know," Jim wrote to Linda that October. "You mentioned this in the letter I got today and it makes me feel helpless, as I am not able to see you and you do not ask." Lest his feelings for her and about their relationship be "some of the things," he proceeded to tell her:

> I remember when I thought it weakness to love to a degree where I considered it impossible to change . . . Now that this has happened and happened is the right word as I did not cause it in myself but rather fought it, it makes me feel stronger instead of the expected weaker because I know I cannot live alone like I thought I could; strong in the sense that when we know we feel the same for each other we are more than two persons because we are then complete.

Jim's attitudes had shifted in only months, since the spring when Peter Snyder had warned him that he was at risk of isolation. But Jim still looked to give himself over to something larger than himself, and he found it, in part, in Linda—the "union of more than two persons." And Linda felt the same way for reasons emerging from her own family, as Jim would later write, like her incredibly difficult mother. "I believe Linda needs this closeness as much as I."

—

With Linda seven hundred miles away, Jim rededicated himself to school, as he had promised his parents, and for the next three quarters undertook a systematized study of literature, completing five surveys and classes in comparative literature, essay writing, and the humanities. He took his second of two dance classes, Beginning Contemporary Dance—a seemingly unlikely activity for Jim, at least at the time, that emphasized fluid movements of the body. (In fact, Jim had grown to like dancing, and it would come to factor heavily in his later fiction as a physical manifestation of joy and fluidity.) For his capstone project, Jim reportedly choreographed his own dance to Stravinsky's *Firebird* suite. His grades improved, and he became resigned to the idea of completing his college degree, if only to appease his parents. "School is a necessary evil, I guess," he'd write to them. "Maybe not even evil as in remembrance I've found that the past year was not without its worth."

The following summer, after spending more than a month with Linda, Jim set off for San Francisco, a city he had long wanted to visit. In July 1959, Winfield drove Jim to the local highway, where he began hitchhiking the roughly twenty-six hundred miles to the coast. By the next day, he had managed to catch a ride outside of Terre Haute all the way to California. The three-day trip along Route 66 took him through Arizona and Southern California and then to San Francisco, where he rented a room at 508 Gough Street. He had missed a reading by Robert Duncan, a poet he deeply admired, at a café in North Beach by only a few weeks. The poetry scene in San Francisco was still thriving, but it had changed, and the founding Beat writers had mostly moved on. Ginsberg, who had just visited San Francisco, had hitchhiked back to New

York City that same month. Kerouac lived with his mother in Queens, and Gary Snyder had moved to Kyoto to study Zen. Neal Cassady was serving time in San Quentin State Prison. Many other writers, however, were still around, including Michael McClure, Philip Lamantia, and Philip Whalen (each of whom had read at the famous Six Gallery in 1955 when Allen Ginsberg first presented "Howl"), along with Robert Duncan, Jack Spicer, Kenneth Rexroth, and Lawrence Ferlinghetti.

Jim had mixed feelings about San Francisco, as he did about all cities at this point in his life. At first, he found the city pleasant, though he was "not overly impressed by the 'beat' section," and he was eager to get out into the countryside, informing his parents that he didn't care for cities like he used to. He wanted to do farmwork. He found the so-called beatniks in North Beach smart but overly affected and narrowly oppositional: "Some are very bright but they go to absurd ends to shield their literacy and would all like to pass as some variety of human criminal not recognizing of course that literacy can be conducted with dignity. I can hold a healthy disrespect for that which represents inane scholarship, 'middle-class' values, 'false christianity,' etc without making my negation a belief, an end in itself." Jim found them mostly "artsy crafty" people, who disliked their families and avoided reality, and he thought their bohemianism more posturing than anything else, "sort of an artifact for commiseration, like Shelley's 'upon the thorns of life I bleed.'" His letters to home were perhaps themselves a bit of posturing. He was eager to distance himself from the hipsters, particularly at a time when he didn't have much to show for his own literary efforts. Rural labor seemed an appropriate antidote to the North Beach scene.

With some initiative and guts, Jim sought out work on farms in nearby Stockton, Modesto, and San Jose. He would jump in the back of a pickup truck before dawn, with little idea of where he'd end up, and head out into the bean fields. "Right now the only visible difference between myself and any other migrant worker is that I don't pick beans as fast," he noted after a few days of work. When given the chance, he opted for the pear-picking jobs because they paid better—one dollar per hour in a ten-hour workday—while picking beans paid only two cents per pound. Given his slowness in picking, he made only about $4.80 a day, barely a subsistence wage. The migrant workers, mostly Mexicans, were only able to live by fielding a whole family. It was tough work; temperatures exceeded ninety degrees every day, and at night he itched from bean dust and pesticides. But he liked the idea of working in "Steinbeck country." After a day in the fields, people in the city treated him "much like a Joad," and though he occasionally met some "Okies," he preferred the "Chicanos' grace and good humor." Beyond the meager pay, the work proved invaluable to him and gave him insight into the lives of a struggling underclass. It placed him light-years from the Co-Existence Bagel Shop, the beatnik hangout in North Beach.

Jim made the most of his time in San Francisco, more so than in Boston and New York. He was a bit older and knew he had limited time if he wanted to get back to Linda. He collected experiences with a voracious appetite, analyzed seemingly everything, formed opinions, read widely, took notes in journals, and worked on poems—all with an urgency. His letters to his parents show him trying (struggling at times) to figure out the world and his place in it and doing so with remarkably bold exertions of energy, courage, and willpower. He was also remarkably candid with his parents, who in turn seemed to appreciate his curiosity and intensity, even when it scratched against their beliefs. He made new friends with "dope addicts, pimps, and whores, etc.," he wrote, "but worry not as I've only spoken to them." He had a fling with a librarian in Berkeley, who was happy when he "read her erudite periodicals and g[a]ve her the tiger eye."

Writing in *Wolf*, Jim would elaborate beyond what he would share with his parents, but it may represent more fiction (or fantasy) than fact. Swanson, the protagonist, takes the librarian to her apartment for sex, and afterward he wears her husband's pajamas; the couple were separated: "She was about thirty-five and a little bit plump for my taste but strangely the best lover I've ever had."

Despite the rich array of new experiences, Jim felt increasingly troubled about San Francisco and city life in general, something he would feel for the rest of his life, even as his reasons would evolve over time. Much of his unease was articulated in terms of religion. "There is something about the city at night that makes me wonder at human beings and I suppose at myself," he wrote in a letter to home, puzzling out his feelings, "because cities once fascinated me. I am not saying 'woe unto you, Babylon,' but it seems unspeakable that these people are made of the same flesh and blood as a Job or David or Isaiah. And I would not even pretend to judge people, only that this product of theirs is corrupt." Jim felt the whole urban project somehow degrading and even complained about the newsstands that sold "practically nothing but obscene magazines"—a surprising gripe, coming from Jim Harrison, who would one day devote a chapter of his memoir to "stripping."

Jim's religion clearly still clung to him, and he supposed that he had become "devout in a different sort of way." What that new way was, he didn't explain, though he still *believed*, and Christianity influenced his view of the world. ("Dostoevsky believed. I must be equal to any unbeliever or I am unworthy to believe.") In one letter to home, he recommended Sir Thomas Browne's *Religio Medici* to his mother and a volume of the letters of Frank Laubach, a Christian evangelist in "the tradition of the great mystics." And he debated theological points with Norma:

> I can't understand how Dr. Pearson could know either what God expects, or what is offensive to Him. Logically enough of course, to be given something to use and not use it seems absurd but, "our ways are not his ways," and knowledge of God must come through revelation not any dialectical disputing and projection of small human logic.

He had had a great deal of time to read and think in San Francisco, he explained. All of this was true even as Jim's new devoutness was clearly permissive—sexually and otherwise—to a degree that would have been unthinkable to him just a few years earlier.

Despite a welcome visit in August from Michigan friend Lisle Earl,

Jim had tired of the city and planned to hitchhike home. It didn't help that a thief had broken into his Gough Street apartment while he was sleeping and snatched his billfold, which included his only means of identification, a Social Security card. If there was any consolation, he felt that if it had happened to him a year before, it would have destroyed his composure, and now he felt only embarrassment. Eager to see Linda, he set off for Michigan that same month. He had barely mentioned her in his letters to his parents, except for the fact that the two corresponded regularly (Linda "writes me every day"). Other times, he included oblique references to his intentions—indeed, proverbs:

> Hold back the foolish tongue that would say tomorrow.
> A man needs a wife before he is able to support one.

Notable for Jim, who was otherwise so candid with his parents. He withheld direct reference to his feelings for her.

His trip back to Michigan was a memorable ordeal. After fighting off a "crazy bum" who intended to rob him (he would later write that he punched the man in his Adam's apple, which left the man choking though visibly alive on the ground) and run-ins with the police, he took a dangerous detour in Fallon, Nevada, that almost killed him. Instead of taking Route 95, Jim took Highway 50, later named "the Loneliest Road" in America by *Life*. Only a few cars passed him in half a day's time—none stopping—and he found himself stranded in the desert heat, sunbaked and dizzy. Finally, a couple pulled over for him and drove him back to Fallon. He would later write a poem, "Hitchhiking," about the experience, which was none too kind to the people of Nevada. Of his breakfast the next morning in Fallon, he wrote that it was "nurtured / by a miraculous hatred."

—

Jim got back to Michigan in time to spend a few weeks with Linda before she returned to Stephens for the fall semester. He would return to MSU and enroll in core English classes—Chaucer, Shakespeare, and Theory of Literature—and one on the Russian Revolution. He also took a job working at a horticultural farm on campus. It was the kind of work that saves a person, as he wrote many years later in the novella "The Seven-Ounce Man," since "if you're troubled in mind you are too wore out at the end of the day to give a shit, period." Linda thought it was a good idea for him to find a job that would keep him busy while they were apart—less time for him to brood. She was taking nineteen credits and working part-time, which kept her going from 8:00 a.m. to 4:00 p.m. most days—also a good thing, she thought, because it would make the year go by more quickly.

This time, their separation was much harder. Before Linda departed East Lansing, she feared she might be pregnant, and the two had debated whether she should return to school at all. She was understandably concerned about the potential upheaval for everyone involved. In the coming weeks, the two wrote obsessively to each other, while Linda feared she had made "some horrible mistake" in going back to Stephens. She felt depressed and scared and alone, and she sought to reassure Jim of her feelings for him: "I wish I knew how I could show you through letters how much I love you. I will try and I hope you know anyway." By this time, they spoke openly about marriage and planned to do it sooner or later, depending on the outcome.

Linda was terrified at the prospect of breaking the news to her parents, especially her mother, and she dreaded the time when she might have to call home. Naturally, she worried about the consequences a pregnancy would have for Jim's education and that he might have to drop out of college altogether to support a baby—an outcome Jim didn't seem to mind, as it would get him out of MSU for a good reason. She didn't write about the consequences for her own education. At other times, Linda wondered if she might not be pregnant at all—some of her college friends didn't think so. "It seems like it is awfully unfair to have things happen like this just because you love someone so much," she complained.

As for Jim, he too sought to reassure Linda of his feelings and intentions: "To be honest, I have liked the idea of the possibility of your being pregnant," he wrote, and then, apparently worried about how that might sound, quickly sought to clarify it: "What I mean is that I'd 'like' it better if you were with me now. Even so, I'd never try to make you pregnant to stop you from going back to school because next fall will be a better time for our marriage."

As they soon discovered, Linda *was* pregnant with their first daughter, Jamie. When she found out, she immediately called Jim, but she could not bear to tell her parents. Winfield advised Jim to go to the Kings' house and tell them the news, but he reminded his son that he did not do this alone: a pregnancy takes two people. Not surprisingly, Margery King took the news badly and began crying hysterically. Bill King, whom Jim generally liked and respected, simply said, "Frankly James, I think you're a bastard," and then went immediately to the phone to call Linda at college to set her mind at rest.

The Kings' reaction was not unexpected. Unlike the Harrisons, they had mostly discouraged the relationship. Winfield and Norma adored Linda but were unsure about the timing of the pregnancy. Given Jim's erratic behavior in the previous months and years, they worried about his ability to take on the role of husband and parent. Linda returned to East Lansing two days later, and on October 10, 1959, just a few weeks after the news came, the couple were married in a small ceremony. With a handful of family and friends in attendance, the reception was held at the Kings', a white, one-story house with pillars framing the front door. Linda, two days short of nineteen, never returned to college to finish her degree. "When we wed I know Linda's parents, for good reason, loathed me!" Jim would write to McGuane many years later. "But out of Decorum and love for her we had a charming though anxious wedding."

Jim's relationship with the Kings, and particularly with Margery, was deeply strained. The Kings had talked openly of abortion, even though it ran counter to their beliefs, or secluding their daughter away for a year at a distant aunt's house. For one, her parents disliked the fact that Jim intended to be a poet, a profession that didn't promise a life of comfort and security for their daughter. In Jamie's estimation, there was "nothing about [my father] that fit the idea of the ideal husband or the ideal American, in fact. So that was a problem." Margery felt that Jim lacked good manners, dressed slovenly, and had no money. She'd sometimes declare that Jim was "white trash" and socially beneath her family, and she held it against him that the Harrisons were comparatively poor, which, measured by disposable income, was true.

The tensions between Margery and Jim were palpable. Jamie recalls Margery's expletive-laden outbursts, which were sometimes directed even at her, her own granddaughter. Once, while visiting the Kings during a break from college, she remembers Margery hurling invectives at her: "You're just a whore and poor white-trash shit, like everybody in your father's family." Margery's paroxysms spoke perhaps as much to her precarious mental health as to anything else, but they were indicative of the kinds of sentiments she would harbor against Jim and his family even many years later. And Jim would do little to dissuade her of her impressions. On the contrary, he would deliberately confront and provoke her. Family dinners could quickly descend into all-out battles, as Jim refused to watch his manners and didn't hesitate to argue back at her. On these occasions, Bill King would simply walk away, Margery would scream, and Jim and Linda would get up and leave. "He would really bring things on," Jamie said, recalling a time when Jim tossed the turkey down the entire length of the table at Thanksgiving dinner.

—

"James, we've always catered to your aberrations," Norma told her son after the wedding, or so Jim remembered. "Now it's time for responsibility." Jim seemed to take her admonition seriously, at least for a time. In marriage, Jim found "something to tie [him] to earth," as he would write. Rather than drop out of MSU, he bore down on his schoolwork, completing almost two years' worth of courses (twenty-three in all) in one year, and he worked up to forty hours a week: winters at the university library and the rest of the year at the horticultural farm. The two jobs appropriately straddled his inclinations—one bookish, the other outside and hands-on. Bleary-eyed and overworked, he seemed to merge his writing with his labor: Rilke with irrigation fields, Wordsworth with root cellars, Lorca with McIntosh apples, Nabokov with fence posts.

Amid it all, Jamie Harrison arrived on May 21, 1960. Jim was thrilled with the baby, and as a bonus, her birth helped to improve his relationship with his in-laws. He completed his undergraduate coursework that summer and, at the encouragement of a few MSU faculty, enrolled in the master's program in English. Due partly to his previously poor grades, his admission was provisional, as was his own commitment to completing the degree. He was still very undecided about his future, but he needed to do *something*, and the program kept him reading and largely in the company of like-minded literary people. That fall, Jim and Linda moved into Spartan Village, a rather bleak brick structure the university provided for married students, which at least gave the new branch of the Harrison clan a temporary home. And Jim found a new job that gave him a bit more time for his own work. A friend of the Kings—Russel Nye, a professor of English—had helped Jim procure an assistantship that paid just over $200 a month and required about only four hours a day of his time. While Jim would make use of the Kings' connections, he refused to take any money from them.

Nevertheless, Jim was more perplexed about his future than perhaps ever before, and he seriously considered giving up writing to become a teacher. It was a remarkable moment for Jim, who would later so adamantly reject academia. The pressures of supporting a new family had weighed heavily against his one-time guiding principle that "a writer's sole responsibility is to his art."

"Perhaps I should teach not write," he had ventured to his mother a full year earlier. "I believe myself to be quite conscientious and under the right circumstances with the right wife I might make a good teacher." But teaching would never take hold of him as writing had, and he would have more than a few chances to test his aptitude and resolve during graduate school.

During the 1961–62 school year, Jim taught English as a second language, and his performance was less than promising. Later, when Jim requested a letter of recommendation for teaching positions, the program director, E. T. Erazmus, did little to hide his disapproval. Erazmus agreed to write Jim a letter, but it turned out to be a terrible one clearly intended to sink his chances. In a letter concealed from Jim in sealed envelopes, Erazmus warned prospective employers away from him. He began by explaining that Jim had started out well enough, but his commitment had deteriorated over the course of the year. His habits of punctuality were poor, Erazmus wrote, and he had "some tendencies to loquaciousness which compromised his effectiveness somewhat." While Jim maintained good discipline in the classroom, he could be overbearing, and he lacked "emotional stability and maturity." While Erazmus had not used the word *arrogant* in his letter, Jim nevertheless thought he had seen it through the envelope—a fact that perhaps speaks volumes about his attitude toward teaching at the time and the program itself.

Erazmus wasn't the only one to voice concerns about Jim's teaching. One student, writing to Jim's supervisor, complained of "the complete irresponsibility of one of your graduate instructors"—that is, Jim, who blamed his poor performance on the program's emphasis on simple repetition. Jim also complained that the students in the program spoke so many different languages that he often couldn't understand them. But that did not address the charge of irresponsibility. As he later confessed, he had once thrown his students' test papers into a dumpster, where they were, he mused, being "saved for research."

Arguably, the most important thing Jim took away from MSU was a lifetime of friendships. There was an extraordinary cohort then working its way through the university, what Tom McGuane would later describe to Jim as that "strange concatenation" that began in East Lansing. It included McGuane, Richard Ford, the sculptor Italo Scanga, Robert Dattila (Jim's future literary agent), and the poets Dan Gerber and J. D. Reed—all of whom would become, at one point or another, friends with Jim. Gerber and McGuane (and Dattila, in his way) would play an outsized role in Jim's life, although those friendships took form years after MSU.* During college, Jim and McGuane knew each other only in passing—that is to say, they knew *of* each other. Both had reputations for their intelligence and literary abilities. Jim knew McGuane only "slightly," in his words, partly because McGuane hung out with a set of people more interested in fiction than poetry. McGuane would recall how Jim first introduced himself as "Kiki the Dog Face Boy" and how, with a remarkable air of self-possession, Jim was followed around by a cast of admirers. It wasn't until 1966, while McGuane was living in Málaga, Spain, years after his graduation from MSU, that the two would begin corresponding. That correspondence, voluminous and rich, would last a lifetime, like the friendship itself.

During graduate school, Jim befriended Clyde Henson, a professor of English (Dan Gerber would later credit Henson with waking him up to Walt Whitman), and more importantly, Herbert Weisinger, a professor of comparative literature, who would become an important mentor to him. Weisinger, who spoke with a Brooklyn accent and wore thick, half-frame glasses, had completed his PhD at the University of Michigan in 1941 and specialized in Renaissance studies. Jim considered him the first truly great man he had ever met, and he marveled at how Weisinger could "topologically see the whole history of the world and its literature and from all different angles: mythographically, historically, economically, scientifically," and he wore his immense learning lightly. Weisinger encouraged Jim's interests in wine, Mozart and Bach, mythology, anthropology, the French symbolist poets, Mexican art, and Shakespeare—a specialty of Weisinger's—among other things. It was Weisinger who would eventually persuade Jim to transfer from English to the comparative literature

* Many of these people overlapped at MSU, but they were not necessarily in the same graduating class; their programs and dates of attendance and graduation vary. McGuane transferred to MSU as an undergraduate in 1960 and graduated in December 1962; Richard Ford attended Michigan State from 1962 to 1966; Jim started as an undergraduate at MSU in 1956 and finished graduate school in 1966.

program, which Weisinger then directed, in part to eschew national traditions for a more comprehensive view of things. It was a viewpoint that Jim would continue to embrace long after leaving MSU.

Despite Henson's and Weisinger's attention, Jim would not take to graduate school any more than he had to undergraduate studies. He began his first year with good grades, taking such classes as Studies in Form and Genre and Methods of Literary Research, but by the spring of 1961, he had flunked out. He despised most of the faculty's cool, clinical approach to literature, and he simply disliked many of his professors. Part of it surely stemmed from his desire to *write* poetry and fiction. And he didn't think academics took books seriously. After a summer of outdoor work, he reenrolled and rebounded, earning mostly As, but by the spring of 1962, he had lost interest entirely and failed every class, an outcome that portended an emotional and psychological crisis.

Soon afterward, without warning to anyone, including Linda and his two-year-old daughter, Jim hitchhiked to New York City, where he stayed with an artist friend. The episode alarmed everyone—Winfield had been worried enough to telephone the state police—but Jim returned in a few days in a state of "teary penance." He was experiencing, as he would later describe it, a "total nervous crack-up," and by June he officially withdrew from school. Luckily, the university allowed him, Linda, and Jamie to remain in their Spartan Village apartment.

With the help of his father and Mr. King, Jim interviewed for jobs, some as far away as Washington, DC, though nothing came of them. In November, when the family was finally evicted from student housing, they moved in with the Kings. Jim and Margery found some common ground playing bridge, but it was uncomfortable for everyone. Weeks later, Jim got invited to interview for a teaching position at a high school in Manton, a small town in northern Michigan. Given his lack of options, it was a relatively appealing prospect that promised a steady income, and he and Linda looked forward to visiting the school. What they didn't know was that their lives were about to change entirely and irrevocably.

5

BLACK THICKETS

(FALL 1962 – SPRING 1965)

Though in the dark, she doesn't sleep.
On cushions, embraced by silk, no lover
comes to her. In the first light when birds
stir she does not stir or sing. Oh eyes can't
focus to this dark.

November 21, 1962, the day before Thanksgiving, was cloudy and breezy, and it was warmer than it had been for weeks—a great start to the holiday weekend. Winfield and Judy bustled about the house, preparing to leave for a deer-hunting trip near Reed City, an annual ritual. Judy liked to hunt and fish as much as anyone. Despite the nice weather, Jim spent the morning debating whether to join them, and by the time he made up his mind not to go, he'd delayed their departure by several hours. He had just returned from a trip up north and wanted to stay around the house. So Winfield and Judy headed off in the early afternoon without him. They drove north on Route 127 over the Looking Glass River and the Bad River and through the rural farmlands of central Michigan. At Mount Pleasant, they turned west on M-20, a residential two-lane roadway, and crossed the Chippewa River, named for the local Saginaw Chippewa (Ojibwa). At the exact same time, James Schumacher roared eastbound at more than eighty miles an hour. When a third car suddenly backed out of a driveway onto M-20, Schumacher swerved into the opposite lane and collided head-on with the Harrisons. Winfield and Judy were killed instantly. The shattering impact snapped in half a shotgun in the Harrisons' trunk. Their deaths would drive Jim into the deepest of depressions ("my world imploded," he wrote) and rattle his confidence in his own sanity.

That evening, while Jim played bridge at his in-laws' house, the phone rang, and Bill King answered: It was Norma. Jim would recall the stricken look on King's face. Something terrible had happened—Winfield and Judy never made it to Reed City. Jim quickly left, lying to Linda that Judy was fine, though he knew otherwise. King drove Jim the five miles to the Harrisons' home, where Jim spoke with his brother John and his wife, Rebecca, in Cambridge, Massachusetts, who decided to drive to Michigan that night, nonstop and over wintry highways. Jim stayed up late with David and Mary, then fourteen and fifteen years old respectively. Norma, clearly stunned, washed and rewashed sets of dishes throughout the evening. Later, from the bathroom, her heaving sobs could be heard above the running water. "The family was so close, and goodness, they loved Judy so much," said Rebecca. "She was such a character. She was going to be like John and Jim for sure. Jim was deeply affected."

The details of the accident made the evening news. If the Kings had had a television, they might have seen the report before getting the phone call. Thirty-two-year-old Schumacher, a father of eight from Mount Pleasant, was drunk and racing to a bowling alley—he also died. Two days later, the *Lansing State Journal* announced Winfield and Judy's funeral services alongside their photos and an article about the dangers of travel on Thanksgiving weekend. Their bodies were taken to Lansing and buried on Saturday in Glendale Cemetery in nearby Okemos. The paper noted that Winfield was nationally recognized for his work in soil conservation. Judy, just nineteen, was a sophomore at Michigan State.

"It has often occurred to me that surviving family members meet violent deaths in an enduring state of recoil," Jim later wrote. "The word 'love' becomes mortally imprecise when the objects of love are torn from us and our love whirls off into the void on their invisible track."

In an instant, Jim had lost two of the most meaningful relationships in his life. In the following hours and days, as reflection began to replace shock, actions prior to the accident took on ominous significance, and Jim blamed himself for delaying them. His wavering on whether to join them had placed them perfectly in harm's way, he thought. "If I had made up my mind about hunting with them a minute earlier, five minutes, moments earlier, my father and sister would have avoided the collision." The thought would haunt him.

But the alternative, the sheer randomness of it, was perhaps even more terrifying.

Just days earlier, things had been looking up. On Tuesday, Jim and Linda had visited Manton, where Jim had interviewed for a teaching position in the English Department of the local high school. He had received an offer, and the couple returned to the Kings' in time for the holiday weekend. The position came with a spacious apartment situated above a storefront and promised a much-needed escape from ongoing tensions, mostly related to money, with both the Kings and Jim's parents. After failing out of graduate school, his unemployment and general lack of direction had become a significant source of stress in the family and a frequent topic of conversation. With a two-year-old daughter and the prospect of mounting expenses, he desperately needed a job. They had planned to move out of the Kings' home the following week, but the accident had changed everything.

Following the funeral, Jim declined the position and moved Linda and Jamie into the Harrison house. He wanted to stay close to his mother and siblings, and he privately doubted his sanity and fitness for the teaching job. Holding his daughter was one of the few things that gave him comfort. To John, he confessed, after finishing off the last of Winfield's bottle of whiskey, "Jamie is comfort because she is of life."

—

"Well, death did it to me," Jim once said when asked about how he had begun writing. "You can see it in my first book, *Plain Song*. If people die then you better get down to business."

He couldn't have uttered truer sentences. The horribleness of it all was the motivation that he needed. In the years that followed the accident, Jim would identify Winfield and Judy's deaths as a kind of poetic genesis stemming from the realization of the fragility of life, though perhaps more accurately, it was a renascence, a renewal of his commitment to live as an artist. It was a cliché, but no less true for being so. He would devote himself to writing and a life lived—fiercely so—on his own terms. A condolence letter from friend J. D. Reed, akin to a call to arms, echoed his new commitment: "I am sending no sympathy cards to you or your mother. Your mother's consolation is Jesus, and yours is life." This was, in retrospect, the most fitting sentiment Jim heard at the time.

In the weeks and months that followed, Jim wrote at a small wooden desk upstairs in the hallway of the Harrison home, sometimes late into the night, with David and Mary asleep below, and he completed some of the first polished poems of his life. His skills would develop with remarkable speed. Months later, he'd reflect on how far he had come, noting in a letter how back in April and May he "wrote so many agonized mediocre poems." But even then, in the winter and early spring, he noticed a definite difference from his earlier attempts at writing—something in him had changed.

To John and Rebecca, he admitted with some surprise his newfound voice. He began having visions like the ones he had experienced in the past, and they came cloaked in spiritual imagery. "I can see Daddy & Judy—" he wrote to them, "first I am in their sight the second of death, then brighter—the huge FACE of God. Holy Holy. Jesus sits on the sofa next to me. We converse in ordinary terms. I search out the facts of my destiny. Humility. It seems strange but I have begun to receive the gift of speech. The truth is always new wine!"

The vision was yet another origin story, but the revelation of it would be slow to come. Months later, Jim was still unemployed and so depressed he was unable or unwilling to pursue anything except writing. It had caused fights between him and Linda and put stress on everyone. The unanimous consensus in the family was that he *needed* to get a job.

There was simply no other choice. Even as he joked with John that he "would much prefer some sort of magic billfold, or a pet Gosehawk [*sic*] that brings me a twenty everyday," the family openly discussed his future and the prospect of sending him to Boston, where he could stay with John and Rebecca while looking for work.

Writing to John in April, Jim admitted that his lack of a job had strained his marriage and asked if he might stay with them. "I will need no financial assistance, only a humble couch to lay my head on and a cup of coffee in the morning. If you consent you will help save my marriage. Which is on the skids." It was a last-ditch effort, he admitted, acknowledging a motif of chronic unemployment and emotional distress in his life: "I am trying to work out of a pattern that has been set for some ten years. I love my wife and don't wish to lose her by sitting on my ass."

He assured John that this was no whim: "All has been coolly and rationally discussed." When John and Rebecca agreed to the plan, and Jim departed, Linda and Jamie moved back in with the Kings. It was decided that once Jim found a job, they would join him in Boston.

—

In the spring of 1963, Boston was on alert. In February, a feature article in *Life* magazine included an eerie photo of a dark wintry street at twilight. The accompanying subhead read, "A chain of sex stranglings haunts the streets and snug apartments of Boston." Nine women had been found dead by strangling in the previous eight months. Jim was arriving at the height of the Boston Strangler scare, and the gruesome murders would play out for yet another year against a backdrop of economic decline in the city and flawed efforts at urban redevelopment. Nevertheless, the new surroundings managed to rattle him free from his depression.

His move to Boston would prove very different from his last one six years earlier, this time living with family who provided hot meals and encouragement. John and Rebecca's apartment was at 64 Kirkland Street in the heart of Cambridge, a pleasant tree-lined street just a short walk from the Swedenborg Chapel, Harvard Square, and the Widener Library, where John worked as a librarian. The furnished second-floor apartment—situated in a large house of more than thirty rooms—with units above and below, included one bathroom, a large kitchen, several closets, a living room, one bedroom, and lots of light from eleven windows. In early May, days after he arrived and despite having caught a cold, the three ventured to Walden Pond. A photo shows John and Jim in jacket and cap, smiling and happy (despite recent events), if a bit self-conscious, with the birch trees in the background still bare from winter. It was the first of many day and weekend trips they'd share, including visits to Concord, where Jim would reflect on the landscapes that had nurtured Emerson and Thoreau. "Thoreau, mon allié, mon garde-frontières," he proclaimed years later.

Once settled, Jim quickly began searching for work. In the mornings, he read the ads in *The Boston Globe*, though he often slipped back into his bed on the couch. He interviewed during the day in suits borrowed from John, and in the evenings, Rebecca typed his cover letters and résumés. Besides scouring the papers, he worked with a "classy employment agency" and felt in somewhat better spirits, although he sorely missed his wife and daughter, admittedly suffering from homesickness. Writing to his mother in May, he complained that the job-hunting process seemed endless, though it made him "realize now how deeply I care for and need my family, my wife and little daughter. The separation is agonizing and makes me feel so greatly your own separation," he added, referring to the accident.

The nearly two months that Jim and Linda would spend apart were difficult for them, perhaps especially so for Linda. Their letters from this time reflect the typical insecurities of a young couple separated by long distances, but ones likely exacerbated by Linda's having to care for Jamie alone (she was three years old now) and by the fact that their relationship had been fraught before his departure. She wrote with news from Michigan, including updates on Jamie and local friends and cheery reassurances about their plans, but she also expressed understandable feelings of distress. She was lonely, sometimes intensely so, and she longed to be with him: "I can't bear waiting to see you when I allow myself to think of it my stomach just feels sick." She was insecure and worried that Jim might somehow settle into the long separation ("don[']t even get used to it as you say you almost could"), and she insisted that the distance between them had not lessened but rather strengthened her feelings: "You mean so much to me and I am surer of it now than ever. I refuse to ever accept us not being together." Moreover, she prodded Jim to share *his* feelings, perhaps because his letters to her, the few that survive, are less demonstrative. In one, Jim left the emotional work to a short poem, one by the eighth-century Japanese poet Yamabe no Akahito: "I wish I were close / To you as the wet skirt of / A salt girl to her body. / I think of you always."

While the distance between them strengthened and clarified their feelings, the fact that Linda was staying with her parents almost certainly made matters worse, as her relationship with her mother had become increasingly strained. "What a day—my mother hit an all time low, or high, whichever you prefer. Actually it has been brewing for several days," she wrote, with subtle references to her mother's imbibing. "Mother had a slight hangover, why it wasn't worse I don't know."

"Oh please, never let me ever get in that condition," she wrote elsewhere. "How she must hate herself when she gets like that." Days later, she complained that her parents weren't even able to discuss anything anymore because her mother would get so mean. "It is sickening to see and hear." By late May, things were getting "quite thick," so bad, in fact, that she would visit the Harrison household in the hope of an invitation to spend the evening just to escape for a time. The stress made her "panicky" to get away and reunite their own family.

Linda was also concerned for Jim's mental health. At one point, referring to his tendency toward self-absorption, she urged him not to let himself get desperate and "worry about [his] sanity." She thought of him constantly and feared that he sounded down, which his mother, too, had noted after speaking with him. Her concerns for Jim may have been heightened by the recent suicide of a friend of theirs, which she reported to him the same week. She encouraged his writing, in part as a therapeutic regimen that had always helped him before. It sounded to her like he was doing much more of it than ever before, and he was. Jim found that writing was one of the very few things that could lift him out of a depression or at least make it temporarily more bearable—then and in the years to come.

Jim's letters to Linda from this time reveal little about his own state of mind. In mid-April, he admitted that things "seemed rather dark the past few days" but had picked up recently, and he acknowledged that John was a "steady kind of influence" on him.

When Jim finally secured a job with Campbell and Hall, a local book wholesaler, it restored his independence. It was clearly demanding work, requiring him to drive up to two hundred miles a day, though John later described it in jest as a "grand tour that took him from one oyster house joint to the next." When he was still at John and Rebecca's, he worked extremely hard at his writing; he would stay up late into the night working in the kitchen, sometimes all night, with only Sylvie, their cat, as company. When he finally received a paycheck, the first in many months, he flew to Michigan to bring Linda and Jamie back with him to Boston.

Within days, they rented a sunny one-bedroom in a four-story walk-up at 5 Bellvista Road in Boston, three miles, as the crow flies, from John and Rebecca's place across the Charles River. Pink tile covered the bathroom walls, and bas-reliefs of fauns framed the fireplace. In the rear of the building, long open-air balconies surrounded a muddy courtyard where Jamie would often play. Jim would arrive home from work as early as two or three o'clock in the afternoon, settle in for a nap, and then take over the kitchen at seven thirty or eight. "He works every evening that he can on his poetry until 2:00 a.m. or later," Linda recounted in a letter to Norma and the family.

Despite Jim's new job, Norma remained skeptical about her son's pursuit of poetry as an occupation given his role as the breadwinner for the family, particularly in light of Winfield's death. Money was scarce. The source of tension, as it had been for years, was Jim's general resistance to a more traditional lifestyle and career. He shared his mother's Midwestern Calvinist work ethic, but he'd direct his energies almost solely to his writing. Jim approached the subject with Norma as a good-natured debate, and he'd describe his single-mindedness in religious terms that seemed tailored for her.

"I only want you to understand that it is more difficult to be a disciple than to merely take a job," he wrote to her from Boston, "that one tries to become a disciple with his entire being in order that the 'word' might be transmitted . . . You feel a calling just like you feel a calling to be a minister. I know that I'll never have more than a vaguely nominal interest in any job."

The trick, which literally kept him up at night, was finding the time to write. As for the stress on his marriage, a concern his mother had voiced, his renewed commitment to his poetry helped it, or so he argued. His marriage was getting along better, not so much because of his new job but because he felt more at "peace with what I am than I have ever been before."

The transmitted word, he hoped, would continue to come to him in visions. After suffering intensely through the previous months with little relief, he wondered whether he was still capable of them. One night, as he lay back on the bed in a dark room, he immediately saw his high school engulfed in flames, and then it became a church. For a half hour or so, thousands of images passed before him. After sensing Jesus and creatures in the room, he saw "a bony angular face" he recognized as that of the poet Arthur Rimbaud, "only much aged and leathery." Then he saw Winfield and Judy. They smiled, and he hugged them. Winfield's eyes seemed to enlarge and darken, and his nose changed into a beak. His head became covered with black feathers, like a hawk's, Jim thought, imagining perhaps a black hawk. He expected Judy to make a funny comment about their father, but instead she herself transformed into a white dove or a pigeon. They beat their wings as they rose through the darkness, avian totems flying off into a spiritual realm. He then entered a thicket he recognized as being near his family's old cabin. Inside, it was fleshy, like a clam, and he descended into it only to fall through. Afterward, he found himself beside a wide, beautiful stream. He felt fresh and clean. The silvery undersides of poplar leaves shimmered around him, and the wind rippled the water's surface. Then Judy's face appeared, "soft and luminous above the water," he wrote, and his body began to shake.

The vision, a kind of rebirth story, bears out Jim's own transformation. The presence of Rimbaud seems to speak to the connection Jim saw between visions and poetry. Rimbaud, one of Jim's early heroes, considered himself a *voyant* and visions as a crucial form of consciousness. The artist's main stock-in-trade is "total consciousness," Jim would tell Norma, "to be one on whom nothing is lost . . . to see through not with the eyes . . . If his vision becomes corrupt or blurred he will fail."

During the spring and summer months, Jim undertook other important work for his career—making connections. One place in particular, Gordon Cairnie's Grolier Book Shop in Harvard Square, had become a de facto headquarters for local poets. The Grolier, which Cairnie opened in 1927, had long catered to independent presses and avant-garde literature. A gruff, cantankerous Canadian (a sign in the store's entrance read, "Close the damn door"), Cairnie had served as a gunner in a Canadian artillery unit in World War I, worked as a potato inspector on Prince Edward Island, and studied landscape architecture at Harvard before opening the bookstore, where he would go on to nurture the careers of many writers.

The Grolier provided Jim with a community at a time when he sorely needed one. He quickly became a regular at the store and usually visited on Saturday mornings. There he met William Corbett, a fellow poet whom he and Linda would see socially; Paul Hannigan; Stephen Sandy; and briefly Jim's own future publisher, Seymour Lawrence, who was then serving as director and editor in chief of the Atlantic Monthly Press.

The city was a good fit for Jim this time around.* He found Boston

* For a discussion of Boston's literary scene from 1955 to 1960, see Peter Davidson, *The Fading Smile: Poets in Boston, 1955–1960, from Robert Frost to Robert Lowell to Sylvia Plath* (Alfred A. Knopf, 1994), 11–31.

"lively with poetry," though the literary scene had mostly transformed from what it had been just a few years earlier. Robert Frost, who had kept a house at 35 Brewster Street in Cambridge, had been the center of literary life until his death in January 1963. Forty-six-year-old Robert Lowell had been a close second. Lowell, who Edmund Wilson claimed had "made poetry out of modern Boston," had held court at his Boston University writing seminar (attended by Anne Sexton and Sylvia Plath) and during tutorials he led at his home in Back Bay. But by 1960, Lowell had quit his job and moved to New York City. Other poets had also departed, including Richard Wilbur, Donald Hall, Elizabeth Bishop, Stanley Kunitz, and Ted Hughes (along with Plath). On a broader stage, a generation of poets largely associated with modernism had begun to die off. E. E. Cummings, Robinson Jeffers, William Carlos Williams, and Theodore Roethke—a Michigander and one of Harrison's favorite poets—all died between 1962 and 1963, as had the young Plath.

Though the academic formalism and New Criticism that had prevailed in American poetry at mid-century was still generally favored at the Grolier, no longer was the city dominated by adherents of this style, for whom T. S. Eliot was a patron saint. New poets like John Wieners, James Tate, Denise Levertov, Michael Palmer, and Clark Coolidge had taken their place, and in one way or another, they all looked to transform poetry. Many of them were linked to the Vancouver Poetry Conference of 1963, a landmark event for "New American" open-form poetics that was co-organized by Robert Creeley. Less a conference than a three-week-long program of readings and workshops for students, it assembled a diverse group of poets who had been largely ignored or vilified by academics and often wrongly lumped together as simply Beats.

One such figure was Charles Olson, a sort of anti-Lowell, whose poetics countered New Critical principles at every turn. Along with Allen Ginsberg, he had co-headlined the Vancouver Conference. Born in Worcester, Massachusetts, Olson was the leading figure and theorist of the Black Mountain poets, a group named after the experimental Black Mountain College in North Carolina, where Olson had taught and that counted among its ranks Creeley, Wieners, Duncan, and more loosely, Levertov. Olson rejected academic verse and espoused instead an open-form poetry where form followed content, experimentation and primitivism were valued, and the poet's breath was privileged over the iamb as a unit of line measurement. Formal poetic meter was largely rejected.

Immense and bespectacled, Olson stood six feet eight inches tall, with dark, prodigious eyebrows, a gray beard, and wispy hair. Jim befriended Olson through Gordon Cairnie and would visit him at his Fort Square apartment in Gloucester. Years later, Bill Corbett remembered first visiting Olson with Jim and Paul Hannigan, a bottle of Cutty Sark in hand. Bringing the whiskey had been Cairnie's suggestion. Olson, Corbett recalled, sat at his kitchen table before "a heap of books, most of them open," with a dozen students surrounding him, smoking cigarettes down to "butts so small he had to hold them between thumb and forefinger for the last drag." Jim remembered Olson as an electrifying "hypnotic talker" who urged him to read dozens of books, including those by Robert Duncan, who would later become a friend and mentor to him. But while Olson filled his ears with ideas about poetry and poetics, Jim remained much more interested in his own more personal, idiosyncratic efforts at poetry than in polemics.

Jim was intensely influenced by these open-form poets, including Olson, whose anti-academic stance naturally appealed to him. Jim was already writing open-form poetry, and although he'd later experiment with traditional forms, he'd ignore strict rules and bend them to his will. And while his poems would often be intensely personal, he'd simultaneously work to avoid writing from a position of ego, yet another concern of these experimental poets.

—

By August, Jim felt confident enough about his new poems to reach out to Denise Levertov, who had once offered to read his work. He sent her a typed letter addressed to her farm in Temple, Maine. He had not published anything, he reminded her, nor studied with anyone, with the exception of Rimbaud, Whitman, Villon, and Neruda, and he asked for some assessment of his work, if only "yes / or no." Perhaps to lower her expectations, he added his own humble, even fearful assessment: "They, the poems, seem sometimes so inbred and slight that I think I may be insane and the poems worthless." His insecurity was understandable: He was nervous and had shown his work only to Linda, an avid, shrewd reader but not a writer, and certainly never to anyone of Levertov's stature. Nonetheless, he concluded his letter in startling bravado with the poem "Word Drunk," which would later appear in his first collection, along with a brief note: "just thot up (with the aid of whiskey) for your benefit."

Levertov, for her part, replied with a sprawling handwritten letter and resounding praise, so much so that Jim showed it only to Linda for fear of jinxing himself. "I am thrilled," she enthused. "It so rarely happens. I read so many MSS. One always hopes for a marvel. Your poems are the real thing." Levertov had recently become poetry adviser for W. W. Norton, and she urged Jim to put together "now all the poems you have" and send them to her, even if he was dissatisfied with them. She would recommend them for publication to a senior editor. She had already arranged to publish the objectivist poet Louis Zukofsky and Joel Sloman, whom Levertov likened to Jim. "There's only one other poet with whom I've had this experience," she told him, "of being really nourished & stimulated by work that comes out of the blue," though she thought Jim had a much better understanding of what he was doing. She also suggested that he pursue publication in other venues, including *Poetry*, *The Paris Review*, the *Quarterly Review of Literature*, and *The Nation*, where she was serving as interim poetry editor. (Jim would publish "New Liturgy" and "Exercise" in *The Nation* in April 1965; these would be among his first published poems.)

Jim and Linda were jubilant. Levertov's judgment, a literary veteran's, carried tremendous weight—affirming, even celebrating, his talent—and she helped, delivering tangible results. By mid-September, in a flurry of work, Jim had collected fifty more poems and sent them to Levertov, who responded with a range of editorial comments and queries. She addressed issues of word choice, emphasis, punctuation, and line breaks, and she suggested dropping several poems from the manuscript "(mostly because they are too slight, occasionally because they are in addition somewhat facile-sounding)." In one instance, she inquired about the internal logic of a poem: "Stanza 3: the girl bends & then stoops—how are you differentiating between the 2 actions? It sounds tautological." For another, "Blue Hawaii," she urged Jim to take more control of the poem: "This is a confused but interesting poem—I think you could do more with it, i.e, either bring it into sharper focus or if it is intended to be out of focus make that work, make one know it must be the way it is, blurred, not leave one wondering if you realize that it is so."

Hers was the most extensive commentary he'd received thus far on his poetry, and it proved an important education for him. "I trust implicitly your judgment," he confessed, accepting her guidance "as a neophyte to a POET," and he responded days later, point for point. Writing about "Blue Hawaii," he agreed with her: "'Blue' was intended to be confused, twisted, blurred, luminous, I will make it more directly what it's supposed to be." Of the poems she would drop, he acknowledged, "'Facile' is a good word." "This has been a new thing for me—to have someone read my work. It's thrown me out of joint but with a certain sweetness." And, speaking on a point that he would demand throughout his life, he accepted her criticism because she had herself created "notable work"—a fundamental qualification, he would insist, for any critic worthy of the name.

Levertov sent Jim's revised manuscript to Norton weeks later and arranged to visit him in Cambridge for dinner in November. Linda found Levertov "a very refreshing and warm person" and thought that she and Jim "seemed to get along easily and their conversation was 'zooming.'" Levertov, whose own sister, Olga, had died in March, would become a sympathetic friend to Jim, and with a Radcliffe Institute Fellowship, she was frequently in the Boston area. She advised Jim on all aspects of professional writing, from sources of funding to the conventions of magazine and book publishing; introduced him to other poets; and continued to advise him on matters of craft.

She may also have lent Jim some ideas about conducting a writerly life. Levertov and her husband, Mitchell Goodman, also a writer, spent summers on their farm in Maine—a rural outpost with a barn, electricity, and no plumbing—a fair distance along a dirt road from the nearest neighbor. Goodman had built a cabin for writing on a nearby hill. "It saves our lives," she affirmed, escaping from New York City. The Harrisons would later arrange their lives in similar fashion.

By December, Jim still had no word on his manuscript, so Levertov fired off a complaint to the head of Norton, and by early January, good news arrived. The standard contract included a graduated scale for royalties based on sales and a $250 advance. More good news followed in the weeks and months ahead. Henry Rago at *Poetry* had accepted five of his poems, and Jim had agreed to write a review of Hayden Carruth's *North Winter*—his first work of criticism. Carruth was a friend of Levertov's, and Jim likely took on the project at her request. The review was difficult to write. Jim thought Carruth's earlier *The Crow and the Heart* so different from *North Winter* that they "weren't written by the same human." Carruth's first collection smacked of the academic, "the sort of book one had learned to expect from the capable assistant professors who wrote within the baroque orthodoxy of the time (1946–59)." The latter book, a single poem in fifty-eight parts, was "poetry of a higher sort." Jim especially admired Carruth's unsentimental treatment of the natural world: "There's nothing in it of 'Vermont Landscapes,' the overweening idea of nature as a constant source of delight."

This was a season of firsts for Jim, and that included a major poetry reading. In February, he was selected as one of four poets to participate in the Poetry Center's Discovery '65 program, a reading series to highlight talented new poets, at the YM-YWHA in New York City. It was an honor, and it linked Jim to a storied tradition of readings and poets, including William Carlos Williams, who read there in 1939 during the center's inaugural season. Poets Nancy Sullivan, Mark Strand, and Robert

David Cohen joined him. Although each received an honorarium of just twenty-five dollars, it was terrific publicity. The center's calendar reached twenty-five thousand people, including a list of professional editors, publishers, and agents, and the event was advertised in *The New York Times* and *The Village Voice*.

The reading was held on April 19. Friends Bill Corbett and J. D. Reed drove with Jim to New York to provide support. In a biographical note in the evening's program, Jim wrote that he had been "occupied with poetry since the age of sixteen, when a teacher introduced me to the Elizabethans, Whitman, Hart Crane, and Pound, though it wasn't until two years ago that I wrote a poem that pleased me."

Jim read thirteen poems that night, eleven of which would appear in *Plain Song*, in a sturdy, quick, confident voice with a Midwestern accent—a bit nasally, vowels overdrawn—and he interspersed his readings with sometimes-humorous commentary. The poem "Hitchhiking" derived from standing eighteen hours in Nevada—"uncharitable people," he quipped—without a ride. After reading "Kinship," a poem about his great-uncle William, he joked that he had "nearly four or five hundred similarly worthless relatives who I can turn into verse like that." Jim Harrison, a poet newly minted, was a name now in circulation.

"Poem," which Jim chose not to read that night, was published in the center's program. That he chose it as a representative work suggested its importance to his developing poetics. The poem spoke to his understanding of the relation between form and content.

Form is the woods: the beast,
a bobcat padding through red sumac,
the pheasant in brake or goldenrod
that he stalks—both rise to the flush,
the brief low flutter and catch in air;
and trees, rich green, the moving of boughs
and the separate leaf, yield
to conclusions they do not care about

or watch—the dead, frayed bird,
the beautiful plumage,
the spoor of feathers
and slight, pink bones.

By including "Poem," in particular, Jim effectively announced his adherence to an open-form poetry that embraced what Levertov called "organic form." Almost a year later, Jim explained his position that "form is never more than an extension or revelation of content," an idea he borrowed from Robert Duncan ("extension") and Levertov ("revelation"). Instead of writing in a received form, like a Shakespearean sonnet, the idea went, the writer's job was to reveal or make manifest the form inherent in the experience.

"That is, form is a dynamic, alive vehicle within which the poem inseparably occurs and lives," Jim wrote, "'alive' things which happen and are given shape within the natural ecology of the poet's brain."

As "Poem" unfolds in deadly action, the poem's form—its physical structure, including line length, rhythms, and rhymes—is commensurate with the content, and it performs its central thesis: Its form and the woods become one: dynamic, interlocked, and kinetic. The poem foregrounds the cycle of life and death and the eerie indifference of nature to the death of a beautiful creature. The poem was a reader's key to the whole collection, and it would appear, appropriately, at the beginning of *Plain Song.*

—

Two months later, desperate for life in the countryside and tired of the city, the Harrisons returned to Michigan. Replicating something like Levertov's arrangement in Temple, Maine—"far north, few people"—they rented an old house in Kingsley, a town just twenty miles from Manton, where Jim had interviewed for the teaching job two and a half years earlier. Jim collected unemployment, earning just thirty-five dollars a month, with only a vague hope that settlement money from the family's lawsuit for the auto accident would come through.

In November, *Plain Song* was published. As some critics would note in the coming months, the collection was intensely autobiographical, ranging from the poet's upbringing to the death of his father and sister. In "David," Jim had used the persona of his younger brother to provide some clarity and the emotional distance to address his father's funeral. He was unable to say anything at the time about the death of his father directly that wasn't "benumbed, cloudy, constricted," as he would later reflect. Of his brother David, he wrote,

> His mind's all black thickets
> and blood; he knows
> flesh slips quietly off the bone,
> he knows no last looks,
> that among the profusion of flowers
> the lid is closed to hide
> what no one could bear—
> that metal rends the flesh . . .

The poem subtly merges the boy's knowledge of hunting and the violence of the woods, the sensations of blood, bone, and flesh with the death of the father. The steel of a car "rends" like the cut of a field-dressing knife. The thickets do not admit sanctuary or reprieve, only darkness and gore.

Other poems, like "A Sequence of Women," addressed Judy's death obliquely, so much so that Jim confessed to not knowing it until after it was written. In "Sketch for a Job-Application Blank," the lines "Light macerates / the lamp infects" echo the gruesome cause of death ("macerated brain") on Winfield's and Judy's death certificates. Reviews for *Plain Song*, which Jim dedicated to Linda, would not appear until the following year.

6

OPERATION STONY BROOK

(SPRING 1965 – 1968)

We'll settle the city question by walking deeply into forests and in reasonably vestal groves eat animal meat and love.

"My friend Michael Palmer just read me your letter and I was pleased to hear you think of me now and then," Tom McGuane wrote to Jim in the early months of 1966. "I sometimes regret not having seen you more in East Lansing, but at the time it didn't seem I could be around anyone who knew what I might be up to in my writing."

McGuane's letter was the first of hundreds that would flow, sometimes on a weekly basis, between him and Jim for the next five decades, and the exchange marked the beginning of their friendship. They had kept their distance from each other during college, both sensing a competitor in the other, and it was a feeling that would never fully go away. McGuane would describe that same feeling in another letter, writing to Jim of their "non-acquaintance" at MSU and a memory from that time, a "glistering image of explication, to wit: you crossing the parking lot at Wylie's bookstore preoccupied as Phillip II at prayer and trailing half a dozen disciples, monks in hot imitation of your gait, speech and predilections; I remember thinking that there was no possibility for myself but collision or steering clear."

Jim had felt similarly, and he'd avoided anyone who "might have reached even the apprentice stage" of writing. "No tarots, little magazines, or public discussions of current 'work.'" The "tarots" referred to MSU's literary magazine *Tarot*, which McGuane had edited.

The two were unalike in many ways: Jim was mostly poor, the son of a county farm agent; Tom, socially polished and well-to-do. But both radiated intellect and energy in a way that drew people to them. Both were extremely driven to write and incredibly well read, and they understood each other in ways others couldn't.

Jim and McGuane's relationship would remain episodic and long-distance. They'd visit with each other at least once a year, mostly in Montana and Key West, often fishing or hunting together. (Jim would credit McGuane with teaching him most of what he knew about fly-fishing.) But McGuane and his opinions would remain ever present in Jim's life, if only as vivid background. McGuane was often a sympathetic sounding board for Jim (and vice versa), and letters ranged from the performative—literary high-wire acts—to the confessional to journal-like documentation of their thoughts and doings. As the years went on, they'd write to each other with the expectation that they were doing so for posterity.

"There is an oddness about our communications—we've only met once," Jim would write of McGuane to friend Dan Gerber in 1968. "But I didn't really know McGuane either before we fished two years ago. It is a question of likeness & empathy. I am also arrogant enough to insist on the success of what I undertake."

Thomas Francis McGuane III was born in Wyandotte, Michigan, in 1939—two years to the day, December 11, after Jim's birth—and grew up in an Irish Catholic household in an affluent neighborhood in Grosse Ile. His father was a tough-minded businessman and auto-parts manufacturer. When McGuane was in his teens and began failing out of school ("I was a very unsuccessful high school student," he admitted), his father yanked him out of public schools and enrolled him at Cranbrook Schools, a private boarding academy in Bloomfield Hills. There McGuane met fellow classmate Edmund White, who had "read all of Proust by the age of twelve" and served as a mentor to him. Like

Jim, McGuane had had a bumpy college career, mostly because he was singularly interested in writing. He attended the University of Michigan (flunked out with a 0.6 grade point average); Olivet College, a small school where Gertrude Stein and Ford Madox Ford had once taught; Harvard for a summer program; and then, finally, MSU.

Back in those days, McGuane was skinny, cocky, "entitled," and a "goddamn genius," said his dorm room neighbor Bob Dattila, and along with his short-cropped hair, he dressed the part of the prep school kid: seersucker suits, ties, tennis sweaters, brogue shoes.* While McGuane's father would go on to make a lot of money, McGuane insisted he didn't grow up with the expectation of having it. If he had a class consciousness, he said, it was because both his parents had college educations. Still, his financial prospects seemed more assured than those of many of his peers, a fact not lost on those around him at MSU. Years later, when McGuane traveled to Ireland to finish a novel, Dattila asked Jim, partly tongue in cheek, why *they* couldn't just set out for Ireland like Tom. "We have no money, Bob," Jim replied simply. Or, as Jim once put it, McGuane was in "the fortunate position of not having to grub for a living."

When McGuane first wrote to Jim in 1966, he had recently completed an MFA in playwriting at the Yale School of Drama—"chiefly avoiding the draft"—and was then living with his first wife, Becky, in Málaga, Spain. McGuane had visited Michigan the previous summer, reportedly fishing Bear Creek and the Boardman River, but he hadn't known that Jim was living in nearby Kingsley and regretted not having seen him. He had read *Plain Song*, and its many references to Michigan made him feel homesick. "I haven't seen such a congestion of good poems," he enthused, "since *RipRap*," referring to Gary Snyder's 1959 collection.

---

* McGuane claims that he never owned a seersucker suit or brogue shoes, and while the comparison sets up a contrast with Jim's modest family economics, his family came with painful problems, chiefly drug and alcohol addiction.

"[Jim] was kind of a lean and muscular guy" in those Kingsley days, recalled local friend Jon Jackson. "He had that bad eye," but he was vigorous and active, and he had a "striding walk," like he was "swinging through life . . . He was on his way to becoming a really recognized poet right from the start."

When the Harrisons moved to Kingsley, a small, tightly knit farming community, in the spring of 1965, they did so at the suggestion of Jim's close friend Lisle Earl, the same friend who had visited him in San Francisco several years earlier. (The poem "Lisle's River" in *Plain Song* is named after him.) Jim and Earl had met at MSU, and for a time, they were practically inseparable. When Jim had moved to Boston, Earl followed him there and tried to get a job at Campbell and Hall, though it didn't pan out, and he eventually returned to Michigan.

A year later, Earl and his family (his wife Marianne and three kids) were living in Kingsley. Earl sounded upbeat, Jim thought, and he was renting a farmhouse (seven rooms and many acres) just a few miles from town for only fifty dollars a month. The idea was too much for Jim to resist, as he and Linda were desperate to escape Boston. The "low overhead" of country living promised freedom from a taxing job and more time to write, or so Jim imagined, and then there was the presence of the Earls and other friends and proximity to excellent bird hunting and fishing. The Harrisons eventually settled in the town of Kingsley on Brownson Avenue in an old farmhouse-like dwelling with a long veranda and a short walk from the local watering holes, the Kingsley Tavern and Kingsley Hotel—Jim's hangouts.

Earl quickly introduced Jim to Pat Paton, a woods-hardened fisherman and hunter, local mason, and all-around handyman who then employed several townspeople. Jim extended him a dainty, limp-wristed handshake, and Paton thought, "Holy shit. What am I into?" He later realized that Jim was sizing him up right then. "Jim never stopped checking people out," Paton said. "I can usually gauge people pretty well. But not him. I thought, this is going to take some work."

Despite their odd first meeting, Jim and Paton became close friends. "I was taken under the rumpled wing of Pat Paton," Jim later wrote, referring to his time in Kingsley and Paton's prosthetic arm. (Paton would lose his arm in a construction accident.) Each morning, Jim would help him with an assortment of jobs, from laying brick and block to roughing in and roofing houses, concrete work, and trimming Christmas trees, all for $2.50 an hour. He vastly preferred the outdoor labor to delivering books in New England, and he liked that Paton paid him at the end of every day. That first summer, he fell into a routine: He worked four hours with Paton, collected his ten dollars, went to the tavern, headed home for a nap, and then wrote. He worked hard at everything. "Whatever he did, he did good and did thorough," Paton said. "There was no slack in that man."

Paton and his wife, Vesper, had moved to Kingsley in 1938 and built their own house ("every inch of it," said Paton). Local farmers referred to the five-foot-seven-inch Paton as a hippie because he wore an earring and had long hair, but Paton never thought of himself as one. After meeting Paton in the late 1960s, Gary Snyder remembered him as dressed "all in black, bearded, with a wrinkled face like a tough old woods-elf." Snyder hadn't forgotten either that Paton had given him a broadax as a gift (a "real boon," he thought).

Despite their differences, Jim and Linda grew to think of Pat and Vesper as family. They were, in a sense, surrogate parents. Paton was ten years older than Jim and not literary in the slightest, and while Jim was "a definite Democrat," Paton was "a righty." But the two had no problems talking about their views and often did so fireside on camping trips.

The Patons had never met anyone like Jim. One evening, the couple were astonished to hear Jim and Lisle Earl analyze Peter Matthiessen's *At Play in the Fields of the Lord*. "And that was the first time I had ever heard that done," recalled Vesper. "It was the most interesting evening we had ever had." The Patons had also never met anyone like Linda (nor had many of the locals), whose parents were well off and politically connected enough to have state police escort her to Lansing. All they knew was that her father was some kind of "big wheel."

Linda, in turn, was equally unused to the Patons' lifestyle. When she first met them, they were living in a rough, unfinished house, and they took Jim and Linda to the hardware store for dinner, where everyone dined on hot dogs and drank cola while employees demonstrated stoves for the customers. "I didn't know how I could possibly move to Kingsley," she later admitted to Vesper. And yet, Linda took to the Patons, in part because their door was always open to her and Jim, and the coffee pot was always on. If Linda couldn't make it to Lansing to visit her family, or Jim was drinking at the hotel bar, which he often did, she could go to the Patons and feel welcomed and at home.*

Jim and Paton shared a love for the woods and rivers of northern Michigan, and that was a large part of their connection; they regularly fished and hunted the area and camped out in the Upper Peninsula. Paton would serve as something of a father figure to Jim, and not a judgmental one. Once, just a few days after they met, Jim sheepishly asked Paton what he thought of his damaged eye, and Paton responded bluntly, "I think it's your goddamn eye. What are you bothering me about it for?"

Jim and Linda loved the Kingsley area, and it reminded Jim of Reed City. It was a landscape that would "appear nondescript and scrubby to those who favor the cordillera of the Rockies," but to him it looked like home. At the time, there was also a buzz about the place to which Jim's presence had contributed. Newcomers flocked to the area, including his friend Jon Jackson, and many were college graduates just out of MSU who moved to rusticate and live out a hippieish country idyll.

The Earls hosted pig roasts at their farmhouse—revelers came and went around the clock, literally all night long—and the whole community would come out. "There was a hog roast last week—they roasted a hundred pound pig which was served along with corn turkey ham etc and endless quantities of beer plus dancing to a hillbilly band," Jim reported to Levertov. "Much drunkenness. I helped to butcher the hog which un-nerved me a bit." Most of Jim's friends were interested in healthy local food and cooking, and they took it seriously. On weekends, Jim

* Years later, when the Patons were planning to move to the countryside outside of Kingsley, Linda drew a detailed sketch of a home in the woods. The Patons would use it as a model for their new home, such was the close nature of their relationship.

and Linda went square dancing or listened to bluegrass. "Been having a hectic week-end," Jim wrote to Norma at one point, highlighting his social schedule. "Linda and I went to three parties in four days & danced a lot which I haven't done for quite a while."

Many of the locals looked on these newcomers with a mix of amazement and derision. Mostly conservative farmers, they didn't look kindly on outsiders or self-proclaimed poets, especially male ones, but Jim never hesitated to declare what he considered his profession. He would go into the Kingsley Hotel and announce, "I'm a poet," said friend Jim Crockett, another Kingsley local. "I heard him say it a million times."

Regardless of the fun, the Harrisons were mostly broke, and it took its toll on them. If Paton did not work, neither did Jim, and he would try to pick up odd jobs where he could. "Woe. Poverty. etc.," he complained to Norma in July 1965, when there was little work to be found. At one point, he considered applying for employment in a canning factory to make ends meet and later in a nearby state hospital for the mentally ill (it was considered a local industry) as a ward attendant but decided against it.

Things got so bad at times that he half regretted leaving Boston, as "a prisoner wishes he was back in the security of his cell block." Things couldn't get much worse. In October, Norma helped out the family with a lump-sum loan that would last them until February, Jim estimated, especially with Linda's "heavy, cold hand on the checkbook." The loan would give him the chance to work under conditions that he felt necessary for an artist, he told his mother, and he would try again to write a novel, which he hoped, if successful, might bring in some money (a "long shot," he realized). The novel didn't work out.

To make matters worse, their rental, forty dollars per month, was cold and drafty, and the house brought with it a large fuel bill. Once, when it was below zero and they ran out of gas, Paton apparently hot-wired a fuel truck and gave them a free tankful. Others chipped in to help out too. At Christmastime, Vic Herman, who owned Horizon Books in Traverse City, started a tab for Jim at the store so he could buy presents. Years later, Jim would return to Horizon many times to do readings, and the store would sell his rare first editions.

—

The release of *Plain Song* in November lifted Jim's spirits, and he became something of a celebrity in the village—and elsewhere. Locals called him "Shakespeare." The poet Michael Palmer, a friend of McGuane's, thought Jim the best-known poet in America under thirty, or so McGuane told Jim, adding that Palmer "reads every last wrinkle." Others—like Al Young, the editor of *Love* magazine, another of McGuane's friends—were surprised to find a poet "who wanted to write poems and not join a school of poetry."

Professional reviews—the first of Jim's life—were mostly positive, with some key exceptions. "[Mark] McCloskey raped me in Poetry," Jim complained to Levertov months after *Plain Song*'s publication. "Sorry it had to happen there & so coldly." McCloskey's review was particularly poignant because *Poetry* "held a strong almost supra-literary effect" on Jim, and he'd been reading it since the age of sixteen. Some poems he found uninteresting, others failed on their own terms. "Mr. Harrison on occasion creates poetry rather than notes toward it," McCloskey had concluded, with more than a little condescension. He cited "David," "Fair/Boy Christian Takes a Break," and "Kinship" as examples.

The Detroit News celebrated *Plain Song* as belonging "neither to the Beat nor to the Academic wing of contemporary poetry," while Bill Corbett, Jim's friend from Boston, praised the collection as emerging from the tradition of Whitman, Williams, Pound, and more lately Theodore Roethke, but not just that, "Li Po, Lorca, Vallejo, Rilke and René Char as well"—smart, given that the latter would remain some of Jim's favorite poets.

Jim read every review he could get his hands on, but he weathered the critical ups and downs and continued writing. "Up to my chin in projects, large and small," he informed his mother. He was still working on a novel that he had begun four years earlier and found in it "nothing salvageable," just a sloppy "gob of prose," and he assured his friends that he had no intention of crowding the ranks of novelists. Mostly he worked on new poems for his second book, *Locations*, and given the poor state of his fiction, he hoped to break into magazine publishing. That would at least bring in money and give him a much broader readership. This he had learned from McGuane, who was already publishing in *Sports Illustrated* and other prominent magazines. Money had become a primary concern.

"There's no freedom in scratching for a living," he wearily admitted to Levertov that fall. "But I'm always possessed by the dreamy idea that something will turn up, as they say."

—

Jim was right—something did turn up. In January 1966, Herbert Weisinger, Jim's former professor, unexpectedly extended an invitation to him to complete his master's degree at MSU, and he provided him with an easy path forward. The two had stayed in touch since Jim had dropped out, and Weisinger had kept tabs on Jim, following closely his success with *Plain Song*. While Jim was still living in Boston, Weisinger had urged him to return to school, insisting that his "métier is teaching and not bookselling"—Jim agreed with the latter—and it followed that he needed a graduate degree. "After all," Weisinger had written, "universities are now the Mycenae of the arts." Weisinger persuaded Jim that a teaching job would demand far less time and energy from him than construction work, and so it would free up his time for the "real work of writing." He had pulled some strings, he told him, and Jim could finish his degree without taking more classes. He would only need to complete a thesis, but that would require him to write only about the composition of *Plain Song* and nothing more.

Given the Harrisons' financial woes, the prospect of teaching sounded more palatable than it had in the past, and Jim accepted the offer. He proudly informed Norma that he had received a "fine letter" from Weisinger that praised his new book and "repeated (aggressively)" the invitation to finish his degree, and he would set about working on the required thesis. "This would at least assure me of a decent teaching job in the Fall," he noted. Meanwhile, Weisinger had taken a leave of absence from MSU to teach at New York University alongside his friend M. L. Rosenthal, and he would oversee Jim's progress from afar. As for teaching jobs, he recommended that Jim begin making inquiries to various schools and, knowing Jim's mind, warned him against getting "over involved with the paper; just get it done," he urged him.

The result of Jim's labor, "A Natural History of Some Poems," was the kind of exercise—an inevitably reductive one—that would make many writers cringe, but it was undoubtedly the easiest way for him to get the degree. "The very real objection that anyone might have is that of honesty," he wrote in its opening pages. "Papers of this sort have always had an air of the unreal to me—the temptation to pose for the picture, to exaggerate, to minimize unpleasant or embarrassing aspects, is great." His reservations notwithstanding, "A Natural History" is a unique document, providing context for the creation of *Plain Song*, a discussion of his influences, the themes of the collection, and the poems themselves, and it provided a snapshot of his budding poetics. It would later appear in *Just Before Dark: Collected Nonfiction* in 1991, though Jim was reluctant to include it. He would insist it was only "juvenilia, of interest only to 'assistant professors,'" and he would leave the proofs of it to his daughter Jamie, who, then in her thirties, would edit the collection.

In August, Jim formally submitted the thesis, and on September 2, 1966, the Comparative Literature Department awarded him the degree of master of arts. Jim observed that he had gone from black sheep to white in the eyes of the faculty, and he chalked it all up to "a pure acknowledgment of the power of New York publishers." *Plain Song* had seemingly changed everything.

Months earlier, as Jim chipped away at the thesis, he and Linda traveled to the East Coast. They had visited with John and Rebecca in New Haven, where John had taken a job as head of the science library at Yale, and they managed to see Levertov and her husband, Mitchell, in Maine. John and Rebecca went along and were very impressed with her—especially Rebecca, herself a poet. In what came as some relief, Levertov assured Jim that publisher George Brockway, the head of Norton, "intended to stick with [him]" and that Norton planned to publish his second book of poetry. *Plain Song* had sold well—about a thousand copies each in hardcover and soft—and it was second in sales for poetry behind only Louis Zukofsky's new collection—not "bad for poetry in five months." Jim was also glad that Levertov herself intended to stick with him. He wrote to her often during this period and still considered her a mentor, in his words, "Apprentice to journeyman, colt to yearling or something like that."

Other things were looking up for Jim too. Western Michigan University had offered to pay him a hundred dollars to do a reading that spring, a nice fee for any poet at the time, and he would buy Jamie a new bike and a puppy, a white English pointer named Missy, with the money. On top of that, Northern Michigan University in Marquette had offered him a teaching position to begin in the fall, once he had his degree in hand. Jim was excited at the prospect of a steady income, and his plan was to teach during the school year and then exhaust himself with work during the summer months. He tended to work in phases anyway, he reasoned, and have dry spells when he could do nothing but revise. For now, he was going through a highly productive period.

"Have no choice but to teach next year," he wrote to Levertov, "but it's a low pressure place way up in the woods on lake Superior . . . Getting so many images & ideas of late that I am glutted . . . I have the feeling of gifts being forced upon me and I have to reshape and uncover them and give them a durable form. If it keeps on I'll have enough work for the rest of the year."

The Harrisons' hopes that they might somehow stay in Michigan seemed secured by the job offer, and Jim and Linda began looking for a place to live in Marquette. But just before they committed to one, Weisinger wrote to Jim with yet another opportunity. He was leaving MSU for good, he explained, and he had accepted a position as chair of English at the University of New York at Stony Brook. He wanted Jim to join him there as his assistant.

The opportunity was simply too good to resist. It came with the chance to work with his college mentor and for good pay, about $9,000 a year—a staggering sum compared with his recent income. It also offered Jim an easy out from having to teach. Weisinger would help to smooth things over with Northern Michigan University, and Jim would work to smooth things over with Linda.

"We're moving to Stony Brook at the end of the week rather than Marquette," he updated Levertov at the end of the summer, "no teaching, good pay, not too strenuous." There are bright people there, he added, as if trying to convince himself of his decision, and he sensed correctly, against his preferences to stay in Michigan, that the move would be a good thing for his work. He was simply too young to retire to the woods.

How Linda felt about following her husband again to the East Coast is not clear. She likely welcomed the increased income if not the unsettledness of it all and the sense of whiplash that accompanied the back-and-forth. The Harrisons would settle directly in the hamlet of Stony Brook in a "grown-up house, a bit run-down but in a pleasant neighborhood," down the street from Long Island Sound.

The State University of New York at Stony Brook had only just opened its doors in 1962, with two academic buildings housing Humanities and Chemistry, and it did so with the hope that it would soon become the crown jewel within the SUNY system.* By 1966 it was a full-fledged campus with more than six academic buildings, a library, and dormitories as well as a fine-arts center and three more buildings in the works. The English Department, hoping to capitalize on the state's generous

* The institution had first opened as the State University College on Long Island at Oyster Bay in 1957. It relocated the majority of its classes and operations to Stony Brook in 1962, at which time it changed its name.

funding and ambitions, had recruited Weisinger, a well-connected and distinguished scholar, to lead it, and Jim would serve as his aide-de-camp. He would assist with a range of administrative details, organize readings for visiting writers, and having Weisinger's ear, help to shape the direction of the fledgling department, which was already staffed by various luminaries. Among them was John Thompson and, later, Louis Simpson, a relatively mainstream establishment poet who had recently won the Pulitzer Prize.

The renowned critic Alfred Kazin taught there ("a strange and distracted person," as Jim described him), along with Blake scholar David Erdman and Philip Roth. (Roth was teaching part-time at both Stony Brook and the University of Pennsylvania and living in the Kips Bay area of Manhattan.) And then there was a roster of notable students, graduate and undergraduate, who socialized often and freely with the faculty—sometimes too much so—including George Quasha, an advanced graduate student who quickly became great friends with Jim and Linda; Quasha would come to think of them as family.

The university would serve as Jim's debut to literary society. He would meet more writers there in a short time (two school years in total) than perhaps at any other point in his life, and he would make incredibly valuable connections. More than anything else, these were the fruits born of the financial exigencies of being a father and husband—the need for a steady job and, ironically for Jim, one in the bosom of academic administration, of all places. The introductions began almost immediately.

At a department meeting on his first day, Jim met the heavy hitters, Kazin and Roth, a rather "heady experience," he recalled, since he had read everything they had written. Neither was particularly friendly, Jim thought, and he mostly disliked Roth and found him standoffish; he had mixed feelings about Kazin. He would recall how, early on, Kazin came into his office and told him he liked his book very much but then began to opine on "alternative ways to write a poem." But Jim admired their intellects, and he thought they contributed to an intensity of discourse in the department that he would credit partly to the many Jewish intellectuals there, like Weisinger himself, who "spoke about ideas as if they were living organisms."

Stony Brook seemed uniquely wired into the American literary scene, particularly so with poetry. Part of this sense derived from Jim's freedom to invite poets to campus—with whom he dined and drank, often at his own house—and organize seemingly countless readings. In his role as Weisinger's assistant, he met Robert Lowell, James Wright, W. H. Auden, and Derek Walcott as well as the composer John Cage. Robert Duncan visited several times, staying at the Harrisons' house, and guest-taught classes, as did Levertov, Galway Kinnell, and Gary Snyder. James Dickey once came to the house for dinner, and Linda reportedly insisted afterward that "'that man' wasn't going to enter her house again," apparently due to his vulgarity and drunkenness. Future writer Eliot Weinberger left Yale to study at Stony Brook because George Quasha had convinced him that the university was "going to be where it's happening in poetry in America." Geoffrey O'Brien, the future editor of Library of America, enrolled for similar reasons. Jim's friend from MSU, J. D. Reed, followed Jim to Long Island and enrolled.

Stony Brook was unrestrained and aggressively countercultural in the mid-1960s, and despite Weisinger's sober, scholarly style, the English Department had an air of the Wild West to it. "It was an incredibly wild place," said one student; there was "a ton of drugs" and even drug busts in the dormitories. One example: On January 17, 1968, 198 policemen descended on student residences at five o'clock in the morning without prior notice to university officials and arrested approximately thirty-five college-aged persons, about half of whom were enrolled there. The police followed a tactical plan titled "Operation Stony Brook."

"Have you read about the raid on campus?" Linda asked Norma. "It even made Walter Cronkite."

There were parties and lots of drinking and booze-filled impromptu trips to the city. Occasionally, when Jim was too hungover to teach, he would ask Eliot Weinberger, his "prized student," to lead his poetry workshop for him. Weinberger, a brilliant undergraduate who was clearly up to the task, was only auditing classes. He wasn't even officially enrolled at the university at the time.

Faculty and staff fraternized with students, and the line between them could become recklessly blurry. Male faculty had seemingly little compunction about sleeping with female students—Jim included, though he was not faculty. One female student remembered walking in on Jim and another female student having sex in a guest bedroom at a raucous party. It was a jarring experience for her, and she recalled the awkwardness of afterward attending his classes. Jim did not seem particularly embarrassed by the incident but rather mildly amused, at least in her perception.

Jim had then (and would continue to have) a surprising callousness about extramarital flings, and "fling" is the correct word. These were casual sexual relationships, full of excitement or passion in the moment, that demanded next to nothing of him emotionally and little of his time. Over the years, they would range from one-night stands to ongoing sexual involvements, and only rarely would they develop into something more.

There was apparently no consent from Linda for such behavior, especially early on, tacit or otherwise—theirs was not an open marriage—though she was not at all naive about the man she had married. She knew about or surmised Jim's infidelities, and the two would sometimes fight about the issue. Jim's relative carelessness meant that his affairs were often hardly a secret, and if he crossed a line, their marriage would hang in the balance. The two would eventually establish a seemingly uneasy truce—a sort of don't-ask-don't-tell resignation and trade-off. But Jim's actions would cause undeniable anguish to Linda and the family. To friends, it seemed that he did not fully register how much he hurt Linda or how hard it could be on her.

At Stony Brook, Jim would cross one of Linda's lines. During his first year, he met Peter and Deborah Matthiessen, as well as William and Rose Styron. That they all drank a good deal helped Jim feel right at home. "Again, this was a startling experience," he would note, because he had read the work of these "literary giants." Jim respected Bill Styron, but he was somewhat infatuated with Rose. Many of his friends knew about his feelings, although he apparently never confessed them to her.

As for Rose, she enjoyed Jim's company enormously. She considered him "very amusing and very smart," she said, and she liked that they were both poets, "so we had that in common." But she insisted that she thought of him only as a friend. It was never sexual. Nor did she find him physically attractive, at least not like she did her own husband or even Peter Matthiessen.

Jim and Rose would correspond in the years to come and see each other socially, mostly in New York. Jim would periodically invite her on trips—to Key West, Montana, and always in the company of his male friends. Rose would graciously decline.

But Linda sensed trouble from the start. Many years later, she would confess to a friend that of all of Jim's infidelities, Rose was the one that almost broke up their marriage—a surprising admission, given that Jim and Rose's friendship had apparently remained platonic and that Jim had had plenty of other sexual relationships throughout the years. A poet, translator, editor, and human rights activist, Rose has an impressive pedigree and charm, along with an array of professional accomplishments, that Linda may have found uniquely threatening.

As if reluctant to open old wounds, Jim would mention Rose Styron only twice, in passing, in his memoirs. But he would also name one of his dogs Rose (coincidentally or not) many years later, and Linda apparently didn't object. She was, after all, an avid gardener.

Jim would forge new friendships from afar as well. In November 1966, Dan Gerber reached out to him with a typed letter addressed to him at the university. Like McGuane's, Gerber's letter marked the beginning of a lifelong friendship. Gerber was a few years younger than Jim, and he had graduated from MSU, but the two had missed each other there. As Gerber observed, "MSU seems to be following you." The impetus for his letter came from Clyde Henson, Jim's former professor, who shared with Gerber a copy of *Plain Song*. "I didn't know you then," Gerber noted, referring to their brief overlapping time at the university, "but I have been so impressed and delighted by your work that I feel I have been introduced to you."

Jim remembered Henson fondly ("he had a sense of 'bearing,' of dignity that is rare," he recalled), and he thought Gerber's name seemed familiar—of course, it did. The son of Daniel Frank Gerber, the founder of Gerber Products Company, Dan then raced cars professionally and taught high school. He was also a poet, and he hoped that Jim would consider visiting him and his wife, Virginia—or Ginny, as she was called—when he was back in Michigan. Gerber was then living in Fremont, Michigan, in the middle of a "virgin forest," he noted, "the type of setting, I would assume from your poems, that you would enjoy."

Already weary of New York, Jim envied Gerber the woodsy setting in his own home state. He was living in a "mega-city, ie," he griped, "all the eastern seaboard being a giant city. I didn't think it would bother me to be here for two years or so, but it only took a week to depress me, especially after Kingsley." The two would finally meet face-to-face a year later, when Jim and Linda stopped by the Gerbers' home on a snowy evening in late December.

Jim's patience with Stony Brook, both the town *and* the job, had quickly worn thin. His position was too administrative for his liking, and although he taught classes and would eventually be offered a position on the faculty, the idea of working as a poet-teacher in academia remained as unappealing as ever. There was nothing romantic about grading and teaching schedules. In June 1967, he applied for a National Endowment for the Arts grant that, if awarded (he had requested $10,000), would enable him to return rather comfortably to Michigan and his writing.

M. L. Rosenthal, who had read *Plain Song*, served as a reference, as did Levertov and Louis Simpson.

Meanwhile, Jim sent off his new manuscript to Norton that same month, and he kept himself busy. He published the poem "Walking" with Pym-Randall Press in April and gave readings at local colleges. He visited Levertov at Vassar and guest-taught her class there, and in September he attended the World Poetry Conference in Montreal, a sort of reconnaissance mission since he and Simpson were planning a World Poetry Conference at Stony Brook for the following spring. While in Montreal, Jim managed to charm the attractive poet and director of literary programs for the NEA, Carolyn Kizer, which could not have hurt his chances for a grant. Kizer would later thank him for all of his "kind courtesy and attentiveness" in Montreal, and the two would stay in touch.

A month afterward, Jim flew with Simpson and J. D. Reed to Washington, DC, to join the Writers March on the Pentagon, led by Norman Mailer and Robert Lowell, both of whom spoke to the crowds that day in protest of the Vietnam War. Allen Ginsberg had plans to "levitate" the Pentagon, a theatrical publicity stunt, and Mailer would later immortalize the event in *The Armies of the Night*. Eliot Weinberger had recently been beaten "black and blue" in another demonstration, which made Jim feel "both timid and obligated" to participate. Jim and Reed allegedly hung back, taking up the rear of the march, and took turns taking shots of whiskey from a flask. Jim later claimed to have helped chase off members of the American Nazi Party who were harassing protestors. He was not above boastful embellishment, but the fact that J. D. Reed was a hulk of a man, who stood roughly six foot five, makes it somewhat more plausible. Jim likely tucked himself behind Reed and followed.

Jim strongly opposed the Vietnam War, but he generally declined to partake in the activism of some of his friends and colleagues, especially when it came to his poetry, and his position placed him squarely between two of his friends, Levertov and Robert Duncan. Jim had grown increasingly friendly with Duncan, and he would eventually be at odds with Levertov. (By 1975, Levertov and Duncan's differing views on the war would contribute to the end of their own friendship.)

While Jim had sent Levertov his poem "Natural World" for her *Out of the War Shadow: The 1968 Peace Calendar & Appointment Book of the War Resisters League*, he did not share her views about the necessity of political activism (however reluctant her own anti-war activities may have been) or the need to write an "absolutely direct anti-war poem," as she had done with "Life at War" and other poems (i.e., "Advent 1966," "Tenebrae," or the book-length journal-poem *To Stay Alive*). Quasha, who was, like Jim, at the center of these discussions, would describe these as Levertov's "shrill political poems." Levertov began giving readings that were themselves activist acts, said Quasha, and Duncan felt they were a betrayal of her talent.

While Duncan wrote poems with politics in them, he felt that taking an ideological position with them betrayed the space of the poem. Jim shared Duncan's convictions that an artist must remain detached from political action to obtain a state of elevated consciousness. War, for Duncan, was an absolute evil, and he felt "helpless outrage at the lies upon which the American policy is run" and the needless deaths and suffering we had inflicted upon Vietnam. Duncan was definitely against the war, and at one point he had black bands sewn on his suit jackets so he could always bear witness. But Duncan also thought that war was an unceasing and inevitable condition of life: "THERE HAS BEEN NO TIME IN HUMAN HISTORY THAT WAS NOT A TIME OF WAR," he had written to Levertov.

Like Duncan, Jim thought that it was "terribly dangerous" for an artist to embrace causes, particularly so in one's poems, and he believed that the role of the artist instead was to bear witness to the underground survival of life during times of war. The *work* was the thing, as it always had been for him. But his position left him uneasy, as he confessed to McGuane. "So my only form of resistance is consciousness, knowing that I somehow must breed, love, and die within a state of total and permanent horror."

Jim had taken up the topic of war in the poem "War Suite," the one he had sent to Levertov for her calendar, but he had not written about Vietnam specifically. "Only total war comes," he explained, in an echo of Duncan's thought that war never ceases. The poem addressed Vietnam only obliquely through images of war from *Gilgamesh* to the Hundred Years' War. As one stanza read:

> The wars: we're drawn to them
> as if in fever, we sleepwalk to them,
> wake up in full stride of nightmare,
> blood slippery, mouth deep in their gore.

"I sing sixty-seven wars," another stanza began, one war for each year of the current century—total war and the inevitability of it. Jim would wait to take up the subject of Vietnam until his second novel, *A Good Day to Die*, a book that, in his words, "came out of the feeling of the late sixties." Its protagonist is a disillusioned Vietnam veteran.

In November 1967, Jim received welcome news: The NEA had awarded him a grant of $7,000. He planned to finish out the school year and requested that the beginning of the grant period be deferred until June, after the school year ended and when he planned to leave Stony Brook for good. He was delighted, and he seemed perfectly at ease with accepting support from the US government. "Re the political question: even the most recalcitrant of revolutionaries accepts the favors of the State he wishes to overhaul," Jim wrote in his acceptance letter to Chairman Robert Stevens.

> I am simply a poet who has driven on federal roads, slept in federal forests, paid federal taxes, and now has been given some federal recognition of his existence as a poet. I accept this recognition with pleasure and wish long life to a government which honors her artists.

His letter endeared him to the NEA and particularly to Carolyn Kizer, who responded to his "beautiful and welcome letter" and asked him to forward copies of it to *The New York Review of Books* and *The Village Voice*, both of which had been critical of the program in light of the war.

Eight months later, the NEA awarded Jim again, this time $500 for the best poem ("War Suite") published in an American literary magazine. Jim remained pragmatic about the award money, and he looked forward to getting back to the Midwest with new funding and time to write. "Any artist is an artist first and a citizen second. Wars we have with us always—bread less often."

7

LOCATIONS

(FALL 1967 – SPRING 1969)

Mind follow the nose
this honey of whiskey
I smell through the throat of the bottle.

. . . .

And the glass is cool,
a sweet cedar post that flames so briskly.

When Jim received his contract from Norton for *Locations* in October 1967, it came as a great relief, as he had long worried it might be rejected. "Denise had assured me that it was coming," he wrote to publisher George Brockway, "but I am generally a creature made up of all sorts of nightmares, so I wondered."

Jim had no special reason to worry, but the long-awaited contract confirmed for him that *Plain Song* had not been merely a fluke. He was not, as he feared, a one-book writer. At Brockway's request, Jim clarified that he wanted his name to remain "Jim Harrison," as opposed to James, for publishing purposes, "inasmuch as that is the name that I am known under and a reputation is an accretive thing in poetry—years of sediment make a name." Jim was still getting over his fury from a mix-up the previous summer when *The New York Times* published his poem "Cold August" and misspelled his name as "Jim Hanison."

"I have never confessed it before but I am violently ambitious," he admitted to McGuane that fall. "Not so much for a reputation—they can change too rapidly—but for a body of work I can sit on without my feet touching the floor—even if it only takes two or three books. Difficult to trace—ultimately to prove that I am not a liar, that my life isn't that of a liar. That my poems when they are good are true poems, not of course in terms of actuality but as part of a body of inescapably true poems given us in the last thirty centuries."

Locations would add a second layer of sediment.

A few months later, in January 1968, Jim sent Brockway two more poems to add to the manuscript—the eponymous "Locations" and "Legenda." As he informed Brockway, the PEN Club in New York City had invited Jim to read there on April 1, the Guggenheim Museum the following night, just before he and the family would head back to Michigan for spring vacation. He also noted that his novel was almost finished, though he felt he was spreading his talent as "thin as shellac." In truth, the unnamed novel, none of which remains today, wasn't really close to being finished, but he wanted to keep it in Brockway's mind and his foot in the door for when it was. He would chip away at it in the months to come but to no avail.

Even as Jim wrote to Brockway at Norton, he had begun networking on behalf of McGuane (and indirectly for himself) at Simon & Schuster, where an instructor friend's wife, Alix Nelson, worked as a junior editor. McGuane, who had had no success placing his first novel, *The Sporting Club*, had recently fired his agent, and he allowed Jim to act temporarily on his behalf. Jim mailed the manuscript to Nelson, who in turn passed it up the ladder to Richard Locke, and within weeks, McGuane had a contract. (McGuane would simultaneously sign with the high-profile agent Candida Donadio.) Jim would say that shepherding a manuscript through a publishing house never worked that well again in his life and that he was thrilled to help out on behalf of his close friend.

In the coming months, Jim would reach out again to Simon & Schuster—and also to Knopf, Atlantic Monthly, and other presses—on behalf of Dan Gerber and J. D. Reed. Simon & Schuster would publish Reed's collection *Expressways* in 1969. It was characteristic of Jim to help out friends and other writers (many people have attested to this) and hoist them up the literary ladder if he could.

—

That spring, Jim and Louis Simpson worked together to organize the World Poetry Conference at Stony Brook, a remarkable undertaking scheduled for June 21–23, 1968. "It was the only attempt in this country, as far as I know," observed the poet Charles Simic, an attendee, "to bring together such a wide range of poets, young and old, from mainstream to avant-garde and those who eluded classification"—108 poets, including international ones, according to Jim's count. Officially, Simpson was the director, though Jim later claimed that he had essentially run the show. It was an important event for the university and a promotional opportunity that even the administration recognized. Stony Brook's president, John S. Toll, touted the "major international meeting" as evidence of the faculty's stature in the literary world. The press release mentioned only Simpson, but Jim had been instrumental in drawing together so many writers, partly because he had cultivated so many relationships in such a short amount of time.

Simpson boasted, and rightly so, that the invitees were absolutely first-rate and the best writers throughout the world. It was a thrilling opportunity for Jim and one that placed him at the center of the poetry universe. The attendees were a veritable who's who of poetry and included Levertov, Duncan, Gary Snyder, Allen Ginsberg, Anthony Hecht, Donald Justice, Galway Kinnell, Mark Strand, and James Tate. Internationally, Giuseppe Ungaretti, Czesław Miłosz, Zbigniew Herbert, Eugène Guillevic, and Nicanor Parra. Carolyn Kizer came—the NEA had provided a grant to support the festival—as did M. L. Rosenthal and Jim's friends Bill Corbett, Gerber, and of course Reed. The festival's sessions were held in conjunction with the Poetry Center of the Ninety-Second Street YM-YWHA (where Jim had read for the first time back in 1965) and the Lincoln Center Festival '68.

The conference was a wild affair that proved a bizarre spectacle even by Stony Brook's standards, and Linda had seen it coming. She had become accustomed enough, in the years she'd been at Stony Brook, to the antics of visiting writers. "Poets and 'literary' people, when they get together are really something else," she wrote to Norma a few months earlier. "I imagine the poetry festival in June will be interesting, if not a bit disgusting." She was right on both counts.

The first evening began well enough with introductions and a sumptuous dinner, courtesy of Jim, of fresh lobster and fine wines for the guests. Most academics would have simply served cold cuts, but Jim spent well beyond the budget and splurged on the event. The generosity managed to sustain good feelings for a time, though as the night wore on, guests began dividing into their respective tribes, semi-hostile poetry-based factions—academic versus open-form poets, and so on—and the more they drank, the more the tensions between them seemed to escalate.

The event then devolved into something resembling a raucous fraternity party. As inebriated poets took over the university dormitories, which served as housing for the event, some got lost and roamed the hallways. Shouting echoed through the concrete corridors late into the night. Drunken guests claimed the wrong rooms and beds. Some got tossed out. Henry Rago, the editor of *Poetry*, whom no one apparently liked, roamed the hallways with a bottle of vodka, trying to get someone to drink with him, as Simic would recall. Other guests hooked up and sought out private (and not so private) places to have sex. Jim recalled tripping over a "coupling couple" in a parking lot, though most people, he claimed, were just getting drunk and throwing things out of windows. In *1968: A History in Verse*, Ed Sanders remembered staying in the dormitories and the poet

> Anselm Hollo
> Trying to hurl a typewriter out a window,
> but the glass was too tough
> whereupon he tossed it down some stairs

a piece of typed-on paper
around the roller.

That was the first night of the conference.

The next day, hungover participants gave readings throughout the morning and afternoon, and even then, factionalism sometimes reared up. At one point, while reading a lengthy poem, Duncan was heckled by another poet, periodically shouting "shit" until he himself was shouted down and told to shut up. Other readings were peaceful and splendid. International poets were accompanied by translators who read the poems in English, and then the poets read in their native tongues. David Ignatow thought Nicanor Parra "the climax" of the day and "entertainingly brilliant." Everyone had the opportunity to meet fellow writers with whom they had corresponded or encountered only in print. "I went away highly stimulated and filled with hope for the future," Ignatow recalled, "with such a diversified gathering of poets willing and able to talk to and with one another, short of bloodletting!"

The bloodletting would come later. The next night, during an alcohol-fueled party at Louis Simpson's house in Belle Terre, a fight broke out over an insult. "You're nothing without your husband," Ed Sanders had overheard one male professor say to the wife of another. When Sanders laughed at the man and taunted him back, saying that he was nothing too, another guest (likely J. D. Reed) came up from behind the man and broke a bottle of champagne over his head. In the fight that ensued, a glass table on the outside patio was broken into pieces, and as guests tried to put a stop to it, they were themselves punched and kicked and drawn into the melee. At one point, Allen Ginsberg reportedly dropped to his knees amid the fighting and chanted Buddhist prayers for peace. Some of the international poets, watching from a safe distance, wondered with glee if this was how American poets always settled their differences. Sanders later blamed the very drunk Donald Hall, a close friend of Simpson's, for the broken table, because he figured Simpson wouldn't stay mad at him for very long. As for Sanders, he admitted he had drunk so much that his liver was "feeling like a Rudi Stern neon." Jim's whereabouts during the fight are anybody's guess, but he was absent from accounts of it. He would never write about that night or the conference in any detail.

The moment apparently demanded a document, as well—a political statement from the conference and the community of poets. The result was a letter to the editor, titled "Poet Power," published in *The New York Review of Books* and signed by thirty-six of the attendees, including Harrison, Duncan, Levertov, Quasha, Reed, and Simpson. Ginsberg was likely its primary author—it was written in his Beat style and spirit: "That police state military tyranny, sexual repression and laws against expansion of consciousness by joyful music naked dance and high natural herbs threaten further evolution of the race," read one line. The letter took aim at everything from "man's usurpation over all nature" to an oppressive state apparatus, and it promoted poets as the standard-bearers of consciousness—a dubious claim, perhaps, at this conference. In fairness, the document admitted that "Poets fighting on suburban lawns drunk is also real."

The conference, for better or worse, was a capstone to Jim's time at Stony Brook, and he left for Michigan immediately afterward. He had accomplished what he set out to do. At a time when the world of poetry was relatively small, he had managed to meet practically everyone. And in the months that followed, people wrote to Jim with their impressions of the weekend. James Tate, only partly in jest, called it the "World Poetry cesspool" and wished he had had more chances to swap poems with people. Simic would later dub the event "The Great Poets' Brawl of '68." To McGuane, Jim privately confessed that "the poesy conference was an unspeakable drunken atrocity," and he hoped it would remain safely tucked away in unrecorded history.

—

At the end of June, the Harrisons moved into a stone farmhouse on Eagle Highway in Lake Leelanau. The property came with a barn and sat on a hill that overlooked cherry orchards and Lake Michigan. "I can see 20 mi at least from the dining room window—Lake Leelanau, Lake Michigan, further out, N + South Manitou," Jim announced to McGuane, Levertov, Brockway, and anyone who would listen.

"You are so smug about your farmhouse that it will serve you right if birds eat all your cherries and keep you awake while they're doing it," Brockway replied.

Jim was thrilled to be out of the big city and back in Michigan, though he was sorely missed at Stony Brook, at least by a few. Before he had left, the faculty had voted to promote him from assistant to assistant professor, as he would appear in the subsequent year's university catalog. It was a last-ditch effort by Weisinger, Simpson, and Kazin, to keep him at the university. Although the department meeting was confidential, Jim later learned that many people had opposed his promotion, but Kazin, who had come to like Jim, overwhelmed them and "won the day by dint of authority and eloquence." But with the NEA grant in hand, the promotion was not enough to keep him there.

Simpson had been vocally reluctant to let Jim go and was concerned about Jim's returning to the wilds of Michigan, where he thought he would feel isolated and remote from other writers. During the poetry conference, Simpson had pulled Dan Gerber aside and urged him to look after Jim: "He's going to be famous, you know." Simpson had also pulled Linda aside and warned her that it would be a very "difficult thing to be the wife of a famous poet!" It was something that Linda had surely already sensed, but she was excited enough to share the comment with Norma. If she had reservations, she kept them to herself.

Jim wrote to Simpson soon after departing from New York. He hoped the aftermath of the poetry conference, which Jim had avoided, hadn't been too strenuous for Simpson and others. "We did it ONCE which is enough," he wrote, still enjoying the afterglow of it and tucked in the safety of his distant farmhouse. "Now that the aggravations have sloughed away it appears splendid in memory." Simpson agreed that the conference was fine, but he didn't plan on the university doing another for about ten years, and he noted that the finances from the first were still not cleared up. Jim had reportedly gone $30,000 over budget for food and wine. He would later claim the number was closer to $50,000—a figure no one doubted given the extravagance of the event—though he was certainly prone to exaggeration, particularly if it enhanced the story, and Jim rarely felt tethered to facts.

Simpson also confessed to having had some kind of spat with Levertov during the conference. She had apparently written to Weisinger seeking an apology for an apparent offense committed by Simpson: "I don't know what she thinks I had to apologize for," he complained to Jim, "and I can't imagine that you told her I did. I think she is insane." Simpson respected Jim's relationship with Levertov, but he made no apology for disliking her, and the feeling was mutual.

"I can't stand Louis Simpson," Levertov had written to Duncan, and she thought him a "miserable or inadequate" versifier.

"Both Denise and Louis could be very outspoken," said Quasha, and Simpson, who was typically diplomatic, tended to drink a lot and could be complicated and difficult. "And Denise wouldn't be forgiving."

Luckily, Jim managed to steer clear of the fray.

—

That spring, Tom McGuane wandered into R. L. Winston's, a famous rod and fly shop in San Francisco. He had recently finished a Wallace Stegner Fellowship at Stanford and had less than $1,000 left over. He figured he had enough money to live and fish for several months, and the guys at the store recommended Livingston, a ranching and railroad town in southwestern Montana on the Yellowstone River. "Of all the fishing towns out there, it actually has some trees," he remembered them telling him. The upper Yellowstone was also one of the best brown, rainbow, and cutthroat trout fisheries in the world.

Weeks later, McGuane and his wife, Becky, rented a place at 130 South H Street for twenty-eight dollars a month, and McGuane was eager to have Jim visit. "Unless conditions change between now and then,

I think you will be deeply engaged with the fishing here," McGuane wrote. "Turns out Montana has better bird hunting than I thought. The best is for 'huns,' Hungarian partridge, splendid birds. There are also plenty of ruffled grouse, sage grouse, Franklin's grouse, blue grouse."

Livingston was then a blue-collar town catering mostly to the railroads. Old West architecture and brash neon signs lined (and still do) the windswept streets of its downtown. A dozen bars kept around-the-clock hours—the Longbranch (the "cowboy bar") and the Wrangler (the "hippie bar")—as did the local brothel, Sally Dollarhide's at the southern end of town. There were small eateries and theaters, all a stone's throw from the Yellowstone River. The Burlington Northern Railroad had long ago established the town as the northern gateway to Yellowstone National Park, sixty-three miles to the south. Dan Bailey's fly shop, a local landmark, had opened in 1938; the Murray Hotel, where Buffalo Bill and Calamity Jane had once stayed, in 1904.

"In 1968 when I was first here," Jim would later write in a poem about Livingston, "there was a cool scent of pines / and melting snow from the mountains / carried by a southwind through the river's / canyon. The scent is still here, / the sure fresh odor of the West."

In Livingston, McGuane quickly befriended Duane Neal, a "tough old leathery cowboy, sweet as can be," McGuane said, and a local fishing and hunting outfitter who lived on a small ranch in Pray. Neal had once worked on B-24 bombers in Guam during a tour of duty, and it had turned him to drink, or so he confessed to McGuane. Neal had recently purchased Black Otter Guide Service and planned to usher fishermen and hunters into the backcountry of the Absaroka-Beartooth Mountains and the Gallatin Range.

That summer, McGuane telephoned Jim and Gerber with a proposition. Neal needed help setting up his elk camps for the coming hunting season and writing a brochure for his guide service. If Jim and Gerber pitched in, Neal would treat them all to a two-week backpacking trip through the Absaroka Mountains. "Ever foolhardy," as Jim put it, he agreed, and that July he and Gerber flew into Bozeman, Montana. (The airport was little more than a clapboard building of about four hundred square feet.) They then drove the roughly thirty miles through the Gallatin and Bridger Mountains and the Bozeman Pass to Livingston. It was the first time Jim set eyes on the town and the state of Montana, and he would fall in love with both.

The group departed days later with nine horses and a mule. They'd travel over 150 mountainous miles in total, many with staggering views of Paradise Valley and the Crazy Mountains to the north. Unlike McGuane and Gerber, Jim had little experience riding, and Gerber, who developed pleurisy during the trip—at first, he thought he had broken a rib—felt every hoof drop. "It was a splendid, occasionally frightening trip," as Jim later described it, partly because of the presence of bears in the area. Once, well into the backcountry, the group encountered a ranger ("Wilderness Dan," he called himself), who warned the group that the park service had recently dispatched troublesome grizzlies into the immediate area, a fact that left everyone on edge. With a .357 Magnum by his side, Gerber slept lightly. He shared a tent with Jim, and whenever Jim snored, he would thrust out an elbow to quiet him down so he wouldn't miss a bear coming into their camp. More unnerving to Jim, besides running out of cigarettes and whiskey, were the "skinny trails across precipitous scree" that they rode, and he on a horse with the "unlikely name of Brother-in-Law." When they finally got back to town, the group stopped first at the Longbranch Saloon and then at Sally Dollarhide's.

The trip was unforgettably beautiful, and it strengthened Jim's friendship with McGuane, as the two had spent little time together. But Jim thought the real value of the trip, other than the purging effects of wilderness, was the relentless talk with McGuane about fiction, a relative rarity for him and a continuation of the marathon telephone conversations the two had carried on between Stony Brook and Palo Alto for the past two years. The trip inspired Jim, and he felt terribly excited because his head was filling up with literature again.

—

"I just ate two smoked chubs and thought of you out there in the Montana night," Jim wrote to McGuane when he got home to Michigan. "Certain moments; first morning of the camp trip, some frost on us, at six am perfect stillness except horses grazing; on the Boulder catching fish"; and the "HUGE" rises. He added to the list Sally's, the Longbranch, Duane, the presence of McGuane's wife, Becky, and "even you shot through as you are with potatoes, centuries of accidental breeding, ancestors whose sole brag is that their land is shorn of snakes."

The trip bore other fruits, as well: Jim and Gerber had decided to edit and publish a literary journal that they would call *Sumac*. It was a smart idea, like hosting an international poetry conference without the factions and fistfights, and Jim and Gerber could choose their own guest list. From the relative wilds of Michigan, Jim could keep his name in circulation among poets and publishers. The journal would trade on Jim's already established reputation and contacts, and Gerber would bear the brunt of the workload—a burden he was happy to shoulder. Both wanted to make it one of "the finest Poetry magazines going." *Sumac* would serve as an important venue for writers, and it would foreground Jim's position on poetry, that is, that the poems themselves, rather than poetic schools and creeds, were of primary importance. He was not interested in sects, and he and Gerber would arrange the journal accordingly, much to the chagrin of some of Jim's friends.

They would model *Sumac* on journals Jim had admired as a teenager (Marguerite Caetani's *Botteghe oscure*; James Laughlin's *New Directions in Prose and Poetry* anthologies; Robert Bly's *The Fifties* and *The Sixties*), and he and Gerber had agreed to serve as coeditors, each with veto power over the other. They would add an East Coast editor, James Randall of Pym-Randall Press, and later McGuane as fiction editor. The title of the journal was a reference to the tough, ubiquitous trees in Michigan, and they liked the sound of *Sumac* and how it looked on a page. It was not, as some readers suspected, "Camus" spelled backward. And it would be "absolutely open" in terms of its acceptance of different kinds of poetry. They would avoid outside money—not really an issue with Gerber's family money in the mix—and keep it independent, resisting a "kind of 'them and us' attitude between East Coast and West Coast, Olsonites and Academics, Deep Imagists and Objectivists, that seemed to be beside the point."

In May, Jim had Henry Rago run an advertisement in *Poetry*, and by late summer they were sorting through manuscript submissions. "A whole shitload of poems in the mail today," Gerber reported from his home in Fremont. The first issue would have a black-and-white photo of bare sumac trees on the cover and include poems by Levertov, Simpson, Quasha, Reed, James Tate, and Nicanor Parra and a lengthy excerpt, "Nights and Days," from Robert Duncan's *The H.D. Book.* Jim and Gerber had included a poem each. The issue's table of contents practically mirrored the attendance list at the conference at Stony Brook, where they had been busy soliciting contributors.

—

In October 1968, Norton published *Locations.* Jim had become bolder and much savvier about the publishing business since *Plain Song*, and he didn't hesitate to share his opinions. He had received the proofs months earlier in April and bluntly admitted to Brockway that he "loathe[d] the decorative aspects, i.e., leaves or whatever they are," on the cover. The design looked like bamboo leaves on a greenish-white background, and despite his objections, Norton kept them. He also thought the print a bit too small, but acknowledged this was a matter of no consequence and reminded Brockway that the book should be submitted to various prize committees. Jim feared he needed another ten years before "such people" would take him seriously.

In *Locations*, a collection comprising seven suites and more than a dozen other poems, Jim had begun working in longer, more open forms than he had in *Plain Song.* The suite form in particular suited him, and he would return to it many times. It was an attempt to get the intensity of the lyric into poems "whose subjects and length tend to resist the lyric mode," he explained to Brockway. By allowing for the "diversionary, a circling effect by which one may drive many wedges into the total metaphor of the poem," it complimented his own digressive style. As a succession of variations on a single theme, moreover, it allowed Jim to imbue his poems with musical structure and melodic units. It was an approach that brought him back to his childhood when he would listen to classical music with Judy and his mother.

The poems concerned themselves with the natural world but not in the usual manner of the "nature poet"—a term he detested, and one he thought made up by people living in cities. The nonhuman world had its own reasons for existence outside human misuse of it. Like many of his poems, these would impress upon his readers the feeling of a "nearly exhausted planet," or so he hoped. It was an idea—"man violently co-existing with nature"—that would cut through his entire life's work and into the very last poem he would ever write.

Jim was generally confident about the collection, but he was nervous about its reception and even about its quality. They were the tormenting doubts of a second book and a topic he had taken up months earlier in a review for *The New York Review of Books.* With *Locations* being readied for publication, the review had betrayed his own insecurities perhaps more than anything else. "It is a sorry mistake to expect that each collection of poems a poet chooses to publish will be consistently better than his former work," he had begun the piece.

> This Calvinistic attitude supposes that art, like science, is a cumulative process, that the previous book is a foundation on which one stands at least an inch more grandly in every direction in anticipation of the new work to come, or as the hymn says, "every rung goes higher, higher."

As Jim surely knew, it was his own attitude he was faulting in the review, as well as the very same metaphor he had once shared with Brockway and McGuane, that of literary accretion and a stack of books. If he had made his own sorry mistake, as he put it, only time would tell.

Critical attention for *Locations* was excruciatingly scant and slow to come. As he complained to Levertov, he thought the book was being ignored, and if it weren't for friends writing to him about it, he would feel even worse—there would be nothing. Levertov praised the book publicly and reassured Jim that she thought the collection much larger than its size. "I have no second thoughts about it," she insisted. "If someone stepped out of a flying saucer & asked me 'What is poetry??' I could hand him your book. 'This.'"

She also encouraged him to stop comparing himself with other poets: "Paul Carroll has written a few minor poems I like & lots of bad ones, & is quite a dear chap (sort of), & is almost a moron. Mark Strand is a highly ambitious, wit-oriented, prime product of the worst years of the Iowa Poetry Workshop. They aren't worth thinking about. Really."

Simpson, too, wrote with reassuring words. "On every page of LOCATIONS there is poetry—there is the precision of language & feel of poetry—and you are merely having post-birth doubts about it. The only bad thing is the three sprigs of leaves, or whatever it is, beside the title—and that, like a mark on the wall after painting, will be visible to no one as much as it is to yourself."

That Jim felt moribund was exactly what he should be feeling, Simpson consoled him. Jim had written himself out, and that deep emptiness in him corresponded exactly to the depth of the poems he'd exacted from himself. The fullness would once again return. "Then, drop by drop, water has to come down again, things have to start."

On a brighter note, *Sumac* was flourishing, but even it came with painful caveats. By January 1969, three editions of the journal were printed or at press. Under the name *Sumac*, Jim and Gerber had also published *5 Blind Men*—a short anthology that included poems by Jim, Simic, Reed, Quasha, and Gerber—which had been well received. (Years afterward, Gerber would get inquiries from graduate students doing studies of "The Five Blind Men School of American Poetry." "What was *that*?" he wondered.) And they had managed to publish a new canto by Ezra Pound, a real rarity. The cover of the Winter 1969 issue advertised the fact in large print over the photograph of a young Linda Harrison.

The feedback Jim received on *Sumac* from friends (Duncan and Levertov, in particular) was less than complimentary. In January, Duncan criticized the journal for its open, nonpartisan approach, and he declined to submit another chapter of his book for the new issue. He thought the first chapter had gotten lost. "I think of my work as being in a scene or a movement," he told Jim, and he favored "obsessional monomaniacal editors," in his words, like Clayton Eshelman of *Caterpillar* or Richard Grossinger of *Io Magazine*, where he had sent his chapter instead. If his heart could somehow change his mind, he added, he would rush something to them. It was a condescending note and contingency that hurt and angered Jim.

Duncan's assurance that his "letting the magazine go by [was] NOT letting [Jim] go by" was perhaps cold comfort. Duncan's heart would not change his mind, and he would never again submit work to the journal.

A few weeks later, Jim responded to Duncan and Levertov, who had written with her own concerns, in a letter addressed to both. His heart ached to get the letters he knew were coming from them, he admitted, and he accepted all the blame, insisting that he did not have the energy or "bounty of soul" that *Sumac* required. "I have been blank for at least eleven months and had nothing to give a magazine let alone myself." If his remarks were contrite, they were also mostly disingenuous. While he agreed with Levertov that the journal needed more editorial presence or "signature," he did *not* agree with Duncan. He hoped to reach more people with *Sumac* than just the "faithful," he explained, and he wanted a dozen new introductions per issue to the "best unknown poems by unknown poets" to be found. "And now that I have managed to retain my balls," he concluded, "I suspect things will happen though perhaps NEVER enough to please you both or separately. In my sluggish way I love you both to the point of worship."

Privately, Jim was deeply disappointed in Duncan. To Levertov, he confessed that he had been terribly hurt and upset by Duncan's letter, and, worse, it caught him at a vulnerable time—during the "total silence" that had met the publication of *Locations*.

To reaffirm their position, Jim and Gerber would take an aggressive editorial stance in the third issue. Yes, they would make changes to the journal, they explained in a note. They would include more essays, reviews, and statements on poetics and letters, as well as fiction of an experimental nature. They would provide more space in the journal's pages to allow the poems to breathe—a concession to Duncan. *But*, and they were vehement on this point, the journal would remain an open space: "We are not *Caterpillar*, *Io*, *Kayak*, *The Sixties*, *Tri-Quarterly* or *Poetry*. If we evolve any distinct personality it will be as a magazine where poets need not worry if their work is 'right for us.' . . . It may be heretical to say so but poems are more interesting than poets, collections of poets, manifestos, main currents and eddies." It was a declaration of independence for the journal and, to some extent, for Jim himself from his mentors.

The journal *Sumac* would continue until the fall of 1971, and Jim and Gerber would publish nine issues and nearly nine hundred poems. The Sumac Press would publish some two dozen volumes. *Sumac* would include Pat Paton's poems alongside Louis Simpson's and Basil Bunting's.

8

WOLF

(SPRING 1969 – 1971)

I don't have any medals. I feel their lack
of weight on my chest. Years ago I was ambitious.
But now it is clear that nothing will happen.

"My book has met total and usual silence except for George's review," Jim complained to Simpson in February 1969, referring to Quasha's review of *Locations* in *Stony Brook,* the single and only review to that point. "I suppose this wouldn't be so if I were a member of some 'scene' or group," he carped, and he blamed the New York literary establishment and the "Robert Lowell conspiracy, a fine poet who not only has bad taste but enforces it." Lowell had nothing to do with the silence surrounding Jim's book, except perhaps as a symbol, in Jim's mind, of a coastal literary cartel, which would assume different faces over time; it dismissed literature written anywhere but on the coasts as regional and of lesser value.

"No one can control, in the long run, what the public will think of his work," Simpson replied, and he encouraged Jim, as Levertov had, to stop dwelling on other poets and the New York scene. "It isn't just Lowell, you know. Your friend Denise—and this is the only and the last word I'll ever say on this subject—has spent a great deal of her life in literary politics, playing as hard as anyone. But I don't want to offend you, so I'll leave that lay."

Simpson was also still bitterly sorry that Jim wasn't coming back to Stony Brook and worried about Jim's community (or the lack thereof) in Michigan: "DO YOU TALK TO THE TREES?" Jim missed Simpson often and admitted to having imaginary conversations with him.

Not only did Jim *not* miss Stony Brook, but he was "totally bent" now on rural existence in Michigan. He *did* talk to trees, in his way, listening to and observing the nonhuman world. He walked the cherry and apple orchards and the forest-rimmed, stony shoreline of Lake Michigan.

The NEA fellowship had allowed him this free time to walk and focus on his writing and—along with the relocation, away from his drinking buddies in New York—a bit more on his health. He was only thirty-one, but his health had become an issue, and his family and some friends were concerned. He had put on weight.

A few months earlier, Linda had reported to Norma that Jim was dieting and doing a pretty good job at it. "That & his long daily walk certainly make him feel a lot better," she thought. "When we left Stony Brook I think his health was really at a dangerous stage." Linda was looking forward to a visit from the McGuanes, whom she liked, and she thought Tom "really a marvelous influence" on Jim, partly because he helped keep his drinking in check. At that time, McGuane drank very little or not at all.

McGuane had also noticed Jim's questionable health, his drinking and smoking and ballooning weight, during their backpacking trip the previous summer, and he told him so. "For your private info," Jim reported to him a few months later, "I have been in a Kingsley drinking place once for one drink in four months." He was working on slimming down and shrinking the gut.

McGuane was very happy to hear of Jim's plans to get his weight down, "reduce the sauce intake and be healthy. I think you realize that I am not a nut on the subject and have not harped on the issue crankishly. I just felt I was accidentally in a position to see something you perhaps couldn't at the time."

Perhaps because he admired McGuane's discipline, or because he wanted McGuane to think well of him, Jim would send updates on his health regularly to his friend, so much so that it would become at times a running joke. Jim would send off letters with news of his health that read like confessional dispatches, most of them centered on booze:

> "At 190lbs now, 30 less than year earlier during trip to MT."
>
> "Quit whiskey; drank half a gallon of wine."
>
> "Re alcohol: I need it, you don't. Most of us don't have that inimitable Irish grace & need grease for social situations."
>
> "Alcohol: Wanted to go play pool but I'm on a little wine per day and didn't want to stare at golden bottles."
>
> "Stunned my brain last night—like throwing dynamite in the aquarium. O liquor . . . I bought an axe and a Johnny Cash record yesterday. Felt very burly and sane and special. Then I went into the bar and got home thirteen hours later, gibbering, slipping in drool. How unlike the gods. I'm very close to being convinced I am a fool."

—

In March 1969, Jim received more good news and some much-needed recognition. He had been awarded a Guggenheim for creative writing in poetry. The sum of $9,000 would be paid in four installments over the next year. Payments would commence in June and pick up roughly where the NEA had left off, and it would allow him to continue his mostly unfettered lifestyle. He would have few obligations because of it, besides his family and writing, and it meant they could remain in Michigan, an outcome desired by everyone.

"I got a guckenheim!" he announced to Levertov that spring. "Which made me, and especially Linda, happy. She doesn't want to move anymore and likes it very much here in the country." Jim used some of the first payment to buy Jamie a big black horse named Thunder, which would occasionally paw the ground and snort like a bull. They kept Thunder in a paddock next to the barn.

Jim had already managed to write nearly seventy-five poems, and he had begun working with the ghazal (pronounced "guzzle"), an "antique form" that dates back to the thirteenth century, which would make up a good portion of his next collection. With an eye to the new book, he took the opportunity to visit New York City in April, where he lunched with Alix Nelson from Simon & Schuster, the editor who had helped to bring McGuane to the publishing house. Jim was hoping to leave Norton, and the meeting with Nelson was an exploratory first step. It went well, but Jim's lingering feeling after the trip was mostly resentment toward the New York literary establishment, and he wondered if he would ever get over the depressing "John O Hariness of all literary pretentiousness" there. He was relieved to get back to Michigan.

That spring, he hosted friends at the farm in Lake Leelanau, including Quasha and Gary Snyder. Jim and Snyder had arranged to read poems together in a local high school as part of a "Poets in the Schools" program, something Jim had done with Quasha, and the experience would further solidify their friendship. Prior to the visit, Jim had been unusually unsettled ("greatly upset," in his words) about the prospect of spending significant time with Snyder because he had placed such hallowed importance on the poet's first books. It made Jim feel shy and nervous and left his heart going "gargurble in [a] funless trance." Snyder was one of the few writers who could make him feel that way.

But Jim and Snyder had a splendid time together. Snyder had recently composed his "Smokey the Bear Sutra" during a Sierra Club conference in San Francisco, and his *Earth House Hold*, a mediation on ecology, would come out a few months later. Jim and Snyder talked poetry, politics, and Zen Buddhism. Snyder enjoyed meeting Linda, sleeping in the Harrisons' home, drinking with Jim's friends, including

Pat Paton, and walking Jim's fields, as he would tell him. And Jim felt an immediate kinship with Snyder. The two seemed to fit together like puzzle pieces.

"Fine two days with Snyder who stayed with us & turns out to be the noblest poet, bar none in America," Jim declared to McGuane. He had reread all of Snyder's works prior to his visit and thought him, along with Duncan, our best practicing contemporary writer, at least in the United States. He placed Snyder side by side with Matthiessen, both of whom he thought "had a firm sense of how to live."

In June, Jim and Linda traveled to Ireland and England—the first time either of them had traveled abroad—with Dan and Ginny Gerber. The group toured Ireland, staying in Dublin for several days, and drove about the country in a rental car before taking a ferry to Liverpool. From there they traveled to the Lake District, visited Tintern Abbey and Keats's house, and walked Hampstead Heath with M. L. Rosenthal, who happened to be staying in the area. "Since Keats was the first germinal poet of my life my skin tingled somewhat childishly to identify the critical 'place' of the poet," Jim would write. The experience helped to spark his lifelong interest in visiting the homes and graves of his favorite writers.

While the literary sightseeing was a high point, Jim's dogged pursuit of culinary pleasures proved a low one, at least for the Gerbers and, at times, for Jim himself. He gorged himself, often ordering multiple dishes from menus and the most outrageous and rich foods he could find. At one point, he literally ate himself sick and had to spend time in bed. Later, during another prolonged meal that upset his stomach even further, Gerber insisted that Jim stop eating. "Okay, that's it!" Gerber exclaimed and left the table.

Jim's hunger for new foods and experiences stemmed almost certainly from his great curiosity and the simple pleasures he derived from eating. What accounted for his overeating is less clear. At times, he didn't just eat a lot; he ate to the point of sickness. It accorded with a saying he liked to repeat, once uttered to him by Jack Nicholson, that "only in the Midwest is overeating still considered an act of heroism." Jim would link his massive appetites to his fear of sudden weight loss, the obvious symptom of many fatal diseases. Overeating served as a buffer against the void. It was an insight that he would come to with the aid of his psychoanalyst. And the particulars of this terror, he would learn, were also linked to childhood trauma: in his case, he thought, World War II and the photos he had once viewed in magazines depicting starving, emaciated figures in concentration camps. But the particulars perhaps stemmed even more so from his own personal trauma—his eye injury and the sudden loss of his loved ones. Eating filled an emptiness, and it was a compensatory reflex against depression and darkness and maybe suddenness itself. As Jim would write, "At no time is this effort [to avoid sudden weight loss] more energetic and heroic than when my system is verging on depression."

England gave Jim "a taste for more," as he wrote—more traveling, yes, and certainly more culinary adventures. He liked the leafy greenness of England, and he found the people there gentler than in the States.

A few weeks after returning, Jim set off once again, this time for Montana to fish with McGuane. Traveling was an antidote to sitting still and writing, as was fishing, but it came at a price, and he later second-guessed his decision. Alfred Kazin was visiting nearby Traverse City, Michigan, at the same time that July, and he had hoped that Jim would show him around town, as the two had previously discussed. Kazin was apparently offended at Jim's having abandoned him, and Jim would claim that they never spoke again. In truth, the two would occasionally speak and write to each other in the coming years, but it was still a lost opportunity to cultivate an influential ally. It was an example of Jim's tendency to ignore the social demands of writing, not to mention the literary politics Simpson had written to him about. For instance, Jim had once had drinks in New York City with Kazin and Gordon Ray, the president of the Guggenheim Foundation, and he could not rule out Kazin's having helped him land the fellowship.

Such opportunities, Jim would gradually realize, often came about largely through social contiguity, and having moved on from New York, he would remain physically distant from the contacts he had made at Stony Brook. Even when he did visit the city, he preferred saloons to literary events or parties. He would not follow in Levertov's footsteps, as Simpson had suggested of his mentor.

Despite some fine fishing on the Yellowstone, Jim still could not shake his bitterness over the "usual silence" regarding *Locations*, and this time, he lashed out at an unlikely target—Levertov. His relationship with her had grown more intimate over time, and she relied increasingly upon their friendship. She shared with Jim her fears over her husband's widely publicized trial (Mitchell Goodman had been indicted on charges of conspiring, along with the "Boston Five," to aid and abet draft resisters), and she confided with him about her year-long infatuation with George Quasha. "That long phone call—it saved my sanity," she had once thanked him. "Blessings on you for evermore." About her feelings, she wondered, "To whom else can I [confide them]?"

Perhaps that's why she felt especially betrayed when Jim accused her of overlooking him for a literary award. From Montana that July, he had written her an honest but blistering note, likely fueled, he implied, by a depression that would not let up. The green mountainsides and cottonwoods and pines of the Absaroka had not managed to lift him out of it, nor apparently had the Guggenheim. Hearing more about the critical acclaim that had met McGuane's *The Sporting Club* could not have helped either.

"I was very upset & unhappy that you didn't give me one of those prizes for my title poem Locations," he wrote. "I am not inordinately vain but thought it might be one of the thirty better poems of the year."

He was mostly broke and feeling low, he told her, and he wondered if she were trying to teach him a lesson in humility: "Actually I am more upset than I want to let on about the prize bit, partly I think because I've acted with rather unstinting generosity toward everyone & have been continuously fucked for it. Or as Pound says in the fragments how can the world be at peace when one's own friends are enemies."

"Wow! You have Poets' Paranoia much, much worse than I ever realized," Levertov shot back. "I would feel ashamed for your having written me this letter, if I didn't know it was a disease—and even so I am embarrassed at you, on your behalf."

Levertov was glad that Jim had been so frank rather than harboring such resentment without her knowing it. But she assured him that she was not in the habit of going around teaching people lessons in humility. "I may be this, that, and the other, but I'm not that goddamned small-minded and officious. Who the hell do you think I am, your mother or something? Shit."

Levertov went on to explain the arithmetic, as she put it, of how she had selected the poets for inclusion in that year's *American Literary Anthology* and the accompanying cash awards to them and the magazines that had published the poems. She thought "Locations" was probably the best poem Jim had published in 1968 and "a very beautiful one." But rather than choosing the year's best poems, a disgusting idea, she thought, she had tried to juggle the poets and magazines and spread the money around to good purpose. "Locations" was a long poem and thus hard to anthologize, and it had already been twice published, once in *Fire Exit* and once in *Stony Brook*.

For Levertov, Jim's letter added to a short but meaningful list of grievances tallied against him that had been building up over the previous months. For one, she was pained that Jim had published the poet Stanley Cooperman in *Sumac*, "a really low sneak of a non-poet," as she put it, and she felt in general that Jim's magazine seemed to be getting worse, not better. But her anger really sprung from the fact that Jim had mishandled some poems that her husband had submitted to him for consideration. Jim had agreed to consider Goodman's poems, then lost them, and then failed to reply to his inquiries. Instead, he had simply ignored him.

"It seemed ironic to me that you hung Mitch up from sending them elsewhere," she complained, "and yet will print stuff like Cooperman—some sort of professional anti-Communist of the kind I find most contemptible." More than once, Levertov had implored Jim to respond to Goodman, at one point pleading with him, "For god's sake answer Mitchell's letter(s)," and telling him not to let on that she had prompted him to do so. "He is getting pretty critical of you, hurt by your non-response. And I hate to have this happen—please."

Jim's reasons for not responding did little to appease her, and his efforts to avoid literary politics in *Sumac* had clearly failed, at least in her eyes. He had not written back to Goodman because he felt ashamed, he told her, and Goodman's letters to him left him feeling worse than ever about the magazine venture and precipitated his "darkest thoughts yet." Jim asked for Goodman's forgiveness, and he hoped he had kept copies of his poems. (Jim had printed one of Goodman's poems in *Sumac*'s inaugural issue, but he would never again do so.) Given Levertov's frustration, Jim's accusations about the award could hardly have come at a worse time.

"I've cared so much for you and your work—" she wrote again, "promoted it, defended it (unknown to you) against criticism, believed you were authentically the poet, a natural, and a human being of warmth and generosity. Please don't turn out to be less than that."

To make matters even worse, it turns out that Levertov had given Jim an award after all—$500 for his poem "Thin Ice," which had appeared in *Hanging Loose* that year, as well as an award to *Sumac* for its publication of a poem by Rebecca Newth (that is, Rebecca Harrison, John's wife). Jim had yet to hear about the awards when he wrote to her, and he would not learn of it until later that month.*

Naturally, Levertov had assumed that Jim had already received news of the awards and that he was upset over her having overlooked the

* Rebecca Newth Harrison's poem appeared in *Sumac* in the Spring 1968 issue. Her name appeared as simply Rebecca Newth, and Levertov had liked and commented on the poem before she knew that Newth was Jim's sister-in-law. The minor secrecy was due to Rebecca's concern over the appearance of nepotism.

poem "Locations" specifically, a mix-up that made Jim appear all the pettier and ungrateful.

"I took it for granted you would be pleased, not peeved, to get $500 for yourself and $250 for the Rebecca Newth poem from Sumac," she marveled. "And what the hell is wrong with Thin Ice, anyway?"

Jim's apology came soon after he heard the news, but the damage had already been done.

"I kiss yr feet assuming a recent shower," he wrote with a "gulp." "I'm especially embarrassed as this is the sort of abraded vanity crap I supposedly hate."

Despite Levertov's assurances that a gulf had not opened between them, their relationship would never fully recover. Months afterward, when Levertov had still not responded to his apology, Jim mailed her another letter, sending his love, and he confessed that her silence broke his heart even though he knew he had caused it.

Through it all, the gathering gloom of Jim's depression had played a key role. And it would be hard for him to see clearly through a haze that was getting thicker and darker by the day.

—

On October 12, Jim received news that Ray Cave at *Sports Illustrated* was interested in one of his article ideas, a piece about heavyweight horse contests in northern Michigan. The moment was not lost on Jim, but he could hardly have anticipated the outsized effect it would have on his career. The article would help to launch him into the world of commercial magazine publishing and introduce Jim Harrison to a vastly broader readership than he would ever have as a poet.

Cave, a tough, sometimes stubborn senior editor at *SI*, had begun as a reporter in 1959 before moving to the editorial side, where he had set about transforming the magazine by filling its pages with color photography and the work of talented writers. Jim was part of that program. McGuane, who was already at work on a piece for *SI* on fly-fishing in the Florida Keys, had talked up Jim's writing to Cave and associate editor Don Anderson. (Jim had pitched an idea to Joseph Carroll a year earlier, but all Carroll could promise at the time was a sympathetic reading, and Jim never pursued it.) McGuane had helped to open this door, and Jim would follow him through it. With the Guggenheim ending in June 1970, he would need the money, and magazine work paid well.

Jim would use the article, "The Real Fun of the Fair Was the Horse Pulling," to introduce himself to readers, and making himself a central part of the story would become a trademark of his nonfiction. He began with his upbringing in northern Michigan and then his father, the agricultural agent, who organized the annual county fair. Horse pulling, we learn, was a favorite event of his dad's and the local farmers. Not unlike the journalism of Tom Wolfe or George Plimpton, the subject matter would be filtered so thoroughly through its author that he would often overshadow it, except Jim would do so from the hinterlands and through his own farm-bred psyche. What was of most interest was less the horse pulling than Jim Harrison observing and commenting on the horse pulling.

In the run-up to the piece, Don Anderson had suggested that Jim's article blend in "nostalgia, some humor, and mild outrage over the training methods (i.e., the electric prods)," which Jim had already planned to do. Although he would downplay nostalgia, these elements would become other signatures of his journalism, whether he was writing about fishing, traveling, driving, or cooking. Of course, he would also employ his poet's ear for language, as in the following line: "Today, as yesterday, most teams are keyed to start pulling by the sound of the clank of the hitch when the hook drops in, rather than by the shout of the teamster."

Days after receiving Anderson's letter, Jim injured his back while hunting, and he would miss his first deadline for *SI*—a rarity for him. He almost never missed deadlines. Jim was bird hunting along the Manistee River with his dog Missy and Nick Reens, a friend from Lake Leelanau, when he stepped along a high, steep bank that appeared dry and sturdy. In fact, it was wet and muddy, and Jim lost his footing, tumbling off the ledge into the shallow water below.

A sharp pain immediately seized his lower back, and it took him more than an hour to crawl and stumble to the car. Still wary of hospitals from his childhood eye injury, he chose to stay home for several days and rest his savaged back by lying prone on the living room floor, dragging himself as needed to the bathroom, and drinking whiskey to quell the pain. Linda soon insisted on telephoning a doctor, who injected Jim with Demerol and sent him to Munson Medical Center in Traverse City, where he was suspended in traction for several weeks. Friends came to visit, and others sent condolences.

Jim's slow recovery was frustrated by his swollen joints from rheumatoid arthritis, and to make matters worse, he had developed a staph infection that the doctors then treated with penicillin. No one knew, including Jim, that he was allergic to penicillin. After returning home briefly in December, he had a severe reaction to the antibiotic: his face and throat swelled, and his blood pressure dropped. When he returned to Munson, he lapsed into a semicoma that threatened his very life. He would later recall that while in his delirium he imagined that Gary Snyder stopped by his hospital room for a soothing chat. Snyder had never left California, he assured Jim years later.

When he finally pulled out of it, he returned home, sapped and shrunken—literally—from the whole experience. He had lost almost forty pounds since the accident and was down to 172 pounds, with "no stomach or ass," he reported. Jim blamed the mediocre hospital food. Because he had managed to tear the muscle away from the lower spine, he was forced to wear a tight corset to protect his back. The uncomfortable contraption stretched from his chest to his hips, and he would have to wear it for a full two years.

At least two good things came from the injury. For one, Jim was happy about the weight loss, an unexpected benefit to almost dying and being tied up in traction. When he was feeling a bit better, he had Gerber take pictures of him standing in bell-bottom trousers, the corset keeping his middle tight and firm. He wanted to "show off his svelte self," said Gerber, before his appetite and weight came roaring back.

Another good thing to come from the accident was the time it gave him to write, since he couldn't do much else. He managed to finish the piece on horse pulling for *SI*, though it would not appear in the magazine until the following summer. Moreover, McGuane had urged Jim to use the long convalescence to work on fiction. What better time would there be? For inspiration, Jim would turn to his early journals and notebooks, and he would begin a novel (what would become *Wolf*) about his journeys between Boston, New York, and San Francisco during his early twenties. Having abandoned the trappings of city life, the story would go, the young protagonist, Swanson, retreats to the wilderness of northern Michigan, where he hopes he might glimpse a wolf in the wild.

He began by diagramming the book without words, "just a picture of the form," and he wrote out portions in longhand—a practice he would never give up—slowly typing with two forefingers on the old Remington his father had once bought him. The writing took him around four to six weeks. He astonished himself with how quickly he wrote it.

"I seem able to write a great deal now and this makes me nervous," he divulged to McGuane, "but I've been fucking with words for fifteen years now. So maybe some facility with it has been earned, but then it is easier to be graceful in a 'false memoir' than it is in a 'made up' story." As a poet, he liked to think he was writing a novel merely to make money.

When he finally finished a draft, he sent it to John to photocopy at Yale so he could save on copy fees, a dollar per page at the time. But he mailed the sole copy of the manuscript at an almost humorously terrible time. While the package was in transit, the US Postal Service went on strike for eight days (March 18–25, 1970), and mail service was shut down nationwide. For a time, the novel was literally lost in the mail. Several anxious weeks passed before John finally dug it out of an overcrowded mail bin at the New Haven post office. Jim credited John's determination and "authoritative presence, to put it mildly," for its ultimate recovery.

Meanwhile, Jim had made up his mind to move from Norton to Simon & Schuster, and Brockway had agreed to release Jim from his option clause. Richard Locke would publish Jim's next collection of poems, *Outlyer and Ghazals*, and Locke was excited about the prospect of Jim's novel ("Let me see! Let me see! Let me see your novel! Type on, O Bard of Leelanau," he had chimed). Levertov, who had also moved on from Norton, agreed with Jim's decision. She thought Norton did a lousy job with poets and did not seem to care about them, and Jim blamed Norton for what he saw as its shoddy promotional efforts for *Locations*.

—

During the summer of 1970, the Harrisons were forced to move from their stone house rental. Their landlord's daughter and son-in-law were returning to the area and needed a place to stay, so the Harrisons were out. Given the short notice, the family moved temporarily into the Patons' garage, at no expense to them, while they searched the area for a place to buy. It was oddly memorable and fun, even in the uncomfortable garage, like stepping back in time: hot, humid summer months in Kingsley, fishing with Pat, drinking with old friends at the hotel bar, writing when and where he could.

The family hoped to find a farm to buy, but there was very little available, and the Harrisons had no money for a deposit. Finally, Gerber stepped in and loaned Jim the $8,500 needed for a down payment on a house and property at 701 South French Road in Lake Leelanau, fifteen miles from Traverse City and about a mile from Lake Michigan. It was the only place available in their price range. Monthly payments were $99.40, an amount that sometimes proved hard to muster.

The house was a bit run-down and needed work, but it came with a post-and-beam barn and granary (he would convert the latter into a writing studio). It had a chicken coop, shed, garage, pond, and a small menagerie of their own making: dogs, cats, chickens, and horses kept in a fenced pasture. There were two bedrooms on the main floor and three upstairs. The ones upstairs were arranged like a shotgun apartment, so you needed to walk through one to get to the other, which would make it sometimes awkward for the soon-to-be teenage Jamie. Jim would use one of these rooms for work at night or when it was too cold in the granary. The upstairs was uninsulated for the first few years, so even these rooms could get quite chilly. There was an enclosed porch, usually filled with Jim's empty Gallo bottles; a small kitchen, which Linda promptly repainted; a dining and living room; a large fireplace; and a back door that led to a garden. There was only one tiny bathroom, with a tub and no shower, for all of them.

Everyone seemed pleased with the move. Linda had always wanted to live on a farm, and Jim and Linda kept their promise to ten-year-old Jamie that the family would stay put and she could remain in her present school district. The Harrisons would call it home for the next thirty years.

"I would move [to Montana] if I didn't know I could visit there a month or two each year," Jim wrote to McGuane. "I am bent on making a liddle home here for my liddle woman and daughter. Jamie once a month exacts a guarantee against moving . . . Earth is foreign to [children] & they crave familiar people & known landscapes."

The Harrisons also received great news: Linda was pregnant with their second daughter, Anna, who had, as Jim later confirmed, been conceived in the Patons' garage during their own "Summer of Love." They would have a new life—a new home, teeming with children and animals, with a garden and hopes for the future.

With the expiration of the Guggenheim in June, money again became a major concern, and with Jim's turn to fiction, he needed an agent. He began with McGuane's and sent the manuscript to Candida Donadio. *Time* had recently described the shy, chain-smoking Donadio as a power player in the industry, whose clients included Philip Roth and Thomas Pynchon, and who had made a specialty out of promoting untried writers. But Donadio and her partner would not connect with Jim's book and declined to represent him.

"It is, as Tom McGuane suggested, a beautifully written book, with flashes of true brilliance in language, lines, images—a natural poet's style," she explained. "But, and the but is a big but, it isn't for either one of us; not a matter of failure of any one aspect of the book, which is far from the case, but a lack of our communication with the dramatic tension of the whole."

As it turns out, McGuane would soon fire Donadio after discovering that she was double-dealing behind his back—"stealing from me," in his words—during the sale of his first novel to a film producer.*

Meanwhile, Richard Locke had suggested other agents to Jim, including Locke's friend Lynn Nesbit, but nothing would come of it. Without representation, Jim sold his novel to Simon & Schuster in September 1970 for $2,500, and he would deliver the manuscript to them in late January 1971, when he would receive half of the advance. There's no reason to think Locke or anyone else took advantage of him, but he needed someone in his corner.

Jim decided to forgo the big New York agents in favor of Bob Dattila, an old friend from MSU. Dattila was a special case, as unlike the Ivy Leaguers in the publishing world as he was from Jim himself. Raised in Corona, Queens, Dattila's childhood was the stuff of Hollywood movies. When he was ten years old, his aunt married the brother of Thomas "Tommy Three-Finger Brown" Lucchese, Manhattan's reigning godfather. The Lucchese family set up Bob's father with a tavern and his mother with a beauty parlor. Dattila's father, John, had apparently been rejected as a mob associate because he was *too* violent, or at least indiscriminately so, and thus bad for business.

A handsome teenager with wavy black hair, Dattila had narrowly avoided jail (he once stole cars from parking lots at LaGuardia) and even death—eleven different times, by his count. Having spent a lot of time at racetracks with his parents, he later enrolled in the pre-veterinary program at MSU, where he met Jim and McGuane. The two heaped so many books on him, he said, that he wound up changing his major to English. After graduation, he did a stint in law school in New York and

* According to McGuane, Donadio had apparently arranged, through a series of covert contracts, to have money paid to her boyfriend in return for the sale of the movie rights to *The Sporting Club*.

then worked for several publishing houses in New York before striking out on his own as a literary agent. Fittingly, he would name his new venture Phoenix Literary Agency.

Dattila had no direct experience as an agent, and he was able to get his first client, Mason Smith, with help from McGuane, who recommended him. Dattila soon managed to sell Smith's novel, *Everybody Knows and Nobody Cares*, to Bob Gottlieb at Knopf. Dattila telephoned Gottlieb from a payphone, told him that he had been in business for exactly one week, and said he would stake his non-existent reputation on the manuscript. Remarkably, Gottlieb invited him to his offices and walked Dattila through the negotiating process. ("This is the part where you tell me how much you want for it, Bob," said Gottlieb. "You say $10,000 and I say $5,000 and then we settle on $7,500.") Against his own interests, Gottlieb later sent Dattila an already redlined contract with all the excisions and demands that a tough agent would make. It was an act of incredible generosity.

Gottlieb never bought another book from Dattila, but Mason's novel went on to become a Literary Guild alternate and was optioned for a movie by David Foster, the producer of *The Graduate*. Jim Harrison, impressed by Dattila's success with Mason, became Dattila's second client. It was a bold move for Jim, signing with an unknown agent, but he preferred to have his friend represent him, and he got a kick out of Dattila's tough Sicilian reputation. The two would work together for decades, and they'd cut an unlikely figure, like the city and the country in league together.

"From then on," Jim wrote, "I depended on Bob Dattila and learned that there were advantages to having a Sicilian agent for reasons of tenacity and the ability to break ordinary rules in our favor."

"Your manuscript is on the way," Dattila wrote to Jim, referring to *Wolf* in January 1971, and he included a check for $1,000 as part of Jim's advance (the novel was still untitled at that point). "I'll keep diplomatically prodding Alix to let me handle the movie and first serial rights for you and Simon and Schuster's benefit," he added, demonstrating his chops as an agent.

Jim's working title for the novel was *Shes: A False Memoir*, though Alix Nelson convinced him to swap it for *Wolf*. "Shes doesn't seem to be either readable (looks like it rhymes with chess) or crisp and significant enough for such a book." She liked the elegance and humor of *Wolf*.

As *Wolf* went through editing, Simon & Schuster was finalizing *Outlyer and Ghazals*. Nelson had provided comments on the poems months earlier. She didn't do much editing; she knew that Jim wouldn't allow her to tinker much with his poetry. But then, Jim tended to accept criticism from women editors more than men. He preferred to work with women and would seek them out as he moved to different publishing houses. Nelson thought the collection a "quite extraordinary book, rich, varied, totally your own, saturated with your humor, perception, sentiment, and that odd laconic lyricism that is your unique gift."

Nelson suggested that Jim cut back on the "device of a triple repeat (each single triplet is fine, but it looks gimmicky the third and fourth time one sees it employed): its mine its mine its mine, yes yes yes, forgive us forgive us forgive us, maps maps maps." Jim often used this pattern of threes, in one form or another, in his poetry and fiction. And she recommended cutting back on the Lauren Hutton references: "Lauren Hutton's lustre began to fade for the same reasons." Jim had referred to Hutton, an actress with whom he had a brief infatuation, multiple times throughout the collection. Finally, Nelson changed the ordering of *Outlyer*, the first section of the collection, to have it more varied ("light and dark") and shifted the locations of a few ghazals, pushing the "Keats ghazal" back from the second poem to the fifth.

"All my suggestions are suggestions only," Nelson added, "intended in the spirit of an empathetic reader acting as a sounding board; they are not to be construed as autocratic, and I do not meddle for the hell of it."

With *Outlyer and Ghazals*, Jim had moved into very new territory. His choice of the ghazal, originally an Arabic and Persian verse form emphasizing rhyme and repetition, marked a sharp departure from the shorter free-form lyric poems of *Plain Song* and the suites of *Locations*. The traditional ghazal had more structure and restrictions than he was used to.*

Jim's answer was to (mostly) shrug off the rules, and he invoked such license in the introduction, quoting from Robert Creeley that "Form is never more than an extension of content." It was a restatement of the claim Jim had made in his MA thesis: that form must be organic and, per Levertov, a "revelation of content." The introduction thus amounted to an assertion of his literary prerogatives: He would abide by form as much or as little as he wished and, presumably, as the content demanded.

While Jim opted to retain the couplets, keeping them self-contained and thematically unrelated, he abandoned the strict metrics and structure, including rhymes and refrains. The result was a loose poetic form with minimal restrictions (arguably a ghazal only in name) that linked the collection to poets he admired, like Rumi and Federico García Lorca, who had written *gacelas*, as well as to Adrienne Rich and her collection of ghazals, *Leaflets*.

Jim had carefully studied Rich's work. He had once tried to meet Rich at a party, but she somehow put him off, either because she was shy or, "more likely," he thought, because he was "loutish & arrogant." Later, after his back injury, he tried writing to her, and this time she was more responsive.

"I <u>really</u> want to see those ghazals," Rich had replied, and she asked him to send her copies. "The idea that you've written them moves me very much."

For Jim, as with Rich, the ghazals were "essentially lyrics," and he sought to shape the poems around whatever aspect of his life seemed to enter his "field of vision. Crude, holy, natural, political, sexual."

---

* The traditional ghazal is composed of five or more self-contained, unrelated couplets, the first of which sets the scheme of the poem. Each couplet then includes a rhyme (the scheme is AA, BA, CA, etc.) and a refrain of one or more words.

On April 6, 1971, Linda gave birth to Anna Harrison at Munson Medical Center in Traverse City. It was a sunny day, and Pat and Vesper Paton came to watch Jamie at the house until Linda's parents arrived later that night. It was a quick birth, and Jim drove fast (something he almost never did) to get to the hospital. "I don't really remember him being hands-on but I'm sure he helped a bit," recalled Jamie of her father, "and he started cooking more in that period." But his help would not last long. Jim left for Key West that month to fish with McGuane—his first of many times doing so there—and left Linda with a colicky newborn. Anna had come two or three weeks later than expected, and Jim's trip had already been planned, although that was likely cold comfort to Linda. At the same time, Jim's work remained paramount, and *SI* kept him busy writing and traveling.

That August, Nelson informed Jim that she had placed ads for *Outlyer and Ghazals* in *Poetry* and *The New York Review of Books*, and she had sent galleys of *Wolf* to John Berger and others for blurbs. She also congratulated him on his most recent appearance in *Sports Illustrated*, "a dandy of a piece," she thought, referring to Jim's "A Plaster Trout in Worm Heaven" about the National Trout Festival in Kalkaska, Michigan. Published in *SI* in May 1971, the article was only Jim's second for the magazine, but he was on his way to becoming a frequent contributor. He had become chummy with Ray Cave, who paid well and covered all of Jim's expenses for the assignment, as well as with Patricia "Pat" Ryan, who was then an editor at *SI*. Ryan had started at the magazine in the 1960s as a secretary and would eventually become *SI*'s first female senior editor. Jim would develop a great working relationship with Ryan, as he would with Alix Nelson, and he trusted her judgment. *SI* featured Jim that May in its "Letter from the Publisher," and it touted his poetry and forthcoming novel.

In "Grim Reapers of the Land's Bounty," which came out in *SI* in October, Jim called out hunters and anglers who cut corners in their sports—those who snag trout with fishing hooks rather than catching them properly or kill more birds than one could reasonably eat—and violate game regulations. He himself could no longer hunt mammals, he explained, because the anatomy seemed too close to that of a human, which made gutting and skinning them difficult—a deer's heart was too much like his own. Grouse and woodcock, yes. Deer, no. Another reason, which he did not mention in the article, was his sensitivity to the suffering of another creature, a fact he was somehow able to overlook with birds and fish.

The writer Joy Williams would note that Jim was no Saint Cuthbert, that he would kill, by his count, a thousand birds, "throwing the tiny meats of woodcock and snipe into the vast presentation of many elaborate meals." That was a likely number, but Jim did so over the course of a lifetime of hunting, and "game hoggery," human greed, unsportsmanlike killing that ignored the rules of fair play, and wanton destruction disgusted him, a position he would embed into his fiction and poetry alike. Few people adored birds as much as Jim. He spotted and watched them, like his mother; spoke to them; dreamed about them; and endlessly admired them.

Cave loved Jim's approach to the article: "novelistic, partly humorous and a hell of a lot of 'textual concretia.'" But in keeping with *SI*'s lighter tone, Cave reminded him that "we aren't the kind of magazine to indulge in a straightforward look at this subject with the oh-my-gosh-those-nasty-rascals-are-ruining-our-shooting bit."

Cave was also interested in another story idea for Jim. This assignment involved sending him to the Soviet Union to write a piece on the "suppressed sport" of horse racing behind the Iron Curtain. *SI* would cover most of the ample expenses, and Gerber, whom Jim had arranged to join him, would help with the rest.

For Jim, the article was more of an excuse to travel to the birthplace of some of his literary heroes—Dostoevsky, Turgenev, Yesenin, Mayakovsky. For Jim, it would be a literary pilgrimage more than anything else.

—

In November, Jim and Gerber departed for London, where they would spend several days before traveling to the Soviet Union. On a whim one day, the two purchased tickets for the new movie, *Isadora*, about the life of Isadora Duncan, starring Vanessa Redgrave. The movie could hardly have been more fitting as they prepared for the next leg of their trip. At one point, after the death of Duncan's children, Duncan wanders about Europe and eventually decides to open a dancing school in the Soviet Union, where she begins a passionate affair with the young, volatile poet Sergei Yesenin, who had long ago captured Jim's imagination.

The film then follows Duncan and Yesenin's relationship; his outrageous and violent behavior, often fueled by heavy drinking; and their eventual divorce. The real-life Yesenin would go on to marry Sofia Tolstoy and, after suffering a series of nervous breakdowns, commit suicide in a Leningrad hotel room. That he cut his wrists and then hanged himself, though not before writing out a final poem in his own blood, made it all the more gruesome and dramatic.

The depiction of Yesenin in *Isadora* gave Jim the idea for a new collection of poetry, what would become his *Letters to Yesenin*. Jim had read Yesenin in his late teens (in a translation by Yarmolinsky), when he was, in his words, "so obsessed with Russian poetry," and he sensed that he shared with Yesenin, "a fool from the country, so essentially a farmboy," a similar background. As Gerber recalled, the movie "really lit the Yesenin fire for Jim." Seeing the poet depicted on the screen, Jim's own depression and thoughts of suicide, the trip to the Soviet Union, it all came together.

The two spent their first week in Moscow at the Rossiya Hotel (now demolished), a massive, rectangular building that once stood adjacent to the Kremlin, and their room overlooked Red Square. The scene reminded Jim of Pasternak's *Doctor Zhivago*, a favorite novel of his. By this point, he and Gerber were used to traveling together, and perhaps to Gerber's relief, this trip would *not* serve as another culinary adventure. In fact, they would have trouble even getting into restaurants in the city, where soldiers stood guard with machine guns in hand and simply turned them away: "Nyet." The widespread presence of automatic weaponry, which thousands of uniformed men seemed to wear as "fashionable accoutrements," naturally unnerved them.

Part of the problem was their very limited Russian vocabulary. Between them, they knew only a few phrases, like, "Could I have some vodka, please? Here are some flowers. I love you. Goodbye," said Gerber. They eventually managed to purchase some excellent vodka, including Stolichnaya—a real rarity in the States and much better, they thought, than the more familiar Popov or Smirnoff—and a decent brown bread sold from street stands. "I fell easily into the local vodka habits," Jim later wrote.

One night, in keeping with their ostensible mission, they visited a crowded racetrack in Moscow. Only the front straight of the track was illuminated, while the back of it remained in darkness, which added to the race's excitement. One could see the horses start out, but then they would disappear into the darkness for a full minute or so. As the tension built, onlookers watched the snow fall, until finally the horses burst at full gallop back into the light. The whole affair was a sort of nod to Western decadence, said Gerber. Small bets of only a ruble or two were permitted, and it was all secretive but tolerated by the government. Jim and Gerber relished the experience, but Jim would learn little about how the sport worked in the Soviet Union, and he would never write the article for *SI*. Gerber would ultimately pick up the expenses to offset *SI*'s investment. Jim did not seem to mind letting down Cave in this instance, though he was generally very diligent in completing assignments, and if Cave was frustrated, he would not dwell on it.

While still in Moscow, Jim and Gerber made a point of reaching out to Soviet poets they admired. For one, they tried to contact the poet Andrei Voznesensky (Louis Simpson had given Jim his contact information) but were unable to arrange a meeting. While initially optimistic, Voznesensky's wife informed them during a second phone call that any meeting would be impossible. "Something had happened," she said, presumably involving the KGB, and Gerber recalled an air of oppressiveness about the exchange and her response. Jim had been earlier warned by their Soviet guide against telephoning Joseph Brodsky, who was himself on the verge of exile. Brodsky would depart the USSR on June 4, 1972.

Indeed, Jim and Gerber had had to disguise their intentions from the start. When they initially arranged the trip, an agent at the State Department recommended that they list themselves as farmers instead of writers for purposes of their visas. To keep up appearances, they visited a tractor museum, but no one believed they were farmers.

Before they departed for Saint Petersburg (then Leningrad), Jim and Gerber purchased photographs of Yesenin and Mayakovsky—prints bent around pieces of cardboard to make them sturdier—from a kiosk at their hotel. Jim was highly impressed that they sold photos of poets rather than of people like "Pamela from *Baywatch*" and that people actually bought them, he later said. Jim looked at the face of Yesenin in the photo, and he felt he knew all about him.

"I really began to know his work," he remembered, "and I thought though he's dead, he's an ideal correspondent because we emerge from the same problematical background . . . And I said if I have to write letters I may as well write them to him. Albeit he can't respond very adequately."

Letters to Yesenin, which would not come out for another two years, would take up that imagined one-sided correspondence. Jim would keep that matted and glossy photo of Yesenin on his desk in the converted granary behind his house, and he would refer to it in the opening lines of the first letter: the poet who "doesn't stare at me," he would write, "he stares at nothing."

Saint Petersburg was generally friendlier than Moscow, and there was an air of disdain there for Muscovites. And since they managed to get into restaurants, they ate better. They both loved the local *shashlik*, a dish of meat skewers marinated and grilled over a wood fire, and they enjoyed staying at the Hotel Europe, where Gerber managed to get them "grand quarters." Gerber's father had once sent food-processing equipment to the city during the famine after World War II, and people still recognized the Gerber name.

There they visited the Hermitage Museum and Dostoevsky's gravesite in Tikhvin Cemetery, and they walked the fabled streets of

Nevsky Prospect, which Gogol had once described as the "very life blood" and "crowning beauty of our capital." Unlike their guide and mandatory chaperon in Moscow, Luba, who was a devoted party follower, their guide in Saint Petersburg, Nina, was much more convivial, treated propaganda with humor and sarcasm, and spoke freely about politics and literature. Before they departed for good, Gerber gave Nina, whose husband was a theater director, his copy of Henry Miller's *Tropic of Cancer*, and she literally cried with happiness. "Whatever you do," she pleaded, "please do not try to send me any books."

Jim and Gerber stopped in Paris for several days on their return. They both looked longingly at the food choices available to them, but they could barely choke down a chicken sandwich, such was the state of their stomachs. Jim had gotten quite sick in Russia, and his bowels were in no shape for rich French foods. On top of that, when they finally arrived at their hotel, Jim had a terrible fight with Linda on the telephone, presumably because of his being out of touch for so long and his plans to extend his stay in Europe. Between his upset stomach and fraught emotions, he hardly got out of bed the rest of the time he was in Paris.

When Gerber flew home, Jim left for the Normandy countryside to meet a friend of McGuane's, Guy de la Valdène, whom Jim had met in Key West the previous summer. Valdène had invited Jim to visit him in Normandy on his family's estate. The two would become the closest of friends.

Guy Winston de Gaillard de la Valdène, a genuine French count and heir to the Phipps steel fortune, had grown up on the estate that included a small castle built in 1642 and a real moat. He was related to Winston Churchill on his mother's side. Probably to appease Cave and take advantage of his trip, Jim had settled on another subject for an *SI* article—stag hunting in northern France. As part of the French aristocracy, Valdène was versed in the sport and would show Jim how it worked. The article would again include a great deal of "textual concretia"—the trappings of the grandeur that was Valdène's life—much to Cave's liking.

—

Simon & Schuster published *Wolf* in November 1971, and it went largely uncelebrated. It would not be broadly reviewed, though two reviews appeared in *The New York Times*. One of these, written by Christopher Lehmann-Haupt, described it as a "poet's novel," "touching and slightly fearful," with more than a little Faulkner in it, like its two-page-long opening sentence. Joyce Carol Oates, who reviewed *Wolf* favorably in *Partisan Review*, would capture something else with her title, one that applied as much to the story as to its author—"Going Places."

Perhaps the most important legacy of *Wolf*, for Jim at least, was Simon & Schuster's unfortunate advertising campaign, which described the novel as being told from the vantage point of "one of the last male chauvinists of his time (see photo below for documentation)." The photo accompanying the advertisement was of Jim, shirtless in striped overalls, standing in a field beside his house, arms out, leaning against a horse, reins in hand, with a cigarette dangling from his mouth—*the last chauvinist*. The campaign, thought up and proposed by women, would haunt Jim Harrison for the rest of his career, and he would never fully live down the impression it made. At the time, Jeanette Mall of Simon & Schuster humorously suggested ("Smart-ass-literary-suggestion-from-liberated-New York-female," she wrote by way of commentary) that they title his next novel, "CONFESSIONS OF AN EX-CHAUVINIST."

9

THE SPORTING CLUB

(SPRING 1971 – SPRING 1973)

A wave lasts only moments
but underneath another one is always
waiting to be born. This isn't the Tao
of people but of waves.

Spring is the time of plans and projects, as Tolstoy wrote, and Jim and the family were true to his words. In February 1972, Jim traveled to Ecuador to write an article on fishing for striped marlin. The outdoors editor of *True* magazine, Peter Barrett, had reached out to Jim in October and expressed his interest in "sending a top writer" there, and the magazine had agreed to pay all of his expenses plus a fee of $1,500.

"Strange now this late in my life that I am known mostly as a SPORTSWRITER a la Bill Stern," Jim marveled to McGuane.

Jim had accepted the offer, and he invited Guy de la Valdène, a serious fisherman and sports photographer, to join him on the trip. The two flew from Miami to Panama, Columbia, and Ecuador, and then—after a dozen or so drinks on the flights—took a drowsy, two-hour taxi ride from Guayaquil to the coast. There, they stayed at a posh inn a short drive from the fishing boat at Salinas. Jim likened Salinas's small harbor, where every dawn the commercial fishing fleets departed alongside sailing dories with two- or three-man crews, to a movie set for *The Old Man and the Sea*. Although exhausted from the traveling, the two were up and fishing, some fifteen miles out toward the Galápagos, within a few hours.

On the first day, the crew spotted a whopping fifty-five marlins. Jim and Valdène caught three and lost three by noon, all on conventional saltwater tackle—overall, an intense, physically exhausting undertaking. "In fact, it can be too much for one man," Jim wrote in the article. "I quickly learned that a billfish takes more out of you than anything I had done except backpacking into the Rockies."

That afternoon, Jim managed to boat a large Pacific sailfish, which had exhausted itself with twenty jumps, including a "long, shattering stretch of tailwalking." His inexperience and bad back forced him to battle the fish from the fighting chair, yet even from there, he could feel himself seemingly levitate when he slipped up the drag. Both Jim and Valdène had hoped to take a striped marlin on a fly rod during the multiday trip, a rare feat that had been accomplished by a mere two or three others at the time, but despite Valdène's expertise and some very close calls, neither would do so.

Jim's article, "The Mad Marlin of Punta Carnero," appeared in *True* in June. Though it extolled the excellent fishing in Punta Carnero, it took up a familiar subject for Jim: a nearly exhausted planet. The fishing crews rarely released fish back into the wild but instead sold them at market. This was born of economic necessity, Jim knew, since it made up a good share of the crew's income. Another part of the problem was the "macho" sensibility attached to the sport, there and elsewhere, a critique he aimed more at the boat's clients than the crew. "I don't like to kill game fish any more than I would want to shoot 20 deer in a week."

The transition from tropical Ecuador back to wintry Michigan was tough for Jim for a range of reasons. Anna, just short of a year old, had chicken pox, and Linda was concerned about scarring ("You cannot tell a baby not to scratch"). He had also neglected to file tax returns for the past several years and faced harsh penalties. The family had made little money, and Jim wasn't used to managing it. But his neglect also resembled his handling of the poems by Levertov's husband. The longer he put off filing returns, the more it precipitated his darkest thoughts, and the more he avoided it. His depression was made worse by the punishing cold and darkness of late February and March (tax time) in northern Michigan. That winter would be the family's last there, he wished, half seriously and without many options. He wanted to spend future Februaries, Marches, and Aprils elsewhere, preferably in Florida, like McGuane, who had begun splitting his time between Montana and Key West.

"I can't spend another whole winter up here no how," Jim wrote to McGuane in March, noting also that he had smoked an "ocean of dope" and drank several quarts of vodka all in a three-day period. "Snow is god's way of telling you that you are living in the wrong place."

On an upbeat note, Jim had received a flattering offer from the University of Arkansas to teach there for a semester, and although he was momentarily tempted because its campus was near the White River, he graciously declined.

"I am only in love with the possibilities my life really doesn't offer," he added to McGuane a few weeks later, referring partly to the Arkansas offer, "ie Fucking fashion models, owning a Sportfisherman & skiff to anchor off Cozumel or Baja, lots of money. A waistline permanently at 33. A youthful grace. Good enunciation. Another eye. Straight teeth. Praise."

As Jim's reputation as a sportswriter grew, he took every opportunity to keep it going. It continued to bring in much-needed money, and it got his name out there. In February and March alone, he had three new articles come out in *SI* and another in *True* in April. He also worked the angles, getting *SI* to pay for fishing trips to Key West in April and Montana in August. Taken together, the articles amounted to an ongoing chronicle (not necessarily an accurate one) of Jim's life in sport and otherwise. The approach would invite a devoted readership to identify with him and his coterie of illustrious friends and to ride along with him on his various adventures. Jim would regularly personalize the pieces (in one, he described ice fishing with Pat Paton) and fill them with details from his own life, making it and his friends a central part of the story, as he had done with Valdène in Ecuador.

Jim had fallen in love with Key West, and it was becoming a regular destination for him, typically during the springtime. McGuane had promised him two years earlier that the island would expand his "flyfishing notions right smartish. I honestly think you will want to include flats fishing expeditions in your life on a regular basis." He was right: Jim did.

The flats referred to the warm, gin-clear flat-bottomed shallows off Key West, which McGuane then fly-fished mostly for tarpon and permit. He owned one of the only skiffs on the island at the time, and he would use a long pole to push off the sandy ocean bottom and quietly scan the flats for fish, visible in schools or rising to the surface, and then cast to them. Tarpon hit hard and fast, launching into the air, tail-dancing across the turquoise surface—it was an explosive thrill. Tarpon are not generally prized for eating, so people fished them mainly for the sport of it. But there was something about the silence of the flats on a skiff, the diaphanous blues, the bright greens of mangrove forests, the shimmering metallic scales and power of the tarpon that approached the spiritual. It was deeply seductive.

The expedition part of the equation would extend beyond the flats to the town itself and its uninhibited nightlife, and through the years, they would feature a revolving cast of characters that included McGuane, Valdène, Gerber, Dattila, the painter Russell Chatham, Brautigan, the writer Tom Corcoran, and a young Jimmy Buffett.

McGuane had visited Boca Grande and the Keys many times as a kid with his family, and his father had taken him fishing there. In college, he had read stories about fishing in the Keys in *Field & Stream* and fantasized about returning. But it wasn't until the late 1960s that he did so, and he began by renting a place on Summerland Key, dividing his year in a winter-summer split that Jim dreamed of emulating.

With the money McGuane made from the sale of the movie rights to his aptly titled novel *The Sporting Club*, he later purchased a house at 123 Anne Street in Key West, just one block from Duval Street, the center of the island's party scene and a little more than ten blocks from Hemingway's one-time residence on Whitehead Street. The small one-story conch house came with porch columns imported from Lexington, Kentucky, where they had once adorned the house of the artist Henry Faulkner.

In the early 1970s, Key West was a sleepy seafaring town of shrimpers and fishermen. Add to that an assortment of hippies, drug smugglers, writers, and a handful of part-time fishing guides. During Prohibition, smugglers ran rum from Cuba; by the '70s, marijuana; by the '80s, cocaine. Hemingway, who largely made Key West famous as a literary enclave, had not lived there for more than thirty years, though his presence still seemed to hover over the island. Tennessee Williams then called it home, as did James Leo Herlihy, the author of *Midnight Cowboy*. James Merrill, Annie Dillard, Judy Blume, Robert Stone, and Philip Caputo would soon follow. The relatively unknown Jimmy Buffett played informal gigs on Mallory Square at sunset and in the bars along Duval. It was a hard-drinking, hard-partying place with a laissez-faire attitude, a tropical island "totally devoid of rules of behavior," as Jim put it, "fueled by sunlight, dope, and booze, as far from Kansas as you could get in America."

Jim would credit McGuane's obsession with his sporting life for fostering a dozen lasting friendships from Key West to Montana, but the core of the group included Jim, McGuane, Valdène, and the painter Russell Chatham (Gerber often joined them). That they met at all was fortuitous and remarkable, all of them artists and dedicated sportsmen, and McGuane was the catalyst. Another friend, Jim Fergus, would later dub them "the Sporting Club," a play on the title of McGuane's novel, in an article for *Outside*, and they *were* a club, one mutually dedicated to serious fishing and—to varying degrees and in various ways—the pursuit of sensual pleasures.

Jim met Valdène during his first visit to the island in 1970 and Russell Chatham during his second in April 1971. Valdène, who had been fishing the Keys since the late '60s, "knew the area very, very well," and he knew the tides and where to find the fish. As with Jim and Valdène, Jim and Chatham realized quickly that they were kindred spirits. Besides their shared interests in eating well and drinking well, carousing, cavorting, fishing, and bird hunting, Chatham, too, was technically blind in his left eye and had suffered the injury at the age of seven (just like Jim). They were also the two people of the four or five who were struggling to make ends meet.

"For my part the pleasure of knowing you in Key West was sublime," Chatham had written to Jim in May 1971, shortly after leaving the island. "It seems not at all unlikely for us to become good friends."

"Russy-of-the-west, Yes, of course" Jim replied, writing to Chatham at his home in Nicasio, California. "When I get rich I'll buy some of your art. At present I'm sweating house payments."

Chatham had been arranging to write a piece for *SI*, and Jim had inquired about it in the same letter, noting that "Tom and GiGi don't bother with such trifles," using a nickname for Valdène, "but it seems we must."

Chatham looked a bit like Balzac but with lighter hair, a longer bent nose, and softer, narrower eyes. Quick to laugh, he had a warm, easy smile and a generous personality. A "big, gentle, one-eyed man," as Valdène described him. He wore a thick mustache and had "a great European nose that preferred one side of his face to the other."

Chatham had grown up in Northern California in Marin County, and he was an absolutely dedicated fisherman from a young age. His parents owned Loop Lumber, a prosperous company in Alameda, and the family had been well off. His father and siblings had all gone to Stanford. But due in part to his father's alcoholism and his parents' very troubled marriage, he had had a rather unhappy homelife. Chatham's maternal grandfather, Gottardo Fidele Piazzoni, was a Swiss-born plein air painter and muralist—he was friends with Diego Rivera—and he encouraged Chatham to paint despite his eye injury. Chatham had no depth perception, which made painting and fly-fishing—and barroom pool, for that matter—a unique challenge. When Chatham was just a boy, Piazzoni gave him his first paint set and boxes, and Chatham would later cite him as the single greatest influence on his work.

McGuane had first met Chatham, a local fly-fishing celebrity, in 1967 in Bolinas, California. Chatham then held the fishing record for the largest striped bass ever caught on a fly. McGuane and his friend, Gatz Hjortsberg, actively sought him out, and McGuane invited him to fish in Key West. Like Jim, Chatham fell in love with the island and planned to return at least once a year; Chatham would soon follow another of McGuane's leads and relocate to Montana.

The friends would continue to meet each year in Key West for more than a decade and then off and on for another one. Rather than overrun the McGuanes' house, where he lived with his wife and child, Jim, Chatham, and Valdène would rent a place downtown, which they would share from roughly mid-May until mid-June each year. The local hippies referred to them as the "Fat Boys," not because they were all fat, Valdène explains, but because each of them was large in his own way, both physically and temperamentally. Their wives would typically join them for the first week or so, and then the group would remain on the island for another few weeks. That's when "all hell would break loose, in a good way," according to Valdène.

The group fished during the day and drank in the bars at night, though not everyone's priorities were always in sync. McGuane fished during the day, but he was otherwise dedicated to his writing on the island—he lived there, and it was not a vacation—and he did not want to exhaust himself at night, at least at first. For a time, everyone just assumed McGuane wasn't going out to the bars, but that would eventually change.

In the mornings, they were on the water as soon as possible, and they fished (mostly but not exclusively) for tarpon until two or three in the afternoon. McGuane and Valdène each had their own skiff, and they often fished together. No one used or needed to employ the few fishing guides on the island. At that time, many of the tarpon had never been fished before, and it was not unusual during the right tide to see "a hundred fish wander slowly out of the Gulf of Mexico into shallow water," easing their way up into the Keys. "Big, silver-colored fish that had never seen a skiff much less a fly before. Jumping seven or eight or nine fish was not a big deal."

The nightlife was wild and exhausting, but the group of friends fished almost every day, sometimes for thirty days straight, however hungover, however sleep deprived. After very long nights, the group might run across the Northwest Channel—a deep-water gap between Key West and the Mule Keys—into the Mule and Archer basin. There they would shelter from the wind, stake a sharp pole into the bottom of the bay, tie it to the bow of the skiff, and go to sleep. By afternoon, they would return to the house for naps and head out, often to the Chart Room, a lively, quirky little place with a long wooden bar and lots of history, which in turn is attached to the Pier House, an upscale resort at the northwest end of Duval. From there, they could look out over Sunset Pier and Mallory Square and see the island's famous sunsets before deciding where to eat. Later stops included Captain Tony's and the Old Anchor Inn.

—

"Right now I crave Key West immoderately," Jim wrote to McGuane in January 1972, anticipating another trip to the island that spring. "Be grand if Chatham were around."

This time, Jim was planning a monthlong trip on *SI*'s dime in return for an article on Key West's fishing guides. Pat Ryan had told him not to do it on the cheap, and he considered splurging on a stay at the Pier House but thought better of it.

Ryan, who had moved into an editorial position at *SI*, was excited about the piece, and she had given Jim the okay for it with one caveat: that he first clear the topic with McGuane, who was still writing for the magazine. "I much like Keys Guide Ambience," she had written to Jim, "but before you launch into it, let me send you Tom's tarpon piece to read so there won't be any overlap, and I suppose since the subject is on his immediate turf, you or I should make sure he doesn't want to do a similar piece." McGuane had once proposed the same topic to her, but she doubted he would actually deliver it.

Ryan's concerns over McGuane's turf were real and, unbeknownst to her, compounded by the fact that Jim had planned to use Key West as the setting for his new novel (eventually titled *A Good Day to Die*). Jim himself feared that McGuane might feel encroached upon since *his* new novel, *Ninety-Two in the Shade*, was also set in Key West and centered around the infighting between fishing guides. They were both writing about what they knew, as the saying goes, but Key West and its fishing guides was a rather narrow slice of life. The sporting life was beginning to get crowded.

McGuane signed off on the *SI* piece, but not without misgivings. He was troubled because he did not like to travel, so his articles necessarily had to focus on local topics, and he had heard from *SI* that the Keys and Yellowstone were being steadily "used up." He assured Jim that he had nothing to claim in terms of territory, but the issue would linger, and the two would go back and forth about it in the months to come.

"I came [to Livingston] five years ago and slept the first week in a wind-storm in Sacajawea park," he wrote to Jim in April, so "wild horses are not going to keep me from writing about Yellowstone trout fishing, even if I have to do it for $160.00 for Field and Stream."

It didn't help that McGuane felt that Gatz Hjortsberg had quite innocently stolen his idea for an *SI* article on floating the Yellowstone, and he still felt that Jim's novel came too close to his own.

"I feel a little funny about publishing a novel a couple of months after yours when both open in Key West, with fishing and back-country details," McGuane wrote again that same month. "Truth is, I don't see what Key West has to do with your book other than that you went there. – But anyway, you asked and I have been thinking about it."

McGuane knew Jim well enough to defuse the tension. "I know with your inordinate sensitivity that you are liable to be upset over the above; but that would be silly because I mean nothing rancorous about it. Just seemed, since you mentioned it, time to respond with plain talk."

Jim forged ahead with the novel with McGuane's concerns in mind, and by midsummer he had made significant progress. He had planned to have a first draft finished by the time he visited Montana in August, and he had whittled away the Key West sections from thirty pages to twenty and then to ten, cutting a long segment where the unnamed narrator roamed about the island. He would write to McGuane about the issue several more times in the coming months.

Part of the problem was that there were simply too many writers in the mix (Chatham, Hjortsberg, Valdène, Gerber), and they were all sportsmen and all gunning for magazine work, especially with *SI* because they paid so well. Understandably, McGuane had some proprietary claims on these places, whether he claimed them or not. In Jim's mind, he needed the money more than anyone else, with the exception of Chatham, though he would never say as much to McGuane. Moreover, after his upcoming articles on grouse hunting and bar pool, Jim himself worried that he had used up Michigan as a topic and would have to travel more. Jim's article about the fishing guides, "Guiding Light in the Keys," would appear in *SI* in December 1973.

—

Jim had begun working on *A Good Day to Die* in the summer of 1971 well before *Wolf* came out. As his first novel with a more traditional narrative, it was a new and difficult undertaking. He had struggled to have the form emerge naturally from the material (in keeping, it seems, with his approach to poetry), and at one point, he spun into a minor crisis and scrapped almost half of it. But by January 1972, he had finished two hundred pages. His goal was to write a "thoroughly 'noir' novel" a la Raymond Chandler and John D. MacDonald, although he felt it was a rather dour attempt at one. "I wanted to tell one of those simple tales that has a great deal of narrative urgency," he later said, "propelled by characters who, once you've met them, you know it's going to be a godawful mess. These are people that nobody wants in their living room."

After reading the novel, Alfred Kazin reemerged and complained to Jim that such characters could not really exist, but of course Jim disagreed. They were just "utterly alien" to almost everyone, including

Kazin, in the book-reviewing media. Jim actually knew "whacked out Vietnam veterans" who had arrived in Key West rather than, say, entering academic life, and he had read about one who had "tried to blow up a dam—this was in 1971." Jim's protagonist would do the same.

A Good Day to Die opens with a brief prologue in the backcountry of Key West with details familiar to Jim from his fishing trips: the local marina (Garrison Bight), the waterbirds (osprey, roseate spoonbills), the marine life (sand sharks, bonefish, a leopard ray), and various features around the islands (Snipe Key basin, the mangroves).

The unnamed narrator awakens hungover on a skiff, "double-anchored off Cudjoe Key," with a woman he met at Captain Tony's, a saloon off Duval. The plot, which involves the narrator's "debut in the realm of ecological violence" or "*sabotage*," follows him and an ex-marine—Tim, a veteran of the Vietnam War—from Key West to Georgia, Arizona, the Grand Canyon (where they initially plan to blow up a dam), Utah, Montana, and finally Orofino, Idaho, where they settle on dynamiting a dam on the Clearwater River.

Along the way, the two men pick up Sylvia, a girl who had fallen in love with Tim prior to the war and who now struggles futilely to recover what they once had. Tim (whose name amusingly combines both Jim and Tom) is too badly damaged from the war to return her affections. A heavy drinker and drug user, Tim is desensitized, emotionally and physically scarred (he bears a large scar on his face), impotent, and implicitly violent.

Like Tim, the narrator is deeply damaged too—depressed, suicidal, mostly aimless, and alienated from his wife and family—but the source of his malady is less clear. While he longs for Sylvia sexually and convinces himself and her that he loves her, he's no more capable than Tim of sustaining a meaningful relationship. Ultimately, Tim may be worse off than the narrator—he doesn't survive the novel—but from the start, both seem somehow fated for destruction, self-inflicted or otherwise. As the narrator observes at one point (in a muted reference to Jim's father and sister), "Almost around the next curve on the highway. A drunk is heading for us at a hundred miles per hour."

At one point, Jim's narrator attributes the saying, "Take courage, this is a good day to die," the inspiration for the title, to the Nez Perce, and the novel links the damage done by Vietnam to the historical violence perpetrated on Native Americans and environmental destruction. Their whole project of eco-sabotage is connected in the narrator's mind with Chief Joseph and the Nez Perce War. The dam, which prohibits steelhead from spawning, becomes a symbol, then, and a literal concrete imposition against the natural flow of the river and the vitality of its ecosystem. In this sense, the dam strikes a blow against the narrator's primary forms of recreation and reprieve, the natural world and fishing. That's when, for a few hours, "all problems—money, sex, alcohol, generalized craziness—disappeared in concentrating on the flow of water."

In narrating the blowing up of a dam to save a river, Jim had helped launch a new genre—ecoterrorism fiction—a fact that is overlooked. Notably, *A Good Day to Die* (a book Edward Abbey admired) preceded Abbey's cult classic *The Monkey Wrench Gang* by two years. Not unlike Jim's novel, Abbey's would follow a group of eco-minded misfits across the West, including a burly Vietnam veteran named Hayduke, as they commit acts of sabotage in the name of the nonhuman world. Their group's goal is the destruction of the Glen Canyon Dam.

Jim sought to downplay the environmental terrorism aspects of the book, noting that his story had little to do with "so mundane an article as sabotage." He did not want to reduce people to meaningful acts in the singular. But the environmentally based rationales behind the characters' plot play a prominent role in the novel, which is even more pronounced in earlier drafts. In one version, the narrator fumes, "We have to have non-personal violence. The only wilderness left is being massacred by the bulldozers & chainsaws of the developer. Every river is being dammed to make lakes for water-skiers . . . The gov't has sat on its ass too long." It's a rant, brief as it is, worthy of Earth First!

—

Jim would travel to New York that September but not before a month-long visit to Montana. He felt tentative and strung out, in his words, after finishing his novel, and he couldn't bear to be more than mildly introspective. Montana would prove a welcome break for him.

McGuane had settled into a "solid farmhouse" about twelve miles south of Livingston that he had named the Raw Deal Ranch. The former dairy farm on Deep Creek came with beautiful acreage and 360-degree views of the mountains—the Absaroka Range to the east and the Gallatin Range to the west—four bedrooms, a garden, two barns, a huge corral, and several chicken houses, which McGuane had transformed into tiny guesthouses. McGuane found the valley "aching beautiful," as he put it, and a "hundred times good enough" for him, and he felt the "temptation in the face of such country" to say, "this is it."

While McGuane had blazed the trail, others quickly caught on to the magic of Livingston and the Paradise Valley, and a steady stream of writers and artists, loosely nicknamed the "Montana Gang," would begin settling in the area. The idea was to live cheaply, focus on writing and art, grow food, raise chickens, and fish and hunt at every possible chance—not unlike Jim's vision for Michigan. And everyone hung out at the McGuanes'. There was not much to do in Livingston then, besides getting together for meals; good food, well prepared and local, was becoming extremely important. A distinct community was actively forming in the wilds of Montana.

Gatz Hjortsberg, who had visited Livingston in 1969 to fish the Yellowstone at McGuane's invitation, took the bait and relocated to Montana with his wife, Marian, and daughter, Lorca. Russell and Mary Chatham had also made the move. In May 1972, the Chathams packed up their rental apartment in Nicasio, California, and drove to Paradise Valley. During a visit there the previous fall, Chatham had leased a former schoolhouse at the very top of Deep Creek, above the McGuanes' property, that rented for sixty dollars a month and included a coal furnace in the basement, wood stoves in the living room and kitchen, and a shed that Chatham converted into a painting studio. "It was hard living," said Lea,

Chatham's daughter, who was born after her family moved in. The pipes often froze in the winter, and they had to haul water up to the house every day from the nearby creek.

After finishing a draft of the novel, as he had planned, Jim visited Montana that August. There was already a crowd at the Raw Deal Ranch, some staying for the summer, others just passing through. Jimmy Buffett and his girlfriend were there, along with Valdène and his wife, Terry, as were Gerber, Dattila, and a good friend from Key West, Benjamin "Dink" Bruce. (Dink's father, Toby Bruce, had been Hemingway's handyman and friend.)

Richard Brautigan was also there. Brautigan would purchase a house and barn down the road from the McGuanes. Friends would call it "Rancho Brautigan." McGuane had first met Brautigan in 1967 at a party in Bolinas and had conveyed to him how much he liked his novella *Trout Fishing in America*, which McGuane eventually reviewed for *The New York Times*. Afterward, McGuane and Brautigan exchanged letters over a period of months, and McGuane eventually invited him to Montana. In the coming years, Jim would come to think of Brautigan as a close friend.

When Jim returned from Montana, he was teetering on the edge of the "most violent of depressions," something that had been building for months and that the air of Montana still hadn't cured. Now at home after months of distraction—traveling in Ecuador, Key West, New York, and Montana, followed by a second stay in New York—he could no longer avoid himself. But he also felt strangely refocused on his art and sensed an opening in "the re-emergence" of it, as he put it—"primary intentions which seem to get lost." Poetry offered the possibility of some relief, and the depression itself seemed to invite the muse.

Jim attributed his depression to a fatigue with the realities of his life, namely the need to write sports journalism and novels instead of poetry to make a living. He had strayed in some sense from the purity of his calling—that monkish, religious devotion to poetry that he had once told Norma about. Those feelings were themselves tangled up with some vague guilt over his cavorting in Key West and elsewhere and his sense of the cheapness of it all—the "vulgarization of sexuality," as he confessed to Gerber, and he vowed to "never touch a woman in my life again unless I sense I could love her." He didn't elaborate, and the offhand remark seemed freighted with more than a little regret. It was a feeling and a side of Jim that he would have been reluctant to show to McGuane. His letters to Gerber tended to strike a more reflective, reverent tone, often Rilkean in cadence and character, than those to almost anyone else, and vice versa.

He determined to put all his energies into the Yesenin project, the conceit of which dovetailed with his fragile and dark mental state. He would continue to write novels, but he no longer wanted to participate in the superficial hustle to make them successful. "I am surprised and pleased at my ability to almost make a living," he confirmed, "but I can't let it overwhelm the helpless dreamer who wrote those little poems seven years ago."

The living he referred to *was* going well, and the family's finances improved even more that fall. His magazine work had paid off, his finances seemed to be "solving themselves," and he expected a "FAT" year on the heels of a rather lean one. He still had not filed a tax return, however, and he would continue to ignore the notices, but the debt would not go away. In early October, the Harrisons had the house painted by two unemployed commercial fishermen, and Jim began renovating the granary and Jamie's room. He also bought a horse named Rachel and a filly from Kingsley friend Jim Crockett. They brought "incomprehensible delight" to Jamie.

Still, cracks had begun to emerge in the Harrisons' marriage. Or, more accurately, the cracks that had been there since at least Stony Brook were now emotional fissures shooting down through their relationship like glacial crevasses. Key West hadn't helped. As Jim would write, the island would precipitate marital problems and the eventual divorces of McGuane, Valdène, and Gerber. Jim and Linda, who had celebrated their thirteenth wedding anniversary on October 10, 1972, had managed to stick it out.

Jim was generally happy in the marriage, and he loved Linda, relying upon her in profound ways. But he was naturally restless, and the tensions between them were sometimes palpable. Earlier in the year, in June, he had mentioned to McGuane that there were problems at home—"domestic difficulties," as he had phrased it—and he complained that his "heart's affections [were] dulled and picklish."

That Jim had been away from home for months out of the year was a big challenge for the two, and his absences sometimes came at particularly sensitive times. In April, Anna had turned one, and Jim was not only missing out on a chunk of his second daughter's childhood but leaving Linda to take up the slack. It was an issue (and a fear) that Jim had projected into *A Good Day to Die*. At one point, the narrator admits that he "couldn't go home to my wife. Six months now." And he wonders, "How long has it been since I've been home? I thought of my little daughter in her Sunday frock skipping in errant circles around the yard. My dog. Would dog or daughter remember their father?" There was "little fire left," Jim wrote, "except the antimechanics of inertia." Married people tend to stay married.

Jim's infidelities, or the prospect of them, had caused problems at home, and Linda was suspicious of him. It was one thing to write a love letter to Lauren Hutton, as Jim had done, and get a laugh out of it (the narrator in *A Good Day to Die* does the same thing and notes that his "wife had thought it very funny") and quite another to have sex with a random waitress or hippie in Key West—or worse, love another woman.

"So much of love is only a localized patriotism," Jim had observed to McGuane a few months earlier, and he claimed he was "non-directionally in love" and hoped it didn't aim itself. His claim synced up with his jest that he had "proposed fucking to an even dozen waitresses but was not taken seriously."

McGuane took up the subject of Jim's marital infidelities most directly in a letter to Gerber rather than to Jim, likely because he felt he could be more candid without causing offense. There were at least two paths in dealing with marriage, in McGuane's view: One, a specific Western tradition involving "compartmentalizing proscribed drives: jacking off in locked bathrooms, lost weekends, buying whores and clandestine affairs," which he acknowledged might be the right way to do things: "There is hardly an existing alternative path." The second, a pioneering path, involved open relationships, which almost by definition risked failure. The "absolute key" to this approach required the extension of all freedoms to one's spouse. The terror and the burden of it, and the "axiom at its center," was that one could not take these freedoms for oneself alone.

Jim had, as McGuane warned, compromised his convictions. He struggled to reconcile his own sexual desires ("the usual niggling desire and itch") with his love for Linda, the still potent vestiges of his Christian upbringing, the conventional marriage modeled by his parents, and the memory of a father he practically idolized. At the same time, he still took seriously Blake's romantic advocacy of gratified desires and the dangers of repressing them, a lesson ingrained in him as a teenager. And there were ample opportunities that would grow along with his acclaim. But he would not, according to many close to Jim and Linda, extend those freedoms to her. They would not have an open marriage by consent.

It wasn't only about the sex for Jim; it was also about the vitality and excitement of falling in love: the flirtations, the electricity of the new, the surrender to impulse and desire, the emotion, the risk.

When the narrator of *A Good Day to Die* falls for Sylvie, the hippie from Key West, he thinks she would make a perfect wife just before realizing that he "already had a perfect wife. What then?" he wonders. "But loving someone at first never seems to involve any questions." At first. The questions come later.

The opportunity to spend time together and reconnect as a couple came for Jim and Linda in February 1973 when they accompanied Gerber and his wife, Ginny, on a trip to Africa. Gerber footed much of the bill. Both had been inspired by Peter Matthiessen, whose book *The Tree Where Man Was Born*, about Matthiessen's travels in East Africa, had come out in 1972. Matthiessen had visited with Jim and Gerber in New York City that September and spoke highly of his travels there.

Their trip started off with unexpected adventures. En route to Nairobi from Amsterdam, where they had spent an evening, their plane was forced to make an emergency landing in Entebbe, Uganda, where Idi Amin had recently launched a coup d'état. When Gerber took a walk to stretch his legs in the early morning, a "very small man" poked him in the ribs from behind with a machine gun and proceeded to push him across the tarmac and back into the plane.

From there, the group went on to Nairobi and then, along with their guide (who supplied them with weed or "bungi"), to the Maasai Mara and across the Serengeti to the Ngorongoro Crater. Hours after descending into the roughly ten-mile-wide, two-thousand-foot-deep caldera to view wildlife, their van struck a rock and broke a drive shaft. As they worked to remove it—periodically stopping to avoid the rare black-maned lions that live there—a large waterspout, a rotating column of air, crossed a nearby body of water and, as if in a choreographed dance, herds of animals responded by running wildly around in circles, stopping as if on cue, and then running again.

For Linda, who was frightened of heights, the ascent out of the crater in only front-wheel drive, accompanied on occasion by slips and slides, was a terrifying ordeal.

Later, they traveled to Olduvai Gorge in Tanzania, where Jim was memorably served a slice of discolored blue ham, which he somehow managed to choke down. The three-week trip was the kind of romantic adventure a la Richard Halliburton that had once distracted him from his grade school studies. On the way home, they stopped in Paris and Rome. Jim would remember staying with Linda at the Hotel Excelsior in Rome, where they both encountered their first bidet, after which they ordered a bottle of wine and pasta to make up for the poor food in Africa.

The trip had done Jim and Linda a lot of good, and it helped to ease his depression, if only temporarily. "I didn't want to stop traveling," he reported to friends, and although he thought he still wanted other women, he claimed he was happier with his wife than ever before.

He was grateful for Gerber's continuing support during the trip and otherwise. He realized that he had been overly optimistic about his financial outlook for the year, and Gerber had made it possible.

"Unfortunately I want everything on the food stamp wages I earn—embarrassing to find out I've been eligible since December," he would write to Gerber. "I would like to say I love you for your thoughtfulness but that has nothing to do with it. When I'm honest I know I've made it so far by the grace of grants and your help. Without the latter it could have been done but scarcely in a tolerable way."

Over the following weeks and months, Jim's mental state plummeted to its lowest point yet. The chart of his emotions had zigzagged up and down for months, but the long trend was downward, and then it dropped precipitously. He admitted to feeling in "greater despair than ever before" but, strangely, "not depressed at all," a perhaps more frightening prospect. This was a "dark period," Jamie said, who was twelve going on thirteen at the time. It was not unusual for her to find her dad crying for no apparent reason. "I mean, that's when I was worried that he would kill himself." Jim had everyone terrified that he might not make it to thirty-six.

There weren't necessarily single events that frightened the family, no one episode, but the possibility of suicide loomed over everything. Both Linda and Jamie read his writing, and Jamie, who sometimes typed his poems for him, saw the idea of self-annihilation everywhere in them.

"All of this darkness," Jim wrote to Gerber in March, made him intensely self-reflective, and he felt that his "brain [was] burning." Perhaps worse, he found he could not "write a single fucking sentence," and every day, he felt "the weight of [his] entire life" crushing down on him. And the frightening letters just kept coming.

In February, another one: "Not writing a sentence . . . emotionally shattered. A peculiar deadness."

And then another: "I'm either going to do something or I'm not and writing you is a quarter's worth of therapy and I've some doubts I'll send this note."

But Jim refused to succumb to it. "You sure have to have balls to stay alive in this racket."

It was the writing of poetry—that "single fucking sentence" he had managed to write—that eventually came through for him. The writing of *Letters to Yesenin* arguably saved his life. While he had thought seriously of ending it, he saw even then something utterly selfish and stupid in the act—"even the next meal is worth waiting for."

And then there was young Anna, whose very presence urged him back from the brink. She was the answer to Yesenin's suicide and what he would write in the final lines of a letter-poem addressed to the Russian poet: "Suicide. Beauty takes my courage / away this cold autumn evening. My year-old daughter's red / robe hangs from the doorknob shouting *Stop*."

10

ZEN AND THE ART OF TARPON FISHING

(SUMMER 1973 – SUMMER 1974)

I was proud at four that my father called me Little Turd of Misery. A special name somehow connected to all the cows and horses in the perpetual mire of the barnyard . . .

"The thief of fire hides in his granary choking," Jim complained to Gerber in June 1973, speaking of the converted granary, his writing studio, behind the house. Along with a picture of Chief Joseph tacked to the wall, Jim kept the souvenir photo of Yesenin on his desk.

"I was out there with you / every day in June and July writing one of my six-week wonders," he would write to Yesenin, "another novel . . . / . . . The horses looked in the window / every hour or so, curious and rather stupid. Chief Joseph stared / down from the wall at both of us, a far nobler man than / we ever thought possible."

Jim's writing of *Letters to Yesenin* may have helped him to fend off actionable thoughts of suicide, but his depression—or despondency, as he had put it—he couldn't fully shake. Just thirty-five, he despaired about his age and what he saw as his mid-career, "easily the most dangerous time." He was no longer a young artist, and he was deeply disappointed that he hadn't achieved the kind of success (after four books, six by the end of the year) for which he had hoped, and Jim measured himself, as always, against McGuane, whose star was quickly rising: *The Sporting Club* had just been adapted into a full-length feature film, and McGuane had completed a screenplay adaptation of his novel *The Bushwhacked Piano* for Robert De Niro, though it would not be produced. His *Ninety-Two in the Shade,* which would be nominated for a National Book Award, came out that year. That was the kind of recognition Jim craved, yet he was happy for his friend.

"Still joyous about your success as I always wanted to know a Famous Artist really well and before it happened," he wrote to McGuane that summer. "Another decade or so and I'll get to tell your biographer-critics many fibs."

To Gerber, Jim would open up about his poor state of mind. He was unable to make real money at writing, and weighed honestly, his dreams of a decade ago hadn't come to much. "I can't make the groceries out of my art [and] it's simply not my fault. An old story . . . That if things go well I can earn a living equal to the local HS typic teacher by writing delicate peripheral essays for a sporting magazine then fine." If things didn't go well, as happened every few years, he lost interest in living. At times, what one wants most is to "take a flensing knife to the universe."

The Harrisons' financial stress was real enough. The family had had trouble paying even their grocery and doctors' bills. During a recent visit from Linda's parents, Bill King sensed something was amiss in the household and secretly slipped Linda some money. When Jim heard about it, he was humiliated, and he literally went upstairs and wept. The career hurdle was supposed to be the second novel—in his case, *A Good Day to Die*—which he had gotten out of the way, though it would not come out yet for several months. But its publication wouldn't change much or alleviate his feelings about a seemingly endless struggle to make ends meet.

That summer, Jim's distress extended beyond his writing and bills to include something resembling a classic midlife crisis. There was a palpable loss of possibilities in his life that left him feeling claustrophobic and old. "To wit, neither of us will become champ ski jumpers, bronc busters," he wrote to McGuane, half seriously. "We are largely what we are, not, though, to revoke fluidity."

Those same sentiments Jim would impart to the protagonist of his next novel, *Farmer*. Joseph (a name the character shares with Chief Joseph) had a lot in common with Jim at the time. He drinks from a bottle of whiskey in the middle of the night, listens to country music until dawn, and has intermittent fits of weeping. As Joseph explains to his love interest, Rosealee, who thinks he has been acting strangely, "Men my age go through a change of life. They know they're going to die without doing what they wanted."

It didn't help that Jim had suffered from minor but persistent ailments that frequently weighed on his body, mostly flus and colds, which were just enough to remind him of his aging. Another was peristaltic colitis. At one point, Ray Cave at *SI* joked with him that, yes, he knew the condition: "It's when you don't give a shit. We used to call it blackass. But the only cure I ever heard of was lots of alcohol and strongly seasoned foods."

For more reasons than the colitis, Jim planned the opposite. He would try again to curb his drinking and especially his intake of hard liquor, but it would be difficult after a decade of heavy consumption. He would avoid the bars, eat at home, and drink more wine. While he would miss "getting poleaxed" on whiskey, at least while his abstention lasted, he found he had more energy. And it vastly improved his sexual abilities and potency, he observed, which frequently suffered as a casualty of the booze.

—

One person who helped to ease Jim's mind was Peter Matthiessen, who was largely responsible for introducing him to Zen Buddhism. Matthiessen was an active practitioner (he would eventually become a Zen monk), and he encouraged Jim to take it up himself, recommended readings, and later introduced him to a number of roshi. The catalyst for Jim's interest, however, had really been Matthiessen's wife, Deborah Love Matthiessen, who had died of cancer in January 1972. Before her death, Deborah had been a member of the Zen Study Society and taught Zen Buddhism at the New School for Social Research; she had inspired Peter's own study and taught him the rudiments of practice. Oddly, Jim would credit her memorial booklet, of all things, dedicated to Deborah's family and friends, for his own enthusiasm.

"Still seems odd that I basically started [Zen] with accidentally coming across your wife's funeral service chapbook four years ago," he later reported to Matthiessen. The booklet, which included short writings by Deborah and Peter, had caught his attention, as did the calligraphy and Zen quotes, like this one: "No snowflake ever falls in an inappropriate place." Or a quote from Deborah's own book, *Annaghkeen*: "I know that the only perfect happiness I have ever experienced has been in nature when in the stillness of an instant I, in perceiving that instant, am the miracle; all the failed moments—on the mountain, on my knees with a rosary, in cathedrals, alone in rooms—were the frustration of the movement of an instinctive direction towards silence."

In the spring of 1973, when he was at work on an article about Matthiessen for *SI*, Jim wrote to him. He had read a quote by Nichiren Daishōnin, a thirteenth-century Japanese monk, and it had centered him that day during his walk. Matthiessen wasn't familiar with Nichiren, but he suggested that the quote probably worked the way any sutra works—it helps to do just that: center you. He also recommended a well-known introduction to Zen, *Zen Mind, Beginner's Mind* by Shunryū Suzuki, which Jim quickly bought and read.

Through the dark days ahead, particularly through the following winter and the publication of *Letters to Yesenin*, Zen helped Jim to find an equilibrium. He had read a half dozen books or so, and he had patiently studied the discipline. It was something of a revelation for him, and the winter of 1974 he would find to be the best of his life thus far. "Self abnegation slugged it out with Anxiety Neuroses and won. Sometimes a single koan equals one hundred hits of valium."

The book that most struck him was Suzuki's, which he would summarize for Valdène and others. More than anything else, Jim's enthusiasm shined through his descriptions of it, and its lessons applied directly to his life: the burdens he felt, the anxieties about his age and career, his fear of entertaining morbid self-attention. Zen had worked its magic on Jim and gave him a scaffold of sorts to climb out of his depression. It helped to refocus him.

"Imagine primal man five hundred thousand years ago, very intelligent but with none of our neuroticisms," he wrote to Valdène. "Eating, sleeping, drinking."

> Zen asks you not to live in the future or the past. It asks you to give all your energies to the present, moment by moment . . . It asks you to stop thinking about your "self" all the time and be conscious of what you are doing on earth, again moment by moment in particular.

He recommended sitting for maybe five minutes a day, for starters, which he had begun doing. It was important to not be ambitious about the practice, because that led to grasping. "Imagine the total absorption of a hawk building its nest or hunting." Best of all, perhaps, it was full of laughter and vitality. The practice would resonate with Jim throughout his life.

Simon & Schuster brought out *A Good Day to Die* in September 1973. Chatham had admired the manuscript and, a few months earlier, had written to Jim to tell him. Jim was less happy with McGuane's response, or the lack thereof, and he suspected that he had remained silent because he did not like the book. In June, Jim complained to him that if you can't get other writers to read your work, you're in trouble, and then extended that admonition to McGuane. "Even you dear friend have been most difficult. Like pulling an elephant tooth to get you to read either of the two novels when in ms [manuscript] or say something to me about them." He felt they no longer discussed literature the way they used to, and he mostly blamed ambition and the business of publishing for it. "Of course," he added, injecting some levity into it, "I know that you've had almost two years of continuous bliss, joy, sparkling jisms, hosannahs, birdy frolics, moon trips, blue buggery, and lunch."

Jim's apprehensions were mostly on the mark. McGuane had been terribly busy, and he responded with a long, bristling letter of seven typed pages. "Yr odd dribbling whimper in hand as I arrive from New England . . . I guess it may be I don't share your 'generosity and attentiveness in literary matters.' I could not summon strength to reconstruct the last 24 months as an excuse; trusting that archaeologists will find their traces on my vertebral remains." He went on to say that while he liked to respond to someone's work with precise remarks, he had had little opportunity to deliver the "full trumpeting waltwhitman [*sic*] yeas of approval." And he took the chance to air some of his own grievances, pointing out that Jim was happy enough to disclaim fiction "as a half-way house between the Sports Illustrated story and the poem" when it suited him, and on the few times when he had offered criticism, he found himself "on testy grounds." His comments betrayed a sore spot—Jim's vocal contempt for having to write fiction instead of poetry when fiction was practically McGuane's religion.

McGuane assured Jim that there was no "great unspoken" about his books, and he proceeded to praise *A Good Day to Die*, though his remarks fell short of Whitmanian yeas. The triumph of the book was that it declared itself as a novel, and it thus marked a leap forward for Jim. "*Wolf*, a wonderful book, is snugly within your gifts . . . But it bids purely on the richness of your language and personality while the present book steps out of the shadows, as a made object." They were measured and insightful remarks, but maybe not quite what Jim had hoped for.

On a (mostly) unrelated note, McGuane also expressed his concern for Jim's mental health. Jim had admitted to feeling isolated and alone after arriving home from another trip to Key West, despite his newfound Zen enthusiasm. Jim himself half joked that his peers thought him some kind of "hermit crank," and even he was beginning to think himself a pretty strange character, tucked away in his rural writing studio day and night. "I'll tell you what you get from hiding out in the granary—lonely."

Jim planned to get out to Montana again in late August and take in some fishing and big sky. What McGuane couldn't understand was why Jim insisted on staying in Michigan if he was so unhappy, judging by the previous two years. "I think you are troubled for peerage and place passion," he wrote. "And I've sensed that your earlier peregrinations have come to be construed as your lifetime budget on that score and that the white cottage is to remain inviolate on its platter no matter what. Are you stuck?" McGuane's note, which echoed Louis Simpson's earlier concerns ("DO YOU TALK TO THE TREES?"), reprised their years of debate about where and how to live. McGuane was worried for his friend.

The response to *A Good Day to Die* was generally positive, but it failed to match Jim's big hopes in terms of sales. Writing for *The New York Times*, critic Christopher Lehmann-Haupt recognized the novel as an evolution for Harrison, who had now written (unlike *Wolf*, which was "almost entirely patched together with scraps of sensibility") a remarkably well-plotted story. Lehmann-Haupt rightly noted its "family resemblance" to James Dickey's *Deliverance*. But writing three days earlier in the same newspaper, an anonymous reviewer wondered why Harrison was "content to waste an excellent narrative talent on this kind of super-machismo a man's-a-man stuff." Together, the two reviews were an example of the sometimes puzzling and polarizing responses critics would have to his fiction. Overall, there were plenty of celebratory reviews to buoy Jim's spirits. For one, *The Washington Post*: "This is a poet's book. Its metaphors are sharp as jagged bone. Its long cadences plead to be read aloud."

Letters to Yesenin followed closely on the novel's heels. Jim had chosen to publish the collection with Sumac Press rather than Simon & Schuster, mostly because it was immediately available to him and came with the promise of having complete control over the book (or so he had thought). *Sumac* had a large mailing list, so the book would assuredly get into the hands of the poets he most cared about. Still, Jim had a terrifying unease over its publication and one that caused some tension, though short-lived, between him and Gerber. Jim thought the collection was probably the best book he had written, and he worried over delays in its final preparation by the printer. He had submitted the corrected page proofs in September and had been assured then that everything was finished except for the cover, which was nearly done. By November, when the book was still not finalized, Jim complained to Gerber that his "own paranoia [was] attaching itself" to the delay. "So that even the word 'Yesenin' sinks to my bowels like cyanide." Zen had not cured all anxiety.

Gerber declined to respond at first and later wrote to Jim that, while their friendship allowed them to be frank, he thought the first two paragraphs of Jim's letter had been merely a "listing of griefs." He felt that Jim was overreacting and unfairly blamed him for the delay, because the book, at this point, was entirely in the hands of the printer. Since they had pushed them all they could, Jim's complaints carried "at least, the innuendo that Jim Austin [the printer] and/or I have delayed or been indifferent to its progress." Sumac had received the manuscript two months late, Gerber added, and Ray Hoagland's ongoing work on the cover art was nevertheless worth waiting for.

Jim, in turn, feared that he had "played the complete asshole again," as he wrote to Gerber in December, and he didn't want the delay or his feelings on the matter to affect their friendship. Yet Jim still took issue, firmly so, with Gerber's characterization of his concerns: "Whatever I've accomplished on earth is largely due to my poetry . . . This book is the most important thing to me on earth." The stakes could not have been higher for him.

Letters to Yesenin came out that same month and included a photo of Yesenin on the cover—the same as Jim's souvenir picture. Rightly so, he dedicated the first poem to Gerber, his travel partner to the Soviet

Union. Jim would later describe that time, during the writing of the poems, as "utterly desperate" and the collection as "an act of desperation and survival." Indeed, the book documents that struggle in thirty letters by Jim to the Russian poet in a one-sided correspondence. The letters are intensely personal and amount to an unflinching, probing account of his daily life during the previous few years. He revisited his trips to Russia, Ecuador, France, Africa, Italy, and Key West, his inability to experience love, his sense of the vast nothingness that confronted him (the word "nothing" is repeated fifteen times in the opening letter alone), and finally his encounter with "something"—"a great river vastly flowing"—an image that obviously corresponded with *A Good Day to Die.*

What kept Jim from committing suicide? He ponders the question. One reason, in addition to his daughter's robe on the door, was the possibility of partaking in culinary pleasures: "Quintuple heaps of caviar and decanters of vodka," for example. "A barrel of nice gravy. Wild boar. Venison, Duck, Partridge. Pig's feet." These are the "magical trifles" that help him to "avoid leaving this physical world," the ones to which Jim, his life hanging in the balance, relentlessly anchored himself. Another is the act of poetry itself, the work that sustained him throughout many a crisis. And his wife and daughters—"Today you make me want to tie myself to / a tree, stake my feet to earth herself so I can't get away. It didn't / come as a burning bush or pillar of light but I've decided to stay."

J. D. Reed, reviewing *Letters to Yesenin* for *The American Poetry Review* in 1976, praised the book and described Harrison as having "pushed the confessional form to the edge, or at least to one of its edges," and he celebrated it as Jim's best volume of poems. Other reviews were painfully few and slow in coming.

Many years later, the poet Hayden Carruth took the opportunity to reassess the volume and consider the lack of attention that attended its publication. Writing in *Sulfur: A Literary Tri-Annual of the Whole Art*, Carruth described *Letters* as "not only [Harrison's] best but one of the best in the past twenty-five years of American writing." As Carruth laments, it was almost completely overlooked by critics and readers, and although it was republished in 1979, once again, "the silence was resounding."

Why did *Letters* meet silence? Carruth thought it demanded too much from its readers: "It says to us that life is unendurable and that we can endure." He would attribute Harrison's turn to fiction to his discouragement over the collection's reception, which was perhaps an overstatement; Jim had already published several novels, and his reasons for continuing to do so were varied. But Carruth's claim captured something. The letdown for Jim was tremendous. He had expected laurels and praise, and the book was undoubtedly worthy of them, as Carruth had suggested. *Letters to Yesenin* should have ushered Jim Harrison into the upper echelon of American poets.

—

By November 1973, Jim had cut back on his drinking yet again. He felt less fuzzy, and he had apparently lost fifteen pounds. His trip to Montana in August had been the high point of his last two years, and it helped to sustain him through the publication of his two books. Now, with yet another novel, *Farmer*, on the horizon and a new long poem in the works, "Returning to Earth," he felt a familiar unease. Dan Green of Simon & Schuster would write in the spring that he couldn't wait to see the new novel, and he was delighted that Jim was already deep into it.

"Fuckin tired of writing a book & worrying the next ten months how it's going to be accepted when I have no control over it," Jim had griped to McGuane.

McGuane was still worried about Jim's state of mind. He would be better off back at Stony Brook than to carry on with this moroseness, he told him, adding that he thought Jim the most gifted artist he ever knew. "You'd better figure out wanting to leap from the station wagon because Wanda Wondell of the NY Times don't like yr. novel. You have to take some abrupt, rough grips on the situation."

As for Jim, he desperately wanted to get back to Key West, with its white sand beaches and coconut palms, and he managed to do it the following spring. "Go away a few weeks, come home, you meet your wife and figure out why you've been married for fourteen years. The food is grand, the daughters lovely, sweet and luminously bright as the dogs are cranky and stupid."

Key West, if anything, had grown wilder since he had begun going there, and the Fat Boys indulged in it all—infamously so. Two years earlier, Jim had confessed that he wanted his future fishing adventures to be more joyful and less "a therapeutic alternative to drinking," but maintaining that level of purity of sport proved challenging, especially as the lines between nightlife and daytime fishing became blurrier.

The group of friends often went fishing well equipped with booze packed in the coolers on the skiffs (usually a quart of rum and a six-pack of Coca-Cola for mixing Cuba libres—mostly because of their proximity to Castro, only ninety miles away, it seemed appropriate, said Valdène). As custom dictated, they would raise their cups above their heads before drinking.

Drugs were not limited to the evenings either. In Jim's "The Sporting Life," later published in *Playboy*, he would describe fishing thirty miles out in the Gulf from Key West, near the Marquesas, on a triple hit of psilocybin and a few joints of Colombian bud. "Why get freaked or trip while you're fishing?" he asked his readers. "Why not? You only do so rarely." He fished to avoid boredom and the habitual, and drugs allowed him to vary the experience.

The list of drugs available was diverse and long: Cocaine, marijuana, crank, MDA, DMT, hash, LSD, TCP, and mescaline.

Even McGuane, when he was on the island, had begun partying with the gang. With his hair grown down below his shoulders, he had adopted the nickname Captain Berserko, a sort of manic alter ego and a moniker that speaks for itself.

—

That same March, Valdène and his brother-in-law, Christian Odasso, began filming a documentary, *Tarpon*, that featured (in addition to the spectacular fish) Harrison, Brautigan, and McGuane; a host of local fishing guides, including Woody Sexton; and Valdène himself. Jimmy Buffett would score the film with original music.

"This will be a messy note because I'm 'thinking' aloud and off the top of my head about your project," Jim had written to Valdène in February. He thought they could easily put together a shooting script in a few days or evenings. But he worried that Valdène's original plan was a bit too orthodox to carry the weight of an hour. The initial idea had been to have the film take place within one twenty-four-hour period, including an arrival and departure from the island by two anglers, and that—without the "filler," in Jim's words—included the whole experience of being on the island.

"People who fish tarpon with fly are rara avis[es]: it's a pilgrimage and the potentialities for the film are fabulous for presenting angling as a total experience," Jim imagined. "Walking around drinking and eating in the evening is a vital part of it . . . Of course you won't have any problem with the angling sequences & backdrops: the Muds, Barracudas, Ballast, the lagoon on the Marquesas."

Jim encouraged Valdène to capture the melting-pot aspects of Key West and the literary angle; he thought they might be able to get a few minutes with Tennessee Williams. His bigger point was that the film needed to be entertaining, and so it should begin with sharks and Hemingway, he suggested. "The almost overbearing macho aspects of it all are a natural."

Jim wanted the film to capture the real look and feel of their yearly ventures on the island, and that included the downtime, which he thought inextricably tied up with the fishing itself: "Visualize Curtis, Woody, Henry Snow, Bob Montgomery [the fishing guides] being filmed eating and talking about tarpon at Louis' Backyard. Get them boozed up first . . . The experience itself is so packed that it will with luck take care of itself, including the boredom of the wait and the explosion of excitement when fish are spotted. No acting will be needed as the camera will be forgotten."

Valdène and Odasso took Jim's suggestions to heart. The resulting film, which wouldn't appear for another two years, was a sumptuous meditation on the beauty and fun of fly-fishing for tarpon on the flats, and it's a mélange of the elements Jim had recommended.

Shot in the cinema verité style for which Odasso was well known, the film included stunning scenes of tarpon, quiet moments spent poling on the skiffs, interviews with guides, and recorded moments of Jim, Brautigan, McGuane, and Valdène enjoying Key West. (Chatham was absent that year.)

The film also advocated (more or less tacitly) for the group's way of fishing: a quiet, graceful, almost spiritual practice combining art with great technical skill, the long-drawn loops and silky ribbons of the fly cast, and an ethic of catch and release. This, in turn, was contrasted with the violent, live-bait fishing of the vulgar, tourist-ridden charter boats.

The film was, finally, an elegy of sorts for a way of life, both culturally and ecologically, that was already disappearing from the Keys. Set against the photography of the island's backcountry and Buffett's guitar, Jim was featured as the film's sole narrative voice, and he used the opportunity to reflect on writing, fishing, and the uniqueness of his island experience: "You never see a painting that reminds you of what you see on the flats," Jim says at one point. "Where in one day the light changes thousands of times. And it's like Brautigan said, layers and layers, strata, lamina in blues and greens, thousands of variations on the bottom from turtle grass, the coral, to clear sand."

The film, hardly ever shown and forgotten for years, enjoyed a new life many years after its creation. It has become an unmistakable homage to the gang of friends in their younger years: hungry, joyful, wild, and inevitably impermanent.

11

FARMER

(FALL 1974 – FALL 1976)

Six days of clouds since
I returned from Montana,
a state of mind out West.
A bleak afternoon in the granary killing flies and wasps.

In August 1974, Jim flew to Paris to help edit *Tarpon*. Valdène had paid for his plane ticket, and Jim divided his time between Paris, where they worked at the Antegor film studio, and Valdène's family estate in Normandy. When he couldn't sleep, he watched the "swans in [the] moat, casting flies at Pike." He had several incredible meals in Paris and caught a "disastrous cold," though his digestion held up, and "that's the important thing." He would later recall the proprietress of a local bistro desperately wanting the flowery cowboy shirt he was wearing and Valdène arranging to trade it for a meal of *tête de veau*, or calf's head, that included the brains, neck, and cheek meat.

He ate well, and he found the work on the film every day long and hard, but he was excited about the process of moviemaking. When he got back to Michigan, he wrote to Valdène that he was still incredibly enthused about his and Odasso's movie, and he thought they would "bring it off splendidly. I suspect the most fun will be in the fine polishing, the final weeks of revision . . . Anyway it was a wonderful trip for me and in an odd way I wish I was still at Antegor." It was a pleasure for Jim to work with others on a creative project—and that in France.

If Jim couldn't make the groceries out of his art, he would live well—indeed, like royalty, at times—off the largess of wealthy friends who were willing to pick up his tab; over the course of his life, Jim gravitated to people with money and vice versa, yet they were real, meaningful friendships. He enjoyed the finer things, as he admitted. The incessant travel away from Linda, Jamie (now fourteen), and young Anna was quite another thing. When, like Ishmael, it was a damp, drizzly November in his soul, Jim took to sea. While it helped with his depression, it came at a real cost.

This time, by going to Paris, Jim had followed again in his friends' footsteps as he sought to get more involved in film projects, like McGuane and Valdène. For one, he had begun working on a script with Dattila (titled *The Prince of Los Angeles* and partially set in Livingston) for Elliott Kastner and had written a full screenplay of *A Good Day to Die* for the producer Fred Wiseman, though neither would make it to the screen. Wiseman had raised money for the film but couldn't find a distributor. Jim would later cowrite *Cold Feet*, initially titled *Razorback*, with McGuane, again for Elliott Kastner.

And then there was the unfinished novel, what would become *Farmer*, that sat on his desk "like a war wound," as he described it to Valdène in August.

Yet even as Jim worked on the novel, his expectations regarding his work as an artist had begun to change, due in large part to his Zen readings. What had started as a wound he attempted to restyle into a pleasure. He had undergone something of a Zen transformation, he fancied, and he would spread the word like gospel among his friends. He would comfortably assume the role of truth-teller, like a guru of sorts, and he genuinely wanted to share his enthusiasm with those closest to him.

"Please try saying fuck art and ambition," he advised Gerber that fall, who had written to Jim with his own problems. "Give it up. I gave it up this winter and consequently got it back, much refreshed and strengthened." In a series of thoughts that applied as much to himself (and that were again drawn from Suzuki's *Zen Mind, Beginner's Mind*), he advised Gerber to try to save his life by new means. "You're thinking about yourself to no particular purpose. You're wringing your neck and life and precipitating a crisis." Jim's diagnosis and prescription obviously drew on his own crises over the preceding months.

He would advise Chatham in December in similar fashion, describing his own state of mind. "What can I say reaching my 37th year without having made an american living?" he wrote four days before his birthday. "I've been very busy this year getting all of me back into the confines of my body, trying in short to banish future and past, hope, despair etc. Also wrote screenplay, articles, a novel and a book of poems." Thanks to Zen, Jim had banished any desire to be someone else or in some other place, or so he insisted, along with "self-pity, self-congratulation, and ALL AMBITION." He wanted to make his art feel fun again. "We like to do ART. That's where we started. Then it was like fishing. That is what we have to return to."

They were wonderful ideas, and they helped Jim finish *Farmer*, but they would remain only as aspirations for him. He would lapse often and securely back into old habits.

Jim had also come to some understanding about his limited finances, at least for the time being, and his feelings seemed in direct relation to the pecuniary abundance of his closest friends. Their immediate circle, Jim had noted to Chatham, made money in the movie business, or they inherited it, or both. He and Chatham and Brautigan, Jim assumed, would never have that kind of money. "What can I say about Tom calling from a posh London hotel wired on snort and a beauteous starlet wrapped around his heels like myrtle (the vine not the girl, kiddo)." Quite a bit, it seems, but the point was this: They needed to forget about their "acute penury with grace."

Jim's new attitude was promptly tested that winter and spring. In addition to suffering for two months from a urethra and prostate infection, coupled with a bad flu and anxiety over a coming "IRS invasion," he had reluctantly accepted a loan from Linda's father to help him write the new novel. Soon after, the family learned that Bill King had lung cancer. And then, in December 1974, Jim crashed his Cortina GT into a cedar tree. Linda was okay but "howling like a banshee" in the passenger seat. She was just shaken up, but Jim suffered lacerations and bone bruises. "The twenty seven drinks relaxed me, as it were," he explained to Chatham.

Added to all this was the troubling news that Simon & Schuster had passed on publishing *Farmer.* "I think you are a wonderful writer," Dan Green wrote to Jim in January 1975, "and I think as one gets into the manuscript the book becomes increasingly moving and lovely, but as I told Bob [Dattila] it seems to me an impossible book to sell." Green thought Jim had not written a novel but rather "a long story, a reverie" and recommended that he shorten rather than lengthen it to commercial proportions.

Jim had carefully cultivated his relationship with Simon & Schuster, and it was an unexpected blow. But things would turn around. Two months later, he was eating littlenecks and striped bass in New York with editor Patricia Irving of Viking and chatting about his novel with the sharp, storied president of the publishing house, Tom Guinzburg, whose father had cofounded it. Guinzburg, a fit ex-marine with a robust sense of humor, had once kicked around Paris with William Styron and had cofounded *The Paris Review* with Peter Matthiessen and George Plimpton. Matthiessen would later describe him as a publisher with no "axes to grind. He just had very good taste." Guinzburg loved *Farmer* and quickly purchased it.

Pat Irving followed up after the meeting with a lighthearted apology for Jim's having to meet-and-greet the executives. "Hope that all that postprandial froth back here at the ranch didn't bring on a permanent case of dyspepsia," she wrote. "You won't have to run the gauntlet next trip, but I did want the big guns to meet you early on. In retrospect I realize that we didn't talk about FARMER half as much as we might have—I mean, in an utterly self-indulgent way, because I like the book so much . . . Anyway, there's plenty of time for that."

Irving would be another in a long line of female editors who would help to publish Jim. Irving proposed that Jim rethink the beginning of the novel, and she did "some housecleaning" on the manuscript. She would give it another close reading, she told him, and they planned for a July 1 delivery date.

—

That summer, after Jim got his manuscript off to Viking, he visited McGuane on the set of *The Missouri Breaks* in Montana. It was simply too appealing to pass up. McGuane had written the screenplay for the Western, which starred Marlon Brando and Jack Nicholson, and his script had reportedly circulated around Hollywood for a full two years before it was purchased by Elliott Kastner. Coming off his work on *Tarpon*, Jim was eager to witness the moviemaking process for a larger-budget production and hang out in Montana. Chatham would join him there, as would Dattila, who seized the opportunity to pitch a few ideas to Nicholson, principally a story about the wheat harvest, which McGuane sarcastically referred to as "*The Big Wheat*, starring Jack Nicholson."

The whole group hung around the set almost every day, so much so that the director, Arthur Penn, kept asking, "Why are these guys here?" Even Dink Bruce, Jim and McGuane's friend from Key West, had secured a production job on the film. Penn couldn't quite figure out who they all were but marveled over "Chatham's pneumatic bottle blondes."

The film was shot mostly at the Bovey Restorations in Virginia City and Nevada City in Montana, restored gold-rush ghost towns, and around Billings on the former sets of the earlier movie *Little Big Man*, also directed by Penn, from early July through mid-September 1975. It was an exciting time, and even the historical film sets felt tied to something urgent happening in the West.

Around the time of Jim's visit, the American Indian Movement members Leonard Peltier and Dennis Banks were fugitives from the law for the shooting of FBI agents on the Pine Ridge Reservation in South Dakota. The two had apparently hidden out at Brando's house in Los Angeles, next door to Nicholson's, and Peltier was later arrested in a motor home owned by Brando. Peter Matthiessen's *In the Spirit of Crazy Horse* would tell Peltier's story, and Jim would share his sympathetic views of Peltier and the American Indian Movement. Brando had declined his Academy Award a year earlier, when Sacheen Littlefeather appeared on stage in his stead.

Jim was deeply inspired by many of the Montana landscapes in the film, especially the vast area of hills, plains, bluffs, and rock outcrops of the Upper Missouri River Breaks that he had surveyed with McGuane and the nearby Big Sag and Choteau. Jim would later use Choteau as the setting for his novella "Legends of the Fall."

During the shooting of *The Missouri Breaks*, Jim and Nicholson would begin a close friendship, one later tied to "Legends," but it would come at no small cost to Jim's relationship with McGuane. One day on set, perhaps sensing an opportunity himself, Jim lent Nicholson his motel room to take a quick shower before watching dailies, and the two got to talking. There was an obvious ease to their conversations, Dattila remembered, like they had known each other for years. Later, Jim gave Nicholson copies of *Wolf* and *A Good Day to Die* (smartly, it seems), and Nicholson sent Jim a postcard and urged him to contact him with any story ideas. Maybe they could work together sometime.

"Usually, people are selling themselves to Nicholson," said Dattila. "Jim never thought of it, I don't think, or maybe he did in the deepest recesses of his mind. But they just hit it off immediately." Dattila's recollection may have been right, but the friendship would nevertheless prove an advantageous one for Jim.

McGuane was not partial to either Brando or Nicholson, and he found both of them "willful and capricious." While he liked Brando's creativity and energy, he didn't much care for Nicholson at all, whom he thought more of a career person, and things got worse when the two had a stern disagreement over the ending of the film. Nicholson felt that his character, Tom Logan, didn't get to follow "through with anything" and that he was "too subdued"; he suggested that Logan should kill the rapacious rancher in the concluding scenes. McGuane disagreed and ultimately refused to change the script, and Nicholson would enlist Jim to intervene on his behalf.

While McGuane was in London editing his first directorial effort, *92 in the Shade*, the film's producers, at Nicholson's insistence (and, according to McGuane, with Jim's full endorsement), brought Bob Townes of *Chinatown* fame to Montana to rewrite the ending. McGuane, whose nerves were already frayed from the whole experience, felt betrayed.

"And Jim took Jack's side," McGuane said. "And it was probably the biggest wound in our friendship . . . I was really really hurt that Jim took Jack's side rather than mine . . . I didn't think he should get into the politics of the set."

Jim wouldn't know just how rankled McGuane was for some time, and he assumed, or so he explained, that he had simply shared his opinion about the ending and nothing more. But Jim's support of Nicholson's position smacked (again) of the opportunistic. Siding with him was certainly to Jim's advantage and worked to draw the actor closer to him at his friend's expense. If Jim had no intention of doing that, it nevertheless revealed an odd blind spot to how certain actions of his might be received.

Meanwhile, another of McGuane's movies, *Rancho Deluxe*, had helped to spread the word about Livingston, which was shaping up into something like an artists' commune. "I can't tell you what a utopian life we're leading here building cooking gardening writing reading hiking and fishing," McGuane had enthused to Jim prior to the Nicholson episode. In addition to McGuane, Chatham, and Hjortsberg, a panoply of other writers and film people had begun settling in the valley.

McGuane had written the original screenplay for *Rancho Deluxe*, again for Elliott Kastner, which would appear in theaters in 1975, a year before *The Missouri Breaks*. The film starred Jeff Bridges and Sam Waterston as hapless cattle rustlers, as well as Elizabeth Ashley and Harry Dean Stanton. (Stanton had also acted in *The Missouri Breaks*.) Jimmy Buffett had a cameo and contributed music to the film, including the song "Livingston Saturday Night." The movie would feature Buffett singing on a stage at the Wrangler Bar and serenading a crowded and rowdy room.

The production for *Rancho Deluxe* took place in Paradise Valley and Livingston in April 1974, and many locals served as extras. During the scene at the Wrangler, Jim had reportedly sidled up to the bar (he didn't make the final cut) while McGuane pretended to play the mandolin on stage beside Buffett. Bridges wound up falling in love with a local girl, Susan Geston, his future wife, and bought a place in the valley. Warren Oates, who had a cameo (playing the harmonica beside McGuane and Buffett), later purchased a cabin and property with Sam Peckinpah on Six Mile Creek near Emigrant.

Rancho Deluxe had kicked off not only an influx of new people to the area—one that was quickly making Livingston a hip, backcountry hot spot for celebrities—but it rattled relationships and marked the beginning of the end for McGuane's first marriage to Portia Rebecca Crockett, or Becky as everyone called her. During the filming of *Rancho*, McGuane had begun an affair (with Becky's knowledge and blessing) with actress Elizabeth Ashley, which continued through the filming of *92 in the Shade*, which starred Peter Fonda, Warren Oates, Elizabeth Ashley, and Margot Kidder, in Key West later that year. Becky, in turn, shared something more than a dalliance with Warren Oates. And by 1975, all bets were off. McGuane and Becky were divorced, while McGuane had called it quits with Ashley and married her costar Margot Kidder. It was a disorienting mash-up.

Even more dizzying, by the time McGuane flew to London during *The Missouri Breaks*, he and Kidder had a daughter, while Becky had split off from Oates and married Peter Fonda; the two would settle in the Paradise Valley. McGuane, in turn, would soon divorce Kidder and marry Jimmy Buffett's sister, Laurie Buffett. This all happened in the span of a year.

Richard Brautigan had purchased his property on Pine Creek in 1973. Gatz and Marian Hjortsberg, along with Lorca and their young son Max, lived next door. Brautigan would live there off and on with his daughter, Ianthe. Jim would sometimes give her fly-fishing lessons, she remembered, and she liked him. "He had a wonderful lingering kind of voice," she later wrote. "When he finished saying a sentence, the last gravelly word remained hanging in the air for a while, much like a good cast."

That September, Jim arrived in town, as did Guy and Terry Valdène, and their visits were the main events of late summer there, when a large group of friends went fishing and hunting together. Jim spent time with Brautigan whenever he was in Montana, and he often slept at his house, where everyone stayed up late drinking and telling stories. Jim used his laid-back voice and style, while McGuane used a "deep, dramatic voice to hold everyone," Ianthe recalled. Though Brautigan didn't cook, Jim, Valdène, and Chatham often prepared elaborate meals of local fish and game. They would also play pranks on one another. Once, Brautigan set up a fake person in Jim's bed, complete with a coconut for a head and pillows for a body. A confused Jim, who had left the party to go to sleep, returned with a bewildered look on his face and never asked who had displaced him. In return, he later slathered Brautigan's doorknob in butter. That same sense of humor spilled over into their correspondence. On one occasion, Brautigan wrote to Jim, "I just thought I'd drop you a line________________________________." Nothing more.

A year earlier, Brautigan had written an article for *Esquire* titled "A Gun for Big Fish" that centered around Jim, though he never referred to him by name. "Big Fish" was one of Brautigan's nicknames for him. The "Big Gun," Brautigan explained, was the new shotgun he wanted to buy for Jim for grouse hunting, which he did—a beautiful twenty-gauge L. C. Smith. Brautigan considered hunting with it himself, but then remembered it was intended for his friend. "I have no business firing it and it's on its way to Michigan right now," he wrote. "Even as I still hold the gun in my hands, it is traveling away from me." The lesson? To actually own something, one needs to give it away.

Brautigan gave other gifts to Jim too. He had lent Jim money to write the novel *Farmer*, and more importantly perhaps, Brautigan had given Jim the title for the story. One night at a bar in Livingston, Jim had asked Brautigan what he thought he should title the book because it was commonly agreed that Brautigan was great at coming up with them. (Just think of Brautigan's *In Watermelon Sugar*, or *Trout Fishing in America*.) After requesting one dollar for the service, Brautigan asked Jim what the book was about.

A Michigan farmer, Jim told him.

Brautigan looked up, paused, and said *Farmer*.

—

For *Farmer*, Jim had mined his childhood memories of his grandfather's farm in Michigan. He had subscribed to the magazine *Michigan Farmer*, and he leafed through old issues at the library. He later wrote that he had based the story on his mother's family, and he imagined that Norma's only brother, who had died as an infant in the 1919 flu epidemic, had actually lived. Jim thus rewrote his uncle's life, he explained. One problem with this account is that Norma never had a brother: Her sister, Irene Dorothy, had died just after birth of erysipelas. It was likely a mix-up on Jim's part, though he rarely let the truth get in the way of a good story.

Jim's imagining of a life not lived applied as much to his own life as to his mother's imaginary dead brother. Joseph, a forty-three-year-old schoolteacher, has an affair with a student, Catherine, in what amounts to an infidelity and betrayal of his longtime partner, Rosealee. The circumstances loosely mirrored an affair Jim himself had had around this time with a graduate student from Arizona. It had begun during his visit there when he had guest-taught a class, and it would continue off and on for decades.

Rosalee, then, would serve as a loose stand-in for Linda, a reading that Jim seemed to both invite and complicate, in part by sexualizing Catherine's horse-riding clothes in an odd reversal of roles. Recall that when Jim saw Linda outside her home in East Lansing, she was dressed in her riding attire. The first time Joseph has an affair with Catherine, she's wearing the same riding clothes, and "going riding" becomes a code and "euphemism for their lovemaking."

Joseph loves Rosalee, and he shudders at the consequences of his affair. "How could he have so nearly destroyed their love like some madman burning a barn or shooting his animals?"

Jim and Linda had struggled with their own marriage during this time and had undergone "local marriage counseling," as Jim put it. Jim had also described a "deep slough" from his own years of infidelities—a state of mind not unlike Joseph's—to the point that he could scarcely function. But Jim had managed to gain, at least for a time, a "deep resurgence," as he wrote to McGuane, by meeting the problem head-on.

The parallels between Jim and Joseph emerge in other telling ways. Joseph's leg was mangled by a farm machine when he was eight, and Joseph's nephew loses an eye in an accident. Joseph drinks too much, loves Keats, dislikes teaching, and at one point, wants to see a coyote, whose howl reminds him of the otherworldly wail of a loon, one of Jim's favorite sounds. Joseph's father dies abruptly in an accident.

Most importantly, however, Jim's response to his own father's death was very different from Joseph's. "Grief makes people lazy because they can't understand why they should go on if they're going to die," Joseph ponders, "but they should go on harder if they understood it." Joseph's truth is Jim's. Unlike Joseph, Jim *had* left the farm, so to speak. He had visited cities and traveled to the coast to see the ocean. Joseph stays on the farm and, in turn, "missed so much of his life. He felt he should have dragged his weary leg around the earth instead of staying on the farm grieving his dead father." What Jim really did in *Farmer* was imagine what his own life might have been had he reacted differently.

—

Pat Irving thought the title *Farmer* "eloquent in its brevity" and "impossible for a potential book-buyer to fumble over! Besides, I just plain like it a lot." She had edited the manuscript, and although she thought her notes were very light and the queries minimal and minor, she fretted over Jim's response. "You didn't phone today," she wrote, "and I know that's a bad sign." Most of her suggestions involved modest reorganization in the first half of the book, and she realized Jim might not agree with the new scheme of things. She had inserted chapter breaks and swapped chapters three and five. "And, please," she added, "fulminate over the phone and not in the manuscript. I can handle any kind of verbal abuse straight on—so for gods [*sic*] sake call and get it out of your system instead of gouging at the script while you seethe. (Only, honestly, I don't think you'll find things that bad.)"

As it turns out, Jim agreed with many of her comments, and he switched the chapters around, thinking her "totally right." He knew what he wanted to say, as he would later tell an interviewer, discounting the work of editors with a bit of bluster. "I've been over it four or five hundred times, so why should I let them fool with it? They're not writers."

Jim had respected Pat Ryan at *SI* and Alix Nelson at Simon & Schuster, and he held Irving in high regard as well. She had earned his trust, a process that required patience and understanding, as the careful framing of her editing remarks reflected. It required an even larger measure of competence, if not genius, for the job. Jim's female editors would meet those marks and earn his loyalty. He would later describe Irving's editing as both "wonderful" and "an extraordinary thing."

Although Jim was delighted with Irving, he would be furious at Viking's rollout of the book. For one, he complained about the summer publication date, and Irving sought to reassure (and breathlessly scold) him on that account.

"Jimmy goddammit you act as if we'd never had one let alone several ANGUISHED conversations about a summer pub date and that summer in *Farmer*'s case meant August and that August meant eve of September which experience has taught us happens to be an extremely good time to put quality fiction on the market," she spewed a la stream of consciousness. "You're entitled to a good wail now and then; you happen to be a model author with a hell of a lot of class, and in a curious way I'm glad to see you stomp around and have a tantrum from time to time—but let's make it a cathartic one."

The marketing of the book, which Jim considered his best novel to date, was another story. In Jim's opinion, *Farmer* had wiped out the previous two novels, which now reminded him of his unprintable poetry prior to *Plain Song*. The relative failure of *Farmer* as a commercial success would break his heart. He felt Viking hadn't done enough to promote the book and later claimed that the extent of their marketing amounted to a ridiculous one-inch advertisement.

Jim's anger at Viking would be made fully clear several years later when the publisher billed him $81.24 for copies of *Farmer* he had once ordered. After Dattila wrote a letter to Michael Loeb, Viking's corporate secretary, on Jim's behalf, Loeb expressed his regret, snidely so, that Jim was "mistakenly dissatisfied with our efforts to publish his book." Loeb claimed that Viking had distributed 484 review copies, which compared favorably, in his opinion, to the total regular sale of 2,890 copies, and he regretted that they had to remainder (that is, liquidate) 3,000 copies.

Following his success with *Legends of the Fall*, Jim sent a biting reply to Loeb. "Talked to Tom Ginsberg [*sic*] in New York over dinner and he admitted you jerk offs did a real bad job with *Farmer* . . . Leave me alone." In a handwritten postscript, he noted that he had made "$560,000.00 last year and I'm still not paying. Please advise if you want to duke it out in court." Viking dropped the fees.

Amazingly, the figure of more than half a million dollars was accurate. Jim's life was about to take a radically new course.

LEGENDS OF THE FALL

(1977–1979)

She says it's too hot,
the night's too short,
that I'm too drunk,
but it's not too *anything, ever.*

In 2002, Jim would tell the story of how "Legends of the Fall," undoubtedly his best-known work of fiction, had come about. The story began with Linda rummaging through the attic of her father's ancestral home, an extravagant fourteen-room house on the Keweenaw Peninsula, where she rediscovered the nineteenth-century journals of her great-grandfather—William Ludlow—which she then gave to Jim, who read them with an eye toward creating fiction. Years later, while visiting the Library of Congress, John Harrison turned up, as if by fate, Ludlow's *Report of a Reconnaissance of the Black Hills of Dakota* from 1875, a detailed account of the man's explorations along the early frontier.

Together, the journals and report would inspire Jim and provide a template for the fictional character "Colonel William Ludlow," the patriarchal landowner and Montana rancher of the novella. While Jim claimed to have used "only a small part of the recorded 'reality'" of Ludlow's life, the materials were "fabulously suggestive," and they derived—or so he thought—from a family relation with a long list of accomplishments to his name—ones of historical magnitude.

But what no one knew at the time was that Jim and the family had inadvertently mixed up two different Ludlows. So, in "Legends of the Fall," Jim wound up merging the lives of two men, only one of them a family relation. The first, an immigrant named William Alfred Ludlow, was born in 1838 in Penzance, Cornwall. He was orphaned and sent to a workhouse, trained as an engineer, and later married in the Upper Peninsula of Michigan. This was the family's Ludlow, the author of the old journals discovered by Linda. In the decades just before and after the Civil War, William Alfred Ludlow traveled widely: He landed in Nicaragua, rounded Cape Horn en route to San Francisco, journeyed to Chile, and ventured to Mexico, where his brother owned silver mines.

The second William Ludlow—no relation to Linda's family—had surveyed lands in Wyoming and Montana, including the Yellowstone region, for the US government and would eventually author the report that John had found. Born in 1843, this Ludlow attended New York University (then known as the University of the City of New York) before enrolling at West Point. Like the character in Jim's novella, he accompanied Colonel George Armstrong Custer on an expedition into the Black Hills of South Dakota, home to the Sioux, where he served as chief engineer alongside George Bird Grinnell, the famous naturalist and anthropologist. Jim admired Ludlow in part because of his opposition to Custer.

Together, the Ludlows' stories held obvious appeal for Jim: They offered themes and places pertaining to the western frontier—exploration, mapping, violence, settler colonialism, Indian removal, and rugged landscapes and wilderness—all elements that would shape his future novella. And then too, there was Linda's ancestral connection, or so he thought.

The truth of the mix-up emerged two decades after the publication of "Legends," and the discovery—made by Jim's daughter Jamie and her son during his work on a high school project—was almost comical. It took only the internet and a few hours of amateur sleuthing to uncover the facts. Once Jamie began writing down the details, connecting the dots, it seemed to her increasingly impossible that these two men were the same person.

"I mean, it wouldn't take a whole lot to think that [these men] are synonymous," she said. Born less than a decade apart, both were named William Ludlow, worked as engineers, and traveled widely in the West. But "it became completely blindingly obvious at some point."

When Jamie told her mother the truth, Linda found it hilarious. "She loved the idea that Dad had been wrong. I just thought it was funny, and it *was* funny, but not funny enough to tell him," Jamie remembered, and so "we just sort of put it off." At one point, years after the discovery, Jamie mentioned in passing to her father that she "wasn't entirely sure that they were the same people."

"What do you mean?" he asked.

"Never mind," Jamie said, and she just left it at that and walked away. "He didn't seem to want to know." At the time, Jim was ravaged by shingles and back pain, and Jamie didn't see the sense in pressing the point. There was simply too much to unravel, despite the humor, and too much explaining to do to unwind the family's own legend.

—

By the early months of 1977, the Harrisons' finances had bottomed out. Jim now had a farm, a wife, two daughters, two cats, and two dogs to support but very little money. The income from *Farmer* was not substantial, and his flurry of work for Hollywood in the previous two years had contributed little up to that point. A screenplay for *A Good Day to Die*, which he had written for the documentarian Fred Wiseman, was still on option, but as Jim noted in an interview that spring, "having a work on option and selling it are two different things. The money doesn't come in until it's sold." His other screenwork had not fared much better.

In February, he had spent several weeks in Florida cowriting the screenplay with Tom McGuane for Elliott Kastner, who had produced McGuane's *The Missouri Breaks* a year earlier. The film, *Cold Feet*, would not be made for another twelve years, and Kastner had yet to send Jim any money for his screenwriting efforts. Jamie visited the mailbox every day for checks that didn't arrive for more than a decade.

Money trickled in from other sources. Valdène's mother, Diana, sent a check to help out, and in April he received an award of $2,500 from the Michigan Foundation for the Arts. Even Jamie, just sixteen, contributed money to the household income. "I worked overtime and I was paying the phone bill and I was paying the electric bill when I was in high school," she explained. But it was still difficult to hold things together financially and otherwise. Jim had not filed a tax return for almost seven years.

"Working on two novels now after recent pratfalls in showbiz, including producer neglecting to pay for work done. A year's livelihood. Beware of Elliott Kastner," Jim fumed to Matthiessen in June. "I want to sleep the dream of apples far from the tumult of cemetaries [*sic*] as Lorca said one afternoon."

Jim desperately needed a break. "A bit dingy of late," he admitted with quite a bit of understatement. He was hoping for a trip to New York, both to fish near Shelter Island, an old haunt at the eastern end of Long Island, and to spend some time with Eido Roshi, one of Matthiessen's Zen instructors, then in residence at Zendo Shobo-ji in New York City.

Matthiessen had continued to encourage Jim's Zen practice, and he remained an important part of his *sangha*, or community of practitioners. Together, fishing and Zen—along with six-year-old Anna, whom Jim described as a balm—helped to lift him from his current funk. He wondered if Matthiessen had finished reading *Farmer*. He had not. Matthiessen had been busy finishing his *Snow Leopard*, a book largely about his own deepening understanding of Buddhist practice. "I don't read anything, goddamn it, but I will," he told Jim, who valued Matthiessen's opinion of his work and noticed the lack of it.

As in the past, Jim kept writing through his depression. He had begun work on a long comic novel about Traverse City, what would eventually become *Warlock*, and he finished *Returning to Earth*, the lengthy poem of sixty-nine stanzas, which he sent that winter to Cecil Giscombe, then the editor of the Court Street Chapbook Series. Court Street, a new imprint of Ithaca House, had accepted only one work to date—a collection of fiction, *Three Times Three*, by Robert Flanagan. Giscombe, who had recently written a favorable review of *Farmer* for the *Chariton Review*, was "awfully impressed" with Jim's poem and offered to publish it, planning a run of five hundred copies. When he wrote in March, he explained that he expected printing to begin in early summer, adding that he and coeditor Scott Sommer had a few "minor suggestions" for revision. They would soon learn of Jim's famous impatience with being edited.

That June, Giscombe enumerated eight editorial requests. In one, he noted that he and Sommer were "slightly bothered" by the line, "'The rower continued his rowing.' It seems weak, weak enough to make the whole stanza suffer for its sin," and then asked if Jim could send them something "more exciting" in its place. In another, he opined, "The description of the crow's wimps & howls ('O jesus / the pain O shit it hurts O god let it end'): we thought you kind of overdid it here. Can we leave out the line I just quoted and make it: 'I barely hear his wimps & howls; / he drags himself through the air mostly landing . . .'?"

Giscombe was only twenty-seven, and his tone a bit presumptuous. Jim was furious and threatened to pull out entirely, while Giscombe, realizing that he had overstepped, quickly sought to walk back his comments.

"We regret that you reacted so strongly to our suggestions," he wrote weeks later. "They were made in a spirit of good will and they were only suggestions." He hoped Jim would reconsider and allow them to publish the book-length poem. His appeal worked, and Jim agreed to stay with Court Street. Giscombe assured Jim that they would publish it "exactly as you sent it to us."

—

Setting aside the future *Warlock*, Jim began work on a sequence of novellas, starting with what would be the collection's namesake, "Legends of the Fall."* (The other novellas, "Revenge" and "The Man Who Gave

* Jim had reportedly discovered the title, "Legends of the Fall," scratched on a piece of paper on McGuane's desk. With his permission, Jim promptly plucked it away and claimed it for his own.

Up His Name," were not yet planned or titled.) He had pondered "Legends" for years, but when he began writing it, it all came quickly; he completed a first draft in just nine days. As usual, he wrote the novella out in longhand on a legal pad. The first draft was shockingly polished, with only minor revisions throughout, mostly inserted words and small changes in phrasing. In the same notepad were pages of preliminary notes, a seemingly disorganized assemblage of quotes and ideas—his common practice when thinking through a work of fiction. On various pages appear words and lines such as,

> "lives becoming history in units of days and nights so fatally private"
>
> "HAUNTED"
>
> "Your husband is dead
> No one knows
> Opium"
>
> "Quotes from journal"
>
> "Autumnal end"

On another page, he listed books that might serve as potential models, including Faulkner's *Sartoris*; Emily Brontë's *Wuthering Heights*; the actor Sterling Hayden's autobiography, *Wanderer*; and Knut Hamsun's *Victoria*. The list provides a remarkable lineage of textual influence, both surprising and strangely obvious (with the exception perhaps of Hayden's book). Jim would adopt Hamsun's use of a distant, "god-like" omnipotent narrator, which he later admitted can sometimes be "too distant," but it worked for "Legends"—"Tristan wouldn't be Tristan if he were a babbler," Jim later insisted.

The writing came sharp and steady, like a "seizure in composition," he later reflected, as if he were "taking dictation from the past." That was the "only time it ever happened like that, the only time anything like that's ever happened to me with fiction. I couldn't stop once I got started."

A part of that directive from the past came from the Ludlow report on the 1874 exploration of the Black Hills, another from the journals of the family's Ludlow—dusty scrapbooks mottled with age. Fragile to the touch, the latter contained sketches, news clippings, ledgers, company stationery from the likes of "Warm Springs Con. Mining Co.," some original verse copied out in longhand, and the names of places and dates:

"Wm. A. Ludlow
Mariposa Dec 28th 1864
California"

Drawing directly at times from these documents, Jim wove their respective stories into his own fictional one, combining the two Ludlows into a composite character.

The novella "Legends" is a hearty brew of historical fact, autobiography, and literary allusion, from Dostoevsky's *The Brothers Karamazov* to Homer's *Odyssey*, the romance of Tristan and Iseult, and the book of Genesis. While Jim often borrowed heavily from family histories and his own life for his fiction—as he had in *Wolf* and *Farmer*—his use of the 1874 report reveals a remarkable willingness to blend fact with fiction and to do so at times without any attribution. He would never again do so to such an extent.

The Ludlow documents provided him not only with basic plot points and details—the architecture upon which he would build his narrative, including the backstory of the fictional Ludlows—but also with language and imagery. In one instance, Jim copied into the novella reportage from the army's Ludlow about swarms of grasshoppers encountered by his exploratory party in the Dakotas:

> Their powers of sustained flight, too, are wonderful . . . they appear able to keep on the wing of a whole day, always moving with the wind, and filling the air to a vast height . . . the wings reflecting the light make them appear like tufts of cotton

> floating lazily in the wind . . . in descending through the slanting rays of the sun, they resemble a fall of huge snow-flakes.

The inclusion of the passage added a literary dimension to the family's aging patriarch and ascribed to him the qualities that Jim so admired in the army's Ludlow: He was, as Jim put it, an "elegant writer," one with both "probity and grace," and a mixture of "literary and scientific" intelligence. Jim borrowed other details and passages from the report: a blood red moon that "fired the beige landscape"; the "doleful cry of a wolf at midday"; "bleached" buffalo skulls; the Cree Indian "One Stab," whom Custer's party took captive and employed as a scout during their exploration of the Dakotas, and the "terse and direct" recommendations on "the Indian question," which the government ignored entirely.

"Legends" can be interpreted in many ways, but on one level, it's unmistakably a document of Jim's rage at the loss of Winfield and Judy. Divided into three chapters—the number three becomes a motif—"Legends" tells the story of the Ludlow family, which mirrors Harrison's own family. But the heart of the story is ultimately Tristan's, the middle son of the patriarch, and it follows him across decades and far-flung seas to multiple continents; through love affairs and world events, including World War I and the Depression; and through several personal tragedies.

When German soldiers kill Samuel, the youngest brother, Tristan is devastated and suffers from guilt reminiscent of Jim's own following Winfield and Judy's deaths. As Jim himself had been following the accident, Tristan is "totally disabled," even suicidal, after his brother's death, and others fear for his sanity, as Jim had for his own. Later, Tristan's wife, named Two, is killed by a stray bullet while sitting in a car, an echo of Judy's death. For Tristan, the loss proves almost too much for him to bear. Jim's claim, writing of Tristan's loss, that "two deaths in fourteen years of loved ones are not all that uncommon except to the mourner who has lost all sense of common and uncommon and is buried in the thoughts of things left out and how it might have been," spoke more to himself perhaps than his fictive character.

As the other novellas in the trilogy would, "Legends" plays out a kind of revenge fantasy wherein the guilty are often made to pay for their actions, sometimes with their lives. This is especially true for Tristan, who seeks to avenge the deaths of his family members. In an essay on the phenomenon of revenge written years later, Jim mused that he once "set out to murder the drunken driver who had killed my father and sister; but he, too, had been killed in the accident." Tristan memorializes his brother by cutting out Samuel's heart with a skinning knife and encasing it in paraffin. Then Tristan inflicts a version of the vengeance that Jim had imagined himself doing: He scalps seven German soldiers, making a necklace from them—a practice inspired by Tristan's spiritual father, One Stab—and one of many examples of American Indian imagery and issues that resonate throughout the novella and Jim's works in general.

Only the ocean and wandering offer Tristan a chance for peace. If there is redemption for him, it might lie with the birth of his children, Three and Samuel. Or perhaps it rests in the realization that there was "no evening the score with the world, because even if he could that would not re-create the woman" he lost or his younger brother.

Soon after Jim finished "Legends," he received a postcard from Toby Carr Rafelson, a well-known and respected production designer, art director, and occasionally, actress. Postmarked "July 5, 1977, Durango, Mexico," it would change his life.

Jim had met Toby through Bob Dattila, and the two became friends. He would sometimes visit Toby and her husband, director Bob Rafelson, at their Hollywood home, which served as a regular hangout and party spot for film-industry friends. A few months earlier, Jim had written to Toby, complaining of his financial troubles and alluding to his depression. By chance, she picked up the letter as she was briefly passing through Los Angeles en route to Mexico; otherwise, the letter would have sat in her mailbox for months.

Toby was then working as a production designer on Jack Nicholson's Western *Goin' South*. Once back in Durango, she approached Nicholson about Jim's problems, and she was the right person to do so. Toby was well liked and known for her generosity, and her husband, Bob, had given Nicholson his big break by casting him in *Easy Rider* and *Five Easy Pieces*. Together, the two devised a plan to support Jim's writing and, provided he was willing, develop a film out of it with a leading role for Nicholson.

"You sounded down," she wrote to Jim in her postcard, "which is understandable, but I have the feeling, after talking with Jack, that things may be looking up. Any chance of your coming down here?" The news could not have come at a better time for Jim.

Perhaps most significantly, Toby's postcard encouraged Jim in unexpected ways. With the eye of a production designer, she provided him, inadvertently it seems, with the setting for his second novella, "Revenge," as well as a key plot feature. In the space of a postcard and with increasingly small handwriting, she essentially scouted a location for him, making a case not only for Jim's visit but for the literary potential of the locale:

> Durango is a 400-yr-old town 6000 ft. high in a wide valley surrounded by brooding blue mountains. The skies are immense and awesome as they fill daily with banks of clouds that finally light up at sunset and then open over the city at night, drenching & cooling everything. The people, quietly dominated by a Mafioso-type family control, are delightful, as are Mexicans in general, and the landscapes are very beautiful.

Then there were the rains, overflowing rivers, miles of mud, and impassable roads, she added. How much of the novella he had already planned at that point is unknown, but like the Ludlow journals, her description of the town inspired him. Jim would set "Revenge" in Durango and use his trip there to gather details for it. He would also borrow the fact of a patriarchal "Mafioso-type"—his character Tiburón, whose name in Spanish means "shark," lords over the region. That Jim chose to nickname the character "Tibey" seems more than coincidence and a fitting, if subtle, tribute to the woman who contributed so much to the birth of the work.

In Mexico, Jim visited movie sets and cavorted with the cast and crew, which included John Belushi, Mary Steenburgen, and Danny DeVito. Toward the end of his weeklong visit, late at night over margaritas, Nicholson finally broached the topic of Jim's debts, and the two agreed on a mutually beneficial plan: Nicholson would serve as a patron to Jim, supporting his writing of at least two novellas, and he would get a "first look" at what Jim wrote and consider it for a possible movie and starring role. Nicholson agreed to give Jim a total of $25,000, and they would split 50/50 any money from the sale of the novellas to film studios. Jim had already discussed his ideas for what would become "Revenge" (at least the broad strokes) with Nicholson and Toby while still in Durango, so Nicholson had an idea of what to expect.

By mid-August, after Jim returned to Michigan, he received the first installment of $5,000, with a check for $10,000 to follow a week later. Taken together, they amounted to more than a typical year's income for the Harrisons. Meanwhile, Nicholson and Toby kept the project in mind. In October, just as *Goin' South* was about to wrap, they scouted locations in Durango for a possible film.

"It's still as beautiful as ever here, weather-and-landscape-wise," Toby wrote to Jim, "and I have taken many more pictures and given Jack several tours of the town with ~~an~~ his eye towards your future project." That she chose to replace *an* with *his* punctuated Jack's involvement.

Due in part to the informal nature of his agreement with Nicholson (no lawyers, Jack insisted), the final details remained hazy. In the coming months, a small battle would ensue between Dattila and Nicholson's people, though the two friends managed to avoid the fray. Nicholson's manager, Robert Colbert, insisted that the payment of $25,000 to Jim meant that the actor owned "all the film rights" to the two novellas, among other things, while Dattila countered that the friends agreed to split evenly "any monies garnered from the studios for the sale of the book rights." At one point, in a letter to Jim, Dattila alleged that Colbert and Nicholson's agent, Sandy Bressler, were trying to boost their commissions at the expense of their client's wishes. (Dattila had not taken any commission on the initial $25,000.)

"It looks like showdown time to me," Dattila declared to Jim, and planned to bypass Bressler and Colbert entirely in communications with the studios.

The hostilities would play out in letters for more than two years, though Dattila's understanding of the arrangement ultimately prevailed: Jim and Nicholson would split all money from the sale of the film rights to "Legends" and "Revenge," and Jim would be compensated separately for any screenplay work he completed.

—

Back at home, Jim began work on "Revenge" and then "The Man Who Gave Up His Name," the remaining two novellas in what would ultimately become the collection *Legends of the Fall*. While he usually wrote in the converted granary behind his house, this time—given the influx of money—he secluded himself at the Jolli-Lodge on Lake Michigan, just a few miles away.

In September, *Returning to Earth* came off press, and despite his initial reaction, Jim had heeded several of Giscombe and Sommer's recommendations. Most important, he retained the second stanza of the poem for the final version, though he had crossed it out entirely in the manuscript.

"On page 1—S. Sommer and I both like that stanza that you crossed out (the one that begins: 'So curious in the middle of America, the only "locus" . . .')," Giscombe had written, urging, "Can you leave it in?"

Why Jim initially chose to delete it is unclear: the stanza orients him geographically in Michigan with other places and things radiating outward in measured distances. He also deleted a question in the final stanza, "At nineteen (was it?) I began to degenerate," revising the line to, "At nineteen I began to degenerate." The change seems relatively minor, though in his handwritten notes for the poem he had marked the age as twenty-four, rather than nineteen, his age in 1962, when Winfield and Judy were killed. Was twenty-four too revealing, given the date of their deaths? Or perhaps age nineteen—that is, most of 1957—was somehow more accurate, the year he suffered a deep depression and hitchhiked across the country, the tumultuous period he recounted in *Wolf.* That he addressed the deaths of his sister and father just two stanzas earlier suggests he had 1962 on his mind.

> O my darling sister
> O she crossed over
> she's crossed over
> is planted now near her father
> six feet under earth's skin—
> their still point on this whirling earth
> now and I think forever.

The final stanza confronts the consequence of this crossing over and loss. For Jim, a "slight smell of death in my gestures" occurred at nineteen—or twenty-four. Either way, the deaths catalyzed some emotional decline or ushered in a more volatile mental state, one marked by an acute sense of his own mortality.

Returning to Earth appeared in abbreviated form in *Ploughshares* a few months afterward and was later paired with *Letters to Yesenin* in a release by Sumac Press. The small chapbook captured very few reviews. Writing for *Harper's Magazine* in June 1978, Hayden Carruth (writing as Jim's advocate once again) considered the poems a much-needed counterforce to "academicism" and the poetry written by "thousands and thousands of 'poets' who have been turned out, 'finished' (as we used to say), perfected in literary decorum and politesse, but with nothing to say and as much like one another as the receiving line at Mme. Porter's cotillion."

Carruth described Harrison's poetry as "hard-boiled," and he read the flow of *Returning to Earth* as a movement away from "despair toward a tentative, tenuous acceptance of the natural world," though the pain remains—"alcoholism, a blind eye, sexual disillusionment, the wrack of the land." For Carruth, Harrison's "degeneration" derives from, among other things, his discovery of the world's degeneration, and what remains—Harrison's poetic "vision" at the heart of it all—is to now live in "primitivism." What that looks like and how one lives in it, Carruth did not venture to say.

—

By the spring of 1978, as Jim completed the manuscript of "Revenge" and began work on "The Man Who Gave Up His Name," Dattila faced a potentially difficult sales job. He had to somehow persuade publishers to take a chance on a collection of novellas, an unpopular and famously tricky genre to market and sell, then especially. Few authors were known for writing them at the time, and publishers were generally wary of the genre even though it had a distinguished track record.* Novellas, the argument went, were an ill-defined form, ranging from several dozen pages to almost two hundred. They were thought too slight for publication as a full book—readers wanted more for their money—yet too lengthy for a magazine. Others shared a vague sense that they were actually unfinished works that required either more substance to make them a novel or "ascetic brevity" and "diligent cutting," as one scholar noted, to make them short stories.

But the genre appealed to Jim, and he enjoyed reading them—Isak

* Think Melville's *Billy Budd*, Mann's *Death in Venice*, Dostoevsky's *Notes from the Underground*, Conrad's *Heart of Darkness*, Kafka's *The Metamorphosis*, James's *The Turn of the Screw*, Faulkner's *The Bear*, Ernest Hemingway's *The Old Man and the Sea*, and Capote's *Breakfast at Tiffany's* for starters, yet most publishers and editors simply did not know what to do with them and thought them somehow a lesser genre.

Dinesen's *Babette's Feast*, Katherine Anne Porter's *Noon Wine*, Hugo von Hofmannsthal's *Reitergeschichte* (*A Tale of the Cavalry*). Years later, he would write to Seymour Lawrence, his future publisher, that he had read Porter "faithfully in late high school as she was my best teacher's favorite," referring to Bernice Smith. "I am sure I wouldn't have been writing novellas if it weren't for *FLOWERING JUDAS* and *PALE HORSE, PALE RIDER*, and *NOON WINE*. She and Isak Dinesen were the true masters of those very long stories that we call novellas." (Lawrence, as it turns out, had published Porter's best-selling and only novel, *Ship of Fools*.)

The novella offered an attractive alternative, a "mid-form, that half-way form between novel and poetry," Jim would say. "I don't like looseness. Maybe that comes from starting as a poet. I love that specific density and compression I can get from the novella form." At the same time, he thought the short story too restrictive. With them, "I don't get to do my divagations, my digressions, which are mostly what's interesting to me because they are the nature of reality." Jim would publish only three short stories in his lifetime.

Then too, the novella was a genre on the periphery of high culture, an appealing idea for Jim, who both reveled in and resented his status as a literary outsider. The novella's "mid-form" was perhaps somehow akin to the Midwest, something closer to home, and he would excel at writing them like few others—penning a whopping twenty-four over the course of his career. The trick was to convince publishers of their promise.

Together, Jim and Dattila struck upon an idea. They would first approach Rust Hills, the well-known fiction editor at *Esquire*, a magazine with a large general readership. If Hills bought one or both pieces, they would be in a much stronger bargaining position with book publishers. It was a smart move. Professorial, polished, a shrewd reader, "Rust had a famous reputation for publishing good literary stuff," Dattila said. At age fifty-four, Hills had worked for years in the magazine business, including several stints at *Esquire* from the 1950s to the 1990s, where he then served as fiction editor, and he was especially practiced at excerpting novels. In the September 1976 issue, he had published "The Seduction of Leslie," an excerpt from Williams Styron's work in progress, *Sophie's Choice*. "He used to say that excerpting was the true editor's art," Richard Ford recalled.

Hills was so impressed by Jim's novellas that he agreed to publish both: "Legends" in full, at twenty-three thousand words, and "Revenge" in a slightly excerpted version, at thirty thousand words, a few months later. "[Rust] was a natural person to do it. It wasn't any brilliance on my part," Dattila admitted. "I was just hoping that he'd like them, and he really did." They were the longest works of fiction the magazine had published in a single issue. By comparison, the Styron excerpt was just over fourteen thousand words.

"The magazine appeared bolder than it had been in years, and Jim seemed to have invigorated American fiction," Terry McDonell would write of the publications. "The traditional four-thousand-word short story, the meat of MFA programs and the staple of all the major magazines, looked claustrophobic in comparison."

Esquire would run the novellas in January and May 1977, respectively, alongside abundant illustrations reminiscent of dime Western novels. And *Esquire* sold them, in part, as such: "It's a tale of high adventure and great romantic obsession," the introduction to "Legends" read, "a spellbinding reading experience that is also clearly a work of literary art." But the challenge of the form remained: Even *Esquire* referred to "Legends" as Harrison's newest "short novel."

With the *Esquire* deal confirmed, Jim and Dattila shopped the stories to several book publishers. Since Guinzburg at Viking still held an option on Jim's next book, he was their first stop, though Guinzburg had no appetite for novellas and Jim didn't want them to publish the collection anyway. He was still furious over their handling of *Farmer*. "Nobody wanted a novella. Nobody liked novellas," Dattila recollected, and that included Viking. Jim decided to withhold from Guinzburg the fact that *Esquire* had already agreed to publish the two novellas, which might have altered his decision to pass. Jim was much more amenable to Dan Green and Simon & Schuster, which had published *A Good Day to Die*, but Green wanted Jim to expand "Legends" into a four-hundred-page novel, which Green insisted would make it "a sure-thing best-seller." Jim promptly refused.

In a move that would spark a long, productive partnership, Jim reached out to Seymour Lawrence, or Sam, a well-dressed and brilliant editor, who then managed his own imprint, Seymour Lawrence Inc., in association with the large New York publishing house Dell and its hardcover division Delacorte. Jim already had a few connections to him, though Lawrence was not as aware of them as Jim. The two had met almost fifteen years earlier at the Grolier Book Shop in Harvard Square, and in 1967 Jim had written to Lawrence on behalf of Tom McGuane, whose *Sporting Club* had yet to find a home, recalling in Lawrence's words their shared "interest in good and original fiction." At the time, Lawrence had even invited Jim to submit a novel of his own, but Jim had nothing to show him at that point.

Lawrence had earlier published Richard Brautigan, beginning with the first combined edition of his works in 1969, a hardcover book that included the novella *Trout Fishing in America*, the poetry collection *The Pill Versus the Springhill Mine Disaster*, and the novel *In Watermelon Sugar*. Brautigan had enjoyed a devoted following, but Lawrence's decision to publish his fiction and poetry together in one edition had carried risks. The book went on to sell three hundred thousand copies in the first year and further introduced Brautigan to a national audience. His bet paid off.

With an instinct for both literary talent and commercial promise, Lawrence took risks that others would not—he then counted Katherine Anne Porter, J. P. Donleavy, and Kurt Vonnegut among his authors—and seemed the logical choice for Jim's collection of novellas. Lawrence enjoyed good wine and food almost as much as Jim, and he tended to become part of his authors' lives, often as a friend as well as an editor and publisher, and Jim was no exception. Friendship would find its way to the center of Jim's professional life.

When Dattila submitted the manuscripts of "Legends" and "Revenge" to Lawrence in April 1978, he explained that he and Jim would like to see both novellas put into one book, "perhaps with some illustrations in a very elegant edition," he suggested, and he noted that they already had an illustrator in mind: Russell Chatham, who would eventually provide the dust jacket art. From then on, Chatham would do all the cover art for Jim's major works.

Dattila also played up Nicholson's involvement in Jim's career, noting that the actor owned a percentage of the novellas and had plans for a theatrical package with himself either directing or acting or both. Lawrence was enthusiastic and promptly invited Jim to join his list of writers. Privately, he doubted the novellas would make the firm any money, but he banked instead on Jim's "bright future."

Writing internally to Ross Claiborne, the editorial vice president, and William Grose, editor in chief of Dell—both of whom shared his excitement over Jim's novellas—Lawrence weighed in on his recommendation to publish: "Yes, emphatically Yes. What a beautiful writer. And a productive one," he opined. "This is an investment and we should go into it with our eyes open. We may lose money on this book, and possibly the next, but not far off we will strike it rich." He also rejoiced that if Nicholson ended up making a movie, they would all be heroes.

After Jim received the good news, he sent a follow-up letter to Lawrence in May, reminding him that they had met several times at Cairnie's Grolier, where, in his words, he "hung out during two mildly indolent & indigent years in Boston." He also explained that he was extremely pleased to be with Delacorte, "knowing that your own imprint takes on few books and does a good job on them and my experiences at Viking had left me with wanting to murder the State." He would finish "The Man Who Gave Up His Name" by the first week of June, he assured Lawrence, and he insisted that he could not imagine a book without the third novella. Speaking of the number of novellas in the collection, and perhaps unintentionally to the motif of threes that occurs throughout them, he noted, "Two is a GM, IBM number; three is grace, euphony, a badger digging for his third ground squirrel, Balzac eating his third bécasse, Catherine the Great approaching her third donkey etc."

In June, Dattila submitted to Lawrence the manuscript of "The Man Who Gave Up His Name." "I think in its own way it is quite beautiful," Dattila remarked, "and along with the other two novellas owns a dead calm view of man in the Twentieth Century." He also reminded Lawrence again that Jim wanted the three novellas published together in the same volume and "feels that they, together, present an integral picture."

Lawrence agreed with both assessments, though he went a step further, planning the publication of three different versions: one edition with art by Russell Chatham, a second with three separate volumes in a white paper-covered slipcase, again with Chatham's work, and a third edition, again with slipcase, though this one with art by John Thompson, the illustrator of the *Esquire* version. The last edition, limited to 250 copies and signed by Harrison, had bronze lettering on the spine and sold for $50.00 (the others sold for $10.95 and $25.00, respectively). As Lawrence intended, both slipcase editions, especially the limited one, looked like instant classics, ready-made for collectors' bookshelves.

"That [was Lawrence] showing the publishing world that [he was] putting [his] taste behind them and risking a bit of money," Dattila suggested, recalling Lawrence's calculation and its effect. "That [was] just saying to everybody this is a classic." And Lawrence's gamble contributed to a kind of cascade effect: The more one person risked and put up, beginning with Nicholson, the more incentive others had to do the same. Nicholson, Lawrence, and Rust Hills, who had also staked his reputation on the novellas' success, were essentially exclaiming, "We all back Jim Harrison." Born of both personal affection and respect for the work, it was an extraordinary show of support for a writer whose books had not yet sold more than ten thousand copies.

In the following months, Jim traveled twice to London, once in the summer and again in late October, while Nicholson was working on *The Shining*. Stanley Kubrick, who liked the control that a soundstage provided, shot interior and snowy exterior scenes at EMI's

Elstree Studios in nearby Hertfordshire. While there, Jim spent time with Nicholson and Anjelica and Allegra Huston, played chess with Kubrick, attended "drunken parties with upper-crust English," and sometimes hung out at the film studio, including the day that Kubrick shot the memorable scene of Jack chopping through a door to get to actress Shelley Duvall.

The trips marked a tremendous change in Jim's life and a transition of sorts to a new one, a life more tied to Hollywood, screenwriting, cocaine, movie stars, and especially money. But Jim's primary purpose for visiting London was to work on a screenplay for "Revenge" in consultation with Nicholson and his almost father-in-law, John Huston, whom Nicholson had suggested as a possible director for the film. (They had imagined Orson Welles for the role of Tibey.) Huston was known as a good screenwriter, and his participation, Nicholson hoped, would help move the script along. Nicholson planned the role of Cochran, the retired fighter pilot, for himself.

Following the publication of "Legends" in *Esquire*, and after news of Nicholson's involvement got out, film studios began calling Jim. Even before he had signed up with Lawrence, Jim had visited with John Calley, the bespectacled chief of Warner Brothers, who expressed interest in both "Revenge" and "Legends," though he apparently had trouble deciding between the two novellas. "The Man Who Gave Up His Name," Dattila explained, was "always the orphan child." In Dattila's opinion, the obvious choice was "Legends," but that required more of an investment because of its vast scope, including war scenes and ocean settings. Of course, they were all "being really nice to me because they had a chance at getting a Jack Nicholson movie out of it. It wasn't all my boundless charm," Dattila admitted. Warner Brothers opted initially for month-long options at $15,000 for each of them—together more money than all of Jim's books had ever made—before purchasing a longer option on "Revenge." MGM eventually optioned "Legends."

Warner Brothers also hired Jim to write a script for "Revenge," which posed serious challenges for him. Not only did Jim need to learn to write screenplays, a genre he had only practiced off and on over the past few years, but his work would now be subjected to even greater scrutiny and control by others, something he wasn't used to and didn't like.

The financial and critical success of *Legends*, which arrived in bookstores in May 1979, was tremendous. The Book of the Month and Quality Paperback Clubs adopted it as an alternate. Reviews were far more numerous and enthusiastic than those for any of Jim's other books to date. The overwhelming feeling among critics was that Jim had come into his own with this collection, like a review in *The New Yorker* that suggested that Harrison had finally caught up with himself, that "his ideas have never quite matched his technical and artistic skills until now."

Other critics situated Jim's accomplishments in a grander context. Bernard Levin, writing for *The Sunday Times* of London, thought "Mr. Harrison may be the man to rescue and revitalize an important American tradition," the novella. Harrison is "a writer with immortality in him." Raymond Carver also chimed in, noting that "The Man Who Gave Up His Name"—the most Carveresque story in the collection—could stand with the "best examples the [novella] form has to offer—those by Conrad, Chekhov, Mann, James, Melville, Lawrence, Isak Dinesen."

But not everyone agreed. One critic found *Legends* exciting to read but facile and skimming "dangerously near the category of thrillers." A few reviewers vehemently criticized the book *and* the author, examples (again) of the polarizing and sometimes ridiculous reactions that Jim's writing and subject matter could elicit. Writing for the *Times Literary Supplement*, Vernon Scannell seethed, "Ill written, trite, and maudlin, all three of these stories would seem to be products of a vulgar, dubiously illiterate and rather unpleasant mind." It was comical—if only Scannell had been in on the joke. Yet other negative reviews struck to the bone, like Peter Prescott's, which accused Jim, along with fellow fiction writer James Salter, of writing "macho fiction," a tag that would follow him for years to come. "Like all good macho writers, their primary concern is for plot, for stories of fear and obsession, of death and mutilation," Prescott declared. These books celebrate masculine self-reliance, the argument went, and subordinate women, often killing them off only to "ennoble" male characters.

"Macho is just an awful, ugly word," Jim responded months later in an interview, though he was largely unresponsive to the specifics of Prescott's arguments. Jim insisted that he rooted his choice of subject matter in his Midwest upbringing. "I write about the preoccupations I was born and raised with, fishing and hunting in the country. Why is that macho? It's the reality I know. In order to eat the pig, you have to slit its throat. Most people maybe never had to do that, but they're still eating pork." These published comments did little to allay his critics, not all of whom were strangers or aloof coastal literati, as it turns out.

Surprisingly, some of the sharpest criticism of the subject matter and its treatment in *Legends* came from Peter Matthiessen. After receiving a copy of the bound galleys, Matthiessen wrote first to Sam Lawrence, expressing his frustration. He thought Jim Harrison "talented as hell," and he explained that he badly wanted to admire the novellas more than he did. "But all three are tainted by that technicolor romanticized media violence that he himself deplores."

In a follow-up letter to Jim, Matthiessen was even more blunt:

> To extend that a little: do you realize what you almost/might have accomplished in 'The Man Who . . .' You almost transformed a cold-fish unlovable non-hero into a real existential modern hero, which has only been pulled off once that I can recall in modern literature—the Consul, in 'Under the Volcano.' When you could be keeping company like that, why do you settle for this prime-time media mock-up tough-sensitive wine-tasting hard-fucking killer-killing Hemingway cum James Bond spit-back who infests all three stories to one degree or another? I don't care about Revenge, which is just an absurd exercise in fantasy

> macho, but Legends could be an interesting full-length novel if you had taken the time and care to develop the scenes and people instead of tossing it off as what boils down to a well-written movie treatment. I suspect that both of these had their inception in the wilds of Benedict Canyon . . . But 'The Man Who . . .' is potentially terrific, a very difficult idea that you are in the process of bringing off by sticking with the near-heroic character you are creating out of your own intelligence and pain and even Zen intuition, and then quite suddenly he turns into Dirty Harry or Kojak or whatever right before our eyes, the cliché anti-hero—Christ, Jim, I get furious writing this.

The letter was startlingly presumptuous and dismissive, particularly of "Revenge," and it amounted to a pointed accusation that Jim was "pissing away" his talent and intelligence for quick money and perhaps fame—for Hollywood, really: Jack Nicholson lived on Mulholland Drive, not far from Benedict Canyon. Made by a close friend and someone whose work Jim deeply respected, the accusations stung mightily. To make matters worse, Matthiessen chose to write (as we've seen) directly to Lawrence, whose respect and admiration Jim surely wanted to preserve. It felt like a betrayal.

Jim shot back a letter to Matthiessen, accusing him of going out of his way to do him "a bad turn" and condemning his criticisms as "gratuitously mean," "intemperate," and "almost rabid" and chastising him, rightly so, for contacting Lawrence about it at all. Jim's reaction, moreover, was fueled by a sense of ingratitude since he had written an enthusiastic review only months earlier of Matthiessen's *The Snow Leopard* for *The Nation*.

Matthiessen responded, in turn, by arguing that his comments derived only from his respect for Jim as a writer. "You missed the spirit of my letter, not to speak of our 'friendship'; if you haven't destroyed it, perhaps you should read it again," Matthiessen suggested. "In the 'lit world' you refer to so bitterly, an honest opinion from a peer is very hard to come by; apparently it isn't what you wanted." Following yet another exchange of letters, Matthiessen eventually acknowledged that despite his good intentions, he might have overdone it. "Perhaps it was me (I?) who wrote the letter with a coke hangover—anyway, I now feel it was too much, and I apologize. I wanted to light a firecracker under you, because I think you're a terrific writer, and I don't agree with practically everybody else . . . that this book is the fulfillment of your talent."

Matthiessen had joked that Jim would make a million from the novellas in Hollywood and then not invite him out on his new "Bertram 36-footer with outriggers and sonar." In truth, he had not been far off in terms of money. By year's end, Jim had received close to $350,000 for "Revenge," which included money from Warner Brothers for an option on the book rights (he would split this with Nicholson) and for Jim's screenwriting services. Producer John Calley also agreed to pay $135,000 plus $15,000 for travel and research expenses per year for a type of first look at all of Jim's work.

Additionally, Jim accepted the assignment of writing a screenplay based on John D. MacDonald's Travis McGee mystery series, for which he would receive between $150,000 and $200,000. Jim had met MacDonald in Sarasota, Florida, while visiting Rust Hills from *Esquire*; Hills and MacDonald were neighbors. Jim had long admired MacDonald and showed him a draft of "Revenge," which in turn led to Jim's assignment. MacDonald was impressed with "Revenge," later writing to Jim that the novella "handles the subjective of violence as well as anything I've ever read."

It all amounted to an astronomical leap forward financially, from an average household income of roughly $12,000 a year to hundreds of thousands, and Jim set about spending it. On visiting the Lake Leelanau property during this time, one journalist reported that the old farmhouse was "aswarm with carpenters and workmen in the midst of remodeling . . . Everything seemed to be in a chaos of sudden change." Jim remodeled the house and built a new kitchen. He hired a personal assistant, Joyce Harrington (later Joyce Harrington Bahle), a friend of Jim's daughter Jamie, who would work with him for the rest of his life. He also bought a new car, a four-wheel-drive Subaru, as well as a small cabin in Grand Marais, Michigan, a secluded fishing village on the southeastern shore of Lake Superior. Both the car and cabin would provide Jim with a valuable means of escape—and especially so from the Hollywood that had allowed him to purchase them. It was a paradox that would haunt him.

Other close friends wrote to congratulate Jim on his newfound success but also to check in on his well-being and offer advice. Valdène, whose mother had sent money to Jim years earlier to support him, wrote with praise. He had loved the book and thanked Jim for the co-dedication in *Legends* alongside Nicholson: "As you said you brought home the bacon! I am deeply happy for you." But he also delivered a warning. He was very worried that John Calley and company would overwork Jim and that screenwork would take its toll on him, if only because of the sheer number of words he'd have to crank out.

Valdène's words were prescient, and in the coming months and years, Hollywood would deliver rich rewards to Jim but strain his mental and physical health, demanding his time and attention and distracting him, to his dismay, from his poetry and fiction. It would prove, in retrospect, something like the proverbial deal with the devil.

13

THE THEORY AND PRACTICE OF HOLLYWOOD

(FALL 1979 – 1982)

Ah, yes. Fame never got anyone
off the hook, it seems . . .

On one of their first trips to Hollywood together, Jim and Dattila were driving through Los Angeles en route to a meeting at Universal Studios. It was a warm, dry day. As they got off the 101 at Universal City, they both noticed a man standing on a nearby balcony overlooking the traffic. The man stood in an open robe, naked, vigorously masturbating.

"Did you see that?" Dattila asked.

"Uh-huh," Jim said. "I wonder if he's waiting for something special to drive by. Like a Facel Vega with a wood ski rack?"

It was, they mused, an inauspicious metaphor of sorts for the Hollywood experience—everyone jerking it, and no one getting off—not unlike another metaphor Jim would employ for the same place, that of being stuck on an elevator, always caught between one floor or another, in transit up or down, and never arriving.

In Hollywood, Jim would learn to seek out places of refuge to recollect himself amid this shuddering of his affairs, thickets in the city that helped recenter him in ways that the concrete channels of the Los Angeles River could not. He loved to stroll the UCLA Botanical Gardens, a natural oasis kitty-corner to the Westwood Marquis, or hole up at Nicholson's estate on Mulholland Drive. From those locales, he mused, he could "relax and see the broadness of the comedy in which I had made myself the featured actor."

A few months before Jim's forty-second birthday in 1979, a reporter for the *Detroit Free Press* observed that for Harrison, "Success, of all things, threatens at every turn." After *Legends*, Jim's life and that of the Harrison family would never again be the same. For one, Jim would now shuttle regularly between the family home in Lake Leelanau and what he called the "urban dream coasts" of New York and Los Angeles, Aspen (where Nicholson had a house), Palm Beach (where Valdène lived), Montana, Key West, and Grand Marais (a retreat from all the above).

His success with *Legends* brought the Harrisons a small fortune and himself a lifestyle radically different from his years of impecunious struggle and months denned up in the granary with only Yesenin and Chief Joseph as company. Twin-engine jets sent from Hollywood now flew to fetch him for negotiations. Newly sought after by well-wishers and the media, he could no longer rely on his privacy.

Pat Irving, interviewed by the *Detroit Free Press*, referred to Jim as a philosopher-poet whom one could count on to never write a "formula novel." Dattila credited Jim's success to his "encyclopedic knowledge of music, cooking, hunting, fishing, art, nature—everything. He's simply the most intelligent person I ever met." In an accompanying photo for the piece, titled "The Wolves Are Howling at Jim Harrison's Door," Jim leaned against the granary doorway (his Airedale, Hud, sitting next to him), attired in shorts and an unbuttoned Hawaiian shirt, appearing relaxed and casually comfortable with his new success. "Jim Harrison can't see Hollywood from the steps of the shed on his nine-acre Leelanau Peninsula farm," read the tagline, "but Tinseltown has him in its sights."

In contrast to Jim's itinerancy, Linda cultivated a rather stationary private existence in Lake Leelanau. She bird-watched, rode horses, gardened, doted on her daughters, and cooked splendid meals (by most accounts, she was a better cook than Jim, though he was happy to take the credit). "Linda was her own person. Very controlled. Very private.

Devoted to her family," according to Molly Phinny, a close friend and neighbor. Molly had married Dan Gerber's nephew, Peter Phinny (an aspiring novelist and Jim's friend), and the two knew each other through their children: Anna Harrison was best friends with Molly's youngest daughter, Morgan, and Linda and Molly had met through the local school. Linda was strong-minded, shy, and seemingly aloof at times, said Phinny, but in a way that masked her shyness, and she was a careful watcher and listener. "She knew everything, but she kept it to herself." Even many years later, after Anna had grown up, Linda would opt to stay at home rather than travel with Jim. He would receive a great deal of attention on the road, and she preferred her privacy and her pastimes. She did not want to follow him around and be the wife in the wings.

But she enjoyed entertaining friends at their French Road home, and the family's increased wealth encouraged, and coincided with, a spate of parties given by the Harrisons and nearby neighbors on the peninsula. Those were supplemented by yearly visits from Valdène, Chatham, Gerber, and sometimes Buffett, who came for grouse season and would split their time, along with Jim, between Leelanau and Grand Marais. Sometimes Hollywood people who would later work with Jim would visit Lake Leelanau, like Sydney Pollack and Harrison Ford. There were lots of parties and lots of food, booze, and drugs, and everyone partook, including Linda. "I realized that I needed to change my life when I was in the barn doing drugs and the kids were in the house," she once admitted to Molly, though by that time Jamie (twenty years younger than her mother) often joined the party. "[Linda] was steady-Eddy in that family," Molly explained, and this was "maybe the wildest time of her life."

Jamie (or "Gertie," as Jim called her) was in her sophomore year at the University of Michigan and studying English in its small honors college. She would graduate with high honors and complete a thesis on the works of Peter Matthiessen. She would often write to her dad, filling him in on the details of her life, including what she was reading ("nearly fell asleep over Herodotus") and eating. "We went to a Chinese restaurant (medium but boring, I think I'm spoiled), and [I had] a caviar omelet that was horribly rich," she would write in one letter, highlighting the importance of food across the family.

Anna was nine going on ten, and Jim would occasionally pen parental letters to her with literary flourish ("Today I went upstairs to look for a book. Horrors! What an indescribable mess, a veritable hog-wallow, a nightmare of sloppiness . . . Certain privileges are in the gravest of peril"). Anna was becoming aware of just how different her family was. Jim had chronicled his life in national magazines—the parties, drugs, sports, women—and people in the community, including at Anna's school, had read all about it. Anna fully knew that her dad wasn't the same as others. Unlike her friends' fathers, she once noted, hers was often still in his bathrobe at 11:00 a.m.

Amid all the gains and changes and craziness that fall, the family also tallied an immeasurable and crushing loss. John and Becky's sixteen-year-old daughter, Gloria, had been hit by a car while riding her bike near Guilford, Connecticut. Gloria lay in a coma for months, and the family would remove her from life support that December. John and Rebecca wanted to wait until after Christmas Day. David Harrison and his wife, Cindy, who were both living in Washington, DC, came to Connecticut right after Christmas. Jim and his sister, Mary, flew to Connecticut together, while Linda and Anna stayed in Leelanau. Norma, who had just had surgery for colon cancer—she would survive it—was unable to make the trip. The memorial service was held on Saturday, December 29, at the Episcopalian church that John and Rebecca attended in New Haven. Everyone would remember the glitter of Long Island Sound in the distance and the cold, piercing wind that blew off it. "The hearts of everyone who loved that beautiful girl were broken," Mary remembered.

Years later, Jim would dedicate a collection of poetry, *The Theory & Practice of Rivers*, to Gloria Ellen Harrison (Ellen had been Judy's middle name), a deeply meditative work that would mourn her death. At one point in the collection, Jim would recall his brother reciting the burial service over "his dead daughter":

I cannot bear this passion and courage;
my eyes turn toward the swamp
and sea, so blurred they'll never quite
clear themselves again . . .

Gloria's death, as real and immediate and painful as anything, inevitably recalled Judy's. "Nothing is harder to deal with than a small casket," Jim would write.

On the way home from Connecticut, Jim and Mary got stuck in Chicago because of a weather delay. Jim was very impatient, and he was walking with some difficulty because of bad back pain, so he paid to charter a plane to take him home and drop Mary off in Alpena, Michigan, where her husband, Nick, and their sons were visiting family. "Money means not having to be inconvenienced," Jim told his sister. He may have been new to having money of his own, but he had been around it enough to know. "And the simple truth of that stuck with me," said Mary.

—

To deal with the growing complexity of his life, Jim would integrate Joyce Harrington Bahle, his new assistant and aide-de-camp, into his family's life and household affairs in a remarkably intimate way.

Bahle, who has big blue eyes and curly hair, grew up in a German Irish family in New York—her father owned a meat-packing business in Manhattan—and moved to the Lake Leelanau area in 1976. There, she worked various jobs, including one as a waitress at the Bluebird, a tavern and restaurant in nearby Leland, where she first met Jim. She recalled Jim holding court at the corner of the bar with his elbows propped before him. She knew he was a writer and a local character, liked to drink, and had a funny sense of humor. "Quirky as hell."

She often saw Jim and the Harrisons at local parties (Jim once brought Jimmy Buffett to a pig roast) and at Dick's Pour House, an unassuming bar and restaurant close to Jim's house. One day at Dick's, Bahle bought a winning lottery ticket, and she used the money (a portion of $10,000) for a trip to the British Isles with Jamie Harrison. Jamie was younger than she, but the two were friendly. Jim would task them both with reading John D. MacDonald novels during the trip. Jamie would talk up Bahle's qualifications, but the Harrisons were already impressed by her assertiveness. Once, during a Harrison family reunion, Bahle noticed smoke emanating from the gears of the door of the garage where everyone was gathered, and she took charge. She snapped the whole clan to attention—not an easy feat—and hustled them out of the structure. If needed, she could command a tough room.

When Bahle and Jamie returned to the States, Jim asked Bahle if she would like to work for him. The two sat down together in Jim's granary, and he laid it out: He didn't really know "how to do life," he told her, and he needed help. If she could manage the everyday details, like assuring that he file yearly tax returns, he could focus on his writing. "We had a good connection after that meeting," said Bahle, and the two agreed to a six-month trial arrangement. Considering Jim's new responsibilities, particularly in the movie business, the two would later form Anna Productions, named after Anna Harrison, in January 1982.

Soon, Jim and Linda granted Bahle power of attorney to conduct financial transactions in their names. She would carry their credit cards and checkbooks and dole out monthly allowances. Bahle recalled how her hands shook on her first trip to the local EF Hutton office to deposit a big check on their behalf. As for Linda, she was more than happy to relinquish control in return for more time (for gardening and the kids) and fewer worries, though Jim's lawyer apparently raised an eyebrow at the arrangement. But Jim trusted Bahle, and over the coming years, she would manage almost every facet of his life. She would become privy to the most intimate aspects of it. She read his fiction and poetry, written out in longhand on yellow legal pads, and typed it for him, and she began reading, typing, and sending (mostly by fax machine) all of his correspondence, including later letters and emails between Jim and his psychologist, Lawrence Sullivan, in New

York. It's hard to imagine a more personal and intertwined business relationship.

When Joyce married and took the name Bahle, it was Jim who encouraged her to keep Harrington and use all three names. He thought it sounded fancy and intimidating: Joyce Harrington Bahle. She would become not only Jim's life manager but a gatekeeper as well. To get access to him, a person would need to go through her, and she was tough and protective of his time.

During the winter of 1979–80, the Harrisons rented a place in Palm Beach, where Valdène and his family then lived, and Bahle came along. She remembered how, when they arrived, Cuban lifeboats and refugees were landing regularly in Florida and even on Palm Beach's golden shores. (One day, Jim found a pair of children's shoes on the beach, which he would hang above his desk, along with other items, as a totem.) Jim was escaping a snowy winter. Linda stayed only for a short time because she had to return to Michigan to attend to her ailing father, who would die of lung cancer that January. The family was devastated by his loss, and in Linda's absence, Bahle helped to care for Anna.

The Harrisons' extravagant Palm Beach rental was one of many expenses that kept their money moving out the door almost as quickly as it came in. Jim was not used to having money—real money, like many of his friends enjoyed—and he spent it, by his own admission, with little regard for the family's future. It had all come too quickly, like an avalanche of riches for a time—an income in the high six figures. And Jim reportedly burned through a solid $20,000 in Florida within the course of a month's time. "I can't tell you where the money went as my brain lacks that orientation," he later wrote. "I have the feeling that the money simply took a bus out of town." More accurately, it took a bus *around* town. In Palm Beach, Anna shuttled to school in a chauffeur-driven town car, and Jim, who made frequent excursions to Key West, shopped lavishly at the most expensive food market in Palm Beach.

Cocaine and fine wines had also become substantial expenses on the family's ledger. Anna once found a pile of cocaine beside a coke grinder under the bed, and the adults told her it was Bahle's "special salts." On top of that, the "pre-bedtime line of coke," Jim wrote, "called out for a vintage Margaux," and the expenses mounted. He had succumbed in those years, as he readily admitted, to something approaching greed. Despite having grown up in a family content with the idea of just getting by, the one-eyed goofy, "the black sheep poet emerging from this gene pool had inadvertently struck it rich."

In June 1980, Jim took Jamie to Manhattan, and the two stayed at the Carlyle, a luxurious hotel and legendary landmark on the Upper East Side where Nicholson regularly stayed. (Jamie would remember sharing an elevator with European royalty.) While there, Jim wrote to McGuane on Carlyle letterhead, announcing that Matthiessen would be in Livingston around July 8 for some fishing and that he had passed along McGuane's number to him. He missed McGuane, he told him, and his "incisive, wrong-headed intelligence!" The two had hardly spoken in months. He also encouraged McGuane to respond to Nicholson, who "seemed mildly upset" that he hadn't called him. "One accrues bruises, but he is a good ally & friend and it wouldn't hurt for you to call when you're out there [in Los Angeles]." Jim was trying to mend fences.

Jim himself was frequently traveling to Los Angeles for film meetings, and he was spending an increasing amount of time with Nicholson (and, by extension, Anjelica Huston, who was then dating the actor). "It was so intense for so long," McGuane said of Jim's relationship with Jack. "I think he mesmerized Nicholson. Jim and Jack were umbilically connected for a while." The two often saw each other in New York, arranged to meet in Aspen, and spent time together in Los Angeles, where they frequented restaurants and clubs together, including Dan Tana's, an Italian eatery next door to the Troubadour, where Nicholson first brought him.

The two often went to On the Rox, Lou Adler's exclusive invitation-only lounge above the Roxy on the Sunset Strip. Adler had had a wildly successful career as a music and film producer, and his place was a regular hangout for celebrities. Adler has said that On the Rox began as a private club with only two members: himself and Nicholson. "We would be the only people that Sherpa's on Everest would not have recognized," Dattila said of visiting the club with Jim. "Everybody else in the room was famous: Mick Jagger, Elton John, etc." Jim and Adler quickly became friends, and when Jim was in Los Angeles, he would sometimes stay at Adler's house in Malibu.

Jim was also spending more time in New York City, often called there for meetings with film executives if not his publishers. He typically stayed at the Carlyle, drank martinis at the hotel's stylish Bemelmans Bar, and dined and drank at Elaine's, the Upper East Side eatery and literary hangout, partly because of Datilla. A faithful patron, Dattila had worked his way into owner Elaine Kaufman's inner circle. Indeed, they would often sit at Kaufman's "family table."

Nights at Elaine's included a bevy of A-list writers, from Norman Mailer and Gay Talese to George Plimpton, Bruce Jay Friedman, Woody Allen, and of course any number of unpredictable guests and events. One night, Federico Fellini invited Jim to dine at his table. Another night, Jeanne Moreau showed up and had a drink with Jim, and Kaufman, who was no stranger to fame, curtsied in her presence. On rare occasions, the room could descend into relative chaos. Once, when Dattila bumped into a well-known actress, he noticed she had cocaine powder sprinkled on her face and neck after a visit to the ladies' room. Glancing down at her neck, he jokingly asked if he could have some, and she apparently thought he meant her breasts. Offended, the actress promptly threw a drink in his face. Dattila proceeded to dump a bucket of ice water on her head, apparently with Kaufman's consent, as the actress's companion tried to kick him in the face with her boots. Meanwhile, Jim stood nearby with two friends from Lake Leelanau, who looked on in disbelief. The event would land Dattila in a New York gossip column.

Food was front and center during Jim's visits to New York City. During the day, he liked to eat at Katz's Deli or J.G. Melon, and he had gotten in the habit, along with Dattila, of eating his way through what he called "the Triple"—first, a knockwurst sandwich at a German deli on Eighty-Sixth Street, followed by a slice of Ray's pizza, and finished off with two hot dogs and a large papaya juice at the Papaya King on Eighty-Sixth Street and Third Avenue, just a few blocks from the office of Jim's new psychologist, Lawrence Sullivan, or Larry, as his friends called him.

The Triple was a windup to the therapy sessions with his "mind doctor." Jim thought Sullivan, a gangly guy who liked to stretch out and lay back in his chair during sessions, a man with an "immense range of practical wisdom." Dattila, also a client, had introduced them. Jim had been initially wary of seeing a psychologist for fear the analysis would tamper in some way with his writing process, but he was more frightened by his "questionable sanity" and the effects on it by his use of drugs and alcohol. Sullivan would help him with that and many other things, and because of their friendship, he would continue to see Jim in a half-professional way until the final months of Jim's life. Sullivan would, in Jim's words, throw him a rope to pull him "out of holes [he'd] dug and fallen into," but the other half of their relationship, the friendship part, was "about food, books, family, the world at large." While New York City tended to sap Jim of energy, his face-to-face meetings with Sullivan were a definite lifeline, sometimes all but literally so.

All of these new demands on Jim's time came with personal costs, and while he strengthened new friendships he strained others. In July 1980, Gerber complained that he hadn't heard from Jim in a month, despite having left multiple messages, including three in the past week, and he wondered if Jim had become bored with their friendship. He also sensed that Jim was somehow less than happy with his new lifestyle. "I'm sorry that you don't seem to be enjoying your success, don't seem to be enjoying today . . . You seem to be taking less and less joy in writing screenplays. Is that work your master or servant?" Almost a year and a half later, Gerber still felt that he had been forced, against his will, to abandon their friendship because he could not go on "maintaining an illusion." He had seen so little of Jim in recent years, he felt, and it seemed that he now needed to beg "for an audience" with him. "Fame can be a more insidious drug than cocaine or booze, its frequently attending lords," he warned him, and he suspected that perhaps Jim enjoyed spending his time with more successful friends: "Success likes successful company, and in my apparent failure as a novelist, perhaps I've become an unwelcome emblem of failure."

While Jim appreciated Gerber's comments on his new novel, *Warlock*, which Gerber had included in the same letter, he found the rest of it "unwittingly cruel" if not unique. "The past few months every close friend I have—you, Pat, Guy, Tom, and Bob—have gone well out of their way to tell me how I have disappointed them," Jim replied. "Everyone, that is, except Russell [Chatham] who neither accepts nor offers criticism." As for an explanation, Jim declined to provide one, and he seemed at a bit of a loss. "I don't have anything substantial to say on any of this. My 'free time' has been tarpon & bird season . . . I miss everyone."

Gerber explained that his letter had not been criticism but a "plea . . . All that's important to be said in that letter or this one is that I miss your companionship and would like to see you."

—

In October 1981, Seymour Lawrence and Delacorte Press brought out *Warlock*, the same comic novel that Jim had begun tinkering with almost a decade ago. The novel's cover displayed a Chatham painting—compliments of Jack Nicholson, who had purchased it—of a wintry landscape with the base of two bare trees anchored in a snowy hillside. Lawrence threw an afternoon launch party at Elaine's on October 29 with cocktails and a luncheon buffet, but the real party happened back at the Carlyle later that evening. Jim found the eight-day trip to New York arduous, and he considered its highlight ("the single moment of pleasure") a lunch with Dattila's father, who cooked an immense Italian "peasant lunch."

As he had done for *Warlock*, Chatham was again at work on cover art for the trade paperbacks of *A Good Day to Die*, *Farmer*, and *Wolf*, the rights to which Lawrence and Delacorte had acquired, and the future cover of Jim's *Selected & New Poems*.* Mostly inspired by Montana landscapes

* Harry Dean Stanton owned the painting used for the cover of *Legends*, and it was

and the Paradise Valley, Chatham's designs would become a hallmark and deeply admired feature of Jim's books. Their partnership amounted to an alchemy of the visual and literary arts that made the physical object of the book greater than the sum of its parts, and the two would become inextricably linked. It didn't hurt for Jim, too, that Chatham's career had begun to flourish, particularly in the light of a landmark show in Livingston in October 1980 (a four-part exhibition of paintings beginning with a private preview at the Danforth Gallery followed by dinner at Chico Hot Springs). Nicholson, who had become an important patron of Chatham's, attended the show and bought several paintings, as did other celebrities.

"Maybe I'm pushing these guys too hard, I don't know," Chatham wrote to Jim in February 1981, speaking of Dell/Delacorte's art department. "However, I do know they are largely feebs and semi-feebs and cannot get this stuff right on their own . . . If you want the books to look as pretty as they should, you must insist they do as I say!" A few days later, Chatham enclosed a page layout and his proposed designs to Chris Kuppig, then editor in chief of trade paperbacks at Dell, which "in my opinion," he noted, "will greatly improve the esthetic quality of the covers, and give them that touch of class they now lack. Naturally, your people needn't follow these drawings to the gnat's ass, but it would certainly be nice if they could come reasonably close." Chatham's alterations included changes to the border around each painting, the dimensions and shape of the image, and the typeface.

"Really wrote Warlock because of a dream in the UP while drying out—huge wild boar talking to me rather merrily in a basso voice," Jim wrote to McGuane in March 1982, though the two were going through what Jim would call another one of their silent periods. "When you don't drink much your dreams become rich & deep." (The character Warlock has a dream and overhears an "oracular baritone [that] came from a water-filled puddle where a tree had tipped over.")

---

used with his permission; Dan Gerber owned the cover art for *Wolf*, Dattila *A Good Day to Die*, and Jim *Farmer*.

Dreams play a central role in *Warlock*, more so than in any of Jim's earlier works of fiction. The plot revolves around a dream had by the protagonist—one that emerges from the details of Jim's own life (as Jim writes in the opening paragraph, "the baby emerged December 11, 1937, at 12:11:37 A.M.," Jim's own birthday). In the midst of the dream, Johnny discovers his own dead body "smack dab in the middle of the kitchen floor." For him, the dream is a symbolic death and rebirth that accompanies the loss of his job at a foundation, and it brings with it the opportunity to revitalize his life and live up to the magic of his secret name, Warlock. The idea would become a central theme of Jim's fiction: that the realization of one's mortality can (and should) propel one into a more vital existence, much like the transformation Jim himself had undergone.

Warlock goes on to become an amateur detective hired by an eccentric inventor, Dr. Rabun, and charged with investigating everything from illegal lumbering in Michigan's Upper Peninsula to blackmailers in Key West. Much of it has overtones of John D. MacDonald's Travis McGee, an obvious influence on Jim. At one point, Jim tips his hand and tells us that Warlock affects "Travis McGee's laconic cynicism."

With *Warlock*, Jim was inadvertently inching closer to the creation of the Brown Dog stories, a set of novellas and backwoods satires that would become cult favorites, beginning with "Brown Dog" in 1990. Like the character Brown Dog,* a down-on-his-luck Native American (of Chippewa-Finnish heritage) from the Upper Peninsula, Warlock is bawdy, tough, reckless, and tends to overindulge in food and booze. He lacks good judgment (at times), gets himself into trouble, has a good heart, and enjoys women. Both Warlock and Brown Dog have a folksy familiarity with northern Michigan and share enough of their author's attributes that the lines between the characters and Jim Harrison become blurry. The similarities would help to earn Jim an almost cultlike status himself among his devoted readers, who imagined—not

* Brown Dog was also a nickname for Jim himself, sometimes shortened by friends to simply "Brown."

entirely incorrectly—that the author and the characters were practically one and the same.

As for Warlock, he's forty-two (he turns forty-three in the course of the novel); lives near Lake Michigan, "only a few miles from any farmhouse on the hilly Leelanau Peninsula"; drinks at Dick's Pour House; spends time in Grand Marais, Palm Beach, and Key West; owns a dog named Hudley (as did the Harrisons); and has a "slight stigma" in his right eye. His last name is Lundgren, a family name on Norma's side, and he's a "Keatsian romanticist." In a sense, Warlock is to Johnny an "alter ego," as Jim is to Warlock or the future Brown Dog.

With *Warlock*, Jim wanted to write a contemporary book without "frayed romance" and "not ruled by Irony, who drags her tired ass, making us snicker cynically rather than laugh out loud; to a certain extent, of course, she is the true Queen of our age."

But his aims were largely lost on his critics, many of whom focused understandably on the novel's comic and detective features and, perhaps inevitably, on the novel's shortcomings in comparison with *Legends*. As one critic ventured, it was most likely a case of success inspiring an overly hasty follow-up. Others criticized its uneven pacing, which John D. Casey, writing for *The New York Times*, described as the book's only flaw. J. D. Reed came to the novel's defense in a review in *Time* that he fittingly titled "Hick Gumshoe."

Notably, years later, David Foster Wallace would emerge as a fan of the book, noting in a letter that Jim's novels were "a big deal" to him. Wallace went on to confess an oddly personal connection to *Warlock*, "the sort of over-intimate, fan-letterish aside that will either amuse you or make you wince," he wrote, which must surely have pleased Jim to no end. It seems Wallace's own "devirgination," as he put it, was made difficult because of his memory of a line from *Warlock* about a female pulling on "W's member as if it were an outboard motor's starter-rope." The image repeated in his head over and over, eliciting from Wallace "during the act creepy and impossible-to-explain giggles, and so on: you can imagine." Wallace wondered why he was burdening Jim with these details.

Warlock went into its second printing in December 1981, just as Jim was reviewing his *Selected & New Poems, 1961–1981*, which Delacorte was publishing in the new year. The dates in the title were omitted from the cover, as Jim preferred, though they would appear on the book's title page. He would later write that such a book was probably premature, but that because of his success with *Legends*, Lawrence was "quite willing to collect [his] poetry." The chosen date range, 1961–1981, reached back to when Jim was writing his first poems in Boston rather than to the publication of *Plain Song* (1965), and it lent the book the heft of two full decades. At the same time, the choice to remove the dates from the cover downplayed the book's retrospective qualities for a poet just forty-four years old.

As usual, Jim was actively involved in the book's production and concerned about its style and presentation. He wanted the ghazals printed two to a page, as they had been in the original Simon & Schuster book—"Having the poems run on from page to page is extremely awkward and makes me cry at night," he wrote to the publishing house—and he wanted the poems from *Yesenin* to be one to a page, "or we simply can't go on with this project and I will be forced to go to the mountains. Or to the sea."

Chatham provided the cover art for the book, which Jim dedicated to John and Rebecca. Twelve sketches by Chatham were also included. Reviews were resoundingly positive, though one stuck out, as Jim boasted to McGuane in June 1982: "Publishers Weekly said ([of] Selected Poems) I was an 'untrammeled, renegade genius' a la 'Whitman, Dickinson, Keats and Rimbaud.'" He didn't believe any of it, he claimed, any more than he did bad reviews. But "untrammeled, renegade genius" stuck to the ribs.

—

The new year was a time of reshuffling and travel for Jim and the family. In the spring of 1982, Jamie graduated from the University of Michigan and moved to New York City. Later that year, John and Rebecca relocated from Connecticut to Fayetteville, Arkansas, where John had accepted a top job with the University of Arkansas library system. It was a grand promotion, but Jim feared his brother was "cracking up" in the aftermath of Gloria's death, as he admitted to McGuane, whose own sister had recently died. "You of all people understand the emotional content of this best."

Gloria's death was still haunting Jim too, and he sought distraction where he could find it. He had begun cross-country skiing that winter, and he would use it to explore some newly purchased acreage around the farm. He spent an astonishing amount of time on the road as well: Costa Rica in January and Los Angeles, La Paz, Denver, and Aspen with Chatham in early April. The trip to La Paz apparently involved a great deal of cocaine and a plan to parlay some of the marching powder into quick cash back in the States through a dealer acquaintance ("to pay for the 'ranch'—prospects pretty good," in Jim's words), but the deal apparently fell through. Jim later described his "two hundred sneezes" in the aftermath of some of the best coke of his life.

Jim would also spend almost four solid months that summer secluded (more or less) at the cabin in Grand Marais, where he was at work on his fifth novel, *Sundog*. The novel was giving him trouble, and by August, roughly three months into the project, he decided to change everything. His complaint was as important and basic as they come; namely, the noble protagonist was starting to "bore the shit" out of him, which he likened to "being locked in with the fucking 'Donkey Serenade' played at spring concerts without irony." Being locked in the cabin, so to speak, may not have helped his feelings—he had set a large portion of *Sundog* at a similar cabin beside a similar river in the Upper Peninsula, the clip-clop, clip-clop, round-and-round of the song echoing in his head—nor probably did the back-and-forth drives between cabin and home. Jim had turned the road trip to the UP into a veritable work-a-day commute of roughly four and a half hours each way, and he planned to remain there through October in seven-day stretches punctuated by three-day visits home. The trip was wearisome and took him away from his family, but it provided a routine for writing and helped to relieve his sense of claustrophobia. Being away from home also provided him with liberties, sexual and otherwise.

One liberty, cocaine, had assumed a prominent role in Jim's life, and his letters from this time are shot through with references to the drug du jour.

> July 1980: "Thirty days away from coke except for one night. First evidence of self-control in years. I wish I didn't love the feeling, the passion with which I regard a quarter bag."

> December 1981: "Before me on the desk is a gram of coke. The hair of the pig that tore at us so savagely last night. I am going to throw it away . . . Here it goes into the stove!"

> March 1982: "Had coke sneezes all night, lasting a total of 12 hours. Could you ask —— if it's possible to become suddenly allergic to this substance?"

> May 3, 1982: "Coke & booze. Both frequently steal your real emotions, supplanting them with those ill fit for anything but inclusion in a parody of a Russian novel: a kind of masturbation & doomed self-absorption where one feels cheated of parades, and lost Teddy Bears, responsible for the deaths of sisters, in short a sump pump for imaginary demons."

Cocaine was another distraction from Gloria and the new "kind of hysteria" that had evolved after *Legends*. Of course, alcohol and drugs had long been a part of his life, but he could now afford to indulge himself in cocaine, and he socialized in places and with people who had access to plenty of it. Cocaine and alcohol worked together in a wonderful and dangerous partnership—one up, one down, with each balancing the other out. Coke allowed him to drink more and later into the evening, which in turn called for more coke, and once again, clip-clop, the Donkey Serenade. For a time, Jim did, by his own admission, "any amount of cocaine that anyone offered," which came with the additional problem of having to drink a lot to subdue the edgy feeling, and the combination inevitably "shot the mornings" for writing.

That he didn't succumb to a full-blown drug addiction he credited to his love for food. Nothing blew the glories of a wonderful meal quicker and more completely than the "stomach-constricting anxious energy" of a few lines. Despite his love for the drug, Jim would not let anyone use coke before a meal when he cooked, because it created "a sort of bubblegum nimbus that slaughters the palate and sensuous capacities, in addition to shrinking the wee-wee and tearing holes in the social fabric." Even in La Paz, Jim had managed to set aside time for splendid meals, apparently between cocaine binges. "In good spirits except for the shits," he had reported to McGuane after the trip, "the last Chatham-Harrison meal in La Paz included platters of t-bones, lobsters, chicken mole etc."

The eating came with its own repercussions, of course, especially given Jim's preferences for seafood and game and other meats high in purines. Gout had begun to plague Jim, a torment he would readily impart to his fictional characters, including several in *Warlock* and the narrator of *Sundog*, who complains of his gout-ridden toes that could barely handle a gas pedal.

But Jim's rapturous meals provided him with a rich new topic for his writing—food and wine—and he would not need to compete with McGuane or his other friends (Chatham perhaps excepted) for the material or territory. It was his alone.

In 1981, with relatively little forethought, Jim began his first food column for *Smoke Signals*, a small literary journal edited by the poet Mike Golden and published out of Brooklyn. It seemed almost like a throwaway, of no particular significance, and neither he nor Golden had any idea what it would become. Jim's "Eat Your Heart Out" marked the first of many installments that would follow. In these letters, as he would term them, Jim would cultivate a new and exuberant voice—comic, self-deprecating, authoritative, wise (and unwise), supremely indulgent, and almost always over the top. (He enjoyed the approach so much that he contemplated using the same voice and tone for a novel.) His epic meals and bacchanalian revelry, undertaken despite gout and other excess-related afflictions, carried with it an air of that heroism Nicholson had once mentioned to him. He encouraged his readers to live vividly. One should live to eat, not the other way around.

"WONDERFUL! MAGNIFICENT! I'm hooked! What can I tell you?" Golden marveled after reading the first of the letters. He knew they were on to something remarkable. "Viki and I rushed out for the ingredients to make Caribbean stew. Holy Mackerel! Jesus! There aren't enough superlatives."

Jim's next contribution, "Food for Thought," published in *Smoke Signals* in 1982, discussed an epic meal he had once enjoyed with Orson Welles at Ma Maison in Los Angeles.* "The two of us were accompanied by a beautiful Hungarian countess who left in either boredom or disgust. You see, Mike," Jim wrote, addressing the letter directly to Golden, "she was slender and could not comprehend our great sad hearts choked as they are with fatty deposits." Readers discover that the first course included a half pound of fresh caviar with an iced bottle of Stolichnaya.

The letters were a smashing success and especially captured the hearts of a particular demographic. That fall, Golden wrote to Jim to tell him as much: "Just for the record, your column's picked up a lot of fans (relative of course to the size and scope of our distribution) . . . As for your readers, your fans, and you've picked up more, from the feedback I've got, than anyone else in the rag, it's a strange thing. There's a whole pocket of 28-29-30 year old guys who have just flipped, run out and bought and read everything they could get their hands on, and then turned all their friends on to you." These same readers would become Harrison fans and follow him, like the Pied Piper, to his other poetry and fiction, but it was the food writing that hooked them. If

* This meal with Welles at Ma Maison was charged directly to Warner Brothers. Welles (later rejected) was briefly under consideration to star alongside Jack Nicholson in a film version of Harrison's "Revenge."

these letters led people astray, the journey was worth it, and if they did not exactly follow in his gout-ridden footsteps, they could still live vicariously through Jim, their hero of heroes.

One of those fans was thirty-five-year-old Barry Gifford, the author of a series of novels about Sailor and Lula, who wrote to Jim to express his admiration for the column. Gifford would later become a friend (the two had corresponded once before, exchanging compliments early in 1981). Gifford found Jim's food letters "accurate, appealing and philosophically & personally agreeable," and he wrote to wish him well. Jim (and Golden, by extension) had hit on something truly special. Jim's joy of eating and sense of humor combined with social commentary and a confessional style to create a voice unique to the genre of food writing and arguably shined even brighter than his sportswriting. With food and wine, Jim was on confident and solid ground.

"I got to admit Big Brown," Golden confessed. "I may be keeping this fly by night rag going just to digest your food letters. Stimulates not only the palette, but the frontal lobe as well."

Selected & New Poems came out in August 1982 and earned good reviews. But it landed in a poetry community that seemed suspicious of Jim's status as a member. Remarkably, *Publishers Weekly*, which had celebrated the collection, noted that Harrison's name did not come up much in "discussions of contemporary poetry" and tagged him as one of the most underappreciated writers in America. The challenge for Harrison was his classification as a novelist, the reviewer argued, "which is not surprising, considering the unclassifiable nature of his poetry." The latter comment apparently referred to Jim's lack of identification, once again, with a particular school or movement.

That his name didn't come up often in poetry circles had become an obvious problem for Jim, and a prejudicial one, and the consequences were anything but abstract. His poems were overlooked for anthologies, and he received less critical attention. Moreover, he lost out on opportunities for awards and prizes—the very things he had so coveted and arguably deserved.

When Jim went on to write *Wolf* and *Farmer*, there was a feeling that he had "left poetry" or even "sold out," observed Jim's former student Eliot Weinberger, a viewpoint that obviously infuriated Jim and about which he was defensive. Jim thought of himself as first and foremost a poet. Novels and screenplays helped to feed his family, a fact he protested to anyone who would listen. But that argument was not entirely persuasive. If he had once done so, the necessity of continuing to do so had lessened since the publication of *Legends*, particularly since his tastes and expenses had grown quite lavish. It took money to eat a half pound of fresh caviar for an appetizer and pay for around-the-clock cocaine. It cost money to finance the impressive wine collection that Jim had dubbed the "Warner Brothers Memorial Cellar" and housed in his basement in Leelanau.

Stony Brook was the last time that Jim was "really considered a poet among poets," claimed Weinberger. After that, Jim was "always considered a novelist, really, even though he published many books of poetry, and obviously there were readers there," he said, "but I don't really think there was that much recognition of Jim as a poet after that period . . . I think there was this image of Jim that, 'Oh well, he's gone off and is hanging out with Jack Nicholson and is just in another world now.'"

Other reviews of *Selected & New Poems*, including by fellow poets, reinforced Weinberger's assessment of the attitudes of at least some in the poetry community. In one, the poet James Humphrey accused Jim of being a sellout, if not in those exact words. Harrison has more "guts and heart than any 50 men," but his true self, and his "real poems," lay hidden behind a facade of the "physical, rugged, rude, violent and even charming" aspects of his poetry, Humphrey wrote, without further explanation. Where to look for the real Jim Harrison? he asked. "Not in his $70,000 kitchen and $50,000 wine cellar." As Humphrey went on to explain, "Due to his friendship with movie actor Jack Nicholson,

Harrison has written two screenplays for a half million each; his first book of poems, *Plain Song*, signed, is now fetching $200 for a first edition."

Humphrey's review was an odd mélange of presumptuous claims and condemnation by innuendo. But his suggestion that money and Hollywood were somehow responsible for what he saw as Jim's shortcomings as a poet reflected a broader ambivalence about Jim's status and loyalties, if not about the poems themselves. What the review didn't register was the broader audience outside of the tightly knit poetry world that Jim's lifestyle and prose was attracting to his poetry.

The sum of money and fame that came to Jim after *Legends* was real enough, and his growing celebrity brought with it new challenges. "Everyone used to leave us alone because few knew we existed," Jim had observed to McGuane. Now, "every jackoff currently wants one's time." Not without some truth, Jim claimed to miss the days when he was "wildly ambitious and anonymous," and he thought it strange to have become the center of so much "grasping neurotic attention." That attention had led him to change his phone numbers and list them as private. And Jim was already worrying again about money. Around February 1982, he had managed to run out of it for the first time in four years, and he still owed vast sums to the IRS.

"Brutal admission," he wrote to McGuane that May. "I've been sorely depressed because I'm absolutely broke with no prospects. I made a little over a mil in the last four years and ALL of it is gone somewhere: charter boats, Australian oil stock, English gambling stock, laser stock, personal loans, coke, gambling, expensive trips, five hundred dollar meals, two hundred dollar whores, Carlyle suites . . . Own partially paid for house, farm cabin. Sixty grand in immediately due debts. They scream on the lawn. O my god, how did I come to this!"

Gerber had earlier advised Jim to pretend that *Legends* hadn't happened at all. "Fix up your house, if you want to, maybe buy better cuts of meat, you know, some better wine, but otherwise, just pretend this didn't happen." But things had gone another way. A year after *Legends*, said Gerber, "Jim [was] three hundred and fifty grand in debt to the

IRS," and he had to employ "Joyce [Bahle] to protect him from himself," to keep him solvent.

Jim took some solace in the fact that Thomas Jefferson and Mark Twain were "worse financial fuckups" than he was, and he eventually worked his way out of the quagmire in the coming months. His hopes hung mostly on a screen project about horse racing for Rastar Films / Columbia Pictures and producer Ray Stark—this he hoped would "save [his] ass."

The Stark project, later titled *Blue Moon in Kentucky*, would save Jim from the IRS, but it required him to leave the cabin and once again set aside his poetry and fiction. That fall of 1982, Jim traveled to Keeneland in Kentucky to research the thoroughbred world. Although the film would never be made, Jim studied the horse-racing business, and it involved two of his favorite things—the country and animals. He met local farm agents and charmed the members of the Kentucky Film Office; he made friends and drank with them and exchanged barbecue recipes. At Claiborne Farms, Jim was cordially introduced to the thoroughbreds Nijinsky, Sir Ivor, Riva Ridge, Spectacular Bid, and Secretariat, whom he found somewhat hostile but of "breathtaking beauty." In a projection of his own feelings perhaps, he learned that the horses didn't want anything to change "i.e., a paddock <u>or</u> pasture change pisses everyone off."

In October, Jim received a check for $38,000 for the treatment, another $12,000 in January for revisions, and $25,000 for finishing the screenplay in March 1983. The topic of the failed film project was so much to his liking that he would repurpose his research for a novella by the same name, "Blue Moon in Kentucky," but he never thought it good enough to publish.

The fame part of the equation came with other opportunities and dangers, at least to his marriage. Jim had grown accustomed to revolving in relatively rarefied circles of celebrity. Around this same time, he began a brief and public romance with the actress Jessica Lange. He had met Lange a year earlier through Nicholson, who had recently starred with Lange in *The Postman Always Rings Twice*, directed by his old friend Bob Rafelson. Jim had attended at least one party at Lange's apartment in New York City, where she then lived with Mikhail Baryshnikov. Jim Fergus, a good friend of Jim's, later told a story about how Jim had lain on the floor during the coke-fueled party while Baryshnikov took a few strides and leapt gracefully over him, clearing most of the room in the process.

Jim and Lange's brief infatuation wouldn't go anywhere. Lange was between relationships with Baryshnikov and Sam Shepard, but for a brief time she dazzled Jim, and vice versa. Lange was a beautiful and famous actress, and Jim was struck by how well read she was. But Lange, perhaps sensing Jim's limitations as a romantic partner, apparently once told him that he wouldn't leave his hunting dogs for her, let alone his wife, or so the story goes. Jim would later confront his marital guilt over the affair, one of his "past sins," as he termed it, that felt like a "blow to the breastbone." In a letter to McGuane, he would recall necking with an actress, her name omitted, "over a dozen martinis at Bemelmans bar at the Carlyle, booted out, tears, can't remember Lord's Prayer because I'm over-coked."

14

UP IN MICHIGAN

(1983–1986)

The days are stacked against
what we think we are.

In the winter of 1983, months before Jim's doctor insisted that he lose twenty pounds and quit smoking, Jim began trying to cut back on his cigarettes, which he described as a "full scale Crimean war" and no fun at all. He had become alarmed enough about his poor health to try to change his behavior.

As in the past, his inspiration came partly from McGuane, who had given up drinking (with a few stutter steps) entirely. The two had recently committed to renewing their friendship and correspondence, both of which had tapered off in the preceding years. They would once again write regularly and arrange to see each other.

In February, Jim briefly gave up smoking entirely ("preposterous anguish"), and he tried moderating his other habits as well, namely alcohol and cocaine, because doing so simply made the world look better. In March, he noted to McGuane that he was on the last three days of his first cocaineless screenplay in years. Not an easy task, partly because he counted on the energy it gave him: "A bowl of this mixture," he noted, "gave me a 13-page day without a shimmer of exhaustion." Booze in any quantity tended to "freeze a personality in an attitude of self-pity or extreme self-absorption," feelings all too familiar to him from past years and ones that he preferred to avoid.

A challenge of cutting back on drinking came from the act of writing itself, or so Jim thought, a connection made clearer for him in those early months of 1983 by Walker Percy's *Lost in the Cosmos* (published that same year). Percy argued that, for writers, reentry into the everyday world (from a place of abstraction and imagination, outside of the here and now) was a fraught and difficult process. Writers, Percy explained, were thus more susceptible than most people to neurosis, alcoholism, drug addiction, suicide, solitariness, and even "florid sexual behavior," among other things. One option available to them to ease the transition, wrote Percy, was to anesthetize the brain with alcohol or drugs.

"That new W. Percy has some good stuff on 're-entry' which is our singular problem," Jim shared with McGuane that July. "He says booze is an attempt to stun the cortex to make re-entry easier." Percy's idea, the reentry problem, rang true for Jim, and he would repeat it in interviews for years to come. It also synced nicely with McGuane's own notion that drinking was the writer's "black lung disease," another idea Jim liked to repeat, and his own sense of the writer as a kind of martyr to his art. To be an artist, one needed to suffer.

Part of his effort to get his health under control involved frequent visits to Larry Sullivan in New York City, and that included paying closer attention to his dreams, under Sullivan's direction, than ever before.* Jim had continued keeping a careful record of them since he had written *Warlock*, even relatively mundane ones: "I dreamt that smoking, hard drinking, and over-eating are the SAME thing," he noted about one.

Larry Sullivan's practice centered around the work of Herbert "Harry" Stack Sullivan—no relation—an influential psychoanalyst in the first half of the twentieth century (he died in 1949). Harry Stack Sullivan drew on Freudian theory and cultural anthropology, and he

* Jim's interest in dreams and their connection to writing was heightened by his reading of James Hillman, the post-Jungian psychologist and progenitor of "Archetypal Psychology." As an epigraph to *Warlock*, Jim used a quote from Hillman's "The Dream and the Underworld," and he referenced Hillman in "The Man Who Gave Up His Name" and later in *Dalva* and "Julip."

espoused an interpersonal theory of psychological development that emphasized personal relationships and social context. This approach was thus a good fit for a novelist whose own business involved close observation of the social and interpersonal.

Larry Sullivan, like his predecessor, was pragmatic and humanistic, and he placed a great deal of importance on the experiences of early childhood. The name Freud never came up in their talks, Jim would say. For both Sullivans, friendship (in its many forms) was a key to happiness and mental health, and Larry, dispensing with the detached, aloof posture of the analyst, worked to develop a relationship with his patients that went beyond the typical patient-doctor dynamic. Jim and Larry discussed literature and books, exchanged recipes, talked politics and movies, and shared stories about their lives.

Jim met with Sullivan face-to-face on average about one week three times a year, and he visited more frequently when he felt he needed the extra energy the sessions released. Initially, he had begun seeing Sullivan because he was struggling with the psychological fallout from his eye injury and the violent loss of his loved ones—the resulting deep depressions that had arisen and seized hold of him over the years, for one, and his self-medicating for them, for another.

"So; certain memories were unpleasantly exhumed and certain patterns were identified," Jim explained to McGuane of his therapy sessions. "I simply can't say that it has worked wonders because it hasn't, but again it has been like a ball player improving his average late in the season. It has kept me rather happily married and ensured a loving family relationship with my children and friends."

In addition to their meetings, Jim frequently wrote detailed letters to Sullivan, and their conversations were thus carried on from a distance in voluminous correspondence. Bahle, who often typed and sent Jim's letters, was thus privy (whether she liked it or not) to some of the intimate details of Jim's psyche.

Jim's drinking and drug use harked back even to his feelings in the 1950s in New York City and his romantic urge to give himself over entirely, often at the expense of everything and everyone, to his art. "I am so aware of that mordant tendency to hand myself over to a kind of martyrdom and its panoply of self-destructive habits," Jim had written to Sullivan back in November 1981, "a sort of literary death urge, to be frank. The traces, as we discussed, which includes a sense of duty far outweighing what is actually required, bourgeois masochism answered by the sedation of alcohol, drugs, sleeping too much, gluttony." Jim would add to that list a "fatuous love affair with the actress [Lange]" and his refusal to abide by a kind of marital and social orthodoxy that left him depressed and sapped of energy.

Art provided Jim with a meaningful reason for self-sacrifice and, at the same time, an excuse for self-destruction. What managed to nurture him and give him a sense of renewal was the "dance of long periods" alone in the natural world—that and his therapy.

In March 1983, Jim reported to McGuane that Lange had officially run off with Sam Shepard; she moved in with Shepard that month. "I ran off with myself! Sometimes it seems strange to be in love with your wife after 24 years." He and Linda would celebrate their twenty-fourth wedding anniversary that year. "I shudder at the close calls."

A month later, Jim, Linda, and Anna traveled together to New York City to visit Jamie, and Jim enjoyed seeing the city through twelve-year-old Anna's eyes. The family cooked a memorable meal of pasta with leeks, sweetbreads, and roasted quail at Jamie's apartment. But Jim also spent twenty hours in meetings about screenwriting revisions in the final days of the visit, which he would compare unfavorably to the fifteen or so pages of poetry he had written in the last month. "NOTHING GOOD" came from the former, except for bittersweet solvency, while the latter brought on feelings of "juice, light, heat, ebullience." People in the city seemed grasping, and he felt everyone was pulling at his sleeves, sometimes literally so.

Grand Marais had become a refuge from such things. Even the journey there and the ritual of crossing the Straits of Mackinac was a transformative experience that Jim equated with freedom. The remote log cabin, which sat in the middle of sixty acres next to the Sucker River and Lake Superior and was a short drive from town, may have been owned by Jim and Linda, but it was fully Jim's retreat. There, he could largely disconnect, write steadily, walk in the woods and along the beach, dream, hunt and fish, drink with friends, and live another life, often with a "local squeeze."

The cabin itself, which Jim borrowed as a setting for *Sundog*, was nine hundred square feet and split into two floors. In the novel, he described it as an "ample, old-fashioned, log house" with an "enormous stone fireplace chimney from which friendly smoke emerged in a plume." Jim kept his grandfather's spittoon, filled with spare change, near the stone fireplace. There was a kitchen table and several chairs in a recent addition, windowed on three sides, where Jim would write, and shelves thick with books, scattered candles, and a Styrofoam cube stuck with bird feathers. Above the fireplace, several arrows pierced the wall, and nearby hung a picture of a lone crow in a snowy landscape. At the foot of Jim's bed was a small bookshelf that held copies of his own works for signing and giving away. Mice were a constant problem and would, if given the chance, infest the kitchen, spilling out of anything without a firmly screwed lid. An intractable colony of bats nested in one of the walls and gave off an odor strong enough to disturb the rare sober guest assigned to the bed pushed up against it. The Sucker River, colored an amber hue by inland cedar swamps, could be heard in the cabin at night, as could Lake Superior roaring in the distance if it was stormy. The place reminded him of his childhood cabin.

Jim's closest friend in Grand Marais was Mike Ballard, the local bartender and owner of the Dunes Saloon. The year that Jim purchased the cabin, Ballard bought the Dunes, and Jim would quickly claim it as his official haunt in town. A former logger, construction worker, and surveyor, Ballard looked the part at six foot two inches tall and well over two hundred pounds. When Jim was away, he served as a caretaker for the cabin and the grounds.

Jim and Linda first met Ballard together at the Dunes, and it was one of the only times Ballard would meet her, so rare were her visits to the cabin. Sitting at the bar, they all got to talking, and Ballard, an avid reader, claimed Richard Brautigan as one of his favorite authors. "That got the ball rolling," said the red-haired Ballard, who wore a thick, droopy mustache at the time, a bit like Brautigan himself. But what cemented his friendship with Jim was their shared love of fishing and bird hunting. Ballard would sometimes show up at the Dunes with an impressive string of trout, and that caught Jim's attention. Jim's trips to New York and LA, Ballard said, would "just beat him up. He'd come up just looking like he was wore right out. He'd come back and say, I want to go fishing."

Most of the people Jim knew in Grand Marais he had met at the Dunes (or at the nearby Sportsman's)—almost everything in the lakeside town is only steps apart—and nightly visits there were part of his routine. His days almost unfailingly began with writing, and his nights often ended at the bar, where he liked to drink Canadian whiskey—VO and water. "[He] never overdid the liquor," insisted Ballard. "At the most, he'd have five drinks in a night, if that. He'd drink wine during the day, and then in the bar he'd drink whiskey." Jim was an "absolute creature of habit," explained another local friend, Rick Capogrossa. "He'd show up at the bar at exactly the same time each night." But even in Grand Marais, Jim could not fully escape from Hollywood. Before he reluctantly purchased a cell phone, he would take calls at the Dunes, which functioned as a remote office, and Ballard and the employees would take names and numbers on bar napkins. "Call Sydney Pollack." "Art Garfunkel wants to know if you are at the cabin." "Call Nicholson." Ballard chatted with Harrison Ford on the bar's telephone.

Jim himself quickly became a minor celebrity in the town, and later a major one. He was the first famous person, or so people considered him, that most locals had ever met. In the years to come, it was not unusual to find twenty people gathered around Jim at the Dunes with four tables pulled together as he held court. Although it wasn't exactly an exclusive club, tossing back a few with Jim Harrison came with bragging rights.

In the fall, Jim hosted his friends at the cabin: Valdène, Chatham, Nick Reens (Jim's friend from Lake Leelanau), Doug Peacock, Phil Caputo, and others. Jim had first met Peacock in 1981, and Peacock had heard of Jim through his friend William Eastlake, who had written a blurb for Jim's *Wolf.* Eastlake, it turns out, had also introduced Peacock to Ed Abbey. (Peacock had served as the inspiration for the character George Washington Hayduke in Abbey's *The Monkey Wrench Gang.*) Eastlake had given *Wolf* to Peacock and said, "This sounds like you!" speaking of the protagonist. Afterward, Peacock and Jim exchanged letters, and then, one day, Peacock called Jim from his parents' house on Thumb Lake in Michigan.

"I'm trying to get hold of Jim Harrison," Peacock said to the man who answered the phone.

"What do you want to get a hold of him for?" Jim asked with his characteristic slow drawl. "Are you from the IRS?"

Peacock then drove the eighty-five miles from Thumb Lake to Lake Leelanau. "There was Chatham, and Guy, and Linda," Peacock recalled, "and all the boys were cooking an elegant entrée for a meal. And I had earlier stopped at Sam's in Chicago, and I bought an off-year Bordeaux, a Petrus. And before I went out the door [that night], Jim tucked a bottle of '71 Lafite under my arm, and that was it." It was the beginning of a beautiful friendship.

Jim had met the writer Phil Caputo during a fishing trip to Key West, and Caputo and his then-wife, Marcelle, would sometimes visit Jim and Linda in Lake Leelanau, including a full month in August 1983. Caputo would become a frequent visitor to Jim's cabin and would get to know Ballard, describing him as the "real thing." Jim thought Caputo wonderful to talk to and enjoyed his company.

During hunting season, when Jim's friends converged on the cabin, there were "feathers everywhere," all over the cabin's lawn, said Mary Capogrossa, who operated the Superior Hotel in town with her husband, Rick.

Where they plucked the birds at a picnic table, it was like down pillows had exploded. Jim had hired Mary in the fall of 1983 to keep up the cabin when his friends were there and at other times. She cleaned the dishes, mopped, made the beds, and did the laundry off-site. "They had a beggars' banquet every night of everything they had caught," said Mary. "So it would be grouse and sharptail and fish." The cabin would be in a cluttered condition in the mornings, with dishes and pots stacked high and a slew of empty wine bottles. On top of the mess, Jim and his friends would sometimes leave *Playboy* magazines, opened to various photos, scattered purposefully about the cabin for her to find. "Oh yeah," said Mary, "on a chair or on the bed I had to make, or on the sink. It was just hilarious. They were just pranksters." Mary would remain silent about it, which drove them all nuts.

Mary truly enjoyed working for Jim, and she would do so until he eventually sold the cabin in 2003. Jim was "never difficult" to work for, she insisted. "He was very dear in how he spoke to me about things." "Diamond Jim," as Rick had nicknamed him, visited the Superior Hotel daily when he was in town, and he would use the hotel fax machine to send whatever he had written that day to Bahle. The Superior Hotel would function as a kind of second office for Jim, alongside the Dunes.

In January 1984, Jim escaped not to the UP but to a "secret clinic" (a "greaseball lard farm," as he described it) in Tecate, Mexico, for two weeks. He had sent off *Sundog* to Seymour Lawrence just days before leaving and, feeling "in extremes," thought the trip would do him some good. A full year had passed since he had set his sights on improving his health, but not much had happened in the interim.

"Where the fitness revolution began in 1940 and is still growing," read an advertisement for Rancho La Puerta, a health spa and nature preserve at the foot of Mount Kuchumaa. La Puerta maintained four tennis courts, served good vegetarian food each night and fish twice a week, kept groomed trails for walking and hiking, and prohibited alcohol use on the grounds. “A lot of people use it for ‘rest’—i.e. they’re not fat etc.,” Jim explained to Gerber, and he thought he and Virginia would like it. But Jim’s first four days without drinking were horrible and turned him into an insomniac. He claimed he did hours of calisthenics every day, cut out drinking, and reduced his smoking to a few cigarettes per day.

In retrospect, Jim found his two weeks at La Puerta a deeply comic experience, and he was surprised with himself that he elected to do something so modern as to attend a health spa. Maurice Stans, “Nixon’s cabinet bag man,” was his neighbor, and a group of heavy-set Republican ladies had apparently taken a shine to Jim. He did his part to stir up some misbehavior. Jim slipped into town a few times for the local swordfish. He secretly drank and smoked and mostly cheated the system, but he probably consumed a lot less there than he would have in Grand Marais. At one point, he sneaked into town with several of the women and got drunk, and he kept a flask filled with booze for sipping around the spa. None of this he admitted to McGuane and Gerber, preferring to project to them his stalwart and healthful self-control: To them, he spoke of twelve-mile day hikes into the mountains. His blood pressure, he claimed, was as near normal as it had been for ten years. Perhaps it was.

“O say a Rowena for me as I am trying mightily to quit smoking!” Jim urged McGuane, who offered to do him one better by giving up on cigars in solidarity, and he shared with Jim his technique for quitting drinking. Each day you go without a drink, you mark a zero in an appointment book. “A pride in the zeros forms. In the end, the zeros win.” For Jim, however, the zeros would never win, at least not for long.

A month after the spa, Jim traveled to Rio de Janeiro with Lou Adler. Adler had hired Jim to write a screenplay for a film about Carmen Miranda, the Portuguese-born Brazilian samba singer and dancer—think “Chica Chica Boom Chic”—and the trip was for research purposes. The project was titled *Samba*, and Adler would produce it. Jim had no other offers at the time, and he needed the money, though he wouldn’t tell Adler that. He liked the project because it was so different from anything he had done before and because the two knew each other so well. "Also it sounds like a gas," Jim wrote. "I could learn to Samba!" That January, he got $50,000, with $10,000 more to come upon completion of the screenplay.

Before leaving, Jim stopped off in Aspen to see Nicholson and confer with Adler about the project. Although Jim claimed he had been drunk only once in the previous thirty days, he didn't waste any time leaping off the wagon. Almost upon arrival in Brazil, he purchased ten grams of rock crystal Bolivian cocaine from a scientist for $120. Jim thought it was the best he had ever had, including in Los Angeles and Aspen, and he washed it down with local wine and cachaça, a distilled spirit made from fermented sugarcane juice. He apparently had to give away a lot of the coke before he left the country. Jim could not quite figure out Brazil, and he thought that life there was tough for everyone except the top 5 percent. The place and the women were beautiful, but the heat was relentless—ninety-five degrees and humid when he left, compared to fifteen degrees in Michigan upon his return home. There he stayed in bed for days, sick with dysentery and a bad cold and suffering from insomnia, with his dogs by his side.

In May, Jim went to Grand Marais to work on the screenplay, but he was worn out: "Sort of wobbling around and along the edge of a 'minor' crackup, psychic exhaustion." The pressures of book publication and the movie were getting to him, and he woke up at 5:30 a.m. in the cabin feeling a "sense of implacable bleakness." Meanwhile, Adler sent a telegram, wondering if the dysentery or voodoo had delayed the script.

"My boss, Mr. Jim Harrison," Bahle responded on his behalf, "is physically and mentally ill but is recovering. The work is slow but relentless." For Jim, he needed to find "the string of thoughts," as he put it, to pull him out of it. Jim blamed the eighteen months of work (not including the time in La Peurta) he had put in before even beginning the screenplay for his poor condition.

—

While Jim wrote *Sundog*, he worked simultaneously on a long poem that would burgeon into a collection he called *The Theory & Practice of Rivers*. The title would make an appearance in *Sundog*, where the character Robert Strang, a master dam builder, explains that he has what he calls a "theory and practice of rivers."

Sundog required Jim to research a range of new topics, including engineering, about which he knew very little. Indeed, like the Carmen Miranda project, that was part of the attraction. For the novel, Jim had generated a large collection of notes and research, two large cartons' worth, covering topics like epilepsy, tropical botany, and dam and irrigation engineering. He traveled to Georgia to view a "big ole dam," subscribed to trade papers that included pictures and specs for assorted engineering projects, and interviewed engineers, including an employee from Bechtel who described to Jim how he managed $200 million worth of heavy equipment. Senator Bill Bradley, a friend and fan of his writing whom Jim had met through Nicholson, had also arranged for Jim to visit the Richard B. Russell Dam, compliments of the Army Corps of Engineers.

In a notebook entry from around this time, Jim described the novel as being about "someone who is totally 'in the world,' the better to contrast with being out of the world," like the poet-novelist, or the person off to the side, as Jim liked to think of himself. The idea would account for his observation in July 1984, a few months after the book appeared, that he had figured out that he was "writing about [his] alter ego, or 'other.'" The idea accorded with Jim's initial desire to write his new poetry collection "under a nom de plume" because he felt fatigued with the restrictions of Jim Harrison, as he put it. In this sense, writing about Strang was a freeing experience, even if a difficult one.

The writing of it had not gone smoothly. Going into it, he had made up his mind to write this novel differently from the way he had others in the past—that is, in a hurried frenzy, he felt—but to his surprise, the slower pace and significant planning did not seem to be working out either. Even after rewriting most of the novel when the protagonist began to bore him, he had considered abandoning it altogether. The problem, he had decided, *was* the overplanning, the extra time, and slower pace, and he determined to set aside his piles of note cards and addenda.

"I know exactly what you mean about these fiction projects that show only intermittent signs of life," McGuane sympathized. "In my opinion, they are usually the victims of planning. We Lit guys are paid to show up and bust our asses, not to make plans nor, especially, outlines. I think the way to do it is [to] get the tone right like Faulkner or Sherwood Anderson did, then gun it."

"You are totally and luminously correct about novels & planning," Jim agreed. "I was emotionally at that point anyhow and what you said tripped the sense of how I wrote well before—I 'mulled' it until I got the tone right."

By November 1983, the new approach (that is, his old approach) had worked, and Jim felt he was "truly cruising." His one regret was that *Sundog* was not turning out to be the long novel he had hoped to write, a personal goal of his, and he was still hunting for that one idea. He would get closer with his next book, *Dalva*.

Meanwhile, after seventeen years with Dell/Delacorte, Sam Lawrence departed for E. P. Dutton after Delacorte declined to renew his contract. "[Lawrence's] imprint fell victim to the economy ax wielded by the troubled management team at Doubleday, Dell's owner," as *The New York Times* later reported. Dutton, where Lawrence would remain for the next six years, had agreed to give him his own imprint and thus to retain his independent status.

At the time, Dattila and Lawrence strategized about how to get Jim out of his contract, as Jim had no intention of remaining there without Lawrence. At Lawrence's suggestion, Jim wrote a bland letter to James R. McLaughlin at Doubleday explaining his situation. He had no ill feelings toward Delacorte, he explained, but because of his personal relationship with Lawrence and his "particular and unique input to the process of publishing [his] books," he felt he should return his advance for his next work (that is, *Sundog*).

Dattila hand delivered the letter to McLaughlin, and he coordinated with other agents who were making similar requests. Dell agreed to release Jim from his contract, and Jim repaid the advance on his next novel ($25,000 plus interest), though Dell retained the rights to softcover editions. Days later, Dutton signed Jim, and they agreed to pay him $70,000 (roughly equivalent to $230,000 in 2024 dollars) as an advance on a graduated schedule. John Macrae III, the president and publisher of Dutton, welcomed Jim with open arms.

Jim and Lawrence had remained close since the publication of *Legends*, and their friendship had in the intervening years blossomed into something like a romance. "Dear Passion Flower: I forgive you, Honey bear," Lawrence addressed him in one letter. "I love you dearly but we at Dutton have always been partial to bears. Why don't you change your name to Jimmy the Pooh." Letters, even those on E. P. Dutton letterhead, were often personal rather than professional and ranged in topics from gossip to dining out, travel, and weight-loss regimens.

"I don't know what it is about that Detroit Free Press interview," Lawrence wrote to Jim in April 1984, referring to a profile of Jim in the paper, "but I now see you in a new light: the sensitive romantic poet living in the woods defiant against the world. Not the guy who holds court at Elaine's surrounded by sycophants, snorting coke with Hollywood superstars, a stretch limo waiting outside to whisk him away to the Carlyle & other luxurious haunts. I like to think of you in rustic simplicity leading the life of Thoreau, lean & hungry & brooding . . . Love & kisses, Big Brown Poet, Sam."

In the same letter, Lawrence noted that reports of advance orders for *Sundog* had totaled fifteen thousand copies, and by June a second printing was underway. Sales stood at nearly nineteen thousand. Lawrence thought they'd pass the twenty thousand mark if Lemuria Books in Jackson, Mississippi (John Evans, the owner, was a friend and devoted reader of Jim's), got to work. The sales figures were considerably greater than those of *Legends* and *Warlock* had been.

In *Sundog: The Story of an American Foreman, Robert Corvus Strang, as Told to Jim Harrison*—the novel's full title—which Lawrence and Dutton brought out in hardcover on May 22, 1984, Jim used a dynamic

1. Winfield, Norma, John, and Jim Harrison, circa 1938

2. Jim Harrison in Grayling, Michigan, 1938

3. John and Hulda Wahlgren with John and Jim Harrison, Rodney, Michigan, 1938

4. Jim Harrison, summer 1940

5. *Left to right:* John, Winfield, and Jim Harrison in Haslett, Michigan, circa 1941

6. Jim Harrison, circa 1948

7. Jim (*center*) with (*clockwise from the top*) John, Mary, David, and Judy Harrison at home in Haslett, Michigan, circa 1954

8. Judy Harrison, circa 1956

9. Jim Harrison playing for the Haslett Vikings, circa 1956

10. The Harrison family—***left to right:*** John, Norma, Winfield, and Jim (*back row*); Mary, Judy, and David (*front row*), Haslett, Michigan, circa 1956

11. Linda King Harrison at the Kings' house, East Lansing, Michigan, 1959

12. Jim, Jamie, and Linda Harrison, Haslett, Michigan, circa 1960

13. J. D. Reed and Jim Harrison, Stony Brook, New York, 1966

14. Jim and Linda Harrison, 1968

15. Guy de la Valdène (*left*), Tom McGuane (*right*), and Richard Brautigan (*foreground*) in Key West, early 1970s

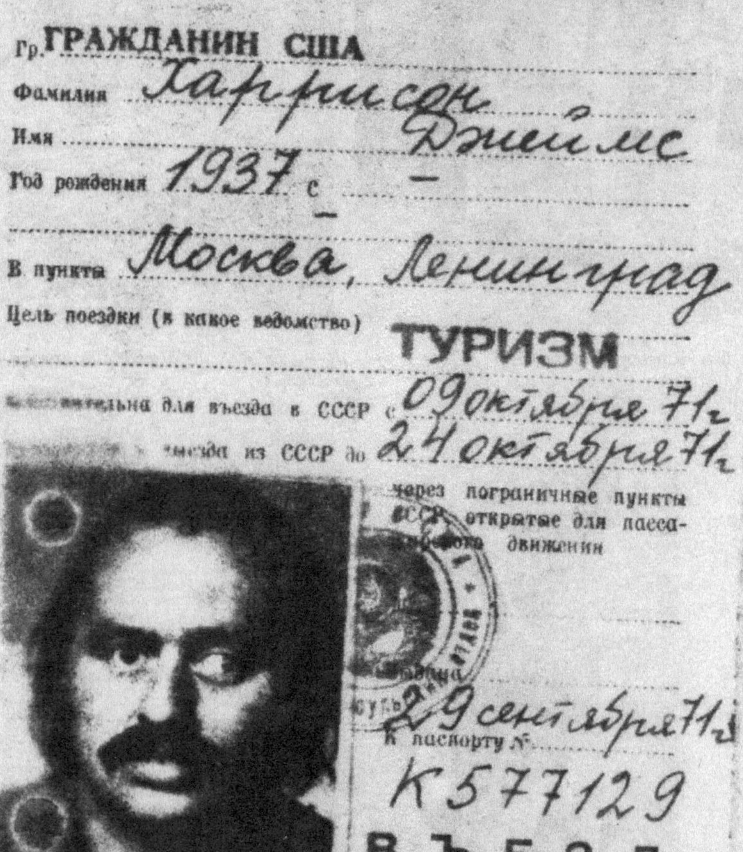

Виза К-1 № 829856

Гр. ГРАЖДАНИН США

Фамилия Харрисон

Имя Джеймс

Год рождения 1937 с —

В пункты Москва, Ленинград

Цель поездки (в какое ведомство) ТУРИЗМ

...тельна для въезда в СССР с 09 октября 71 г

...выезда из СССР до 24 октября 71 г

через пограничные пункты СССР, открытые для пасса-...ного движения

29 сентября 71 г

К паспорту № K577129

ВЪЕЗД

16. Jim Harrison's Soviet visa, 1971

17. Jim Harrison, France, 1971

18. Tom McGuane on a skiff in the Florida Keys, 1972

19. Jim Harrison at his writing desk, Yesesnin's portrait nearby, 1972

20. Jimmy Buffett and Dan Gerber on Deep Creek, Montana

21. Lake trout catch, Lake Leelanau, early 1970s

22. Jim Harrison and Pat Paton, circa 1973

23. Jim on the running board of Russell Chatham's truck, mid 1970s

24. Jim, Jamie, Linda, and Anna Harrison, circa 1977

25. Joyce Harrington Bahle and Jim Harrison outside the writing studio (the granary) in Lake Leelanau, Michigan, early 1980s

26. Russell Chatham (*left*) and Robert Dattila (*right*)

27. Dan Lahren and Jim Harrison on the banks of the Yellowstone River, 1987

28. Jim Harrison and Guy de la Valdène hunting in Michigan

29. Jim Harrison and Peter Lewis at the Lannan Foundation's Readings & Conversations series in Santa Fe, New Mexico, 2002

30. Dan Lahren, Jim Harrison, and Peter Matthiessen at Pine Creek boat launch on the Upper Yellowstone River, September 2003

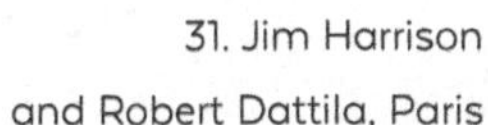

31. Jim Harrison and Robert Dattila, Paris

32. Jim Harrison at the estuary at Grand Marais, Michigan, in the early afternoon fog and drizzle

33. Jim and Linda Harrison at the casita in Patagonia, Arizona, circa 2010

Laura Wilson

34. Jim Harrison in Patagonia, Arizona

similar to that of *Warlock*, pairing a relatable, if flawed, character with a more mysterious one. As with Lundgren in *Warlock*, who works as an undercover investigator for the nefarious Dr. Rabun, the narrator of *Sundog* (named Jim Harrison) undertakes the writing of a biographical work on the enigmatic but brilliant engineer Robert Strang. Like Lundgren, the narrator is a gourmand and glutton, struggles with his weight and an overactive libido, suffers from gout (as well as a high pulse rate and blood pressure), and finds himself in the midst of a midlife crisis. Like Lundgren, the novel's Jim Harrison longs to do "something truly different in [his] life, something totally unexampled."

Part of Jim's interest in Strang had to do with the character's energy and capacity for work. These were traits that Jim certainly shared with his fictional alter ego. Although Strang suffers from "petit mal" epilepsy, or absence seizures, and later from paralysis of his legs, the character has had a highly productive career with "no time allowed for vacations" in thirty years. Strang's opinion, the reader learns, is that people suffer because they live without energy. "They can't get anything done," Strang says at one point. "It's the real and secret source of their anguish." Jim had often discussed this topic with George Quasha and McGuane and many others: Genius *was* energy, and personal contentment and professional success derived from a laser-focused use of it—undissipated by life's many distractions. That was Jim's guiding principle.

That Strang lives his life without any sense of dread, unlike the narrator Jim Harrison and the author himself, was also an appeal. He wanted to create a hero who was free from dread, Jim would say of Strang. "Dread and irony have gotten to be literary addictions. And I noticed there are people that live without it," an idea vocalized in the novel through Strang, who notes that "cynicism along with irony is a device, a set of blinders, to keep the world in its place."

Reviews of *Sundog* were mixed and garnered familiar love/hate reactions from critics. Michiko Kakutani, writing for *The New York Times*, insisted that Harrison's execution had gone "seriously awry" and, predictably, thought the novel celebrated a "macho esthetic." Writer Judith

Minty saw it as a brilliant "book of the spirit" and, building off Jim's own comments about the book, found it to be the conclusion of a "spiritual autobiography" for Harrison that had begun with *Wolf* and went through *Farmer* and "The Man Who Gave Up His Name."

Ed Abbey praised the novel, but he was deeply disappointed with Jim's portrayal of Strang. "SUNDOG is a splendid novel," Abbey wrote to Jim months after the book appeared, "your best so far, and I enjoyed every page of it. It was only in retrospect, succumbing to my obsessions, that I began to resent your making a hero of a goddamned dam-builder. Ungrateful bastard!: his life is saved by a flowing river."

From the start, Abbey was absolutely furious at Jim for writing the book, as Doug Peacock remembered, and had held back in his letter to Jim. Privately, while Jim deeply admired his *Desert Solitaire*, he found Abbey preachy and condescending and put little stock in his literary opinions.

Sundog was an odd and even contradictory follow-up to *A Good Day to Die* and its militaristic defense of free-flowing rivers. But it was also in keeping with Jim's tendency to dismiss what he saw as quixotic idealism in favor of the practical necessities of the world, particularly those involving the labor of farmers and blue-collar workers, the very people who make the human world work. Few now know where electricity or their food comes from, but "many educated people find it unpleasant that either comes from any place," wrote Jim in *Sundog.* "It is a philosophical inconvenience that rivers be diverted and controlled or animals destroyed."

Still, Jim tried to balance even his own competing beliefs. Strang finds it pathetic to build a dam where there shouldn't be one, which he thinks is often a purely political decision. Strang also believes that the Glen Canyon Dam—an anathema and rallying cry for Abbey and other environmentalists—"shouldn't have been built any more than we would allow NASA to dye half the moon pink for research."

—

In September, Jim learned terrible news. Richard Brautigan had taken his own life. On the 16th, he had climbed the stairs to the second-floor living room of his Bolinas home and, as he looked out at the Pacific Ocean, shot himself with a .44 Magnum. Jim found the news "terrifying but somewhat expected," given Brautigan's depression.

Strangely, one obituary had blamed Brautigan's suicide on Montana and the culture in Livingston. In "The Big Sky Fell In on Brautigan," Warren Hinckle had argued that Brautigan's death was fueled by the toxic macho culture of the state. "Up there you had a bunch of artistic weirdos living in rancher country," Hinckle wrote, quoting the words of Ken Kelley, an acquaintance of Brautigan's. "And the artists seemed compelled to compete in macho terms against the cowboys, and then tried to out-macho each other."

Jim and Brautigan's other friends were disgusted by the piece. Chatham responded to Hinckle in no uncertain terms, describing the obituary as a "piece of festering tripe" that Hinckle had the poor judgment to publish. "You should have your pathetic face slapped from here to kingdom come," Chatham added. "You know absolutely nothing about Livingston or Richard's relationship to the region . . . The word macho should be sculpted out of used razorblades and rudely rammed up the ass of every insensitive moron like yourself, who misunderstands and mis-applies it every time they are called upon to discuss art or artists who are not domesticated or properly shelved and labeled." Chatham shared his letter with Jim, and Jim approved wholeheartedly, though the violent language of the letter may have inadvertently done more to support Hinckle's argument than undermine it.

Months later, in April 1985, after thinking over "those post-mortmots being printed on Richard," Jim wondered again "if [Brautigan] were a suicide who became a writer, or vice versa," a topic he had once discussed with Brautigan himself. Perhaps drawing on his own experiences, especially through the writing of *Yesenin*, Jim would attribute much of Brautigan's suffering, and even his death, to alcoholism. "It seems to me that the brain's major work is to adjust itself gracefully to the brutish impermanence of life," Jim would write. "Other than in modest amounts, alcohol is utterly contrary to this intent . . . It's extraordinary what great work alcoholics do before the disease wears them out. What sadness."

It was a lesson close to his own heart and one he dearly hoped to put into practice for himself, if only he could.

—

By November 1985, Jim was again casting about for work in Hollywood to replenish the family's coffers. That past June, he had been fired from a screen project about the photographer and ethnologist Edward Curtis for Columbia Pictures. Jim had put a lot of work into it and felt personally connected to it. "I was swindled out of it after seven months & low pay," he complained a few months later, just as the big money was about to come in for revisions.

The producers wanted to try another writer with a "different perspective" on dialogue and action description, though they assured Jim it would always be his project, whatever that meant.

In truth, it was probably a mixed blessing for Jim, given that a few months earlier he had felt uncontrollable anger at having to set aside his poetry to work on the screenplay. As he wrote in his journal that July, "the most destructive thing in my life is the unwritten poem."

As another upside, some of the research he had done dovetailed with the subject of his new novel, *Dalva,* the story of a part-Sioux woman and her family and the legacy of settler-Indian violence. Jim had conceived of the book in various forms, including as a collection of themed short stories and later as a trilogy of novels on the order of a much longer *Legends.* That summer, freed of his obligations, Jim and Linda took a road trip to Nebraska, the primary setting of the novel, to do more research. Then, in late July, they rushed to Michigan for a visit from Jamie. By that fall, Jim had completed the first third of the book, about 180 pages, and he sent it off to editor Leslie Wells at E. P. Dutton, whom Jim had first met in the fall of 1983. She worked with Lawrence and had helped to edit *Sundog.* Wells, who would edit *Dalva,* was thus one more female editor who would help to shape Jim's career.

Dattila had tried in vain to negotiate a $100,000 advance with Lawrence and Dutton for the book, but Lawrence, despite his love for Jim—his "Sweet Pea," his "Big Brown Bear"—couldn't match that number. The economics of it didn't work out. Dutton had printed 22,500 copies of *Sundog,* and 19,000 had been distributed. Lawrence claimed to have spent over $20,000 in advertising. The book had sold very well in the Midwest, Los Angeles, and certain areas of the South, like at John Evan's Lemuria, but in other areas of the country, it had moved slowly. ("If we had 500 Lemurias in America good writing could survive," Lawrence later wrote to Jim. "They sure sold a lot of your books.") Lawrence's best offer was $60,000 payable at $2,500 per month for two years. But Lawrence assured Dattila that he thought Jim's audience was growing and that his next book "may be his breakthrough." Dattila understood the significance of the numbers—Dutton had paid $70,000 for *Sundog,* and the book did not earn back that advance—so Jim accepted the deal.

—

"Art and duckheads are long," Jim's brother John wrote to him in May 1986, referring to Jim's new collection of poetry, *The Theory & Practice of Rivers.* "I believe E[zra] Pound said that and even though most of his work remains beyond me that statement does not. A long poem and a river poem to boot." John was moved that Jim had chosen to remember his daughter, Gloria, in the poems, and he felt nourished by the collection. "I am pleased at age 50 that I still love my brother."

Norma, who had moved to her parents' old farm in Rodney, was also touched by the poems. Jim had sent the book to her as a surprise, and she wrote to him, saying she had enjoyed it immensely, "feeling that I was seeing you a bit and loving sentences like 'I'm trying to become alert enough to live' . . . and your reference to John reading the funeral service." Jim had once mentioned to her that she might find it difficult to read his work, as it so often dealt with the deaths of family members, but the reverse seemed true.

Jim had chosen to publish the collection with Winn Publishing, who had brought out Chatham's *Russell Chatham—Deep Creek*, a collection of paintings, in May 1984. Jim had contributed a short and humorous essay to that book extolling, or rather roasting, his friend, Russell. Although he rarely dealt with Jim's poetry, Dattila had managed to negotiate a relatively lucrative deal for Jim's book, and Winn had planned for a deluxe version as well, with Chatham's prints included. Larry Winn, the president of the publishing house, hoped Jim might do some readings to help promote it, but he knew Jim "found such things as exciting as pounding copper nails in [his] head during a lightning storm."

Winn published *The Theory & Practice of Rivers* in May 1986, and it would sell out. The collection of eleven poems, dedicated to Gloria Ellen Harrison (1964–1979) and anchored by the long, almost book-length poem "The Theory & Practice of Rivers," dealt with familiar themes to Harrison's readers, including loss and death, this time in the shadow of Gloria's. Jim later wrote that the collection was an attempt to render "what could keep one alive in a progressively more unpleasant world." For him, the answers lay in his family and the natural world—as he would write, "the rivers of my life: / moving looms of light," "wolf prints in alluvial fan," "the sun the moon the earth"—and in Jamie's visits home.

In December 1986, Jim sent his mother a copy of Gretel Ehrlich's *The Solace of Open Spaces*, a book he liked. Norma read it in one sitting, and she enjoyed "all of it, every word of it, completely." It made her want to visit the West in the spring, she wrote, hoping to see states like Wyoming, Montana, and Idaho "with different eyes." Yet even Ehrlich wasn't beyond correction, as Norma pointed out. Ehrlich had made a mistake, "speaking of the new moon in the morning before the beginning of the sundance. We see the new moon only in early evening—hers would have been the waning moon." It was perhaps a pedantic observation but the kind of detail that would not escape Norma's sharp eye, the same one she had so often cast on Jim.

Her thoughts then slid into reflections that must have struck close to the heart for Jim. "Blessings to you as you start your 50th year of life," she wished her son. "Life is full of such valleys and peaks and only time gives us a glimpse of what growth and changes there are in our selves. I've only started even liking myself the last couple years, or at least forgiving myself for inadequacies & mistakes. I hope you handle this at a younger age. And may our Lord bless you and keep you and make his face to shine upon you and give you peace."

Even from the Wahlgrens' farm, Norma remained a strong presence in Jim's life, as did his entire family. Her sentiments were a potent echo of his childhood. If Norma found the luminous in the Lord, as Jim once had, Jim now found it in nature and the rivers, the "moving looms of light" he had written about in his poems. Finding forgiveness and peace was another story, a difficult (perhaps impossible) ascent into more rarefied climes.

15

DALVA

(1987–1988)

> *O god all our continents are only rifted magma welled up from below. We don't have a solid place to stand.*

At the start of 1987, Jim paused to take stock of his work, timely now as age fifty loomed: "7 buks of pomes, on 7th novel, on 16th screenplay, 29th article, etc, all in 20 years, buried financially & little critical response etc but generally am overwhelmed with the pleasure of composition of late, of sheer 'making up.'"

Jim enjoyed writing *Dalva* (initially titled *Earthdiver*) and particularly the sections in a woman's voice. On a personal level, he felt some companionship, strangely, in the creation and company of the actual character of Dalva, a one-eighth Sioux woman in her mid-forties: "I am creating this heroine," he had recorded in his journal, "because I'm lonely and wish to have someone I can utterly love." He would refer to her, on more than one occasion, as being like a twin sister separated from him at birth, a claim that, intentionally or not, suggested the loss of Judy. His use of a cross-gender voice inevitably countered his critics' claims that he wrote only macho fiction, and again it helped him get away from the limitations of "Jim Harrison," as he had hoped. There's no character in *Dalva* that clearly mirrors Jim himself, like the parodies he invented for *Warlock* and *Sundog*. Jim found the writing of the novel engrossing and, again, a much-needed opportunity to do something completely new. By late February, he was two-thirds of the way through the book, and by March it was going quite well, he thought, but then he had been making "notes & effusions" for the project for over three years.

To research *Dalva*, Jim had driven extensively throughout Nebraska, visited the Stuhr Museum of the Prairie Pioneer in Grand Island, Nebraska, and he spent time in Lincoln, where he worked with John Carter, folk historian and curator of the Nebraska State Historical Society. (It was Carter who would introduce Jim to poet Ted Kooser during this time, with whom Jim would share a correspondence that would practically rival his and McGuane's in sheer volume, and the two would later coauthor a collection of poems. Through Carter, Jim would also meet friend Beef Torrey, a psychologist from Crete, Nebraska.)* Jim's research left him saddled with the "nearly insufferable burden of knowing what happened in the 19th century," as he put it, namely, the destruction of "Indian civilization." But he enjoyed his visits to Lincoln, where he stayed at the Cornhusker Hotel and frequented the Night Before Lounge, his "favorite strip club in America," which he often visited with prominent academics from the nearby university who used him as an excuse to go.

Jim explored parts of Arizona, which would also feature prominently in the novel, with Doug Peacock, a relentless hiker, as Jim called him, and someone who knew intimately the geology and history of the area and its plants and animals. Jim and Peacock would later hike the Sonoran coastal wilderness and Cabeza Prieta—the area between Ajo and Yuma, Arizona. Prior to their excursions, Peacock would assure Jim, who tended to prefer milder hikes and camping with good food and wine, of "prime picnic spots and soft champagne hikes." The two kept bottles of Bordeaux stowed in their packs and bone-in rib eyes for the campfire.

Jim piggybacked on his road trips by agreeing to write articles for *Automobile* magazine, an unlikely venue for him since he was no "car

* Beef Torrey would eventually cofound the Jim Harrison Society along with Bob DeMott, Aaron Parrett, Patrick Smith, and Gregg Orr.

freak or maven" and had not even washed a car since he was in his teens. He had never met anyone who thought he drove well. But he would imprint on the pieces his own breezy brand of nonfiction, which is exactly what editor David E. Davis wanted.

A huge fan of *Legends of the Fall*, Davis didn't want a typical road test but a "Harrison yarn about roaming over the American steppes—what you saw, what it was like, who you ran into, what you ate, the state of frozen life in the Republic's breadbasket, as you experienced it." He wanted for *Automobile* what Jim had done for *Sports Illustrated* and a half dozen other magazines. For the piece that Jim would title "Log of the Earthtoy Drifthumper," Davis outfitted Jim with a Subaru, a four-wheel-drive turbo station wagon that was basically a new version of Jim's own 1981 model, and Jim documented his travels from the Upper Peninsula to Nebraska and back. He liked the car and was intrigued by the engine, even though Linda quipped that he didn't know what "turbo" meant. The only thing he disliked was the car's trip computer, which distracted him from the essentials of what he was seeing—and much of that was for the book, like the passing landscapes, its windbreaks, and shelters, and the possible "soul history" of the Dismal, the Middle Loup, and the Niobrara Rivers.

In the coming years, Jim would continue writing articles about driving for *Automobile* and *Outside*, and he deeply enjoyed the road trips, often taken with Linda or Gerber or Peacock, more than ever before. For Jim, driving had become something akin to walking, another topic he wrote about during this time, and he described the urge to hit the road as a "religious impulse, a craving for the unknown."

Driving seemed to help Jim, as long as it did not depend on actually getting anywhere. The trick was to avoid computing time and distance, he counseled, and instill a certain aimlessness into the trip. He would provide readers with tips on how to do so, imprinting on the art of road-tripping his own signature, like the need to steer clear of interstates. "Avoid irony, cynicism, and self-judgment," he wrote, advice that could just as easily have applied to his more recent theories of fiction.

He encouraged his readers to do some research before they travel too, so they'd know, for instance, that "Crazy Horse, He Dog, American Horse, Little Big Man, and Sitting Bull took the same route when it was still a buffalo path." The hardest advice, at least for Jim, was to pretend to not care about food, since the options on the road were limited.

Jim would bring in thousands of dollars writing these articles, much of it spent to finance the travel, and the road trips would factor into much of his future fiction, characters lighting out for the territories to discover themselves along the way and perhaps America itself. The only trouble with having to write the articles was that "you have to write fifty to equal a screenplay!"

—

Jim sent Lawrence sections of *Dalva*, three in total, as he finished them, beginning with part one in January 1987. Lawrence was "bowled over" by the manuscript, and he thought Jim had accomplished something extraordinarily difficult by writing in Dalva's voice. "The first book has infinite range, sensuality, mastery of language and a tragic view of life," he wrote via Western Union.

The second installment arrived in March, and after retreating to Grand Marais to finish the book, Jim sent the third off in June. Lawrence again assured Jim that the book was magnificent, insisting that it would be an international success, and he prepared a special edition consisting of a self-sustained section from the book, thirty or forty pages, to be sent in advance to booksellers across the nation. According to Lawrence's plan, Jim would autograph the editions, and Lawrence would include a letter to each bookseller saying what he felt about the book, "that it is a major work of fiction, etc." Lawrence thought the sampler would no doubt become an instant collector's item and sell on the rare book market. While Leslie Wells edited, Camille Hykes, who worked for Lawrence, would see *Dalva* through the production process.

Six months before its publication, *Dalva* was still titled *Earthdiver*, a reference to the character Northridge rather than to Dalva, though the folks at Dutton intervened. "At the risk of shooting your blood pressure sky high," Lawrence wrote to Jim, anticipating pushback, "several people have asked what the title EARTHDIVER means and whether you would consider a different title. My own feeling right along is that this is Dalva's book and the title should be hers: DALVA. She is such an extraordinary woman, so beautifully created, and she dominates the narrative as she dominates our imagination." Lawrence had consulted a title expert, or so he claimed, and this person had agreed with him. It was a typical Lawrence maneuver, Dattila said, that is, citing an anonymous expert, but Jim did not put up a fight this time and agreed with Lawrence's assessment: *Dalva* it was.

Lawrence really wanted to push *Dalva*—he thought this book was the *one*—and he had arranged for a host of readings, including at Lemuria and Square Books in Oxford, Mississippi, run by Richard Howorth, "a great fan of yours," Lawrence wrote, "and one of the most intelligent booksellers in the South."

To bolster advance sales, Lawrence brought Jim along as the guest of honor to the NAL/Dutton sales conference in San Juan, Puerto Rico, a gathering of salespeople in the book business, later in the year. It was a chance for Lawrence and Jim to market and pitch the book. Jim would say a few words about *Dalva* to the assembled representatives and attend some informal group sessions.

Lawrence also had his eye on foreign sales; making deals abroad, particularly at the Frankfurt Book Fair, was one of his great strengths. "[Lawrence] was known for it throughout the industry," explained Dattila. "He was just a great dealmaker." If Lawrence was involved, people felt confident they were getting "a quality literary product." In October, Lawrence returned from Frankfurt, where he went, as he boasted to Jim, with "fire in my eye, hunger in my soul, and DALVA in my hand. When it was all over we emerged triumphant." Lawrence had managed to sell *Dalva* to Century Hutchinson in England, Otava in Finland, and most importantly for Jim, to Christian Bourgois in France. The Bourgois sale marked the beginning of an important relationship that would bolster Jim's reputation in France, and Lawrence expected offers in the coming weeks from publishers in Germany, Holland, Norway, and Sweden, a fact he conveyed to Al Silverman of the Book of the Month Club. In May, Lawrence assured Jim, "I'm your publisher till death do us part."

If that was not enough, in September Lawrence reassured Jim about his future plans for him. "BD," or Brown Dog, Lawrence wrote via Western Union, "we love you truly, truly dear. We will pay you 100 grand for your next masterpiece. Love, Uncle Sam, EP Dutton."

—

About the time Jim was finishing up a draft of *Dalva* in the spring of 1987, Jamie and her boyfriend and future husband, Steven Potenberg, were packing their car for a move to Livingston, Montana. The two would live at Russell Chatham's old place on the North Fork of Deep Creek in Paradise Valley. After a stint at *Rolling Stone* with Jann Wenner, followed by another with actor Michael Douglas, Jamie had already made more money than Jim had by the age of forty, as he bragged to McGuane. Jamie was first-rate at editing and computer work, he added, and he suspected she would like to ride a horse when she got there. She had read and commented on the first half of *Dalva*, and Jim thought she had done "a wonderful go through." He and Linda planned a trip to visit her in Montana in July. "Curious that 3 of my friends (about half) live there, plus my daughter."

That April, before Jamie and Steve departed Michigan, the family vacationed in Key West for ten days. Lawrence had given Jim the keys to his house on Vernon Avenue, "Sams-by-the-Sea," as he called it, a lovely, multiunit building on the beach. The town itself was a bit of a letdown, Jim found, and only vaguely similar to the one he had once known: "It's a Princeton preppy imitating a lumberjack for reasons he doesn't understand." But the ocean was the same, and Jim managed to squeeze in a few afternoons of fishing with guides Gil and Linda Drake, old friends of Valdène's.

The Gulf Stream water was reportedly cold, and the tarpon sleepy and slow to take a fly. At one point, Jim cast to a record fish in a pastel green crater near Archer Key, as he would inform friends, but he could not get one to bite. For the relatively poor fishing, Gil mostly blamed Jim. Gil found him a very interesting person, but he thought Jim far too talkative for sight fishing—basically, visually locating fish and casting to them—which requires an incredible amount of attention. "Guiding Jim was difficult because he was always turning around and looking at me and talking," said Gil.

The trip to the Keys was restorative, but upon sending *Dalva* off to Dutton in June, the same month that Jamie left for Montana, Jim felt worn out once again. His pace of work and poor health were catching up to him, and he found that "shaking the continuing virus" of exhaustion was an almost constant struggle.

As Jim turned fifty, he would later reflect, Linda had become "quite seriously, if irrationally," concerned about the financial well-being of their daughters, a fact that kept Jim working as hard as he did in spite of the exhaustion. According to Jim, Linda feared that Jamie and Anna, despite their ample talents, would somehow be left destitute if anything happened to them. Of course, Jim had his own demons that drove him to work beyond tiredness. For one, he felt "guilty and vulnerable," and producing work that earned income for the family was a way of atoning for his past sins. His need for self-sacrifice, or at least the feeling of it, as well as the "bourgeois masochism" and overextended sense of duty he had discussed with Sullivan were now well-worn grooves of habit. His exhaustion from work, in turn, led to an assortment of colds and flus, and he had recently sought treatment for hypothyroidism and a perforated eardrum caused by a neglected viral sinus infection. He would spend hours in the dentist's chair to have a tooth removed to drain his sinuses. He needed a change.

"A pause at the thought," he wrote to McGuane that June. "Our art told us, or so we thought, to give up our bodies for it, and to ingest the 1000 grams of <u>cocacaine</u> or cocaine, the thousands of cases of booze &

cigarettes, also to stick your brain in the vise everyday beginning with the wake-up call. You seem to have made some attempts to reverse the process and I think I'll have a go at it."

Jim began by quitting cocaine, and it happened rather suddenly. During a night at Elaine's, Dattila had offered his friends at the table a vial of coke. Jim took it and went off to the bathroom, while Gerber declined and headed back to the Carlyle, where he was staying with Jim. "I was sitting up reading when Jim walked in," Gerber recalled. "He lifted what was left of the vial of coke in the air, walked across the room, opened the double hung window, and dropped it into the early spring night." With that gesture, Jim vowed to never use it again, and he was apparently good to his word.

Years later, Jim would repeat the story to Dennis Hopper, who would star in *Carried Away*, a movie based on *Farmer*. "A present friend said," Jim wrote, speaking of Gerber and the vial, "'What if a kid finds it?' and I said, 'Fuck 'em, it's their problem now.'" The impetus to quit may have come from his waking up one recent morning at the Carlyle with his face stuck to his pillow. In the night, he had suffered a nosebleed, and the coagulated blood had glued his face to the linen. But more likely, it stemmed from his simple desires to eat well, write well, and live vividly—things that cocaine tended to disrupt and diminish.

Jim's relationship to alcohol was much more complex. Of course, he knew only too well that drinking affected his health and sleep and thus his dreamlife, which he valued so highly. But drinking—like the act of smoking, which he did incessantly while he wrote—was intimately connected to his creative process. Alcohol, as George Quasha speculated, was an ally to Jim—a spiritual and shamanic ally, like psylocibin to shamans. If drinking was a matter of reentry for the writer into the everyday world, as Jim had imagined, it was also totemic, sacred, and profound, and it seemed to connect Jim to his imagination. The trick was to survive it—to eat and drink, as Jim once wrote about food, and not die from it—for the simple reason that otherwise it would be the end of your eating and drinking.

Still, drinking did not always work for Jim, especially when done to excess, and at times it short-circuited his creativity. During the writing of *Dalva*, Jim had noticed that his writing had slowed down because his heroine would not talk to him if he had been drinking. If he had more than a little bit, Dalva went quiet—she "escapes, evades me," he had noted in his journal, "the voice just beyond hearing." Even the slightest trace of a hangover would send her into hiding.

But as Jim curtailed certain vices, he mourned the slow passing of his wilder days. He had become, at fifty, he felt, "a pretty nice tame ole' 4-H steer that no one got around to taking to auction." His own "bottomless pit" remained the "vertiginous passage of time, longing for the unlived life, mourning for lost vices—adultery & drunkenness out the breezy cold window."

—

"Two life-saving screenplay offers I can't do anything about because of the fucking strike!" Jim complained in March 1988. He was referring to a strike by the Writers Guild of America that began on March 7 after the organization had rejected the final offer of the Alliance of Motion Pictures and Television Producers. The strike would not be settled until August, and its effects were reaching his "vitals (gizzard & spleen rather than heart)." Even after it ended, Jim still felt "waves of anger," though the strike had provided him with a five-month break from screenwriting, time he would devote to writing poetry, fishing, and taking long walks. For that he was grateful. Jim came from a very labor-friendly family, but the strike had stopped all movie income at a time when he felt pressured to make even more.

Jim had his hands in all sorts of movie projects, and the money was rolling in, at least before and after the strike. For one, he had written a movie treatment for Sydney Pollack's Mirage Enterprises and Universal Pictures. Like most projects, it would not actually be made, but with Pollack's permission, Jim would again capitalize on his research and transform the idea into a novella, "Sunset Limited." Pollack loved Jim, and the two would spend time together socially.

Jim had also sold a heavily discounted film option for *Farmer* to acquaintances from Michigan—one of the buyers was related to the owner of a butcher shop in Warren. Dattila thought they had stolen it from Jim, but Jim really liked the butcher's sausages, so he had given them a break. Pollack would later purchase the same option for considerably more money. And later that year, Jim signed a contract with Harrison Ford and Columbia Pictures for a full-length feature film for which he would receive a cool $100,000 for a first draft.

And then there was *Cold Feet* (or *Razorback*, its working title), the movie he had cowritten with McGuane. That movie's fate was still up in the air, though McGuane would reach out periodically with updates. "Yr Razorback phone call gave me a dose of melancholy," Jim replied to McGuane in October, recollecting painful memories about the writing of the screenplay and the delayed compensation. "A great deal of any grace we earn on earth comes from being able to purge our griefs & resentments." The delayed money had come just after *Farmer* had been "utterly ignored," and the missing $12,500 he had been owed at the time represented a year's living.

By December 1987, McGuane had become so frustrated with the project that he'd decided to drop it altogether. He could not seem to get it to work, and he complained that he had spent five weeks trying to get a response to a deal memo. In case Jim had any interest in trying, McGuane told him, he sent along the number for Jeff Berg at ICM Partners, who was handling the deal. Jim had not moved on it, but a month later, the movie began to get traction. ICM had a check waiting for Jim, McGuane wrote, and he had begun revising this "humongous piece of shit," in his words, that "we put our names to a decade ago. You may laugh up your sleeve over this."

By May, when McGuane returned to Livingston from a fishing trip in the Marquesas, the production of *Cold Feet* was underway in town. The film, which starred Keith Carradine, Tom Waits, Bill Pullman,

Sally Kirkland, and Rip Torn, with a brief cameo by Jeff Bridges, would be released a year later by Avenue Pictures. McGuane observed how the actors had caused quite a stir in town, and some "celebrity sycophancy" had begun. The Fondas, Peter and Becky, McGuane's ex-wife, were hosting barbecues for the actors with "the persistence of lab rats at the pellet lever," he observed. "I have never understood why the world which could hardly be bothered with a page of the script upon which the uproar is based seems to have an air hammer parked on its G-spot the day the production office opens."

Nonetheless, everyone seemed to join in the fun. McGuane took a small acting role as "Cowboy #1," and his wife, Laurie, got a credit as an animal coordinator. Dattila's son worked as a production assistant, as did McGuane's, and Jim scored a credit as music editor.

—

E. P. Dutton brought out *Dalva*, the story of four generations of the Northridge family, in March 1988. By using journal entries to tell the story, Jim had returned to a familiar literary device (at points in the novel, there are journals *within* journals), the same one he had used so successfully in *Legends*. The novel follows the fortunes of Dalva Northridge; Michael, a well-meaning, brilliant, and egotistical historian; and Dalva's great-grandfather, John Wesley Northridge, an agricultural missionary to the Oglala Sioux in the late 1800s. The elder Northridge was once given a Sioux name, which means "earthdiver," because he was "forever digging holes and inspecting root systems of trees to determine their hardiness in certain soils."

Jim had also gone back to a familiar historical moment and theme: the late nineteenth century in the United States and the "Indian question." At one point, John Wesley Northridge records in his journal meeting Colonel William Ludlow—along with Grinnell, Custer, and the Cree scout One Stab—in South Dakota. Similar to the Ludlow of "Legends," Northridge fought in the Civil War, disliked Custer, befriended Crazy Horse and

He Dog, and later attempts to buy up land to resettle Sioux families in Nebraska; his sympathies earn him the contempt of his neighbors. The character Michael hopes to mine Northridge's "first-hand, intimate" journals to secure himself tenure at Stanford. In Michael's words, Northridge was "a witness to the twilight of the gods," and he was there when things "became dark, absolutely dark," in this country.

But the novel is really Dalva's, as Lawrence had rightly pointed out, and her voice bookends the novel in its first and final sections. Her name comes from a Brazilian samba, "Estrela Dalva"—a name Jim had likely held in reserve since his work on the Brazilian samba project—and translates as Morning Star. Her name and physical appearance almost certainly came, as well, from the Brazilian painter Dalva Duarte, a beautiful woman and Buffett family friend who Jim spent time with in Key West. It's through the character Dalva's voice, so compelling and spirited, that the novel's themes are amplified: history, time, and memory; loss and suffering; the nature of consciousness; longing; and the deep "irrationality involved in love."

When we first meet Dalva, an intelligent and elusive character, she works at a clinic for teenagers with drug and alcohol problems in Santa Monica, California. Her first journal entry is written to her missing son, whom she had given up for adoption when she was just fifteen. The remainder of the novel is largely framed around her search for her son and the backstory of her relationship with the child's father, Duane Stone Horse. By the novel's end, Dalva has come to realize something similar to what Derek Walcott had once pronounced: that "for every poet it is always morning in the world. History a forgotten, insomniac night . . . the fate of poetry is to fall in love with the world, in spite of History."

Jim had branched out geographically in *Dalva*, with portions of the novel set in or featuring southern Arizona, Baja, the Dakotas, and the land between Cherry and Keya Paha Counties in Nebraska. He had grown to love the sandhills of the state and the Niobrara Valley, and he thought that Route 12 from Springview to Valentine was one of the most beautiful roads in the country.

Doug Peacock had introduced Jim to much of Arizona, as well as to the nearby Baja Peninsula (San Carlos and Loreto), and Jim had hired him to draft field notes (of the Growler Mountains, the Cabeza Prieta, and the Loreto areas) as research for the novel. Jim had used some of Peacock's materials verbatim, Peacock said. At one point, Jim incorporated Peacock's notes into a letter in the novel written by Paul, Dalva's uncle, and his friend Douglas (a fictional alias for Doug Peacock). Jim characterized Douglas, who spends his summers with grizzly bears, with Peacock in mind. Both are veterans, and Peacock had lived among grizzlies.

Jim brought other friends into the novel, including his former mentor, "the fabled Weisinger," and Mike Ballard, whom Jim did little to disguise (the character is named Ballard, and he is the inept captain of the *Ashtabula*, a schooner manned by "drunken louts").

"Early reviews in daily NyTimes & Wash Post fairly promising but who the fuck knows," Jim wrote to McGuane in March. Jim had dreaded Michiko Kakutani's review for *The New York Times* (she had panned *Sundog*), but hers was largely positive. Kakutani observed that, following some "less ambitious works, Harrison had returned to some of the themes and narrative methods that served him so well in 'Legends.'" Her praise was mildly qualified, but she described Jim's storytelling instincts as "nearly flawless" and the characters as "full-blooded individuals." She especially admired his descriptions of the land. Writer Louise Erdrich gave the book a hearty blessing, though she complained of the novel's "virtual saturation" with descriptions of drinking.

Surprisingly, neither Kakutani nor Erdrich took up the subject of Jim's writing in a woman's voice. That would be left mostly to a man: John Blades, writing for the *Chicago Tribune* in a clumsily titled piece, "'He' Writing as 'She.'" Harrison's choice had not only managed to subvert his "Bluto image," Blades argued, "but to literally transform himself into a feminist heroine." Others thought Harrison "could win a whole new readership. He certainly deserves it."

—

The remainder of 1988 would bring several milestones for Jim and the family. In May, Jamie Harrison married Steve Potenberg at the Riverside Inn in Leland, Michigan. Guy and Terry Valdène and Russ and Suzanne Chatham came early for "a serious cooking week." A high point was shad roe brought by Chatham. Jim was jubilant, and he threw open the doors to the Warner Brothers Cellar. No bottle was off-limits: a '61 Lafite, a '47 Meursault, a '69 Château d'Yquem, and several '68 Heitz Martha's Vineyards. By the day of the ceremony, everyone was "pretty much ruined" from the previous days, remembered Jamie. Dattila came, as did Bahle, Paton, Lisle Earl, and many others. Gerber presided over the ceremony.

A few months later came another milestone of sorts. Jim's good friend, the writer Jim Fergus, profiled Jim for *The Paris Review*'s Art of Fiction series. It was the culmination of a process that had begun five years earlier, in 1983, when Fergus had first asked Jim if he might write something about him.

Jim and Fergus first met in 1979 in Palm Beach, where Fergus was working as a tennis instructor, and the two began corresponding. The first article Fergus wrote on Jim was for the *Saturday Review*, and it landed him on the cover. But just as the piece was about to go to press, the magazine gave way to financial insolvency, and it disappeared "into the muck of time," as Fergus termed it. Then, in July 1986, Fergus was asked by George Plimpton (at Jim's recommendation) to write a piece on Jim for *The Paris Review*. "Don't feel old," Fergus assured him, "Truman Capote and William Styron both did their interviews back in 1957 for the very first series and they were just kids."

For the interview, Fergus spent five days at the farm in Lake Leelanau in mid-October, right in the heart of bird-hunting season. Valdène and Chatham were visiting. They all spent an enormous amount of time planning, cooking, eating, and discussing each meal, Fergus remembered.

And there was yet another milestone that fall. Jim contributed his first food essay to the premier issue of *Smart*, a magazine founded by Terry McDonell. *Smart* enjoyed a much larger readership than *Smoke Signals*, the literary journal where Jim had first published his food column, and this would translate into a large new roster of Harrison devotees. McDonell had worked with Jim in 1977 at *Outside*, a magazine founded by Jann Wenner and run by Will Hearst (formally William Randolph Hearst III).

Back then, McDonell had edited Jim's "Safety Without Portfolio" for *Outside*, a piece about fishing in Key West with Gil and Linda Drake. As McDonell would recall of that time, he had suggested to Jim that his lede for the piece was actually the second paragraph and the first paragraph his second. He had then read *Farmer* but otherwise knew little about Jim Harrison and his impatience for editing. Predictably, when Jim heard the suggestion, he immediately hung up the phone, and a moment later, Dattila called to ask if McDonell wanted to proceed with the piece.

McDonell said he did.

"We just want to be on the record about what a dumb shit you are," said Dattila, followed by a short pause. And then, he added, "But Jim can be difficult too."

McDonell went ahead and switched the paragraphs anyway, and no one discussed it again.

Despite the initial friction, McDonell learned a few things from Jim, and Jim was a big influence on the way he thought about pieces going forward. "I realized that they could be far more eccentric than anyone would have thought," he said, "as long as they were sort of within touching distance of something that was important, like Key West and/or fly fishing."

Jim and McDonell's working relationship, as well as their friendship, would flourish in the coming years, and it would keep building, said McDonell. "It was easy to work with [Jim], because he was always so hungry for the work, he always wanted the assignment, always wanted to do more, make more money."

Jim's initial essay for *Smart*, "Sporting Food" (later published as "Eat or Die"), was the first in a long series of food essays that would follow. "Small portions are for small and inactive people," he began. "The idea is to eat well and not die from it—for the simple reason that that would be the end of my eating."

16

PATAGONIA

(1989–1992)

What beauty
can I imagine beyond these vast rock walls
with caves sculpted by wind where perhaps
Geronimo slept quite innocent of television
and when his three-year-old son died
made a war these ravens still talk about.

In January 1989, Jim returned to Rancho La Puerta in Tecate, Mexico, compliments of Valdène. He had gifted Jim a two-week stay at the spa so that Jim could tend to his health and relax. Like McGuane and others, Valdène was concerned about Jim's smoking.

"Between Literature and Hollywood my health is in severe disarray," Jim had confessed to Sam Lawrence prior to his departure. "I'm tired of banging my head against the barn for temporary relief."

In Mexico, Jim hiked five to seven hours a day, or so he claimed, and found bobcat dens, followed puma tracks, and lost "a bunch of fat," though he realized he was not a mountain climber as the hiking down the mountain proved "real difficult."

Jim would describe a fictional spa near Tecate in an upcoming novella, "The Woman Lit by Fireflies," noting that it had "vastly upgraded its facilities" from a decade earlier and describing the clientele as "a bit more hard and glitzy" than they had been. As for results, "it was a break, not a cure, a shifting into a pleasant neutral where the body's exhaustion supplanted the brain's dreary machinations." Jim's character, it seems, would fare better than he did.

Jim was hopeful that this time he would kick the smoking habit for good, and he kept a list of his incentives—"my family, religion, art, hunting & fishing etc"—but his reactions to the retreat were not what he expected. While he claimed to have stopped smoking at the spa with the help of Nicorette, the time spent alone also had him reevaluating his priorities.

"The bottom that fell out down in Tecate wasn't cigarettes," as he had expected, "but literature," he reported to McGuane that February. "Hadn't been really alone in five months to think things over & everything bad that ever happened to me made a little visit. Now that my life is, at the very least, two thirds over, I wasn't ready to have literature as a 'support system' take a powder. Goodbye, she said."

The crisis derived in part from his feeling that *Dalva*—his second act, as he put it—had, like his other novels, been terribly misunderstood and ultimately ignored. While he took comfort in his other support systems, as he called them—the natural world, his family and dogs, and the fact that he was earning a good living—literature had let him down. Jim did not elaborate about what he meant by "ignored," but it apparently had to do with the New York literary establishment. *Dalva* had been well reviewed, including by New York papers, but it had not earned him the accolades he might have wanted—no National Book Award, no National Book Critics Circle Award, no nominations even. *Dalva* was Jim's *big* book, the one he had hoped would break through. How many more did he have in him? he wondered. His dreams of literary fame, as he had once imagined it, were receding over the horizon.

"I felt ursine, damp, betrayed. Have to deal with this. Since this is dread of a different color it's been quite a challenge to counter it," he wrote at the time, but "I feel <u>no</u> self-pity."

But if New York had overlooked Jim, he was becoming something of a cult hero in other parts of the country and even around the world, a phenomenon that had its own momentum. That spring, Avenue Pictures released *Cold Feet* (abortively, as Jim described it), and its reception was tepid: it grossed less than $290,000. By comparison, the movie *Road House*, released that same day, would gross $30 million in the United States. That film's lead character, Dalton—a tough, city-savvy drifter who smokes cigarettes, practices tai chi, opts to live in a barn loft amid the fragrance of nature, and works as a "cooler," or head bouncer, in a roadhouse bar—might have stepped from the pages of a Jim Harrison novel. At one point in the movie, a shirtless Patrick Swayze, in the starring role, conspicuously reads *Legends of the Fall*. The significance, though subtle, was not lost on Harrison fans. Dalton is macho and tough, yes, but sensitive and smart, at ease in country and city, and a man like that reads Jim Harrison.

The director of *Road House*, Rowdy Herrington, had loved the novella and had "passed it on to everybody" on set to read and put it in Swayze's hands for the shot. For Herrington, it was an opportunity to "show the character reading something serious," he said, and it was Herrington's favorite book. Dalton, a very smart guy with a degree in philosophy, is involved in "furthering his own consciousness" by reading the novella.

At the same time, Jim was finally getting one of his stories, the novella "Revenge," made into a feature film. Almost a decade after the publication of "Legends," the film was in production after languishing for years in "development hell," as Jim put it, and even he had lost interest in it. Ray Stark and Rastar Films, in conjunction with Columbia Pictures, had purchased the rights from Warner Brothers, and Tony Scott, the director of *Top Gun*, was slated to direct it. The film would star Kevin Costner as Jay Cochran, Anthony Quinn as Tiburon "Tibey" Mendez, and Madeline Stowe as Miryea.

"Getting 'REVENGE' into production has made me an old man very quickly," Ray Stark had written to Jim in the spring of 1988. The crew began shooting in August in various Mexican cities, including Puerto Vallarta, where Stark had once worked with John Huston on Tennessee Williams's *The Night of the Iguana*. Stark remembered it as a "decent little village" and was surprised they allowed him to return. The film, *Revenge*, was based on a screenplay by Jeffrey Alan Fiskin, though Jim had written a version of it back in 1979 for Warner Brothers along with twelve different endings.

Despite his crisis, Jim had not stopped writing fiction, even amid the movie hoopla, and he had migrated, along with Lawrence, from E. P. Dutton to Houghton Mifflin, Lawrence's new publishing home. Jim planned a sequel to *Dalva* and a new collection of novellas. As early as February of 1989, just after Tecate, Jim had sent Lawrence rough drafts of three novellas for the new collection: "Brown Dog," "Sunset Limited," and the namesake work, "The Woman Lit by Fireflies." Lawrence was eager to assemble a collection of Jim's articles as well, and he hoped it would include illustrations by Chatham, "that guy with the funny beak." He would publish the book between the collection of the novellas and the *Dalva* sequel, though Jim had plans to take his time with the latter. A decade would separate *Dalva* from its sequel.

That December, Jim became a grandfather. Jamie and Steve Potenberg's first child, Will, was born on Jim's birthday, the 11th. "Strange to be a grandpa," he expressed to McGuane, "and on our birthday—William James P." He had felt thrilled to lend money to Jamie and Steve for a down payment to buy a home in Livingston for their new family. The fact that he had nine books being reissued in April meant nothing to him, he claimed, by comparison. "Actually, less than nothing."

What did mean something to him was that Anna Harrison, now eighteen, had begun her freshman year at Lawrence University in Wisconsin and had officially left home. Jim and Linda had visited the campus for parents' weekend in October. Jim had cried a bit about his second daughter going off, as he admitted to friends—"Quite a lot actually."

In truth, Anna's departure from Lake Leelanau would hit him hard. His work, in the movie business especially, had often kept him away from home during much of Anna's childhood, much more so than during Jamie's, when he was a mostly housebound poet. It was an absence that fell disproportionately hard on Anna. "Anna Productions," the company created in the wake of *Legends*, would thus carry an inescapable irony.

—

"They pretty much shot the novella," Harrison told a reporter, speaking of the movie *Revenge*, which Columbia Pictures released on February 16, 1990. The film opened in about 1,400 theaters nationwide and would earn more than $15 million from the domestic box office. Stark had sent Jim a print.

"I was so swept away by it that I cried—I really did. And I'm not known for crying." If Jim was being honest about the film, he apparently changed his mind, because months (and years) later, he would complain about it. Perhaps his tears had something to do with seeing one of his works of fiction on the big screen for the first time, or perhaps it was the moment when Cochran first sees Miryea, his love interest; she's dressed in jodhpurs, just like Linda was when Jim first met her.

Even though most critics disliked it, *Revenge* marked the beginning of a string of big-budget movies linked to Jim Harrison in the 1990s that would help to boost his reputation in Hollywood and beyond. A reviewer for the *Los Angeles Times* blamed the failures of the movie mostly on Tony Scott, whose opening scene, he argued, tried "to induce flashbacks in the audience of his last aerorama epic, 'Top Gun.'"

Roger Ebert, who gave it a pitiful two and a half stars, explained that the movie was "based on a novella by Jim Harrison, the 1940s pulp macho king, who had been rediscovered" by a range of directors, including Sam Peckinpah. Ebert had mistaken Harrison for the writer Jim Thompson, whose books had earlier been adapted into popular films like *The Getaway* and *The Grifters*.

In "What If . . . ? New Movies in Other Hands," Janet Maslin, writing for *The New York Times*, wondered publicly what many did privately, including Jim—that is, how the novella might have been handled by another director, namely John Huston, who had once cowritten a draft of the screenplay and met with Costner and Stark, Huston's close friend. For one thing, she observed, Huston "surely would have brought more seedy vitality" to the story, less prettiness and more danger.

Jim later admitted that his own vision of the material was "improbably darker and grittier than the director's," and he confessed that his main problem with the movie was the hundreds of lit candles when Costner and Stowe first make love in a remote cabin, a detail that Maslin found at best distracting and at worst a fire hazard. "Where did all the candles come from?" Jim wondered. "No one owns that many candles except a candle store and we're in an isolated cabin in the Sonoran Mountains."

To promote the film, Jim had traveled to Puerto Vallarta a month earlier for a press junket. Don Safran, the executive vice president of marketing for Rastar, told him to forget the demands of the press. Stark just wanted them to know that there "really is a Jim Harrison, not that they need to pester you." He also assured him that while Ava Gardner, Deborah Kerr, and Sue Lyon will not be in Puerto Vallarta, "there will be a lot of other women in handkerchief size swim suits with little to do and open to suggestion."

Jim eventually agreed to go, apparently thinking it was more like a movie premiere, and he solicited a contribution from Stark for the American Indian College Fund in return for his going. He was misinformed. "It wasn't a 'premiere' in Puerto Vallarta," he groused to McGuane in February. "It was more like date rape. I thought I might have a chat with a few news folk under a cabana, but instead did <u>29</u> tv interviews in a day and a half." Years later, in his memoir, *Off to the Side*, Jim described the experience as a premiere party, which no doubt sounded better than the "shit monsoon press junket" it really was.

Jim liked Kevin Costner and thought him "a fine sort," and he would boast (or fib or fabulize) to a few friends that he had had a fling in Mexico with Madeline Stowe. When he got back to Michigan, Jim thought of ways to leverage the movie in his favor, and he encouraged Pocket Books at Simon & Schuster to market the softcover of "Revenge" in conjunction with the movie release. It looked "more and more like a big number," he wrote of the film, and he recommended a flyer or wraparound band or ad in *Publishers Weekly* to remind people that the novella was in *Legends of the Fall*. "I say this not as yet another nitwit author but as an ex–book salesman (1963–1965)."

That February, a busy month, Jim received some welcome news. The Society for the Study of Midwestern Literature had honored him with the Mark Twain Award for his distinguished contribution to Midwestern literature, and that spring, Jim would travel to MSU to accept it in person. "I got a modest 'award' (my first!)," he announced to friends.

While in East Lansing, Jim was asked about the "flowering in the old days," meaning him, McGuane, Richard Ford, Carolyn Forché, and others who had attended the school. "So you see how these things get started," he wrote to McGuane, referring to the assumption that they were all friends at MSU or somehow constituted a coherent group. It was odd to be back in his college town, not far from Haslett, with late-night streets choked with drunken students and pretty girls everywhere, whom he felt he no longer understood. His hotel windows wouldn't open, which Jim hated, and he felt "sealed & melancholy."

Meanwhile, Jim had a flurry of other film projects in various stages of development. Ed Zwick, the director of *Glory*, and TriStar Pictures had purchased "Legends of the Fall," and Zwick had already announced it as his next movie. On top of that, Sydney Pollack and Mike Ovitz were interested in "The Man Who Gave Up His Name," and Mirage had optioned *Farmer*. Jim was also working on a Western titled *Catledge* set in Omaha in the 1920s for Harrison Ford and producer Doug Wick.

Ford had introduced Jim to Wick—Ford and Wick had done *Working Girl* together—and the two first met in person in the Salt Lake City airport en route to Ford's ranch in Jackson, Wyoming. Jim's efforts on the screenplay would go on for years, and it would never make it to the screen, but Jim formed lasting friendships with Wick and his wife, Lucy Fisher, who then worked as an executive vice president for Warner Brothers.

Wick reminded Jim of Woody Allen, especially on the phone, and Wick found Jim physically imposing, "like a pirate with one eye" and "built like a linebacker." He knew of his reputation as a macho outdoorsman. But then an announcement came over the airport speakers that their flight had been delayed, and Jim softly exclaimed, "What about Little Jimmy?" That was when Wick fell in love with Jim and his sense of humor and what Wick saw as the remarkable, gentle, sensitive inner life that contrasted with Jim's gruff exterior.

Ford took to Jim too, and Jim was especially close with Ford's wife, Melissa Mathison, a producer. Ford and Mathison would later name a cabin on their property "Little Jimmy" and stock it with "Little Jimmy" letterhead. Jim would even serve as godfather—more of a symbolic and secular (or at least nondenominational) one—to one of their children.

At the same time, Jim was at work on a screenplay and film treatment for Wick that would become the movie *Wolf* (no relation to Jim's first novel). Directed by Mike Nichols and starring Jack Nicholson and Michelle Pfeiffer, *Wolf* would not come out until 1994, but by the summer of 1990, the original screenplay was beginning to take shape.

—

That fall, Bob Dattila wrote to Jim to thank him for his continuing friendship and "all the good times we have had and continue to have together." He was grateful that Jim had remained a faithful and loyal friend through the years and "all the siren songs of fortune and fame."

Jim had stuck with Dattila since the beginning, and their relationship as agent and writer had lasted longer than many of their friends' marriages, almost twenty years and running. Both had benefited from the arrangement. Between January and October 1990, Jim netted about $487,000 from a combination of magazine and film work and royalties, including $100,000 for his screen work on *Wolf* and, as a nice surprise, roughly $20,000 from *The New Yorker*. Dattila had negotiated a deal with the magazine for Jim's entire novella "The Woman Lit by Fireflies," which editor Robert Gottlieb published in its entirety that July.* The lengthy story sprawled across twenty of its three-column pages.

Jim was thrilled with the sale but less so with the process, or so he blustered to McGuane. "Copyeditors at New Yorker could turn Faulkner into 'Talk of the Town.' Doubt I'd do it again unless strapped. I told

* Back in the 1960s, Jim had met Gottlieb through Stony Brook connections, and Gottlieb had asked Jim if he might be interested in writing a biography of William Carlos Williams. Jim politely declined.

them that the human voice was a rich instrument, an infinite cello, as it were, and shouldn't be diminished into an anal-compulsive's tin drum."

Honestly, Jim could hardly have been happier. The publication had surprised him. It was a coveted accomplishment, a victory, he thought, and a rare affirmation from the "dream coasts" and a storied magazine. It was also his first publication in *The New Yorker*, an odd omission from his résumé that was due in no small part to his unwillingness to write short fiction.

"The New Yorker is a great break for you, for us, for the book," Lawrence opined, and Houghton Mifflin had agreed to delay the publication of the collection from June to August 22 to better align with the magazine's timeline. "My lucky number is 11 and I chose that date because of double 11s," Lawrence explained. "Who said publishing isn't a science?"

Lawrence had suggested the arrangement of novellas for the collection: "Brown Dog," the first of the series of novellas that would include Brown Dog as protagonist; "Sunset Limited," a story about the limits and obligations of love and friendship; and then "The Woman Lit by Fireflies," a clean, sharply rendered novella—arguably one of Jim's best. Lawrence thought it beautifully conceived, and he saluted the "Maestro." Houghton had paid Jim a $125,000 advance, a sign of how far they had come together.

Jim thought "The Woman Lit by Fireflies" "pure Chekhovian and delicate," and with another finger in the eye of his critics, he had once again chosen to write in the voice of a woman—this time, a middle-aged one named Clare.

Disillusioned by her marriage, Clare secretly escapes from her husband, Donald, one day at a highway rest stop and takes refuge in a cornfield across the street ("curled in a thicket"), where she spends an entire night. There, she imagines a conversation with her daughter, Laurel, and she reflects on the recent deaths of her friend Zilpha, "killed" by cigarettes, and her dog, two weeks later, by cancer. She rethinks, too, her relationship with her ex-hippie-become-businessman husband and her past romances.

In his journal, Jim had described the story as one of "death and transfiguration, baptism, the ~~disillusion~~ dissolution of marriage and the discovery of religion." Like the character Warlock or the writer in *Sundog* or the narrator of *Wolf,* Clare undergoes a baptism and a kind of rebirth in the earth itself—in her case, a slide into the "sluggish, dark brown water" of the field, "an inadvertent baptism by immersion," as Jim wrote, that returns her "solidly to earth." It's an image and trope that resonates with almost all of Jim's works and that arguably recalls his own rebirth, so to speak, as a writer following the deaths of Winfield and Judy.

By many measures, the collection was a great success, and by August, advance sales were over twenty thousand, and the limited edition had sold out. It made the *Los Angeles Times* bestseller list and was named a Notable Book of the Year by *The New York Times Book Review*. Houghton had taken out a full-page ad later that August, complete with a large photo of Jim. "We couldn't ask for better reviews or better space," Lawrence raved.

Arranging book tours with Jim was a delicate negotiation—in general, he hated them, increasingly so—and the one for *The Woman Lit by Fireflies* proved no exception. To help win him over, Lawrence agreed to give money to the American Indian College Fund ("the equivalent of 2 bottles of Lafite Rothschild") if Jim agreed to do a limited book tour. Houghton had a network system that worked directly with independent booksellers, and Lawrence insisted that it would make "a big difference" in terms of sales. While he assured Jim that the schedule wouldn't be too demanding, Jim thought otherwise.

Sounds like "an ass-fucking plague ridden nightmare," Jim shot back that spring. "Relatively speaking, and unlike your other writers I don't give a fuck about my 'career.' That's because I know enough about literary history, the fragility thereof, and how book tours don't figure very large. What figures very large is the truth of the heart's affections and the imagination."

Jim reluctantly agreed to go, but not without some more complaints and threats of cancellation. Lawrence insisted that Jim was actually getting off easy: Tim O'Brien had recently made forty-two stops, and McGuane fourteen. "We want you to do 6." Lawrence also floated the idea of planning a trip to London and France in the spring of 1991. He had sold *The Woman Lit by Fireflies* to Christian Bourgois for $10,000 and to the publishers Weidenfeld & Nicolson in London (through Allegra Huston, Anjelica Huston's sister).

One of the first stops was Elliott Bay Book Company in Seattle ("the Lemuria of the Northwest," as Lawrence dubbed it), where McGuane and Chatham had both done signings in the past. Jim liked Elliot Bay, and it would become a regular stop for him. Other shops on the tour included Horizon Books in Traverse City—Jim's home field—the Tattered Cover in Denver, Webster's in Milwaukee, Odegaard in Minneapolis, and Lemuria in Jackson, Mississippi. John Evans of Lemuria had ordered forty copies of a limited edition and five hundred of the trade edition.

Mississippi would become something like a home way from home. Jim had first traveled there for *Dalva* in April 1988 (Chatham had joined him), and he did signings at Lemuria and at Square Books in Oxford, where Jim was feted and chaperoned by owners Richard and Lisa Howorth. Jim got to know Richard Howorth and Evans years earlier at the American Booksellers Association convention in Atlanta. Lawrence had organized a dinner for Jim at a spiffy restaurant, and he had invited specific booksellers. Evans went because he had sold so many copies of *Legends*. Jim would travel to Oxford eighteen different times and to Jackson for practically every one of his books from *Dalva* onward. "That's one of the reasons that Jim had such a fan base here," said Howorth. Jim put in the time in Mississippi, and Mississippi's "social currency is interactive, you know people, or you know people who know people. People up here [in Oxford] were getting to know Jim Harrison."

It helped that Lawrence himself had purchased a home in Oxford and lived there part-time with the writer Joan Williams, his partner. Williams had once been romantically involved with William Faulkner, and Lawrence seemed to enjoy telling people this fact whenever he had the chance.

Preparations for Jim's visits to Mississippi, not surprisingly, often involved food. "Everybody loved to party and eat and drink with Jim," said Howorth. Jim typically flew into Memphis, and he liked to stop for barbecue at Betty Davis Grocery, a small roadside restaurant, on the drive to Mississippi. In Oxford, dinners at the Ajax Diner and the upscale City

Grocery became obligatory, both of which served local cuisine, and Jim got a lot of attention at each. Through the years, he would meet up with Barry Hannah, Larry Brown, and Willie Morris, all of whom called Mississippi home. Hannah was "always around," according to Lisa Howorth, and coincidentally, it was Sam Lawrence who had discovered him.

After his first visit to Jackson, Jim wrote to thank John Evans and his wife, Mel, that "despite a mild hangover," he was "full of the power of trout, lamb, beef and asparagus."

The pilgrimage to Mississippi became so predictable that Lawrence called it the "I-55 Tour," referring to the interstate that stretches between Oxford and Jackson.

That summer, Lawrence promised Jim that they'd celebrate the success of *The Woman Lit by Fireflies* in Jackson with "fried oysters, frogs' legs, [and] rib-eye steaks" at Crechale's Cafe, a traditional steak and seafood restaurant that opened in 1956. It was one of Jim's favorite stops, and it helped assuage the pain he felt over the tour.

It's safe to say that Jim loved Mississippi, and Mississippi loved him back. Thanks in large part to Evans and Howorth, locals bought and read a lot of his books.

—

At the end of 1990, McGuane confronted Jim again about his health—a topic that was practically ever present in their correspondence now, and one that McGuane took seriously. This time, his direct approach would land the two in a quarrel.

"I've been thinking about your health which is horrible and maybe you don't give a shit," he wrote to Jim in October. "But you ought to do something about it and here, welcomed or not, are my suggestions."

McGuane proceeded to outline a diet and regimen that included only healthy foods during the week (no "critter fat"), with weekends reserved for "grotesque feasting." He suggested that Jim drink two bottles of good wine with each weekend meal and "go to bed plastered," if that's what he wanted, but skip the wine during the week. After opining about smoking and how to quit, he then took a shot at Jim's walking: "Walk all the time," he wrote, "and stop fibbing to people about the distances. Don't tell anyone at all about your walking or how far it is. Tell yourself the truth as to the real distances but no further spouting off about distances, experiences, equipment, circling with the blind eye, etc." And there was more. Forget about walking as something that "characterize[s] you . . . No explanation or poetry is required during a walk." As he and almost everyone knew, Jim fibbed a great deal about his walking and hiking.

McGuane was blunt with Jim in a way that few others would or could be, and if he had stopped at Jim's eating, drinking, and smoking, the pill might have gone down without incident. The walking advice, on the other hand, set Jim off, and McGuane had smartly braced for an explosion.

"I would not dream of telling you what I think is wrong with your life," Jim snapped back, "unless I were directed a specific question. For instance, all of my poetry & fiction comes from the essential 'blankness' of my walks, so that your near parodic description of my walks betrays either a disrespect or at very least, a disinterest in the integrity of the poetry and fiction. Of course this is <u>not</u> intended but I am reading the letter word by word."

Jim went on to suggest that perhaps distance had made them unfamiliar with each other's feelings, and he chided him that this was no way to address an old friend "one has any respect for," a point he punctuated in his conclusion to the letter: "As of this moment you might try utterly giving up control of the world and all of its inhabitants. All good influence is by way of grace, heat, example. We are different folks."

McGuane wondered how Jim ever found "all that" in his letter and apologized. "I promised myself <u>two years ago</u> that I would stop trying to jar you into taking better care of your health," he confessed, and hoped (a bit tongue in cheek, it seems) that this would teach him a lesson.

Oddly enough, it was Jim's excessive eating and drinking, along with his fibbing (his mother's word for his storytelling) that had helped to catapult his nonfiction to a new level, despite its effects on his health. Jim

Harrison was quickly becoming a renowned food writer, and in the new year, he would continue to dispense his own gratuitous lifestyle advice.

Jim had stopped publishing his food column with *Smart* months earlier and had followed Terry McDonell to *Esquire*, where McDonell then worked as editor in chief. There, Jim had begun a new food series, the Raw and the Cooked, which McDonell published monthly. The title was a play on Claude Lévi-Strauss's book by the same name (*Le cru et le cuit* in French).

Jim had published roughly fifteen pieces of nonfiction in 1990, everything from a preface to Chatham's *One Hundred Paintings* to "Poetry as Survival" in *Antæus*, and roughly fourteen pieces in 1991, ten of which were for *Esquire*. As with *Smart*, Jim's column for *Esquire* was appropriately named, as the pieces themselves were seemingly raw *and* cooked, balanced somewhere between wild (at times, vertiginous) and controlled, polished prose, and they thrilled readers with hearty servings of humor and wit. Jim rightly described his style as oracular and the column as a way of amusing himself, a pleasure that seemed to shine through it. McDonell would write that Jim was "giving America its appetite back."

Jim's counsel on food and drink often included candid and intimate details drawn from his own life, and he provided readers with hard-won (and sometimes not so hard-won) wisdom on good living. We discover that Jim's favorite meat is venison, "by far," though he preferred not to hunt deer, and that puttanesca is "the great restorative." Based primarily on his experiences in Mississippi, he tells us that "down south they drink like they do in Russia." And he's critical of "eco-ninnies" and the "lifestyle Nazis afoot prating about what one should drink, eat, read."

We also learn that book tours and visits to Los Angeles and New York had taken a serious toll on his health. He reportedly gained fifteen pounds during his last one. His accounts of his travels and meals are a dizzying whirlwind of rich game meats, purine-rich seafoods, and wines, and he consumed these with such visceral joy and confidence as to be inspiring, despite their ample effects on him ("the perils of public eating," as he referred to them).

In "One Foot in the Grave," a morbid pun, Jim addressed his third bout of gout, which, as "severe as the pain was," he wrote, "does not deserve a soupçon of sympathy. Barring the cases where the sufferer is a victim of bad genes or simple ignorance, the disease is earned and totally devoid of emotional resonance."

More of Jim's nonfiction would follow under bound cover. During the summer of 1991, Russell Chatham's Clark City Press collected some of the best of Jim's published nonfiction in a beautiful volume titled *Just Before Dark*. Chatham had begun the press in 1987 in a small building on Main Street in Livingston, with the idea of publishing inspired writing in exceptionally edited and designed books.* *Just Before Dark* would serve as a testament to the remarkable breadth and depth of Jim's writing, dating as far back as 1965. But it was a risky decision for Jim to forgo Houghton for the hardcover, and he hoped he would not later kick himself for it. By publishing with Clark City, he had given up on a big advance that might cost him as much as $120,000, or so he thought. At the same time, he knew that nonfiction sold well, and Houghton could have sold three times the number of volumes. By publishing with Clark City, which was struggling financially, he had done Chatham and the press a big favor. To McGuane, he privately confessed that he simply could not bear to publish another New York book with its attendant publicity and tours. He was worn out.

But Jim would not get away that easily. Houghton had purchased the paperback and worldwide rights to the book and by late July was already finishing up its own *Just Before Dark*. Moreover, Lawrence had sold foreign rights to Christian Bourgois in France, and Jim and Lawrence were expected to visit London and Paris the following spring for signings and media. Jim balked at the idea, but rather than admit to his poor health and fatigue, he concocted what sounded like an improbable excuse.

* Jamie became an editor at Clark City in 1988, and Jim began discussing the possibility of such a volume soon afterward.

His brother David had spoken with officials in the State Department, he told Lawrence, and they had discouraged him from traveling on any commercial flight because of the Gulf War. He did not "wish to be on a plane," though he did not seem to have a problem taking domestic flights, which he still did often during this time. "Widespread terrorist vengeance could begin momentarily, so I'm told."

Lawrence pushed back a bit, but he was understanding. "Oddly enough I'm not in doubt about London and Paris," he replied, "but who can predict the unpredictable. If you're in doubt that's all we need," and he told Jim they could go for the next book.

As it turned out, Jim's argument would get some help from *The New York Times*, which published an article in February 1991 titled "Shadow of War over Paris: Empty Stores and Restaurants, Heavy Security, a Peace March and a Bombing." The reporter, Alice Furlaud, would note that the city seemed to be "waiting for something to happen. The atmosphere recalls photographs of Paris during the occupation of World War II, the city deserted." The police were reportedly receiving 160 bomb-threat calls a day.

Knowing Jim, Lawrence pointed out that, because of the scare, they could probably get into all of the four-star restaurants, but they might not live to tell the tale. He was 60/40 in favor of going.

Christian Bourgois was cordial about the news but didn't hide his disappointment. "I cannot comment on the reasons for Jim Harrison's absence!" he wrote, complete with exclamation point. "The author's absence, after we announced to all the world his coming, will not facilitate things, but we remain confident."

Jim and Lawrence saved Paris for another day.

—

During the winter of 1991–92, Jim and Linda escaped Michigan for Patagonia, Arizona, a small village couched in the shadows of the Patagonia and Santa Rita Mountains, a short drive from the San Rafael Valley and Nogales on the US-Mexico border. Jim had grown quite fond of Arizona from his trips with Peacock, and he and Linda had considered it as a possible retreat away from Michigan winters.

As it turns out, Peter Phinny, Gerber's nephew, and his wife, Molly, had purchased land in Patagonia a year earlier. In addition to a five-thousand-square-foot main house, "the Creek Ranch" included a small casita, which the Harrisons would rent that winter and later buy outright. They would return to Patagonia almost every year for the rest of their lives, typically departing from Michigan (and later Montana) after Thanksgiving and returning in April.

The casita, a little brick cowboy house on the edge of Sonoita Creek, nudged up against the Circle Z, a dude ranch that permitted the Harrisons to walk the vast property. Back in April, Peter had written to Jim about it: "You're a lock. I think the place will suit you. I'm glad you'll be here and we can touch base when we return to Michigan in May/June if you have any questions."

Bob Bergier, a local rancher and artist, had agreed to let Jim and Peter write each day at a house on his property he called "the Hard Luck Ranch." "I don't moo as loud as his cows and I won't bug you if you don't bug me," Phinny had assured Jim. Jim would later boast of his daily commute along a remote dirt road past old cottonwoods and desert scrub to his office on the Hard Luck.

Patagonia was a good fit for the Harrisons; Jim would hunt Mearns quail in the nearby San Rafael Valley, and the Patagonia-Sonoita Creek Preserve (owned by the Nature Conservancy) provided habitat to over 275 species of birds, including gray hawks and fourteen species of hummingbirds—a bird-watching mecca. The hummingbirds frequently buzzed about the casita, and Jim and Linda were always on the lookout for new birds.

"Saw 22 species of birds while barbecuing chicken thighs the day before I left my beloved Patagonia," Jim wrote to McGuane in April 1992, adding that he had had a splendid winter: No television, mail only once a week, almost no bar time, and lots of walking, he had noted.

"Like Montana you never see anyone while you're out walking. Gray hawks on [the] San Pedro [River]."

Jim spotted vermilion flycatchers, phoebes, towhees, warblers, and the very rare "(first time in this country) blue Mexican mocking bird," which lived in the Harrisons' front yard—a fact that had tourist birders often gaping over their fence.

Patagonia improved his mental and physical health, Jim claimed. The escape from Michigan winters had helped the seasonal sinus infections that had tormented him for the past five years, though his continual smoking obviously aggravated them. His doctors had ordered him to undergo a CAT scan to better understand them and urged him to cut back on the cigarettes. At the same time, they worried that his high blood pressure would not permit him to get a nicotine patch.

Jim wrote to McGuane that their friendship had endured some "raw spots but we still trudge on etc," referring partly to their back-and-forth about his health. Jim owed McGuane money, $7,000 from years earlier, and the two had tied Jim's repayment to his quitting smoking. "I have never paid you back that seven grand because <u>I CAN'T admit to YOU</u> that I can't quit smoking because I'm sure I can, just haven't be[en] able to <u>so far.</u>"

Jim was also feeling a bit better about literature overall. By June, he felt he had mostly kicked his "continuing lit sickness" and was working on three new novellas that would comprise *Julip*, one of which was a new addition to the Brown Dog series. By November, he was at work on new poems. It was a breakthrough Jim credited partly to McGuane, who had reminded him "why we wrote in the first place," and also to a saying that he attributed to the writer Simon Ortiz: "There are no truths, only stories." The latter was an idea that Jim loved, and it inspired him.

That November, Jim returned to MSU for the Michigan Writers Symposium, an annual event that this year was honoring him, Richard Ford, Dan Gerber, and Ted Weesner; McGuane was finishing a book tour and couldn't make it. Jim did not feel a "soupçon of sentiment" at the reunion, but he was thrilled that Weisinger showed up for three days. He also enjoyed his time with Richard Ford, who had kicked off the festivities with a reading from his novel *The Sportswriter.* Jim had generously encouraged Ford's writing years earlier, and Ford felt the same way about Jim. As Ford recalled fondly, Jim appeared for the honorary dinner dressed in only a terry-cloth robe.

17

ENTRE CHIEN ET LOUP

(1993–1996)

At Hard Luck Ranch the tea is hot,
the sky's dark blue. Behind me
the jaguar skin from the jaguar
who died so long ago from a bullet
while perched on a calf's back
tells me the same old story.

The winter of 1992–93 was uneventful for Jim and Linda, who spent the season in Arizona. One exception was when Linda had been bucked off a horse that had panicked in thick mud. Her face had turned black and blue, and she had suffered a spinal bruise, but she would be okay. Her mother was another story; Margery King stopped eating and had withered away to a mere seventy-seven pounds. She would barely last the year.

Back in Montana, Jamie had left Clark City Press, where she had worked as managing editor. Clark City had failed to make its financials work and shuttered its offices. Meanwhile, Jamie had begun writing a novel of her own, the first of many to come; she would, in this sense, follow in her father's footsteps. Anna had moved away to Minneapolis, where she interned at Graywolf Press and worked for an indie book distributor.

As for Jim, the return from quiet Patagonia that spring set off a flurry of meetings and events, and April was an especially busy month.

On the 7th, he traveled to New York for meetings with Mike Nichols for the movie *Wolf*. "Looks like show biz is investing 80 mil on two of my movie fibs this year," Jim wrote to McGuane, speaking of *Wolf* and the film *Legends of the Fall*.

Although Jim liked Nichols—he was impressed by his improbable wit and charm—the two had very different visions for the movie. After screening it many months later, Jim confessed to friends that he "really only liked the first half, before the director lost faith in the material" and it became "yuppiefied." Years later, he would carp to an interviewer that he had wanted "Dionysian, but [Nichols] wanted Apollonian. He took my wolf and made it into a Chihuahua."

A week later, Jim traveled from New York to Oxford, Mississippi. Lawrence had donated his personal collection of publishing materials to the University of Mississippi, which in turn had dedicated a special reading room to him and planned a weekend of events, including a visit to Faulkner's home at Rowan Oak for him and his authors. Festivities kicked off with cocktails at Lawrence's home, followed by dinner at Richard Howorth's parents' house. A black gospel group sang at supper, and UM cheerleaders did a couple of cheers. On Saturday morning, Jim spoke in a panel discussion on the craft of writing.

A photo commemorating the dedication of the reading room shows a Faulknerian Lawrence holding a wooden cane in one hand and a cigarette in the other, dressed in a gray suit with pocket square and tie, and surrounded by more than a dozen of his authors: Tim O'Brien, Tom McGuane, Gish Jen, Jayne Anne Phillips, Frank Conroy, Susan Minot, and others. Jim, standing next to Lawrence, rests his hand on his shoulder. The photo reflected the influence Lawrence had in publishing and his friendships with his authors, who had traveled to the Deep South to enjoy the celebration with him. "This was a big to-do for Sam, whose health was in decline," said Howorth. "I think he essentially wished to enjoy a last hurrah before he left this world. He was loyal to his writers and they to him." Sadly for Jim and many others, Lawrence would not see another April.

That same month, in between trips and while on the road, Jim began writing "The Beige Dolorosa," the third of three comic novellas that would make up the collection *Julip*. (The second novella, "The Seven Ounce Man," was a Brown Dog story he had finished in Patagonia that winter.) The novella was about a world Jim had chosen to miss, as he put it—namely, academia. The central character, Phillip Caulkins, is a fifty-year-old professor who thinks he has Alzheimer's and begins "losing interest in himself"—a feeling familiar to Jim.

"The Beige Dolorosa" is a comic send-up of the excesses of 1990s "political correctness," a target at which Jim had taken frequent aim. Caulkins, who is hauled into the dean's office (the dean is named Ballard) for a series of comically non-PC misfires, winds up losing his tenured position, which itself becomes a blessing. "This has become a society of so many raw issues that no one can be thought to behave well," Caulkins observes at one point. Jim would finish "The Beige Dolorosa" that summer, along with the book itself.

In May, before he had time to take a breather, Brice Matthieussent and the film director Georges Luneau visited Jim at his home in Lake Leelanau. The two had arranged to film Jim for a French-based documentary called *Entre chien et loup* (a title that Matthieussent translated as *Just Before Dark* but whose literal meaning is "between dog and wolf," a French idiom referring to twilight, when one can't tell the two apart). Jim had agreed to participate mostly for Lawrence and Christian Bourgois because the film would air in France and arguably help with publicity. He would also come to like and trust Matthieussent, who would become the lifelong translator of his works in France. He had already translated *Sundog* and *Dalva*.

Matthieussent, a debonair and erudite Frenchman educated at the École Nationale Supérieure des Mines de Paris, where he studied engineering, grew up speaking English in India even before his native French. His father was fascinated by "everything which came from the States," and his mom loved English literature. Matthieussent had begun working for Christian Bourgois at age twenty-three, and he had first recommended that Bourgois publish Harrison's *Sundog* (You "must absolutely buy this book," he told him). Despite Bourgois's success at publishing anglophone authors—he had published Rushdie's *Satanic Verses* in 1989, despite the fatwa threats—he did not speak or read English and relied on the recommendations of his wife and friends. Matthieussent had thought *Legends* a tour de force, and while *Sundog* might not sell millions of copies, he argued to Bourgois, Harrison was certain to write "wonderful things" to follow. On his advice, Bourgois purchased the rights to *Sundog* and *Dalva*.

To say that Jim already enjoyed a devoted readership in France would be an understatement—he had become wildly popular there—and Matthieussent and Luneau were eager to get Jim on film for French audiences. *Entre chien et loup*, which begins and ends with Jim lying by a campfire at night, barely visible, somewhere in the north woods, his dog Tess by his side, both reflected and contributed to his mystique.

The film included an interview with Jim and shows him going about his everyday routines: foraging for mushrooms, walking in the woods with his dogs, drinking and playing tabletop shuffleboard at Dick's Pour House, driving to Grand Marais, fishing with Russ Chatham, and cooking with Chatham and Ballard at the cabin. At one point, we oversee Jim at his writing desk in the granary reading a poem into a Dictaphone—stanzas from the poem "Sonoran Radio," which would appear in *After Ikkyū*—for Joyce Bahle to type. It amounted to a day in the life of Jim Harrison.

But despite the quotidian, the film managed to project Jim as a somehow larger-than-life figure and as a mysterious backwoods poet and philosopher through whom "the physiognomy of a country emerges," as Matthieussent and Luneau tell us in the film, "its wide spaces, its myths and roots." This was at least a part of Jim's attraction in France: his perceived connection to the woods and wilderness and the history of the American frontier.

Less than a month later, Jim flew to Paris, where he would stay at the Hôtel Lenox, near Bourgois's office and Les Deux Magots, from June 14 to 19. It was the first time Jim had met Bourgois, so neither really knew what to expect, and Lawrence had worked as an advance man.

"We like the sound of your proposed publishing program: 'restaurants & bistros,'" Lawrence had written to Bourgois in March. "I might add 'with no discussions whatsoever of literature.' 'Wine, women & song' will be our theme." Lawrence noted that Jim "hated pretense" and could discuss with authority an endless variety of subjects: "vintage wines, haute cuisine, beautiful women, poetry, hunting & fishing, the American Indian, and endangered species such as toi et moi . . . He is one of the most intelligent men I know with an incredible sense of comedy & the ludicrous."

At Bourgois's request, Jim sent along his food and wine preferences in advance, noting that he preferred simple places, one-star restaurants. In the past, he had enjoyed La Terne, Bellecour, and Le Voltaire, but he admitted that he didn't know enough to decide where to eat. "I tend to enjoy food of provincial specialties rather than classic haute cuisine," Jim wrote. "The same with wines. I have drunk enormous quantities of Grand Crus and while I enjoy them the expense vitiates the experience." He liked to eat in relaxed circumstances rather than dine in "cathedrals of good taste."

Bourgois assured Jim that they might not have bear stew in France, a dish that Jim had apparently cooked for Matthieussent during his visit to Lake Leelanau, but he promised some great "gastronomique" feasts.

Sadly, Lawrence would not make the trip. While he had intended to join Jim for the tour and festivities, his poor health and a recent foot operation had him getting around only by wheelchair. "I'm sorrier than you know," he told his friend.

Jim was a bit reluctant to visit France without Lawrence and anxious about the demands of *any* book tour, let alone an international one. "Have thought for years of visiting my European publishers, esp where I'm somewhat popular, in Finland and France," Jim had written to McGuane several years earlier. "I've never felt too comfortable in France as it reminds me, strangely, of NYC."

But Jim's feelings about France would quickly change, and he would come to think of it almost as a second home, at least partly due to the generous welcome he received there. Things were going almost too well, as he reported to Lawrence during the trip. He was averaging about seven interviews a day, along with photographs, "so it wouldn't have been much fun for you!" he consoled him. And he had signed about two hundred books in Lyon—"quite a mob show with lots of truffles for dinner . . . Strange to feel overappreciated." He considered his meals in Lyon the high point of his trip.

In short, France had won him over. That August, he would reflect that his week "in Gay Paree (they don't like you to call it that) with a day in Lyon were good for [his] black and blue soul." He was tempted to move to a country that seemed to appreciate him. "It is a tonic to meet this many people who are obsessed with Literature with scarce mention of side issues like movies, Kulture, etc." "Even girls (belle dames) tried to get close" to him.

That summer, Matthieussent wrote to Jim with news of *Entre chien et loup*. The editing was nearly over, and he thanked Jim again for his cooperation with the "fucking Frenchie." He also invited Jim to come to France again in October for four days for the film's opening. That way, they could talk about Jim's books in person. Jim went again and enjoyed the experience immensely.

—

By November 1993, the Raw and the Cooked column had come to an end, mostly because Terry McDonell had left *Esquire* for *Sports Afield*. Oddly, Jim had been offered a biweekly food column by *The Wall Street Journal*, which surprised him, but he turned it down.

Before McDonell's departure, Jim had published a few essays that year for a special edition of *Esquire Sportsman* and a total of four essays for the Raw and the Cooked. In his very last one, "A Huge Hunger in Paris," Jim reflected on his recent trips. After taking a shot at political correctness in America, a "nation struggling for its soul against legions of politically correct dweebs in high and low places, where the simplest notions of vigor, humor, and jubilance are scorned and proscribed," he rhapsodized about Parisian life, architecture, and French cuisine, beginning with a dinner at La Mère Brazier in Lyon. Life seemed different in France. There he had fruits, cheeses, *crêpes aux truffles*, a *volaille de Bresse demi-deuil*, a specialty of the establishment, and lots of Côte de Beaune. The dish, *volaille de Bresse demi-deuil*, or half-mourning chicken, gets its name from the slices of black truffles stuffed under the skin. The truffle against the white flesh is said to resemble a mourning veil. The meal was not an elaborate one, but it overshadowed all but a few others in his life.

Meanwhile, Houghton was readying *Julip*, which Jim had dedicated to Lawrence, for an April launch. Lawrence was touched by the gesture and got "literally choked up." Lawrence had served in part as a mediator between Houghton's publicity team and Jim regarding a spring book tour, which they had already largely planned. Lawrence wanted Jim to consider a trip to England in the spring of 1995, when they planned to publish *Julip* there ("I want to see you lionized in London the way you are in Gay Paree"), and he hoped that Jim would attend a second reunion of his cohort of writers in Charlottesville, Virginia, in April. It would be a "weekend of conviviality tied in with a traveling exhibit of highlights from the Ole Miss Reading Room."

Jim was not enthusiastic about the prospect of attending the Charlottesville fete in the midst of his book tour, which included trips in April and May to Los Angeles, San Francisco, Chicago, and other cities, as well as the usual locales in Mississippi, not to mention his obligations for the two movies coming out, *Wolf* and *Legends of the Fall*. On top of that, he had plans to begin his "Great Big Novel" in the winter, and he wanted to preserve as much time for that as possible as May had always been the beginning of his most productive writing periods, as he told Lawrence. "During all of this there has to be some blank spaces where I take on oxygen and fuel and perform the tasks that I truly care about, the art for which I am best designed."

None of it would matter. On January 4, 1994, the plans for the Mississippi trip came to an abrupt halt when Sam Lawrence died of heart failure. Jim was in Los Angeles for meetings when he found out, and the news fell on him like a butcher's cleaver.* He had lost a dear friend, and Lawrence's death came with professional implications. It felt like the end of an era. With his bespoke white suits, Harvard pedigree, and literary affect, Lawrence seemed the epitome of old-school publishing, and he had an air of the upper class about him that he had imparted indirectly to Jim through his advocacy of his work. In future trips to France, Jim would, on occasion, leave off his T-shirts and Western vest and don a white suit, as if in subtle tribute to Lawrence.

Two days later, Jonathan Warner, editorial director at Houghton, wrote to Jim with his condolences and reassured him of their commitment to him: "I know that you and he were close and understand that it must be both dismaying personally and disconcerting professionally that his friendship and advice is now lost to you." Houghton arranged to hold a memorial tribute for Lawrence at the Harvard Club of New York City on February 14. In a show of support, Bourgois and his wife, Dominique, sent condolences to Jim, and Dominique flew to New York to attend the memorial. She and Jim would have lunch together in the city, and Jim would set aside time for much-needed sessions with Larry Sullivan.

A full three years later, after Lawrence's last will and testament had made its way through probate, Jim received a letter from a law firm. Lawrence had left Jim $2,000 from his personal estate, as he had each of his sixteen authors.

The publication of *Julip* in April, coupled with the release of Jim's films that summer and fall, brought with it a storm of publicity, so Jim had little time to dwell on the loss of his friend. The book tour, with its dinners,

* Sam Lawrence died while visiting McGuane in Boca Grande, Florida. Lawrence left the Gasparilla Inn on a stretcher, promising to "be right back," as McGuane recalled, and wearing a Yellowstone Angler / Livingston, Montana hat. McGuane would speak at his memorial at the Harvard Club of New York City.

parties, and all manner of interviews, extended from April until the end of May. In the short term, at least, Jim had decided to stick with Houghton. He liked Joe Kanon, executive vice president, and thought no one else seemed quite as "bright & trustworthy," but he was considering his options.

At the same time, Linda's mother died from pancreatic cancer in early May. She had been getting thinner and thinner and had refused to eat after her rest home companion died two months earlier. By the time Jamie arrived in Michigan, a few days after Jim and Linda, who had made the drive from Arizona, Margery King's system was shutting down from a lack of food; she had stopped eating entirely. Between scheduled appearances, Jim bid her a prayerful goodbye. Marge King—or Mimi, as she sometimes went by—died a week later. As for Linda, she was left with mixed feelings. She had been heartbroken over the loss of her father, but her relationship with her mother had been such a fraught one, not unlike fictional Julip's relationship with her own mother, Margaret, from whom she flees at age fourteen. "Margaret," Jim wrote, "was totally without talent or instinct for motherhood due to a panoply of neuroses."

Roughly two months later, the movie *Wolf* came out. The making of it, for Jim—for everyone, really—had been a rocky road. Mike Nichols marveled at how weirdly "painful this movie has been for all of us. For Jack [Nicholson], because of his private pain, which was not helped by having hair pasted all over him most mornings (ask me). For you, because of having your baby in the hands of nannies," as he wrote to Jim. "And for me, who never felt on my game for the whole fucking thing."

Jim had expressed his concerns to Nichols about the direction the movie was taking. He had long-held anxieties about losing control of his work, a concern that hardly ever applied to his fiction and poetry but was ever present in the movie business. With Hollywood, his work was subject to revision—to doctoring, as they called it—reworking it, at times, beyond recognition, and contractually there was little he could do about it.

"Now, looking at it, inchoate, slowly forming, I have no idea what it is," Nichols confessed back in October, referring to the movie. "I have no idea how close to or far it is from your original dream, or mine, for that matter. Some days I like it, some days I hate it. I'm always afraid I've fucked up royally, and occasionally not without some slight satisfaction in parts of it." Nichols was more concerned about their feelings toward each other, or so he claimed, and he insisted that Jim had more grace and kindness than anyone he had ever worked with on a screenplay. Whether sincere, Nichols's sentiment was very diplomatic.

Jim had long been interested in the original idea for the film, which dated back roughly to his first novel, *Wolf* (though, again, the novel had no direct relationship to the film). Jim told Columbia Pictures and producer Doug Wick that the film had originated a dozen years earlier, when Anna had challenged him to write something that would frighten her. He couldn't come up with anything at the time because it was life itself that most frightened him.

But then, one night in his cabin, he suffered what he termed a modest "attack of lycanthropy" (the delusion that one has become a wolf). He woke up, jumped out of his bed, tore off the doors of the cabin, rubbed his hand over his face, and felt fur on it. He also felt a snout. The episode lasted about twenty minutes. "My dogs didn't forgive me for a week. It was not pleasant and not something I particularly want to experience again."

Back in 1986, Jim had elaborated on the story to Jim Fergus, reflecting that perhaps the episode derived from some anger coming out of him. He had dreamed he found a wolf on the road and her back was broken. He hugged her, and "she went all the way into me," he said at the time, "and I remember thinking humorously in the dream—God, I've been trying to lose weight all summer and now I have to carry this she-wolf around in my body." It was a "shamanistic thing," Jim ventured, "a process that occurs in your dream life." After it happened, Jim told Wick about the experience, and later Nicholson, before he sent them both a treatment for the film. It was the first and only time Jim would work in the horror genre.

From 1990 to 1992, Jim worked on five different drafts of the screenplay. He enjoyed working with Wick and thought him a good friend, but the process was difficult and draining. In February 1991, Wick's Red Wagon Productions sent Jim a lengthy memo with dozens of revision notes for the then-current draft. They were optimistic about the story but had reservations. Jim needed to strengthen the romance plot and simplify and improve upon the overall structure, the memo read, and the script was overly detailed and overburdened with subplots.

Jim complained to Wick that a literal execution of these notes would be "a contortion that would certainly kill the patient," while Wick hoped that the notes would have more of an aggregate effect. "Think of a big wave washing over you, pushing you in a certain direction," Wick had replied.

By that April, Jim assured the studio folks that his new version was a "good deal more commercial, and generally less moribund, moody, blurred, lump-in-the-throat."

Still, Wick thought the final act lacked a sense of what the stakes were for the story and that Jim still needed to pare away "extraneous sub-plots" (what Jim termed "certain striations of fat"). "We need a clear conflict which defines the stakes and propels the plot of Act III," Wick wrote in May. By October, Wick had scheduled meetings in New York with Mike Nichols.

Jim thought Nichols had directed some brilliant movies, but even then, he had serious doubts about this one. All the truly wild behavior he wanted in the film, Nichols had ultimately rejected. By May 1992, Jim submitted his final version of the script, after which he officially resigned from the project. The studio agreed to bring in script doctors to revise what remained. By that fall, the studio had hired Wesley Strick, who had written the screenplay for Scorsese's *Cape Fear*, and then Elaine May (at Nichols's request) to rework Jim's draft. Jim would receive a screenwriting credit alongside Strick, though he was less than happy about the results.

"I'm sure you're not thrilled about having been rewritten," Strick commiserated with Jim. "You probably feel I wrecked your work—and then Elaine May delivered the coup de grace." Strick had taken the job because he respected Jim and liked his screenplay, thinking it idiosyncratic and the dialogue refreshingly formal, and then, despite this, "proceeded to schematize it, and colloquialize the characters," by his own admission. But he did so with all due respect, he told Jim, whose work was important to him.

Jim's anger about the process came perhaps less from Strick and May than from not receiving sole writing credit for the film, a contractual requirement for receiving a bonus for attaching Nicholson to the project. Now, there would be no bonus, which Jim blamed on "contractual deviousness," as he complained to Sid Gains, the vice chairman of Columbia Pictures. And his long-ago hope of "preparing the most frightening movie ever by keeping it close to our hearts," as he had once assured Wick, had also vanished. His feelings were vindicated when the movie was released to lukewarm reviews, but it wasn't really a victory: His name was still attached to the project, and his original dream for it had mostly disappeared.

Jim may have had a much grittier, darker vision for the film—a better one—but his screenwriting efforts never quite delivered it. Jim's screenwork had always been hindered by his literary soul, said Wick, who likened Jim's struggles on that front to F. Scott Fitzgerald's, noting that Billy Wilder had once commented on his friend's work as a screenwriter by saying that it was like "a great sculptor who is hired to do a plumbing job. He did not know how to connect the pipes so the water could flow." And so it was with Jim, who could never fully let go of the poetic.

According to Dattila, who often worked as an intermediary between Jim and the studios, Jim simply refused to learn the form and adapt his creativity to the genre. Jim thought it was somehow beneath him, Dattila suggested—something he did purely for the money. For Jim, screenwriting was always an unfortunate necessity because he was unable to make a living—at least one that suited his preferred lifestyle—solely on his novel writing or magazine work, let alone his poetry.

Jim would later muse that he should have tied himself to directors more sympathetic to his writing, but of course, that was much easier said than done, and Jim had tried. "The relationship between Hollywood and the writer is basically adversarial," he later wrote, and he would mark his experiences with *Wolf* as the official end of his screenwriting career—"Good-bye to all of that." In fact, Jim would hang on for several more years, though not very successfully, teaming up with Jamie as a writing partner and chasing that dream of sympathetic directors and the truly great movie that seemed always to have eluded him.

—

Six months later, *Legends of the Fall* appeared in theaters (December 1994 in the US). The movie would receive four Golden Globe nominations, including one for Ed Zwick as best director, and three Academy Awards. TriStar Pictures released a memo in March 1995 announcing that the film opened to "Blockbuster Numbers Overseas," and they anticipated the film would gross more than $100 million at the international box office.

Jim had written two early versions of the screenplay (they were infinitely inferior to the final version, he admitted), but Zwick never saw them, and apparently, because Jim declined to petition the Writer's Guild, he would never receive a partial writing credit.

The latter screenplay would work its way through multiple people and iterations. Zwick had first worked with screenwriter Alvin Sargent, but Sargent didn't think he could crack it, said Zwick, and he preferred to give the money back. Zwick turned next to Bill Wittliff, who had adapted Larry McMurtry's *Lonesome Dove* for the television miniseries, and then to Susan Shilliday, wife of the producer Marshall Herskovitz. Shilliday had collaborated with Zwick in the past and was more willing than Wittliff to take certain liberties with the novella for adaptation purposes.

Jim had once said to Zwick that "a man's life is the sum of his grief." It was a "really resonate thing to say, and it absolutely pertains to *Legends of the Fall*," thought Zwick at the time. "I felt that [idea] gave me a kind of license, and if I was being true to that, to that sort of deepest intention, then some of the changes or compressions of plot or whatever we did were okay, and in fact that was how Jim reacted."

Jim had declined to visit the film sets, which were mostly in Alberta and Vancouver, Canada, but he assured Zwick that he would watch the movie one rainy afternoon with a magnum of Bordeaux to calm his nerves since he had "nearly bit the big one over *Wolf*." Instead, Jim arranged to have a print sent to him for a screening at the Bay Theater (owned by Joyce Bahle's husband, Bob Bahle) in Suttons Bay, Michigan.

The screening celebrated several occasions: Linda's birthday, October 10, and Jim and Linda's thirty-fifth wedding anniversary, October 12. "We were married as children in a midwestern version of a Hindu ceremony designed for sexually hyperactive youngsters, otherwise known as a *shotgun marriage*," Jim jested to Zwick. It also had special resonance for Jim, as the movie of the book that had changed his life. If Jim Harrison was not quite a household name, people knew and would remember the movie *Legends of the Fall*.

Among other things, the movie solidified the career of Brad Pitt, who won his first Golden Globe nomination for the part of Tristan. Roger Ebert, who gave the movie a thumbs-up and three stars, mused (inexplicably) that Jim Harrison "must be mighty surprised how much his stuff adapts to the screen just like Margaret Mitchell and John Jakes." Did Ebert still have Jim Harrison mixed up with Jim Thompson? (Ebert had made no mention of Jim Harrison in his review of *Wolf*.)

Despite its commercial success, Zwick was frustrated by the reviews and particularly those "shitty notices" that compared the novella to the movie and purported to speak for Jim. "Bad reviews I can take," he wrote. "But when they presume to speak for you . . . It just pisses me off."

Zwick was referring to two reviews in particular. In "Grit vs. Good Looks in the American West," Janet Maslin had assailed Zwick's *Legends* as being (again) overly prettified ("Mr. Zwick goes for the Kodak moment at every opportunity, drowning out dialog with swelling music and sweeping scenery"), so much so that he missed the opportunity to bring "Mr. Harrison's tough, brooding novel to life."

Kenneth Turan, writing for the *Los Angeles Times*, shared Maslin's view: "Although it retains the name of the Jim Harrison novella, as admired a piece of American writing as the last 20 years has produced, the most telling thing about 'Legends' is how little it has to do with its nominal source material." In an echo of Maslin, he added that the movie turned "the masculine Harrison into a latter-day Edna Ferber, the patron saint of panoramic Western romances."

Zwick loved the novella and had first read it in *Esquire* when he was a film student. Shortly afterward, he bought the book and even annotated it at age twenty-three with notes on how he might one day adapt it. Throughout the project, Zwick had gotten to know Jim. The two had fished the Yellowstone River together; visited Butte, Montana; and driven through the Gallatin and Absaroka Ranges talking about and scouting possible locations for the film. So he felt comfortable asking Jim if he might be willing to help out and fire a shot over the critics' bows, as he put it. Jim had liked the movie (mostly), and he liked Zwick, and he hoped to work with him again in the future, so he obliged. (Jim would softly pitch *Dalva* to Zwick, and Zwick had read an adaptation of "The Man Who Gave Up His Name.")

"I was disturbed to see that Janet Maslin used my novella, 'Legends of the Fall,' as a club to batter the director of the splendid movie version, Ed Zwick," Jim responded to *The New York Times*. "Writers habitually carp about the treatment of their work in Hollywood, but I found 'Legends' to be thoroughly wonderful as a movie and specifically faithful to the essence of the novella." It was a good turn for Zwick, surely, but Jim's defense would go overboard. At one point, he described Maslin's attitude as akin to Newt Gingrich sneering over his shoulder at the poor—rough words for a critic who had praised him and his novella by comparison.

Turan got the lesser of it perhaps, but Jim still referred to him as offering "minimalist fern bar witticisms" and as being so fatigued and overburdened by his job that he could not "rise to the nature of his work." Again, it was a surprising and practically inexplicable response to a critic who clearly revered Jim's fiction. Perhaps Jim wanted to win

Zwick over to his side, or perhaps Jim simply enjoyed taking it to a critic—any critic. Either way, no one could say that Jim's defense of the film wasn't robust.

"I actually liked the movie. To love it was impossible because, once again, the film was destined to fall short of the resonance of my interior vision," Jim would later write of Zwick's *Legends*, faintly echoing the same reviewers he had lambasted. "Like Nicholson I thought the film should have been far grittier." Then, in 1999, Jim practically adopted aspects of Maslin's argument, telling interviewers that the film should have been grittier and that "the art director got a little out of hand, you know, and everyone looked too pretty."

But if Jim had more to say, he held his tongue. He admired Wittliff's screenplay and really liked his *Lonesome Dove*, calling it the best program on television that dealt with the Western movie. He appreciated Zwick's intelligence and his attention to historical detail, and the film was arguably the most faithful rendering of Jim's work to date, a fact that Larry Sullivan had recognized. "At last something of yours has been translated to the screen with consummate artistry, and with the consistent respect and dignity which the material deserves." As much as anyone, Sullivan knew how distraught Jim had been over the treatment his work had received in Hollywood; indeed, Sullivan had carefully helped him through those moments.

On January 22, 1995, the Sunday edition of *Good Morning America* featured Jim as part of a special episode dedicated to *Legends* (they would do two interviews with Brad Pitt and one each with actors Henry Thomas and Aiden Quinn). The film received a lot of press coverage. Interviewed from his living room in Patagonia, Jim kept a cigarette burning in his hand. He lauded Wittliff's work and admitted to liking Zwick's *Legends* "infinitely more" than either of the other films attached to his name, "if you get what I mean," he said with a knowing smile. "This is definitely the best served I've been."

—

"A nice satori yesterday when I caught my dick in a zipper," Jim joked to McGuane in April 1995. Zen had been much on his mind since he began writing the Zen-inspired poems that would make up *After Ikkyū and Other Poems*. There were other proverbial zippers too—namely, film and book events—that kept Jim on the road, writing his Zen poems between trips. Back in November, Jim had traveled to Paris (compliments of Columbia TriStar) to promote *Legends* with the Hollywood Foreign Press, and he returned again in May for *Julip*.

Jim had mixed feelings, not surprisingly, about his business trips to France, which he was now making about twice a year. On the one hand, he sorely needed to be liked for his books, as he put it, "after seven years of spinning drafts, solidly, quite a hole in the ole life." Readers in France treated him as a "Living Artiste."

At the same time, he hated the airports and flights and book-tour obligations. When he returned in May, he had a cold and felt "about all Paris-ed out." Minus the language differences, he found the book touring and "*Legends* hoopla" remarkably like that in the States. "Pynchon & Salinger seem more rational every day."

In June, Jim took a road trip to Nebraska to research what would become *The Road Home*, his follow-up to *Dalva*, and refocus himself. He brought with him a half dozen nature guides to "puzzle out the surroundings" and, with John Carter's help, pored over old ranching magazines from about 1895 to 1935 at the Nebraska State Historical Society, scrolling for hours through microfiche. The work was slow going, and he would think about the book for months. He had hoped to begin writing in July and vowed to write it *very* slowly, and by August, he hadn't written a sentence. He was on a "brain diet," he explained to McGuane, and "thinking things over slow. I nap between paragraphs." He was also trying to lighten up a bit, as he put it, perhaps reinspired by Zen, and take himself less seriously: "If I don't get to be happier in this life when will I?"

—

That August, Jim and Linda traveled to Montana to help Anna prepare for a September wedding. Anna had recently moved back to Livingston, and Jim and Linda would spend most of the month there. Jim took the opportunity to fish with Dan Lahren, a local fishing guide, focusing on stretches of the Yellowstone that were far from the frenzy of tourist-fishermen, or "Orvisoids," as Jim called them. Anna's ceremony was held on an island in the river. Chatham and Valdène attended, as did Matthiessen, who officiated as a Buddhist priest. Jamie rang a Tibetan bell while Anna walked, and Peacock caught the bouquet. A dinner was held afterward at the Murray Bar, and Jim was a bit irked that McGuane had not attended.*

"I was upset and a bit embarrassed, frankly, that you did not attend the wedding dinner to which so much time, energy (and money) had been given," Jim wrote to him a few months later. But he said he understood "all the ghosts that form parts of our lives," and he apparently didn't hold a grudge. "I think of you as my oldest friend."

As of November, he had written a total of two sentences for the new novel, one following the other. Jim was apparently still on a brain diet.

Months later, the film *Carried Away* (based on *Farmer*) was released, and it marked a sort of trifecta for Jim, three of his works brought to the big screen in a relatively short amount of time. The film starred Dennis Hopper, Amy Irving, and Hal Holbrook and was directed by Bruno Barreto (Irving's then-husband) and produced by New Line Cinema. Jim would later write that the film "drowned without notice," but he thought the movie tasteful and honorable, in a way very few are, and he gushed to Hopper that his performance was utterly brilliant. Jim had not worked on the screenplay and would not get a writing credit.

Siskel and Ebert lauded the film for its maturity and risk-taking, and as Siskel said on their television show, it was "the kind of movie that we say never gets made in America with some real ideas about sex." *Variety*,

* McGuane skipped the wedding for several reasons. Most importantly, he did not hold the groom in high regard and preferred not to celebrate the marriage.

of all sources, would describe it as "an explicitly told tale culled from a Jim Thompson novel"—Thompson, Jim's apparent alter ego. Had the writer consulted Roger Ebert's old reviews? Jim never mentioned the mix-up, but it must have irritated him to no end, and it harked back to the old days when *The New York Times* had misspelled his name as "Jim Hanison." As he had long ago made clear to George Brockway of Norton, "years of sediment make a name," and the repeated confusion suggested that his name would never be secured in Hollywood.

His name in the world of poetry was a better bet and vastly more important to him. Shambhala Publications would publish *After Ikkyū and Other Poems*, and Jim thought Shambhala, a specialized press focused on Buddhist-oriented literature, a class act, far removed from the "summer dream of NY publishing." Chatham's painting, "First High Snow Above Deep Creek," would adorn the cover. Jim wanted the book printed in a smaller, cozy size, like a pocket edition, and the press obliged.

Shambhala's Dan Barrett convinced Jim to record an audio version of the collection for Random House, which he did in June 1996 at Narwood Productions in New York City. For the three-hour session, which followed an early morning appointment with Larry Sullivan, Jim requested that a bottle of wine be ready in the studio, even at the hour of 10:00 a.m., "to clear my resonant baritone." It was the only recording of his work in a studio that he would ever do.

That evening, Jim joined Barrett and Morgan Entrekin of Grove/Atlantic for dinner at Daniel, a French restaurant in the city. Jim had decided to leave Houghton and sign with Entrekin, who would become his publisher for the remainder of his life and thereafter, and Entrekin would inherit Jim's long-awaited *The Road Home*. Like Lawrence, Entrekin was especially good at the "foreign stuff," and Jim's works were now published in seventeen countries.

By early August, Shambhala sent Jim paperback copies of *After Ikkyū and Other Poems*, and by October, editor Peter Turner wrote with an update: Sales of the book were good, with 800 cloth editions and 6,500 copies in paperback already shipped, and those numbers without a single review. "Further proof that the poetry mafia doesn't have a strangle hold yet."

Barrett and Turner had gently floated the idea of a book tour, but Jim agreed only to a very abbreviated one. He would visit only Books & Company in New York and Elliott Bay in Seattle. Linda had encouraged the trip to Seattle and would join him, so there was no way he could say no. "This is a woman that you couldn't get to go to NYC or Paris at gunpoint."

In the preface to the poetry collection, Jim noted his Zen influences, which included Snyder, Gerber, and Matthiessen, among others, though he clarified that he did not "remotely consider [himself] a Zen Buddhist." His lifelong obsession was art rather than religion, and he was only too aware of our tendency to "spin webs of deceit out of our big hanging asses, whether with Jesus or the Buddha."

But Jim knew that Zen (especially the teachings of the "Chinese oldtimers"), along with Larry Sullivan and his Christian prayers, had helped to save his life. Without them, he would have been as "dead as a railroad spike."

18

THE SHAPE OF THE JOURNEY

(1997–2000)

> *A modern man, I do not make undue connections*
> *though my heart wrenches daily against the unknow-*
> *able, almighty throb and heave of the universe against*
> *my skin that sings a song for which we haven't quite*
> *found the words.*

While Jim Harrison wasn't exactly a household name in the United States, he would come closer in France. Strangers recognized him on the streets of Paris. Fans lined up outside and around the corner at his book signings. Many brought gifts: Domaine Tempier Bandol Cuvée La Tourtine, foie gras, cheeses and charcuterie, Calvados.

But things had changed, even in the States, since his movies came out, so much so that he placed a sign outside of the Michigan farmhouse: "Do Not Enter This Driveway Unless You Have Called First!" He had achieved a new level of fame, and he was more in demand from various media than at any other time in his life. It was an experience he was eager to share with friends.

"In the middle of the night I was thinking about yr book and airplanes," Jim wrote to Jimmy Buffett, speaking of Buffett's new book, *A Pirate Looks at Fifty*. "I was thinking that perhaps . . . yr airplanes were the free floating equivalent of my cabin in the U. Peninsula, places that ~~you~~ one could get away from the apparent success that you have created.

We both know that you have to have an actual life to go along w/ the success or it's simply not worth it."

The idea of a getaway had long been important to Jim. He liked to escape from the public, routines, prying eyes, and Hollywood and business obligations, but he now found himself adding to the list the surreality and "imponderable violence of success." His actual life included "children, wives, and houses full of art and the good food we dream up," as he explained to Buffett. "Anyway, it occurred to me that our old gang has done rather well."

Jim returned to France again that May, but he intended to mostly avoid the spotlight and book business and spend the bulk of his time in Arles. He had arranged to meet Valdène there for a five-day country drive highlighting food and wine. But Valdène had developed a post-operative staph infection and didn't want to travel with a "dangling rubberoid tube" protruding from him.

At Bourgois's request, Jim had agreed to do a few promotional events in Paris and Saint-Malo, a medieval walled city jutting out into the English Channel, for the Étonnants Voyageurs Festival International du Livre, where he was a featured participant. The excellent seafood in Saint-Malo ("the best ever in my life") helped with his irascibility over having to publicize his own work yet again. But the best part of visiting the seaside city were his rainy morning walks at dawn, when he would study the Fundy-like tides that he could hear roaring from his hotel room window.

He also traveled to Burgundy to visit Gérard Oberlé, where he would spend four days at Oberlé's Manoir de Pron, a roughly twenty-room countryside estate built in the 1770s that then housed a library of some thirty thousand volumes. The manor was once owned by a wealthy family that sold cattle to Napoleon's armies. Oberlé had purchased it in 1976. Jim loved to walk Oberlé's dog, Eliot, around the grounds. The German shepherd would literally lead him around the manicured forests and past the white Charolais that grazed the Morvan, where "Julius Caesar was one of the first prominent local residents," Jim liked to tell people. And Oberlé kept many fine wines in the cellar and prepared exquisite meals. "There is a tendency to eat too much here at the Manoir de Pron, an amount, in fact, that can't be walked off by an older man and an old dog."

Oberlé had first met Jim in Saumur, France. Oberlé and some friends were sitting outside their hotel along the Loire, eating a breakfast of red wine, rillettes, charcuterie, and cheeses at 6:00 a.m. It was a cool morning, and Oberlé noticed a man with a cane walking alone in the fog—it was Jim. Oberlé had read all of Jim's novels, and he recognized him.

"What a nice breakfast!" Jim said as he passed by, and Oberlé, who looked like a well-dressed monk or a dapper version of Brando's Colonel Kurtz, invited him to join them for a glass of wine. Jim liked Oberlé right away. Educated in the classics at the Sorbonne and by Jesuits at Fribourg, Oberlé was a true Renaissance man: a dealer in illuminated manuscripts, a musicologist, an expert in insurance fraud (dealing with private libraries lost to fires), and an expert in salami. "I simply have to visit you," Jim declared that morning, or so Oberlé recalled, and the two would arrange for future visits when Jim was in the country.

Once back in the States, the writing of *The Road Home* would consume Jim's time and attention for most of the rest of 1997. By July, he had drafted two out of three sections of the novel in Grand Marais during a stretch at the cabin and still felt mired in its guts. "To be frank, I couldn't quite figure out what I was doing," he admitted to McGuane. "I almost left it to heaven" and took up whiskey again, which he claimed to have left alone now for eighteen months. "I wish to die as a modest wino with garlic breath."

Jim sent off the second section to Entrekin, Bourgois, Matthieussent, and even Larry Sullivan, hoping for feedback but mostly for encouraging praise to keep him going. The third section was a mixture of three voices and served to tie things together and provide clarity. Voice novels were certainly more difficult to write, he found, speaking of the multiple first-person narrators in the book, but he found them more engaging ("sometimes believing Rilke's question, 'Who is this 3rd person anyway?'").

Oberlé, Valdène, and Chatham visited Jim in October for bird-hunting season, a time that typically served as a break from writing. Jim was so excited about Oberlé's visit that he put the novel aside and gathered a veritable king's feast of ingredients: wild pig, grouse, woodcock, quail, pheasant, chukar and Hungarian partridges, venison, and a case of Muscovy thighs. Linda had made several containers of herb-and-garlic–roasted tomato sauce from the garden, and Oberlé had sent ahead some fantastic wines for them to pair with the meals. Oberlé is "bigger than we are," Jim explained to a friend, "more than an amateur glutton, and doubtless the best cook I know. I'm beginning to think we have too much to eat?" Jim had a splendid time, and the group surely rose to the occasion in terms of food.

Before they departed Michigan for Patagonia, Jim and Linda had a goodbye dinner with Anna, which Jim thought a bit melancholy as Anna had recently split with her husband. Moreover, his dog Tess, a thirteen-year-old English setter, was not doing well and would die in the coming months. Her hips had gone out twice, and the image of her pulling herself from the swamp and ferns by her forelegs haunted him. But then Jim was not everything he had once been in the field either. He now had astigmatism in his good eye, and it was the "kind of distortion that makes birds safer," he noted.

Patagonia that winter was a boon. The casita was remote and quiet, with only the sound of Sonoita Creek in the near distance, and Jim worked in the mornings and evenings at the Hard Luck, taking "modest quail jaunts in the afternoon." After finishing *The Road Home* in March, and feeling a bit depleted, he headed off to the desert in Cabeza Prieta for a restorative dose of the Sonoron flora. One of the bigger thrills of the season was Jim's sighting of an elegant trogon, a rare and prized bird ("the girl I always wanted"). The grayish female, with a reddish belly and white teardrop behind its eye, appeared at the window the very moment he wrote Dalva's death.

On top of that, Jim now had a new puppy, Rose, a Labrador retriever. Rose tended to mope around and send him dramatic, longing looks, he observed, whenever he would run her for any length of time. But he would fall in love with her.

—

In May 1998, another Rose, Rose Styron, invited Jim to attend a PEN dinner in New York City. She was the only reason he went. He found the city sad overall, but he enjoyed his time with Rose and his long walks, appointments with Sullivan, and plenty of hot dogs and pizza slices. But he found the PEN dinner even worse than the city itself and "quite mordant" compared to the Hollywood shindigs he had attended, like "[Warren] Beatty's thing after Bulworth. Must say I felt alien."

Jim had finished *The Road Home* in March in Patagonia, and by May he was copyediting the manuscript for Grove. He was also at work on a new book of poems, *The Shape of the Journey: New and Collected Poems*, which Copper Canyon, an independent poetry press headquartered in Port Townsend, Washington, planned to publish that fall. With Jim's two new books—one fiction, one poetry—he had begun two new relationships with publishers, Grove Press and Copper Canyon Press. Jim would stay with both, and they, in turn, would shape the contours of his future publishing career.

"I woke up screaming a lot while copy-editing my thickish novel and thickish collected poems," Jim wrote in June to Judy Hottensen, the director of publicity at Grove. His sole demand for Grove, he noted, was that their "putative figure for an advertising budget" allow for ads in *The Bloomsbury Review* and the now defunct *Hungry Mind Review*, his old advertising staples. "I certainly enjoyed being around you," he added, referring to his visit to Grove during his trip to New York City, and he hoped that the folks at the press would learn to "pat [him] on the head now and then." That was Little Jimmy speaking.

Entrekin would oblige with more than a generous pat from time to time. When Jim and Linda returned to Livingston, they found a case of Échezeaux waiting for them, compliments of Grove. "My all time favorite," Jim told Entrekin, "that disappeared from my life, of course when I quit writing screenplays to write a novel for you!" The exquisite Burgundy was an elixir and helped Jim, at least theoretically, get through the editing process.

Entrekin had first met Jim back in 1978, when he was an up-and-coming assistant editor working at Delacorte Press with Sam Lawrence. (Entrekin would describe Lawrence as a model for how he wanted to work, as "one individual and his personal vision" in publishing, a phrase he attributed to Sam.) Back then, Lawrence had asked Entrekin to read the *Legends of the Fall* manuscript, which deeply impressed him. Before Lawrence died, Jim had apparently asked him whether he should go with Sonny Mehta at Knopf, who had been courting him, or Morgan Entrekin, and he recommended Entrekin without hesitation. Lawrence probably had a bit of a rivalry with Mehta, but he felt sure that Jim would be more important to Grove.

Jim's coming to Grove was very impactful, said Entrekin. Grove had had a great heyday, but despite a few exceptions—Milan Kundera, for one—it had diminished a bit in its ability to attract big-name contemporary authors after its founder, Barney Rosset, sold the press in the mid-1980s. Jim helped to move the press back to a level of publishing where they were once again a good alternative to Farrar, Straus and Giroux or Knopf or Scribner. Jim helped rebuild their "literary bona fides," said Entrekin. Jim was one of the first writers from Lawrence's list to move to the publishing house, and he would encourage others to follow, like Barry Hannah. Charles Frazier, too, had felt especially reassured when Jim signed with Grove, because he was part of a list that included one of his literary heroes. (Entrekin would publish Frazier's *Cold Mountain*.) Grove wouldn't make a huge amount of money on Jim's books, partly because they paid him a lot, but over time, with the backlist and steady sales, they did well. And Jim delivered his books regularly and on time.

As for Jim, he liked Grove's more "artisanal form of publishing," as opposed to the bigger houses, and Entrekin had agreed, unusually so, to pay his advances in monthly installments over a period of two years instead of in one big chunk, as Jim preferred and as Lawrence had done for him. And then there was Grove's literary legacy, which must have thrilled Jim. Rosset had been an outspoken champion of the Beat poets and, through his unwavering persistence, had almost single-handedly challenged obscenity laws in the United States. Rossett would prevail against multiple federal book bans and successfully publish D. H. Lawrence's *Lady Chatterley's Lover*, Henry Miller's *Tropic of Cancer*, and later William S. Burroughs's *Naked Lunch*.

—

Later that summer, Jim and Linda traveled to Livingston to visit their second grandchild, John Potenberg, on his second birthday. Jim really felt like a grandfather now, and all the more so because he had arrived in such poor condition. Before they had left Michigan, Jim had cooked a deer liver, a doe's, brought by a friend to celebrate his two upcoming books, and now he was suffering from a terrible case of gout. It was so painful that he had to walk on the sides of his feet to keep the pressure off his toes, and he had trouble getting in and out of the drift boat when he fished with Dan Lahren. His feet felt like crab claws, he told Lahren. Jim didn't like taking his gout medication, allopurinol, because it made him feel goofy, as he would say, so he would rarely take it as a prophylactic—only after the fact, when he was already in pain.

Lahren had become Jim's go-to fishing guide in Montana. While they typically fished the Yellowstone, they soon branched out to the Boulder, Madison, and Missouri Rivers, as well as to the Big Hole, Jim's favorite, a sexual river, as he would say, which they floated down to Notch Bottom. A smart, tough Montana native—also a bit wild and prone to storytelling, like Jim—Lahren had attended thirteen different schools in four states before finishing high school in Manhattan, Montana, where his mom and stepdad owned a bar. Later, he had worked as a logger on the Olympic Peninsula before becoming a tackle salesman and guide for Dan Bailey's fly shop in Livingston. Anthony Bourdain would one day describe him as a "jack of all trades and the man to know in these parts," speaking of Livingston. Jim had profiled Lahren in a short piece about his favorite fishing guides in the *Big Sky Journal*'s fly-fishing issue in 1997, noting that Lahren could read the river better than anyone he knew. The two got along well (mostly)—Lahren could be "irascible and opinionated," Jim wrote, "but then so am I"—and he committed to booking him for fishing expeditions until he dropped dead.

Jim had finalized the details for *The Road Home* with his new editor at Grove, Amy Hundley, and following the trip to Montana, he was eager to get to his cabin before the book tours began. He had dedicated the novel to Peter and Molly Phinny, and he chose a photo of him and his dog Tess that would take up the entire back cover. The front of the jacket included faint cloudlike formations—a suggestion of constant change, the designers thought—alongside the solid depth of Chatham's "Twilight in Eastern Montana." Images of historical maps of Nebraska, found by John Carter and copied from an 1885 atlas, were used for the book's endpapers. Jim got his first look at the final design at the tavern after a day of bird hunting, and he was jubilant. "How utterly beautiful!" he wrote to Grove. "Please kiss everyone involved."

The Road Home, which appeared first in France in September 1998 as *La route du retour*, was published by Grove in October. The novel served as a sequel (and a prequel, of sorts) to *Dalva*, and it continued the story of the Northridges. The first two hundred pages is written entirely in the voice of the elderly John Wesley Northridge II, a section that Jim would describe (again) as Chekhovian in style; he wanted it to carry the reader away with its details and meandering narrative. The second section is narrated by Nelse (Dalva's son), and the third by three characters: Naomi (Dalva's mother), Paul (Dalva's uncle), and Dalva herself. To get the voices right, he had had to reread *Dalva*, which he found an excruciating exercise because he hated rereading his work. But it helped him to make sure that the voices and characters fit together as a whole.

A full decade earlier, standing outside his cabin one morning at

5:00 a.m., Jim had pondered the idea that the earth and its "soul history" were the proper subject of the writer, and he had written *The Road Home* with that in mind. As he would tell his friend Robert DeMott, *The Road Home* deals with "the soul history of our country." For Jim, this meant, partly, the sordid, bloody history of settler-Indian violence and its legacy. If you put a sheet over the American continent, he would say, "you can see all the places where the blood soaks through." It was that same history that troubled his sleep during the researching and writing of the book. The soul history also meant our strained relationship to the nonhuman world, a world we have largely abandoned, Jim would say. The book had captured, he hoped, that "character of longing for a life that would have been at peace with the landscape if we could have done things right from the start."

—

Jim flew to France on September 6, and by week's end, he had run a gauntlet of thirty-nine interviews, dinners, book signings, and all manner of adoration. On the 12th, Joan Buck, the editor of *Vogue Paris*, had thrown a party in Jim's honor in Paris, and the guests had included Christian and Dominique Bourgois, Michel Braudeau, Valdène, Oberlé, and the actress Jeanne Moreau, with whom Jim had become quite friendly (the two had met before at Elaine's in New York City). On the eve of his return to the States, Bahle suggested that everyone call him "Ralph or Fred or some such thing, so he can get out of his skin for a few days before having to commit to the Jim Harrison name again."

Jim's name carried a lot of weight in France, and it would become oddly imbued with the history, if not exactly the *soul* history, of the American West and its folklore. To coincide with his tour, *Le Monde* had done a two-page profile of him, "Jim Harrison, le grizzly du nord du Michigan," written by Michel Braudeau, who had ascribed to Jim a wilderness mystique similar to the one portrayed in *Entre chien et loup*. Jim is a man of Rabelaisian stature, the piece reads, and an adventurer with a bandit-like mustache and a lumberjack cabin in the woods. That same month, *L'express* labeled Jim "le Mozart des grandes plaines," a name that would stick with him, and playfully mythologized him as "Big Jim," a wilderness recluse in a trapper's cabin, a writer with the biceps of a lumberjack and "moustaches de Viking." Jim was especially proud of the prominent coverage he had received in *Le Monde*, one of France's papers of record, and he made a point of bragging about it to McGuane, Buffett, and others.

"Welcome home. I hear you are quite the celebrity in France—the cover of the paper? I'm impressed," Hottensen wrote to Jim, referring to *Le Monde*. Entrekin chimed in as well: "I heard Paris was a triumph." By September 16, the book hit number four on the bestseller list in France. By October 19, it would reach number two. In November, Hottensen informed Jim that the book was in its fourth printing, and she expressed delight over a recent review in *The New York Times*: "To read this book is to feel the luminosity of nature in one's own being."

Of course, the critics were not uniformly positive—this was a Jim Harrison book, after all—but *The Road Home* would receive consistently better reviews than any of his previous books. Later that month, Jim found out that the novel was selected as the Editor's Choice for *Booklist* and was voted number eight in *The Village Voice*'s ten best books of the year, one spot behind Philip Roth's *I Married a Communist.* One happy customer on Amazon touted the novel as the "culmination of my existence [as] an American . . . If I could rearrange the charter of my life, I would request to be friends with him, Jim Harrison, Fisherman, Poet, Writer, Human Being." This was the kind of public praise to be savored.

On October 13, a day after Linda's birthday, Jim set off for a six-week US book tour, which included the obligatory visits to Mississippi (Entrekin joined him there) and Elliott Bay in Seattle. In New York City, Jim did a signing at Books & Company, owned by his friend Jeannette Watson—another one of his regular stops—and he spent a day walking around the city with two Dubliners, as he had described them, one of whom was Colum McCann. Jim would remember eating a monstrous

Irish breakfast of bacon, ham, sausage, potatoes, grilled tomatoes, and eggs at an IRA-inclined pub as one of his best days in the city in years.

McCann had long admired Jim's writing, and he had first met him back in 1995. At that time, McCann, who had just finished writing *This Side of Brightness*, heard that Jim was in town and telephoned him at the Carlyle. Jim invited him out for a drink at the Gramercy Tavern, McCann recalled, and while Jim waited for Entrekin, the two ended up "getting toasted." McCann later wrote to Jim to thank him for the evening and for the signed copy of *The Theory & Practice of Rivers* that Jim had given him. Afterward, Jim would often spend time with McCann whenever he was in New York, and the two would meet up in France on occasion.

By the time the book tour ended, Jim was already at work on a collection of novellas. He was happy to be at home, and the prospect of writing one of them, "Westward Ho," another Brown Dog novella, cheered him, as he was trying to readjust his mood after being on the road. He enjoyed writing the Brown Dog novellas; the character always lifted his spirits. The process of composition was a delight compared to bookselling and the "suspicious accoutrements of success."

In January 1999, McCann wrote with a New Year's greeting of sorts and congratulations on *The Road Home* and *The Shape of the Journey*, which had come out concurrently. "Anyway, this is just a letter to let you know that on this first day of the year that you annoy the shite out of me—" McCann joked with him, "I mean, a delicate fuck-you really, because how is one man supposed to write fiction and poetry and make them both work? But you do and all kudos to you as they say."

—

Copper Canyon had published *The Shape of the Journey* a month earlier in November. By the beginning of 1999, Jim was already complaining that it had barely gotten reviewed, but that would quickly change. Unlike his *Selected & New Poems*, *The Shape of the Journey* was soon getting reviewed everywhere, it seemed, and much more so than any of his other books of poetry. "It would sell around eleven or twelve thousand copies," said Joseph Bednarik, "which is great for poetry." *Booklist* would name it a "Top Ten Book of the Year," and it became a finalist for the Los Angeles Times Book Prize for poetry. It would become one of the press's bestsellers. Copper Canyon later sent Jim a royalty check for $20,000, the first he had ever received for a book of poems, and he went out and bought his mother a nice used car with the money.

Jim had gotten to know Sam Hamill, one of the founders of Copper Canyon Press, through Shambhala, where Hamill had done translations of Chinese and Japanese poets, and Hamill had long been interested in doing a book of Jim's. Copper Canyon was well known as a letterpress house, and Hamill, along with cofounder Tree Swenson, had a reputation for being very focused on the poems. "Sam was a legendary figure," said Bednarik. "A cranky, classic publisher [who came] up in the 70s with an independent streak, a no-bullshit attitude, and a love of poetry." Hamill famously resisted reading fiction at all. "I've read virtually no fiction in the last twenty years," he once wrote to Jim. "Somebody, maybe Bill Kittredge or Jim Welch, was needling me about not reading novels written by friends, and I told him, 'I'll read your novel when you read Chinese.'"

Back in 1996, Hamill had proposed the idea of doing a book of Jim's collected poems. He thought it would "make a killer book," and he wanted Copper Canyon to do it. "If we begin to plan now," he wrote, "there'd be time for your Shambhala book to have its run," speaking of *After Ikkyū*, and we'd bring all that wonderful stuff into big wraps. And you get pocket money for a month."

Jim had agreed, and Hamill paid him a $2,000 advance, but of course Jim's decision wasn't about money, at least not when it came to poetry. He trusted Copper Canyon to take good care of his poems and keep the book in print, and he had good, well-established relationships there. In addition to Hamill, he knew editor Michael Wiegers, and he had a connection to Copper Canyon through his friend Peter Lewis, the Seattle restaurateur, who served on the press's board.

"While the advance isn't much," Hamill told Jim at the time, "you will have the best book design and books *in print* well down the pike. As we have with Hayden [Carruth], Kizer, Merwin, Neruda, et al." Michael Wiegers, then managing editor, would edit the book.

As plans for the collection came together, Joseph Bednarik had agreed to type Jim's manuscript and prepare it for delivery to Copper Canyon. Bednarik had interviewed Jim for a small literary magazine years earlier, and he had edited *The Sumac Reader*. Jim had been impressed with his work, and he knew that Bednarik took poetry *very* seriously and with monkish devotion. Almost concurrently with passing along the manuscript to Copper Canyon, Bednarik accepted a position there as associate editor, and he would assist Wiegers in ushering Jim's manuscript through to publication. That made Copper Canyon doubly attractive to Jim because he knew his poems were in good hands.

For Bednarik, the work on Jim's new collection amounted to the creation of a standard edition of Jim's poems. *The Shape of the Journey* would bring together eight books of poetry as well as new and uncollected poems under one cover. Bednarik checked and double-checked the poems against original publications, noted all the variations, questioned typos and different line breaks, and allowed Jim to reflect on how he ultimately wanted his poems represented, "because every time you move up stream, this is now the standard, and now we've established this as the standard," said Bednarik. Going through that process together helped to strengthen his and Jim's relationship, and Jim was soon referring to Bednarik as his little brother. Soon after Bednarik's wife delivered surprise twins, Bednarik received a card from Jim. When he opened it, out fluttered a check for $2,000, along with a note: "You're going to need this."

"I've written a goodly number of novels and novellas," Jim said in the introduction to the collection, "but they sometimes strike me as extra, burly flesh on the true bones of my life," by which he meant his poetry, his first and primary love. *The Shape of the Journey* would do him a valuable service. By this point, Houghton Mifflin's *Selected & New Poems* had slipped out of print, and except for Clark City's version of *The Theory & Practice of Rivers* and *After Ikkyū*, there was very little out there. "All the early work you had to hunt down," Bednarik said, "so this for him was a fantastic thing, and we recognized the honor it was to do it." With this book, Jim was "being seen as a poet again, being considered as a poet."

Before her death on December 20, 1997, Denise Levertov wrote to Sam Hamill about Jim's connection to Copper Canyon. She was thrilled that they got Jim Harrison's poems, and she thought it a "perfect fit!" Hamill was a close friend of Levertov's, and after her death, while he was busy preparing her memorial and funeral, he promptly wrote to Jim about it. It had been her last letter to Hamill before she died, he told Jim, and it seemed a fitting tribute from his early mentor. Coming on the eve of the publication of his collected poems, her note and death seemed, appropriately so and sadly, to bookend the whole experience—that is, "the portion of my life that means the most to me"—the whole shape of Jim's journey.

That spring, Jim and Linda left for France together. It was a typical trip for Jim, except for the fact that he was again being honored at the literary festival in Saint-Malo, and it was a big deal for Linda to join him. As Jim wrote to Michel Le Bris, the director of the festival, "this trip will be the 1st time my wife has consented to come to Europe w/ me in 25 years." It was an even bigger deal because Linda had had a series of serious health concerns, though she was doing better. A year earlier, she had been hospitalized in Tucson (flown there by helicopter) because of a life-threatening case of severe asthma, a "terrifying illness," as Jim had characterized it, and in early September had undergone a series of tests for related concerns. The whole process left Jim feeling "semi-shattered," though Linda reportedly passed the tests and performed well enough to travel. "Scarcely a sniffle in 38 yrs of marriage and this past year has been real hard," Jim wrote to McGuane. "I smoke outside now with vastly reduced intake due to weather," or with "head and shoulders well in the fire place."

After these health scares, it was especially nice for Jim and Linda to get away together. The air quality was too poor for Linda in Paris, so they spent four days in Saint-Malo and a week at Oberlé's in Burgundy. In Saint-Malo, they stayed at Le Grand Hôtel des Thermes, a beautiful belle epoque building with panoramic views of the sea. Altogether, they would spend two weeks in France. Jim refused to do any interviews or photos, though he made an exception for a few at the Christian Dior lingerie department for a piece he had written on underpants for *Vogue Paris*.

Following the French leg of the trip, Linda returned to Michigan and Jim flew to Barcelona alone to research a new novella he intended to write, fittingly titled "I Forgot to Go to Spain." When he got back to the States, he wrote to thank Oberlé for his hospitality. Jim and Linda had gifted him a Weber grill, and Jim assumed that he had already become an "expert of experts on the matter," though he'd still need some lessons from Jim himself to reach the top of the grilling profession. "Frankly, I'm home sick for France and would live there if I weren't so addicted to wild natural beauty, shooting birds and catching fish, the grand pelvic gorges that rivers cut in the fleshy earth."

Jim had finished "Westward Ho," the Brown Dog novella, in Patagonia that January, and "The Beast God Forgot to Invent," another "Chekhovian tale," over the spring and summer of 1999. That one required an "unflinching gaze into the soul of wildness," as he put it, through the brain of an injured character. "I Forgot to Go to Spain," a story about a person who works too hard and its consequences, was much closer to his own experience. It recalled a time for him, as he told Entrekin, when he had quit screenwriting several years earlier after writing eleven versions of three different screenplays.

Jim had turned sixty-two that December, and roughly two weeks after his birthday, he received the kind of news that makes one feel his years. His mother had died unexpectedly. When Norma hadn't answered the phone, Mary, Jim's sister, went to check on her and found her body slumped over at the kitchen counter. She died in the house she had had built on the property of the Wahlgrens' old farmhouse, where she had lived for years. Mary called Jim and Linda in Patagonia to tell them the news, and Jim flew back to Michigan to attend the service, along with Jamie. Jim would suggest that the family have a stained-glass window made for the United Church of Big Rapids, where her memorial was held, and he insisted that the window be of a bluebird. She had been an intrepid birdwatcher. The design included leaves, dark russet-colored branches, magnolia blossoms, and purple and creamy yellow irises, and it would be installed in the east-facing window.

Her death left Jim feeling deeply out of sorts. The day before Norma's service, he wrote an anxious note to Hottensen, at one point stating that her silence about his novellas was "ominous," and then informing her that he might have to go to New York to see Larry Sullivan. "My mother died and I am not sure I like being an orphan," he told her. "I hear from my publisher so rarely. I wonder if I am welcome in Gotham."

In the months that followed, Jim could not shake the stomach-sinking feeling over her death, and then he had his own health concerns to worry about. In January, he landed himself in the emergency room in Nogales for kidney stones, nineteen to be exact. Jim had passed number nineteen during a long night in the hospital with the aid of three hypodermic needles full of morphine ("I had the feeling that I gave birth to a concrete block through my weenie"). He found a new doctor and friend in Alfredo "Che" Guevara, the urologist who helped with the stones.

There was also the debilitating gout, a recent cold and flu, recurring severe back pain, and an elbow injury. And that spring, he would suffer from three abscessed teeth that were then extracted, with subsequent infections requiring four sequences of antibiotics that enlarged his lips to a cartoonlike extent. He would bury his pulled teeth by the graves of his dogs Tess and Sand. By August, Jim was fitted for new teeth—a bridge, which he often opted not to wear at all, leaving him looking far more haggard than his years.

Despite his health issues, Jim's poetry writing was thriving. "I am always amazed at your most tired times how the poems flow," Bahle had once written to Jim, and the same seemed to apply to times of crisis.

To friends, Jim would claim that 1999 and 2000 were the best years he had ever had for writing poems, and if he did not have to also earn a living, he would devote himself solely to poetry—along with birds and dogs and fishing.

Traveling served as a restorative of sorts, so long as it wasn't associated with a book tour, as did fishing, and Jim did a lot of both in the coming months. That April, he stayed in France for an entire month, and he set aside nine days to travel by himself, something he had never done before; Linda had decided not to join him this time. Jim visited Oberlé in Burgundy, Matthieussent in Marseilles, and he stayed at Nord-Pinus in Arles. But if the traveling helped with his mental health, his emotions still seemed raw. One night, as Oberlé and Jim were heading out to dinner, Jim began crying in the taxi. At first, Oberlé thought Jim was drunk, because he wouldn't stop crying. When he pressed him about it, Jim told him that his mother had died. Naturally, Oberlé thought it had happened very recently, but it had been months.

"Oh, stop now," Oberlé said to Jim in a thick French accent. "If you want, you can call me mommy. I will be your mom." Later, Jim sometimes referred to Oberlé as "Mommy, dear."

"He was a mixture of great sensitivity, extreme sentimentality," Oberlé said, reflecting on Jim's character. "It's very weird."

More travel followed. In June, Jim took Steve Potenberg and Dan Lahren to Zihuatanejo for a fishing trip, and Dan Gerber joined them. Jim had been interested in rooster fish since he read Van Campen Heilner and spoke to sportsman Kip Farrington in the 1970s, both of whom had been associated with Hemingway in one way or another. The group fished for three days and caught black tuna and roosters. The latter was a strong fish that took long runs, which Jim found brutal work in ninety-five-degree heat and 100 percent humidity. At night, the group frequented a local strip club. With its "huge surf, volcanic rocks, fecund sea, [and] multitudinous birds," Jim thought the coast even more beautiful than Costa Rica or Ecuador. They ate portions of their daily catch at lunch under palm fronds.

In September, Jim was back in Livingston and fished the Yellowstone with Lahren and Peter Matthiessen. They had a twenty-five-fish day, Jim recalled, and they talked about fishing, birds, and girls. Both Jim and Lahren knew that if you got Matthiessen talking about women and sex, his casting would invariably go to hell. They both thought it terribly funny.

In October 2000, Grove brought out Jim's children's book, *The Boy Who Ran to the Woods*, and the novella collection *The Beast God Forgot to Invent*, and the book tours and publicity began yet again, the cycle of life for Jim.

Death was still very much on his mind. "I find myself quite confused about death," Jim had written to McGuane months earlier. "I assume it will be a no-smoking situation?"

19

THE ROVING GOURMAND

(2001–2003)

Everyone thought I'd die
in my twenties, thirties, forties, fifties.
This can't go on forever.

By the end of 2000, *The Beast God Forgot to Invent* was named a *New York Times* Notable Book of the Year and a *Los Angeles Times* Best of the Year. *The Dallas Morning News* referred to Jim as "one of our finest living writers." A critic writing for *Salon* used the occasion to take stock of Jim's four decades of writing, noting that he had managed to avoid the "snares of critical reduction," including such tags as "macho" and "regional." Harrison had created a body of work "so lushly idiosyncratic as to thwart even the greatest efforts at classification."

Jim *was* difficult to categorize because of his facility with different forms and genres. Indeed, it's hard to name a writer who had been as proficient and prolific as Jim was with poetry, fiction, and nonfiction as well as screenwork, which could be both a curse and a blessing. The poetry community tended to forget he was a poet.

Moreover, he had mostly managed to elude comparisons to Hemingway, though he arguably shared more things with him—fishing, hunting, Michigan, Key West, a romanticized immoderation, and so on—than his peers Updike, Roth, DeLillo, Stone, McCarthy, and even McGuane, who was himself burdened by Hemingway's ghost. Jim's fiction was incomparably more lyrical, satirical, and joyful, and not as exactingly concise. Jim's own feelings about Hemingway were complicated, and although he praised him on many occasions (one example: Hemingway wrote about war "as beautifully as any man in our century"), he understandably distanced himself from Papa at almost every chance, lest he become a mere satellite to his system, as many writers feared. Almost all writers of his generation had to contend, one way or another, with Hemingway's legacy as well as with Faulkner's and their long modernist shadows. Writers had to fight for their own place in the sun.

Part of the comparison with Hemingway came from the "macho" tag that still clung to Jim, despite the claims in *Salon*. Of course, he had railed against that particular descriptor for years, and his decision to write in a woman's voice had helped to dispel it. "I couldn't be a good writer if I was a 'tough guy,'" he would insist to Amy Hundley.

"Could a tough guy have written Dalva?" Hundley asked in reply.

It was an idea worth pondering, even if those same female narrators would expose him to other criticism, mostly from a small chorus of anti-appropriation critics who disapproved of a man writing in a woman's voice. To the latter critique, Jim would respond that he tended to "think of art as essentially androgynous" and gender as "a biological rather than a philosophical system."

In a review of *The Beast God Forgot to Invent* for *The New York Times*, Dwight Garner rightly pointed out that Jim hadn't done himself many favors in regard to the macho tag. In the past, Jim had labeled feminist detractors as "brie brains," as Garner noted, and once, in a 1983 *Esquire* piece, remarked, "Even now, far up in the wilderness in my cabin, where I just shot a lamprey passing upstream with my Magnum, I wouldn't have the heart to turn down a platter of hot buttered cheerleaders." Setting aside the fact that the invasive sea lamprey had been enormously destructive to Great Lakes fisheries, the comment seems all bravado; Jim wasn't above perpetuating a macho image, particularly earlier in his career. And to be fair, Jim's "hot buttered cheerleaders" quote was from twenty years earlier, and a lot had changed culturally and personally for him in the intervening decades. Jim hated shooting most things: deer, antelope, and increasingly even game birds. After wondering why Harrison hadn't done even a slightly better job of defending himself, Garner took up the task by pointing out that Jim's "subversive and deft" satire is almost always aimed directly at his "aggressive, but somehow bewildered, antiheroes," all men, and while those men are louts, "they're tender, easily wounded louts."

But if Jim was difficult to categorize, it was not for lack of effort. Despite the relative success of *The Beast God Forgot to Invent*, he noticed an irritating trend in the way some critics described his work, including in a review by Malcolm Jones in *Newsweek* that referred to him as "our greatest nonwriterly writer." Jim wondered what the hell that meant, as he carped to Hottensen, and he was tempted to respond. Hottensen assured Jim that Malcolm Jones loved him, and she took it to mean he wasn't an "MFA bullshit New York writer," an interpretation that Jim surely appreciated whether he believed it or not.

Another reviewer referred to Jim as "a cult writer," as he complained to McGuane, "which isn't too encouraging" and a clear condescension. Still others labeled him a historical writer (in a review of *The Road Home*) and a regionalist writer, "an admission," Jim insisted, "of abject failure as an artist." (He would note in his journal that anything written outside of New York City was considered regional.) Perhaps worse were those critics who labeled him an outdoor writer or a nature writer—"a first-rate" one, claimed *The Wall Street Journal.* "Women, nature, and food," Jim marveled, "[are] evidently thought to be rare items in some circles."

"If you go outside you will not be taken as seriously as if you stayed inside feeding on yr own brain snot . . . At least the French don't seem to mind if you go outside."

—

A year earlier, Jim had signed up with *Men's Journal* to write an essay on the problems along the US-Mexico border, and Patagonia provided him some firsthand experience. He had become a contributing editor to the magazine in 1999 and since then had published a handful of pieces on food (French and soul food) and fishing, including his account of the Zihuatanejo trip. But by January 2001, he was regretting his choice of topics. "A month of research uncovers incomprehensible suffering. Don't have enough teeth to gnash. I'm too old for this."

The nexus of his research was the death of a twenty-year-old Mexican woman, Ana Claudia Villa Hererra, a story that he would set off in italics and weave throughout the piece; Hererra would put a face to the grueling statistics. Herrera grew up in the city of Córdoba in the state of Veracruz and died crossing the US-Mexico border on July 28, 1998. She was traveling with her child, whom she carried in her arms, and her brother. The family walked together up a dry wash for forty miles until Hererra dropped dead of acute dehydration in the desert east of Sells, Arizona, her "fallen body wrenched into a question mark." Miraculously, her child lived. She was only twenty when she died, Jim told friends, "like thousands of others in the last decade, out in Papago country trying to reach the promised land. Summer ground temp 150 plus."

In early 2001, Jim traveled to Veracruz to do research and see "where the dead girl came from." The resulting essay, "Life on the Border," published July 2001, was unusually political for *Men's Journal* and also for Jim, who announced in its opening pages his political stripes as a liberal and left-wing Democrat. The piece detailed the excruciating poverty and desperation of migrants—the kind that would make a young woman leave a place as beautiful as Veracruz—and the suffering and deaths on the border (official figures that year were 369, though the real number was possibly triple that, Jim noted). Jim concluded the essay with a simple but poignant assertion: "Ana Claudia Villa Herrera. What a lovely name."

"Life on the Border" took "a lot of bluster" out of his life, and it led to what he would term "a mental crack up" that winter, a depression that felt different from others because it came from the outside rather than within. "I had not only pulled the rug out from under myself. I had also removed the floor and basement." His feeling stemmed from his conflation of Herrera with his sister Judy, who had been killed at roughly the same age, and the young Mexican woman almost shared a name with his own Anna. He had no control over the issue either and felt fatigued by the idea that all he could do was to "shine a tiny penlight on this hell," the power and constraints of any writer. His next two pieces for *Men's Journal* stuck to safer topics: "A Man's Guide to Drinking" in October and "Naked Women Dancing" in December.

Jim had a tough time shaking "the blues" throughout 2001, but he pressed ahead on a new novel (later titled *True North*) and a memoir, *Off to the Side*, about which he had the deepest questions. For one, he wondered if everything he had to say was already in his writing, and for another, he worried that reliving certain early times would be "harrowing indeed." The writing would be difficult, as he had feared, and as he recounted his life, it would confirm his suspicions that he had never been "real strong at mental balance." It made him wonder about his future perhaps as much as his past.

His mood shifted from day to day and chapter to chapter: "Mentioned in memoir our early Absaroka trip, Summerland Key, the Palo Alto–Stony Brook calls," he wrote McGuane with some evident pleasure in his tone. "How excited we were about literature! It was almost as good as fishing." Other times, his mood would clearly darken, as he would be forced to confront his past actions: "Much anguish in certain periods when the egregious asshole spun the wheel upending those aboard his tugboat. You know what I mean." On yet another occasion, "What an asshole, I kept thinking."

That spring, Jim canceled his usual trip to France and opted to stay close to home in Patagonia. The rare wildflowers, dozens of varieties he had never seen before, and the vivid greenery from ample rainfall the previous winter had prompted him to stick around—that and the fact that he could not face another literary festival, even for a free airplane ticket. In April, he would accompany Bob and Gail Bergier, the owners of the Hard Luck Ranch, to the Avra Valley, which borders the west side of Tucson, and then to the Buenos Aires Ranch in Sasabe, a border town in Pima County, to view the beautiful landscapes. Soon afterward, Anna visited the casita with her future husband, Max Hjortsberg, the son of Gatz Hjortsberg, and he was happy to have her close to him.

Jim and Linda returned to Michigan from Arizona in mid-April, just before Linda, Jamie, and Anna left for a trip to England and Ireland. With the house empty, Jim went to Grand Marais. After much discussion that winter, he and Linda had decided to sell the Lake Leelanau farmhouse and resettle in Montana, mostly to be closer to their daughters, son-in-law, and grandchildren. They would also soon sell Jim's cabin in the Upper Peninsula. In reality, as Jim knew, he simply would not be able to visit it often enough to warrant keeping it, and he had considered purchasing a cabin somewhere in Montana instead, a short drive's distance from Livingston. But it would still be another year before they pulled up roots and made the trek westward.

That August, Aralia Press brought out a chapbook of poems by Jim and Ted Kooser titled *A Conversation*. Ever since John Carter, the historian in Nebraska, had introduced them, Jim and Kooser had been writing to each other continually, exchanging both letters and poems. Whenever Jim visited Nebraska, the two would drive around the state and talk about books and local history and lore.

"It was in ways an improbable friendship," said Kooser, "me quite retiring, shy and sober, and Jim neither of those. I learned early not to challenge him, and he liked my deference. He always wanted the last word."

But neither of them quite got the last word in poetry. They'd shoot poems back and forth to each other for years—some of which would make up *A Conversation*—and it was, finally, a solidly two-sided one.

Back in 1998, Kooser had been recovering from surgery and radiation treatments for a near-fatal cancer and was grappling with depression. As part of his therapy, he had begun taking daily two-mile walks each morning along country roads near Garland, Nebraska. He had been told to stay out of the sun for a whole year due to the radiation therapy, so he walked in the early mornings before sunup. At one point, he began writing poems (really haiku) based on those walks, and in keeping with their earlier exchanges, pasted them on postcards and mailed them to Jim. Jim loved them and thought Kooser had opened "a whole new vein of creativity" in the process. Kooser would collect and publish them with Carnegie Mellon University Press in 2000 as *Winter Morning Walks: One Hundred Postcards to Jim Harrison.*

In January 2001, the editor of Aralia Press, Michael Peich, reached out to Jim and Kooser. Peich had already spoken to Kooser, who had told him about their exchanges of poems and haiku over the years. Peich's idea, which he pitched to them both, was to publish something like the improvisational call-and-response of jazz music but with poems. Peich asked them to put together fifteen pages of two haiku per page, though he intended the chapbook to be about ten pages of text in total. The poems would be unsigned, so there would be no attributions. Some would be Jim's, some Kooser's, but readers wouldn't know.

By the end of January, Kooser had "picked out 14 pair, mostly Jim/Ted but some Ted/Jim and one Jim/Jim to add to the bafflement" as he put it. Even Kooser got a bit confused as he assembled the poems, at one point jotting down "Jim (I think)" next to one of them in the manuscript. To introduce the poems and the idea behind them, Kooser sketched out an introduction and sent it off to Peich. The document represented a kind of manifesto for the chapbook.

"It plays to our western point of view to assign a literary work some part of its value on the virtue of its author's name," Kooser wrote. "If Olive Oyl is touched by the poem she finds in the spinach can, should she care whether it was written by Popeye or Bluto? This little book is an assertion in favor of poetry and against credentials." Jim was likely the Bluto of the equation.

It was an idea that liberated Jim, in a sense, from thoughts about the business of literature—the "credentials"—that sometimes inevitably occupied his mind. And it also freed him from the limitations and burdens of being Jim Harrison. A larger collection of their haiku, *Braided Creek: A Conversation in Poetry*, would be published two years later by Copper Canyon.

—

That fall, Jim and Linda were in Montana, scouting for possible properties and homes, and Jim managed to get out on the Yellowstone for his yearly fishing trip. The fishing had been poor for five days straight, but it picked up on September 11, 2001, of all days. Jim and Lahren and Steve fished the river that day. "Everyone was pretty quiet," recalled Lahren.

"I was fairly gasping when I fled the house for the river," Jim wrote in his memoir, almost contemporaneously, "the brain whirling with tears and shed blood." When he stepped off the McKenzie drift boat at the end of the day, the "consciousness of what had happened blossomed with the charm of the mushroom cloud we had all memorized as children." Matthiessen was flying to Montana that same day to join them, but his plane was forced to land in Michigan, along with all other commercial flights. He wouldn't make it out to Livingston for another two days.

The Raw and the Cooked: Adventures of a Roving Gourmand came out two months later in November 2001. Grove had toyed with the idea of subtitling it "Adventures of an Infamous Gourmand"—both were fitting. The book was a compilation of food essays drawn from Jim's *Smart* and *Esquire* columns, as well as a few from *Men's Journal*, *Brick*, the *Kermit Lynch Wine Merchant* newsletter, and food-related correspondence between Jim and Oberlé. Jim had traveled to Oxford, Mississippi, to have his cover photo taken at the Ajax Diner. Taken by Maude Schuyler Clay, a Mississippi-born photographer, the picture shows a happy-looking Jim Harrison seated at a table surrounded by sundry Southern dishes. The collection's humor and joie de vivre would come as a welcome distraction for Harrison readers from news of the recent tragedy. Wherever he went, Jim would tell Terry McDonell, he was asked by thousands of people if he was ever going to write about food again. This book would give them something to chew on.

"I absolutely love *The Raw and the Cooked*," McGuane wrote to Jim in October. "I think you'll have success with it too. I also think Grove-Atlantic did a great job of making it a delightful object. Anyway, it's so high-spirited and heedless I found it irresistible." Many readers felt the same—irresistible was a good word.

Jim was pleased by the book. After rereading a few of the pieces in preparation for an NPR interview, he laughed over his own colorful freewriting style. The best press for the book was perhaps, again oddly, *The Wall Street Journal*, which referred to Jim as the "Henry Miller of food writing"—high praise for him, given his love of Miller. It wasn't the only comparison either. Jeffrey A. Trachtenberg argued that Jim, by virtue of his talent, could "sit at the same table as A. J. Liebling and M.F.K. Fisher." That situated Jim in the upper echelons of food writing.

There was no formal book tour for *The Raw and the Cooked*, mostly at Jim's urging and for some of the usual reasons: "A tour instills self-importance," he remarked to Hottensen, "the arch enemy of good writing, because wherever you go you are the center of attention which is further amplified by crowds, newspapers, reviews, and interviews," all of which adds up to a "misbalance far from the heart's affection and the truth of the imagination."

Although he did not mention it to Hottensen, Jim's health may have had something to do with it. While he traveled to France that same month, free and clear of all publicity encumbrances, he suffered a terrible spike in his blood pressure soon after arriving, and following two weeks of fear and discomfort, flew to San Francisco to see a cardiologist and get an exhaustive physical. In fact, he had been concerned about his blood pressure even before he left for the trip. It would turn out that his doctor discovered a contraindication with his medications that had apparently been at least partly responsible.

"Heart, lungs, kidneys, liver etc fine," he informed McGuane of the results, without further elaboration, a few days before his sixty-fourth birthday. "They wouldn't let me smoke during nuclear renal test of 3½ hours. Fucking Californians."

—

In January 2002, Jim and Linda hosted the publisher Will Hearst at their casita in Patagonia. They had a wonderful dinner of doves, quail, and antelope, including a dessert course of flan, and they drank a panoply of fine wines brought by Hearst: Clos de la Roche, Margaux, Lafite, and Montrachet. Jim and Hearst had more in common than literature and publishing and were on their way to becoming fast friends. The world-class wines helped him to write better, or so Jim later joked with the folks at Grove.

He was almost finished with *Off to the Side* and had sent the first two hundred pages to Hundley—and only to her. Jim had become frustrated with Grove's copyeditor, who he thought had no business correcting his stylistic idiosyncrasies, like his use (or nonuse) of commas, and he found her overly enthusiastic. He knew he would need editorial help with the memoir, so he asked that Hundley be the only person at Grove to see the manuscript through the process. "In Hollywood, everyone wants to be involved with what they call creative input, a loathsome word," and he did not want to replicate that. He admitted to wandering too much in the memoir, and he was struggling to keep focused in "a life relatively without focus, except in the arena of the imagination."

When Jim traveled to Santa Fe in February for a reading and public interview conducted by his friend Peter Lewis, the topic of the memoir inevitably came up. People wanted to know. Dressed in a black shirt and his signature brown leather vest, Jim smoked freely on stage and sipped from a bottle of Domaine Tempier in front of a crowd of over one thousand people. "I'm not writing one of those tell-all things," Jim said of the book, "I mean, tell some."

It was a question shared by his friends and family. How much of his life did Jim plan to share? they asked with some trepidation. He had already assured his friends that he would leave out any sexual adventurism and indiscretions. When he first brought up the idea to his family, Jamie had asked him nervously, "You're *not* writing a memoir?"

"Yes, I guess I am," Jim replied. "This is why you drink nice wine too." He agreed (jokingly) to send her to Europe on publication day and told her not to worry. "I'm not writing *that* kind of memoir." In fairness, Jamie had also urged him to be honest.

Jim's efforts to dredge up the past would coincide—or rather, collide—with the move to Montana, which the Harrisons completed in April 2002. "I am here, so is Linda, as of yesterday," he announced to McGuane upon his arrival. "We came in late and stayed at a Bozeman [hotel] in deference to the raging snowstorm which made the landing dicey indeed." A truck with their belongings would follow. But the snow had been the least of their worries, as the move had been full of daunting hurdles. The farmhouse had taken a long time to sell, due in large part to the uneasy aftermath of 9/11, and then the Harrisons had been involved in a nasty surveying dispute with their neighbor.

Leaving behind his home of thirty-five years was easier than Jim had expected and mysteriously unemotional, or so he told himself. He chalked it up to the fact that he could no longer afford to buy his farm, since the price per acre had gone up so much in the county. His heart had moved out long ago, he would say. There were too many corporate types and rich people moving into the area and too much money talk, an idea he would express even in his poetry. When folks at the Bluebird Tavern talk of "Lucent Lucent Lucent," he wrote in "Bars," he goes to Dick's Pour House, "where actual working men talk of fishing, / crops, bankrupt orchards, the fact that the moon / is a bit smaller than it used to be. No one says Lucent."

Still, in an article Jim wrote for a local magazine the following January, he told a different story. When earlier asked, as he often was ("several times a day"), why he was moving, Jim said it had only to do with his daughters and grandchildren, not the area. That was the "only immediately suitable or acceptable answer." But he knew, he wrote, that that answer concealed a certain amount of pain, "an emptiness or vacuum that will present plenty of room for future homesickness." That's a natural pain, he explained, after living in Michigan for sixty-three years. He would keep a presence in Leelanau, if only out of his own fear of moving away. His business address would remain as Leelanau County, and his assistant of twenty years, Joyce Bahle, who lived near their old farmhouse, would continue to run nearly all of his life except the writing, hunting, and fishing. Montana had become the subject of his daughters' dreams, as northern Michigan once had for him, and he would follow them there out of "simple human, family affection." His affection for Michigan, however, would stay with him: "On thousands of walks throughout Leelanau County I learned my own life."

McGuane seemed to heartily approve of Jim's decision, and he sensed there was more to it than price per acreage. "Welcome to the fair Yellowstone valley!" he chimed that April. "I'd bet that the painlessness of leaving the 'farm' has less to do with the deterioration of the neighborhood than it's just being time to move and do something else. I think you've done just the right thing, indeed it's full of rightness. As thoroughly as I love this ranch, I can imagine moving on, especially in the direction of my grandchildren. I suppose the last look down the driveway would be awful. But much is awful."

By June, sure enough, Jim had begun feeling the emotional effects of the move. Naturally, he felt dislocated, and it did not help that he was wandering down memory lane daily as he worked on the memoir, revisiting every aspect of his life from his childhood in Reed City onward. He found himself making lists of what he now missed: the farm, the pond by the garden that had been built for Linda, the baby grouse in the mulberry tree, the heron that sometimes walked up the steps and sidewalk to their front door, and the fact that "looking at the Manitous on a winter walk"—islands in Lake Michigan that form part of Sleeping Bear Dunes National Lakeshore—"is worth any self-help book save the Bible."

Paradise Valley, Montana, as the name suggests, would be good compensation, however, and Jim and Linda loved their new home. They now had a two-story, four-bedroom house on about ten acres of land along the Old Yellowstone Trail. Adjacent to the main house was another tiny one, like the granary in Michigan but nicer, which Jim used as a writing studio. Beside his metal desk, which faced the wall rather than the view of the mountains, he kept a twin bed for taking naps. Flanked by the cordillera of the Absaroka in the east and the foothills of the Gallatin Range in the west, the house faced the Yellowstone River and the almost eleven-thousand-foot peak of Black Mountain. Junipers, ashes, willows, spruce, and cottonwoods stood by the roadside out front. Behind the house, Hogback Ridge arced westward beside Antelope Butte. It was an idyllic setting.

—

Off to the Side came out in November 2002, another of Jim's books that would make the French bestseller list and become a *New York Times* Notable Book of the Year. Grove (via Hottensen) described it to reviewers as a "testament to a life—albeit only to middle age so far—lived fully and deeply, a celebration of nature, childhood, love and marriage, and literature." The road to the book's success had been bumpy, however. Amy Hundley had done her usual "dance of the seven hundred commas," in her words, referring to Jim's idiosyncratic use of the mark, but there were larger problems to deal with. At Jim's request, Bednarik had read the uncorrected proof as late as July, and he had worried that the manuscript still needed a lot of work, as he conveyed to Grove. "It's a challenging book to edit," he wrote to Hundley, "especially working with someone who resists editing. But the book (as far as this sympathetic reader is concerned) really needs work . . . But if he doesn't see it, someone needs to make him see it."

Bednarik relished Jim's writing and thought him brilliant, but he knew that Jim did not have the patience to work it all out. Certainly, no one doubted Jim's work ethic, but as he had gotten older, his attention to the granular had begun to wane. Jim would turn sixty-five in December. Even at his best, as Dwight Garner had once observed,

Jim had never been "the most exacting writer on the planet." He was, for instance, prone to repeating "the same adjectives (notably 'otiose,' a longtime favorite of his)," but these were minor sins compared to the many wonderful things about his writing.

Rather than confront Jim directly, at least at first, something he knew would not work out well, Bednarik pursued back channels to express his concerns. Jim's drinking and poor health often made him less patient and increasingly diminished his attention to the nitty-gritty, including dates and names and issues of continuity and word repetition, he told Bahle. Hottensen and Hundley had agreed with him. "But somebody somewhere has to have the balls and/or ovaries to have the conversation [with Jim]." Bednarik insisted. "Believe me, it is 10000 times easier for me to keep my mouth shut but I care about Jim's work."

The answer to editing this book and future ones would take a village, so to speak, and it would rest largely on Bednarik's and Hundley's close relationship with Jim. For future books, they would typically fly to Montana to work with him side by side on edits and revisions. That process would expedite things, and despite the long days cooped up together, it would prove less taxing on Jim. It would also fall to Bahle, who would assist Jim whenever she could with the editing process, drawing his attention, as best she could, to whatever needed work.

As with many of his books, Jim had divided *Off to the Side* into three sections: "Early Life," "Seven Obsessions," and "The Rest of Life." Each of the sections he then split into titled chapters, seven of which addressed his obsessions, as he called them: (1) "Alcohol," (2) "Stripping," (3) "Hunting, Fishing (and Dogs)," (4) "Private Religion," (5) "A Short Tour de France," (6) "The Road," and (7) "Nature and Natives." The title, *Off to the Side*, referred to the necessary position of a writer, in Jim's mind: hidden and well off to the side, observing. Much of the book reads like Jim's journalism, particularly his "Seven Obsessions" section, which explores its topics with similar humor and wit (most of these chapters were first published by *Men's Journal* under different names), though none of these chapters are particularly personal or candid.

In the more strictly autobiographical sections of the book, Jim proceeded in a roughly chronological manner with plenty of digressions. It was his strong preference not to write anything overly chronological, as he had once advised Sam Lawrence about his own memoir project: "The most boring memoirs are those that are merely chronological and have an aura of the ABCDEFG about them. I think if you stuck to your high points, i.e., the most vivid periods of your life you would be better off . . . In all of our lives there are both brilliant periods and dead spots, the latter of which are called 'clean lifts' in Hollywood."

Jim had followed his own advice, mostly, and stuck to what he saw as the high points: his childhood, time on the road, the deaths of his father and sister, Boston, Kingsley, Stony Brook, MSU, and so on. That almost half of the last section, "The Rest of Life," was devoted to Hollywood rather than to poetry and fiction was perhaps attributable to his belief that everything he had to say was already in his writing. In truth, Jim spent remarkably little time covering the things that were arguably the most important to him. He rarely discussed his family, and when he did, it was only obliquely. "There is no self-destructiveness without the destruction of others," he wrote at one point, speaking of drinking. "We are not alone." But there was no mention of who or how. As his friend Bob DeMott once observed of an interview with Jim, "Much of him remain[ed] protected and set apart for his family and for his work," and that rang true for *Off to the Side*.

Jim would do an eleven-city book tour during October and November of 2002. A highlight included a signing in Marquette, Michigan, at the Landmark Inn, which had designated one of its rooms the "Jim Harrison Suite." "They'll have to decorate it with empty wine bottles and used condoms," he had joked when he heard the news. After appearances in San Francisco and Austin, he and Linda headed off to Patagonia for the winter.

—

In April 2002, Copper Canyon published Jim and Kooser's *Braided Creek: A Conversation in Poetry*. Like *A Conversation*, their earlier chapbook, *Braided Creek* had its origin in Jim and Kooser's correspondence. Kooser took over the initial process of selecting and arranging the poems, though Jim thought the collection should start out with two pages of "Strong Ones and end thusly," or so Denise Levertov told him thirty-seven years ago.

Kooser had all of the poems typed out and, to establish their order in the book, had laid them in pairs down the entire length of his house and moved them around until they felt right: "Worked 12 hours yesterday on the arrangement, and a couple of hours this morning," he informed Jim. "Cut up the print run you sent back and spread the individual poems out from the north wall of the downstairs bedroom and to the south end of the living room, two long rows, shuffled and shuffled them all day and then taped them together."

Kooser had tried to suggest some themes "running under the surface" of the collection, and he tried to separate the long poems and mix them up with shorter ones. He wanted the reader to feel that the whole piece had "a subtle thread to it, and comes around toward a full circle at the end." Kooser made little attempt to alternate his and Jim's poems, and sometimes several poems by the same author ran on in a row. "Anyone starting the book figuring that he or she can figure out who's who," Kooser noted, "will wind up pissing down their leg."

It was Jim's idea to not provide attributions to the poems, Kooser insisted, but it's clear they were both invested in the idea. While Kooser's poems are more imagistic and figurative than Jim's, whose poems are closer to conversational speech—"strong speech," said Kooser—it's difficult to tell the difference between them in the book. To have a name on every poem, Jim thought, called far too much attention to the poet and distracted from the poetry. Years later, there were a few poems that he could not identify if he tried. That anonymity led to some funny results, like one critic who argued that anyone familiar with Harrison and Kooser could easily tell which poems were whose. He then cited one poem as an example, claiming it as Harrison's, but of course it was Kooser's.

The two dedicated the book to Dan Gerber, whom Jim described in a letter to Copper Canyon as an influence and friend, and Chatham provided (once again) the cover art (*Afternoon on Sweetgrass Creek*). In the brief "About the Authors" section, Jim suggested simply, "This book is a rather avian triangulation of their brotherhood."

Jim had initially brought the idea for the book to Copper Canyon, and it was the first of Kooser's works the press would publish. Jim had also suggested the title. He wanted the poems to be interwoven, much "like the myriad little channels in [the] Platte River." Bednarik had wanted it to be a smaller-sized book, "to make it abundantly portable. I know I want to carry it in my satchel for those poetic spaces during the day." It would go on to be extensively reviewed, especially in "metro dailies, from Kansas City to Wichita to Philadelphia to Houston to Memphis, newspapers that aren't really widely known for reviewing poetry." By October, Copper Canyon sold out of the first printing of *Braided Creek*, including a 276-copy run of a signed limited edition.

Copper Canyon had agreed to publish Kooser's next book of poems, and it hoped to grow his readership through the publication of *Braided Creek*. Jim's readership was significantly larger at the time, and as executive editor Micheal Wiegers had written to Jim in February 2002, "size does matter." Wiegers wanted to use the cowritten book to introduce Jim's readers to Kooser's work, and he planned to bring out Kooser's book of poetry six months later. That book, Kooser's *Delights & Shadows*, would win the Pulitzer Prize for poetry in 2005, and by that time, Kooser had become the poet laureate of the United States. It was the kind of success and recognition that had passed Jim by, large readership or not.

By March 2003, Jim was about halfway through his newest novel, *True North*, and he had become "a maniac (nothing new)" about drafting the manuscript by May 1. The pace of work would leave him unable to shake a post-novel fatigue and the feeling that he desperately needed a break. He would visit the cabin, but even that provided little solace because he and Linda had decided to sell it, and he knew it was coming. As Jim put it, "I'd rather sell my kidneys to a republican."

In August, John and Rebecca visited Montana, and Matthiessen arrived soon afterward for fishing. John had recently retired from his position as dean of libraries at the University of Arkansas, and this visit would be his last. John would die a few months later. The remainder of the year, with a few bright exceptions, would be a downward spiral. That same month, August, a rattlesnake in the Harrisons' yard bit Jim's dog, Rose, in the face, and she lost sight in her right eye. "A fang was stuck in the corner," Jim told McGuane. "Now it jogs like a milky sparrow in its socket. Amores perros." And then, in September, Linda had a terrible asthma attack at a fundraiser and a month later landed in the hospital.

Jim would continue to write through it all that fall. Fortunately, he was working on yet another Brown Dog novella, "The Summer He Didn't Die," which managed to brighten his mood a bit: "When I fully enter his problems, mine are somewhat absolved." But nothing could shake the lingering fear he felt for Linda.

That summer, Jim had become the food editor of Michael Ondaatje's literary journal, *Brick*, and he was thrilled to be back at the food writing. And then, in November 2003, he traveled to France for "A Really Big Lunch"—the thirty-seven-course meal designed by Oberlé and prepared by Chef Marc Meneau and his staff at L'Espérance in Saint-Père-sous-Vézelay. Jim would chronicle the events (held on November 17) for *The New Yorker*, though the piece would not appear in the magazine for almost a year. He would celebrate the experience and his own transgressive brand of excess involving both pleasure and digestive pain. "Is there an interior logic to overeating," Jim asked, "or does gluttony, like sex, wander around in a messy void, utterly resistant to our attempts to make sense of it?"

Jim would note briefly in the essay that certain quarrels had arisen over the lunch and that some attendees thought the food and service disappointing. To Treisman at *The New Yorker*, Jim admitted to being in a "ticklish situation right now between 2 friends over the event as a 'scandal' occurred." Oberlé insisted that the meal had been "a fake."

Meneau had been an exceptional chef for many years, said Oberlé, and the two of them had been close friends. Meneau had cooked an elaborate meal for Oberlé's fortieth birthday. For his fiftieth, Oberlé and Meneau recreated the Roman banquet from *Satyricon*. Jim admired Meneau's cooking, and he and Oberlé (and even Linda) had had amazing meals at L'Espérance. But by the time of the big lunch, Meneau's restaurant had gone downhill, and according to Oberlé, Meneau owed a lot of money to a lot of people.

As for the big lunch, Meneau made changes to the planned menu and doubled the prices, adding all sorts of extra expenses to the bill, and he invited his own friends to join the meal—many came just to meet Jim—though Oberlé and Valdène were paying for it all. Worst of all, the food was poorly prepared, said Oberlé. It was apparently so bad that two people who worked in Meneau's kitchen were scandalized enough to later quit in protest. The lunch would put an end to Oberlé and Meneau's friendship, and afterward Oberlé told everyone he knew about what had happened. Meneau would go bankrupt and close the restaurant soon afterward.

Jim said he declined to criticize the meal, rightly so, because he had not paid for it.

Later, other scandals emerged around the lunch. At one point, Meneau had reportedly tried to force himself on Valdène's daughter, Valerie, who was serving as an intern for the chef, and she apparently fought off his advances. No one ever told Valdène, for fear he might kill Meneau.

A month later, the meal and the scandals seemed but a distant memory. On December 15, while Jim and Linda were in Patagonia, they received the devastating news. John had died of a heart attack at the age of sixty-seven. John's memorial was held on December 19 at St. Paul's

Episcopal Church in Fayetteville. Jim had relied on John as a steady, constant figure in his life. He had been Jim's "lifelong companion," as the Reverend Lowell Grisham, who presided over the memorial, said to Jim, and John had served as a kind of father figure to him in Winfield's absence. John had helped, like Linda, to anchor him to earth.

As Jamie would later say of John's loss, "Somehow feels in hindsight like the beginning of the end."

20

MORTALITY IS GRAVITY

(2004–2007)

It's after midnight in Montana.
I test the thickness of the universe, its resilience
to carry us further than any of us wish to go.
We shed our shapes slowly like moving water,
which ends up as it will so utterly far from home.

The mid-2000s would be astonishingly productive for Jim, so much so that Morgan Entrekin at Grove would eventually insist that they stop publishing books for a time and space them out. The market had become saturated with Jim Harrison. In January 2004, Jim was sixty-six years old, and the older he got, the more desperately and doggedly he seemed to write. He knew that time was running out, that there was, looming somewhere over the Montana horizon, a permanent deadline. These were the years when Jim would set his affairs in order. He had not only the creative impulse to write but the muscle memory and reflex and repetition of a lifetime of literary labor, as well as his continuing desire for acceptance and recognition. Then, too, he also had the perceived need to accumulate money for his family while he still could. Between 2004 and 2007, Jim would publish more works than at any other time in his life: the novels *True North* and *Returning to Earth*; a collection of novellas, *The Summer He Didn't Die*; and a collection of poetry, *Saving Daylight*—all in this four-year span. He'd also begin new projects; write a third novel, *The English Major*; publish almost fifty pieces of nonfiction (some reprints and excerpts), including ones for his food column in *Brick*; and write a short work of fiction—*short* being the real challenge.

"I wrote my first real short story," Jim announced to McGuane at the beginning of 2004. "I started it in August and finished it yesterday. I'm a master of divagation so it was real hard to practice this peculiar economy." Jim had his eye on *The New Yorker*.*

Jim had earlier submitted his Brown Dog novella, "The Summer He Didn't Die," for consideration to the magazine, but Deborah Treisman didn't think it could be easily cut back to work at magazine-length and had urged him to fulfill his one-time promise to submit a short story. (Her maximum word count was roughly twelve thousand, and that was only for the special fiction issue; the average length of fiction in their pages was five to six thousand words.) Jim had first met Treisman at the *New Yorker* offices when he was there meeting with then–fiction editor Bill Buford, and the two had had lunch occasionally since then, when Jim was in the city.

"Father Daughter," the short story (the title an echo of Turgenev's *Fathers and Sons*), was an arduous task for Jim because it "allowed no room to show off, dress up, mark time, fool around," as he explained to Treisman. "Since we've all read a thousand stories it was strange to have my mind turn to earlier models—Mansfield, Chekhov, Cheever."

Jim had wanted to make the story longer—eighty-five pages longer, to be exact—and he thought that in terms of the time he spent writing it, it was the least profitable project in twenty-seven years, except for his service to "the Bride of Hell, poetry." He doubted privately that he would ever write another one. "It pays better to write 'How I caught a modest Fish' for Field and Stream."

Jim had always thought of his novellas as elongated short fiction, with three to a book, but there was something different about the short story. He was most comfortable with the compression of poetry, and his

* Jim had published a short story once before. His "No Man Is in Iceland" appeared in 1987 in *Caliban* 2, 70–74.

fiction could pack a lot in a little space, but the canvas of short fiction was simply too small for his digressive narratives and structure.

In February, Jim spent a week in Mérida, Mexico, as a getaway. After John's funeral, he had caught another flu and a severe chest cold, and he was in a "brother-death-slump," as he described it. In the Yucatán, he swam in jungle pools and ate roasted hog fish, wild turkey, a baby pig, and octopus ceviche for breakfast, all in a somewhat depressive state, but it helped him to get his mind off John. Still, he had managed to write some twenty new poems, and he returned from the Yucatán with good news: *The New Yorker* had agreed to publish his short story. It brought Jim "a silly amount of pleasure" to sell one to them. Treisman loved the story and planned to run it as soon as possible.

"Father Daughter," the second of only three short stories Jim would ever publish, appeared in the March 29, 2004, issue. While the story explores the strained and tentative relationship of a middle-aged father and his daughter—Norton and Laura—at its heart, it's a tale of loss, change, time, and age.

Treisman thought the story cried out for the present tense, partly because it unfolded gradually and information was "revealed too informally perhaps, for the finality of past tense," but she recognized that Jim might not like that approach. She also thought the story should end with Norton, the father, rather than his daughter.

"O prescient one, how did you know I didn't like purely present tense stories?" Jim asked. "They're always too breathless." But he agreed with Treisman about the ending of the story, and he worked up several versions of endings and sent them to her, noting the one he liked best. It ended on the following line: "Right now he wasn't sure if he was landing or taking off but was confident that he could proceed with grace."

Treisman liked the new concluding paragraph, but she still questioned the last line. She thought it too confident for the character of Norton and suggested swapping out its second half for a separate sentence with a more qualified note: "He was simply *trying* to proceed with grace."

Jim liked it: "How many times I have said, 'Simply trying with no confidence!'"

—

A week before "Father Daughter" appeared, *True North* was published in the United States by Grove. Once again, Bourgois brought out an edition in France a few weeks earlier. Grove's first run was thirty-seven thousand copies, a hearty number, but Jim felt so unsure of the book that he didn't bother sending it to McGuane, even though he thought it more purely a novel than anything else he had written. He had tried to restrain himself from his tendency toward divagation and the parenthetical.

Jim first had the idea for *True North*, a story about a "UP predatory family," fifteen years earlier. It came to him one day during a long walk with Dan Gerber on the Kingston Plains in the UP amid about twenty thousand acres of white pine stumps. At one point, Gerber said, "I'm glad Grandpa didn't do this," speaking of the clear-cutting, and Jim began wondering how a young man might have felt if his own family had done such a thing, had been so predatory and rapacious. How might a family deal with that inheritance?

The almost complete eradication of white pines across Michigan had long been on Jim's mind, and in a funny way, the story brought him full circle, back to the day of his birth in a lumberman's former mansion. It evoked, too, the humbler work of his own grandfather, Carty Harrison, as a cook on a logging boat. And it seemed timely, given what Jim saw as the imponderable greed in America during the previous twenty-five years and the dot-com bubble.

True North tells the story of David Burkett and his sister Cynthia, who at the age of fourteen takes up with a Finnish Native American. Both David and Cynthia grapple with how to deal with their family's destructive legacy, a depraved wealthy father, and a pill-popping alcoholic mother benumbed to it all.

Jim had spent a great deal of time in the UP doing research for the novel, including at the Peter White Library in Marquette, and as he had with *Dalva* and *The Road Home*, he found the subject at times overwhelming. "U.P. history is so naked," he wrote to McGuane. "Re research, a quote: 'Mich. woke in 1915 and found itself the not so proud owner of 13 million acres of stumps.' Think of all those rivers before they were log gouged! Anyway, I'm flooded by guilt producing galleys."

Jim sensed this novel had the potential to reach a broader audience than his previous books, but he downplayed his expectations. His old friend Bill Corbett, who reviewed it, smartly recognized it as "an elegy for the Michigan country in which Harrison had spent more than 60 years and thus a continuation of his memoir by other means." David Burkett, he observed, shares the history that Jim once wrote about in his early "Sketch for a Job-Application Blank," along with Jim's youthful religious ardor.

The book tour for *True North* began in early May in Hailey, Idaho, (notably, the same town where Ezra Pound was born) and passed through another eighteen cities. Unsurprisingly, and with characteristic overstatement, Jim described the thirty-six-day tour as "fundamentally inhumane," but he made the best of it. In New York City, he bookended his five-night stay with dinners with Mario Batali, a new friend, and Judy Hottensen. (Jim had once had a wonderful meal at Batali's Babbo—easily the best he had had at an American restaurant, he noted—which set in motion their friendship.) In between, Entrekin threw a cocktail party for Jim at Elaine's, where the guest list included Paul Auster, Eliot Weinberger, and Tom Brokaw, whom Jim knew through McGuane. An eleven-day book tour in France followed that fall ("ball smashing").

Reviews of the book wound up being mixed, and after all the on-site promotion, he was angry to learn that Grove had apparently not purchased ads in his typical reviews and newspapers. *True North* had "whistled ad-less into the void," he thought. Much of it boiled down to miscommunication and apparently an internal mix-up at the publishing house. Jim had made clear that he thought ads in *The New York Times Book Review* were a waste of money—"a vanity plate," as he called it—largely because many of his readers west of the Mississippi did not follow the literature media of the East Coast. Instead, he had urged Eric Price at Grove to advertise in smaller publications, like *The Bloomsbury Review, The Ruminator* out of Minneapolis, the *Los Angeles Times*, and the Denver papers.

Hottensen thought Grove had done a "damn good job publishing TRUE NORTH without advertising," and she noted that the book had strong sales—"stronger than the previous books." They had managed to find the novel's market in the Midwest and throughout the country, she thought, in no small part due to the book tour. Jim eventually calmed down, but it felt to him like an opportunity lost, and he would hold a grudge, still referring to the incident years later. "Life is short," he wrote to Entrekin and Hottensen. "True North is the only True North I'll ever write." Whether Jim was right or not about the advertisements, his frustration had become a motif in his life: He would never shake the feeling (sometimes with merit and based on past experience) that the business side of publishing had somehow held him back from success.

Nonetheless, Jim thought Grove was "as good as it gets," and he felt himself well out of the world of corporate publishing. As he told Dattila, they were lucky to be with them.

In October 2004, Jim received some distressing medical news, the kind that, once again, reminds one of the shortness of life. He was diagnosed with type 2 diabetes, after which he committed to a "radical self-designed diet" that apparently backfired and helped to wreck his stomach. The latter eventually resulted in an ambulance ride to the hospital for a suspected heart attack and further diagnoses of gastritis, duodenitis, and esophagitis (these were related to his special diet, as he said then, but as he would later admit, they also derived from his overall lifestyle). The conditions, which would take several months to begin to clear up, caused significant discomfort. His doctor insisted that he cut way back on his drinking. "All of which has created a sense of exile," Jim would report months later, "and I have not fully inhabited this new country where there is no serious food and drink."

To Sullivan, Jim wrote that "a downshift is in order . . . Less, less, less wine." He was permitted only four ounces of his "beloved red" a day until he got "the big D" under control, which, he felt, ruined the bottle before it was even consumed. There was nothing worse than leaving an unfinished bottle all alone overnight.

Jim felt understandably compelled to broadcast the news. Along with his other conditions, diabetes would affect his life in substantial ways and require some explanation. To Hundley and Hottensen, he blamed it for his "fatigue, anger, anguish," and he asked them to put on "kid gloves and only touch me with pom-poms." To Dominique Bourgois, Christian's wife, he mourned the loss of "[his] lovers—Bandol, Vacqueyras, Gigondas etc who have left me. Is life worth it without this love? Time will tell."

Jim's doctor thought the book touring had contributed significantly to his diabetes, and it was hardly surprising news. Jim inevitably ate more and drank more on tour (performing "Jim Harrison" for his fans) and slept less. Added to that were the physical and emotional stress of interviews, appearances, dinners, parties, and the like, what his doctor had called the "fright and flight," which caused extreme stress and blood-sugar spikes. Then again, as Jim fessed up, he had already been on the "mortal edge for quite a while," and food and drink had long been his main sport—one he played daily.

In the last seven years or so, since he quit working in Hollywood, his drinking had become "truly problematical," as he confessed to McGuane. It was an unusual admission for Jim and particularly so to McGuane, to whom he often preferred to project an image of self-control. He had recently cautioned his readers that what people say about alcohol is almost always "deeply suspect," a fact he knew only too well about himself: Jim would regularly lie about the amount of his drinking. He'd taper down for a time and then relapse. He'd sneak drinks. He'd pour bottles of booze down the drain. At times, drinking seemed to him a slow form of suicide.

To compound things, Jim had come to resent the business of

literature, the "lit biz," more than ever. "I don't seem to believe in Literature anymore," he shared with McGuane. "I believe in certain novels and poems, certain authors. What we think of Literature comes from outside, a kind of consensus of folks outside the creation of it."

Months shy of his sixty-eighth birthday, Jim had the overwhelming feeling, as he had in the past, that he had somehow failed to achieve literary success, at least in the United States, and everything besides the actual composition had become an irritation. Even his food writing, he thought, was "too off brand" to be broadly accepted, and he felt "totally 'off to the side,'" as he put it, in this case, marginalized by the establishment. And yet it felt good to meet people who thought otherwise. And yet it seemed silly to complain of being ignored, he knew, when he was receiving almost a thousand dollars a page for his writing and could afford to extend his daughter a car loan. In the aftermath of *True North*, and in light of his serious health concerns, the lingering depressions and darkness, and the loss of his brother, he had grown increasingly bitter and self-absorbed.

When John died, Jim had a moment of clarity about his literary ambition. "One of the central, if not the central, urges for me to succeed," he realized, "was [John's] concern that I had been somewhat overlooked." John had become a kind of stepfather to him, as he put it, and he wanted to make him proud. Now, the core of his personal hopes came down to money. With John gone, he had determined to make enough of it to quit most of the things in his life except for "fishing and Virgil's rustication." But Jim would never let go of the work itself, nor completely of the ambition. Those grooves had simply been worn too deeply.

—

Jim was busy at work on *Returning to Earth*, a sequel to *True North*, and his pace was the slowest he'd ever written. He planned this to be his last work of fiction, or so he told friends and perhaps even himself, and anything more could be "engineered by [his] heirs after his demise." If he was being honest, he had vastly underestimated himself: He would go on to write three more novels and more than half a dozen novellas. So much for Virgilian rustication. He would settle instead for more trips to France, even if they were work related.

During the spring of 2005, Jim visited the Mediterranean seaport town of Collioure in southwestern France, just north of the Spanish border. He imagined writing a series of essays that would document pilgrimages to the graves of his literary heroes, like Antonio Machado, who died in Collioure. Jim concocted a plan to search the town for Machado's missing manuscripts, a valise of poems that the poet lost after escaping Franco's Spain with his family in 1939. An admittedly quixotic plan, Jim was "deadly serious" about it, as he told Michael Wiegers at Copper Canyon.

An even bigger incentive for Jim was to visit with Christine Campadieu, a winemaker in Collioure. Jim had met Campadieu and her then-husband Vincent Cantié through Kermit Lynch, who imported Campadieu's wine, and Jim had written a nice piece about their winery, Domaine La Tour Vielle, for Lynch's newsletter. Jim had watched and rewatched *Wine from the Heart*, the documentary about the village and winery, and it had captured his imagination. On different occasions, Jim and Campadieu would travel together in Spain and around France, and he would sometimes refer to her as his French daughter. Campadieu was the same age as Jamie.

Before he left for France, Jim had finished writing his collection of novellas *The Summer He Didn't Die*, which included the autobiographical "Tracking," written in the third person, which he referred to as a "re-version" of his memoir. "Tracking" retells much of *Off to the Side*, and although Jim wrote it to correct lacunae, as he'd say, the fictionalized version didn't add a whole lot to the story. But it kept Jim replaying his life, so to speak, remembering his people and places and his loved and lost ones. It also added a novella to the collection; Jim knew as well as any writer how to package and repurpose his research and ideas in almost mercenary fashion.

At times, the book reads almost like an adult fairy tale, akin to *The Boy Who Ran to the Woods*, and the writing of it made him wonder how he was "always rushing ahead of [himself] and trying to eat all aspects of the world," a clear-eyed acknowledgment of his volcanic appetites. The process brought to mind the experience of watching a film of his own life, which he would write about in the poem "The Movie." Building on one of his favorite sayings, "There are no truths, only stories," Jim reflected:

> It's not truth that keeps us alive
> but invention, no actual past but the stories
> we've devised to cover our disappearing
> asses.

The Summer He Didn't Die made it to bookstores by mid-July. The namesake novella continued the Brown Dog series. Jim had joked that he once told his psychologist that Brown Dog was his alter ego, and his doctor replied, "No, it's closer than that." It was perhaps more accurate to say that Brown Dog was Jim's UP Freudian id, stripped of family and other responsibilities and set loose in the North Woods. The comic mode appealed to Jim, and his readers loved the books. Letters about Brown Dog accounted for a good share of his fan mail.

"The true subject here is not really autobiography," Jean Thompson wrote of the collection in *The New York Times*, referring partly to the inclusion of "Tracking," "but the mystery of physical place and how it marks consciousness." What was perhaps most remarkable about the book was Jim's return, yet again, to the novella form; he had now published fifteen, which amounted to roughly one novella every twenty months since the release of *Legends of the Fall* in 1979. No writer had worked with the form as often and as successfully as he had. As Thompson noted, one of the pleasures of reading Jim Harrison's fifth collection of novellas "is the reminder that this intermediate, unloved and ostensibly unpublishable form is capable of great range and vitality."

—

A few months after the release of *The Summer He Didn't Die*, Jim ended his professional relationship with Bob Dattila. It was in keeping with Jim's plan to better attend to his personal and financial matters, but it would be a difficult breakup. The two had worked together for more than thirty years. Dattila had stopped putting forth full effort in his role as agent, Jim thought, and he complained that Dattila had made a mess of things by not keeping accurate records. Dattila didn't fully disagree with him; he was tired of the work.

What bothered Dattila was that Jim ended the relationship with a letter—and only a letter—rather than in person, which was arguably better than an angry confrontation, the way things were heading. That didn't make it much easier for Jim, who found the writing of it "absurdly difficult with outlines, drafts, etc," though his intentions remained "firm as a railroad rail." It carried both legal and personal implications. Still, Jim was anxious for a clean break; he would work instead with Stephen Sheppard, a named partner in a New York City law firm, who would function as his agent.

Jim mailed the letter to Dattila in July. It began simply, "Dear Bob, We're parting company." Jim would elaborate on his reasons only briefly. He hadn't been happy with the way things had been going for quite some time, he explained, and following the death of his brother, who died at Jim's then current age, he felt compelled to get his affairs in order. He was one of only three Harrisons left from his family: Jim, David, and Mary. He would no longer have "an agent as such."

The letter was notably impersonal, and Dattila was hurt by it. He had expected more, really a conversation, after so many years. Dattila would work with Sheppard on the transition, though, and Sheppard published notices in *Publishers Weekly* and other trade papers. But Jim and

Dattila's friendship would never be the same again, and they wouldn't talk for more than a year afterward. They would eventually bump into each other at Glenn's Bar in Livingston, one of Jim's hangouts, and although the two would sit together and catch up, neither said a word about the split. "We were both too proud," said Dattila.

—

That October, Jim and Linda traveled to Italy together. Like the protagonist of his earlier novella, "I Forgot to Go to Spain," Jim had forgotten to go to Italy, as it were, and he had the rare chance to travel to Europe again with his wife. Linda preferred not to stay in five-star hotels, so they opted for two- and three-star ones instead, as Jim often did in France. Before they left, Valdène and Batali visited them in Montana, and Batali prepared a "gastro plan" for their trip. Jim had apparently forgotten his new diet, as well.

Jim, like Linda, had never been to Italy, except for their brief stopover in Rome following the Africa trip many years ago, and he had an almost childlike excitement about it. He considered buying a dark suit to wear around in the evenings. He had held back on traveling there, he'd say, because his publisher in Milan hadn't paid a single cent on two of his novels that had landed on the bestseller list.

Once there, both wrote regularly to friends and family with updates and details about the trip. With jet lag, Jim read on the toilet at night while Linda slept. In Florence, the two stayed two hundred feet from Dante's house. "A relentlessly wonderful trip," Jim penned to friends.

> Dulcet, graceful, polite people who laugh more than we. Incomprehensible beauty of paintings heretofore only seen in art books . . . churches where I actually lit candles for troubled friends. Nearly dreamscape. Walking up foggy mountain to see 9th century ruins of Mathilde's castle with five chickens following me. Returning pleasantly to earth tracking the 25

> restaurants Mario B[atali] advised us to visit in Parma, Reggio, Modena, and Florence. Improbably direct and wonderful food—little stuffed tagliarini with olive oil, butter, fresh parm and white truffles. Zampone, a boned stuffed pig leg. A Florentine t-bone with baby beet greens. No backspin.

Jim kept good records of his dining experiences, as his letter suggests, and he sent Batali updates on practically every meal he ate, from breakfast to dinner. During one lunch at Cocchi, a restaurant in Parma, Jim noted that a "200 kilo (immense) man" sitting next to them had the complete *bollito misto* including *zampone* and a slab of fat jowl, "tongue in copious amounts," and other things. "I envied his greatness."

In between meals and sightseeing, Jim managed to put a few finishing touches on his newest collection of poetry, *Saving Daylight*, his first solo collection in over ten years, and by November, once back in the States, it was done. More traveling would follow.

In January, Jim did a reading with Ted Kooser at the Lannan Foundation in Santa Fe that, at $7,500 per person, would pay for twenty-eight days of fishing, he figured. He then headed back to New York City, where he met with Sullivan, in part to discuss a complicated psychological issue related to his new novel, *Returning to Earth*. During another session, he and Sullivan took a forty-block walk that ended at Aquavit, a Scandinavian restaurant on East Fifty-Fifth Street, where they ate three servings of herring, brisket soup, and calf's tongue with anchovies. Jim attended a dinner at Diane von Fürstenberg's—but left fairly quickly, wishing he were back in Montana—one at Terry McDonell's in the West Village, and five different meals at Batali's Casa Mono (cuttlefish, fresh sardines, langoustines, guinea hen thighs, salt cod croquettes with aioli). Casa Mono had recently supplanted Babbo as Jim's favorite restaurant, partly because he had a crush on the hostess there. (Whenever he saw her, he had a peculiar but evidently endearing custom of politely taking her by the hand and brushing it against his bad eye.) He was *still* "trying to eat all aspects of the world" and with some apparent success.

One downside of the trip to New York was the meetings with his new agent-lawyer and his colleagues. It wasn't Sheppard who was the problem but the emphasis on his will that got to him. "My three days with Steve Sheppard wore my emotions very thin (gossamer)," he later wrote. "Hearing the sentence, 'After Jim's demise' is no fun after 300 times by 3 lawyers but then one doesn't want to leave a mess."

In March, while Jim was at work on a lighthearted comic novel he would title *The English Major*, he continued his literary pilgrimages, this time visiting Spain and the grave of García Lorca with Christine Campadieu. He flew into Paris and finally to Seville and Granada to see where the poet was shot, and he slept in Lorca's favorite hotel room, the whole thing a fun and slightly comic idea. But it had been a rough trip. Jim caught the flu and reportedly felt dizzy during interviews, including a four-hour session with Radio France (*The Summer He Didn't Die* had made it to number eight on the French bestseller list). Then, at some point in Spain, he caught viral dysentery. By the time he reached Chicago, homeward bound, he was so ill that he had to spend a very long evening in an emergency room at the Hospital of the Resurrection. With IVs in each arm, he prayed to see his family and dogs again. It would take him weeks to get back to normal.

In April, Copper Canyon brought out Jim's *Saving Daylight*. Bednarik had asked Jim to sign sets of limited editions. They had produced 250 numbered copies, 26 lettered copies, and a dozen hors d'commerce copies for donors and board members. "I recognize that you're not enthusiastic about such things," Bednarik acknowledged, "but a special edition helps us underwrite the project and provides our sales reps with something special for their key literary accounts."

The book was broken into four sections, each thematically cohesive, and Wiegers recommended separating the sections with a simple ornament, rather than a label, to allow for a pause between them. It would include several Spanish translations of his poems, and Bednarik liked that there was no discussion about why the translations were there in the first place: "They're simply *there*."

In the face of the deaths of his mother and brother, Jim seemed to have gone on record in this collection, with the poems offering up a bold array of definitions and conclusions. "Mortality is gravity, the weight we bear up under daily," he told the reader in "Paris Television," and a few lines later in the same poem, the "source of all religion is incomprehension." Quoting Emily Dickinson, Jim observed that "The Brain is just the weight of God" ("The Little Appearances of God"), and he attributed a quote to Norma: "If you want to understand mortality look at birds" ("Mother Night"). In another, he revealed, "Time means only the irretrievable" ("Buried Time").

Time, or the experience of time, is a dominant theme in the collection, as the title, a kind of reversal of *daylight savings time*, suggests: "Clocks leak our invisible / blood in invisible increments," Jim wrote in "Modern Times."

> I'd rather say,
> "sun is up, high brutal noon, sun is down,
> night comes," in rhythm with the bird's superior
> clock. I can no longer reshape the unbearable
> world and have given up to count birds.

—

In "Late Works: Writers and Artists Confronting the End," published in *The New Yorker* in June 2006, John Updike wrote that at least for him, an aging reader, "works written late in a writer's life retain a fascination. They exist, as do last words, where life edges into death, and perhaps have something uncanny to tell us." Jim found the essay intriguing, and he read and reread it. He didn't particularly care for Updike's work, but this essay was another story. Updike had captured something, how we get winnowed by time. The piece left him contemplating the possibilities of his own late style as he approached his seventieth birthday.

He had the Updike essay in mind at Christmastime that year, when he finished writing *The English Major* (it had taken him about one year to write), which Jennifer Egan would later describe as "tragedy recast as comedy." The comic, Jim reflected, had to come after these "melancholy tales" of the Midwest, like *Returning to Earth*, which he thought a lovely but somber book.

A full year later, in December 2007, he was still talking about the Updike essay, and he had decided, after ruing the idea that Oprah Winfrey was the major force in American literature, that he was only going to write comic novels from this point forward. Indeed, Jim's late style would be decidedly comic. As he shared with Treisman, he surely did not want to become "an embittered codger" like Richard Yates; Jim had a drink with Yates the year before his death, and he was apparently appalled at his poor condition: "Literature is an art, not a life," he'd say of Yates, in a statement that could just as easily have applied to himself, though he seemed to miss the point. What he meant, as he later clarified, was that it was horrid to finish "your writer's life that embittered."

Meanwhile, Jim planned to hold on to *The English Major* for a while, rather than rushing it to publication. He agreed with his publisher's concerns that he was getting ahead of his market and he considered "bank[ing] a few" novels for his daughters for after his death. There was already a bottleneck forming. While Jim was editing *The English Major* in early February 2007, *Returning to Earth* had been in bookstores for only a little more than a month.

At the same time, Entrekin was looking for ways to increase Jim's advance for his next two books, and they would settle on a bonus schedule. Many writers were being asked by their publishers to take lower advances due to industry pressures, Entrekin explained to Jim and Steve Sheppard, but he agreed to keep Jim's advance the same, $400,000 for the next two books, one novel and one collection of novellas, paid out as usual as an allowance: $10,000 a month for forty months. The bonus schedule offered an additional $50,000 per book based on sales targets. Even accounting for inflation, Jim had come a long way from his days with Sam Lawrence, when an advance of $100,000 for a book seemed an uncertain hurdle.

Entrekin's main concern, as he made clear, was that Jim was simply publishing too many books too quickly, and he insisted that Jim not publish any new fiction soon after *Returning to Earth*. As part of their new contract, Entrekin built in a publishing schedule. The earliest Jim could publish his next hardcover book was spring 2008, and the next in fall 2009. "It is hurting sales," Entrekin explained, "to have so many books in the marketplace with so little time between them." Jim agreed to the new schedule, but he was unhappy about it and a bit paranoid; he wondered what his publisher was doing behind his back. Grove would hold off on publishing *The English Major* until October 2008 and a new collection of novellas would follow a full year after that.

Entrekin thought *Returning to Earth*, which had an official publication date of January, was Jim's best novel, and Grove did an initial print run of fifty thousand copies. Jim felt the same way about it, though he thought it would be a triumph if the book sold half as many copies in the United States as it would in France.

The novel would arguably earn Jim some of the best reviews of his life. *Returning to Earth* picked up the story of Cynthia, the daughter from *True North*, and her husband Donald, a middle-aged Chippewa Finnish man who is slowly dying from Lou Gehrig's disease. Over the course of the novel, Donald, a lifelong resident of the UP, documents his family's history for posterity, a history that would be otherwise lost. At one point, Donald calmly explains, "I'm forty-five and it seems I'm to leave the earth early but these things happen to people," a remarkable gesture and an acceptance of the inevitable. After he dies, Cynthia and David, Cynthia's brother, manage to revisit and ultimately redeem their troubled past. David, it turns out, has made it his life's mission to prevent Mexican border crossers from dying in transit, an atonement for his family's legacy and a nod to Jim's own attempt to raise awareness of the issue through the story of Ana Claudia Villa Herrera.

One critic wrote that it might be Jim's "'breakout' book," an almost comical observation at this point in his career. Will Blythe, writing for

The New York Times, rightly recognized that the novel represented a new direction in Jim's novelistic inquiry: "Whereas his fiction generally wrestles with the nature of a good life, this novel explores the theory and practice (to steal a favorite phrase of the author's) of a good death."

—

In mid-January 2007, Jim found out that he had been elected to the American Academy of Arts and Letters. Norman Mailer, William Styron, and Peter Matthiessen had recommended him. The "seduction" into the academy, as Jim would put it, was a long time coming. At one point, Matthiessen had told Jim that a certain contingent in the academy had held back his nomination for unspecified reasons. To Treisman, Jim would joke that "Judith Regan ha[d] [him] trapped in the nominating committee for a decade because [he] love[d] corned tongue and herring and she presumed [he] was Jewish." Regan, a controversial editor who had her own imprint at HarperCollins, was not a member of the academy, but she had recently been fired from the publishing house for allegedly making anti-Semitic remarks. That Jim would even make the joke suggests how closely he followed publishing gossip along the dream coasts. His acceptance into the academy brought with it the kind of formal recognition he had long sought.

Jim quickly shared the good news with Sullivan, who recognized its importance. "I know you don't like the fluff of awards," Sullivan replied, "but this one must speak to the deepest part of you . . . I feel jubilant for you—and Linda." Jim was delighted, and it did seem finally a vindication of sorts. His brother John would have been proud of him.

On May 13, Jim boarded a flight to New York City for the induction ceremony. He had a dinner with Dwight Garner and Jonathan Miles, and one with Hottensen at Casa Mono. And he kept almost daily appointments with Sullivan, who would attend the event as Jim's guest.

The ceremony was held on a stormy afternoon on May 16. Jim managed to have a short conversation with Updike about his "Late Works," and Jim promised to send him a poem. A description of Jim's contribution to the arts noted that his "stories, novels, and novellas (a form he has brilliantly rescued almost single-handedly) make up as significant a body of work as that of any living US fiction writer." Jim, in turn, read a short comic poem, which he'd written a month earlier in Patagonia:

Lying curled and naked in bed,
just like baby Jimmy
sixty-nine years ago,
I can't find the key
to the door between then and now.

That night, Batali and Entrekin hosted a big dinner at Batali's Del Posto Ristorante, and remarkably, Jim ate *too* much: "I puked at 2am and felt better," he confessed to Laurie McGuane. "How did this happen?" The dinner was extravagant: seven courses of eighteen different dishes, including foie gras truffle, turbot with Sangiovese, lardo with pine shoots and peppercorns, and Babbo's "Pig Foot alla Milanese." But the roster of attendees rivaled the meal: Matthiessen, James Salter, Charles Simic, Russell Banks, Garrison Keillor, Richard Ford, Terry McDonell, and Dan Halpern, among others.

The remainder of the year would be a whirlwind of travel and celebrations and, for a change, no book publications. Jim traveled again to Collioure to visit Machado's grave, this time with his friend Peter Lewis. They would also seek out the graves of Camus and René Char and then visit Colette's and Apollinaire's in Père-Lachaise in Paris. That November, during the trip and just weeks before his seventieth birthday, Jim received the Medal of the City of Lyon, another prestigious honor. Though there was less need for vindication in his beloved France, it was yet more welcome recognition, not to mention a chance to eat some great meals. Any adherence to a strict diet had gone out the window.

For Jim's birthday in December, Batali made a surprise visit to

Patagonia. He had planned a big feast to celebrate Jim's seventieth. Batali arrived with two renowned chefs from New York City to assist with food preparation. The writer Phil Caputo, who lived nearby, joined the party, as did Jim Fergus, Lewis, and Valdène. Jim had been feeling "forlorn," as he'd say, despite the medals and honors, mostly because of the season and the momentous occasion of this birthday. But Batali's "little birthday dinner" lifted Jim's spirits. "After 5 hours 'at table' we were full indeed."

21

ANTELOPE BUTTE

(2008–2010)

I hope to define my life, whatever is left,
by migrations, south and north with the birds
and far from the metallic fever of clocks,
the self staring at the clock saying, "I must do this."

In late December 2007, Christian Bourgois, Jim's longtime French publisher, died at the age of seventy-four following a long illness. *Le Monde* reported that Bourgois had made his reputation publishing great foreign authors such as Ginsberg, Burroughs, Tolkien, Rushdie, and Harrison. Although deeply saddened by Christian's loss, Jim opted to put himself up for bid in France rather than remain with the Bourgois publishing house, which would now be run by Dominique. Jim had long thought that he could do better financially in France, but he felt a loyalty to Christian that didn't necessarily extend to his wife. The best of five bids, €500,000 (roughly $735,000), came from French publishing house Groupe Flammarion—an unheard-of sum in France in those days, explained Dominique—and Jim felt confident that he'd recover about 60 percent of that in the next two years or so. ("Odd to think of the French paying my Montana mortgage," he mused.) Dominique's bid fell short by a full €150,000, but she still felt betrayed and hurt by Jim.

Jim had been with the Bourgois publishing house for almost twenty years, and Dominique needed him now perhaps more than ever to stick with her. For Jim, the parting of ways was not necessarily strictly business but also personal. The two had spent a lot of time together in France, though their personalities were very different. Dominque deeply admired Jim's writing, and she thought him incredibly intuitive and observant, but she also found that he could be unreasonably difficult. She wondered if people misread him because, behind his sense of humor and social performance, he was one of the most depressed and anxious people she knew. Jim had adored Christian and their son, Mathieu, but he felt less comfortable with her, who unlike her husband didn't drink. "I was not the right person after 6:00 p.m.," reflected Dominique. "I think he respected me. I think he knew he could trust us." Jim did respect and trust her, but he thought Dominique could be overbearing, and he was privately ready to move on. The difference in the bids gave him a relatively easy out. "It was awful," said Dominique, speaking of his decision to leave. "Of course I was furious." She would never see him again.

Jim's life was slowly filling up with ghosts, and yet his sister's death remained on his mind as much as ever. "Like my sister Judith the final unanswerable koan that follows us through our lives," he remarked to McGuane, referring to Christian's death. "Nearly fifty years later I have no real response though the question is always on the tip of the tongue."

In January 2008, Jim finished writing his newest essay, "Rage and Appetite," for his food column in *Brick*, Eat or Die, which he did now four times a year. He would attribute the style of his food writing partly to the comic fiction of Flann O'Brien. Back in the '60s, when McGuane was still at Stanford, he had sent Jim a copy of O'Brien's novel *At Swim-Two-Birds*, which greatly influenced him and that he thought helped "muddy [his] Scandinavian side," his tendency toward the heavy and lugubrious, which could "loom so big and dumb" at times. He would credit O'Brien often, and the very idea of literary influence was much on his mind these days (it was the primary topic of a book he planned to write on literary pilgrimages), as he shifted his focus almost exclusively to comedic fiction.

In February, Jim was busy writing his fifth Brown Dog novella, which he thought would probably be his last ("Get nearly as much pleasure doing so as a dog does hunting," he said of the writing process), but by late March, as he neared the finish line, he didn't have the heart to end the series conclusively. To put an end to Brown Dog was akin to losing an old friend or retiring a fictionalized facet of himself.

At the same time, Jim was having what he described as by far the most productive year of his life as a poet, thirty-five poems in the past few months. He found it surprising that he already had enough for another collection, and many of these would make up *In Search of Small Gods*, a medley of meditations on death, old age, nature, and the passing of time. It's possible that as the ghosts piled up, Jim had flourished more than ever before in the realm of poetry, or that his age and infirmities, his own mortality, increasingly inspired introspection, but it's equally true that the relative absence of book tours and screen projects had freed up his time for his first love. Notably, his lighthearted fiction—Brown Dog, for one—seemed to work as a counterbalance to the melancholy of the poems. Despite the pleasures he claimed to get from writing fiction, he still fantasized about quitting it altogether.

Jim would need as much pleasure as he could get, because by early spring he faced another medical setback. By February, he was preparing for a highly unpleasant medical procedure to address another buildup of kidney stones. The doctor would pulverize the stones with an instrument inserted through the urethra, a "version of the roto-rooter up the dick to sand blast stones in the kidney," as he described it. Jim initially failed his pre-op test to proceed with the surgery due to a "fuzzy EKG," coupled with his diabetes, but he managed to have the surgery on April 8 with the aid of his Writer's Guild insurance. He suffered horribly in the aftermath: "Post op renal stones convalescence in the top 3 horrid body experiences," he wrote to McGuane with excruciating detail. "Pecker gouting blood all over the toilet for five days. Felt betrayed by weenie that had given pleasure then turned on me like a toy pet bull. Doc after a week had to pull a slender blue foot and a half tube out of innards. Looked like a Cambodian snake . . ."

Jim addressed the EKG after recovering from the surgery, and on May 3, he headed off to San Francisco for two days of heart analysis with his "ace cardiologist." The news was not great. He failed the San Francisco workup, and he acknowledged, somewhat euphemistically, that his heart was no longer "a totally successful organ." Rather than slow him down, his health uncertainties had him working even harder—overworking, really—and irrationally determined to pay off the mortgage at all costs, a pace that would backfire if his health gave way under ever-greater pressure.

In July, Jim set aside his health concerns for a reunion with McGuane and Richard Ford at MSU; if it wasn't exactly restful, it was a chance for Jim to spend time with McGuane in person. The three authors gathered at the Wharton Center for Performing Arts and answered questions from an overflow audience. Some of Jim's old friends who had admired his success from afar traveled from Haslett to see their old high school buddy honored by the university. Asked what got him first interested in literature, Jim replied half seriously that it mostly came during the hormonal frenzy of fourteen when he was reading good literature and wanted to use poetry to woo girls, but he also recalled how a farmer had once committed suicide and hadn't left a note for his wife and kids. When Jim asked his father why not, Winfield explained that the man did not have the language. Jim remembered thinking how he wanted always to have the language.

But that language was becoming harder for Jim to master. "I must say that this last novella was my most difficult which, of course, doesn't mean it's any good," he observed to McGuane the following month, referring to "The Games of Night." "Maybe I've lost my fluency. I need clearer notes these days to find my way." An exception to his new comic rule, "The Games of Night," a mostly transparent take on Jim's own compromises in the wake of his diabetes diagnosis, tells the story of a retired werewolf who struggles to lead a normal life after being misdiagnosed with a rare blood disorder. Jim managed to finish it by the end of August.

Unlike with his poetry, Jim had trouble sustaining the patience and attention required for fiction, and his struggles would extend to his next novel, *The Great Leader*, as it had also to his third and final short story, "Outcast," which *The New Yorker* had recently rejected. Eventually published by *Best Life*, a magazine spin-off of *Men's Health*, the story was anemic, Jim thought. He had written it soon after his brother died when he was "surging with deep emotions" that hadn't translated well to the page.

Jim found it a bit easier to write an introduction to a new edition of James Welch's 1979 novel *The Death of Jim Loney*. Welch, a good friend of Jim's who had grown up within the Blackfeet and A'aninin cultures, had lived in Missoula at the time of his death in 2003. Jim admired Welch's work, and the Harrison family remained close to his widow, Lois, a professor of English with grand intellectual capacities, as Jim once described her.

"Recently while rereading *The Death of Jim Loney*," Jim began the piece, "I wanted to write or call Jim Welch in Missoula and talk about his novel but he's dead." He went on to recall the memory of visiting Welch in 1970 with McGuane, when the two drove to Missoula in McGuane's Porsche, "which wouldn't start unless you pushed it, an ambiguous fruit of his success." Almost thirty-five years later, Jim attended Welch's funeral. He had sent him a letter that unfortunately arrived a day after his death and hugged him only three weeks earlier, during a visit, when Welch said of his fatal illness, "These things happen to people." It was a jaw-dropping sentiment, and Jim considered it one of his favorite sentences, a statement he would credit to "Native American stoicism." He had saved it for later use by his character Donald in *Returning to Earth*.

At the conclusion of the funeral, a Blackfeet man made a succession of "diminishing calls of a disappearing owl," which symbolized Welch's spirit flying away. The image also resonated with Jim, who years earlier pictured his own death in the poem "Counting Birds," where he entreats the birds to carry *himself* away into the "*marvel of this final night.*"

—

Grove released *The English Major* in October 2008 again with a sizable print run of fifty thousand copies. Like many of Jim's stories, *The English Major* is a road novel, one about freedom, discovery, and self-recreation on the open highway—aimless driving was one of Jim's favorite restorative pastimes. The novel would go on to become a *New York Times* Notable Book of the Year and a *San Francisco Chronicle* Best Book of the Year. William Kittredge, writing for *Orion*, described it as a book about curiosity, "getting out and around, sizing up the world as it is." While he didn't consider it one of Harrison's major efforts, he thought it reintroduced us to his enthusiasm for "common sense pleasures like food and wines and bird watching and flowers and the consoling psychic usefulness of devotion and ecstatic physical lovemaking." Kittredge, who taught writing at the University of Montana, knew Jim well and shared his passions.

Armed with a doctor's note, Jim would forgo a book tour for the novel. "I think I've pretty much canceled the idea of a book tour after having another physical," he told Bednarik. Doctor's orders. He had also twisted his knee in thick sacaton while grouse hunting with Valdène and limped about the house that holiday season. For the new year, he had resolved to write only half the day, a schedule he had been trying to keep now for several years and one that typically freed up his afternoons for hunting or fishing. A half day was plenty, he reasoned, because he smoked too much when he wrote anyway, so the truncated schedule gave his lungs a break. Writing all or most of the day also tended to disturb his sleep because he couldn't stop his mind from turning over the material in bed. At other times, he found it difficult to work the voice of a character out of his head, which sometimes took months, or to stop creating sentences in his head.

With the passing of John Updike in January 2009, Jim began reflecting on the lives and careers of living authors, with his own legacy foremost in his thoughts. "Mailer Updike Styron dead as doornails," he wrote to McGuane in February. He admired Mailer and Styron, a bit less so Updike (a good writer, he thought, but he found his characters were "never as goofy as people actually are"), and even less so Philip Roth. "I guess Roth is my Stegner whom I also can't read," Jim mused, referring to McGuane's dislike of the author. Jim thought Stegner overrated, and he remembered Roth during his first year at Stony Brook as "the stuffiest prick in the dept. with an improbable level of condescension to everyone. Probably just trying to protect himself but I find a remoteness to the ordinary human in his work." Jim described Stegner as "a cold fish pretending to be a warm fish," and as someone with a heroic view of himself not warranted by his work. "Amusing when Harold Bloom was bleating about Roth not getting the Nobel instead of [Doris] Lessing, a far better writer."

Another writer that bothered Jim was Cormac McCarthy, somewhat surprisingly given McCarthy's off-the-grid geography and subject matter. Jim thought little of his fiction, or so he claimed, and he had once pissed off Gary Fisketjon, the former editor and vice president of Knopf, when he insisted that he wasn't taken by McCarthy's Border Trilogy. Publicly, Jim supported McCarthy's *All the Pretty Horses*, likely at Fisketjon's request, and he had blurbed the first-edition hardcover, along with Matthiessen, calling it a "superb book" that would bring McCarthy the "attention he had long deserved." It's possible that Jim had admired *All the Pretty Horses* but less so the other novels. He couldn't finish *No Country for Old Men*, he told his friends, because McCarthy grossly exaggerated the violence along the border: "In the 17 years we've been [in Patagonia] no one has been murdered along our border—the 50 miles between Nogales and Sierra Vista. No one wants to know that El Paso is a great deal safer than DC. Who can give a fuck about these drug cartels killing each other? McCarthy has blood on his brain."

As for Jim, he thought that nearly all writers were "eliminated in the last act," and on Herman Melville's birthday in August, a seemingly fitting occasion, he opined about his own legacy: "I suspect that if I 'last' at all it will be for my verses though 'Legends' and 'Dalva' are still selling and I get a fair amount of mail for my alter ego Brown Dog."

As for lasting, Jim feared increasingly that his own death was close at hand, a topic that became the central theme of his next collection of poetry, *In Search of Small Gods*. At age seventy-one, Jim felt old, though he joked that he could easily pass for seventy. He was almost always short of breath and prone to severe fits of coughing and choking due to aspiration. He could launch into severe coughing spasms that would alarm every patron in a restaurant. He walked with a cane and limp, especially after his knee injury the previous fall. And despite his interest in women, he had lost his sexual capacity years earlier.

While he claimed to have given up most of his drinking, he still consumed wine and vodka daily, the latter in steady, significant quantities (Harrison's "daily infusions," as Charles McGrath of *The New York Times* had noted during a visit to Patagonia), and he smoked upward of two packs of cigarettes a day, a habit that was dangerously problematic for his wife's asthma. ("Rarely without a cigarette," observed McGrath.) When Jim smoked in the house, which he continued to do despite Linda's serious condition, he would try to lean into the chimney to blow the smoke out, but even this small consideration was hardly an unbreakable rule, much to the frustration and sometimes absolute fury of family and friends.

At the same time, the death of family and friends seemed increasingly to haunt him. In the poem "Hard Times," included in his new collection, he imagined walking up Antelope Butte, the stretch of land beyond the pasture behind his home in Montana, while his "thumping chest recites the names / of a dozen friends who have died in recent years." Sometimes their presences could seem almost palpable. Jim imagined seeing Judy and, walking in the woods or by the river, his dog Rose. He pictured Judy and Winfield showing up at the door in their hunting clothes. Or he saw his niece Gloria sledding down a big hill near the stone house in Lake Leelanau. He took some solace, he'd say, in the fact that life seemed to exist in a continuum: "It's my own conviction from a summer dawn vision in a hotel that no one is born and no one dies. This seems possible in a cosmos of [a] hundred billion galaxies and trillions, trillions, trillions of stars." But he couldn't fully sustain that belief.

At other times, his Christian upbringing would resurface. That God or gods were on his mind was evident from the title of his newest poetry collection. He would demur about how exactly he felt about Christianity, but he would also claim that he still said his prayers every morning, as he had been taught as a child, and he continued to believe in the Resurrection. "I imagine I'm one of the few Am[erican] lit writers who believes" in it, he shared with friends. "I feel it palpably on Easter." What Jim meant, and whether he believed in the Resurrection literally or metaphorically, he didn't say. It was a statement at odds with many of his other assertions over the years.

Not since his childhood had Jim subscribed to any specific religion, and at times he had often noted the strain of not being a true believer. He found spiritual sustenance—"gods"—in the winter and summer solstice and in the small gods of his new book: the "Water gods, moon gods, god fever, / sun gods, fire gods" that he had once summoned to "give this earth-diver / more songs before I die." He relied on Zen, and he admired and borrowed from various American Indian spiritual practices too. Jim avowed that formal religion was "a suffocating box. Give me William Blake," he once said, who had himself created his own mythology wedded to poetry.

As for the dead, Jim thought there wasn't much left to do after all. The "pitiless aspect" of mourning, he found, was that we seek for conclusions and answers when there are "none whatsoever except for loss. Perhaps here I envy the true believer."

—

In late February 2009, Jim headed off to Will Hearst's ranch in San Simeon. Both he and Hearst had arranged to make a documentary film about Gary Snyder, which they'd shoot over the course of three days. Jim and Hearst would produce it together, and John Healey would direct it. As Jim and Snyder strolled the hills, the film crew would record them talking.

By that point, the scenic coastal landscape was familiar to Jim, if it wasn't to Snyder. Jim had visited the ranch several times over Memorial Day weekends for an annual gathering organized by Hearst for his friends. The weekends were a cross between a dude ranch, a spa retreat, and an intellectual salon in the hills. They almost always included Terry McDonell, sometimes McGuane and Chatham, the likes of scientists and mathematicians, and practically anyone else who impressed Hearst.

Hearst would typically invite about six couples for horseback riding and camping, and the festivities were always accompanied by excellent food and wine. Linda joined Jim only once; the other times he attended stag, as would others. Jim's one stipulation was that he preferred not to ride horses. The first time Hearst invited him, Jim told him that he had once been bucked from a horse and spent three days in a coma, so horse riding was utterly out of the question. When Hearst later told Chatham the story, Chatham asked, "What horse? That's bullshit!" Jim had made it up. But his aversion to riding was real enough, so Hearst would accommodate him, if need be, with Jeep rides around the vast property.

Hearst, a devoted fan of Snyder, was the catalyst for the documentary, which shared its title, *The Practice of the Wild*, with an earlier collection of Snyder's essays. For Hearst, Snyder was nothing less than Japhy Ryder, the original "dharma bum" of Kerouac's novel, and an American icon. Hearst described him as "the poet laureate of the American West," a man who bridged the Beats and our present moment. Jim deeply respected Snyder, though he once joked that if you're an actual dharma bum, you wouldn't exactly go around telling people.

One day, while Jim and Hearst were driving about the ranch, Hearst mentioned to him that Snyder deserved a profile or perhaps a documentary film, and Jim agreed, noting that he knew Snyder personally. Jim also quipped that he and Snyder were "the only true writers that can go from Zen to pussy in one sentence," a remark that would stick in Hearst's brain.

Hearst also knew Snyder. He had published lengthy essays by him in the *Oakland Tribune*, and he had visited with him a few times in the Bay Area. But it was Jim who talked to Snyder about the project. Snyder was cautious about the whole thing, and neither he nor Jim wanted to do anything sensational.

They'd keep it all, Snyder recalled, "on a high level of discussion." The clincher, at least for Snyder, was that he'd get to visit the vast Hearst Ranch, a segment of California from Monterey to San Luis Obispo amid the Santa Lucia Mountains that very few people got to explore.

The property is a "closed system," as Hearst put it. "You can visit the castle and see the tapestries, but you can't go onto this incredible ranch on eighty thousand acres along the California coastline. So that was the Faustian bargain that Jim engineered," Hearst explained. "We would get three days with Gary, if Gary could wander around the inner part of the central coasts of California at the Hearst Ranch." The result combined biography, the natural world, and food and wine (Domaine Tempier Bandol sits on the table during a recorded dinner with members of the cast and crew), and it brims with the wide-ranging conversation between two old friends reunited. Promotional events would follow in the United States and abroad.

The following month, with the documentary behind him, Jim traveled to Paris to meet with his new publisher and editor from Flammarion, Patrice Hoffman. While there, he was also subjected to the typical battery of interviews and photos. He wound up catching a bad cold, tried to recover while staying in Narbonne, where he spent several days with *Brick* editor Michael Redhill, then traveled to Barcelona. With a 1,200-square-foot balcony, a hundred yards from the Boqueria, which Jim thought the most splendid market in the world, he had a wonderful stay; he ate fifteen different tapas one evening. Jim had a succession of books appearing in both Spanish and Catalan, and he'd meet with his Spanish publisher while there. But with a lingering cold, he returned to Arizona in diminished condition.

In April, Copper Canyon brought out *In Search of Small Gods*, which Jim had dedicated to Dan Gerber and Ted Kooser. Many of the poems in the collection had already been sent to friends, including a year earlier to Bednarik and Wiegers. Joyce Bahle had begun distributing Jim's newest poems, freshly written, to a growing email list, like an invitation-only poem newsletter. Some people would reply with comments or suggestions or simply gratitude. "They really do sustain one through all the daily issues," wrote Wiegers.

"Of all the poems Jim has sent along in recent months," Kooser responded to one email, "I think I like Poor Girl[s] the best. Ninety-nine percent of our contemporaries, elitist fuckers that they are, couldn't write a poem like this without a sneer, though they'd do their best to hide it. Jim has managed to place himself among the poor girls in the almost invisible way that I find attractive, the way in which Hopper looked at his subjects." Jim's poem, "Poor Girls," which appeared in *In Search of Small Gods*, exemplified his attempt to forgo irony, as Kooser suggested.

Jim's emails to friends—to Bednarik, Lewis, Gerber, Kooser, and others—and their responses (like Kooser's) seemed to help fuel his productivity, and he would build them into his writing process, using the emails as a way to work through certain poems. For example, Jim worked out much of his thinking for the poem "The Golden Window" in email exchanges. A lengthy, seven-page poem, and written as a suite, "The Golden Window" presented Jim with "difficulties nearly beyond [his] reach," as he had confessed to Bednarik and Peter Lewis. "Of course a poem is not a revelation but a process of revelation," Jim had written in another email, and he suspected that what he was looking for were "forms of light not previously recognized" to counterbalance his own feelings of despair. "What is more tentative than our voices in the dark? This is the voice of a man trying to melt the ice within him." What he wanted to expunge was any aspect of the therapeutic, "the ironical 'schlep' that plagues the poetry of our time. We're these fleshy little rockets and irony fuels no trajectory."

Jim had flown Bednarik out to Livingston the previous July, putting him up at the Murray Hotel, and the two had worked together on revising *In Search of Small Gods.* Jim had grown to prefer face-to-face conversations for the final editing process, as he now did with Amy Hundley at Grove. The social aspects of the meetings took the edges off the tedium, and he could better focus on the revision process.

"You two work perfectly together," Wiegers wrote of the visit, "so I'll wait for the dust to settle before offering what will likely be an unnecessary opinion."

Jim trusted Bednarik wholly, because he took the work so seriously. Bednarik considered *The Shape of the Journey* one of the "central texts" of his life. His copy of *Selected & New Poems*, read countless times, was held together by duct tape. Both Jim and Bednarik shared a sense of poetry as a spiritual process, and it's not a stretch to say that Bednarik saw Jim's poetry as a sacred text. Such was the solemnity with which he read and contemplated Jim's work, and Jim knew this.

—

If Jim's legacy had been much on his mind recently, two television shows would go a long way toward promoting it that spring. Both would lionize Jim as something approaching a national treasure and icon, and his poetry was at the heart of it all.

The first was Anthony Bourdain's *No Reservations*, whose production crew arrived in Livingston in May. The episode was devoted to Montana, but especially so to Jim Harrison, whom Bourdain openly idolized. "There aren't that many people that I really look up to in this world," Bourdain would say, "but Jim Harrison, I want to be him when I grow up."

The feelings were mutual. Jim liked Bourdain and thought him "a real good guy," surprisingly well read, and "graceful and polite."

Back in 2002, Jim had sent Bourdain a copy of *The Raw and the Cooked*, and Bourdain had tried numerous times to get Jim on the show. Bourdain's initial idea was to film Jim for a bird-hunting sequence, but Jim had politely declined: "I'm not so sure about that as it is simply impossible to shoot with a camera crew," Jim wrote. "When the New York Times was out last winter, my dog became so disgusted that she jumped in a water tank and wouldn't get out." Jim's hunting abilities had declined by this time; he simply wasn't the walker and shooter he had once been, a fact that may have accounted for his reluctance to televise it.

Bourdain claimed to understand Jim's desire "to steer clear of the pain and indignities of television." "Your dog," he wrote back, "is clearly smarter than I am."

But Jim eventually warmed to the idea of being on the show. That spring, Bourdain stayed in the spacious Sam Peckinpah suite at the Murray Hotel, where the famous film director had once lived for a time. "Tony was infatuated with Jimmy," according to Dan Lahren, who took Bourdain trout fishing, cooked for him on several occasions, and guided him about town. The Yellowstone River was still blown out with spring runoff, so Lahren took him to nearby Burns Lake, where Bourdain caught the first fish of his life on a fly rod.

Jim would host Bourdain at his house on May 20 for dinner, and Lahren did most of the cooking. ("Made him dinner, grilling two dozen doves, then an elk stew," Jim told McGuane, seemingly taking credit for the meal.) In lieu of a hunting sequence, the crew had earlier filmed Jim, Lahren, and Bourdain plucking the feathers off doves at a picnic table outside Jim's house as if they had just returned from the field. (The doves, actually hunted in February, had been sent from Florida, frozen in the round, guts and all, by Valdène.) Bourdain was impressed by the town and would add the Murray to his list of top hotels. Of Livingston, Bourdain later wrote that you're "just as likely to see a cowboy foraging for fresh morels as an ex-hippie in a pick-up with a gun rack . . . Livingston confounds any attempt to stereotype the West."

In June, Jim wrote to Bourdain to see whether he had made it to a restaurant that he had recommended—Igou's, at Nord-Pinus in Arles—and he told him again how grand it had been to have some time together in Livingston. Jim hoped it would happen again.

Bourdain hadn't yet made it to Igou's, but he noted that he kept thinking about "[Jim] and Livingston and how nice it was to wake up in the Peckinpah chamber every morning. Been experiencing a strange half life / dream life of clips and bits of your books, The Wild Bunch, 70s, Key West."

The episode aired on the Travel Channel on August 24, and Jim loved it and the exquisite cinematography. Arguably more than the cooking or fishing or hunting, Jim and his poetry turned out to be the real star of the show. His readings of "Larson's Holstein Bull" and "Barking," both from the new collection, would bookend the episode and provide a dreamy voice-over to shots of the Montana landscape.

"My hero," Bourdain wrote to Jim after its airing. "You looked good up there. Absolutely gobsmacked so many poetry and lit fans out there in TV land. Reaction overwhelmingly good for a slow, relatively (for us) thoughtful show. Reason to live."

Jim's poetry would make another large impression on television audiences that spring. Right on the heels of the Bourdain visit, Jeffrey Brown interviewed Jim at his home in Montana for *PBS NewsHour* as part of a program focusing on American poetry and underwritten by the Poetry Foundation. Jim thought it remarkable and certainly heartening that *In Search of Small Gods* had occasioned the visit and interview: Poetry did not usually make the evening news. Reason to live, as Bourdain had put it.

"Now seventy-one, Jim Harrison is a Falstaffian figure," Brown announced at the beginning of the segment, "blind in his left eye from a childhood accident, chain-smoking his American Spirit cigarettes, part wild man, part cultivated literary lion who peppers his speech with talk of birds and great poets of the past." Brown's dramatic characterization of Jim echoed Bourdain's elevation of him to iconic status. During the segment, Jim and Brown wandered the grassy fields beneath Antelope Butte with the Harrisons' dogs—Zilpha, an English Labrador retriever, and Mary, a cocker spaniel—running ahead.

During the episode, Jim explained the origin of the title of his new collection: "You sense those spirits in certain, often remote places," he said, "whether it's the spirit of animals, the spirit of trees. So those are the small gods," and they would appear to him on his daily walks, like the Chihuahuan ravens he'd known for nineteen years. The episode concluded with Jim reading from his poem "Hard Times" and a shot of him walking off toward Antelope Butte.

—

At the end of September, Jim and Linda celebrated their fiftieth wedding anniversary with a trip to Calgary. Jim had initially suggested returning to Italy, but Linda demurred, which ended up saving them a bundle of money. The plan was to "escape the anniversary nonsense," as Jim put it, because Linda didn't want anyone to know it was their fiftieth. On their way, they stopped for a night in Choteau, Montana, so Linda could see the Bob Marshall Wilderness (or "the Bob," as it's called), approximately one million acres of roadless federal land along the Continental Divide. They spent three nights in a fine hotel in Calgary and a night in Lewistown on the way home. Of course, they ate well: Thai, Japanese, Chinese, and excellent fish in Calgary.

Before the two departed for home, Jim had reached page 270 on his new novel *The Great Leader*, which he had been writing since the beginning of May. "My hero will be misunderstood," he predicted, "as he is an intelligent old (65) lout from the UP and will be unsympathetic to modern readers on the coasts." The darkly comic novel would revolve around a retired detective named Sunderson, who investigates a cult leader for crimes that are never fully known (presumably for having sex with underage girls), and it would take Sunderson through some familiar landscapes: The UP, a border town in Arizona, and Nebraska. Jim wondered more than once why he was even writing the goofy semi-comic mystery novel, as he described it, except that he wanted to. The time of his dirges was over.

Meanwhile, *The Farmer's Daughter* came out in January 2010. Again, there was no book tour for its release—doctor's orders—and it would earn mixed reviews. Writing for *The New York Times Book Review*, Liesl Schillinger basically reduced the book's three novellas to masculinized fantasy. ("What an unbearably stupid and condescending review," Jim snapped to Hundley in response, "a pure product of NYC culture. That's why I'd rather go to Calcutta.") But other critics celebrated it. For the *Chicago Tribune*, Alan Cheuse took a novel approach. Writing his review as a letter to President Obama, Cheuse nominated Harrison for the post of "secretary of quality of life": "I don't know a better antidote to all of the foolish repressive ideas and customs generated in our neo-puritanical society than reading the beautifully narrated and vital fiction of Jim Harrison."

Seven months later, in September, Jim was still revising *The Great Leader*. He rewrote the manuscript three different times and claimed to have never had so many problems with a book. "I've been going without food, water and sleep in your service," he wrote to Entrekin. That he often wrote while on the road surely did not help matters. Jim had worked on it during a visit to Valdène's property in Florida in June. He worked on it during two separate trips to France, one in late August and one in early September between interviews and publicity for *The Farmer's Daughter* (twenty-seven by his count). And he worked on it in Lyon, where he attended the premiere, along with Snyder, of *The Practice of the Wild*.

All the while he traveled, Jim felt extremely anxious about being away from Linda, who struggled throughout the year with serious health problems. Back in March, she suffered from heart problems that had him "moving freely between acute panic and acute anxiety." Her lungs were the main problem. Jamie had even gone to Patagonia to help out, while Jim ran errands and walked the dogs. When Jim and Linda returned to Livingston in late April, Linda continued to have severe asthma attacks. By late May, she was getting better and by mid-June needed an oxygen tank only occasionally, but the issues would linger.

While Jim was terrified much of the time, it hadn't stopped him from traveling. Linda, rightly consumed by her own problems, and with her daughters nearby, might not have minded having her needy, chain-smoking husband out of the house during her convalescence.

"You can read a lot about impermanence and suffering but it's just reading," Jim thought aloud to McGuane. That said a lot, coming from a writer.

22

PARTS UNKNOWN
(2011–2013)

In the Upper Peninsula of Michigan
and mountains of the Mexican border
I've followed the calls of birds
that don't exist into thickets
and up canyons. I'm unsure
if all of me returned.

In January 2011, as Jim hiked along Sonoita Creek in Patagonia, he felt an insect or spider bite him on the shoulder—he wasn't sure which, he told his friend and urologist, Alfredo Guevara, someone he liked to consult on any manner of medical issues. When he checked his back in the mirror a few days later, he was startled to find a virulent red mess of rashes. Linda applied various lotions to it, but it didn't help, while a rancher friend told him it looked like the shingles he had once had. It *was* shingles, and he would also develop postherpetic neuralgia, a common and painful complication associated with the virus. Jim's would be especially painful, and the condition would turn out to be the great torment of his late life. It would not go away. Blistering rashes itched and burned, like a boiling itch, as Jim would liken it, and simply wearing a shirt irritated his newly sensitive skin. He would often choose to go shirtless.

"On my second week of 'shingles' and hadn't imagined anything could be so ghastly," he shared with friends, "reminiscent of the couple weeks I spent as a child totally blinded because of surgery."

A week later, he decided it was worse even than his eye and kidney surgeries, worse than thirty days in traction and his depressive mental torments of the past. He suffered bouts of insomnia, when, as he put it, because of the pain, "everything became confused in my blender brain and will never be clear."

By February, the red rashes on his back were fading, but the pain remained ever present. It came in a jolt every few minutes, like "electrical strokes." He couldn't write, because he couldn't get any flow, and it worried him, as he told Guevara. The one upshot was that it left him with the feeling of a not unpleasant blankness.

Following a visit to a pain clinic in Tucson in March that brought with it a "frolic of hypodermics," his condition improved a bit, and he was able to work in small increments and walk the dogs again. But the pain had "knocked the shit out of [his] fabled memory," he complained, and he had trouble remembering what the doctors were even doing to him. His memory was in a folder, he told McGuane, and he was worried about how his condition would affect him in the long run. The pain had the added consequence of further excluding almost any interest in literature, which, except for poetry, was already very low. His handwriting had become shaky and tentative.

Meanwhile, the family was reading widely about Jim's condition. Jamie sent her father reams of information, and Linda was worried enough about his chronic pain that she asked Lahren to hide Jim's guns. People with the condition are at risk of suicide, she had read. Jim owned a .357, a rifle, two double-barreled shotguns, and a .22 pistol, which he typically filled with birdshot for shooting rattlesnakes. Lahren hid them all.

"This is certainly merciless," Jim wrote to Guevara. "I can well imagine how some dogs enjoy euthanasia . . . the itching is a form of madness." The shingles and postherpetic neuralgia were almost certainly brought on and exacerbated by Jim's exhausting pace of writing and travel, as his doctors had strongly suggested about his diabetes. Jim would admit as much in his later poem "Dead Man's Float," where he'd write that "Dr. Gucvara said that I'm hollow-eyed / and exhausted from writing too much. / I should take a break but I don't know how."

Amid his suffering, Jim turned to an old, familiar source of relief, asking Entrekin to send him one of his fancy wine catalogs. He planned to treat himself to some fine wines. He had also begun working again in earnest, alternating in three-hour shifts—three on, three off—reviewing his newest novel, *The Great Leader*, but the schedule was not working well for him. At one point, Bahle had to intervene and spoke with Hundley about possible ways to ease pressure on Jim to make the editing and writing process even easier. Bahle and Hundley agreed to first discuss any editorial questions among themselves before putting them to Jim, so Bahle could help him. Hundley could field easier questions herself and bypass Jim entirely. When Grove set the manuscript in galley form, Jim would have another chance to go over any changes.

Although he was making progress on the novel, and he was a third of the way through the new Brown Dog novella, Jim was only too aware of his limitations. In addition to the pain, his vision was deteriorating, and he wondered how Aldous Huxley—who wore eyeglasses with lenses that seemed an inch thick—managed his own galleys.

A moment of relative normality came for Jim in May, when he had the chance to travel to France for the Banquet Littéraire at the Cent Quatre in Paris. The festivities included about two hundred people sitting at tables eating a lunch of cream of asparagus soup and Madagascar prawns, purslane salad, and cakes. After opening remarks by Jim and Jay McInerney, who joined him on stage, actors read extracts from their works. Whatever joy the visit brought would be short-lived: it would be Jim's last trip abroad, and the family and he would face a new set of problems soon after his return to Montana.

In August, the Harrisons were buffeted again, this time due to Linda's health. After suffering labored breathing, she was admitted to the local hospital only to be transferred to St. Vincent in Billings after a diagnosis of pneumonia and sepsis, the origin of which would never be fully known. News of her illness spread swiftly among their friends, as her condition deteriorated. Matthiessen put Linda on the "be-well prayer list" chanted during the Zen services at his small Zendo. Linda was fully sedated in the intensive care unit in guarded condition, where she would remain for several weeks. The family took turns driving the two hours from Livingston to Billings to stay by her side. "I admit I've been stretched thin by panic and the strain of so much being undiagnosed," Jim shared with a small group of friends. "It's a huge ICU and full of maddening electronic noises. We're so lucky to have two daughters who hover around the bed non-stop day after day . . . Sometimes I inevitably lose my hopeful feeling but then the world grows too dark to handle."

By the 17th, Linda began showing small signs of improvement, but her condition was still so serious that Jim and the family faced the prospect of the unthinkable. "I certainly don't know whether to be hopeful," he wrote that day. "It occurs to me absurdly to ponder my own physical decline with these 7 months of shingles but not to care in the face of her condition." For much of it, Jim was practically in a panic.

"It scared the shit out of Jim," Lahren recalled, "because he said, 'I never thought she would die before me.'" No one did. With Jim's habits of eating the world, there was simply no question about it.

Miraculously, two days later, Linda was awake, talking, and stable, though she'd have a slow recovery, including spending almost two weeks after ICU in a rehabilitation facility before returning to Livingston in mid-September.* The scare for the family would remain, and no one could take Linda's health or even her long-term survival for granted. Compounded by Jim's own health problems, Linda's near-death experience added to his feelings that he was losing control of his life.

* Linda had suffered septic shock and spent two weeks intubated. She suffered from an ICU paralysis syndrome, and her body had been flooded with saline. She would have to relearn how to walk, such was the seriousness of her condition.

"So strange to have a life of language and no way to use it," Jim wrote to friends after Linda was safely home, at least for now. Language and stories saved his life in the past, though now language couldn't quite conjure another reality.

A few weeks later, Jim did a reading with Matthiessen, Peacock, and Lois Welch for Elk River Books in Livingston to raise funds for a film of James Welch's novel *Winter in the Blood*. It was the only time Jim would share the stage with Matthiessen, and it would be his last public reading. Recent events had visibly worn Jim down. He looked haggard, preoccupied, worried, even confused at times. He had another two teeth pulled that same morning, and he walked and talked with effort, although he managed to get steady laughs from the crowded room. Listeners were quick to help him out with ready applause and evident affection. Jim read several selections from Welch's poetry, and he did so slowly, with shaky hands and the aid of a magnifying glass. "I said to my actual dentist this morning," he told the crowd, "'amongst mammals, it's the eyes and teeth that go first,' which is obvious to a lot of us." He made no mention of Linda. At one point, again to laughs, he said, "Seems like just a year ago, I could read."

Even as Jim had begun losing some control of his life, his work seemed to take on a fresh life of its own: it was more popular than ever, even though the quality of his late fiction, as some critics pointed out, was not quite as sharp as it once had been. Jim won the PEN Oakland Josephine Miles Book Award in 2011, along with Gary Snyder, and at the beginning of October, his novel *The Great Leader* came out. Influenced by the detective fiction of Raymond Chandler, John D. MacDonald, and others, the novel received good (even excellent) reviews and would sell better than any other of Jim's novels for Grove. As Jim told various friends, he had tried in the novel to figure out the complex relationship between religion, sex, and money (an act of "silly hubris," he admitted). The topic hearkened back to Jim's early obsession with fundamentalist Christianity and its influence on his teenage sexual development. Throughout the novel, Jim has the protagonist, Sunderson, reflect on the triptych. Overall, Jim thought detective fiction had to deal in some way with redemption, and it arguably comes for Sunderson by the book's conclusion.

Some of Jim's familiar fans praised the novel. Tim McNulty celebrated it in *The Seattle Times*, and so did Tom Bissell in *Outside*. At one point, Bissell labeled Harrison "America's greatest living writer." Praise also came from less familiar quarters, like Sally Ketchum's description in the *New York Journal of Books* of Harrison as the "Philosopher King of earth" and *The Great Leader* as among Harrison's best works.

Grove was, of course, delighted by the book's success. "Guess who's a Heartland Indie Bestseller and PNBA Bestseller (number ten on both lists)," Hundley announced to Jim that month, "as well as NYTBR Editor's Choice!" Entrekin was obviously very pleased that the book had broken into the *New York Times* bestseller list, and he assured Jim that it continued to sell nicely. More marketing ads were to come.

Jim's poetry was also flourishing. *Songs of Unreason*, Jim's second collection of poems in eighteen months, came out close on the novel's heels. This book, dedicated to Hearst, served as a testament to Jim's astounding productivity in poetry over the past few years. It included sixty-six poems and a lengthy one, "Suite of Unreason," that Jim and Copper Canyon divided into single stanzas and spread across the entire collection, appearing only on the unnumbered left-hand pages in a different font from the others. "Suite of Unreason" and other poems in the collection pondered the limits of rational thought and language itself, a topic that was especially on Jim's mind after recent events. As he wrote in one poem, he now "see[s] today that everyone on earth / wants the answer to the same question / but none has the language to ask it. / The inconceivable is clearly the inconceivable." The sentiment anticipated Jim's own thoughts at Linda's hospital bedside.

In November, *Songs of Unreason* reached number one on the Poetry Foundation's bestseller list, one ahead of Seamus Heaney's newest book.

On the strength of the book's success, *In Search of Small Gods* wound up back on the list at number twenty. To folks at Grove, Jim boasted that his new poetry book "leads the USA in poetry sales," which it did. Hundley was happy for him and realized its importance. "It must be your year—" she wrote, "which you certainly deserve after the less pleasant parts leading up to it." The remarkable success of his work, especially that of his poetry, was a redemption of his own, if only he could manage to fully enjoy it.

—

That December, in 2011, Jim was taking Route 89 from Livingston to the Harrisons' house in Paradise Valley. He was driving slowly, as he always did, a psychological vestige from Winfield and Judy's car accident. (Jim would often ask drivers to slow down when he was a passenger.) That day, someone driving behind Jim's car telephoned the police to report a reckless driver, and an officer pulled him over. Jim had been at Glenn's bar in town and had had a few drinks, but his blood-alcohol level was still within the legal limit, as the officer verified. When asked if he took any pain medications, Jim said he had stopped taking them, but the officer reported it differently, describing Jim as an impaired driver and ascribing his poor driving to medication. The state would suspend Jim's license, which amounted to yet another blow to his independence and sense of self-control.

It wasn't until spring that Jim's local doctor confirmed his competency to drive, and Steve Potenberg—Jamie's husband, as well as Jim's close friend, fishing and cooking partner, and confidant—petitioned the court to get him a temporary license. The written test would pose all sorts of problems for Jim, mostly humorous ones, but he eventually passed it. The comedy of a lifelong intellectual and writer struggling with a state driving exam didn't escape him, but it was just the kind of bland bureaucratic task that he despised. And he was in no physical condition, with shaky hands and poor eyesight, to concentrate and read fine print.

More challenges followed. A few months later, Jim's shingles were flaring again and causing him excruciating pain. He found his Lidoderm patches "only slightly helpful," and it was wearing him out. Guevara had prescribed strong pain relievers (gabapentin), but Jim didn't like them, because they made him feel strange, he said. He couldn't deal with the "zombie effect of the whopper pills," and that included Valium. Worse, the medications disrupted his writing and didn't mix with alcohol, which proved a serious problem for him. Alcohol and smoking were not negotiable, even at the expense of worse pain. At one point, Guevara instructed Linda to not let Jim drink late at night prior to taking the medication, which Jim invariably did anyway. Better to go without the pills. Jim would try laser therapy and acupuncture and everything from OxyContin to "Latino tree bark" lotion.

To make matters worse, that summer, Jim was diagnosed with spondylolisthesis and spinal stenosis. By August, he could barely walk, and he was forced to put off a planned trip to France. But Jim still clung to the idea that he could somehow keep up with his busy (and increasingly former) lifestyle, and he planned a rigorous travel schedule for the spring. There was the annual drive from Arizona to Livingston; a trip to Seattle to visit Elliott Bay Books and see his grandson, Will, graduate from college; and his yearly stay at Hearst's ranch over Memorial Day weekend. Bahle and others thought it was *too* rigorous.

"IT IS YOUR IDEA TO THINK SMALL so I am encouraging it!" Bahle told him. She knew Jim got exhausted from flying, and she thought the trips were a sure way to exacerbate his neuralgia. Hearst would send a private plane to retrieve Jim, so that was perhaps the least stressful option. "Things that help you," she reminded Jim: "fishing, writing poems, walking the dogs, go for MT drives with Linda, listen to cello music, practice your self-hypnosis, eat pig hocks, lardo, and cook, cook, cook! . . . Isn't France on your mind? SAVE LITTLE JIMMY FOR WHAT HE REALLY WANTS TO DO."

What Jim wanted was to go to France, but there was simply no way he could reasonably do so. The French Ministry of Culture had recently honored him as an officer of the Ordre des Arts et des Lettres, and Jim had hoped to attend the induction ceremony in September. Few things meant as much to him, and the prospect brought with it a feeling of relative normality. Still, no one thought it was a good idea, including eventually Jim himself. It was yet another instance of a disconnect between his aspirations and the realities of his new life. France came to Jim instead. Patrice Hoffman and three French journalists visited him that month in Livingston, and even Larry Sullivan flew out to Montana to meet with Jim face-to-face.

Jim had scheduled spinal surgery for October, which he hoped would ease his back pain enough to allow for future travel, and he kept up a breakneck pace of writing, working on a new collection of novellas. It was perhaps a testament to his new limitations that he would settle on two novellas for the book, rather than his trademark three—"The River Swimmer," which he casually referred to as his "Water Baby," and "The Land of Unlikeness." Both novellas were already in the hands of Hundley and Entrekin, and Jim began work on *The Big Seven*, a novel about the Seven Deadly Sins. Adding to *The Great Leader*, *The Big Seven* would be another Sunderson novel. Not unlike Brown Dog, Sunderson gave Jim some "extra access to the world, in short, freedom," as he would say, and that's what he desperately needed now. It wasn't *all* about the money.

—

That October, Jim checked himself into Bozeman Deaconess for spinal surgery. Given his health conditions, he had been instructed by his doctors to cut back severely on alcohol consumption and cigarettes prior to surgery, but he had continued to both drink and smoke and didn't inform his doctors. On the 10th, Jim and Linda's fifty-third wedding anniversary, Jim went into surgery. It was a "long and invasive procedure," as Linda would describe it. His continued drinking and smoking compromised his system to a dangerous degree, and his body could hardly withstand the trauma of an operation. At one point, Jim's blood pressure dropped so low while on the operating table that he almost died. He remained in the ICU for a full week, all the while suffering delirium tremens.

Bahle wrote to Linda on the 12th—Linda's birthday, as it turned out—to express her concerns over how she, Jamie, and Anna would deal with Jim during his difficult and prolonged recovery, during which he would be restricted by his doctors from drinking: "Jim's way is his only way," Bahle wrote, speaking from experience. It was a serious concern, and caring for him in the midst of recovery and withdrawal was more difficult than anyone could have expected. The family arranged for professional twenty-four-hour care. Following the surgery, Jim's mental and physical health deteriorated to an astonishing degree. On the physical side, he became frail and could hardly walk on his own. He wanted to drink, and he would plead with reluctant friends to sneak alcohol into the house in spite of the risks and against the obvious wishes of the family. His bouts of delirium from withdrawal left him confused and disoriented.

By late October, Linda hardly knew where to turn and pleaded with his family doctor in Livingston for guidance. "I can't keep this up," she insisted. "Jim is simply not capable of recognizing what he has become." She wondered, could Jim drive? Could he smoke? Could he drink? Wine? Vodka? Nothing? It was a tremendous burden on the family and especially on Linda, who had her own health to worry about.

As the situation got increasingly urgent, Tom Brokaw, McGuane's good friend, pulled some strings and got Jim admitted to the Mayo Clinic in Rochester, Minnesota, where he would receive a full medical workup. Mayo solved multiple problems. It took pressure off the family to care for him. It allowed Jim to convalesce and stabilize from withdrawal under medical supervision and ensure his sobriety while there. And for a time, Jim seemed to appreciate his stay. In a letter to the CEO of Mayo and copied to Brokaw (Brokaw sat on the board of the hospital), Jim noted that it had been "a grand 2 week stay. One day I suddenly could walk again! After a month of being unable."

But Jim felt increasingly trapped there against his will. While he had intended to leave and return to Montana, his doctors denied him permission and refused to sign a release. "I had assumed attendance here was voluntary," Jim complained to the staff, "both arrival and departure," and he informed everyone that he considered any further delay legally actionable. The experience brought back painful memories of being restrained against his will as a boy following his eye injury. For someone who valued freedom as much as Jim, it was a terrifying feeling and, finally, the ultimate loss of control.

Part of the reluctance to release him came from a series of unexpected diagnoses. During extensive examinations, doctors discovered signs of brain disease caused by multiple factors, including small strokes that affected his ability to reason and concentrate. The condition, they found, might involve anything from personality changes and memory loss to confabulation—a neuropsychiatric disorder that could lead to false or distorted memories—and continued delirium.* This condition, in turn, was exacerbated by withdrawal symptoms. For a time, it was not clear to anyone, including his family, that he *should* be permitted to leave Mayo, and they considered whether enforced sobriety might be the best thing for him. Jim became furious and lashed out at anyone he deemed complicit in his continued hospitalization. His medical team had also agreed that Jim, even if released, should no longer be permitted to drive. Finally, after careful consultation with the family, the doctors agreed to release him and allow him to return home. Hearst sent a private plane to Rochester to pick up Jim and the family, as well as Bahle. The whole ordeal was a whirlwind and difficult for everyone. The family took the added steps of hiring various employees to take care of him, which he very much needed.

Jim would refer to Mayo as that "Pentagon of medicine," and he informed Hoffman and Entrekin that the hospital didn't want to let

* The official diagnosis was Korsakoff's syndrome, a neurological disorder linked to chronic alcoholism. His memory issues were linked almost exclusively to alcohol addiction. He would later believe that he truly was drinking less and smoking less, so that he could ask for a glass of vodka and honestly believe it was his first. As Jamie Harrison asked, How does someone quit if they truly believe they already have?

him go. Hearst, he suggested, had somehow broken him out of hospital prison by sending a plane for him, but in fact he had already been released. What he didn't tell them was that Mayo had written to the State of Montana, citing ongoing cognitive dysfunction, to request that Jim's driver's license be revoked once again. The state complied. The hospital had confiscated his physical temporary license ("purloining my license from my wallet," as Jim would refer to it angrily). This was trouble of a different sort, and Jim was facing the prospect of never driving again, a potential outcome that struck him to the core. Driving and its freedoms had defined him for many years, and at times, movement across space on the open road rose for him to an almost spiritual level of self-discovery.

Jim now described his experience at Mayo as a "horror," and he complained that all he got out of his stay was a lost license. In the coming months, he wrote letters to the state of Montana and implored his local doctor to intervene on his behalf: "I can't be condemned to experience life with a driver. Talk about premature aging," he complained. "My life can't end this way."

No one, including his family, thought Jim should be driving, at least not at this point, for his sake and that of others. For his part, Jim retorted that except for the one in December 2011, he had not received a ticket in sixty years of driving. He would also note that the neurologists at Mayo told him that it wasn't especially unusual for a person his age to show some signs of small strokes in an MRI, and they had told him that he had "lots of undamaged brain 'leftover' for life purposes." Eventually, many months later in the summer of 2013, as Jim's condition stabilized, he would get his driver's license back. He would have to pass annual driving tests and medical exams, but he would once again be mobile.

Just weeks out of Mayo, Jim began putting pen to page, and the first poem he wrote, "Hospital," which he had finished by December 19, is a detailed account of his saga. The prose poem reads like a diary entry. During his surgery, he wrote, he recalled delusions of being in Paris at his favorite food store buying cheese; he overheard his own wailing cries at night and the "thousand electronic gizmos beeping" in and around the operating room; he imagined people entering his room for tests. "There was no red wine and no cigarettes," he noted, "only the sick who tore at the heart." As for the doctors, they tended toward the "smug and arrogant. Hundreds of doctors looking for something wrong are suspicious."

There had always been a network of people aiding Jim and facilitating his writing, but now more than ever they found ways to help him write. Bahle, for one, shared Jim's sense of mission and, as much as possible, helped to clear the way for him to work, though Jim's health would inevitably limit his availability for many tasks. As Bahle wrote privately to Linda that month, it is Jim's "new book that is sacred," referring to *The Big Seven*, "and to have him writing again is all we want. HE WANTS . . . We know he has a great desire to sit and write." Bahle was committed to protecting Jim's energy for what mattered most. "We know exhaustion has been a big part of these past two years," she added, but "we couldn't slow him down." Bahle was right about Jim's desire. The new novel *was* his "main anchor" to the world, and it was what he could control, the work itself and the world within it.

In November, Jim headed to Patagonia, though Linda would hold off until late January because she was completing a battery of health procedures, including oxygen tests, for herself. Jim was happy to escape the Montana cold and the need to shuffle through snow from the house to his writing studio; his walking had devolved into a shuffle, which embarrassed him. "Now that the horror is past I'm so relieved to be among my creek and birds," he wrote with some newfound joy to McGuane. Arizona felt like a fresh start, and he managed to get outside and do some half-hearted hunting. Jim still had a full-time nurse attending to him, but he was getting closer to taking care of himself, or so he felt.

McGuane was happy to hear about the bird hunting, even if Jim didn't shoot a single bird and took frequent spills in the mud. "I called the other day not knowing you'd flown the coop," he wrote. "Had a nice talk with beautiful Linda. I'm glad you're wallowing in the mud and doing normal things under the sky . . . Keep pushing your mobility and stick to red wine!"

That same month, Grove brought out *The River Swimmer*. Entrekin had decided not to offer any interviews because of Jim's health, but he held out hope for a big one if the opportunity presented itself. The book received dozens of good reviews, a balm for Jim, and after three weeks it was posting great numbers, particularly given that it was a book of novellas.

"Funny thing about all of these grand reviews," Jim wrote to McGuane, "is that you doubt they will be reflected in sales." At seventy-five, he didn't feel indelible, as one reviewer had described him. "In short all the praise makes you feel good briefly, then you're back to the shingles!"

Hoffman and Flammarion were concerned that there were only two novellas in the new collection, but they agreed to add a third, the newest Brown Dog novella, "He Dog," to the French release, so Jim could "pay [his] nurses," as he told them. Hoffman again hoped to get Jim to Paris in April, though Jim's ability to travel was still highly questionable, perhaps more so than seven months earlier. Jim had been experiencing dizzy spells in the mornings, and Linda insisted that if he did go, he not do it alone. Unfortunately, his frequent travel companion, Peter Lewis, couldn't join him this time. "I miss Paris terribly, especially the wandering around aimlessly, thinking about Rilke and Proust and others," Jim replied to Hoffman. He had even made plans to meet with the poet René Char's widow in France, with whom he had been corresponding. But by late March, he was forced to cancel his plans yet again, and it was beginning to dawn on him that he might never again get back to France.

There were other *lasts* occurring too. By the spring, Jim was more than a hundred pages into *The Big Seven*, and that also would be a last—his last novel. At first, he was writing it "very fast," and he couldn't stop himself, he said. "It is partly about an evil country family; a case of genetic mayhem," he explained to McGuane. But soon the writing became much more difficult, and he questioned its quality. He felt he was blundering along, worn out by it all, and confused about its direction, especially the ending. "Run it into a bridge abutment at 100 mph?" he contemplated. "Everyone in novel admirably perished to avoid hitting an errant gopher." By late summer, he put the finishing touches on it, and he couldn't decide if he liked it or not. It couldn't go on forever, he told Hundley. He had to simply end it. His "old brain" had been on an "accelerated hot spin cycle for 100 days" and he longed to go fishing.

In September, while Jim worked on a poem sequence titled "Solstice Litany"—even the poems were giving him a tough time—Matthiessen came out to fish with him and Lahren, their usual ritual. Matthiessen's health was very poor. He was suffering from leukemia and had undergone extensive chemotherapy, and he had needed help getting in and out of the boat. But then so did Jim, who was simultaneously delighted to have Matthiessen in Montana and torn up inside about his illness. Matthiessen was eighty-six, and he would not make it out to Montana again—another last. He would die less than a year later.

The remarkable success of Jim's work would continue to buoy him. He was already at work on a collection of novellas, what would become *The Ancient Minstrel*, when the new Brown Dog collection, *Brown Dog*, came out in November 2013. It included five previously published novellas and the new one, "He Dog." On November 11, Hundley wrote that the book was a *Publishers Weekly* Best Book of 2013. The character Brown Dog had become a literary icon, at least in certain circles. As John Freeman wrote in *The Boston Globe*, "Every guy who bellies up to a diner with a hangover and just enough change for a cup of coffee ought to be given a copy of 'Brown Dog.'" He would compare the character to the Big Lebowski, Alexander Portnoy, and Cochise rolled into one. The *Daily Beast* referred to Brown Dog as an American hero, and Jim, as B.D.'s alter ego, wasn't far behind in the affections of readers.

"I know I've been hysterical about money and am worried about impending depression," Jim had written to Bahle before his birthday that year. "One of my worries is that I need a break. Can't continue working like this at 75." He had saved money for the future but wondered if maybe that future was *now*. "Was thinking mostly about Linda but I'm here too. But I don't think I can continue at this speed."

When Valdène visited Arizona that December to celebrate Jim's seventy-sixth birthday, Bahle encouraged Jim to enjoy himself: Take a moment to relax, she told him, take a drive with the windows down, listen to an aria, eat a tomato sandwich with your feet in the river. Valdène and Jim took in some bird hunting.

But the break didn't last long. Hundley followed soon after, visiting Jim a month later to work on revisions to *The Big Seven*, and it was back to work. Jim wanted Linda to be able to keep both houses if something happened to him, and he had every expectation of going before her. His back pain had him shuffling again when he walked, something he thought he had mostly corrected through physical therapy, though it now seemed his new destiny—the shuffling gate. Linda made him carry a cell phone in case he took a serious spill. The weight of mortality, he concluded, writing to his old friend McGuane, is indeed heavy.

23

COUNTING BIRDS

(2014–2016)

Where Is Jim Harrison?

He fell off the cliff of a seven-inch zafu.
He couldn't get up because of his surgery.
He believes in the Resurrection mostly
because he was never taught how not to.

By early February 2014, Jim was scheduled to arrive in Paris on the 16th of the month. Given his advancing age (seventy-six) and declining health, he knew it was likely his last chance. He purchased plane tickets, and Grove sent copies of his books to his hotel in Paris for him to sign for Flammarion. He was determined to do a book tour with "the power of cane," or "cane power," as he called it, to help him get around the city: a cane, that is, not cocaine. The trip would serve as a reclamation of sorts, a reassertion of the person he was prior to the hospital stays and daily humiliations, and he would get to bask again in his celebrity there one last time. He was practically giddy at the idea.

Jim had an ambitious fourteen interviews in fourteen days scheduled for the visit. In preparation, he had reread *The River Swimmer* and some of his other books, because the interviewers often remembered them better than he did. Even a book tour now excited him, though privately he felt timid about traveling. He knew his limitations.

His excitement spilled over in letters to friends. To McGuane, he boasted that there was a picture of him on the wall at the Ritz Hotel and asked if he knew of this. Jim rarely went to the Ritz when he was in Paris, he would say, but his apparent fame there clearly excited him. Notably, the head bartender at Bar Hemingway would later single out Harrison as the most interesting person he had ever served. Jim Harrison was "so Hemingway[-like]," he would say, a charismatic man who could drink Crown Royal until it was "coming out his ears—he walked in the same way he walked out, it had no effect on him."

And still, despite the trip's momentum, caution prevailed. As the trip drew nearer, the family urged Jim to cancel. Given his health, there was simply no way for him to make the trip and meet his obligations, and Jim conceded. "Had to cancel Paris trip due to my illness, prostate, bowels, back," he admitted to McGuane. "Had so looked forward to it." With more than a little optimism, he wound up rescheduling the trip for September, though he knew he would likely back out yet again. The temporary hope outweighed the inevitable disappointment.

By mid-March, Jim's ongoing depression was threatening to overwhelm him. He asked Bahle to send him all the poems he had written since his last book, and he contemplated quitting prose for a month or so and working only on the poetry manuscript, what would become *Dead Man's Float*. Bahle encouraged the idea. She thought fiction had become too much of a grind for him. Poetry was his joy as it had always been, and the grind could wait until after he spent more time on self-care, as she put it. She reminded him that he was taking a low dose of medication for depression and could boost it with his doctor's permission.

But Jim's mental health wouldn't much improve. To borrow from the title of his friend Tom Hennen's collection of poetry, in the months ahead, darkness seemed to stick to everything. News of deaths was mingled with a monotony of editing sessions and social visits as his health seemed to decline even further, and his work remained a steady throughline.

On April 5, Peter Matthiessen died of leukemia at his home in Sagaponack, New York, at the age of eighty-six. It was a terrible blow to Jim. The next morning, he woke up early and was thinking about him. "Don't quite know what it means," he wrote to friends. "So obvious I can't quite see it. Put on mud boots and walked Zilpha across creek ford which she likes to do . . . Peter was grand. Last September he had doubts he would make it another year. Fishing was only so-so but two years ago he got a 5 lb brown in fast water which made him glow."

"He was a great bird of passage," McGuane chimed in.

"Doing the 'dead man's float' and only working on poems as I get exhausted writing a novel and novella this year," Jim wrote, thinking now of himself and his own mortality. He wouldn't settle on the title for the collection for a few more months. "You remember the stroke. I couldn't do it well as I had muscle density back then."

The swimming stroke, which involved floating on your stomach with very little movement, was a fitting metaphor. Having grown up swimming, he knew that during moments of exhaustion, the dead man's float (its name a metaphor of its own) could save one's life. Jim's own strength and stamina were in short supply. Poetry kept Jim afloat and alive. But there was also the potent image of a dead man floating in deep open water at the mercy of strong currents. By October, he would tell Gary Snyder: "I'm calling [the collection] 'Dead Man's Float' after the old swimming stroke. In my journal I wrote 'We're all in a death row in cells of our own devising.'"

Joseph Bednarik drove out to Livingston in late July (his wife, Liesl, came along) for another "2-day on-site intensive" editing session with a follow-up visit in Patagonia in mid-January 2015. More than ever, Jim required the on-location visits to assist with the editing and revision, and together they could choose poems and decide how to arrange them. Bednarik had been in touch with Jim about publishing a new collection since at least January 2014, when he observed that Jim's "new-poems file" had reached critical mass. Copper Canyon planned to publish the new book as their lead title in September 2015. And there was also the social aspect of the visit. The two got to spend some valuable time together.

Jim had counted 107 pages of new poems. He thought there were more open-form poems in this collection than in the previous two books, and he couldn't find any to throw out: "Of course these are my children and I don't mind birthmarks. Even big ones." What became the final manuscript for *Dead Man's Float* required more editorial attention than any of Jim's previous poetry titles, said Bednarik. "I knew Jim would question me over line edits and why I wanted to remove so many poems. He listened to my reasons and mostly agreed." Jim and Bednarik worked on a total of 117 poems, 93 of which would wind up in the collection. In keeping with their shared sense of the hallowedness of the occasion, Bednarik had brought with him a broadside for Jim to sign that featured a quote from Jim, "Poetry at its best is the language your soul would speak if you could teach your soul to speak."

Jim was sending the Murray Hotel a steady supply of business, as Hundley followed Bednarik by a few weeks. "We cannot abandon this great book that battles against, and exposes, evil in the northern Midwest!" Jim joked with her, referring to *The Big Seven*. Similar to the work Jim and Bednarik had done, the two did a line-by-line edit and review of the entire book.

Despite the visitors, including a welcome visit by friend Bob DeMott and his partner Kate Fox in August, the darkness was unrelenting. On the 13th, Jim's dog Zilpha died. She had a half dozen severe seizures and was put down. Jim felt like he had lost a child, though he knew those feelings were perhaps absurd. "Nothing could be done," he wrote to Kooser. "So fast. No warning." And he added a Faulknerian epitaph:

Pause here
son of sorrow
remember death.

Then, on the 30th, the writer Charles Bowden died in Las Cruces, New Mexico. Bowden had regularly stayed at the Harrisons' casita during the summer months, when Jim and Linda were in Livingston, and Jim and Bowden had become close friends. The two first met at Doug

Peacock's house many years ago with Ed Abbey, and they loved to talk about writing and birds. Bowden, who wrote extensively about drug cartel violence along the US-Mexico border, died of unknown causes following a sudden illness. Family members had requested an autopsy, and some feared murder (by the cartels or even the CIA).

By September, months after Linda got a new puppy—a black cocker spaniel she named Folly, a brief ray of light—Jim still felt he had not yet regained his equilibrium. He was also writing poorly and slowly, and he was averaging four to six hours of naps a day. Linda would often tuck Jim into bed for his naps, a detail few people knew, and Jim found it comforting. He felt he was aging precipitously, and he didn't have the stamina or even the eyesight to read new proofs. At times, Bahle would review the manuscript and direct Jim's attention to the important pages. Other times, Bahle took it upon herself to write sentences and even passages into the manuscript in response to revision requests from Grove, an idea that Jim detested and resisted. Jim had seen his doctor earlier in the summer about his condition, but there were no clear markers in his blood tests to indicate any specific medical cause beyond the haze of those previously diagnosed.

"I think it's age and exhaustion from writing too much without wrestling with pretty girls," Jim speculated, along with a lack of outdoor activity. "Haven't fished much this year due to lack of energy."

As for his drinking, Jim had cut back on vodka once again, he claimed to friends, but only to the point of absolute boredom: "When Raymond Chandler quit drinking to avoid death he said, 'Life has lost its Technicolor.'" He claimed to have emptied the house of big bottles of vodka and stuck to red wine at dinner, as his doctors had advised, with a single drink in the evening rather than four or five.

Come late November, as the winter solstice approached, the darkness remained. As Jim told Sullivan, this was the time of year that drove him batty. It was the season of "death anniversaries," and it reminded him of the loss of his father, sister, and mother. "On particular days in late November I'm back there in the shroud of funerals," he wrote, and afterward, he felt a palpable sense of extended mourning in his chest and brain. He was relieved to have Valdène visit in December for his birthday. He needed friends about him more than ever.

In February 2015, Grove brought out *The Big Seven*. Entrekin sent a case of Châteauneuf-du-Pape to properly thank him for signing 1,500 copies, many of which landed at Lemuria with John Evans. "I'm so grateful for the lavish gift of wine," Jim thanked Entrekin in early March.

The wine was well-timed because a truckload of visitors funneled through the house that April, including Peter Lewis and his wife, Johnna; David and Cindy Harrison; and Anna, Max, and their young son, Silas. Jim and Lewis also drank an '82 Petrus, sent by Hearst, which Jim mused he could have sold and put his grandson through college. He was training Folly and writing steadily, a page and a half a day or so between naps, but the struggles continued. He had begun a new novel that was giving him trouble, and he had dreamed up a new Brown Dog novella, but he wouldn't finish either of them. He simply couldn't carry their weight, he explained. "Still could use a sabbatical though it's apparent it will come under ground."

By June, Jim described himself as having the "king of sleep disease." During the day, he couldn't stay awake for long stretches of time, and every night, tubes up his nose, he was connected to a noisy oxygen machine. His shingles continued to bother him; his hands were shaky, even after drinking; and his coordination was failing him. He would spill coffee on his papers at his desk, and he had earlier fallen outside the Wagon Wheel in Patagonia, a spill he attributed to pilot error that left his face bruised and bleeding.

Dead Man's Float was still slated for release in the fall, and despite his bewildering late-life productivity and commercial success, he couldn't shake the feeling of overall failure, even on the fiftieth anniversary of the publication of *Plain Song*. It was an honor, he would tell friends, that the Academy of Arts and Letters had compared his success at both poetry and prose with that of Robert Penn Warren. The problem was he didn't much care for Warren's poetry. Where did that leave him?

As the visits tapered off that summer, Linda's health took a dark turn. She was having trouble breathing and reliant on supplementary oxygen, and her condition had been precarious since late July. While the focus was solely on her, Jim's current and past behaviors weren't far from everyone's minds.

Jamie and Anna had long felt frustrated with their father's refusal to give up smoking, despite their mother's condition. "I get the sense that you feel like this is something people are doing to you, that people are being cruel," Jamie wrote to Jim on September 26. "I understand you would never deliberately hurt her, but your smoking hurts her." The latter point had been repeatedly hammered home to him. Even his close friends were surprised and deeply disturbed by his willingness to smoke around Linda and in the house: His smoking killed her, many would later say. Jim still blew smoke up the chimney on occasion, smoked in his writing studio and bedroom with the door propped open, and when Linda wasn't present, smoked downstairs in other rooms of the Livingston house. If Linda wasn't in sight, he seemed to think it would be okay. In the Patagonia casita, he had set up air purifiers in the hallway outside his studio-bedroom, but the smoke nevertheless circulated about the house and inevitably found her.

Jim was in deep denial about the issue and unable to grasp the consequences of his actions, as the doctors at Mayo had earlier observed, and he tended to bend reality to suit his narrative. Indeed, the phrase he repeated (attributed to Ortiz), "There are no truths, only stories," seemed to collide in frustrating and infuriating fashion with the hard facts of Linda's health. The fact that Jim's own limitations had more to do with damaged brain function than with moral failing, as some objectively realized, made it no less maddening. And then Jim would have to break an almost sixty-year addiction—furthermore, one that was inextricably tangled up with his creative process, as he smoked a lot when he wrote.

Jim's smoking became such a touchy issue that Linda considered living elsewhere at the urging of almost everyone who cared about her, and she doubted Jim's repeated promises that he would only smoke outside. Even if he did, there was still the issue of the secondhand smoke that clung to his clothing—a real concern, as Linda's doctors made crystal clear. Jim had to quit; that was the ultimatum.

"You told me, 'I'll do anything,' and the obvious thing to do is quit, period. Go to a clinic, go to a hypnotist, do it cold turkey, do it now," Jamie insisted in a letter. "We all know how strong you can be."

Meanwhile, Linda's condition had deteriorated even further, and she was hospitalized in Billings. Her condition quickly became dire. When Linda realized that her chances of survival were very low even with intubation, she chose to have it removed, and her death became a certainty. On October 2, almost before anyone could fully come to terms with what was happening, and just six days after Jamie's letter to Jim, Linda King succumbed to lung disease at age seventy-four. In a sense, it occurred suddenly—the disease had progressed slowly, gradually, over many years, and then, so very quickly, she was gone. She passed calmly with Anna, Jamie, and Bahle by her side. Jim, who had visited the hospital daily, may not have fully comprehended the fact that she was going to die. He was alone at home when it happened, and Jamie called to tell him the news. Linda had no doubts about the end, and she was not scared, she said.

When Jamie told her mother that she was doing it all so well, Linda asked simply, "What's my choice?"—a faint, bold, and beautiful echo of "These things happen to people," the line from James Welch.

Of course, her death came as a great shock to everyone, even if not exactly a surprise. She had come back from the brink in the past. She had worked very hard at just surviving, and no one had expected Jim to outlive her, least of all Jim himself. Their fifty-sixth wedding anniversary was just days away.

Linda's obituary would describe her as an intensely private person and "graceful in all things." She was a horsewoman, gardener, natural architect, artist, reader, and a phenomenal cook. "She had a fine sense of humor and did not suffer fools gladly, but no one has ever been kinder." It also quoted a "poet she loved," a passage from Jim's poem "Spring":

> I could say that we are released, but I don't know, in our private night when our souls explode into a billion fragments then calmly regather in a black pool in the forest, far from the cage of flesh, the unremitting 'I.' This was a dream and in dreams we are forever alone walking the ghost road beyond our lives.

"You're not unaccustomed to heartache," McGuane wrote to console Jim that month. "Nor am I and our age gives it a hollow and painful quality it didn't always have . . . I don't have any idea how you reconcile yourself to a loss like your loss of Linda. At 55 years neither of you were cheated. And our age, it's reasonable to feel something has to give. I think we may feel that writing will let us throw the ball a bit further and you have to believe in human immersion, life and death, not the abyss. It's a matter of faith. Your life and work haven't been about despair. I wouldn't try it now. In your case, it would be unseemly."

"No 'despair' isn't the problem," Jim replied simply. "She was very ill and 8 pulmonologists couldn't save her. The problem is loneliness for her." It was the loneliness that he would never get past.

—

The remainder of October was mercifully busy for Jim, and no one knew quite what was best for him. Just a week after Linda's death, he traveled to Boston to be inducted as a fellow into the American Academy of Arts and Sciences. Linda's seventy-fifth birthday, Monday, October 12, was just a few days after the ceremony. Jamie had discouraged the trip because of Jim's health and the timing, and she was hoping to cook something together to honor her mother's birthday.

"If you had another few months of rehab, if you didn't have to give a speech, if you were traveling with someone who knew you and could anticipate your needs and could help you carry your things," Jamie wrote, "it might seem doable and survivable, but right now crossing the yard to your study, with J.K," the family's caretaker and assistant, "seems hard enough."

If Jim was going to travel, he should go to Paris, or New York, or LA, she thought, where he had close friends he wanted to visit. At the last minute, Bahle arranged to join Jim on the trip, which solved a lot of the problems and Jamie's concerns. Jim seemed to enjoy the experience in Boston as much as anyone could under the circumstances. He was appropriately feted, once again, and his life's work was formally recognized by his peers. If he still felt like an overall failure, a feeling that seemed to disappear or lose its importance with Linda's absence, this was at least one more arrow in his quiver of awards and honors.

A few weeks after the ceremony in Boston, Anthony Bourdain showed up again in Livingston with a film crew, this time for his show *Parts Unknown.* Jim rallied for the occasion, but he looked sadly frail and worn hollow. He would read the entirety of his poem "Seven in the Woods" during the episode, as well as excerpts from "Time" and "Wolves of Heaven," all from his upcoming *Dead Man's Float.* Bourdain joined a mining team in Butte, he bird hunted with locals and his friend Joe Rogan, and he again featured the town of Livingston, where he drank with Dan Lahren at the Mint Bar before returning to Jim's house for another dinner. This time it was spatchcock Hungarian partridge, a liver loaf made of elk and pork fat, beets, quail in aspic, a morel and chanterelle mushroom risotto, smoked trout, and elk carpaccio.

At one point, Bourdain asked Jim if writing was any way to make a living. Jim replied no, not unless one was willing to be "completely tenacious and write in disregard for every outside circumstance that there is." That sounded like Jim, Jim at seventy-seven, and Jim at seventeen. And then he pulled out one of his favorite quotes. Most people look in the mirror and say, "I'm getting old," Jim said. "But Shakespeare, the poet, said, 'Devouring Time, blunt thou the lion's paws.' That's a little better, huh?"

In the concluding minutes of the episode, Bourdain and Jim—one of "America's greatest poets," as Bourdain celebrated him—took a drive (Bourdain behind the wheel) in Jim's faded old red Toyota Land Cruiser, which had been washed and cleaned for the show. The two drove through the valley and stopped and talked next to a dirt road with mountains in the background, as Bourdain looked on with admiration. The episode would show a lone coyote running off across the autumnal landscape of dry grasses. It was indeed a farewell, as Bourdain surely knew, to a man who had, in the chef's words, "lived a life that can only be imagined." The two would not meet again.

In late October, the family and Bahle gathered at the B-Bar Ranch in Montana in Tom Miner Basin (on the border of Yellowstone Park) to spend time together. On November 1, they held a memorial gathering for Linda at the house. The McGuanes came, as did the Peacocks, Scott McMillion and his wife Jennifer, Lois Welch, Becky Fonda, Lahren and his son Rob, Jim's old friend Jon Jackson (from Jim's Kingsley days), Bob Dattila, and others—more than fifty people total.

Later that month, Lahren drove Jim and Linda's dog, Folly, to Arizona, and he helped Jim get set up at the casita. He would return in April to pick him up, as was their custom. Because of his health, Jim would require regular oversight, and Bahle and the family arranged for assisted care and physical therapy for most days of the week. Every Wednesday, Jim had telephone appointments with Sullivan, who was now living in Florida. Several people would cook meals for him and stop by in the evenings, and Jamie, Anna, and Bahle arranged for regular visits. Lahren visited again at Christmastime so Jim wouldn't be alone for the holidays.

Despite the company, Jim wasn't doing well mentally and felt terribly lonely, but he tried to keep to his routines. He'd started a new novella, "The Woman Who Loved Trees," inspired by Linda, and he was still writing poems. Almost every afternoon, he reported to the Wagon Wheel Saloon at 4:30 p.m. sharp (or 4:31 p.m.—he hated even numbers).

Copper Canyon published Jim's collection *Dead Man's Float* in December, and *The Ancient Minstrel* appeared in bookstores in February. In between, the family held a second memorial for Linda in January, this time in Arizona. Batali had planned the meals, and he brought with him Anthony Sasso, a chef from Casa Mono, and Chef Chris Bianco from Phoenix, both of whom Jim knew and liked. Together, they cooked rib eye steaks, sausage and peppers, paella, and *fideuà* (a Spanish seafood dish), and they ate an entire kilo of Osetra caviar with *jamón de Jabugo.* Batali would surprise Jim with his favorite lunch, a *bollito misto.*

"Jim was sad," Batali later wrote, and he dearly missed Linda. He was in a "dream state, a fugue, a funk," but food and the love of his friends helped to draw him back toward life, he thought. The two made plans to finish a food book they had planned to write together, and Jim talked openly about returning one more time to France that spring.

But after the television crews left and the rush and condolences were over, when everyone had returned to their lives, there was just Jim, alone at the casita with his thoughts, the silence of the inactive air purifiers he no longer needed, the burble of Sonoita Creek during the long nights, and the overgrown garden. He was incredibly lonely, he wrote to Jamie in February. Jamie and Anna had their families, he recognized, and he did too, but his family, his daughters and siblings were remote from him. His friends at the Wagon Wheel, the locals, and his hunting companion J.B. couldn't begin to fill the cosmic hole in his life.

"So it's acute loneliness," he told Jamie. "I miss Mom every hour of everyday," adding that he spoke to her in his dreams. "Like it or not I have to live some sort of life without her."

"The whole fabric of your life has been ripped away," Jamie replied, who was only too aware of his feelings, and she knew fully what her mother's absence meant to him. "You were 22 when you started living together. All the times you were alone before it was with the idea that you could fall back into this safe place and that you could talk to someone who might be angry but who knew you absolutely. There was nothing to explain." Now she was gone.

On Friday, March 25, Jim ventured out to the Wagon Wheel Saloon. It was a beautiful afternoon, seventy-five degrees and sunny, and a group of people sat outside. Jim Fergus stopped by for a visit, as did Phil Caputo,

Laura Chester, and a host of regulars—eight or ten people revolving in and out as usual. At one point, Jim presented a mock marriage proposal to Chester's attractive niece that got everyone laughing.

A few hours later, Fergus walked Jim out to the car. Jim had drunk conservatively, at least for him. He didn't want to lose his driver's license again. Fergus apologized that evening for not being more attentive to him, which Jim seemed to understand because Fergus had been working under deadline on a novel. But Fergus promised to prepare a *pintade* (guinea fowl) for Jim and stop by in the coming days.

Later that night, at the casita, Jim telephoned Lahren. He told him that he had purchased a pot roast at Dickmen's Meat and Deli in Tucson. The weather was getting hot, and he was looking forward to getting back to Montana. When Lahren returned to Arizona in a few weeks in April, they would cook the pot roast and cut up the rest for sandwiches for the journey home.

The next day, Jim sat down to write a poem at his desk in his studio-bedroom. He was alone with his work, as he was most mornings. He bent over his notebook on the desk in front of him. As he wrote, he smoked and crushed out smoldering cigarettes in a crowded ashtray, and then lit another one. His smoke wouldn't intrude on anyone. He began writing:

> In unease the earth turned itself inside
> out when its gravity fled. All of us
> fell off the earth. I was in Africa
> at the time and fell near an elephant.
> I made my way to her and stretched
> out on her stomach for protection
> from the polar cold of the high atmosphere.
> I caught a couple of passing
> tomatoes to eat and a bottle of whiskey.
> The earth used to be God's body
> but he took too many wounds and abandoned it.

He left us with the husk we made
of the body like a wasp's nest.
Man shit his pants and trashed God's body

Jim died after writing that poem. Mortality is gravity, he had once written, and it fled somewhere amid the dreams of geologic upheaval and the continent of Africa, which he had once visited with Linda almost fifty years earlier. He suffered cardiac arrest, perhaps during the writing of the poem's final lines, which dwindled to mere scratches on the page. He added no period to the end of the poem, no full stop. An American Spirit burned to a frail ash on the desk. His body slumped off the writing chair onto the floor, where he lay on his side. He was still holding a pen in his hand. He looked peaceful, people would say, the few who saw him in the back room before his body was taken off to the hospital. Folly was still roaming the house.

—

A local friend found Jim's body. She had been cooking for him, and she'd brought him a chicken pot pie, one of his favorites, that afternoon. He had lain on his side for perhaps a few hours, and he felt cool to the touch. He was shirtless, as usual, because of his skin condition. She telephoned the local clinic in town that had helped to care for Jim and then called the EMTs. Jim's urologist, Dr. Guevara, made the thirty-minute drive from Nogales to Patagonia to declare him dead and sign the death certificate. Guevara, who had covered Jim's body with a bed sheet, suspected that a piece of plaque in Jim's arteries had broken free and blocked his blood flow. His heart would have fluttered, Guevara said, and he would have felt increasingly dizzy as he wrote to the end of the poem. He would not have felt much pain.

Guevara called Phil Caputo, who lived close by. When Caputo heard Guevara say he had bad news, he knew it was Jim. Guevara needed help, so Caputo went to the casita, where the two waited for an ambulance.

It wouldn't arrive until after dark, sometime around 8:00 p.m., and in the intervening hours, several locals stopped by to pay their last respects, including Laura Chester and her niece.

As news spread, a small crowd gathered, and it was an awkward situation. "I think Jim would not have been happy," said a friend, referring to all the people. He would not have wanted so many people around him at such a time. A few knelt by Jim's body, prayed, and left; others milled about and talked. The woman who first found his body had since left, and no one felt they had the authority to tell others to leave.

Several people were struck by the notebook on Jim's desk and the handwritten poem that devolved almost into illegibility. Everyone agreed that the manner of his death was fitting—a poet's death—"like a warrior dying in battle," said Caputo.

When Jamie heard the news, she informed the rest of the family, including Anna, who was at a movie with her son Silas. They were celebrating his tenth birthday that same day. The weather was nice in Montana, and Lahren floated the Jefferson River with Callan Wink, one of Jim's fishing guides. Around the time of Jim's death, Wink caught a beautiful brown trout as if on cue. Doug Peacock was traveling from his winter retreat in Arizona to the Paradise Valley at the time. Will Hearst got a note from Joyce Bahle. Peter Lewis canceled the hotel and plane reservations he had made with Jim for their last trip to France. Jamie also called McGuane, and he telephoned Valdène, who knew what McGuane was going to tell him as soon as he picked up the phone. Dan Gerber was at his house in California when he heard the news. He had spoken to Jim about a week earlier, and Jim had confided to him that he wasn't enjoying much of anything anymore.

Gerber would recall the last time he saw his lifelong friend. He and Jim had been fishing the Yellowstone River down by Big Timber. Afterward, Jim wanted to stop and have a drink in Livingston, and he had driven his truck from the valley into town to meet Gerber there. Jim was practically naked, his shirt off and his pants falling down. "He had shrunk," Gerber said. "He had a goatee and a cane, and he'd become gnomelike."

They had a drink or two, and then Gerber walked Jim to his truck. Jim got in, and before he left, he turned and stuck his head out of the window. "You know, we ought to meet up again and take another one of those road trips across the country, like we used to," Jim told him, like the many he and Gerber had taken over the years with a Best Western hotel guide in the glove compartment. The two would talk about their lives as the countryside rolled by.

"Yes, we should," Gerber said, knowing that they would never do it. "Yes, we should." Jim grinned—a big smile, teeth missing, eyes aglow, luminous—and he drove away into the Montana night.

ACKNOWLEDGMENTS

I owe a tremendous debt of gratitude to the Dumsch, Harrison, and Potenberg families. While *Devouring Time* is not an authorized biography, they have been remarkably forthcoming and generous. David and Cindy Harrison, Mary Harrison Dumsch and Nick Dumsch, and Rebecca Harrison welcomed me into their homes and readily shared their insights and memories. My first email for this project went to Jamie Harrison Potenberg, who offered her unwavering support, as did Steve, along with some splendid meals. She weathered many interviews with me and never shied away from difficult questions and memories. Anna Harrison Hjortsberg provided her ongoing support as well. Buck Harrison graciously shared his memories about Winfield's family. For this and more, I thank them.

I am immensely grateful to Joyce Harrington Bahle. She has been a pillar of support from the beginning. She granted me access to a wealth of Harrison materials, connected me with Harrison's colleagues and friends, and generously put me up at her beautiful Birdhouse for months at a time. It was with her assistance that I got to know the Lake Leelanau area, and the Birdhouse served as a home base for forays to the Upper Peninsula and Traverse City. I am lucky to call her a friend.

Thanks to the wonderful archivists at Grand Valley State

University—Annie Benefiel, Leigh Rupinski, Diana Page, and Robert Beasecker—for their tireless assistance during my seemingly countless hours at Seidman House. Their good spirits and conversation—and Friday lunches—made my time there memorable and enjoyable. The Jim Harrison Papers are in the best of hands.

I owe a special thanks to the editorial, marketing and publicity, and production teams at Blackstone Publishing, especially Haila Williams and Marilyn Kretzer. Thanks to Michael Krohn and Michael Signorelli for their diligent editorial work.

At Grove Atlantic, Morgan Entrekin, Judy Hottensen, Amy Hundley, and Deb Seager shared their stories about Jim and readily provided assistance. Likewise, I am indebted to Michael Wiegers and Joseph Bednarik at Copper Canyon Press. My wonderful conversations with Joseph, who has been a relentless and enthusiastic advocate for this book, helped to shape my understanding of Jim Harrison's life and poetry.

To Tom McGuane, who shared his memories of his longtime friend and granted me access to their remarkable correspondence, I remain incredibly grateful. Dan Gerber, ever gracious, was seemingly always available to answer my questions. I benefited from countless conversations with Bob Dattila and Dan Lahren, and I thank them for their friendship.

This book would not have been possible without the more than one hundred people who agreed to be interviewed for it. The list is long, but I wish to extend a special thanks to a number of people in particular who helped bring this book to fruition: Mike Ballard, Rick Bass, Mario Batali, Bob and Gayle Bergier, Marc Beaudin, Jean-Claude Boulet, Dominique and Mathieu Bourgois, Rick and Mary Capogrossa, Phil Caputo, Lea Chatham, Jim and Scruffy Crockett, Jill Eggers, John Evans, Jim Fergus, Lucy Fisher, Richard Ford, Charles Frazier, Barry Gifford, William Randolph Hearst III, Vic Herman, Patrice Hoffman, Richard and Lisa Howorth, Jon Jackson, Pamela King, Ted Kooser, Peter Lewis, Brice Matthieussent, Column McCann, Terry McDonell, Gerard Oberlé, Geoffrey O'Brian, Pat and Vesper Paton, Doug and

Andrea Peacock, Molly Phinny, George and Susan Quasha, Toby Carr Rafelson, Amy Reynolds, Gary Snyder, Rose and Susanna Styron, Deborah Treisman, Frederick Turner, Eliot Weinberger, Lois Welch, Doug Wick, and Edward Zwick.

To my intrepid agent, Philip Turner, as well as to his son and partner, Ewan, I owe many thanks. Your support and insights over the years have meant a lot to me. You have rarely been more than a phone call away. Thanks for helping me see this through.

Thanks to my dear family, George and Lee Goddard, Gary, Linda, Oscar, and Sophie. To Natalie I owe more than I can say—thank you for your love and support. More than anyone else, you have lived and breathed this project from the beginning. Thanks also to Sam and Vicki Jackman.

The following people have provided support in various forms over the years. Some have read drafts or accompanied me on trips, assisted me with research, or simply offered their friendship at difficult times. Others have offered wisdom. My heartfelt thanks to Marc Beaudin, Brent and Kara Beckman, Christine Campadieu, Abra Fortune Chernik, Erin Cousins, Todd F. Davis, Michael Goode, Nathan Gorelick, Chris CW Johnson, Brian and Dawn Kempisty, Bret Lucas, Jon Margolis, Scott McMillion, Max Rankenburg, Lance Richardson, Justo Sanchez, and Brian Whaley. Nancy McKeon's shrewd, critical eye made this a better book. Robert DeMott, especially, provided me with many insights into Jim Harrison's life and work. His wonderful collection of Harrison interviews proved a valuable resource. Gregg Orr and Beef Torrey's comprehensive bibliography of Harrison's works was another incredibly valuable resource, and Orr readily shared updates with me from his forthcoming addenda.

Thanks to the members of my dedicated biography group for their conversation and support. The late Ken Silverman, my professor at New York University, served as a mentor to me and, along with Frederick R. Karl, got me hooked on biography. The prolific Carl Rollyson has frequently advised me on all manner of questions pertaining to the field. Utah Valley University provided me with sabbatical funding and a talented cast of librarians. UVU's librarians, including Annie Smith, helped to locate a number of hard-to-find books and articles. Frederick Courtright and Christopher Wait arranged for an array of permissions.

Finally, I owe special thanks to Leslie McRoberts at Michigan State University and to the Archives and Special Collections at Montana State University Library. Many other libraries and librarians have also assisted with this project, including the Archives and Special Collections, UC-Davis Library; Howard Gotlieb Archival Research Center, Boston University Libraries; Oregon State University Special Collections; Rare Book & Special Collections, Library of Congress; Special & Area Studies Collections, University of Florida; Special Collections at The Ohio State University; The University of Mississippi Libraries, Department of Archives & Special Collections; Special Collections, Stanford Libraries; Southwest Collection / Special Collections Library at Texas Tech University; The Harry Ransom Center at the University of Texas at Austin, and the University of Arizona Libraries–Special Collections.

Any errors of fact or misinterpretations are entirely my own.

NOTES

ABBREVIATIONS

BD	Bob Dattila
DG	Dan Gerber
DGP	Dan Gerber Papers, Special Collections, Michigan State University Libraries
DL	Denise Levertov
DLP	Denise Levertov Papers, series 4, box 48, Department of Special Collections, Stanford University Libraries
JH	Jim Harrison
JHB	Joyce Harrington Bahle
JHP	Jim Harrison Papers, Special Collections & University Archives, Grand Valley State University
LH	Linda Harrison
OTS	*Off to the Side* (Grove Press, 2003)
RC	Russell Chatham
SL	Seymour Lawrence
TM	Thomas McGuane
TMP	Thomas McGuane Papers, Merrill G. Burlingame Special Collections, Montana State University Library

PREFACE

xiv ***"My place of grace":*** JH, "Hospital," in *Dead Man's Float* (Copper Canyon Press, 2016), 6.

"addicted to wild natural beauty": JH to Gérard Oberlé, August 26, 1999, JHP.

xvi ***"the true bones":*** JH, introduction to *The Shape of the Journey: New and Collected Poems* (Copper Canyon Press, 1998), 1.

xviii ***"Jim would give you":*** Mike Ballard, in discussion with the author, July 20, 2018.

"the General": Jim Fergus, in discussion with the author, February 11, 2023.

1 THE LEGEND OF LITTLE JIMMY

1 ***"Go, my songs":*** JH, "Credo After E.P.," in *Jim Harrison: Complete Poems*, ed. Joseph Bednarik (Copper Canyon Press, 2021), 35.

"Life is a near death": JH, "A Really Big Lunch," *New Yorker*, September 6, 2004, 78.

2 ***"tempestuous French chef":*** Marc Meneau Obituary, *Times* (London), December 18, 2020, https://www.thetimes.com/uk/article/marc-meneau-obituary-32hvqt0m8.

"Courage": JH, "A Really Big Lunch," *New Yorker*, September 6, 2004, 78.

"I am going again": JH to Deborah Treisman, November 4, 2003, JHP.

"a thrill to have [the piece]": Deborah Treisman to JH, August 12, 2004, JHP.

3 ***"likely cost as much":*** JH, "A Really Big Lunch," *A Really Big Lunch: The Roving Gourmand on Food and Life* (Grove Press, 2017), 59.

"It's a long road": JH, "A Really Big Lunch," *A Really Big Lunch: The Roving Gourmand on Food and Life* (Grove Press, 2017), 60.

"a Swedish Lutheran": JH, "A Really Big Lunch," *A Really Big Lunch: The Roving Gourmand on Food and Life* (Grove Press, 2017), 67.

5 ***"Germans and Swedes":*** Norma Harrison, "Childhood Memories of the Farm," unpublished manuscript, JHP.

"ideas, to argument": Norma Harrison, "Life and Times of Some Harrisons: 1928 to 1950 or So," JHP.

"there was no money": Norma Harrison, "Life and Times of Some Harrisons: 1928 to 1950 or So," JHP.

7 ***"true Swede autocrat":*** JH, *OTS*, 9.

"John was laconic": Mary Harrison, in discussion with the author, May 1, 2020.

"trying to make too much": David Harrison, in discussion with the author, October 27, 2021.

8 ***"From my ancestors":*** JH, "Sketch for a Job-Application Blank," in *Jim Harrison: Complete Poems*, ed. Joseph Bednarik (Copper Canyon Press, 2021), 6.

"exquisite quilter": Mary Harrison, in discussion with the author, May 1, 2020.

"Your dad was never": Norma Harrison, "Childhood Memories of the Farm," unpublished manuscript, JHP.

9 ***"I grew up within that framework":*** JH, "Writer Jim Harrison: Work, Booze, the Outdoor Life—and an Absolute Rage for Order," interview by Kathy Stocking, *Detroit Free Press*, June 5, 1977, 21.

"out near the pigpen": JH, "Tracking," in *The Summer He Didn't Die* (Grove Press, 2005), 189.

"Farm children then": JH, "A Memoir of Horse Pulling," in *Just Before Dark: Collected Nonfiction* (Mariner Books, 1999), 98.

"Smoking in a barn": JH, "A Memoir of Horse Pulling," in *Just Before Dark: Collected Nonfiction* (Mariner Books, 1999), 99.

10 ***"Finally we were to stay":*** Norma Harrison, "Life and Times of Some Harrisons: 1928 to 1950 or So," JHP.

11 ***"the nineteenth century in a small":*** JH, "A Memoir of Horse Pulling," in *Just Before Dark: Collected Nonfiction* (Mariner Books, 1999), 98.

"basically an obnoxious": JH, "Writer Jim Harrison: Work, Booze, the Outdoor Life—and an Absolute Rage for Order," interview by Kathy Stocking, *Detroit Free Press*, June 5, 1977, 21.

"something of a populist": JH, "Creating Habitat for the Soul: An Interview with Jim Harrison," interview by Robert DeMott and Patrick Smith, 1997/1998, in *Conversations with Jim Harrison, Revised and Updated*, ed. Robert DeMott (University Press of Mississippi, 2019), 154–55.

"as Indians": Ernest Thompson Seton, from the subtitle of *Two Little Savages: Being the Adventures of Two Boys Who Lived as Indians and What They Learned* (Grosset & Dunlap, 1903).

12 ***"farmers in a hopelessly unfertile":*** JH, "A Memoir of Horse Pulling," in *Just Before Dark: Collected Nonfiction* (Mariner Books, 1999), 98.

13 ***"In the parking lot":*** Mardi Suhs, "This Is How Jim Harrison Lost His Eye: Harrison Describes Impact of Events on Author's Life," *Cadillac News*, March 29, 2016, https://www.cadillacnews.com/news/local/this-is-how-jim-harrison-lost-his-eye/article_5c6a7b9f-05f2-56d3-9724-104157f40fe4.html.

"The Harrisons' family friends": Norma Harrison, "Life and Times of Some Harrisons: 1928 to 1950 or So," JHP.

"mosquito-bite scab": JH, "Then and Now," in *Just Before Dark: Collected Nonfiction* (Mariner Books, 1999), 15.

"first sexual experience": JH, "Lake Effect: Talking with Jim Harrison," interview by Edward C. Reilly, December 1991, in *Jim Harrison* (Twayne Publishers, 1996), 2.

"the blind eye shone": JH, "Then and Now," in *Just Before Dark: Collected Nonfiction* (Mariner Books, 1999), 15.

"one-eyed goofy": JH, *OTS*, 251.

14 ***"wild and unruly":*** JH, *The Boy Who Ran to the Woods* (Atlantic Monthly Press, 2000).

15 ***"were long-range":*** JH, *OTS*, 18.

"They would take the rowboat": Norma Harrison, "Life and Times of Some Harrisons: 1928 to 1950 or So," JHP.

16 ***"a world where he felt":*** JH, *The Boy Who Ran to the Woods* (Atlantic Monthly Press, 2000).

2 HASLETT

17 ***"A little life":*** JH, "The Existentialist," in a letter to John Ciardi, July 1956.

"unhealable rupture": JH, "Tracking," in *The Summer He Didn't Die* (Atlantic Monthly Press, 2005), 197.

19 ***"These were hunters":*** David Harrison, in discussion with the author, June 6, 2020.

20 ***"widely if erratically":*** JH, "Tracking," in *The Summer He Didn't Die* (Atlantic Monthly Press, 2005), 196.

"Well, we have eighteen": David Harrison, in discussion with the author, June 6, 2020.

"a wonderful smelly old": JH, *OTS*, 74.

21 ***"Now get to work!":*** Mary Harrison, in discussion with the author, May 5, 2019.

"the emotional center": David Harrison, in discussion with the author, May 5, 2020.

23 ***"religion stuck fast":*** JH to Dr. Jill Paláez Baumgaertner, March 31, 2015. Jim sent Baumgaertner some of his poems that dealt with religious themes. Letter accessed while in possession of JHB, November 20, 2020.

"piss off [his] parents": JH, *True North* (Grove Press, 2005), 15.

"a Bible-thumping": JH, *OTS*, 118.

"actual emotions": JH, *OTS*, 44.

24 ***"Everybody loved [Roost]":*** Ralph Morr, in discussion with the author, July 1, 2021.

"suspense, death and comedy": Haslett (MI) High School, *Dixit* (1956), JHP.

"young and pretty": Jean Marr, June Marr, and Irma Lilrose, in discussion with the author, July 7, 2021.

"real hard as my leading man": JH to Harrison Ford and Doug Wick, January 2, 1989, JHP.

25 ***"highly confident":*** Ralph Morr, in discussion with the author, July 1, 2021.

"I liked him": June Marr, in discussion with the author, July 7, 2021.

"[Jim] was head and shoulders": Ralph Morr, in discussion with the author, July 1, 2021.

"I don't know if I ever": Jean Marr, in discussion with the author, July 7, 2021.

26 ***"Critics are continually harping":*** JH, "A Study of the American Novelist, Thomas Wolfe," 1956, JHP.

"The 100 Greatest Books": David Harrison, in discussion with the author, April 13, 2019.

"could recite any verse": Ralph Morr, in discussion with the author, July 1, 2021.

"I finally realized": JH, "The Man Whose Soul Is Not for Sale: Jim Harrison," interview by Hank Nuwer, in *Conversations with Jim Harrison*, ed. Robert DeMott (University Press of Mississippi, 2002), 47.

27 ***"pallid and drudgery-ridden":*** JH, *OTS*, 27.

"about the nicest looking": JH to Norma, Winfield, and Harrison family, July 26, 1954, JHP.

"a flatlander": JH, "Tracking," in *The Summer He Didn't Die* (Atlantic Monthly Press, 2005), 201.

"the world's biggest": JH to Norma, Winfield, and Harrison family, August 2, 1954, JHP.

28 ***"very thrifty":*** JH to Norma, Winfield, and Harrison family, n.d., JHP.

"little affair": JH to Norma, Winfield, and Harrison family, July 14, 1954, JHP.

"resolved his virginity": JH, "Tracking," in *The Summer He Didn't Die* (Atlantic Monthly Press, 2005), 202.

"just for the fun": JH to "Mother, Dad, John, Mary, and David," n.d., JHP.

29 ***"Not only did we not know":*** David Harrison, in discussion with the author, May 12, 2020.

"Green Witch Village": JH, *OTS*, 27.

"We were more immediately": JH, *OTS*, 27.

30 ***"My left eye is blind":*** JH, "Sketch for a Job-Application Blank," in *Jim Harrison: Complete Poems*, ed. Joseph Bednarik (Copper Canyon Press, 2021), 6.

31 ***"Thus, exhorters of the spirit":*** John Ciardi, "Poverty on Parnassus: The Economics of Poetry," *Saturday Review*, July 28, 1956, 8.

"Your article was depressing": JH to John Ciardi, July 1956, JHP.

32 ***"those irrationalities":*** John Ciardi, "Poverty on Parnassus: The Economics of Poetry," *Saturday Review*, July 28, 1956, 8.

"Ford Motor Plants": JH, "Poet and Fiction Writer Jim Harrison," interview by Lindsay Ahl, 2006, in *Conversations with Jim Harrison, Revised and Updated*, ed. Robert DeMott (University Press of Mississippi, 2019), 231–236.

"truck driver, a proctologist": JH, *OTS*, 53.

"require one year": JH, "When I'm Thinking About Two Hours," interview by Casey Walker, 1997, in *Conversations with Jim Harrison, Revised and Updated*, ed. Robert DeMott (University Press of Mississippi, 2019), 132.

"strong opinions": John Ciardi to JH, August 6, 1965, JHP.

"I am eighteen": JH to John Ciardi, n.d., JHP.

"the tweed school": JH to "Dear Father, Mother," n.d., JHP.

3 ON THE ROAD

34 ***"Hot, hungry, eighteen and reading":*** JH, "NYC," in *Jim Harrison: Complete Poems*, ed. Joseph Bednarik (Copper Canyon Press, 2021), 795.

35 ***"had a lively wildness":*** JH, "Tracking," in *The Summer He Didn't Die* (Grove Press, 2005), 208.

"rich stew of oil paints": JH, "Tracking," in *The Summer He Didn't Die* (Grove Press, 2005), 209.

"for not feeling good": JH to "Mother, Father, Judy, Mary, David," n.d., ca. July 1957, JHP.

"mental torture barracks": JH, "Tracking," in *The Summer He Didn't Die* (Grove Press, 2005), 210.

"couldn't stand college": JH, "Words from the Woods," interview by Gregory Skwira, *Detroit Free Press*, March 25, 1984, 17.

"sitting inside insides": Kenneth Falor to JH, n.d., ca. 1957, JHP.

36 ***"the center of cosmopolitan":*** JH, *Wolf: A False Memoir* (Delta, 1981), 181.

"She was blond": JH, *Wolf: A False Memoir* (Delta, 1981), 185.

"No more than a supermarket": JH to "Mother, Father, Judy, Mary, David," n.d., ca. July 1957, JHP.

37 ***"a vast night ocean":*** JH, "Tracking," in *The Summer He Didn't Die* (Grove Press, 2005), 209.

"quite drunk with language": JH, *OTS*, 63.

"future great poet": JH, *Wolf: A False Memoir* (Delta, 1981), 59.

"yokel, a clyde": JH, *Wolf: A False Memoir* (Delta, 1981), 59–60.

"good about being in": JH to "Mother, Father & Family," August 22, 1957, JHP.

***"obviously daft* poet":** JH, *OTS*, 57.

"free donuts [and] radical": JH, *OTS*, 57.

"I am not especially looking": JH to "Mother, Father and family," n.d., ca. July 1957, JHP.

38 ***"the Castle":*** High School of Music and Art (New York), *Mosaic* (June 1957), 7.

"Put me in a system": High School of Music and Art (New York), *Mosaic* (June 1957), 56.

"She is undoubtedly one": JH to "Father, Mother, & Family," n.d., ca. August 1957, JHP.

"First three doubles at": JH, *Wolf: A False Memoir* (Delta, 1981), 193–94.

39 ***"way ahead of [him]":*** JH, *OTS*, 56–57.

"everything that was cheap": JH, *Wolf: A False Memoir* (Delta, 1981), 195.

"It was wonderful": JH to "Family and Judy," n.d., ca. spring 1957, JHP.

"she is Jewish": JH to "Father, Mother & Family," n.d., ca. August 1957, JHP.

"shabby beatnik": JH, *OTS*, 56.

"completely shot": JH to "Mother, Father & Family," Sunday afternoon, ca. September 1957, JHP.

40 ***"Do not be so absurd":*** JH to "Mother, Father, Judy, Mary, David," n.d., ca. July 1957, JHP.

"I can't say I am especially": JH to "Mother, Father & Family," August 22, 1957, JHP.

"I shall try to compensate": JH to "Father, Mother & Family," n.d., ca. August 1957, JHP.

41 ***"St. Petersburg of the United":*** JH, *Wolf: A False Memoir* (Delta, 1981), 41.

"My story is completely ready": JH to "Family," n.d., ca. winter 1958, JHP.

42 ***"wisdom based on experience":*** Winfield Harrison to JH, n.d., ca. winter 1958, JHP.

43 ***"And that something could be":*** Winfield Harrison to JH, n.d., ca. winter 1958, JHP.

"If I had wanted to": JH to Winfield Harrison, n.d., ca. winter 1958, JHP.

"even if it wasn't condonement": JH to "Mary, Dad & Mother," n.d., ca. February 1958, JHP.

44 ***"awfully snobbish":*** JH to "Dear Family," Tuesday, ca. March 1958, JHP.

"the first actual novelist": JH to "Dear Pa & Ma," Wednesday, ca. March 1958, JHP.

"I am developing into": JH to "Dear Father, Mother and Family," 1958, JHP.

"I am sick of trying": JH to "Father, Mother and Family," n.d., ca. April 1958, JHP.

45 ***"much too IDEALISTIC":*** Peter Snyder to JH, June 2, 1958, JHP.

46 ***"I would be very morose":*** JH to "Family," n.d., ca. spring 1958, JHP.

"overwhelmed with love": JH, *Wolf: A False Memoir* (Delta, 1981), 166.

"I feel as though I": Billy Meisner to JH, n.d., JHP.

"Would like to talk to you": Carol Snyder to JH, March 31, 1958, JHP.

47 ***"more morose and inward":*** JH to "Dad & Mother," n.d., ca. March 1958, JHP.

"quite homesick": JH to "Dear Father and Mother," n.d., ca. April 1958, JHP.

4 SOMETHING TO TIE ME TO EARTH

48 ***"The boy followed the girl":*** JH, "Love," in *Jim Harrison: Complete Poems*, ed. Joseph Bednarik (Copper Canyon Press, 2021), 746.

"He was only attracted": Dan Lahren, in discussion with the author, July 24, 2020.

"just really, really fell": Jamie Harrison, in discussion with the author, June 15, 2020.

"with the desperation": JH, "The Beige Dolorosa," in *Julip* (Houghton Mifflin, 1994), 203.

49 ***"marriage is, and should be":*** JH, "What Jim Harrison Taught Me About Marriage," interview by Rose DeMaris, *Millions*, April 29, 2016, https://themillions.com/2016/04/jim-harrison-taught-marriage.html.

"Journalist": JH to TM, n.d., ca. 1984, TMP.

50 ***"really was a wonderful":*** Jamie Harrison, in discussion with the author, June 15, 2020.

"essentially a kind man": JH, *OTS*, 65.

"very kind and very": Penny McClure, in discussion with the author, November 6, 2020.

"really, really difficult woman": Jamie Harrison, in discussion with the author, June 15, 2020.

51 ***"I wish that you would":*** JH to Linda King, October 17, 1958, JHP.

"I believe Linda needs": JH, *OTS*, 67.

52 ***"School is a necessary evil":*** JH to "Father, Mother," n.d., ca. July 1959, JHP.

53 ***"not overly impressed":*** JH to "Ma, Pa and family," Wednesday, ca. July 24, 1959, JHP.

"Some are very bright": JH to "Father, Mother," n.d., ca. July 1959, JHP.

"sort of an artifact": JH to "Father, Mother, family," n.d., ca. July/August 1959, JHP.

"Right now the only": JH to "Father, Mother, family," n.d., ca. July/August 1959, JHP.

"Okies": JH, *Wolf: A False Memoir* (Delta, 1981), 128.

54 ***"dope addicts, pimps":*** JH to "Father, Mother," n.d., ca. July/August 1959, JHP.

"She was about thirty-five": JH, *Wolf: A False Memoir* (Delta, 1981), 126.

"There is something about": JH to "Father, Mother," n.d., ca. July/August 1959, JHP.

55 ***"devout in a different":*** JH to "Father, Mother," n.d., ca. August 1959, JHP.

"the tradition of the great": JH to "Family," n.d., ca. winter 1958, JHP.

"writes me every day": JH to "Father, Mother," n.d., ca. August 1959, JHP.

56 ***"crazy bum":*** JH, *OTS*, 64.

"the Loneliest Road": *Life*, July 1986, 28.

"if you're troubled": JH, "The Seven-Ounce Man," in *Julip* (Houghton Mifflin, 1994), 131.

57 ***"some horrible mistake":*** Linda King to JH, n.d., ca. September 13, 1959, JHP.

"It seems like it": Linda King to JH, Sunday, ca. September 13, 1959, JHP.

"To be honest": JH to Linda King, September 21, 1959, JHP.

58 ***"Frankly James, I think":*** JH, *OTS*, 65.

"But out of Decorum": JH to TM, June 30, 1995, TMP.

"nothing about [my father]": Jamie Harrison, in discussion with the author, June 15, 2020.

59 ***"You're just a whore":*** Jamie Harrison, in discussion with the author, June 15, 2020.

"James, we've always": JH, *OTS*, 65.

"something to tie [him]": JH, *OTS*, 66.

60 ***"a writer's sole responsibility":*** JH to "Father, Mother, and Family," n.d., ca. April 1958, JHP.

"Perhaps I should teach": JH to "Dear Mother," Monday, ca. 1958, JHP.

61 ***"some tendencies":*** E. T. Erazmus to Mr. H. Shotwell, Superintendent of School, Manton, Michigan, November 16, 1962, JHP.

"the complete irresponsibility": Anonymous complainant to supervisor of JH, Michigan State University, n.d., JHP.

"saved for research": JH, *OTS*, 177.

"slightly": JH, *OTS*, 178.

"Kiki the Dog Face Boy": TM, "Thomas McGuane Remembers His Friend, Jim Harrison," April 12, 2017, Literary Hub, https://lithub.com/thomas-mcguane-remembers-his-friend-jim-harrison.

62 ***"topologically see the whole":*** JH, "MSU's Gang of Four Showcased on Campus," interview by Barry Gross, *MSU Alumni*, April 1, 1993, https://alumni.msu.edu/stay-informed/alumni-stories/feature-msus-gang-of-four-showcased-on-campus. See also JH, "Herbert Weisinger: A Personal Remembrance," *Muses*, 1998–99, College of Art and Sciences, Michigan State University.

63 ***"teary penance":*** JH, *OTS*, 179.

"total nervous crack-up": JH, *OTS*, 178.

5 BLACK THICKETS

64 **"Though in the dark":** JH, "A Sequence of Women," in *Jim Harrison: Complete Poems*, ed. Joseph Bednarik (Copper Canyon Press, 2021), 10.

"my world imploded": JH, *OTS*, 182.

65 ***"The family was so close":*** Rebecca Harrison, in discussion with the author, November 17, 2018.

"It has often occurred": JH, *OTS*, 183.

"If I had made": JH, *OTS*, 190.

66 ***"Jamie is comfort because":*** JH to John and Rebecca, n.d., JHP.

"Well, death did it": JH, "An Interview with Jim Harrison," interview by Kay Bonetti, 1984, in *Conversations with Jim Harrison, Revised and Updated*, ed. Robert DeMott (University Press of Mississippi, 2019), 35.

67 ***"I am sending no":*** J. D. Reed to JH, n.d., JHP.

"wrote so many agonized": JH, unaddressed letter, September 19, 1963, JHP.

"I can see Daddy & Judy": JH to John and Rebecca Harrison, n.d., Rebecca Newth Harrison Papers, Special Collections & University Archives, Grand Valley State University.

"would much prefer some": JH to John Harrison, n.d., JHP.

68 ***"I will need no":*** JH to John Harrison, n.d., JHP.

"All has been coolly": JH to John Harrison, n.d., JHP.

"A chain of sex stranglings": *Life*, February 15, 1963, 16.

"Thoreau, mon allié": JH, "Jim Harrison: 'Thoreau, mon allié, mon garde-frontières,'" interview by Martin Duru, *Philosophie Magazine*, July/August 2011.

69 ***"classy employment agency":*** Rebecca, John, and JH to Norma Harrison and family, May 5, 1963, JHP.

"realize now how deeply": JH to John Harrison, May 14, 1963, JHP.

"I can't bear waiting": LH to JH, April 20, 1963, JHP.

"don[']t even get": LH to JH, May 11, 1963, JHP.

"You mean so much": LH to JH, n.d., JHP.

70 ***"What a day":*** LH to JH, May 11, 1963, JHP.

"Oh please, never let": LH to JH, May 14, 1963, JHP.

"It is sickening": LH to JH, May 22, 1963, JHP.

"quite thick": LH to JH, postmarked May 27, 1963, JHP.

"worry about [his] sanity": LH to JH, n.d., JHP.

71 ***"seemed rather dark":*** JH to LH, postmarked April 19, 1963, JHP.

"grand tour": JH, quoted in *Jim Harrison*, by Edward C. Reilly (Twayne Publishers, 1996), 10.

"He works every evening": LH to "the Harrisons," May 27, 1963. JHP.

72 ***"I only want you":*** JH to Family, n.d., JHP.

"peace with what I am": JH to Family, n.d., JHP.

"a bony angular face": JH, "Note Re: Judy and Winfield," journal entry, September 19, 1963, JHP.

73 ***"total consciousness":*** JH to Norma, n.d., JHP.

"Close the damn door": Rhoda Feng, "House of Poesy: At the Grolier Poetry Book Shop," *Paris Review* (blog), February 26, 2013, https://www.theparisreview.org/blog/2013/02/26/house-of-poesy/.

"lively with poetry": JH, *OTS*, 202.

"made poetry out of modern": Edmund Wilson, *The Bit Between My Teeth: A Literary Chronicle of 1950–1965* (Farrar, Straus and Giroux, 1965), 547.

75 ***"a heap of books":*** William Corbett, "A Letter from William Corbett," *Minutes of the Charles Olson Society*, no. 26 (June 1998), https://charlesolson.org/Files/Corbett.htm.

"hypnotic talker": JH, *OTS*, 202.

"yes / or no": JH to DL, n.d., DLP, folder 35.

76 ***"I am thrilled":*** DL to JH, September 15, 1964, JHP.

"mostly because they are": DL to JH, September 15, 1964, JHP.

77 ***"I trust implicitly":*** JH to DL, n.d., DLP, folder 36.

"a very refreshing": LH to "the Harrisons," n.d., ca. November 1964, JHP.

78 ***"It saves our lives":*** DL to JH, September 15, 1964, JHP.

"weren't written by": JH, "The Northness of North," review of *North Winter*, by Hayden Carruth, *Nation*, February 15, 1965, 180.

79 ***"occupied with poetry":*** JH, biographical note, in "Discovery '65 Program" (Poetry Center, YM-YWHA of New York, NY, 1965).

"uncharitable people": JH, reading, Poetry Center, YM-YWHA of New York, NY, April 19, 1965.

"Form is the woods": JH, "Poem," in *Jim Harrison: Complete Poems*, ed. Joseph Bednarik (Copper Canyon Press, 2021), 5.

80 ***"form is never more":*** JH, "A Natural History of Some Poems," in *Just Before Dark: Collected Nonfiction* (Mariner Books, 1999), 215.

"That is, form is a dynamic": JH, "A Natural History of Some Poems," in *Just Before Dark: Collected Nonfiction* (Mariner Books, 1999), 215.

"far north, few people": JH to DL, n.d., DLP, folder 36.

81 ***"benumbed, cloudy, constricted":*** JH, "A Natural History of Some Poems," in *Just Before Dark: Collected Nonfiction* (Mariner Books, 1999), 199.

"His mind's all black": JH, "A Natural History of Some Poems," in *Just Before Dark: Collected Nonfiction* (Mariner Books, 1999), 199.

6 OPERATION STONY BROOK

82 ***"We'll settle the city question":*** JH, ghazal XXVIII, in *Jim Harrison: Complete Poems*, ed. Joseph Bednarik (Copper Canyon Press, 2021), 158.

"My friend Michael": TM to JH, n.d., ca. March 1966, JHP. Letter misdated by archive as 1962, though McGuane is writing to Jim from Málaga, Spain.

"non-acquaintance": TM to JH, March 15, 1968, JHP.

"might have reached": JH to TM, March 18, 1968, JHP.

83 ***"There is an oddness":*** JH to DG, n.d., ca. 1969, DGP.

"I was a very unsuccessful": TM, in discussion with the author, November 3, 2021.

84 ***"entitled":*** BD, in discussion with the author, May 11, 2021.

"the fortunate position": JH to DG, ca. 1968, DGP.

"chiefly avoiding the draft": TM, interview by Dexter Westrum, July 25–26, 1988, in *Thomas McGuane* (Twayne Publishers, 1991), 2.

"I haven't seen such": TM to JH, n.d., ca. March 1966, JHP. Letter misdated by archive as 1962, though McGuane is writing to Jim from Málaga, Spain.

85 ***"[Jim] was kind of a lean":*** Jon Jackson, in discussion with the author, December 12, 2019.

"Holy shit": Pat Paton, in discussion with the author, September 14, 2020.

"I was taken under": JH, *OTS*, 203.

"Whatever he did": Pat Paton, in discussion with the author, September 14, 2020.

86 ***"every inch of it":*** Pat Paton, in discussion with the author, September 14, 2020.

"all in black": Gary Snyder to JH, February 7, 1969, JHP.

"a definite Democrat": Pat Paton, in discussion with the author, September 14, 2020.

"And that was the first": Vesper Paton, in discussion with the author, September 14, 2020.

"big wheel": Pat Paton, in discussion with the author, September 14, 2020.

"I didn't know how": Pat Paton, in discussion with the author, September 14, 2020.

87 ***"I think it's your":*** Pat Paton, in discussion with the author, September 14, 2020.

"appear nondescript and scrubby": JH, *OTS*, 203.

"Linda and I went": JH to Norma Harrison, January 2, 1996, JHP. Letter misdated "Jan 2, 65."

88 ***"I'm a poet":*** Jim Crocket, in discussion with the author, September 21, 2020.

"Woe. Poverty. etc.": JH to Norma Harrison, July 10, 1965, JHP.

"a prisoner wishes": JH to Norma Harrison, July 10, 1965, JHP.

"heavy, cold hand": JH to Norma Harrison, October 16, 1965, JHP.

89 ***"reads every last wrinkle":*** TM to JH, August 1967, JHP.

"who wanted to write": TM to JH, November 25, 1966, JHP.

"[Mark] McCloskey raped me": JH to DL, n.d., ca. August 1966, DLP, folder 36.

"Mr. Harrison on occasion": Mark McCloskey, "Five Poets," *Poetry* 8, no. 4 (1966): 272–76.

"neither to the Beat": Joseph J. Waldmeir, "Just Good Poetry, Not Bear of Folksy," *Detroit News*, May 29, 1966.

"Li Po, Lorca, Vallejo": William Corbett, "One Redskin," review of *Plain Song, Harvard Advocate*, March 1966, 34.

"Up to my chin": JH to Norma Harrison, n.d., ca. 1965, JHP.

"nothing salvageable": JH to DL (letter begins "Dear People"), n.d., ca. fall 1965, DLP, folder 36.

90 ***"After all":*** Herbert Weisinger to JH, April 6, 1965, JHP.

"fine letter": JH to Norma Harrison, January 2, 1966, JHP. Letter misdated "Jan 2, 65."

"over involved": Herbert Weisinger to JH, n.d., ca. spring 1966, JHP.

91 ***"Papers of this sort":*** JH, "A Natural History of Some Poems," in *Just Before Dark: Collected Nonfiction* (Mariner Books, 1999), 199.

"juvenilia": JH, introduction to *Just Before Dark: Collected Nonfiction* (Mariner Books, 1999), xi.

"a pure acknowledgment": JH, *OTS*, 209.

"intended to stick with [him]": JH to DL, May 1966, DLP, folder 35.

"bad for poetry in five": JH to TM, May 1966, TMP.

"Apprentice to journeyman": JH to DL, August 1966, DLP, folder 35.

92 ***"Have no choice":*** JH to DL, May 1966, DLP, folder 35.

93 ***"no teaching, good pay":*** JH to DL, August 1966, DLP, folder 35.

"grown-up house": JH, *OTS*, 213.

94 ***"heady experience":*** JH, *OTS*, 212.

95 ***"'that man'":*** JH, *OTS*, 219.

"going to be where": Eliot Weinberger, in discussion with the author, June 11, 2021.

"It was an incredibly wild": Ruth Lepson, in discussion with the author, December 14, 2021.

"Have you read about the raid": LH to Norma Harrison, n.d., ca. January 1968, JHP. See also D. S. Greenberg, "'Pot' and Politics: How They 'Busted' Stony Brook," *Science* 159, no. 3815 (1968): 607–11.

"prized student": JH, *OTS*, 220.

96 ***"Again, this was a startling":*** JH, *OTS*, 213.

97 ***"very amusing":*** Rose Styron, in discussion with the author, September 25, 2021.

"MSU seems to be": DG to JH, n.d., ca. January 1967, JHP.

"I didn't know you then": DG to JH, n.d., ca. 1966, DGP.

98 ***"he had a sense":*** JH to DG, n.d., ca. 1966, JHP.

"virgin forest": DG to JH, November 18, 1966, DGP.

"mega-city": JH to DG, n.d., ca. November 1966, JHP.

99 ***"kind courtesy":*** Carolyn Kizer to JH, September 15, 1967, JHP.

"black and blue": JH, *OTS*, 223.

100 ***"absolutely direct anti-war":*** DL to Robert Duncan, January 25, 1966, in *The Letters of Robert Duncan and Denise Levertov*, eds. Robert J. Bertholf and Albert Gelpi (Stanford University Press, 2004), 519.

"shrill political poems": George Quasha, in discussion with the author, February 9, 2022.

"helpless outrage": DL to Robert Duncan, January 25, 1966, in *The Letters of Robert Duncan and Denise Levertov*, eds. Robert J. Bertholf and Albert Gelpi (Stanford University Press, 2004), 490.

"THERE HAS BEEN NO TIME": Robert Duncan to DL, October 4, 1971, in *The Letters of Robert Duncan and Denise Levertov*, eds. Robert J. Bertholf and Albert Gelpi (Stanford University Press, 2004), 661.

"terribly dangerous": JH, "The Art of Fiction: Jim Harrison," interview by Jim Fergus, 1986, in *Conversations with Jim Harrison, Revised and Updated*, ed. Robert DeMott (University Press of Mississippi, 2019), 65.

"So my only form": JH to TM, n.d., ca. fall 1967, TMP.

101 ***"Only total war comes":*** JH to TM, n.d., ca. fall 1967, TMP.

"came out of the feeling": JH, "The Art of Fiction: Jim Harrison," interview by Jim Fergus, 1986, in *Conversations with Jim Harrison, Revised and Updated*, ed. Robert DeMott (University Press of Mississippi, 2019), 53.

"I am simply a poet": JH to Roger L. Stevens, December 5, 1967, JHP.

102 ***"Any artist is an artist":*** JH to Roger L. Stevens, December 5, 1967, JHP.

7 LOCATIONS

103 ***"Mind follow the nose":*** JH, "Dawn Whiskey," in *Jim Harrison: Complete Poems*, ed. Joseph Bednarik (Copper Canyon Press, 2021), 93.

"Denise had assured me": JH to George Brockway, October 18, 1967, JHP.

"inasmuch as that is": JH to George Brockway, October 18, 1967, JHP.

"I have never confessed": JH to TM, n.d., ca. 1967, TMP.

104 ***"thin as shellac":*** JH to George Brockway, January 5, 1968, JHP.

105 ***"It was the only attempt":*** Charles Simic, "The Great Poets' Brawl of '68," *New York Review of Books*, April 23, 2014, https://www.nybooks.com/online/2014/04/23/great-poets-brawl-68/. See also JH, "Jim Harrison: An Interview with Joseph Bednarik," interview by Joseph Bednarik, 2000, in *Conversations with Jim Harrison, Revised and Updated*, ed. Robert DeMott (University Press of Mississippi, 2019), 183–200.

"major international meeting": Stony Brook University Office of University Relations, press release, May 3, 1968, Stony Brook University Special Collections.

106 ***"Poets and 'literary' people":*** LH to Norma Harrison, n.d., ca. spring 1968, JHP.

"coupling couple": JH, *OTS*, 224.

"Anselm Hollo / Trying to": Edward Sanders, *1968: A History in Verse* (Black Sparrow Press, 2000), 155.

107 ***"the climax":*** David Ignatow to JH, August 13, 1968. JHP.

"You're nothing without": Edward Sanders, *1968: A History in Verse* (Black Sparrow Press, 2000), 155.

"feeling like a Rudi Stern": Edward Sanders, *1968: A History in Verse* (Black Sparrow Press, 2000), 155.

108 ***"That police state":*** "Poet Power," *New York Review of Books*, August 22, 1968.

"World Poetry cesspool": James Tate to JH, December 22, 1969, JHP.

"The Great Poets' Brawl": Charles Simic, "The Great Poets' Brawl of '68," *New York Review of Books*, April 23, 2014.

"the poesy conference": James Tate to JH, December 22, 1969, JHP.

"I can see 20": JH to TM, n.d., ca. summer 1968, TMP.

109 ***"You are so smug":*** George Brockway to JH, July 24, 1968, JHP.

"won the day": JH, *OTS*, 224.

"He's going to be": DG, in discussion with the author, May 13, 2021.

"difficult thing to be": LH to Norma Harrison, n.d., ca. spring 1968, JHP.

"We did it ONCE": JH to Louis Simpson, n.d., July 1968, JHP.

110 ***"I don't know what she":*** Louis Simpson to JH, August 14, 1968, JHP.

"I can't stand Louis": DL to Robert Duncan, March 9, 1961, in *The Letters of Robert Duncan and Denise Levertov*, eds. Robert J. Bertholf and Albert Gelpi (Stanford University Press, 2004), 293.

"Both Denise and Louis": George Quasha, in discussion with the author, February 9, 2022.

111 ***"In 1968 when I":*** JH, "Livingston Suite," in *Saving Daylight*, Copper Canyon, 2006, 21.

"tough old leathery cowboy": TM, in discussion with the author, November 3, 2021.

"Ever foolhardy": JH, *OTS*, 230.

112 ***"It was a splendid":*** JH, *OTS*, 230.

"skinny trails across precipitous": JH, *OTS*, 230.

113 ***"I just ate two":*** JH to TM, n.d., ca. August 1968, TMP.

"the finest Poetry magazines": DG to JH, March 9, 1968, JHP.

"absolutely open": JH to TM, n.d., ca. June 1968, TMP.

"kind of 'them and us'": DG, introduction to *The Sumac Reader*, ed. Joseph Bednarik (Michigan State University Press, 1997), xv.

114 ***"A whole shitload":*** DG to JH, October 13, 1968, JHP.

"loathe[d] the decorative aspects": JH to George Brockway, April 8, 1968, JHP.

"such people": JH to George Brockway, May 29, 1968, JHP.

"whose subjects and length": JH to George Brockway, March 19, 1968, JHP.

115 ***"nature poet":*** JH to George Brockway, March 19, 1968, JHP.

"It is a sorry mistake": JH, "Fresh Usual Words," *New York Times Book Review*, April 28, 1968, 6.

116 ***"If someone stepped out":*** DL to JH, September 12, 1968, JHP.

"Paul Carroll has written": DL to JH, September 12, 1968, JHP.

"On every page": Louis Simpson to JH, September 12, 1986, JHP.

"Then, drop by drop": Louis Simpson to JH, September 12, 1986, JHP.

117 ***"I think of my work":*** Robert Duncan to JH, January 8, 1969, JHP.

"letting the magazine go": Robert Duncan to JH, January 8, 1969, JHP.

"bounty of soul": JH to Robert Duncan and DL, January 22, 1969, DLP, folder 38.

118 ***"We are not* Caterpillar*":*** "Editorial Note," *Sumac* 1, no. 3 (1969): 106.

8 WOLF

119 ***"I don't have any medals":*** JH, letter 2, in *Letters to Yesenin* (Copper Canyon Press, 2007), 5.

"My book has met": JH to Louis Simpson, February 1969, JHP.

"No one can control": Louis Simpson to JH, February 12, 1969, JHP.

120 ***"DO YOU TALK":*** Louis Simpson to JH, February 12, 1969, JHP.

"totally bent": JH to TM, n.d., ca. October 1968, TMP.

"That & his long": LH to Norma Harrison, October 12, 1968, JHP.

"For your private info": JH to TM, n.d., ca. October 1968, TMP.
"reduce the sauce intake": TM to JH, October 15, 1968, JHP.
121 ***"At 190lbs now":*** JH to TM, Friday 13, ca. 1969, TMP.
"Quit whiskey": JH to TM, n.d., ca. 1968, TMP.
"Re alcohol": JH to TM, n.d., ca. 1966, TMP.
"Alcohol: Wanted to go": JH to TM, n.d., ca. 1970, TMP.
"Stunned my brain": JH to TM, n.d., ca. January 1969, TMP.
"I got a guckenheim!": JH to DL, July 19, 1969, DLP, folder 35.
122 ***"antique form":*** JH, "Notes on the Ghazals," in *The Shape of the Journey: New and Collected Poems* (Copper Canyon Press, 1998), 127.
"John O Hariness": JH to DL, April 1969, DLP, folder 35.
"greatly upset": JH to DL, n.d., ca. April 1969, DLP, folder 35.
"gargurble": JH to TM, n.d., ca. April 1969, TMP.
123 ***"Fine two days":*** JH to TM, n.d., ca. spring 1969, TMP.
"Since Keats was the first": JH, *OTS*, 232–33.
"Okay, that's it!": DG, in discussion with the author, June 21, 2021.
"only in the Midwest": JH, *A Really Big Lunch: The Roving Gourmand on Food and Life* (Grove Press, 2017), 23.
124 ***"a taste for more":*** JH to DL, June 2, 1969, DLP, folder 35.
125 ***"That long phone call":*** DL to JH, December 2, 1969, JHP.
"I was very upset": JH to DL, July 19, 1969, DLP, folder 35.
"Actually I am more": JH to DL, July 19, 1969, DLP, folder 35.
126 ***"Wow! You have Poets' Paranoia":*** DL to JH, July 24, 1969, JHP.
"I may be this": DL to JH, July 24, 1969, JHP.
"a very beautiful one": DL to JH, July 24, 1969, JHP.
"a really low sneak": DL to JH, July 24, 1969, JHP.
127 ***"It seemed ironic":*** DL to JH, July 24, 1969, JHP.
"darkest thoughts yet": DL to JH, February 1969, JHP.
"I've cared so much": DL to JH, July 24, 1969, JHP.
128 ***"I took it for granted":*** DL to JH, July 24, 1969, JHP.
"I kiss yr feet": JH to DL, July 25, 1969, DLP, folder 35.
129 ***"nostalgia, some humor":*** Don Anderson to JH, October 12, 1969, JHP.

"Today, as yesterday": JH, "The Real Fun of the Fair Was the Horse Pulling," *Sports Illustrated*, August 31, 1970, 55–56.

130 ***"no stomach or ass":*** JH to TM, December 5, 1969, TMP.

"show off his svelte": DG, in discussion with the author, December 27, 2021.

131 ***"just a picture":*** JH, "The Art of Fiction: Jim Harrison," interview by Jim Fergus, 1986, in *Conversations with Jim Harrison, Revised and Updated*, ed. Robert DeMott (University Press of Mississippi, 2019), 62.

"I seem able to write": JH to TM, n.d., ca. fall 1969, TMP.

"authoritative presence": JH, *OTS*, 236.

"Let me see!": Richard Locke to JH, n.d., ca. 1969, JHP.

133 ***"I would move":*** JH to TM, n.d., ca. summer 1969, TMP.

"It is, as Tom": Candida Donadio to JH, April 13, 1970, JHP.

134 ***"stealing from me":*** Tom McGuane, in discussion with the author, April 6, 2022.

135 ***"This is the part":*** BD, "Fractured Narratives: A Memoir in Stories," unpublished manuscript, 60. JHP.

"From then on": JH, *OTS*, 236.

"Your manuscript is": BD to JH, January 15, 1971, JHP.

136 ***"Shes doesn't seem":*** Alix Nelson to JH, January 27, 1971, JHP.

"quite extraordinary book": Alix Nelson to JH, June 11, 1970, JHP.

"device of a triple": Alix Nelson to JH, June 11, 1970, JHP.

"All my suggestions": Alix Nelson to JH, June 11, 1970, JHP.

137 ***"Form is never more":*** JH, "A Natural History of Some Poems," in *Just Before Dark* (Mariner Books, 1999), 215.

"more likely": JH to DL, 1966, DLP, folder 35.

"I really want": Adrienne Rich to JH, December 9, 1969, JHP.

"essentially lyrics": JH, "Notes on the Ghazals," in *Jim Harrison: Complete Poems*, ed. Joseph Bednarik (Copper Canyon Press, 2021), 129.

138 ***"I don't really remember":*** Jamie Harrison, in discussion with the author, June 15, 2020.

"a dandy of a piece": Alix Nelson to JH, August 4, 1971, JHP.

139 ***"throwing the tiny meats":*** Joy Williams, "A Holy Terror Dancing with Light: On Jim Harrison," *Paris Review* (blog), October 21, 2021, https://

www.theparisreview.org/blog/2021/10/21/a-holy-terror-dancing-with-light-on-jim-harrison/.

"game hoggery": JH, "Grim Reapers of the Land's Bounty," *Sports Illustrated*, October 11, 1971, 38–48.

"novelistic, partly humorous": Ray Cave to JH, October 18, 1970, JHP.

"suppressed sport": JH, *OTS*, 244.

140 ***"so obsessed with Russian":*** JH, "Jim Harrison: An Interview with Joseph Bednarik," interview by Joseph Bednarik, 2000, in *Conversations with Jim Harrison, Revised and Updated*, ed. Robert DeMott (University Press of Mississippi, 2019), 190.

"really lit the Yesenin": DG, in discussion with the author, September 2, 2020.

"fashionable accoutrements": JH, *OTS*, 128.

141 ***"Could I have some Vodka":*** DG, in discussion with the author, September 2, 2020.

"I fell easily into": JH, *OTS*, 244.

"Something had happened": DG, in discussion with the author, September 2, 2020.

142 ***"Pamela from* Baywatch*":*** DG, in discussion with the author, September 2, 2020.

"I really began to know": JH, "Jim Harrison: An Interview with Joseph Bednarik," interview by Joseph Bednarik, 2000, in *Conversations with Jim Harrison, Revised and Updated*, ed. Robert DeMott (University Press of Mississippi, 2019), 190.

"doesn't stare at me": JH, letter 1, in *Letters to Yesenin* (Copper Canyon Press, 2007), 3.

"grand quarters": DG, in discussion with the author, September 2, 2020.

"very life blood": Nikolay Gogol, "Nevsky Prospekt," in *"Diary of a Madman," "The Government Inspector" and Selected Stories*, trans. Ronald Wilks (Penguin Books, 2005), 79.

"Whatever you do": DG, in discussion with the author, September 2, 2020.

144 ***"poet's novel":*** Christopher Lehmann-Haupt, "The Woods Are Ugly, Cold, Wet," *New York Times*, November 24, 1971.

"Going Places": Joyce Carol Oates, "Going Places," review of *Wolf*, by JH, *Partisan Review* 39, no. 3 (Summer 1972): 462–463.

"one of the last": Advertisement for *Wolf*, JHP.

"Smart-ass-literary-suggestion": Jeanette Mall to JH, January 8, 1972, JHP.

9 THE SPORTING CLUB

145 ***"A wave lasts only moments":*** JH, "Waves," in *Jim Harrison: Complete Poems*, ed. Joseph Bednarik (Copper Canyon Press, 2021), 551.

"sending a top writer": Peter Barrett to JH, October 14, 1971, JHP.

"Strange now this late": JH to TM, March 17, 1972, TMP.

146 ***"In fact, it can":*** JH, "The Mad Marlin of Punta Carnero," *True* 53, no. 421 (1972): 88–94.

"long, shattering stretch": JH, "The Mad Marlin of Punta Carnero," *True* 53, no. 421 (1972): 88–94.

"I don't like to kill": JH, "The Mad Marlin of Punta Carnero," *True* 53, no. 421 (1972): 88–94.

"You cannot tell a baby": JH to TM, March 21, 1972, TMP.

147 ***"I can't spend another":*** JH to TM, March 9, 1972, TMP.

"I am only in love": JH to TM, March 20, 1972, TMP.

148 ***"flyfishing notions":*** TM to JH, January 14, 1969, JHP.

149 ***"totally devoid of rules":*** JH, *OTS*, 242.

"knew the area": Guy de la Valdène, in discussion with the author, July 8, 2020.

150 ***"For my part":*** Russell Chatham to JH, May 12, 1971, JHP.

"Russy-of-the-west": JH to Russell Chatham, June 7, 1971. Letter accessed while in possession of Lea Chatham.

"Tom and GiGi don't": JH to Russell Chatham, June 7, 1971. Letter accessed while in possession of Lea Chatham.

"big, gentle, one-eyed": Guy de la Valdène, "1974," in unpublished notes sent to the author.

151 ***"all hell would break loose":*** Guy de la Valdène, in discussion with the author, July 15, 2020.

"a hundred fish": Guy de la Valdène, in discussion with the author, July 15, 2020.

152 ***"Right now I crave":*** JH to TM, January 25, 1972, TMP.

"I much like Keys Guide": Pat Ryan to JH, December 23, 1971, JHP.

153 ***"used up":*** TM to JH, n.d., ca. April 5, 1972, JHP.

"I came [to Livingston]": TM to JH, n.d., ca. April 5, 1972, JHP.

"I feel a little funny": TM to JH, April 5, 1971, TMP.

"I know with your": TM to JH, n.d., ca. April 5, 1972, JHP.

154 ***"thoroughly 'noir' novel":*** JH, "The Art of Fiction, No. 104," interview by Jim Fergus, *Paris Review*, no. 107 (Summer 1988): 52–97.

"utterly alien": JH, "The Art of Fiction, No. 104," interview by Jim Fergus, *Paris Review*, no. 107 (Summer 1988): 52–97.

155 ***"double-anchored off Cudjoe":*** JH, *A Good Day to Die* (Dell/Delta Publishing, 1981), 13.

"Almost around the next": JH, *A Good Day to Die* (Dell/Delqta Publishing, 1981), 119.

156 ***"all problems—money, sex":*** JH, *A Good Day to Die* (Dell/Delta Publishing, 1981), 121.

"so mundane an article": JH to TM, June 20, 1972, TMP.

"We have to have": JH, early draft of *A Good Day to Die*, in green spiral notebook, JHP.

157 ***"solid farmhouse":*** TM to JH, October 23, 1969, JHP.

"aching beautiful": TM to JH, n.d., ca. July 1969, JHP.

"It was hard living": Lea Chatham, in discussion with the author, May 5, 2021.

158 ***"most violent of depressions":*** JH to DG, September 12, 1972, DGP.

"vulgarization of sexuality": JH to DG, September 12, 1972, DGP.

159 ***"I am surprised":*** JH to DG, September 12, 1972, DGP.

"solving themselves": JH to TM, September 1972, TMP. See also JH to TM, October 1, 1972, TMP.

"incomprehensible delight": JH to TM, October 1, 1972, TMP.

"domestic difficulties": JH to TM, June 13, 1972, TMP.

160 ***"couldn't go home":*** JH, *A Good Day to Die* (Dell/Delta Publishing, 1981), 27.

"How long has it been": JH, *A Good Day to Die* (Dell/Delta Publishing, 1981), 44.

"little fire left": JH, *A Good Day to Die* (Dell/Delta Publishing, 1981), 70.

"wife had thought it": JH, *A Good Day to Die* (Dell/Delta Publishing, 1981), 40.

"So much of love": JH to TM, September 1972, TMP.

"proposed fucking": JH to TM, July 8, TMP.

"compartmentalizing proscribed drives": TM to DG, July 13, 1972, DGP.

161 ***"the usual niggling desire":*** JH, *A Good Day to Die* (Dell/Delta Publishing, 1981), 46.

"already had a perfect": JH, *A Good Day to Die* (Dell/Delta Publishing, 1981), 102.

162 ***"very small man":*** DG, in discussion with the author, June 21, 2021.

"I didn't want to stop": JH to DG, March 1973, DGP.

163 ***"Unfortunately I want everything":*** JH to DG, June 6, 1973, DGP.

"greater despair than ever": JH to DG, March 1973, DGP.

"dark period": Jamie Harrison, in discussion with the author, September 7, 2019.

"All of this darkness": JH to DG, March 14, 1973, DGP.

"Not writing a sentence": JH to DG, n.d., ca. February 16, 1973, DGP.

"I'm either going": JH to DG, n.d., ca. February 17, 1973, DGP.

164 ***"You sure have to":*** JH to DG, n.d., ca. February 16, 1973, DGP.

"even the next meal": JH, "The Art of Fiction, No. 104," interview by Jim Fergus, *Paris Review*, no. 107 (Summer 1988): 52–97.

"Suicide. Beauty takes my": JH, letter 3, in *Letters to Yesenin* (Copper Canyon Press, 2007), 6.

10 ZEN AND THE ART OF TARPON FISHING

165 ***"I was proud at four":*** JH, letter 12, in *Letters to Yesenin* (Copper Canyon Press, 2007), 23.

"The thief of fire": JH to DG, June 6, 1973, DGP.

"I was out there": JH, letter 8, *Letters to Yesenin* (Copper Canyon Press, 2007), 13.

"easily the most dangerous": JH to DG, March 17, 1973, DGP.

166 ***"Still joyous":*** JH to TM, August 15, 1973, JHP.

"I can't make the groceries": JH to DG, June 6, 1973, DGP.
"To wit, neither of us": JH to TM, July 2, 1973, TMP.
167 *"Men my age go"*: JH, *Farmer* (Dell/Delta Publishing, 1976), 49.
"It's when you don't": Ray Cave to JH, December 12, 1971, JHP.
"getting poleaxed": JH to TM, March 16, 1973, TMP.
168 *"Still seems odd"*: JH to Peter Matthiessen, n.d., JHP.
"I know that the only": Deborah Love Matthiessen, *Annaghkeen* (Random House, 1970).
"Self abnegation slugged it": JH to TM, March 1974, JHP.
169 *"Imagine primal man"*: JH to Guy de la Valdène, August 1974, JHP.
"Imagine the total": JH to Guy de la Valdène, August 1974, JHP.
"Even you dear friend": JH to TM, June 1974, JHP.
170 *"Yr odd dribbling whimper"*: TM to JH, June 1973, JHP.
"great unspoken": TM to JH, June 1973, JHP.
"hermit crank": JH to TM, June 1973, TMP.
171 *"I think you are troubled"*: JH to TM, June 1973, TMP.
"DO YOU TALK": Louis Simpson to JH, February 12, 1969, JHP.
"almost entirely patched": Christopher Lehmann-Haupt, "Old Monsters Never Die," review of *A Good Day to Die*, by JH, *New York Times Book Review*, September 13, 1973.
"content to waste": Sara Blackburn, review of *A Good Day to Die*, by JH, *New York Times Book Review*, September 9, 1973, 4.
"This is a poet's book": William Crawford Woods, "What a Strange Accomplishment," *Washington Post Book World*, September 9, 1973, 4.
"own paranoia": JH to DG, November 1973, DGP.
172 *"listing of griefs"*: DG to JH, December 5, 1973, JHP.
"played the complete": JH to DG, December 6, 1973, DGP.
"utterly desperate": JH, introduction to *The Shape of the Journey: New and Collected Poems* (Copper Canyon Press, 1998), 4.
"a great river": JH, letter 1, in *Letters to Yesenin* (Copper Canyon Press, 2007), 4.
173 *"Quintuple heaps of caviar"*: JH, letter 24, in *Letters to Yesenin* (Copper Canyon Press, 2007), 47.

"pushed the confessional form": J. D. Reed, "One of the Beasts," review of *Letters to Yesenin*, by JH, *American Poetry Review* 5, no. 4 (1976): 37.

"not only [Harrison's] best": Hayden Carruth, "Carruth on Harrison," *Sulfur: A Literary Tri-Annual of the Whole Art*, no. 7, (1982): 157–60.

174 ***"It says to us":*** Hayden Carruth, "Carruth on Harrison," *Sulfur: A Literary Tri-Annual of the Whole Art*, no. 7 (1986): 159.

"Fuckin tired of writing": JH to TM, n.d., ca. fall 1973, TMP.

"You'd better figure out": TM to JH, November 28, 1973, JHP.

175 ***"Go away a few weeks":*** JH to TM, November 28, 1973, JHP.

"a therapeutic alternative": JH to TM, Match 7, 1972, TMP.

"Why get freaked": JH, "A Sporting Life," *Playboy*, January 1976, 144–46, 214, 216–17.

176 ***"This will be a messy":*** JH to Guy de la Valdène, February 1974, JHP.

"People who fish tarpon": JH to Guy de la Valdène, February 1974, JHP.

"The almost overbearing": JH to Guy de la Valdène, February 1974, JHP.

177 ***"You never see a painting":*** JH, *Tarpon*, dir. Guy de la Valdène and Christian Odasso, UYA Films, 1973.

11 FARMER

178 ***"Six days of clouds since":*** JH, "Weeping," in *Jim Harrison: Complete Poems*, ed. Joseph Bednarik (Copper Canyon Press, 2021), 291.

"swans in [the] moat": JH to DG, illegible date, ca. August 29, 1974, JHP.

"bring it off splendidly": JH to Guy de la Valdène, August 1974, JHP.

179 ***"like a war wound":*** JH to Guy de la Valdène, August 1974, JHP.

"Please try saying fuck": JH to DG, September 10, 1974, DGP.

180 ***"What can I say reaching":*** JH to Russell Chatham, December 15, 1974, JHP.

"What can I say about Tom": JH to Russell Chatham, December 15, 1974, JHP. In McGuane's memory, he was staying in a cheap rental in London provided by the "scurrilous" Elliot Kastner, while he edited his film.

"IRS invasion": JH to Russell Chatham, December 15, 1974, JHP.

181 ***"I think you are":*** Dan Green to JH, January 9, 1975, JHP.

"axes to grind": Peter Matthiessen, quoted in "Thomas Guinzburg, Paris Review Co-Founder, Dies at 84," by Bruce Weber, *New York Times*, September 10, 2010.

"Hope that all": Patricia Irving to JH, March 13, 1975, JHP.

"some housecleaning": Patricia Irving to JH, March 13, 1975, JHP.

182 ***"Why are these guys":*** TM, in discussion with the author, November 3, 2021.

183 ***"Usually, people are selling":*** BD, in discussion with the author, September 6, 2019.

"willful and capricious": TM, *Variety*, May 11, 1976.

184 ***"And Jim took Jack's side":*** TM, in discussion with the author, November 3, 2021.

"I can't tell you": TM to JH, June 1973, JHP.

186 ***"When he finished saying":*** Ianthe Brautigan, *You Can't Catch Death: A Daughter's Memoir* (St. Martin's Press, 2000), 76.

"deep, dramatic voice": Ianthe Brautigan, *You Can't Catch Death: A Daughter's Memoir* (St. Martin's Press, 2000), 76.

"I just thought I'd drop": Richard Brautigan to JH, n.d., JHP.

"I have no business": Richard Brautigan to JH, October 9, 1973, JHP.

187 ***"going riding":*** JH, *Farmer* (Dell/Delta Publishing, 1976), 62.

188 ***"How could he have":*** JH, *Farmer* (Dell/Delta Publishing, 1976), 8.

"local marriage counseling": JH to TM, February 1974, TMP.

"deep resurgence": JH to TM, June 1974, TMP.

"Grief makes people lazy": JH, *Farmer* (Dell/Delta Publishing, 1976), 97.

"eloquent in its brevity": Patricia Irving to JH, June 3, 1975, JHP.

"You didn't phone": Patricia Irving to JH, October 10, 1975, JHP.

189 ***"I've been over it":*** JH, "The Art of Fiction, No. 104," interview by Jim Fergus, *Paris Review*, no. 107 (Summer 1988): 52–97.

"an extraordinary thing": JH, "The Art of Fiction, No. 104," interview by Jim Fergus, *Paris Review*, no. 107 (Summer 1988): 52–97.

"Jimmy goddammit": Patricia Irving to JH, January 14, 1976, JHP.

190 ***"mistakenly dissatisfied":*** Michael Loeb to BD, July 23, 1980, JHP.
"Talked to Tom Ginsberg": JH to Michael Loeb, n.d., ca. July 1980, JHP.

12 LEGENDS OF THE FALL

191 ***"She says it's too hot":*** JH, "Returning to Earth," in *Jim Harrison: Complete Poems*, ed. Joseph Bednarik (Copper Canyon Press, 2021), 267.
"only a small part": JH, *OTS*, 248.

192 ***"I mean, it wouldn't":*** Jamie Harrison, in discussion with the author, September 7, 2019.

193 ***"She loved the idea":*** Jamie Harrison, in discussion with the author, September 7, 2019.
"What do you mean": Jamie Harrison, in discussion with the author, September 7, 2019.
"Never mind": Jamie Harrison, in discussion with the author, September 7, 2019.
"having a work on option": JH, quoted in "Whiners? Writer Discounts Complaints of Hollywood, Success," by David Averill, *Traverse City Record-Eagle*, March 4, 1977, 15.

194 ***"I worked overtime":*** Jamie Harrison, in discussion with the author, September 7, 2019.
"Working on two novels": JH to Peter Matthiessen, March 8, 1977, JHP.
"awfully impressed": Cecil Giscombe to JH, March 8, 1977, JHP.

195 ***"slightly bothered":*** Cecil Giscombe to JH, June 19, 1977, JHP.
"We regret that you": Cecil Giscombe to JH, June 28, 1977, JHP.

196 ***"lives becoming history":*** JH, notes for draft of "Legends of the Fall," n.d., ca. 1978, JHP.
"god-like": JH, "Creating Habitat for the Soul: An Interview with Jim Harrison," interview by Robert DeMott and Patrick Smith, 1997/1998, in *Conversations with Jim Harrison, Revised and Updated*, ed. Robert DeMott (University Press of Mississippi, 2019), 144.
"seizure in composition": JH, *OTS*, 250.

197 ***"Wm. A. Ludlow / Mariposa":*** Original journal in possession of the Harrison family.

"Their powers of sustained": See JH, *Legends of the Fall* (Grove Press, 2016), 201. See also William Ludlow, *Report of a Reconnaissance of the Black Hills of Dakota, Made in the Summer of 1874* (US Government Printing Office, 1875), 12. Jim slightly misquotes the passage.

198 ***"elegant writer":*** JH, "Lake Effect: Talking with Jim Harrison," interview by Edward C. Reilly, December 1991, in *Jim Harrison* (Twayne Publishers, 1996), 78.

"fired the beige landscape": JH, *Legends of the Fall* (Grove Press, 2016), 201–202; cf. William Ludlow, *Report of a Reconnaissance of the Black Hills of Dakota, Made in the Summer of 1874* (US Government Printing Office, 1875).

"totally disabled": JH, *Legends of the Fall* (Grove Press, 2016), 215.

"two deaths": JH, *Legends of the Fall* (Grove Press, 2016), 249.

199 ***"set out to murder":*** JH, "Revenge," in *Just Before Dark* (Mariner Books, 1999), 271.

"no evening the score": JH, *Legends of the Fall* (Grove Press, 2016), 215.

200 ***"You sounded down":*** Toby Rafelson to JH, July 4, 1977, JHP.

"Durango is a 400-yr": Toby Rafelson to JH, July 4, 1977, JHP.

201 ***"first look":*** Robert S. Colbert to JH, August 20, 1977, JHP.

"It's still as beautiful": Toby Rafelson to JH, October 21, 1977, JHP.

"all the film rights": Robert S. Colbert to JH, August 20, 1977, JHP.

"any monies garnered": BD to JH, January 23, 1979, JHP.

202 ***"It looks like showdown":*** BD to JH, March 5, 1979, JHP.

"On page 1": Cecil Giscombe to JH, June 19, 1977, JHP.

"At nineteen I began": JH, "Returning to Earth," notes and drafts, JHP.

203 ***"O my darling sister":*** JH, *Returning to Earth* (Ithaca House, 1977).

"academicism": Hayden Carruth, "The Passionate Few," *Harper's Magazine*, June 1978, 86–89.

204 ***"hard-boiled":*** Hayden Carruth, "The Passionate Few," *Harper's Magazine*, June 1978, 86–89.

"ascetic brevity": Graham Good, "Notes on the Novella," *Novel: A Forum on Fiction* 10, no. 3 (1977): 197–211.

"faithfully in late high school": JH to SL, August 20, 1990, JHP.

205 ***"mid-form, that half-way":*** JH, "Creating Habitat for the Soul: An Interview with Jim Harrison," interview by Robert DeMott and Patrick Smith, 1997/1998, in *Conversations with Jim Harrison, Revised and Updated*, ed. Robert DeMott (University Press of Mississippi, 2019), 144.

"Rust had a famous": BD, in discussion with the author, September 6, 2019.

"He used to say": Richard Ford, quoted in "L. Rust Hills, Fiction Editor at Esquire, Dies at 83," by Bruce Weber, *New York Times*, August 13, 2008. *Esquire* published the excerpt of Styron's *Sophie's Choice* in September 1976.

206 ***"[Rust] was a natural":*** BD, in discussion with the author, September 6, 2019.

"The magazine appeared bolder": Terry McDonell, *The Accidental Life: An Editor's Notes on Writing and Writers* (Vintage, 2017), 153.

"It's a tale of high": Foreword to *Legends of the Fall*, by JH, *Esquire*, January 2, 1979, 35.

"Nobody wanted a novella": BD, in discussion with the author, September 6, 2019.

"a sure-thing best-seller": JH, *OTS*, 250.

207 ***"interest in good":*** SL to JH, February 9, 1967, JHP.

208 ***"perhaps with some illustrations":*** BD to SL, n.d., Seymour Lawrence Collection, box 39, file 18, Archives and Special Collections, J. D. Williams Library, University of Mississippi.

"bright future": SL to Ross Claiborne and William Grose, "Office Memorandum," April 17, 1978, Seymour Lawrence Collection, box 39, file 18, Archives and Special Collections, J. D. Williams Library, University of Mississippi.

"Yes, emphatically Yes": SL to Ross Claiborne and William Grose, "Office Memorandum," April 17, 1978, Seymour Lawrence Collection, box 39, file 18, Archives and Special Collections, J. D. Williams Library, University of Mississippi.

"hung out during two": JH to SL, n.d., Seymour Lawrence Collection, box 39, file 18, Archives and Special Collections, J. D. Williams Library, University of Mississippi.

209 ***"I think in its own way":*** BD to SL, "Dear Sam," n.d., Seymour Lawrence Collection, box 39, file 18, Archives and Special Collections, J. D. Williams Library, University of Mississippi.

"That [was Lawrence]": BD, in discussion with the author, September 6, 2019.

"drunken parties": JH, *OTS*, 261.

210 ***"always the orphan child":*** BD, in discussion with the author, September 6, 2019.

211 ***"his ideas have never":*** Review of *Legends of the Fall*, by JH, *New Yorker*, July 30, 1979, 89.

"Mr. Harrison may be": Bernard Levin, "Hair on His Chest," review of *Legends of the Fall*, by JH, *Sunday Times*, January 27, 1980.

"best examples the [novella]": Raymond Carver, "Rousing Tales," review of *Legends of the Fall*, by JH, *Chicago Tribune*, May 13, 1979.

"dangerously near the category": Review of *Legends of the Fall*, by JH, *Atlantic*, September 1979, 92.

"Ill written, trite": Vernon Scannell, "Willfully Waffling," review of *Legends of the Fall*, by JH, *Times Literary Supplement*, March 21, 1980.

"Like all good macho writers": Peter Prescott, "The Macho Mystique," *Newsweek*, July 1979, 92.

212 ***"Macho is just an awful":*** JH, "With Stunning Violence, Author Weaves Tales of Man and Nature," interview by Frederick Burger, *Miami Herald*, June 22, 1980.

"talented as hell": Peter Matthiessen to JH, n.d., JHP.

"To extend that a little": Peter Matthiessen to JH, n.d., JHP.

213 ***"a bad turn":*** JH, quoted in a letter by Peter Matthiessen to JH, May 11, 1979, JHP.

"You missed the spirit": Peter Matthiessen to JH, May 11, 1979, JHP.

"Perhaps it was me": Peter Matthiessen to JH, ca. May 1979, JHP.

214 ***"Bertram 36-footer":*** Peter Matthiessen to JH, n.d., JHP.

"aswarm with carpenters": Fred Lutz, "Jim Harrison: Legend of the Fall," *Toledo Magazine,* October 7, 1979, 7.

215 ***"As you said":*** Guy de la Valdène to JH, n.d., JHP.

13 THE THEORY AND PRACTICE OF HOLLYWOOD

216 ***"Ah, yes. Fame":*** JH, "Clear Water 3," in *Jim Harrison: Complete Poems,* ed. Joseph Bednarik (Copper Canyon Press, 2021), 289.

"Did you see that": BD, in discussion with the author, May 11, 2021.

"relax and see the broadness": JH, *OTS,* 253.

217 ***"Success, of all things":*** Paul Magnusson, "The Wolves Are Howling at Jim Harrison's Door," *Detroit Free Press,* September 16, 1979.

"Linda was her own": Molly Phinny, in discussion with the author, November 11, 2021.

218 ***"I realized that I":*** Molly Phinny, in discussion with the author, November 11, 2021.

"nearly fell asleep": Jamie Harrison to JH, October 30, 1978, JHP.

219 ***"Today I went upstairs":*** JH to Anna Harrison, n.d., ca. 1978, JHP.

"The hearts of everyone": Mary Harrison, in discussion with the author, July 7, 2020.

"his dead daughter": JH, *The Theory & Practice of Rivers* (Winn Books, 1986), 5.

220 ***"Nothing is harder":*** JH, *OTS,* 259.

"Money means not": Mary Harrison, in discussion with the author, July 7, 2020.

"Quirky as hell": JHB, in discussion with the author, November 22, 2020.

221 ***"how to do life":*** JHB, in discussion with the author, November 22, 2020.

"We had a good": JHB, in discussion with the author, November 22, 2020.

222 ***"I can't tell you":*** JH, *OTS,* 83.

"I have the feeling": JH, *OTS,* 83.

"special salts": JHB, in discussion with the author, November 22, 2020.

"pre-bedtime line": JH, *OTS*, 84.

"the black sheep poet": JH, *OTS*, 251.

223 ***"incisive, wrong-headed intelligence":*** JH to TM, June 1980, TMP.

"It was so intense": TM, in discussion with the author, November 3, 2021.

"We would be the only": BD, in discussion with the author, August 30, 2020.

225 ***"immense range of practical":*** JH, *OTS*, 257.

"out of holes [he'd] dug": JH, *OTS*, 302.

"I'm sorry that you": DG to JH, July 20, 1980, JHP.

226 ***"unwittingly cruel":*** JH to DG, November 12, 1981, DGP.

"plea . . . All that's important": DG to JH, November 9, 1981, JHP.

"the single moment": JH to DG, November 7, 1981, DGP.

227 ***"Maybe I'm pushing":*** Russell Chatham to JH, n.d., ca. February 1981, JHP.

"Really wrote Warlock": JH to TM, n.d., ca. March 1982, JHP.

228 ***"the baby emerged December":*** JH, *Warlock* (Dell/Delta Publishing, 1982), 3.

"smack dab": JH, *Warlock* (Dell/Delta Publishing, 1982), 3.

"Travis McGee's laconic cynicism": JH, *Warlock* (Dell/Delta Publishing, 1982), 78.

229 ***"only a few miles":*** JH, *Warlock* (Dell/Delta Publishing, 1982), 5.

"Keatsian romanticist": JH, *Warlock* (Dell/Delta Publishing, 1982), 40.

"alter ego": JH, *Warlock* (Dell/Delta Publishing, 1982), 32.

"frayed romance": JH to TM, January 1982, TMP.

"not ruled by Irony": JH, jacket copy for *Warlock*, Delacorte Press, fall/winter 1981–82, JHP.

"a big deal": David Foster Wallace to JH, November 20, 2004, JHP.

230 ***"quite willing to collect":*** JH, introduction to *The Shape of the Journey: New and Collected Poems*, (Copper Canyon Press, 1998), 5.

"having the poems run": JH to Tom Condon and Mike Carney, November 19, 1981, JHP.

"*Publishers Weekly* said": JH to TM, June 1982, TMP.
"cracking up": JH to TM, n.d., ca. 1982, TMP.
231 ***"to pay for the 'ranch'":*** JH to TM, April 14, 1982, TMP.
"bore the shit": JH to TM, August 19, 1982, TMP.
232 ***"Thirty days away":*** JH to TM, July 2, 1980, TMP.
"Before me on the desk": JH to TM, December 1981, TMP.
"Had coke sneezes": JH to TM, March 1982, TMP.
"Coke & booze": JH to TM, May 3, 1982, TMP.
"kind of hysteria": JH, *OTS*, 144.
"any amount of cocaine": JH, *OTS*, 255.
233 ***"stomach-constricting anxious energy":*** JH, "Eat Your Heart Out," *Smoke Signals* 2, no. 2–3 (1981): 13.
"In good spirits": JH to TM, April 14, 1982, TMP.
234 ***"WONDERFUL! MAGNIFICENT!":*** Mike Golden to JH, September 9, 1982, JHP.
"The two of us": JH, "Food for Thought," *Smoke Signals* 2, no. 4 (1982): 72–74.
"Just for the record": Mike Golden to JH, September 9, 1982, JHP.
235 ***"accurate, appealing":*** Mike Golden to JH, December 7, 1981, JHP.
"I got to admit": Mike Golden to JH, December 7, 1981, JHP.
"discussions of contemporary": Review of *Selected & New Poems 1961–1981*, by JH, *Publishers Weekly*, June 25, 1982, 114.
236 ***"left poetry":*** Eliot Weinberger, in discussion with the author, June 11, 2021.
"really considered a poet": Eliot Weinberger, in discussion with the author, June 11, 2021.
"guts and heart": James Humphrey, "Harrison's Hide and Seek," *Greensboro Daily News/Record*, September 5, 1982, 4.
237 ***"Everyone used to leave":*** JH to TM, December 16, 1982, TMP.
"wildly ambitious": JH to TM, August 9, 1982, TMP.
"grasping neurotic attention": JH to TM, November 1, 1981, TMP.
"Brutal admission": JH to TM, May 17, 1982, TMP.
"Fix up your house": DG, in discussion with the author, May 13, 2021.

238 ***"worse financial fuckups":*** JH to TM, August 1982, TMP.
"save [his] ass": JH to TM, August 19, 1982, TMP.
"breathtaking beauty": JH to TM, December 5, 1982, TMP.
239 ***"past sins":*** JH to TM, October 1986, TMP.

14 UP IN MICHIGAN

240 ***"The days are stacked":*** JH, "The Theory & Practice of Rivers," in *Jim Harrison: Complete Poems*, ed. Joseph Bednarik (Copper Canyon Press, 2021), 307.
"full scale Crimean war": JH to TM, August 1983, TMP.
"preposterous anguish": JH to TM, February 1983, TMP.
"A bowl of this": JH to TM, May 25, 1983, TMP.
"freeze a personality": JH to TM, September 21, 1983, TMP.
241 ***"florid sexual behavior":*** Walker Percy, *Lost in the Cosmos: The Last Self-Help Book* (Picador, 1983), 142.
"That new W. Percy": JH to TM, July 1983, TMP.
"I dreamt that smoking": JH to TM, November 1983, TMP.
242 ***"So; certain memories":*** JH to TM, October 29, 1982, TMP.
"I am so aware": JH to Larry Sullivan, November 12, 1981, JHP. The letter was accidentally first sent to Dan Gerber, who urged Jim to see his problems through the lens of Zen Buddhism.
243 ***"dance of long periods":*** JH to Larry Sullivan, November 12, 1981, JHP.
"I ran off with myself!": JH to TM, postmarked 1983, TMP.
"I shudder at the close": JH to TM, September 1984, TMP.
"NOTHING GOOD": JH to TM, March 6, 1983, TMP.
244 ***"local squeeze":*** JH to TM, July 1983, TMP.
"ample, old-fashioned": JH, *Sundog* (E. P. Dutton, 1984), 22.
245 ***"That got the ball":*** Mike Ballard, in discussion with the author, July 20, 2018.
"[He] never overdid": Mike Ballard, in discussion with the author, July 20, 2018.
246 ***"This sounds like you!":*** Doug Peacock, in discussion with the author, May 13, 2021.

"Chatham, and Guy": Doug Peacock, in discussion with the author, May 13, 2021.

"real thing": Philip Caputo, *In the Shadows of the Morning: Essays on Wild Lands, Wild Waters, and a Few Untamed People* (Lyons Press, 2014), 147.

"feathers everywhere": Mary Capogrossa, in discussion with the author, July 23, 2018.

247 ***"never difficult":*** Mary Capogrossa, in discussion with the author, July 23, 2018.

"Diamond Jim": Rick Capogrossa, in discussion with the author, July 23, 2018.

"secret clinic": JH to TM, November 22, 1983, TMP.

"greaseball lard farm": JH to TM, February 3, 1984, TMP.

"Where the fitness revolution": JH to DG, postcard, Rancho La Puerta, n.d., ca. 1980s, DGP.

248 ***"Nixon's cabinet bag man":*** JH to TM, February 3, 1984, TMP.

"O say a Rowena": JH to TM, December 30, 1984, JHP.

"A pride in the zeros": TM to JH, December 30, 1984, JHP.

"Also it sounds like": JH to Lou Adler, December 16, 1983, JHP.

249 ***"Sort of wobbling":*** JH to DG, May 29, 1984, DGP.

"My boss, Mr. Jim": JHB to Lou Adler, May 25, 1984, JHP.

"the string of thoughts": JH to DG, May 29, 1984, DGP.

250 ***"theory and practice":*** JH, *Sundog* (E. P. Dutton, 1984), 5.

"big ole dam": JH to TM, August 1983, TMP.

"someone who is totally": JH, personal notebook, circa 1983, accessed while in possession of JHB.

"writing about [his]": JH to TM, July 9, 1984, TMP.

251 ***"I know exactly what":*** TM to JH, September 4, 1983, JHP.

"You are totally": JH to TM, September 21, 1983, TMP.

"truly cruising": JH to TM, November 1983, TMP.

"[Lawrence's] imprint fell": Richard D. Lyons, "Seymour Lawrence, 67, Publisher for a Variety of Eminent Authors," *New York Times*, January 7, 1994.

"particular and unique input": BD to JH, July 28, 1982, JHP.

252 ***"Dear Passion Flower":*** SL to JH, May 20, 1983, JHP.

"I don't know what": SL to JH, April 4, 1984, JHP. SL was referring to a profile and interview by Gregory Skwira: "Words from the Woods," *Detroit Free Press,* March 25, 1984.

"something truly different": JH, *Sundog* (E. P. Dutton, 1984), 1.

253 ***"no time allowed":*** JH, *Sundog* (E. P. Dutton, 1984), 11.

"Dread and irony": JH, "An Interview with Jim Harrison," 1985, interview by Kay Bonetti, in *Conversations with Jim Harrison, Revised and Updated,* ed. Robert DeMott (University Press of Mississippi, 2019), 32.

"seriously awry": Michiko Kakutani, review of *Sundog,* by JH, *New York Times,* May 21, 1984.

"book of the spirit": Judith Minty, "Sex, Adventure, Food: A Novel of Survivors," review of *Sundog,* by JH, *San Francisco Chronicle,* June 3, 1984.

254 ***"SUNDOG is a splendid":*** Ed Abbey to JH, November 11, 1986, JHP.

"many educated people": JH, *Sundog* (E. P. Dutton, 1984), 45–46.

"It is a philosophical": JH, *Sundog* (E. P. Dutton, 1984), 45.

"shouldn't have been built": JH, *Sundog* (E. P. Dutton, 1984), 73.

255 ***"terrifying but somewhat expected":*** JH, *OTS,* 59.

"Up there you had": Warren Hinckle, "The Big Sky Fell in on Brautigan," *San Francisco Chronicle,* October 27, 1984, 4.

"piece of festering": Russell Chatham to Warren Hinckle, November 1, 1984, JHP.

"those post-mort mots": JH to TM, April 1985, TMP.

256 ***"I was swindled":*** JH to TM, July 1985, JHP.

"different perspective": Taylor Hackford to JH, June 26, 1985, JHP.

"the most destructive thing": JH to TM, January 5, 1985, TMP. See also Jim's July journal, accessed while in possession of JH .

257 ***"If we had 500":*** SL to JH, March 4, 1986, JHP.

"may be his breakthrough": SL to BD, September 6, 1984, JHP.

"Art and ducksheads": John Harrison to JH, May 7, 1986, JHP.

"feeling that I was": Norma Harrison to JH, May 19, 1986, JHP.

258 ***"found such things":*** Larry W. Winn to BD May 22, 1985, JHP.

"what could keep one": JH, *The Shape of the Journey: New and Collected Poems* (Copper Canyon Press, 1998), 5.

"the rivers of my life": JH, "The Theory & Practice of Rivers," in *The Theory & Practice of Rivers* (Winn Books, 1986), 3.

"all of it, every": Norma Harrison to JH, December 1986, JHP.

259 ***"Blessings to you":*** Norma Harrison to JH, December 1986, JHP.

15 DALVA

260 ***"O god all our continents":*** JH, "The Times Atlas," in *Jim Harrison: Complete Poems,* ed. Joseph Bednarik (Copper Canyon Press, 2021), 338.

"7 buks of pomes": JH to TM, January 19, 1987, TMP.

"I am creating this": JH, *Dalva* journals, JHP.

261 ***"nearly insufferable burden":*** JH to TM, December 26, 1986, TMP.

"prime picnic spots": Doug Peacock to JH, January 7, 1987, JHP.

"car freak or maven": JH, "Log of the Earthtoy Drifthumper," *Automobile Magazine,* July 1986.

262 ***"Harrison yarn about roaming":*** David E. Davis to JH, January 27, 1986, JHP.

"religious impulse, a craving": JH to TM, February 1988, TMP.

"Avoid irony, cynicism": JH, "Going Places," *Outside,* June 1987.

263 ***"you have to write":*** JH to TM, March 1987, TMP.

"bowled over": SL to JH, January 29, 1987, JHP.

"that it is a major": SL to JH, August 4, 1987, JHP.

"At the risk of shooting": SL to JH, August 4, 1987, JHP.

264 ***"a great fan":*** SL to JH, August 10, 1987, JHP.

"[Lawrence] was known for": BD, in discussion with the author, February 18, 2023.

"fire in my eye": SL to JH, October 26, 1987, JHP.

"I'm your publisher": SL to JH, 1987, JHP.

265 ***"We love you truly":*** SL, September 10, 1987, JHP.

"a wonderful go through": JH to TM, January 1987, TMP.

"Curious that 3": JH to TM, June 10, 1987, TMP.

"It's a Princeton preppy": JH to TM, May 1, 1987, TMP.

266 ***"Guiding Jim was difficult":*** Gil Drake, in discussion with the author, February 18, 2023.

"shaking the continuing virus": JH to TM, June 10, 1987, TMP.

"quite seriously, if irrationally": JH, *OTS*, 46.

"guilty and vulnerable": JH, *OTS*, 46.

"A pause at the thought": JH to TM, June 10, 1987, TMP.

"I was sitting up": DG, in discussion with the author, March 23, 2002.

267 ***"A present friend said":*** JH to Dennis Hopper, August 20, 1995, JHP.

268 ***"escapes, evades me":*** JH, "From the *Dalva* Notebooks, 1985–1987," *Antæus* 61 (Autumn 1988): 211.

"a pretty nice tame": JH to TM, February 7, 1987, TMP.

"Two life-saving screenplay": JH to TM, March 1988, TMP.

"vitals (gizzard & spleen": JH to TM, last of June 1988, TMP.

"waves of anger": JH to TM, late August 1988, TMP.

269 ***"Yr Razorback phone":*** JH to TM, October 1987, TMP.

"humongous piece": JH to TM, January 1, 1988, TMP.

"celebrity sycophancy": JH to TM, January 1, 1988, TMP.

270 ***"forever digging holes":*** JH, *Dalva* (E. P. Dutton, 1988), 124.

"first-hand, intimate": JH, *Dalva* (E. P. Dutton, 1988), 137.

271 ***"irrationality involved in love":*** JH, *Dalva* (E. P. Dutton, 1988), 234.

"for every poet it is": Derek Walcott, "The Antilles: Fragments of Epic Memory," Nobel lecture, December 7, 1992, https://www.nobelprize.org/prizes/literature/1992/walcott/lecture/.

272 ***"the fabled Weisinger":*** JH, *Dalva* (E. P. Dutton, 1988), 141.

"Early reviews in daily": JH to TM, March 1988, TMP.

"less ambitious works": Michiko Kakutani, "Epic America in 'A Woman's Quest,'" Book of the Times, *New York Times*, March 9, 1988, 84.

"virtual saturation": Louise Erdrich, review of *Dalva*, by JH, *Chicago Tribune*, March 19, 1988.

"but to literally transform": John Blades, "'He' Writing as 'She,'" *Chicago Tribune*, March 7, 1989.

"could win a whole": Georgia Jones-Davis, "The Literary Seductions of a Macho Woman," review of *Dalva*, by JH, *Los Angeles Times*, April 10, 1988.

273 ***"a serious cooking week":*** Jamie Harrison, in discussion with the author, February 4, 2023.

"into the muck": Jim Fergus to JH, May 8, 1984, JHP.

"Don't feel old": Jim Fergus to JH, August 12, 1986, JHP.

274 ***"We just want to":*** BD, quoted in Terry McDonell, *The Accidental Life: An Editor's Notes on Writing and Writers* (Vintage, 2017), 8–9. The book is an excellent account of McDonell's work and friendships with Harrison, McGuane, Hunter Thompson, Peter Matthiessen, and many others.

"I realized that they": Terry McDonell, in discussion with the author, September 13, 2021.

"It was easy to work": Terry McDonell, in discussion with the author, September 13, 2021.

"Small portions are for": JH, "Sporting Food," *Smart* 1, no. 1 (1988): 68–70.

16 PATAGONIA

275 ***"What beauty / can I imagine":*** JH, "Portal, Arizona," in *Jim Harrison: Complete Poems*, ed. Joseph Bednarik (Copper Canyon Press, 2021), 537.

"Between Literature and Hollywood": JH to SL, January 11, 1990, JHP.

"a bunch of fat": JH to TM, February 1989, TMP.

"vastly upgraded its facilities": JH, *The Woman Lit by Fireflies* (Houghton Mifflin, 1990), 234.

276 ***"my family, religion, art":*** JH to TM, n.d., ca. January 1989, TMP.

"The bottom that fell": JH to TM, February 1989, TMP.

"I felt ursine, damp": JH to TM, February 1989, TMP.

277 ***"passed it on":*** Rowdy Herrington, in discussion with the author, February 4, 2023.

"development hell": JH, quoted in "Hollywood Harrison," by Pat H. Broeske, *Los Angeles Times*, February 18, 1990.

"Getting 'REVENGE' into production": Ray Stark to JH, March 2, 1988, JHP.

"decent little village": Don Safran to JH, December 20, 1989, JHP.

278 ***"that guy with the funny":*** SL to JH, February 10, 1989, JHP.

"Strange to be a grandpa": JH to TM, December 18, 1989, JHP.

"Quite a lot actually": JH to TM, October 31, 1989, JHP.

279 ***"They pretty much shot":*** JH, "'Revenge' Is Author's Reward," interview by Pat H. Broeske, *Akron Beacon Journal*, February 21, 1990, 47.

"I was so swept away": JH, "'Revenge' Is Author's Reward," interview by Pat H. Broeske, *Akron Beacon Journal*, February 21, 1990, 47.

"to induce flashbacks": Peter Rainer, "Saga of Ex-Navy Pilot Flies off the Mark in 'Revenge,'" review of *Revenge*, dir. Tony Scott, *Los Angeles Times*, February 16, 1990.

"based on a novella": Roger Ebert, review of *Revenge*, dir. Tony Scott, *Chicago Sun-Times*, February 2, 1990.

"surely would have brought": Janet Maslin, "What If . . . ? New Movies in Other Hands," *New York Times*, March 11, 1990.

"improbably darker and grittier": JH, *OTS*, 283.

280 ***"really is a Jim Harrison":*** Don Safran to JH, December 20, 1989, JHP.

"there will be a lot": Don Safran to JH, January 2, 1990, JHP.

"It wasn't a 'premier'": JH to TM, February 7, 1990, TMP.

"shit monsoon press junket": JH to John Evans, February 8, 1990. Letter accessed while in possession of John Evans.

"a fine sort": JH to TM, February 7, 1990, TMP.

"more and more like": JH to Pocket Books, n.d., JHP.

"I got a modest 'award'": JH to TM, May 1990, TMP.

281 ***"flowering in the old days":*** JH to TM, May 1990, TMP.

"So you see how": JH to TM, May 1990, TMP.

"sealed & melancholy": JH to TM, May 1990, TMP.

"like a pirate": Doug Wick, in discussion with the author, March 28, 2022.

282 ***"all the good times":*** BD to JH, November 13, 1990, JHP.

"Copyeditors at New Yorker": JH to TM, June 20, 1990, TMP.

283 ***"The New Yorker is a great break":*** SL to JH, April 10, 1990, JHP.

"Maestro": SL to JH, January 9, 1990, JHP.

"pure Chekhovian and delicate": JH to SL, May 24, 1990, JHP.

"curled in a thicket": JH, "The Woman Lit by Fireflies," in *The Woman Lit by Fireflies* (Houghton Mifflin, 1990), 215.

"death and transfiguration": JH, "Novella notes: The Woman Lit by Fireflies," JHP.

"sluggish, dark brown water": JH, "The Woman Lit by Fireflies," in *The Woman Lit by Fireflies* (Houghton Mifflin, 1990), 200.

284 ***"we couldn't ask for better":*** SL to JH, August 21, 1990, JHP.

"the equivalent of 2 bottles": SL to JH, March 28, 1990, JHP.

"an ass-fucking plague": JH to SL, May 24, 1990, JHP.

"We want you to do 6": SL to JH, May 9, 1990, JHP.

285 ***"the Lemuria of the Northwest":*** SL to JH, May 9, 1990, JHP.

"That's one of the reasons": Richard Howorth, in discussion with the author, February 25, 2023.

"Everybody loved to party": Richard Howorth, in discussion with the author, February 25, 2023.

"always around": Lisa Howorth, in discussion with the author, February 26, 2023.

286 ***"despite a mild hangover":*** JH to John Evans, April 21, 1988. Letter accessed while in possession of John Evans.

"fried oysters, frogs' legs": SL to JH, August 21, 1990, JHP.

"I've been thinking about your health": TM to JH, October 20, 1990, JHP.

"critter fat": TM to JH, October 20, 1990, JHP.

287 ***"I would not dream":*** JH to TM, November 4, 1990, TMP.

"one has any respect": JH to TM, November 4, 1990, TMP.

"all that": TM to JH, November 15, 1990, JHP.

288 ***"giving America its appetite back":*** Terry McDonell, *The Accidental Life: An Editor's Notes on Writing and Writers* (Vintage, 2017), 155.

"by far": JH, "What Have We Done with the Thighs?" The Raw and the Cooked, *Esquire,* February 1991, 47.

"the great restorative": JH, "The Days of Wine and Pig Hocks," The Raw and the Cooked, *Esquire,* March 1991, 58.

"lifestyle Nazis afoot": JH, "What Have We Done with the Thighs?" The Raw and the Cooked, *Esquire,* February 1991, 47.

"the perils of public eating": JH, "The Days of Wine and Pig Hocks," The Raw and the Cooked, *Esquire*, March 1991, 58.

289 ***"severe as the pain":*** JH, "One Foot in the Grave," The Raw and the Cooked, *Esquire*, April 1991, 65.

290 ***"wish to be on a plane":*** JH to SL, February 15, 1991, JHP.

"Widespread terrorist vengeance": JH to SL, February 22, 1991, JHP.

"Oddly enough I'm not": SL to JH, February 15, 1991, JHP.

"waiting for something": Alice Furlaud, "Shadow of War over Paris," *New York Times*, February 10, 1991.

"I cannot comment": Christian Bourgois to SL, March 11, 1991, JHP.

291 ***"You're a lock":*** Peter Phinny to JH, April 26, 1991, JHP.

"I don't moo": Peter Phinny to JH, April 26, 1991, JHP.

"Saw 22 species": JH to TM, April 1992, TMP.

292 ***"(first time in this country)":*** JH to TM, April 1992, TMP.

"raw spots but we": JH to TM, March 24, 1992, TMP.

"continuing lit sickness": JH to TM, May 1992, TMP.

"why we wrote": JH to TM, June 23, 1992, TMP.

"There are no truths": JH, "First Person Female," *New York Times Magazine*, May 16, 1999, 98–99, 101.

17 ENTRE CHIEN ET LOUP

294 ***"At Hard Luck Ranch":*** JH, poem 11 from "After Ikkyū", in *Jim Harrison: Complete Poems*, ed. Joseph Bednarik (Copper Canyon Press, 2021), 363.

"Looks like show biz": JH to SL, n.d., ca. spring 1993, JHP.

295 ***"really only liked the first":*** JH to Les Valmadre, November 7, 1994, JHP.

"Dionysian, but [Nichols] wanted": JH, quoted in "A Writer at Life's Banquet," by Susan Salter Reynolds, *Los Angeles Times*, November 24, 2002.

"This was a big to-do": Richard Howorth, email message to author, May 15, 2023.

296 ***"This has become a society":*** JH, "The Beige Dolorosa," in *Julip* (Grove Press, 2008), 231.

"everything which came": Brice Matthieussent to JH, July 29, 1993, JHP.

297 ***"the physiognomy of a country":*** Brice Matthieussent and Georges Luneau, "Jim Harrison Entre chien et loup," posted May 12, 2022, by Georges Luneau, YouTube, https://youtu.be/LfjRs5xuQuY.

298 ***"We like the sound":*** SL to Christian Bourgois, March 19, 1993, JHP.

"I tend to enjoy": JH to Hilary Liftin, April 27, 1993, JHP.

"gastronomique": Christian Bourgois to JH, December 7, 1992, JHP.

"I'm sorrier than you": SL to JH, June 2, 1993, JHP.

"Have thought for years": JH to TM, November 1989, TMP.

"quite a mob show": JH to SL, June 1993, JHP.

299 ***"in Gay Paree":*** JH to TM, August 6, 1993, TMP.

"fucking Frenchie": Brice Matthieussent to JH, July 29, 1993, JHP.

"nation struggling for its soul": JH, "A Huge Hunger in Paris," The Raw and the Cooked, *Esquire*, December 1993, 70–71.

300 ***"literally choked up":*** SL to JH, October 8, 1993, JHP.

"I want to see you lionized": SL to JH, November 16, 1993, JHP.

"During all of this": SL to JH, October 5, 1993, JHP.

301 ***"I know that you":*** Jonathan Warner to JH, January 6, 1994, JHP.

"bright & trustworthy": JH to TM, n.d., ca. 1995, TMP.

302 ***"Margaret," Jim wrote:*** JH, *Julip* (Grove Press, 2008), 4–5.

"painful this movie has been": Mike Nichols to JH, October 28, 1993, JHP.

"Now, looking at it": Mike Nichols to JH, October 28, 1993, JHP.

303 ***"attack of lycanthropy":*** JH, press materials for Columbia Pictures' *Wolf*, 1994, JHP.

"she went all the way": JH, "The Art of Fiction, No. 104," interview by Jim Fergus, *Paris Review*, no. 107 (Summer 1988): 52–97.

304 ***"a contortion that would":*** Doug Wick to JH, March 8, 1991, JHP.

"extraneous sub-plots": JH to Doug Wick, April 24, 1991, JHP.

"We need a clear conflict": Doug Wick to JH, Red Wagon Productions, interoffice communication, May 15, 1991, JHP.

"I'm sure you're not thrilled": Wesley Strick to JH, January 4, 1994, JHP.

305 ***"contractual deviousness":*** JH to DG, n.d., ca. 1991, JHP.

"a great sculptor who is hired": Doug Wick, "My Adventures with Jim, and Part of the Jim Harrison in Hollywood Story," unpublished manuscript. These and other comments were read by Wick at a Jim Harrison tribute in Livingston, Montana. Notes were provided to the author.

"The relationship between Hollywood": JH, *OTS*, 294.

306 ***"Blockbuster Numbers Overseas":*** TriStar Pictures, "'Legends of the Fall' Opens to Blockbuster Numbers Overseas," news release, March 15, 1995, JHP.

"a man's life": Ed Zwick, in discussion with the author, March 3, 2022.

307 ***"nearly bit the big one":*** JH to Ed Zwick, September 2, 1994, JHP.

"We were married": JH to Ed Zwick, October 3, 1994. JHP.

"must be mighty surprised": Roger Ebert, review of *Legends of the Fall*, dir. Edward Zwick, *Chicago Sun-Times*, January 13, 1995.

"shitty notices": Ed Zwick to JH, n.d., ca. December 1994, JHP.

"Mr. Zwick goes for": Janet Maslin, "Grit vs. Good Looks in the American West," review of *Legends of the Fall*, dir. Edward Zwick, *New York Times*, December 23, 1994, 62.

308 ***"Although it retains the name":*** Kenneth Turan, review of *Legends of the Fall*, dir. Edward Zwick, *Los Angeles Times*, December 23, 1994.

"I was disturbed to see": JH to the *New York Times* art editor, December 28, 1994, JHP.

"minimalist fern bar witticisms": JH to the *Los Angeles Times* editors, December 28, 1994, JHP.

309 ***"I actually liked the movie":*** JH, *OTS*, 285.

"the art director got": JH, "Interview with Jim Harrison," interview by Carrie Preston and Anthony Michel, *Red Cedar Review* 35, no. 2 (2000): 37. See also *Conversations with Jim Harrison, Revised and Updated*, ed. Robert DeMott (University Press of Mississippi, 2019), 176.

"At last something of yours": Larry Sullivan to JH, February 23, 1995, JHP.

"infinitely more": JH, interview, *Good Morning America*, aired January 22, 1995, on ABC.

310 ***"A nice satori yesterday":*** JH to TM, April 1995, TMP.

"after seven years": JH to TM, April 1995, TMP.

"about all Paris-ed out": JH to TM, July 22, 1995, TMP.

"puzzle out the surroundings": JH to TM, May 9, 1995, TMP.

311 ***"Orvisoids":*** JH to TM, August 14, 1995, TMP.

"I was upset": JH to TM, November 30, 1995, TMP.

"drowned without notice": JH, *OTS*, 245.

"the kind of movie": Gene Siskel, review of *Carried Away*, dir. Bruno Barreto, *Siskel & Ebert*, released March 30, 1996, Buena Vista Television.

"an explicitly told tale": Leonard Klady, review of *Carried Away*, dir. Bruno Barreto, *Variety*, January 28, 1996.

"years of sediment": JH to George Brockway, October 18, 1967, JHP.

312 ***"summer dream of NY publishing":*** JH to Dan Barrett, n.d., ca. 1996, JHP.

"to clear my resonant": JH to Dan Barrett, May 13, 1996, JHP.

"foreign stuff": JH to TM, November 30, 1995, TMP.

"Further proof": Peter Turner to JH, October 22, 1996, JHP.

313 ***"This is a woman":*** JH to Peter Turner, June 13, 1996, JHP.

"remotely consider [himself]": JH, preface to *After Ikkyū and Other Poems* (Shambhala, 1996), viii.

"Chinese oldtimers": JH to TM, June 1994, TMP.

"dead as a railroad spike": JH to TM, June 1994, TMP.

18 THE SHAPE OF THE JOURNEY

314 ***"A modern man, I do not":*** JH, poem 10 from "Geo-Bestiary," in *Jim Harrison: Complete Poems*, ed. Joseph Bednarik (Copper Canyon Press, 2021), 417.

"In the middle of the night": JH to Jimmy Buffett, dictation, September 3, 1998, JHP.

315 ***"imponderable violence of success":*** JH to TM, February 7, 1985, JHP.

"Anyway, it occurred to me": JH to Jimmy Buffett, dictation, September 3, 1998, JHP.

"dangling rubberoid tube": JH to TM, June 1997, TMP.

"the best ever": JH to TM, June 6, 1997, TMP.

"Julius Caesar": JH, *OTS*, 139.

"There is a tendency": JH, *OTS*, 140.

316 ***"What a nice breakfast!":*** Gérard Oberlé, in discussion with the author, May 27, 2022.

"To be frank": JH to TM, July 24, 1997, TMP.

"sometimes believing Rilke's question": JH to Morgan Entrekin, dictation, September 1, 1997, JHP.

317 ***"bigger than we are":*** JH to Les and Marina Valmadre, dictation, October 14, 1997, JHP.

"kind of distortion": JH to TM, December 22, 1997, TMP.

"modest quail jaunts": JH to TM, November 5, 1997, TMP.

"the girl I always": JH to TM, March 9, 1998, TMP.

318 ***"quite mordant":*** JH to TM, May 28, 1998, TMP.

"I woke up screaming": JH to Judy Hottensen, dictation, June 3, 1998, JHP.

"I certainly enjoyed": JH and Judy Hottensen, dictation, n.d., ca. June 1998, JHP.

"My all time favorite": JH to Morgan Entrekin, n.d., ca. August 1998, JHP.

319 ***"one individual and his":*** JH, "Jim Harrison," in *Seymour Lawrence, Publisher: An Independent Imprint Dedicated to Excellence* (Seymour Lawrence, 1990), 38. This was a privately published tribute.

"literary bona fides": Morgan Entrekin, in discussion with the author, September 15, 2021.

"artisanal form of publishing": Morgan Entrekin, in discussion with the author, September 15, 2021.

320 ***"jack of all trades":*** Anthony Bourdain, *Anthony Bourdain: No Reservations,* season 5, episode 17, "Montana," aired August 24, 2009, on Travel Channel.

"irascible and opinionated": JH, "Danny Lahren," *Big Sky Journal*, Fly Fishing 1997, 71.

321 ***"How utterly beautiful!":*** JH to Grove Press, n.d., ca. 1998, JHP.

"soul history": JH to TM, December 9, 1990, JHP.

"the soul history of our country": JH, "Creating Habitat for the Soul:

An Interview with Jim Harrison," interview by Robert DeMott and Patrick Smith, 1997/1998, in *Conversations with Jim Harrison, Revised and Updated*, ed. Robert DeMott (University Press of Mississippi, 2019), 157.

322 ***"Ralph or Fred":*** JHB to Judy Hottensen, September 13, 1998, JHP.

"Jim Harrison, le grizzly": Michel Braudeau, "Jim Harrison, le grizzly du nord du Michigan," *Le Monde*, September 5, 1998.

"Big Jim": Clavel André, "Harrison, le Mozart des grande plaines," *L'Express*, October 9, 1998.

323 ***"Welcome home":*** Judy Hottensen to JH, September 14, 1998, JHP.

"I heard Paris": Morgan Entrekin to JH, September 18, 1998, JHP.

"To read this book": Thomas McNamee, "O Pioneers!" review of *The Road Home*, by JH, *New York Times Book Review*, November 8, 1998, 11.

"culmination of my existence": Anonymous customer, November 17, 1998, comment on *The Road Home*, by JH, Amazon, https://www.amazon.com.

324 ***"getting toasted":*** Colum McCann, in discussion with the author, September 29, 2021.

"suspicious accoutrements of success": JH to TM, December 15, 1998, TMP.

"Anyway, this is just": Colum McCann to JH, January 1, 1999, JHP.

"It would sell": Joseph Bednarik, in discussion with the author, October 28, 2021.

325 ***"Sam was a legendary":*** Joseph Bednarik, in discussion with the author, October 28, 2021.

"I've read virtually no": Sam Hamill to JH, June 11, 1997, JHP.

"make a killer book": Sam Hamill to JH, January 15, 1996, JHP.

"While the advance isn't much": Sam Hamill to JH, March 5, 1997, JHP.

326 ***"because every time":*** Joseph Bednarik, in discussion with the author, October 28, 2021.

"You're going to need this": Joseph Bednarik, in discussion with the author, October 28, 2021.

"I've written a goodly": JH, introduction to *The Shape of the Journey: New and Collected Poems* (Copper Canyon Press, 1998), 1.

"All the early work": Joseph Bednarik, in discussion with the author, October 28, 2021.

327 ***"perfect fit!":*** DL to Sam Hamill, December 20, 1997, JHP. Sam had forwarded this letter to Jim.

"the portion of my life": JH, introduction to *The Shape of the Journey: New and Collected Poems* (Copper Canyon Press, 1998), 1.

"this trip will be": JH to Michel Le Bris, dictation, May 11, 1999, JHP.

"terrifying illness": JH to TM, May 29, 1998, TMP.

"Scarcely a sniffle": JH to TM, September 5, 1998, TMP.

"I smoke outside now": JH to TM, November 16, 1998, TMP.

"head and shoulders well": JH to TM, December 15, 1998, TMP.

328 ***"expert of experts":*** JH to Gérard Oberlé, dictation, August 26, 1999, JHP.

"Chekhovian tale": JH to TM, November 1, 1999, TMP.

329 ***"My mother died":*** JH to Judy Hottensen, January 8, 2000, JHP.

"I had the feeling": JH to TM, January 10, 2000, TMP.

"I am always amazed": JHB to JH, dictation, April 8, 1998, JHP.

330 ***"Oh, stop now":*** Gérard Oberlé, in discussion with the author, May 27, 2022.

"He was a mixture": Gérard Oberlé, in discussion with the author, May 27, 2022.

"huge surf, volcanic rocks": JH to TM, n.d., ca. June 2000, TMP.

331 ***"I find myself quite confused":*** JH to TM, January 7, 2000, TMP.

19 THE ROVING GOURMAND

332 ***"Everyone thought I'd die":*** JH, *Braided Creek*, in *Jim Harrison: Complete Poems*, ed. Joseph Bednarik (Copper Canyon Press, 2021), 441.

"one of our finest": Richard Kilgore, "The Beast Within: Harrison's Short Stories Examine Shifting Personalities of His Characters and Himself," review of *The Beast God Forgot to Invent*, by JH, *Dallas Morning News*, January 24, 2001.

"so lushly idiosyncratic": Jonathan Miles, review of *The Beast God Forgot to Invent*, by JH, *Salon*, October 19, 2000, https://www.salon.com/2000/10/19/harrison_3/.

"as beautifully as any": JH, "Hemingway Fished Here," *Esquire*, July 1977, 40.

333 ***"I couldn't be":*** JH to Amy Hundley, July 26, 2002, JHP.

"Could a tough guy": Amy Hundley to JH, July 26, 2002, JHP.

"think of art": JH, "First Person Female," *New York Times Magazine*, May 16, 1999, 98–99, 101.

"brie brains": Dwight Garner, "Sauternes and Spaghetti," review of *The Beast God Forgot to Invent*, by JH, *New York Times*, October 29, 2000.

334 ***"our greatest nonwriterly writer":*** JH to Judy Hottensen, December 5, 2000, JHP.

"MFA bullshit New York": Judy Hottensen to JH, December 6, 2000, JHP.

"which isn't too encouraging": JH to TM, July 26, 2000, JHP.

"an admission": JH to TM, January 8, 1998, TMP.

"If you go outside": JH to TM, October 2000, TMP.

"A month of research": JH to TM, January 23, 2001, TMP.

335 ***"fallen body wrenched":*** JH, "Life on the Border," *Men's Journal*, July 2001, 99.

"like thousands of others": JH to TM, January 23, 2001, TMP.

"where the dead girl": JH to TM, January 23, 2001, TMP.

"Ana Claudia Villa Herrera": JH, "Life on the Border," *Men's Journal*, July 2001, 99.

"a lot of bluster": JH, OTS, 124.

"shine a tiny pen-light": JH to TM, April 11, 2001, TMP.

336 ***"the blues":*** JH to TM, June 1, 2001, TMP.

"Mentioned in memoir": JH to TM, February 2002, TMP.

337 ***"It was in ways":*** Ted Kooser, in discussion with the author, January 26, 2021.

"a whole new vein": Ted Kooser, "Winter Morning Walks: A Conversation with Ted Kooser," interview by Jay Meek, *North Dakota Quarterly* 68, no. 1 (2001): 9–24.

338 ***"picked out 14 pair":*** Ted Kooser to JH, January 25, 2001, JHP.

"It plays to our": Ted Kooser to Mike Peich, January 25, 2001, JHP.

339 ***"Everyone was pretty quiet":*** Dan Lahren, in discussion with the author, July 24, 2020.

"I was fairly gasping": JH, *OTS*, 113.

340 ***"I absolutely love":*** TM to JH, October 31, 2001, JHP.

"Henry Miller of food": JH to TM, November 13, 2001, TMP.

"sit at the same table": Jeffrey A. Trachtenberg, review of *The Raw and the Cooked*, by JH, *Wall Street Journal*, October 26, 2001.

"A tour instills self-importance": JH to Judy Hottensen, January 2001, JHP.

"Heart, lungs, kidneys, liver": JH to TM, December 8, 2001, TMP.

341 ***"In Hollywood, everyone wants":*** JH to Amy Hundley, April 10, 2001, JHP.

"I'm not writing one of those": Jamie Harrison, in discussion with the author, February 4, 2023.

"You're not writing": Jamie Harrison, in discussion with the author, February 4, 2023.

342 ***"Yes, I guess I am":*** Jamie Harrison, in discussion with the author, February 4, 2023.

"I am here": JH to TM, April 17, 2002, TMP.

"Lucent Lucent Lucent": JH, "Bars," in *Saving Daylight* (Copper Canyon Press, 2006), 51–52.

"several times a day": JH, "On Leaving Leelanau County," *Traverse, Northern Michigan's Magazine*, January 2002.

343 ***"Welcome to the fair":*** TM to JH, April 19, 2002, JHP.

"looking at the Manitous": JH, "On Leaving Leelanau County," *Traverse, Northern Michigan's Magazine*, January 2002.

344 ***"testament to a life":*** Judy Hottensen, Grove promotional materials for *Off to the Side*, 2002, JHP.

"dance of the seven hundred": JH to Amy Hundley, n.d., ca. August 2002, JHP.

"It's a challenging book": Joseph Bednarik to Amy Hundley, and then JHB, July 30, 2002, JHP.

"the most exacting writer": Dwight Garner, "Sauternes and Spaghetti," review of *The Beast God Forgot to Invent*, by JH, *New York Times*, October 29, 2000.

345 ***"But somebody somewhere":*** Joseph Bednarik to JHB, July 31, 2002, JHP.

346 ***"The most boring memoirs":*** JH to SL, January 28, 1991, JHP.

"There is no self-destructiveness": JH, *OTS*, 81.

"Much of him remain[ed]": Robert DeMott, "Creating Habitat for the Soul: An Interview with Jim Harrison," interview by Bob DeMott and Patrick Smith, 1997/1998, in *Conversations with Jim Harrison, Revised and Updated*, ed. Robert DeMott (University Press of Mississippi, 2019), 135.

"They'll have to decorate": Ray Numi to Jim Barnes to Judy Hottensen, October 17, 2002, JHP.

347 ***"Worked 12 hours yesterday":*** Ted Kooser to JH, February 22, 2002, JHP.

"running under the surface": Ted Kooser to JH, February 22, 2002, JHP.

"strong speech": Ted Kooser, in discussion with the author, January 26, 2021.

348 ***"This book is a rather":*** JH, "About the Poets," in *Braided Creek: A Conversation in Poetry* (Copper Canyon Press, 2007), 87.

"like the myriad little": JH to Ted Kooser, 2020, JHP.

"to make it abundantly": Joseph Bednarik to JH, April 3, 2002, JHP.

"metro dailies": Joseph Bednarik, "Braided Creek Anniversary Celebration," Zoom meeting, January 21, 2023, posted February 2, 2023, by Copper Canyon Press, YouTube, https://youtu.be/eZocwjLaKNM&t=507.

"size does matter": Michael Wiegers to JH, February 6, 2002, JHP.

"a maniac (nothing new)": JH to Ted Kooser, March 2003, JHP.

"I'd rather sell my kidneys": JH to Ted Kooser, August 2003, JHP.

349 ***"A fang was stuck":*** JH to TM, August 2003, TMP.

"When I fully enter": JH to TM, August 16, 2003, TMP.

"Is there an interior logic": JH, "A Really Big Lunch," *New Yorker*, September 6, 2004, 78.

"ticklish situation right now": JH to Deborah Treisman, November 24, 2003, JHP.

"a fake": Gérard Oberlé, in discussion with the author, May 27, 2022.

350 ***"lifelong companion":*** Reverend Lowell Grisham, eulogy for John Harrison's funeral, December 19, 2003, JHP.

351 ***"Somehow feels in hindsight":*** Jamie Harrison, email message to author, July 6, 2023.

20 MORTALITY IS GRAVITY

352 ***"It's after midnight in Montana":*** JH, "Cabbage," in *Jim Harrison: Complete Poems,* ed. Joseph Bednarik (Copper Canyon Press, 2021), 484.

353 ***"I wrote my first":*** JH to TM, January 2004, TMP.

"allowed no room": JH to Deborah Treisman, January 27, 2004, JHP.

"the Bride of Hell": JH to Deborah Treisman, January 29, 2004, JHP.

"It pays better": JH to TM, March 15, 2004, JHP. Letter misdated by JH as May 15.

354 ***"brother-death-slump":*** JH to TM, March 15, 2004, JHP. Letter misdated by JH as May 15.

"revealed too informally perhaps": Deborah Treisman to JH, March 5, 2004, JHP.

"O prescient one": JH to Deborah Treisman, March 7, 2004, JHP.

"Right now he wasn't sure": JH to Deborah Treisman, March 7, 2004, JHP.

"He was simply* trying*": Deborah Treisman to JH, March 8, 2004. JHP. Italics mine.

355 ***"How many times I":*** JH to Deborah Treisman, March 8, 2004, JHP.

"UP predatory family": JH, "Jim Harrison at the Wallace Stegner Center," reading, University of Utah, March 24, 2005, posted September 5, 2016, by the Montana Experience: Stories from Big Sky Country, YouTube, https://youtu.be/3hgdNpKopnQ.

"U.P. history is so naked": JH to TM, February 18, 2004, TMP.

356 ***"an elegy for the Michigan":*** William Corbett, "Living Large," *Providence Phoenix,* May 14–20, 2004.

"fundamentally inhumane": JH to Tom and Laurie McGuane, June 29, 2004, TMP.

"whistled ad-less": JH to Amy Hundley, December 14, 2004, JHP.

"a vanity plate": JH to Eric Price, August 20, 2004, JHP.

357 ***"damn good job":*** Judy Hottensen to JH, November 24, 2004, JHP.

"Life is short": JH to Judy Hottensen and Morgan Entrekin, November 26, 2004, JHP.

"as good as it gets": JH to BD, February 2005, JHP.

"radical self-designed diet": JH to TM, October 2004, TMP.

358 ***"a downshift is in order":*** JH to Larry Sullivan, n.d., ca. fall 2004, JHP.

"beloved red": JH to TM, November 1, 2004, TMP.

"fatigue, anger, anguish": JH to Judy Hottensen and Amy Hundley, n.d., ca. fall 2004, JHP.

"[his] lovers—Bandol, Vacqueyras": JH to Dominque Bourgois, n.d., ca. October 2004, JHP.

"fright and flight": JH to TM, March 22, 2005, TMP.

"truly problematical": JH, "A Man's Guide to Drinking," *Men's Journal*, December 4, 2017.

"lit biz": JH to TM, May 16, 2006, TMP.

359 ***"too off brand":*** JH to TM, September 3, 2004, TMP.

"One of the central": JH to TM, April 19, 2004, TMP.

"engineered by [his] heirs": JH to TM, December 19, 2005, TMP.

360 ***"deadly serious":*** JH to Michael Weigers, February 17, 2005, JHP.

361 ***"always rushing ahead":*** JH to TM, February 10, 2005, TMP.

"There are no truths": JH, "First Person Female," *New York Times Magazine*, May 16, 1999, 98–99, 101.

"It's not truth that keeps": JH, "The Movie," in *Saving Daylight* (Copper Canyon Press, 2006), 16–17.

"No, it's closer": JH, "Jim Harrison at the Wallace Stegner Center," reading, University of Utah, March 24, 2005, posted September 5, 2016, by the Montana Experience: Stories from Big Sky Country, YouTube, https://youtu.be/3hgdNpKopnQ&t=4135.

"The true subject here": Jean Thompson, review of *The Summer He Didn't Die*, by JH, *New York Times Book Review*, August 7, 2005, 11.

362 ***"absurdly difficult":*** JH to Steve Sheppard, July 26, 2005, JHP.

"Dear Bob, We're parting": JH to BD, July 26, 2005, JHP.

"We were both too proud": Bob Dattila, in discussion with the author, August 29, 2000.

363 ***"gastro plan":*** Mario Batali to JH, August 25, 2005, JHP.

"A relentlessly wonderful trip": JH to TM, November 10, 2005, TMP.

364 ***"trying to eat all aspects":*** JH to TM, February 10, 2005, TMP.

365 ***"My three days with Steve":*** JH to TM, May 13, 2006, TMP.

"I recognize that you're": Joseph Bednarik to JH, April 2005, JHP.

"They're simply *there*": Joseph Bednarik to JH, November 14, 2005, JHP.

366 ***"Mortality is gravity":*** JH, "Paris Television," in *Saving Daylight* (Copper Canyon Press, 2006), 40.

"The Brain is just": JH, "The Little Appearances of God," in *Saving Daylight* (Copper Canyon Press, 2006), 72.

"If you want to understand": JH, "Mother Night," in *Saving Daylight* (Copper Canyon Press, 2006), 55.

"Time means only": JH, "Buried Time," in *Saving Daylight* (Copper Canyon Press, 2006), 36.

"I'd rather say": JH, "Modern Times," in *Saving Daylight* (Copper Canyon Press), 2006, 12.

"works written late": John Updike, "Late Works: Writers and Artists Confronting the End," *New Yorker*, August 7–14, 2006.

367 ***"tragedy recast as comedy":*** Jennifer Egan, "Go West, Old Man," review of *The English Major*, by JH, *New York Times*, October 17, 2008.

"melancholy tales": JH to TM, January 2006, TMP.

"an embittered codger": JH to Deborah Treisman, August 16, 2006, TMP.

"bank[ing] a few": JH to TM, November 29, 2006, TMP.

368 ***"It is hurting sales":*** Morgan Entrekin to Steve Sheppard, September 25, 2006, JHP.

"I'm forty-five": JH, *Returning to Earth* (Grove Press, 2007), 3.

"'breakout' book": JH to TM, January 30, 2007, TMP.

"Whereas his fiction": Will Blythe, "Food for the Soul," review of *Returning to Earth*, by JH, *New York Times Book Review*, Feb. 11, 2007.

369 ***"seduction":*** JH to Deborah Treisman, March 13, 2007, JHP.

"I know you don't": Larry Sullivan to JH, January 21, 2007, JHP.

"stories, novels, and novellas": American Academy of Arts and Letters, citation, Jim Harrison, May 16, 2007, JHP.

370 ***"I puked at 2am":*** JH to Laurie McGuane, May 22, 2007, TMP.

"forlorn": JH to TM, December 24, 2007, TMP.

21 ANTELOPE BUTTE

372 ***"I hope to define my life":*** JH, "The Golden Window," in *Jim Harrison: Complete Poems,* ed. Joseph Bednarik (Copper Canyon Press, 2021), 626.

"Odd to think": JH to TM, July 17, 2008, TMP.

"I was not the right": Dominique Bourgois, in discussion with the author, May 23, 2022.

373 ***"Like my sister Judith":*** JH to TM, July 17, 2008, TMP.

"muddy [his] Scandinavian side": JH to TM, February 2, 2010, TMP.

374 ***"Get nearly as much":*** JH to TM, March 23, 2008, TMP.

"version of the roto-rooter": JH to TM, February 25, 2008, TMP.

"fuzzy EKG": JH to TM, March 23, 2008, TMP.

"Post op renal stones": JH to TM, May 3, 2008, TMP.

375 ***"ace cardiologist":*** JH to TM, May 3, 2008, TMP.

"a totally successful organ": JH to TM, May 15, 2008, TMP.

"I must say that": JH to TM, August 20, 2008, TMP.

376 ***"surging with deep emotions":*** JH to Deborah Treisman, August 2, 2004, JHP.

"Recently while rereading": JH, introduction to *The Death of Jim Loney,* by James Welch (Penguin, 2008), ix.

"diminishing calls": JH, introduction to *The Death of Jim Loney,* by James Welch (Penguin, 2008), xiii.

"marvel of this final": JH, "Counting Birds," in *Jim Harrison: Complete Poems,* ed. Joseph Bednarik (Copper Canyon Press, 2021), 356.

377 ***"getting out and around":*** William Kittredge, review of *The English Major,* by JH, *Orion,* March/April 2009.

"I think I've pretty": JH to Joseph Bednarik, September 15, 2008, JHP.

378 ***"Mailer Updike Styron":*** JH to TM, February 19, 2009, TMP.

"never as goofy": JH to TM, January 28, 2009, TMP.

"the stuffiest prick": JH to TM, March 6, 2008, TMP.

"superb book": JH, jacket endorsement for *All the Pretty Horses*, by Cormac McCarthy (Knopf, 1992).

"In the 17 years": JH to TM, February 25, 2008, TMP.

379 ***"eliminated in the last":*** JH to TM, August 2, 2010, TMP.

"daily infusions": Charles McGrath, "Pleasures of the Hard-Worn Life," *New York Times*, January 25, 2007.

"thumping chest recites": JH, "Hard Times," in *In Search of Small Gods* (Copper Canyon Press, 2010), 8.

"It's my own conviction": JH to TM, December 2010, TMP.

380 ***"I imagine I'm one":*** JH to TM, January 14, 2010, TMP.

"Water gods, moon gods": JH, "The Theory & Practice of Rivers," in *The Theory & Practice of Rivers* (Winn Books, 1986), 23.

"a suffocating box": JH to TM, December 2010, TMP.

"pitiless aspect": JH to TM, January 3, 2011, TMP.

381 ***"What horse?":*** William R. Hearst III, in discussion with the author, January 24, 2023.

"the poet laureate": William R. Hearst III, in discussion with the author, January 24, 2023.

"the only true writers": William R. Hearst III, in discussion with the author, January 24, 2023.

382 ***"on a high level":*** Gary Snyder, in discussion with the author, October 3, 2020.

"closed system": William R. Hearst III, in discussion with the author, January 24, 2023.

383 ***"They really do sustain":*** Michael Wiegers to JH, May 29, 2008, JHP.

"Of all the poems": Ted Kooser to JH and DG, May 21, 2008, JHP.

"difficulties nearly beyond": JH to Joseph Bednarik and Michael Wiegers, March 11, 2008, JHP.

"Of course a poem": JH to Peter Lewis and Joseph Bednarik, January 2, 2008, JHP.

"the ironical 'schlep'": JH to Joseph Bednarik and Michael Wiegers, March 11, 2008, JHP.

384 ***"You two work perfectly":*** Michael Wiegers to JH, July 2008, JHP.

"central texts": Joseph Bednarik to JH, December 2006, JHP.

"There aren't that many": Anthony Bourdain, *No Reservations*, season 5, episode 17, August 24, 2009.

"a real good guy": JH to TM, May 6, 2009, TMP.

"I'm not so sure": JH to Anthony Bourdain, April 20, 2007, JHP.

385 ***"to steer clear":*** Anthony Bourdain to JH, April 30, 2007, JHP.

"Tony was infatuated": Dan Lahren, in discussion with the author, July 24, 2020.

"Made him dinner": JH to TM, May 30, 2009, TMP.

"just as likely to see": Anthony Bourdain, "Big Sky . . . Thick Jungle . . . Zero Tolerance," blog post, August 22, 2009, Travel Channel, http://anthony-bourdain-blog.travelchannel.com/read/big-sky-thick-jungle-zero-tolerance-and-diane-saves-the-day.

"[Jim] and Livingston and how": Anthony Bourdain to JH, June 21, 2009, JHP.

386 ***"My hero":*** Anthony Bourdain to JH, August 26, 2009, JHP.

"Now seventy-one, Jim Harrison": Jeffrey Brown, "Writer, Poet Jim Harrison Is a Determined 'Outsider,'" interview of JH, *PBS NewsHour*, aired July 9, 2009.

"You sense those spirits": JH, "Writer, Poet Jim Harrison Is a Determined 'Outsider,'" interview by Jeffrey Brown, *PBS News Hour*, aired July 9, 2009.

387 ***"escape the anniversary nonsense":*** JH to TM, September 2009, TMP.

"My hero will be misunderstood": JH to TM, September 2009, TMP.

"What an unbearably stupid": JH to Amy Hundley, December 16, 2009, JHP.

"I don't know a better antidote": Alan Cheuse, review of *The Farmer's Daughter*, by JH, *Chicago Tribune*, December 16, 2009.

388 ***"I've been going without":*** JH to Morgan Entrekin, April 14, 2010, JHP.

"moving freely between acute": JH to TM, March 6, 2010, TMP.

389 ***"You can read a lot":*** JH to TM, March 31, 2010, TMP.

22 PARTS UNKNOWN

390 ***"In the Upper Peninsula":*** JH, "Suite of Unreason," in *Jim Harrison: Complete Poems*, ed. Joseph Bednarik (Copper Canyon Press, 2021), 693.

"On my second week": JH to TM, January 11, 2011, TMP.

391 ***"everything became confused":*** JH to TM, January 11, 2011, TMP.

"electrical strokes": JH to Alfredo "Che" Guevara, February 8, 2011. Letter accessed while in possession of JHB.

"frolic of hypodermics": JH to TM, March 18, 2011, TMP.

"This is certainly merciless": JH to Alfredo "Che" Guevara, January 18, 2011. Letter accessed while in possession of JHB.

"Dr. Guevara said that I'm": JH, "Dead Man's Float," in *Dead Man's Float* (Copper Canyon Press, 2015), 44.

392 ***"be-well prayer list":*** Peter Matthiessen to LH, August 14, 2011. Letter accessed while in possession of JHB.

"I admit I've been stretched": JH to TM, Ted Kooser, DG, Guy de la Valdène, et al., August 11, 2011. Letter accessed while in possession of JHB.

393 ***"It scared the shit":*** Dan Lahren, in discussion with the author, August 15, 2023.

394 ***"So strange to have a life":*** JH to TM, Ted Kooser, DG, Guy de la Valdène, et al., August 19, 2011. Letter accessed while in possession of JHB.

"I said to my actual dentist": JH, reading, Elk River Books, Livingston, MT, September 7, 2011, posted March 31, 2016, by ElkRiverBooks, YouTube, https://youtu.be/3o6lyzsFguM&t=56.

"Seems like just a year": JH, reading, Elk River Books, Livingston, MT, September 7, 2011, posted March 31, 2016, by ElkRiverBooks, YouTube, https://youtu.be/3o6lyzsFguM&t=533.

"silly hubris": JH to TM, March 23, 2009, TMP.

395 ***"America's greatest living writer":*** Tom Bissell, "The Last Lion," *Outside*, August 31, 2011, https://www.outsideonline.com/culture/books-media/last-lion/.

"Philosopher King of earth": Sally D. Ketchum, "The Great Leader," *New York Journal of Books*, https://www.nyjournalofbooks.com/book-review/great-leader.

"Guess who's a Heartland": Amy Hundley to JH, October 7, 2011, JHP.

"see[s] today that everyone": JH, "A Puzzle," in *Jim Harrison: Complete Poems,* (Copper Canyon Press, 2021), 719.

"leads the USA in poetry": JH to Judy Hottensen, Amy Hundley, and Deb Seager, November 14, 2011.

"It must be your year": Amy Hundley to JH, November 20, 2011, JHP.

397 ***"only slightly helpful":*** JH to Alfredo "Che" Guevara, February 26, 2011. Letter accessed while in possession of JHB.

"zombie effect": JH to Alfredo "Che" Guevara, January 24, 2011. Letter accessed while in possession of JHB.

"IT IS YOUR IDEA": JHB to JH, March 6, 2012. Letter accessed while in possession of JHB.

398 ***"extra access to the world":*** JH to Morgan Entrekin, April 7, 2012, JHP.

"long and invasive procedure": LH to list of recipients, sent by JHB, October 17, 2012. Letter accessed while in possession of JHB.

399 ***"Jim's way is his":*** JHB to LH, October 12, 2012. Letter accessed while in possession of JHB.

"I can't keep this up": LH to Douglas Wadle, MD, October 25, 2012. Letter accessed while in possession of JHB.

"a grand 2 week stay": JH to Dr. John Noseworthy and Tom Brokaw, n.d. Letter accessed while in possession of JHB.

"I had assumed attendance": JH to Dr. John Noseworthy and Tom Brokaw, n.d. Letter accessed while in possession of JHB.

400 ***"Pentagon of medicine":*** JH to Patrice Hoffman and Morgan Entrekin, November 2012. Letter accessed while in possession of JHB.

"purloining my license": JH to Dr. Douglas Wadle, February 12, 2013. Letter accessed while in possession of JHB.

401 ***"horror":*** JH to Dr. Douglas Wadle, February 4, 2013. Letter accessed while in possession of JHB.

"lots of undamaged brain": JH to Dr. Douglas Wadle, February 14, 2013. Letter accessed while in possession of JHB.

"thousand electronic gizmos": JH, "Hospital," in *Dead Man's Float* (Copper Canyon Press, 2016), 4.

402 ***"new book that is sacred":*** JHB to LH, December 16, 2012. Letter accessed while in possession of JHB.

"Now that the horror": JH to TM, January 8, 2013. Letter accessed while in possession of JHB.

"I called the other day": TM to JH, January 8, 2013. Letter accessed while in possession of JHB.

403 ***"Funny thing about all":*** JH to TM, January 18, 2013. Letter accessed while in possession of JHB.

"pay [his] nurses": JH to Patrice Hoffman, March 22, 2013. Letter accessed while in possession of JHB.

"very fast": JH to TM, March 22, 2013. Letter accessed while in possession of JHB.

"Run it into a bridge": JH to TM, June 25, 2013. Letter accessed while in possession of JHB.

"old brain": JH to Amy Hundley, August 27, 2013, JHP.

404 ***"Every guy who bellies":*** John Freeman, "'Brown Dog' by Jim Harrison," *Boston Globe*, December 19, 2013, https://www.bostonglobe.com/arts/books/2013/12/19/book-review-brown-dog-novellas-jim-harrison/74ehJyf7pgSzbnVsJwIj3I/story.html.

"I know I've been hysterical": JH to JHB, October 30, 2013. Letter accessed while in possession of JHB.

"The weight of mortality": JH to TM, March 28, 2013. Letter accessed while in possession of JHB.

23 COUNTING BIRDS

406 ***"Where Is Jim Harrison?":*** JH, "Where Is Jim Harrison?" in *Jim Harrison: Complete Poems*, ed. Joseph Bednarik (Copper Canyon Press, 2021), 769.

"the power of cane": JH to TM, January 31, 2014. Letter accessed while in possession of JHB.

407 ***"so Hemingway[-like]":*** Colin Field, "Off the Record: Bar Hemingway's Colin Field," interview by Danielle Snyder, Dannijo (blog), March 5,

2018, https://dannijo.com/blogs/style/colin-field-bar-hemingway-ritz-paris.

"Had to cancel Paris": JH to TM, February 14, 2014. Letter accessed while in possession of JHB.

"Don't quite know what": JH to TM, April 6, 2014. Letter accessed while in possession of JHB.

408 ***"He was a great":*** TM to JH, April 6, 2014. Letter accessed while in possession of JHB.

"Doing the 'dead man's float'": JH to TM, April 7, 2014. Letter accessed while in possession of JHB.

"I'm calling [the collection]": JH to Gary Snyder, October 8, 2014. Letter accessed while in possession of JHB.

"2-day on-site": JHB to JH, January 9, 2014. Letter accessed while in possession of JHB.

"Of course these are": JH to JHB, April 8, 2014. Letter accessed while in possession of JHB.

"I knew Jim would question": Joseph Bednarik, in discussion with the author, May 20, 2025.

"Poetry at its best": JH, "Poetry as Survival," in *Just Before Dark: Collected Nonfiction* (Clark City Press, 1991), 294.

409 ***"We cannot abandon this":*** JH to Amy Hundley, July 29, 2014. Letter accessed while in possession of JHB.

"Nothing could be done": JH to Ted Kooser, August 14, 2014. Letter accessed while in possession of JHB.

410 ***"I think it's age":*** JH to Guy de la Valdène, September 22, 2014. Letter accessed while in possession of JHB.

"When Raymond Chandler quit": JH to Terry McDonell and Will Hearst, September 23, 2014. Letter accessed while in possession of JHB.

"death anniversaries": JH to Larry Sullivan, n.d., ca. November 2014. Letter accessed while in possession of JHB.

411 ***"I'm so grateful":*** JH to Morgan Entrekin, March 3, 2015. Letter accessed while in possession of JHB.

"Still could use a sabbatical": JH to TM, April 10, 2015. Letter accessed while in possession of JHB.

"king of sleep disease": JH to Joseph Bednarik and Michael Wiegers, June 23, 2015. Letter accessed while in possession of JHB.

412 ***"I get the sense":*** Jamie Harrison to JH, September 26, 2015. Letter accessed while in possession of JHB.

413 ***"You told me":*** Jamie Harrison to JH, September 26, 2015. Letter accessed while in possession of JHB.

"What's my choice?": Jamie Harrison to JH, January 19, 2016. Letter accessed while in possession of JHB.

"graceful in all things": Linda Harrison King obituary, October 8, 2015, JHP.

414 ***"I could say that we":*** JH, "Spring," in *Jim Harrison: Complete Poems*, ed. Joseph Bednarik (Copper Canyon Press, 2021), 736.

"You're not unaccustomed": TM to JH, October 23, 2015. Letter accessed while in possession of JHB.

"No 'despair' isn't the problem": JH to TM, October 28, 2015. Letter accessed while in possession of JHB.

"If you had another": Jamie Harrison Potenberg to JH, n.d., ca. October 2015. Letter accessed while in possession of JHB.

415 ***"completely tenacious and write":*** JH, *Anthony Bourdain: Parts Unknown*, season 7, episode 4, "Montana," aired May 15, 2016, on CNN.

"America's greatest poets": JH, *Anthony Bourdain: Parts Unknown*, season 7, episode 4, "Montana," aired May 15, 2016, on CNN.

417 ***"Jim was sad":*** Mario Batali, introduction to *A Really Big Lunch: The Roving Gourmand on Food and Life*, by JH (Grove Press, 2017), xi.

"So it's acute loneliness": JH to Jamie Harrison, n.d., ca. February 2016. Letter accessed while in possession of JHB.

"The whole fabric": Jamie Harrison to JH, January 19, 2016. Letter accessed while in possession of JHB.

418 ***"In unease the earth":*** JH, untitled poem, in *Jim Harrison: Complete Poems*, ed. Joseph Bednarik (Copper Canyon Press, 2021), 891.

420 ***"I think Jim would not":*** Nancy Droegger, in discussion with the author, April 6, 2022.

"like a warrior": Philip Caputo, in discussion with the author, February 10, 2023.

"He had shrunk": DG, in discussion with the author, March 23, 2002.

421 ***"You know, we ought":*** DG, in discussion with the author, March 23, 2002.

"Yes, we should": DG, in discussion with the author, March 23, 2002.

Davidon life, 16ar-

INDEX

A

Abbey, Edward, 156, 246, 254, 410
academic formalism, 74
Adler, Lou, 223, 248
After Ikkyū and Other Poems (Harrison), 297, 312
Afternoon on Sweetgrass Creek (Chatham), 348
Agricultural and Applied Science (Michigan State University), 34
agriculture, 4, 9
Ajax Diner (Mississippi), 285
Allen, Woody, 224, 281
Alliance of Motion Pictures and Television Producers, 268
All the Pretty Horses (McCarthy), 378
American Academy of Arts and Letters, 369
American Academy of Arts and Sciences, 414
American Booksellers Association, 285
American Indian College Fund, 280, 284
American Indian Movement, 183
American Literary Anthology, 126
Amin, Idi, 162
Ancient Minstrel, The (Harrison), 404, 416
Anderson, Don, 129
Anderson, Sherwood, 26, 36
Annaghkeen (Matthiessen), 168
Anna Productions, 278
Antelope Butte, Montana, 379
Aquavit (New York City), 364
Aralia Press, 337
Arizona, 261
Armies of the Night, The (Mailer), 99
art history program (Michigan State University), 35
Ashley, Elizabeth, 184, 185
Atlantic (magazine), 45
Atlantic Monthly Press, 104
At Swim-Two-Birds (O'Brien), 373
Auden, W. H., 95
Auster, Paul, 356
Automobile (magazine), 261
Avenue Pictures, 270, 276

B

Babbo (New York City), 356, 364
Bahle, Bob, 307
Bahle, Joyce Harrington, 214, 220, 249, 322, 343, 383, 397, 399, 402, 404, 407, 410
Ballard, Mike, 244, 272, 297
Banks, Dennis, 182
Banks, Russell, 370
"Barking" (Harrison), 386
Barreto, Bruno, 311

Barrett, Dan, 312
Barrett, Peter, 145
"Bars" (Harrison), 342
Baryshnikov, Mikhail, 239
Basilica of Sainte-Marie-Madeleine, 2
Batali, Mario, 356, 363, 364, 370, 416
Beast God Forgot to Invent, The (Harrison), 328, 332
Bednarik, Joseph, 325, 326, 344, 365, 383, 408
Bednarik, Liesl, 408
Beginning Contemporary Dance course, 52
"The Beige Dolorosa" (Harrison), 296
Belushi, John, 201
Bemelmans Bar, 224
Berg, Jeff, 269
Berger, John, 138
Bergier, Bob, 336
Bergier, Gail, 336
Best Life (magazine), 376
Betty Davis Grocery (Mississippi), 285
Bianco, Chris, 416
Big Seven, The (Harrison), 255, 398, 402, 403, 405, 411
Bishop, Elizabeth, 74
Bissell, Tom, 395
Black Mountain College (North Carolina), 74
Black Mountain poets, 74
Black Otter Guide Service, 111
Blades, John, 272
Blok, Aleksandr, 37
Bloom, Harold, 378
Bloomsbury Review (magazine), 318
"Blue Hawaii" (Harrison), 77
Blue Moon in Kentucky (film), 238
Blume, Judy, 149
Bly, Robert, 113
Blythe, Will, 368
Bob Marshall Wilderness, 387
Books & Company (New York), 313, 323
Boston, Massachusetts, 68, 414
Boston Strangler scare, 68
Bourdain, Anthony, 321, 384, 415
Bourgois, Christian, 264, 284, 289, 290, 296, 322, 355, 372
Bourgois, Dominique, 322, 372
Bovey Restorations, 182
Bowden, Charles, 409
Boy Who Ran to the Woods, The (Harrison), 14, 361
Bradley, Bill, 250
Braided Creek: A Conversation in Poetry (Harrison and Kooser), 339, 347
Brando, Marlon, 182, 183
Braudeau, Michel, 322
Brautigan, Richard, 158, 176, 186, 207, 245, 255
Brecht, Bertolt, 39
Bressler, Sandy, 202
Brick (literary journal), 349, 373

Bridges, Jeff, 184, 270
Brockway, George, 92, 103, 104, 109, 131, 312
Brokaw, Tom, 356, 399
Brontë, Emily, 196
"Brown Dog" (Harrison), 278, 283
Brown Dog (Harrison), 404
Brown Dog series, 228, 292, 361, 374, 403
Brown, Jeffrey, 386
Brown, Larry, 286
Browne, Sir Thomas, 55
Bruce, Benjamin "Dink", 158, 182
Bruce, Toby, 158
Buck, Joan, 322
Buffalo Bill, 111
Buffett, Jimmy, 148, 149, 158, 176, 184, 218, 220, 314
Buffett, Laurie, 185
Bunting, Basil, 118
"Buried Time" (Harrison), 366
Burlington Northern Railroad, 111
Burroughs, William S., 320
Bushwhacked Piano, The (McGuane), 166
Buxton, Caroline, 24
Byron, George, 26

C

Cabeza Prieta, 261
Caetani, Marguerite, 113
Cage, John, 95
Cairnie, Gordon, 73, 75
Calamity Jane, 111
Caldwell, Erskine, 26
Calgary, Canada, 387
Calley, John, 210, 214, 215
Camp Barakel, 24
Campadieu, Christine, 360, 365
Campbell and Hall, 71
Cantié, Vincent, 360
Capogrossa, Mary, 246
Capogrossa, Rick, 245, 246
Captain Tony's (Key West), 152
Caputo, Philip, 149, 246, 371, 417, 419
Carlyle Hotel, 223, 224
Carnegie Mellon University Press, 338
Carradine, Keith, 269
Carried Away (film), 267, 311
Carroll, Joseph, 129
Carroll, Paul, 116
Carruth, Hayden, 78, 173, 203
Carter, John, 261, 310, 337
Carver, Raymond, 211
Casa Mono (New York City), 364
Casey, John D., 229
Cassady, Neal, 53
Castro, Fidel, 37
Cather, Willa, 26
Catledge (film), 281
Cave, Ray, 128, 138, 139, 167
Céline, Louis-Ferdinand, 37, 39
Centerville, Iowa, 8
Century Hutchinson, 264

Chandler, Raymond, 154, 394, 410
Chart Room (Key West), 152
Chatham, Lea, 158
Chatham, Mary, 157
Chatham, Russell
  advice for, 180
  at Anna's wedding, 311
  artwork by, 208, 209, 226, 230, 348
  Clark City Press of, 289
  competition with, 154
  cooking by, 186
  film appearance of, 297
  friendship of, 149
  A Good Day to Die and, 169
  home of, 184, 265
  hunting by, 317
  at Jamie's wedding, 273
  in Key West, 148, 149
  relocation of, 157
  on Richard Brautigan's obituary, 255
  travels of, 381
  visits by, 218, 246
Chatham, Suzanne, 273
Cheboygan, Michigan, 10
"Chekhovian tale" (Harrison), 328
Chester, Laura, 418
Cheuse, Alan, 388
Chicago, Illinois, 7
Churchill, Winston, 44
Ciardi, John, 31, 36
Circle Z, 291
City Grocery (Mississippi), 285
Claiborne, Ross, 208
Clark City Press, 289, 294
classical music, 27
Clay, Maude Schuyler, 339
Cloisters, 39
cocaine, 222, 224, 231, 232, 236, 240, 249, 266
Cohen, Robert David, 79
Colbert, Robert, 201
"Cold August" (Harrison), 103
Cold Feet (film), 269, 277
Cold Feet (Harrison), 179, 193
Cold Mountain (Frazier), 319
colitis, 167
Collioure, France, 360, 370
Colombian bud, 175
Columbia Pictures, 269, 277
comic novels, 367
commercial magazine publishing, 128
Comparative Literature Department (Michigan State University), 91
Congregationalist church, 22
Conroy, Frank, 295
Conversation, A (Harrison and Kooser), 337
Coolidge, Clark, 74
Cooperman, Stanley, 126
Copper Canyon Press, 318, 324, 347, 365, 383, 395, 408
Corbett, William, 73, 75, 79, 89, 105, 356
Corcoran, Tom, 148

Costner, Kevin, 277, 280
"Counting Birds" (Harrison), 377
County Normal, 5
couplets, 137
Court Street, 194
Cranbrook Schools (Bloomfield Hills), 83
Crane, Hart, 36, 37
Creeley, Robert, 74, 75, 137
Crockett, Jim, 88
Crockett, Portia Rebecca "Becky", 185
Crow and the Heart, The (Carruth), 78
cultural anthropology, 241
Cummings, E. E., 74
Curtis, Edward, 256

D

Daishōnin, Nichiren, 168
Dalva (Harrison), 251, 256, 260, 268, 270, 276, 321
Dan Tana's, 223
Daniel (New York City), 312
Dattila, Robert
  actress and, 224
  drug use by, 267
  on fame, 224
  friendship of, 61, 134, 183, 282
  Jim as ending relationship with, 362
  Jim's collaboration with, 179
  on Lawrence, 264
  letter from, 190
  at Linda's memorial, 416
  in Los Angeles, 216
  negotiations by, 251, 257, 258
  as salesman, 204
  on Thomas McGuane, 84
  Toby Carr Rafelson and, 199
  visits from, 148, 158
  on *Wolf*, 305
"David" (Harrison), 81, 89
Davis, David E., 262
De Niro, Robert, 166
Dead Man's Float (Harrison), 407, 411, 415, 416
Death of Jim Loney, The (Welch), 376
Debs, Eugene, 25
Del Posto Ristorante (New York City), 370
Delacorte Press, 207, 226, 251
Delights & Shadows (Kooser), 348
Dell, 207, 251
DeMott, Robert, 322, 409
Desert Solitaire (Abbey), 254
Detroit News (newspaper), 89
DeVito, Danny, 201
Dickey, James, 95, 171
Dickinson, Emily, 366
Dick's Pour House, 220, 297, 342
Dillard, Annie, 149
Dinesen, Isak, 205
Discovery '65 program, 78
Domaine La Tour Vielle, 360
Donadio, Candida, 104, 133

Donleavy, J. P., 207
Dostoevsky, Fyodor, 197
Doubleday, 251
Douglas, Michael, 265
Drake, Gil, 274
Drake, Linda, 274
Dramatics Club, 24
dreams, 228, 241
drug abuse, 175, 222, 224, 231, 232, 240, 249, 266
Drums of Death (play), 24
Duarte, Dalva, 271
Duncan, Isadora, 140
Duncan, Robert, 52, 53, 75, 95, 99, 105, 107, 108, 117
Dunes Saloon, 244
Durango, 200
Dust Bowl, 12

E

Earl, Lisle, 55, 85, 86, 87
Earth House Hold (Snyder), 122
Eastlake, William, 246
"Eat Your Heart Out" (Harrison), 233
Ebert, Roger, 279, 307
Ecuador, 145
Edmonds, Walter, 26
Ehrlich, Gretel, 258
Elaine's, 224, 226, 356
Eliot, T. S., 74
Elk River Books (Livingston), 394
Elliason, Charlotte, 8
Elliason, John, 8
Elliott Bay Book Company (Seattle), 285, 313
English Major, The (Harrison), 353, 365, 367, 377
Entre chien et loup (documentary), 296
Entrekin, Morgan, 312, 318, 352, 356, 367, 370, 395, 403
environmental terrorism, 156
E. P. Dutton, 251, 252, 257, 270
Erazmus, E. T., 61
Erdman, David, 94
Eshelman, Clayton, 117
Esquire (magazine), 205, 206, 288
Esquire Sportsman (magazine), 299
Evans, John, 252, 257, 285, 286
Everybody Knows and Nobody Cares (Smith), 135
"Exercise" (Harrison), 76
"The Existentialist" (Harrison), 33
Expressways (Reed), 104

F

"Fair/Boy Christian Takes a Break" (Harrison), 89
Farmer (Harrison), 167, 179, 187, 188, 193, 195, 269, 281
Farmer's Daughter, The (Harrison), 387
FarmHouse fraternity, 20
Farrington, Kip, 330
Fat Boys, 151, 175

"Father Daughter" (Harrison), 353, 354
Fathers and Sons (Turgenev), 353
Faulkner, William, 26, 36, 45, 196
Faunce, Roland, 5
Fellini, Federico, 224
Fergus, Jim, 149, 239, 273, 303, 371, 417
Ferlinghetti, Lawrence, 53
Finnegans Wake (Joyce), 37
Fire Exit (Harrison), 126
"First High Snow Above Deep Creek" (Chatham), 312
fishing, 124, 145, 148, 152, 245, 266, 274, 320, 330, 339
Fisketjon, Gary, 378
5 Blind Men, 116
Five Spot Café, 44
Flanagan, Robert, 194
Fonda, Becky, 416
Fonda, Peter, 185
"Food for Thought" (Harrison), 234
Forché, Carolyn, 281
Ford, Ford Madox, 84
Ford, Harrison, 25, 218, 269, 281
Ford, Richard, 61, 206, 281, 292, 370, 375
form, in poetry, 137
Foster, David, 135
Fox, Kate, 409
France, 264, 297, 314, 315, 322, 327, 349, 360, 392, 397
Frankfurt Book Fair, 264
Frazier, Charles, 319
Freeman, John, 404
Freudian theory, 241
Friedman, Bruce Jay, 224
Frost, Robert, 74
Furlaud, Alice, 290

G

Gains, Sid, 305
"The Games of Night" (Harrison), 375
Gardner, Ava, 280
Garner, Dwight, 333, 369
Gerber, Dan
advice from, 237
awards of, 292
and death of Jim, 420
dedication to, 348, 383
divorce of, 159
in *5 Blind Men*, 116
friendship of, 62, 83, 97, 104, 105, 109
Jim's advice to, 179
Jim's collaboration with, 113
on Jim's friendship, 225
in Key West, 148, 149
loan from, 132
in Montana, 158
review from, 172
as sports writer, 154
travels of, 111, 123, 140, 161, 330
viewpoint of, 355
visits from, 218

Walt Whitman and, 62
Gerber, Ginny, 123, 161
Geston, Susan, 185
ghazal, 122, 137
Gifford, Barry, 235
Ginsberg, Allen, 52, 74, 99, 105, 107, 108
Giscombe, Cecil, 194, 202
Glenn's Bar (Livingston), 363
Gogol, Nikolai, 37
Goin' South (film), 200
Golden, Mike, 233
"The Golden Window" (Harrison), 383
Good Day to Die, A (Harrison), 101, 153, 154, 161, 169, 170, 171, 179, 193
Good Morning America (TV show), 309
Goodman, Mitchell, 78, 92, 125, 127
Gottlieb, Robert, 135, 282
Grand Marais, Michigan, 215, 231, 244, 247, 249, 316
Gränna, Sweden, 8
Grapes of Wrath, The (Steinbeck), 12
Grayling, Michigan, 4
Graywolf Press, 294
Great Depression, 6
Great Leader, The (Harrison), 376, 387, 388, 392, 394
Green, Dan, 181, 207
Greenwich Village, New York City, 38
"Grim Reapers of the Land's Bounty" (Harrison), 138
Grisham, Lowell, 351
Grolier Book Shop, 73, 207
Grose, William, 208
Grossinger, Richard, 117
Groupe Flammarion, 372, 403
Grove Press, 318, 339, 341, 352, 356
Guevara, Alfredo "Che", 37, 329, 419
Guggenheim, 121
"Guiding Light in the Keys" (Harrison, 154
Guillevic, Eugène, 105
Guinzburg, Tom, 181, 206

H

Hall, Donald, 74, 107
Halliburton, Richard, 162
Halpern, Dan, 370
Hamill, Sam, 325, 327
Hamsun, Knut, 196
Hanging Loose, 127
Hannah, Barry, 286, 319
Hannigan, Jim, 75
Hannigan, Paul, 75
"Hard Times" (Harrison), 379
Harrison, Amanda Diller, 19
Harrison, Anna
  birth of, 138
  childhood of, 160, 164, 194, 219, 222
  concerns of, 412

at death of her father, 420
divorce of, 317
education of, 278
illness of, 146
marriage of, 311
travels of, 243
visits from, 411
work of, 294
Harrison, Arthur, 6, 11, 15, 18
Harrison, Cindy, 219, 411
Harrison, David, 8, 17, 19, 20, 26, 29, 65, 219, 290, 411
Harrison, Gloria, 219, 231, 257, 258
Harrison, James Thomas (Jim)
accident of, 181
activism of, 99
affairs of, 96, 160, 238, 243
ambition of, 103, 359
American Academy of Arts and Letters and, 369
awards of, 121, 280, 292, 306, 332, 344, 370, 377, 394
birth of, 4, 6
book tours of, 284, 313, 323, 356
in Boston, 41, 68, 414
characteristics of, 85, 86, 217, 247, 332, 373, 386
childhood of, 7, 9, 12, 20
connections of, 73, 94
as considered a poet, 236
criticism of, 211, 235
death of, 419
dog of, 317, 321, 349, 386, 409
drug and alcohol abuse of, 95, 120, 121, 167, 175, 222, 225, 231, 232, 236, 240, 241, 242, 248, 249, 266, 267, 358, 379, 398, 410
early writing days of, 41, 44, 67
earnings of, 54, 60, 78, 86, 93, 101, 121, 127, 134, 135, 145, 190, 194, 201, 214, 238, 249, 252, 257, 269, 282, 283, 325, 367
education of, 11, 24, 34, 40, 47, 52, 56, 59, 63, 90, 281
employment search of, 69
eye problems of, 13, 30
fiction writing origin of, 131, 133
financial challenges of, 67, 84, 90, 110, 166, 180, 193, 201, 237
as food writer, 233, 273, 288, 299, 339, 349, 373
forebears of, 20
in France, 297, 315, 322, 327, 349, 360, 370, 392
friendships of, 61
as grandfather, 320
grief of, 65, 66, 198, 231, 328, 354, 359, 366, 379, 414, 417
health of, 120, 147, 167, 240, 247, 275, 286, 292, 313, 317, 320, 329, 340, 345, 354, 359, 374, 377, 379, 382, 386, 390, 396, 398, 407, 410, 411, 416
in Hollywood, 216

home of, 10, 17, 36, 41, 44, 60, 66, 71, 85, 93, 108, 122, 132, 159, 165, 337, 339, 342
illness of, 1, 35
injuries of, 129
interests of, 27, 62
in Key West, 148, 175, 265
lasts of, 403
legacy of, 384
on life, 1
life fatigue of, 158
Linda May King and, 47, 48, 56
in London, 209
on love, 160
marriage of, 159, 188, 307
on a memoir, 341
mental health of, 30, 46, 65, 70, 128, 146, 158, 162, 163, 165, 166, 167, 170, 173, 179, 180, 193, 194, 249, 266, 289, 303, 365, 407, 410, 417
in Mexico, 201, 354
mission of, 45
moving of, 10, 17
in New York City, 36, 43, 63, 122, 224, 243, 295, 323, 364, 369
nonfiction writing by, 288
overeating by, 123, 224, 233, 370
in Paris, 178, 382
in Patagonia, 290, 317, 336, 370, 402
as peacemaker, 223
personal challenges of, 117, 146
poetry intentions of, 29
poetry reading by, 78
poetry viewpoint of, 32
as political writer, 334
popularity of, 62, 237, 238, 245, 314, 322, 407
privacy of, 49
productivity of, 352, 374, 383
reading by, 12
readings by, 364, 394
re-entry of, 241
religion of, 22, 27, 29, 55, 67, 167, 179, 194, 310, 313, 380
reputation of, 147, 279
reviews regarding, 89, 211, 217, 332, 395
review work of, 78
romantic relationships of, 28, 38, 46, 96
in San Francisco, 52
as screenwriter, 256, 268, 281, 302
self-destruction of, 243
sexuality of, 159, 161
smoking by, 120, 240, 248, 267, 275, 287, 292, 398, 412
spending spree by, 214, 222, 236
as sports writer, 128, 145, 147, 152, 274
as teacher, 61, 63, 92
therapy of, 225, 241, 364
thesis of, 91
travels of, 27, 29, 36, 41, 52, 56, 63, 91, 111, 123, 140, 145,

152, 157, 161, 174, 178, 209, 214, 217, 223, 231, 243, 248, 256, 261, 280, 285, 290, 295, 297, 300, 310, 315, 320, 322, 327, 328, 341, 349, 354, 360, 363, 365, 369, 370, 382, 387, 388, 392, 414
as travel writer, 261
unemployment of, 67, 88
visions of, 67, 72
work of, 41, 44, 53, 57, 59, 60, 71, 86
write-up of, 2
writing challenges of, 376
Harrison, Jamie
at Anna's wedding, 311
birth of, 60
childhood of, 69
comfort from, 66
concerns of, 163, 412, 414
at death of her father, 420
education of, 218
on her parents' relationship, 48
home of, 159, 243
on John Harrison's death, 351
Joyce Harrington Bahle and, 221
on *Legends of the Fall*, 192
life transition of, 230
on Margery King, 50, 59
marriage of, 273
motherhood of, 278
moving by, 265
travels of, 223
work of, 265, 294
writing by, 294
Harrison, John, 17, 65, 68, 91, 191, 219, 230, 257, 349, 350
Harrison, John Arthur, 6
Harrison, Judith Ellen, 11, 17, 27, 64, 67, 72, 203
Harrison, Lena, 19
Harrison, Linda May King
background of, 49
challenges of, 160
characteristics of, 48, 49, 217
concerns of, 70, 146, 266, 398
death of, 413
on Denise Levertov, 77
drug use by, 218
education of, 51, 57
family journal of, 191
grief of, 302
health of, 388, 392, 402, 412
home of, 60, 71, 85, 93, 108, 132, 159, 218, 337, 339, 342
illness of, 327, 349
injuries of, 294
introduction to, 47
Jim's affairs and, 96
on Jim's health, 120
on Kingsley, 87
marriage of, 58, 159, 188
memorial for, 416
personal challenges of, 70
pregnancy of, 57, 133
privacy of, 217

on the separation, 69
travels of, 91, 123, 161, 243, 256, 290, 320, 327, 363, 387
on World Poetry Conference, 106
Harrison, Mary, 8, 17, 65, 219, 220
Harrison, Mary (great-grandmother), 18
Harrison, Norma Olivia Wahlgren
background of, 5, 7
characteristics of, 21, 259
concerns of, 29, 40, 42, 59, 71
death of, 328
on Gloria's poem, 257
grief of, 65
home of, 10, 17
illness of, 219
interests of, 27
pregnancy of, 4
religion of, 22
on *The Solace of Open Spaces*, 258
values of, 20
Harrison, Rebecca, 65, 68, 91, 127, 219, 230, 349
Harrison, Sprague, 18
Harrison, Walter, 11, 15, 19
Harrison, Winfield
advice from, 12
background of, 19
characteristics of, 21
concerns of, 40, 42
death of, 64, 203
education of, 20
home of, 15, 17
in Jim's vision, 67, 72
leadership of, 22
on Linda's pregnancy, 58
marriage of, 5
parenting style of, 43
on reading, 11, 19
religion of, 22
relocation of, 4
values of, 20
work of, 10, 16, 18
Haslett Baptist Church, 24
Haslett, Michigan, 16, 17
Haslett Rural Agricultural High School, 17, 24
Hayden, Sterling, 196
"He Dog" (Harrison), 403, 404
Heaney, Seamus, 395
Hearst, William Randolph, III, 274, 341, 381, 420
Hecht, Anthony, 105
Heilner, Van Campen, 330
Hemingway, Ernest, 36, 149, 332
Henson, Clyde, 62, 98
Herbert, Zbigniew, 105
Hererra, Ana Claudia Villa, 335
Herlihy, James Leo, 149
Herman, Vic, 88
heroine, 268
Herrington, Rowdy, 277
Herskovitz, Marshall, 306
high culture, 205
High School of Music & Art (New York City), 38

Hinckle, Warren, 255
"Hitchhiking" (Harrison), 56, 79
Hjortsberg, Gatz, 151, 153, 154, 157, 184, 186
Hjortsberg, Lorca, 157, 186
Hjortsberg, Marian, 157, 186
Hoffa, Jimmy, 50
Hoffman, Patrice, 398, 403
Holbrook, Hal, 311
Hollywood, 216, 256
Hollywood Foreign Press, 310
Homer, 197
Hood & Gale Lumber Company, 5
Hopper, Dennis, 267, 311
Horizon Books (Traverse City, Michigan), 88
horse racing, 141, 238
"Hospital" (Harrison), 401
Hotel Europe (Saint Petersburg), 142
Hottensen, Judy, 318, 323, 356, 369
Houghton Mifflin, 278, 284, 300
Howorth, Lisa, 285, 286
Howorth, Richard, 264, 285
"A Huge Hunger in Paris" (Harrison), 299
Hughes, Ted, 74
Humphrey, James, 236
Hundley, Amy, 321, 333, 341, 344, 384, 404
Hungry Mind Review (magazine), 318
hunting, 22, 64, 81, 111, 129, 138, 143, 186, 212, 245, 246, 317, 377, 385, 402
Huston, Allegra, 210, 285
Huston, Anjelica, 210, 223, 285
Huston, John, 210, 279
Hutton, Lauren, 136, 160
Huxley, Aldous, 37, 392
Hykes, Camille, 263

I

"I Forgot to Go to Spain" (Harrison), 328
ICM Partners, 269
Ignatow, David, 107
In Search of Small Gods (Harrison), 374, 379, 383, 384, 386, 396
In the Spirit of Crazy Horse (film), 183
In Watermelon Sugar (Brautigan), 207
Indian question, 270
Irving, Amy, 311
Irving, Patricia, 181, 188, 217
Isadora (film), 140
Italy, 363
Ithaca House, 194

J

Jackson, Jon, 85, 416
Jean-Christophe (Rolland), 26
Jeffers, Robinson, 74
Jefferson, Thomas, 238
Jen, Gish, 295
J.G. Melon, 224
"John Severin Walgren, 1874–1962" (Harrison), 8
Jones, Malcolm, 334

Jones, Marylin, 11
Joyce, James, 26, 37
Julip (Harrison), 292, 296, 300
Just Before Dark (Harrison), 289
Justice, Donald, 105

K

Kakutani, Michiko, 253, 272
Kanon, Joe, 302
Kastner, Elliott, 179, 182, 184, 193
Katz's Deli, 224
Kaufman, Elaine, 224
Kazin, Alfred, 94, 109, 124, 154
Keats, John, 26, 27
Keillor, Garrison, 370
Kelley, Ken, 255
Kenton, Stan, 27
Kentucky Film Office, 238
Kerouac, Jack, 39, 44, 53
Kerr, Deborah, 280
Ketchum, Sally, 395
Key West, Florida, 148, 155, 175, 265
Kidder, Margot, 185
Kierkegaard, Søren, 38
Kilmer, David, 13
Kilmer, Vera, 13
King, Harry, 50
King, Margery "Mimi" (Moulton), 50, 58, 63, 70, 294, 302
King, Martin Luther, Jr., 23
King, William "Bill" Ludlow, 49, 58, 59, 65, 181
Kingsley, Michigan, 85
Kinnell, Galway, 95, 105
"Kinship" (Harrison), 79, 89
Kirkland, Sally, 270
Kittredge, William, 377
Kizer, Carolyn, 99, 102, 105
Knopf, 104
Kooser, Ted, 261, 337, 347, 364, 383
Kubrick, Stanley, 209
Kundera, Milan, 319
Kunitz, Stanley, 74

L

La Paz, Bolivia, 231, 233
Lahren, Dan, 311, 320, 330, 331, 339, 385, 404, 416
Lahren, Rob, 416
Lake Leelanau, Michigan, 108, 122, 214, 217, 220, 246, 273, 296, 337
Lamantia, Philip, 53
"The Land of Unlikeness" (Harrison), 398
Lange, Jessica, 238, 243
Lannan Foundation, 364
"Larson's Holstein Bull" (Harrison), 386
"Late Works" (Harrison), 369
Laubach, Frank, 55
Laughlin, James, 113
Lawrence, D. H., 320
Lawrence, Seymour (Sam)
  as agent, 367
  Barry Hannah and, 286
  book tours of, 284

Dalva and, 263, 271
death of, 300
description of, 319
donation by, 295
Entre chien et loup and, 296
home of, 265
Jim's letters to, 205
on Jim's success, 283
Julip and, 300
Just Before Dark and, 289
publishing work of, 278
work of, 207, 226, 251, 257
Le Bris, Michel, 327
Leaflets (Rich), 137
"Legenda" (Harrison), 104
Legends of the Fall (film), 306
Legends of the Fall (Harrison), 183, 190, 191, 195, 197, 202, 206, 211, 217, 237, 281
Lehmann-Haupt, Christopher, 144, 171
Lemuria Books (Mississippi), 252, 257, 285
Letters to Yesenin (Harrison), 140, 142, 164, 171, 172, 203
Levertov, Denise
conflict with, 110
on Copper Canyon, 327
death of, 327
friendship of, 99, 105
Jim's anger at, 125
Jim's collaboration with, 75
on *Locations*, 116
as new poet, 74, 75
on Norton, 132
political statement of, 108
as reference, 99
in *Sumac*, 114
visits with, 92, 95, 99
Levin, Bernard, 211
Lewis, John L., 25
Lewis, Johnna, 411
Lewis, Peter, 2, 325, 341, 370, 383, 403, 411, 420
"Life at War" (Levertov), 100
Life (magazine), 68
"Life on the Border" (Harrison), 335
Lincoln Center Festival '68, 105
Lincoln, Robert Todd, 7
"Lisle's River" (Harrison), 85
"The Little Appearances of God" (Harrison), 366
Little Big Man (film), 182
Littlefeather, Sacheen, 183
Livingston, Montana, 110, 157, 185, 265, 311, 320, 384
"Livingston Saturday Night" (song), 185
"Locations" (Harrison), 90, 103, 104, 114, 119, 125
Locke, Richard, 104, 132, 134
Loeb, Michael, 190
"Log of the Earthtoy Drifthumper" (Harrison), 262
London, 209
Lonesome Dove (TV show), 309

Long Day's Journey into Night (O'Neill), 43
Longbranch Saloon (Livingston, Montana), 111, 112
Loop Lumber, 150
Lorca, Federico García, 36, 137, 365
Los Angeles, California, 223
Los Angeles Times (newspaper), 284
Lost in the Cosmos (Percy), 241
Lowell, Robert, 74, 95, 99, 119
Lucchese, Thomas "Tommy Three-Finger Brown", 134
Ludlow, William Alfred, 50, 191, 270
Luneau, Georges, 296
Lynch, Kermit, 360
Lyon, Sue, 280

M

MacDonald, John D., 154, 214, 228, 394
Macrae, John, III, 252
"The Mad Marlin of Punta Carnero" (Harrison), 146
Mailer, Norman, 99, 224, 369
Mall, Jeanette, 144
Mallory Square (Key West), 152
"The Man Who Gave Up His Name" (Harrison), 196, 202, 208, 210, 211, 281
Manhattan, 223
Manoir de Pron, 315
"A Man's Guide to Drinking" (Harrison), 336
Marc Meneau, L'Espérance, 1
Mark Twain Award, 281
Marr, Jean, 26, 28
Martin, Dean, 27
Maslin, Janet, 279, 307, 308
Mathison, Melissa, 282
Matthiessen, Deborah, 96, 167
Matthiessen, Peter
- analyzing of, 86
- at celebration meal, 370
- criticism from, 212
- death of, 407
- fishing by, 331, 349
- friendship of, 96
- health of, 404
- inspiration of, 161
- *The Paris Review* and, 181
- readings of, 394
- recommendation from, 369
- travels of, 404
- works of, 183
- Zen Buddhism of, 167, 194, 311

Matthieussent, Brice, 296
May, Elaine, 304
Mayo Clinic (Minnesota), 399
McCann, Colum, 323
McCarthy, Cormac, 378
McCloskey, Mark, 89
McClure, James, 25
McClure, Michael, 53
McDonell, Terry, 206, 273, 288, 299, 339, 364, 370, 381
McGuane, Becky, 110

McGuane, Laurie, 370
McGuane, Thomas
awards of, 166
characteristics of, 175, 186
Cold Feet and, 269, 270
conflict of, 184
and death of Jim, 420
as director, 184
divorce of, 159, 185
in documentary, 176
encouragement from, 131, 174, 402
fame of, 165
on fiction, 133, 251
friendship of, 61, 82
grief of, 231, 414
health of, 240, 248
home of, 110, 148, 157
infidelity of, 185
Jack Nicholson and, 183
Jim's advice to, 223
Jim's debt to, 292
on Jim's moving, 120, 160, 286, 343
on Key West, 148, 149, 151
at Linda's memorial, 416
Marlon Brando and, 183
at Michigan State University, 281
The Missouri Breaks (film), 182
networking for, 104
on Peter Matthiessen, 408
on *The Raw and the Cooked*, 340
reunion of, 375
review from, 170
Richard Brautigan and, 158
in *Sports Illustrated*, 128, 152
success of, 165
travels of, 381
at University of Mississippi, 295
McInerney, Jay, 392
McInerney, Jim, 392
McLaughlin, James R., 251
McMillion, Jennifer, 416
McMillion, Scott, 416
McMurtry, Larry, 306
McNulty, Tim, 395
Mehta, Sonny, 319
Meisner, Billie, 38, 43, 45, 46
Meneau, 350
Men's Journal (magazine), 334
Mérida, Mexico, 354
Merrill, James, 149
Metropolitan Museum of Art, 39
Mexico, 201
MGM, 210
Michigan State College of Agriculture and Applied Science, 5
Michigan State University, 34, 375
Michigan Writers Symposium, 292
migrant workers, 53
Miles, Jonathan, 369
Miller, Henry, 38, 320
Miłosz, Czesław, 105
Minot, Susan, 295
Minty, Judith, 254
Mirage Enterprises and Universal Pictures, 268

Miranda, Carmen, 248, 250
Mississippi, 285, 295
Missouri Breaks, The (film), 182, 193
"Modern Times" (Harrison), 366
Monkey Wrench Gang, The (Abbey), 156, 246
Montana, 124, 157, 182, 192, 226, 255, 311, 320, 339, 386, 420
"Montana Gang", 157
Montgomery, Bob, 176
Moreau, Jeanne, 224, 322
Morr, Ralph, 24
Morrill Hall (Michigan State University), 34
Morris, Willie, 286
mortality, 203, 228, 366, 374, 405, 419
"Mother Night" (Harrison), 366
Mule Keys, 152
Murray Hotel, 111
Museum of Modern Art, 39

N

Nairobi, Kenya, 162
"Naked Women Dancing" (Harrison), 336
Nation, 76
National Endowment for the Arts, 98, 101, 105
National Trout Festival, 138
"A Natural History of Some Poems" (Harrison), 91
"Natural World" (Harrison), 100
Neal, Duane, 111
Nebraska, 261
Nebraska State Historical Society, 310
Nelson, Alix, 104, 122, 136, 138, 189
Nesbit, Lynn, 134
Nevada City, Montana, 182
New Criticism, 74
New Line Cinema, 311
Newhouser, Hal, 13
"New Liturgy" (Harrison), 76
New School for Social Research, 168
New Testament Christians, 23
New York City, 29, 43, 63, 122, 157, 224, 243, 295, 312, 318, 323, 364, 369
New Yorker (magazine), 2, 102, 103, 108, 138, 144, 211, 283, 284, 290, 333, 349, 354, 366, 376, 377
Nichols, Mike, 282, 295, 302, 304
Nicholson, Jack, 182, 183, 200, 201, 208, 209, 210, 223, 236, 238, 282
Night Before Lounge, 261
"Nights and Days" (Duncan), 114
92 in the Shade (film), 184, 185
Ninety-Two in the Shade (McGuane), 166
No Reservations (TV show), 384
North Winter (Carruth), 78
Northern Michigan University, 92
Northridge, Dalva, 270
Northwest Channel, 152
novellas, 204, 353, 361
Nye, Russel, 60

O

Oates, Warren, 185
Oberlé, Françoise, 2
Oberlé, Gérard, 2, 315, 317, 322, 328, 349
O'Brien, Flann, 373
O'Brien, Geoffrey, 95
O'Brien, Tim, 284, 295
Odasso, Christian, 176
Odegaard (Minneapolis), 285
Off to the Side (Harrison), 336, 341
Old Anchor Inn (Key West), 152
Olduvai Gorge (Tanzania), 162
Olivet College (Michigan), 84
Olson, Charles, 74
Olsson, Hannah, 7
Olsson, Sven, 7
On the Road (Kerouac), 44
On the Rox (New York City), 223
Ondaatje, Michael, 349
"One Foot in the Grave" (Harrison), 289
open-form poetry, 80
organic form, 80
Otava, 264
Out of the War Shadow (Levertov), 100
"Outcast" (Harrison), 376
Outlyer and Ghazals (Harrison), 132, 136, 138
Outside (magazine), 262, 274
Ovitz, Mike, 281

P

Palm Beach, Florida, 222
Palmer, Michael, 74, 82, 89
Papaya King, 225
Paradise Valley, Montana, 227, 343
Paris, France, 143, 178, 290, 297, 310, 382
Paris Review, 181, 273
"Paris Television" (Harrison), 366
Parra, Nicanor, 105, 107, 114
Parts Unknown (TV show), 415
Patagonia, Arizona, 290, 317, 336, 371, 402
Paton, Pat, 85, 118, 123, 132, 138
Paton, Vesper, 86, 138
PBS NewsHour (TV show), 386
Peacock, Doug, 246, 254, 261, 272, 311, 394, 416, 420
Peckinpah, Sam, 185, 279
Peich, Michael, 338
Peltier, Leonard, 182
PEN Club, 104
PEN dinner, 318
PEN Oakland Josephine Miles Book Award, 394
Penn, Arthur, 182
Percy, Walker, 241
Pfeiffer, Michelle, 282
Phillips, Jayne Anne, 295
Phinny, Molly, 218, 321
Phinny, Peter, 218, 291, 321
Phoenix Literary Agency, 135

Piazzoni, Gottardo Fidele, 150
Pier House (Key West), 152
Pill Versus the Springhill Mine Disaster, The (Brautigan), 207
Pitt, Brad, 307, 309
Plain Song (Harrison), 66, 79, 81, 84, 89, 92, 237, 411
"A Plaster Trout in Worm Heaven" (Harrison), 138
Plath, Sylvia, 74
Plimpton, George, 129, 181, 224
Ploughshares (Harrison), 203
Pocket Books, 280
"Poem" (Harrison), 79
"Poet Power", 108
Poetry (magazine), 78, 89, 138
Poetry Center's Discovery '65 program, 78
Poetry Foundation, 386
"Poets in the Schools" program, 122
politics, artist detachment from, 100
Pollack, Sydney, 218, 245, 268, 281
"Poor Girls" (Harrison), 383
Porter, Katherine Anne, 205, 207
Postman Always Rings Twice, The (film), 238
Potenberg, John, 320
Potenberg, Steven, 265, 273, 278, 330, 339, 396
Potenberg, Will, 278
Pound, Ezra, 116, 257
"Poverty on Parnassus: The Economics of Poetry" (Ciardi), 31
Practice of the Wild, The (documentary), 381, 388
Price, Eric, 357
Prince of Los Angeles, The (film), 179
Prohibition, 149
psilocybin, 175
psychological development, 242
Publishers Weekly (magazine), 235, 404
Puerto Vallarta, 280
Pullman, Bill, 269
Pym-Randall Press, 99
Pynchon, Thomas, 133

Q

Quasha, George, 94, 95, 100, 108, 110, 114, 116, 122, 267
Quinn, Aiden, 309
Quinn, Anthony, 277

R

Radcliffe Institute Fellowship, 77
Rafelson, Bob, 239
Rafelson, Toby Carr, 199
"Rage and Appetite" (Harrison), 373
Rago, Henry, 78, 106, 114
Rancho Deluxe (film), 184
Rancho La Puerta, 247, 275
Randall, James, 113
Random House, 312
Rastar Films/Columbia Pictures, 238, 277
Raw and the Cooked: Adventures of a

Roving Gourmand, The (Harrison), 339
Raw Deal Ranch, 157, 158
Ray, Gordon, 124
Raymond, Gary, 24
"The Real Fun of the Fair Was the Horse Pulling" (Harrison), 129
"A Really Big Lunch", 349
Red Wagon Productions, 304
Redgrave, Vanessa, 140
Redhill, Michael, 382
Reed City, Michigan, 10
Reed, J. D., 62, 67, 79, 95, 99, 104, 105, 108, 114, 116, 173, 229
Reens, Nick, 129, 246
re-entry, 241
Religious Studies Department (Michigan State University), 34
Report of a Reconnaissance of the Black Hills of Dakota (Ludlow), 191
Resettlement Administration, 4
Returning to Earth (Harrison), 194, 202, 352, 359, 367
Reuther, Walter, 25
Revenge (film), 277, 279
"Revenge" (Harrison), 195, 200, 202, 206, 210, 213, 214, 277
Rexroth, Kenneth, 53
Rich, Adrienne, 137
Richard B. Russell Dam, 250
Rilke, Rainer Maria, 37
Rimbaud, Arthur, 36, 37, 72
Rio de Janeiro, Brazil, 248
RipRap (Snyder), 84
"The River Swimmer" (Harrison) 398
River Swimmer, The (Harrison), 403
Rivera, Diego, 150
R. L. Winston's (San Francisco), 110
Road Home, The (Harrison), 12, 310, 312, 316, 318, 321, 323
Road House (film), 277
Rodney, Michigan, 5
Roethke, Theodore, 74
Rolland, Romain, 26
Roost, Chuck, 24
Rosenthal, M. L., 91, 99, 105, 123
Roshi, Eido, 194
Rosset, Barney, 319
Rossiya Hotel (Moscow), 140
Roth, Philip, 94, 133, 378
Rumi, 137
Russell Chatham—Deep Creek (Chatham), 258
Rust Hills, 205
Ryan, Patricia "Pat", 138, 152, 189

S

"Safety Without Portfolio" (Harrison), 274
Safran, Don, 280
Saint Petersburg, 142
Sally Dollarhide's brothel (Livingston, Montana), 111, 112
Salter, James, 211, 370
Samba (film), 248
"Sams-by-the-Sea" house, 265

San Francisco, California, 52
Sanders, Ed, 106, 107
San Francisco Chronicle (newspaper), 377
Sargent, Alvin, 306
Sasabe, Arizona, 336
Sasso, Anthony, 416
Satanic Verses (Rushdie), 297
Saving Daylight (Harrison), 352, 365
Scanga, Italo, 61
Scannell, Vernon, 211
Schillinger, Liesl, 388
Schumacher, James, 64, 65
Scott, Randy, 29
Scott, Tony, 277, 279
"The Seduction of Leslie" (Hills), 206
Selected & New Poems, 1961–1981 (Harrison), 230, 235
"A Sequence of Women" (Harrison), 81
Seton, Ernest Thompson, 12
"Seven in the Woods" (Harrison), 415
"The Seven-Ounce Man" (Harrison), 57, 296
Sexton, Anne, 74
Sexton, Woody, 176
Seymour Lawrence Inc., 207
Shambhala Publications, 312, 325
Shape of the Journey: New and Collected Poems, The (Harrison), 318, 324, 384
shashlik, 142
Shepard, Sam, 239, 243
Sheppard, Steve, 365, 367
Shilliday, Susan, 306
short story, 353
Silverman, Al, 265
Simic, Charles, 105, 106, 116, 370
Simon & Schuster, 104, 131, 134, 144, 169, 171, 181, 207
Simpson, Louis, 94, 99, 105, 107, 108, 109, 114, 116, 118, 119
Siskel and Ebert, 311
"Sketch for a Job-Application Blank" (Harrison), 31, 81
Sloman, Joel, 76
Smart (magazine), 273
Smith, Bernice, 25, 205
Smith, Mason, 135
Smoke Signals (literary journal), 233, 273
"Smokey the Bear Sutra" (Snyder), 122
Snow, Henry, 176
Snow Leopard, The (Matthiessen), 194
Snyder, Gary, 53, 84, 86, 95, 105, 122, 382, 394
Snyder, Peter, 44, 45, 51
Society for the Study of Midwestern Literature, 280
Solace of Open Spaces, The (Ehrlich), 258
"Solstice Litany" (Harrison), 404
Sommer, Scott, 195, 202

Songs of Unreason (Harrison), 395
"Sonoran Radio" (Harrison), 297
Sophie's Choice (Styron), 206
Spain, 365, 382
Spicer, Jack, 53
Sporting Club, The (McGuane), 104, 125, 148, 165
"Sporting Food" (Harrison), 274
Sports Illustrated (magazine), 128, 138, 147, 152
Square Books (Mississippi), 285
Stampa, Gaspara, 37
Stanley Hotel, Estes Park, Colorado, 27
Stans, Maurice, 248
Stanton, Harry Dean, 184
Stark, Ray, 238, 277
Steenburgen, Mary, 201
Stegner, Wallace, 110, 378
Stein, Gertrude, 84
Steinbeck, John, 12, 26
Stephens College (Columbia, Missouri), 51
Stevens, Robert, 101
Stone Horse, Duane, 271
Stone, Robert, 149
Stony Brook (Harrison), 119, 126
Stowe, Madeline, 277, 280
Strand, Mark, 78, 105
Strang, Robert, 253
Stravinsky, Igor, 52
Strick, Wesley, 304
strike, 268
Stuhr Museum of the Prairie Pioneer (Nebraska), 261
Styron, Rose, 97, 318
Styron, William, 97, 181, 206, 369
suicide, 163, 173, 255
"Suite of Unreason" (Harrison), 395
Sullivan, Herbert "Harry" Stack, 241
Sullivan, Lawrence, 221, 225, 241, 301, 364, 369, 398
Sullivan, Nancy, 78
Sumac (literary journal), 113, 116, 126
Sumac Press, 118, 171
Summer He Didn't Die, The (Harrison), 349, 352, 353, 361, 365
Sundog (Harrison), 231, 250, 257, 296
"Sunset Limited" (Harrison), 278, 283
Sunset Pier (Key West), 152
Superior Hotel, 246
Suzuki, Shunryū, 168, 180
Swayze, Patrick, 277
swimming, 408

T

Talese, Gay, 224
Tanzania, 162
Tarot (magazine), 83
Tarpon (documentary), 176, 178
Tate, James, 74, 105, 108, 114
Tattered Cover (Denver), 285
Tecate, Mexico, 247, 275

"The Theory & Practice of Rivers" (Harrison), 219, 257, 258
"Thin Ice" (Harrison), 127
Thomas, Henry, 309
Thompson, Jean, 361
Thompson, Jim, 279
Thompson, John, 94, 209
Three Times Three (Flanagan), 194
time, 366
"Time" (Harrison), 415
Toll, John S., 105
Torn, Rip, 270
Torrey, Beef, 261
Trachtenberg, Jeffrey A., 340
"Tracking" (Harrison), 360
Travis McGee mystery series (MacDonald), 214, 228
Tree Where Man Was Born, The (Matthiessen), 161
Treisman, Deborah, 2, 353, 354
The Triple, 225
triple repeat, 136
TriStar Pictures, 281, 306
trogon, 317
Trollope, Anthony, 26
Trout Fishing in America (Brautigan), 158, 207
True (magazine), 145, 147
True North (Harrison), 23, 336, 348, 352, 355
Turan, Kenneth, 308
Turgenev, Ivan, 37
Turner, Peter, 312
Twain, Mark, 238
"Twilight in Eastern Montana" (Chatham), 321
Two Little Savages (Seton), 12

U

UCLA Botanical Gardens, 216
Uganda, 162
Ungaretti, Giuseppe, 37, 105
University of Arkansas, 147
University of Mississippi, 295
University of New York at Stony Brook, 93, 105
Updike, John, 366, 369, 378
US-Mexico border, 334
US Postal Service, 131

V

Valdène, Guy de la
 at Anna's wedding, 311
 competition with, 154
 and death of Jim, 420
 divorce of, 159
 in documentary, 176, 178
 friendship of, 2, 143, 149
 home of, 151, 222
 hunting by, 317
 illness of, 315
 at Jamie's wedding, 273
 at Jim's birthday party, 371
 in Paris, 322
 praise from, 215
 travels of, 145, 363

visits from, 148, 158, 186, 218, 246
Valdène, Terry de la, 158, 186, 273
Valdène, Valerie de la, 350
Valéry, Paul, 37
Van Gogh, Vincent, 39
Vancouver Poetry Conference, 74
Veblen, Thorstein, 25
Vietnam War, 99
Viking, 181, 190, 206
Village Voice, 102
Virginia City, Montana, 182
Vogue Paris (magazine), 328
von Fürstenberg, Diane, 364
von Hofmannsthal, Hugo, 205
Vonnegut, Kurt, 207

W

W. W. Norton, 76, 77, 131
Wagon Wheel Saloon, 416, 417
Wahlgren, Evelyn, 7
Wahlgren, Grace, 5, 7
Wahlgren, Hulda Severina Elliason, 7, 8
Wahlgren, Inez, 5, 7
Wahlgren, Irene Dorothy, 7
Wahlgren, John Severin, 6, 7
Wahlgren, Marjorie, 7
Waits, Tom, 269
Walcott, Derek, 95, 271
"Walking" (Harrison), 99
Wall Street Journal (newspaper), 299, 334, 340
Wallace, David Foster, 229
war, 99
"War Suite" (Harrison), 101
Warlock (Harrison), 194, 226
Warner Brothers, 210, 214, 277
Warner, Jonathan, 301
Warren, Earl, 28
Warren, Robert Penn, 411
Washington Post (newspaper), 171
"Water Baby" (Harrison), 398
Waterston, Sam, 184
Watson, Jeannette, 323
Webster's (Milwaukee), 285
Weesner, Ted, 292
Weidenfeld & Nicolson, 285
Weinberger, Eliot, 95, 96, 99, 236, 356
Weisinger, Herbert, 62, 90, 109
Welch, James, 376
Welch, Lois, 376, 394, 416
Welles, Orson, 210, 234
Wells Lake, 15, 16
Wells, Leslie, 256, 263
Wenner, Jann, 265, 274
Wesley, John, 270
Western Michigan University, 92
"Westward Ho", 324, 328
Whalen, Philip, 53
White, Edmund, 83
Whitman, Walt, 26, 62
Wick, Doug, 281
Wiegers, Michael, 325, 348, 383, 384

Wieners, John, 74, 75
Wilbur, Richard, 74
Wilder, Billy, 305
Williams, Joy, 139
Williams, Tennessee, 149
Williams, William Carlos, 74, 78
Wilson, Edmund, 74
Wilson, Roger, 25, 28
Wine from the Heart (documentary), 360
Winfrey, Oprah, 367
Wink, Callan, 420
Winn, Larry, 258
Winn Publishing, 258
Winter in the Blood (Welch), 394
Winter Morning Walks: One Hundred Postcards to Jim Harrison (Kooser), 338
Wiseman, Fred, 179, 193
Wittliff, Bill, 306
Wolf (film), 282, 302
Wolf: A False Memoir (Harrison), 36, 46, 54, 135, 138, 144
Wolfe, Thomas, 26, 129
"Wolves of Heaven" (Harrison), 415
Woman Lit by Fireflies, The (Harrison), 275, 278, 282, 283, 284, 416
"Word Drunk" (Harrison), 76
Working Girl (film), 281
Works Progress Administration, 10
World Poetry Conference, 99, 105, 109
World War II, 11
Wrangler bar (Livingston, Montana), 111
Wright, James, 95
Writers Guild of America, 268
Writers March on the Pentagon, 99

Y

Yates, Richard, 367
Yellowstone National Park, 111
Yesenin, Sergei, 37
YM-YWHA, 78, 105
Young Progressive Socialists, 37
Youth for Christ, 24

Z

Zen Buddhism, 167, 179, 194, 310, 313
Zen Mind, Beginner's Mind (Suzuki), 168, 180
Zen Study Society, 167
Zukofsky, Louis, 76, 92
Zwick, Ed, 281, 306